AMERICA'S MUSIC

BY GILBERT CHASE

America's Music
The Music of Spain
A Guide to the Music of Latin America
Introducción a la música
  americana contemporánea

EDITOR OF:
Music in Radio Broadcasting
Yearbook of the Inter-American Institute
  for Musical Research
The American Composer Speaks:
A Historical Anthology, 1770–1965

TRANSLATOR OF:
A Concise Cultural History of Latin America,
by Pedro Henríquez Ureña

GILBERT CHASE

America's
music

FROM THE PILGRIMS TO THE PRESENT

Revised second edition

McGRAW-HILL BOOK COMPANY

New York   Toronto   London   Sydney

73

This book is dedicated to my sons:

Paul, Peter, John

αἰχμὰς δ᾽ αἰχμάσσουσι νεώτεροι, οἵ περ ἐμεῖο
ὁπλότεροι γεγάασι πεποίθασίν τε βίηφιν.
HOMER, ILIAD, IV, 324

tu ne cede malis, sed contra audentior ito
qua tua te fortuna sinet.
VIRGIL, AENEID, VI, 95

I' mi son un, che quando
Amor mi spira, noto, e a quel modo
ch'e' ditta dentro vo significando.
DANTE, PURGATORIO, XXIV, 52

Preface *to the second edition*

The most conspicuous feature of this revised edition is an entirely new chapter on the musical scene in the 1960s. The new chapter does not attempt to cover every aspect of the current scene, but rather concentrates upon creative trends and the changing circumstances in which they are manifested. Its main thesis is that the American composer—in revolt against the cultural-commercial establishment "which had no place for us and for which we had no use" (to quote an Angry Young Man of the new generation)—has taken matters into his own hands. With the university as a stronghold, and with support from private foundations, the composer has found his strength in union for a common purpose: to achieve for music the freedom of expression and communication that literature and the visual arts have long enjoyed. Shortly after this chapter was written came the announcement of the formation of "The American Society of University Composers," which was scheduled to hold its First Annual Conference in New York during April, 1966. The formation of such a Society—widely representative in its membership—confirms the significance of the present decade as a dynamic moment in the development of America's music.

Since it was decided that the second edition should be no bulkier than the first, the addition of a new chapter entailed the deletion of another. Hence the chapter on "Indian tribal music" was eliminated—not without some regret. Personally, I would have preferred to sacrifice MacDowell; but a more objective judgment prevailed. Indian tribal music, though a fascinating subject in itself, is marginal to the mainstream of musical history in the United States. The chapter on Charles Ives has been placed in its proper chronological sequence—insofar as this is possible with a composer whose major creative activity ended around 1920 but whose most important symphony received its first ꞏ ꞏ ꞏ ꞏ ꞏ ꞏ ꞏ ꞏ ꞏ ꞏ ꞏ ꞏ ꞏ ꞏ ꞏ ꞏ ꞏ ꞏ 1965.

The most extensive revisions have been in Part Three, where several chapters—notably those on jazz and on experimental music—have been almost completely rewritten. In the former I have made amends to Duke Ellington—one of the great musicians of our time—to whom I was manifestly unfair in the first edition. At that time I was unfortunately under the influence of Rudi Blesh's *Shining Trumpets*—surely one of the most bigoted books ever written about jazz, in its narrow definition of "the real musical values that jazz represents." Today we see more clearly that jazz represents many values, that it is a changing universe of musical discourse, an "open end" type of music upon which no arbitrary limitations can or should be placed. I yield to no one in my love for traditional New Orleans jazz, to which I have listened with joy night after night in historic Preservation Hall, where the spirit of that old-time music is kept alive by such fine players as George Lewis, Jim Robinson, Louis Nelson, "Punch" Miller, "Kid" Howard, "Cie" Frazier, Billie and "DeDe" Pierce—and others equally remembered though not mentioned. But this attachment to the past no longer prevents me from appreciating the artistry of an Ellington or the new developments of jazz in the post-Parker era—even unto Mingus and beyond.

There has been a tremendous growth of interest in American music since this book was first published. One evidence of this is the number of books that have been written on the subject; another is the reprinting of many older works, such as Billings' *Continental Harmony*, Gottschalk's *Notes of a Pianist*, Ives' *Essays Before a Sonata*, and Cowell's *American Composers on American Music*. Among the most valuable of the newer publications are Hans Nathan's *Dan Emmett and the Rise of Early Negro Minstrelsy*, Irving Lowens' *Music and Musicians in Early America*, Samuel Charters' *The Country Blues*, Richard J. Wolfe's monumental bibliography, *Secular Music in America, 1801–1825*, and the historical anthology edited by Marrocco and Gleason, *Music in America*. I have profited from these publications, as well as from the work of other scholars in the field of music: their endeavors demonstrate that American music no longer suffers from neglect—that it has indeed attracted the interest of an ever-increasing host of admirers and devotees. I am proud to be in that number.

Gilbert Chase

"Sabine Farm" Chapel Hill, N.C.
January 1966

was able to reconcile the two points of view and achieve popular music in the large traditional forms.

America's Music for perhaps the first time attaches importance impartially to all the currents of musical thinking which have influenced our development. We are ex-Europeans, to be sure, and as such have responsibilities to the preservation and continuance of European culture, but we are also a race—and a vigorous one—and it is increasingly evident that we are capable of developing cultural traditions of our own.

Douglas Moore

INT

exp

w

fie

b

i

music and opportunities were rare for the training and development of individual talents. When sufficient numbers of professional musicians had arrived to establish centers of serious musical culture our role as a backward province of European music was firmly established. It was only natural that the imported arbiters of taste would regard any deviation from European musical thinking as deplorable savagery to be resolutely put down. Our emerging talent was packed off to Europe to learn civilized ways. Our wealthy patrons, as they invariably do in a frontier society, regarded the European label as the only sure means of achieving cultural prestige.

Small wonder, then, that a serious dichotomy developed in the field of American composition. Our educated young people, fresh from German or French influences, did their loyal best to write good German or French music. For subject matter they turned to "remote legends and misty myths" guaranteed to keep them from thinking about the crudities of the land which they found so excruciating upon their return from abroad. They did, however, bring back with them a professional competence which was to be their significant contribution to the American scene.

Meanwhile the uneducated creator, finding good stuff about him, carried on a rapidly developing music speech which was a blend of European folk music, African rhythm, and regional color, and discovered that the public liked his music and was ready to pay for it handsomely. As a result via the minstrel ballad, through ragtime into jazz, a genuine popular American music made its appearance and was given every encouragement by the entertainment industry. European musicians were quick to recognize the originality and value of this music and, beginning with Debussy, accepted it as a new resource.

The American serious group, however, anxious to preserve their new-found dignity, nervously dismissed this music as purely commercial (a lot of it was and is), and until it was made respectable by the attention paid to it by Ravel and Stravinsky there were only occasional attempts to borrow from its rhythms and melodies. The highly successful popular group, on the other hand, has developed the notion that the technique of composition is not only unnecessary but an affectation. Such needs as may arise for their concerted numbers, ballets, and orchestrations they can well afford to pay for from the hacks (the underprivileged literate musicians). Gershwin's contribution to the American scene is significant beyond his music itself in that he

Foreword

A serious study of American music is arrestingly important at this time. Music has become one of our leading industries; our performing standards are probably now higher than anywhere else in the world, and we are making rapid strides in music education. How large a part in all this activity is our own music to play? How good is it? How does it differ from European music?

There are many signs of an awakened interest in American composition. More of it is being performed, published, and recorded than ever before. This interest is not confined to the United States alone. During the past few years Europeans who have always liked our popular music have discovered that we have several composers in the serious field well worth their attention. As for the foundations, fortunes are being spent to discover, to train, and to encourage our native talent.

In *America's Music* Gilbert Chase, a musician and scholar who understands and enjoys all kinds of music, has collected all the strands that have gone into the fabric of our musical speech–and a fascinating web of incompatibles they turn out to be. Who could imagine a pattern which would include Billings, Foster, Gottschalk, Chadwick, and Gershwin? Each of them contributed substantially to our musical tradition, and when we can grasp their interrelationship we perceive that there is indeed an American music, a hardy one just beginning to feel its strength and destined to stand beside our other contributions to world culture.

There have been many problems, but apparently lack of public appreciation has not been one of them. From the time of the Pilgrims our people have liked music and made it a part of their lives. They have played and sung and fashioned their own songs for all occasions. There were, however, no European courts for the cultivation of art

Contents

Introduction

According to Santayana, "There can be no history without a bias, because the bias determines the history." It is precisely because he has a bias different from that of his predecessors that the historian decides to retell a thrice-told tale. True, he may have some new facts to offer; but more than likely these are old facts that he presents in a new light: and his bias is what determines the nature and direction of the light that he sheds upon the facts. For my own part, I am fortunate in having an eloquent and far-sighted precursor—Arthur Farwell—an American composer and writer who more than half a century ago formulated the principle upon which my bias rests:

What a new world, with new processes and new ideals, will do with the tractable and still unformed art of music; what will arise from the contact of this art with our unprecedented democracy— these are the questions of deepest import in our musical life in the United States. (Introduction to *Music in America*, August, 1914.)

When I first read that sentence, I remember how impressed I was by that bold phrase, "the tractable and still unformed art of music," which seemed to demolish a thousand years of history at one stroke. Yet I soon perceived that this characterization of the art of music was not a denial of the past but rather an affirmation of the possibilities inherent in "the contact of this art with our unprecedented democracy." As a creative individual looking toward the future rather than the past, Farwell put his questions in terms of what *will* America do with this tractable art of music; what *will* arise from the contact of this art with our democracy. As a historian, I had simply to convert this to the past tense, asking what America—and by this I mean the American people—*had* done with the art of music. I was also interested in the How? and Why?—and this, in brief, is the bias of my history.

Naturally, others before me have undertaken to write the history of American music or of music in America—we must suppose there is a difference of meaning or implication in those terms. Some seventy years ago, Frédéric Louis Ritter (1834–1891), an Alsatian musician who came to America in 1856, published the first comprehensive history of music in the United States, titled *Music in America* (New York, 1883). Divided into six "periods," it began with the "low state of musical culture" in New England, devoted much attention to the establishment of musical societies and orchestras, the rise of oratorio and opera, and "progress of vocal and instrumental music" in the large cities. In his last chapter, Ritter dealt with "The Cultivation of Popular Music." He stated roundly that "the people's song . . . is not to be found among the American people." And he asked rhetorically, "How are we to account for this utter absence of national people's music and poetry in America?" He accounted for it by the Puritanical "repression" of early New England. "From the hearts of such people, in whose eyes an innocent smile, a merry laugh, was considered a sin, no naïve, cheerful, sweet melody could spring. His [the American colonist's] emotional life was stifled and suppressed: therefore there are no folk-poetry and no folk-songs in America." The only concession that Ritter would make to "a people's song" in the United States was to acknowledge the existence and merit of "the songs of the colored race."

The History of American Music by Louis C. Elson appeared in 1904 and gave relatively more attention to composers than to musical institutions. It bestowed a condescending chapter on "the folk-music of America," made a gallant bow to "American women in music," and concluded with an appraisal of the "qualities and defects of American music"—a procedure that might be described as a prenatal postmortem. Out of the 423 pages of his book, Elson devoted sixteen to "The Folk Music of America," declaring, "It must be admitted that in this field America is rather barren." Six pages of this chapter dealt with Stephen Foster as "the folk song genius of America," and eight pages with Indian music. Elson concluded that "American folk song in its true sense can only be derived from Indian or plantation life."

Music in America, compiled by Arthur Farwell and W. Dermot Derby, was published in 1915 as volume four of a composite work called *The Art of Music*. A critical and interpretative study, it was the best treatment of the subject up to that time and the first work to show a grasp of the cultural foundations and creative trends of American music. In his introduction to this work, Farwell wrote:

> The chief danger which threatens the American composer is the tendency to accept and conform to the standards of the centers of conventional and fashionable musical culture . . . and to fail to study out the real nature and musical needs of the American people.

This danger still exists, perhaps will always exist; but it is less of a threat to the creative vitality of American music today than it was fifty years ago, because the deep currents of the American musical vernacular have been so powerfully set in motion that they can counteract the tendency toward conventional stagnation. Speaking of these vital currents in America's music, Farwell concluded:

> The new movement will call forth new and larger efforts on the part of American composers, who, with their present thorough assimilation of the various musical influences of the world, will lead the nation into a new and mature creative epoch.

In this passage Farwell proved that he was a true prophet: what he foretold has come to pass.

In 1931 the late John Tasker Howard brought out his book *Our American Music,* in which, out of eighteen chapters, one was assigned to "Our Folk-Music," including the music of the North American Indian (which, strictly speaking, is not "folk" but "ethnic" music) and a section on "Composers Who Have Used Our Folk-Songs." The character of this work was aptly summed up by Dr. Carleton Sprague Smith, who remarked of the author, "His approach is highly respectable, and implies that we have made aesthetic progress."

My own approach to America's music is not at all respectable—my bête noire is the genteel tradition, and I take my stand with that Connecticut Yankee, Charles Ives, whose most damning adjective was said to be "nice."

As for the doctrine of aesthetic progress, which, in the guise of a firm belief in "progressive improvement" has hitherto dominated the historical criticism of American music, I hold it to be fallacious. According to this doctrine, the music of one period—let us say the "fuguing tunes" of the eighteenth century—was surpassed and made obsolete by the "improved" products of the next age—let us say the hymns of Lowell Mason. And we can observe the implications of this doctrine at work in many other directions. For example, in the belief that the smoothly mechanized performances of the big "name bands" were an improvement over the small-band improvisations of early New Orleans jazz. The important thing, it seems to me, is to be aware, as T. S. Eliot says, "of the obvious fact that art never improves, but that the material of art is never quite the same."[1] Or, as stated by Wilhelm Worringer: "The stylistic peculiarities of past epochs are not to be explained by lack of ability, but by a differently directed volition."[2] To study objectively the peculiarities of style in a given phase of America's musical past—as Mr. Charles Seeger has done so perceptively in his study of "Contrapuntal Style in the Three-voice Shape-note Hymns"[3]—is to discover not merely a deficiency in knowledge (as might be supposed from the persistent use of "incorrect" progressions), or a product which should be either discarded as obsolete or improved by correction, but rather an authentic musical style, with "a rigorous, spare, disciplined beauty" of its own. To discoveries, perceptions, and appreciations of this kind, reaching into the very core of America's music, the present work is chiefly dedicated.

Art changes, and it is the business of the historian to record those changes, to understand them if he can, to accept them whether or not he understands them, and not to presume to establish the pattern of his prejudices as objective truth. I have my definite likes and dislikes in music, as in everything else. I never try to admire what it is merely respectable to admire. I prefer "Beale Street Blues" to *Hora Novissima*. I do not think I am prejudiced in favor of our folk-popular music simply because I believe it has been the most important phase of America's music. And if you ask what do I mean by "important," I will answer, in this case, "different from European music." And if we are now beginning to sense that difference in American art-music also, that is because of the subtle but pervasive influence of our folk-popular idioms; the American musical vernacular has been on the march through all these generations, and even our most academic composers are catching up with it, or being caught up by it.

In this book, some fifteen chapters deal, in whole or in part, with

---

[1] In "Tradition and the Individual Talent," *Selected Essays, 1917–1932*.
[2] In *Abstraction and Empathy* (1908). English translation by Michael Bullock (London, 1953), p. 9.
[3] In *The Musical Quarterly*, October, 1940.

various phases of American folk, primitive, and popular music. This is in line with Charles Seeger's dictum that "when the history of music in the New World is written, it will be found that the main concern has been with folk and popular music." And this dictum, in turn, implies the recognition of historical and cultural factors that are discussed later in this Introduction. I make no apology for devoting much attention to types of music, such as the revival hymn and ragtime, that have hitherto not been regarded as "important" or worth the serious attention of the musical historian. What seemed "cheap and tawdry" to a writer yesterday may serve as material for some of the "best" music of today—as witness the skillfully creative use of gospel-hymn tunes by such composers as Ives, Cowell, and Thomson. A passage from the autobiography of the composer Nicolas Nabokov seems to me to express, better than anything else I have seen, the importance of exploring all kinds of music in a historical work that aspires to approximate the complexity and the movement of human life:

> . . . It seems to me that music came into my life in the way it came to the lives of most composers; through the illicit communication with that fertile subsoil, that vast underground of life where musical matter of all degrees of beauty and ugliness lives freely and is constantly being reinvented, rearranged, transformed and infused with new meaning by a universe of memories and imaginations.[4]

This work is not a conventional history, though it is based on historical principles. It is not a book about the performance of music or about musical institutions, though these matters may be touched upon incidentally. It is above all an attempt to understand, to describe, to illuminate, and to evaluate, the vital processes and factors that have gone into the making of America's music. When I say that it is based on historical principles, I mean that its form and content, the order and organization of its material, follow and are dependent upon the historical processes that determined the growth and direction of musical culture in the United States. This means, for example, that the first part of the book, and the earlier sections of Part II, are concerned largely with the various religious trends and impulses that dominated our musical expression for over two centuries and that continued to

[4] *Old Friends and New Music*, by Nicolas Nabokov. Copyright 1951 by Little, Brown & Company, Boston, Mass.

be powerfully felt even after the rise of secular music in the second half of the nineteenth century. Furthermore, until the closing decades of the nineteenth century, the emphasis in America's music was upon song, upon vocal music in its simpler and more popular manifestations, rather than upon instrumental music; and this emphasis, too, is reflected in the book.

The twentieth century is characterized primarily by the rapid development of instrumental music, both in the popular and "serious" fields. It is, indeed, extremely interesting to observe the rise of ragtime, jazz, and the popular "name bands," paralleling that of our instrumental art music in both the smaller and larger forms, ranging from the piano sonata to the symphony. If jazz may be regarded as our most original and far-reaching contribution to the world's music, this should not blind us to the fact that our "serious" or fine-art music is at present capable of holding its own with most of the contemporary music that is being composed anywhere. And if the influence of jazz has succeeded in making some of our art music a little less "serious," that is all to the good. Certainly, we have not relinquished our search for the sublime in music; but we no longer consider it necessary to be completely solemn about the matter. And that, perhaps, is an encouraging sign of our musical maturity.

In the course of a historical work of such scope as the present one, an author inevitably accumulates many obligations to the scholarly writers who have preceded him. Specific acknowledgments of sources are made elsewhere in this book. But I wish here to pay tribute to the memory of such men as Oscar G. Sonneck, William Treat Upton, and George Pullen Jackson, who dedicated their industry, their talent, and their enthusiasm to exploring virtually unknown tracts of America's musical history. And it is impossible to handle such an impressive work of imaginative scholarship as Benson's *The English Hymn* without profound admiration and respect. Here, too, I should like to mention the admirable writings of Constance Rourke, especially *The Roots of American Culture* and *American Humor*, which, it seems to me, must always remain a source of inspiration to anyone trying to grasp what is really native and traditional in our culture. In a more specialized field, Percy Scholes, in his work on *The Puritans and Music in England and New England*, has made a valuable contribution, by which I have fully profited.

There are many aspects of America's music that I should like to plore further; and I hope that the reader, after finishing these pages, will also feel the urge to further exploration in this vast and fascinating field. I do not claim that this work is either perfect or complete (no book on American music will ever achieve completeness; the subject is too large and diversified), but in it I have sincerely endeavored to present my vision and my understanding of the growth of America's music. I trust that the reading of this book will prove to be an adventure less arduous, but no less stimulating and rewarding, than was the writing of it.

one

The stone which the builders refused is become the head stone
of the corner.

PSALM 118.

chapter one

Puritan psalm singers

Musick is an Art unsearchable, Divine, and Excellent . . . that rejoyceth and cheareth the Hearts of Men.
PLAYFORD, AN INTRODUCTION TO THE SKILL OF MUSICK, 11TH ED., 1687.

The Puritans who settled New England have been held up to history as haters of music, so that the story of America's music has always been darkened at the outset by the shadow of this sinister cloud. Ritter, in his *Music in America*, wrote: "The Puritans, who landed in 1620 at Plymouth Rock, brought with them their psalm-tunes and their hatred of secular music." The first part of this statement is true—the Puritans were psalm singers by tradition and predilection—but the second part is contrary to the facts: love of psalmody did not necessarily imply hatred of other kinds of music. The average Puritan was by no means as severe or ascetic as is generally supposed. Enjoyment of fine clothes, good food, wine, books, sociability, and music, was readily reconcilable with the Puritan conscience.

In order to clear away some prevalent misconceptions, it would be well to begin by making the acquaintance of a typical New England Puritan. We may meet one in the person of Judge Samuel Sewall (1652–1730), B.A. and M.A. at Harvard College; ordained minister; justice of the peace; member of the New England Council; member of the Court of Assistants (hence involved in the Salem witch trials); Chief Justice of Massachusetts from 1718; and father of fifteen children. It is easy for us to become intimately acquainted with Judge Sewall, to learn of his tastes and occupations and interests, because throughout nearly the whole of his long and busy life he kept a detailed diary that has come down to us just as he wrote it. From the pages of this diary emerges, not a Saint-Gaudens statue of gloom-ridden pride, but the lifelike portrait of a very human person.

3

First of all, the Judge—he weighs 193 pounds with his light coa[t]
—will want good food, and plenty of it. Note with what relish he
cords a dinner in Cambridge, England: "Mr. Littel dined with us [at]
our inn: had a Legg Mutton boiled and Colly-Flower, Carrets, Rost[e]
Fowls, and a dish of Pease." Back home in New England there was n[o]
lack of good fare, including that famous apple pie, as the diary testifies on October 1, 1697: "Had first Butter, Honey, Curds and Cream[.]
For Diner, very good Rost Lamb, Turkey, Fowls, Aplepy." Once,[ ]
when the Judge stayed in the Council Chamber "for fear of the Rain,"[ ]
he "din'd alone upon Kilby's Pyes and good Beer." Besides beer, th[e]
Judge enjoys wine (both sack and claret), ale, and a dram or two [of]
that "Black-Cherry Brandy" that Madam Winthrop gave him wh[en]
he was courting her (after the death of his first wife, he courted fou[r]
widows in succession, and married two of them). He prefers to dine
and drink with a numerous and convivial company. Witness the diary
for August 25, 1709: "In the even I invited the Govr. and Council to
drink a glass of Wine with me; about 20 came. . . . Gave them variety of good Drink, and at going away a large piece of Cake Wrap'd
in Paper."

Judge Sewall would be pleased to have some books at hand for
leisurely browsing. He writes of a visit to a friend in Narragansett:
"Din'd at Bright's: while Diner was getting ready I read Ben Jonson,
a Folio." The play from which he read was Jonson's *The Poetaster*,
and he quotes some lines from it in his diary:

> Wake, our Mirth begins to dye,
>   Quicken it with Tunes and Wine.
> Raise your Notes; you'r out, *fie, fie,*
>   This drowsiness is an ill sign.

This introduces the subject of music, which was very near to Sewall's
heart. For him, no entertainment was complete without music. Once
he was invited to a Council Dinner, and notes with disappointment:
"Had no musick, though the Lieut. Govr. had promised it." On the
occasion of the dinner in Cambridge, already mentioned, the music did
not fail: "Three Musicians came in, two Harps and a Violin, and
gave us Musick." During a visit to Coventry, on the same English
trip, he notes: "Had three of the City Waits bid me good morrow
with their Wind Musick." While in London he took the opportunity
to attend a public concert: "Mr. Brattle and I went to Covent Garden

heard a Consort of Musick." But the Judge was not content
ely to listen to music: he loved to raise a good tune himself. Re-
ring to a former classmate at Harvard, he wrote: "We were Fel-
ows together at College and have sung many a tune in Consort,"
which would be the early New England variety of barbershop harmony. In later life, Judge Sewall continued to enjoy part singing, as
indicated by an entry in his diary for May 11, 1698: "In the new
Room with the widow Galis and her daughter Sparhawk; sung the
114th Psalm. Simon catch'd us a base" (i.e., Simon sang the bass part).
The Judge was fond of psalm singing, especially with widows.

Judge Sewall's fondness for psalm singing was shared by his fellow
Puritans, both in old and new England. But here it is necessary to
correct two prevailing misconceptions: one, that Puritans sang only
psalms; two, that only Puritans sang psalms. The singing of metrical
versions of the Psalms of David in the vernacular was a heritage shared
by all Protestants outside of Germany, where the Lutheran chorale
prevailed. Among the French Huguenots, in Switzerland, in the Low
Countries, in Scotland and England, the use of psalmody was widespread. In England psalms were sung by both Puritans and "Cav-
aliers," that is, by nonconformists and by adherents of the established
church. In 1559 Queen Elizabeth granted formal permission for psalms
and spiritual songs to be sung in English churches "for the comfort-
ing of such as delight in music." In the following year appeared an
enlarged edition of a famous English psalter destined to play an important role in the musical life of New England:

> Psalmes of David in Englishe Metre, by Thomas Sternhold and
> others: . . . Very mete to be used of all sorts of people privately for
> their godly solace & comfort, laying aparte all ungodly songes &
> ballades, which tende only to the nourishing of vice, and corrupting
> of youth.

Long before this psalter was brought to Massachusetts by the
Puritans, English psalms were heard in America, and in a manner confirming that they were indeed "used of all sorts of people." In the year
1577, Sir Francis Drake sailed from England on his celebrated voyage
around the world. In June, 1579, he landed on the coast of northern
California, and lay there for five weeks, while his men camped ashore.
The Indians proved friendly and frequently visited the encampment.

This is what we find in an account of the voyage written by Dɪ chaplain, Francis Fletcher:

> In the time of which prayers, singing of Psalmes, and reading of certaine Chapters in the Bible, they sate very attentively: and observing the end of every pause, with one voice still cried, Oh, as greatly rejoycing in our exercises. Yea they took such pleasure in our singing of Psalmes, that whensoever they resorted to us, their first request was commonly this, *Gnaáh*, by which they intreated that we would sing.

It has been suggested that the word *Gnaáh* was intended to be an imitation of the English singing through their noses—a habit allegedly transmitted to New England somewhat later. Be this as it may, the passage quoted above will serve to dispel the notion that psalm singing was the exclusive preoccupation of Puritans.

As to whether the Puritans sang secular songs as well as psalms, that is a question bound up with the Puritan attitude toward music as a whole, into which we shall now inquire.

"Musick is a good gift of God"

The black legend of the Puritan hatred of music has been strangely persistent. Here is a sampling of American opinions on this subject ranging over the past fifty or sixty years: the Puritan looked upon music as fashioned by the evil designs of the Tempter; the Plymouth Pilgrims brought with them a hatred of music unparalleled in history; in the early days in New England, instrumental music was looked upon as a snare of the devil; secular music of all kinds was sternly interdicted as a menace to the salvation of souls; the Puritans were forbidden to invent new tunes; in the early days of the New England colonies psalm singing was the only note of music heard. And so on— one might fill several pages with similar excerpts. It would be nearer the truth to say that music as an art was cherished by the Puritans, but its abuse was not tolerated, and it was regarded as having its highest use as an aid to worship.

In other words, the Puritan attitude toward music was not antagonistic or intolerant, but it *was* moralistic. That is, they judged music according to the way it was used. They considered it wrong to sing bawdy or obscene songs—and a great many of these circulated in those times—and they objected to music as an incentive to wanton or lascivious dancing, of which there was also a great deal in those times. Their objection to instrumental music in churches was based on religious grounds: it smacked of the "ceremonial worship" and "popery" against which they stood. To the use of instrumental music on social occasions, or in the home, they did not object. To mention only a few prominent cases, John Milton was an amateur organist, Cromwell had a private organ and engaged a large band of musicians for his daughter's wedding, and John Bunyan had a "chest of viols" for his recreation.

Now, the judging of music according to its uses was by no means peculiar to the Puritans. This was the view held, for example, by the noted music publisher, composer, and theorist, John Playford, who brought out numerous widely used collections of secular music, both vocal and instrumental, including the often-reprinted *English Dancing Master* and Hilton's *Catch that Catch Can*. In his *Introduction to the Skill of Musick* (London, 1655), Playford writes:

> The first and chief Use of Musick is for the Service and Praise of God, whose gift it is. The second Use is for the Solace of Men, which as it is agreeable unto Nature, so it is allow'd by God, as a temporal Blessing to recreate and cheer men after long study and weary labor in their Vocations.

After lamenting that "our late and solemn Musick, both Vocal and Instrumental, is now justl'd out of Esteem by the new Corants and Jiggs of Foreigners" (a theme upon which every age makes its own variations), Playford concludes by saying, "I believe it [music] is an helper both to good and evil, and will therefore honour it when it *moves* to *Vertue*, and shall beware of it when it would *flatter* into *Vice*."

No better statement of the Puritan attitude toward music could be found; yet it was stated by a man who was not himself a Puritan, though his publications, including the one from which we have just quoted, were well known and highly esteemed by the Puritans, including those of New England. Philip Stubbs, a writer often cited as holding "puritanical" views, in his *Anatomie of Abuses* (1583), warns that music "allureth to vanitie," yet adds:

I grant that Musick is a good gift of God, and that it delighteth bothe man and beast, reviveth the spirits, conforteth the heart and maketh it redyer to serve God; and therefor did David bothe use Musick himselfe, and also commend the use of it to his posteritie, and being used to that end, for man's privat recreation, Musick is very laudable.

One of the most rabid ranters against worldly amusements, William Prynne, in his *Histrio-Mastix* (1633), affirms that "Musicke of itself is lawfull, and usefull and commendable."

In New England, we find the Rev. Increase Mather, in his *Remarkable Providences* (1684), praising "the sweetness and delightfulness of Musick" for its natural power to soothe "melancholy passions." In the poems of Anne Bradstreet (1612–1672), the most notable New England poet of the early colonial period, we find numerous references to music, mentioned in such a way as to make it obvious that this Puritan bluestocking had both an understanding and a love of musical art. Here is an example:

> I heard the merry grasshopper then sing,
> The black glad Cricket bear a second part,
> They kept one tune, and plaid on the same string,
> Seeming to glory in their little art.

Music was loved and skillfully practiced by that band of Separatists whom we call "Pilgrims." The founder of the Separatists was a certain Robert Browne, known to be very fond of music and reputed to be "a singular good lutenist." One of the Pilgrim Fathers, Edward Winslow, has left us an account of their departure from Holland, when they took leave of their exiled brethren:

> They that stayed at Leyden feasted us that were to go, at our pastor's house, being large; where we refreshed ourselves, after tears, with singing of psalms, making joyful melody in our hearts, as well as with the voice, *there being many of our congregation very expert in music;* and indeed it was the sweetest melody that ever mine ears heard.[1]

We may conclude, then, that among the New England settlers there were as many music lovers as one finds in the average group of

[1] Winslow, *Hypocrasie Unmasked* (1646), quoted in Pratt, *The Music of the Pilgrims*. (Italics added.)

normal human beings; and that, while they had a predilection for psalm singing, they cultivated other types of music as far as circumstances permitted. Instrumental music and secular songs were by no means unknown to them.

Black legends and blue laws

Contrary to popular belief, instrumental music was not anathema to the Puritans, nor did they ever pass any laws, in Connecticut or elsewhere, forbidding the use of certain instruments. Instrumental music in religious worship was frowned upon because it smacked of "popery," but, as stated by the Rev. John Cotton in his *Singing of Psalms a Gospel Ordinance* (1647), "the private use of any Instrument of musick" was not forbidden. Specific references to musical instruments in New England before 1700 are rare, yet they *are* mentioned several times. The will of Mr. Nathaniell Rogers, of Rowley, Massachusetts, dated 1664, mentions "A treble viall" (viol), valued at ten shillings. The Rev. Edmund Browne, of Sudbury, at his death in 1678, left a "bass Vyol" and several music books. The Boston printer and engraver John Foster, a graduate of Harvard (1667), owned a guitar and a viol. On December 1, 1699, Judge Samuel Sewall noted in his diary, "Was at Mr. Hiller's to enquire for my wife's virginal." The virginal (or virginals) was a fashionable keyboard instrument of those times, and this Mr. Hiller must have been a tuner and repairer of musical instruments. It is unlikely that he would have long remained in business had Mrs. Sewall been his only client.

The alleged enactment of 1675 "that no one should play on any kind of music except the drum, the trumpet and the jewsharp," is, like many of the so-called "blue laws," a pure fabrication concocted by the Rev. Samuel Peters and originally published in his *General History of Connecticut* (1781), a work as fanciful as it is malicious.[2] The reason Peters exempted the drum, the trumpet, and the jew's-harp from the imaginary ban was that these instruments were so widely known and used in New England. Drums and trumpets were used for military and civil purposes, and the jew's-harp was a favorite item of barter with the Indians. The jew's-harp may also have served as "the poor man's viol," for it was inexpensive and easily carried about.

[2] See Scholes, *The Puritans and Music*, pp. 370–373.

Although antimusical laws never actually existed in New England, there are instances when music and dancing figure in court proceedings of that period. In such cases, however, the music is only incidental to what we would call "disorderly conduct," generally combined with drunkenness. Here are a few typical examples. In Salem, Massachusetts, in 1653, one Thomas Wheeler was "fined for profane and foolish dancing, singing and wanton speeches, probably being drunk." In July, 1678, Josiah Bridges deposed that he saw "an Indian drunk on brandy and cider" in Mr. Crod's house, and that "one night while he was there, there was music and dancing when it was pretty late." In 1679, also in Salem, Mary Indicott deposed that "she saw fiddling and dancing in John Wilkinson's house and Hue drinking liquor there." For one such case that came to the attention of the authorities, there were doubtless dozens or even hundreds that went unnoticed. Hence these court records testify that there *was* fiddling and dancing and profane singing among the common people of New England in early colonial times.

If we wish to know what kind of music they played and danced to, we have only to look into Playford's *The English Dancing Master* (1651; many later editions), a collection of the favorite popular tunes of that time, including such famous ones as "Sellinger's Round," "Trenchmore" and "Green-sleeves." These were tunes that circulated in oral tradition long before they got into print: we can be certain that the people of all the American colonies knew them well.

The Puritan attitude toward dancing was not sweepingly condemnatory. The Rev. John Cotton, very influential in New England, wrote in 1625: "Dancing (yea though mixt) I would not simply condemn. . . . Only lascivious dancing to wanton ditties and in amorous gestures and wanton dalliances, especially after great feasts, I would bear witness against, as great *flabella libidinis.*" The Puritans' dislike of May Day celebrations was due not only to the fact that these were of pagan origin, being survivals of the Saturnalia of the ancients, but also to the fact that the Maypole dancings frequently led to sexual excesses of the most licentious character. (The Maypole itself is of phallic origin.) Romantic sentimentalism has made the Maypole a symbol of innocent merriment, but contemporary accounts give a more realistic picture. This point is mentioned here because of the widely diffused legend of "Merry Mount," the name given to Thomas Morton's settlement at Mount Wollaston (now Quincy, Massachusetts), which has been held up as a bright example of Cavalier freedom and gaiety contrasted with Puritan severity and gloom. In his tale *The Maypole of Merry Mount*, Hawthorne describes the May Day festivities at Merry Mount in the most glowing colors, and then goes on to say: "Unfortunately, there were men in the new world, of a sterner faith than these Maypole worshippers. Not far from Merry Mount was a settlement of Puritans, most dismal wretches, who said their prayers before daylight, and then wrought in the forest or the cornfield, till evening made it prayer time again." Unfortunate indeed that our country was settled by dismal wretches who believed in prayer and hard work!

William Bradford, in his *Of Plimmoth Plantation*, set forth some of the complaints of the Plymouth colonists against the settlement at Mount Wollaston:

They also set up a May-pole, drinking and dancing aboute it many days together, inviting the Indean women, for their consorts, dancing and frisking togither (like so many fairies, or furies rather), and worse practises. . . . Morton likewise (to shew his poetrie) composed sundry rimes and verses, some tending to lasciviousness. . . .[3]

One of the songs used in the revels at Merry Mount has been preserved by Thomas Morton himself, in his *New English Canaan*, where he also tells us in what manner it was sung:

There was likewise a merry song made, which, (to make their Revells more fashionable,) was sung with a Corus, every man bearing his part; which they performed in a daunce, hand in hand about the Maypole, whiles one of the Company sung and filled out the good liquor, like gammedes and Iupiter.

The Songe

Drinke and be merry, merry, merry boyes;
Let all your delight be in Hymens ioyes;
Jo to Hymen now the day is come,
About the merry Maypole take a Roome.

Make greene garlons, bring bottles out
And fill sweet nectar, freely about,

[3] Bradford, *Of Plimmoth Plantation*, ed. by W. C. Ford (Boston, 1912), vol. II, pp. 48–49.

Vncover thy head, and feare no harme,
For hers good liquor to keep it warme.
Then drink and be merry, etc.
Io to Hymen, etc.[4]

This conventional drinking ditty may well have come under the heading of "harmless mirth," as Morton claimed, but all was not harmless at Merry Mount, either morally or politically. The Puritans undoubtedly had ample reason for disapproving of the immoral conditions at Merry Mount; yet their main grievance against Morton was that he sold firearms to the Indians and instructed them in their use, thus creating a serious threat to the very existence of the newly established colonies. This was a grave crime that fully justified Morton's arrest and deportation.

Another phase of the anti-Puritan black legend is that these "dismal wretches" had no interest in artistic or intellectual matters, apart from theology. Yet the *Mayflower*, on its voyage to America, was well stocked with books, and not all of them were religious tracts. History, philosophy, travel, poetry, and music were all represented. Among the three hundred volumes in the personal library of William Brewster, one of the original Pilgrim Fathers, was a celebrated musical work by one of the most notable composers of the Elizabethan period, Richard Allison (or Alison). The title is worth quoting in full:

The Psalmes of David in Metre, the plaine song beeing the common tunne to be sung and plaide upon the Lute, Orpharyon, Citterne or Base Violl, severally or altogether, the singing part to be either Tenor or Treble of the instrument, according to the nature of the voyce, or for foure voyces. With tenne short Tunnes in the end, to which for the most part all the Psalmes may be usually sung, for the use of such as are of mean skill, and whose leisure least serveth to practize. . . . (London, 1599).

This title is in itself an informative commentary on the musical practice of those days, and it indicates that Allison's book could be used for a wide variety of musical purposes, ranging from concerted vocal and instrumental performance to the simplest psalmody. Although the Plymouth settlers were certainly among those "whose leisure least

[4] Morton, *New English Canaan*, ed. by C. F. Adams (Boston, 1883), pp. 279–280.

serveth to practize," we know from Winslow's testimony that they were not among "such as are of mean skill." Whatever use Brewster and his companions may have made of Allison's volume, it unquestionably forms a direct link between them and the finest contrapuntal art of Elizabethan England.

The lute, orpharion, and cittern mentioned by Allison were elaborate, delicate, and costly stringed instruments scarcely practical for use in a frontier community. By the beginning of the eighteenth century, such wind instruments as the flute, flageolet, and oboe (then spelled haut-boy) came into general use, along with the violin, and were soon imported by the American colonies. In 1716, an advertisement in the *Boston News* announced the arrival of a shipment of instruments from London, consisting of "Flageolets, Flutes, Haut-boys, Bass-viols, Violins, bows, strings, reeds for haut-boys, books of instruction for all these instruments, books of Ruled Paper. To be sold at the Dancing School of Mr. Enstone in Sudbury Street near the Orange Tree, Boston." So by this time Boston had a fully equipped music store, and located in a Dancing School at that! The mention of ruled paper raises a question in my mind. Ruled paper is for writing music. If the paper was advertized it was probably sold, and if it was sold it was probably used. By whom and for what? Amateurs who studied instruction books for various instruments would perhaps carry their interest a step further and begin writing "Lessons" or other pieces for their favorite instrument. This supposition is strengthened by the fact that treatises on musical composition were available, *and were used in New England*, from the earliest times.

In 1720 the Rev. Thomas Symmes, of Bradford, Massachusetts, published an essay, *The Reasonableness of Regular Singing, or Singing by Note*, in which he writes, among other things, of music at Harvard (founded in 1636). Speaking of what he calls "Regular Singing," Symmes says:

It was studied, known and approved of in our College, for many years after its first founding. This is evident from the Musical Theses which were formerly printed, and from some writings containing some tunes, with directions for singing by note, as they are now sung; and these are yet in being, though of more than sixty years standing; *besides no man that studied music, as it is treated of by Alstead, Playford and others, could be ignorant of it.*

The musical theses and writings to which Symmes refers were subsequently destroyed when the library of Harvard College burned. The passage I have italicized is what concerns us particularly, for Symmes clearly takes it for granted that educated men in New England would be familiar with the theoretical works on music that he mentions. The author whom he calls "Alstead" was Johann Heinrich Alsted (1588–1638), and the work in question is undoubtedly his *Templum Musicum: or, The Musical Synopsis, of the learned and famous J.H.A., being a compendium of the rudiments both of the mathematical and practical part of musick, of which subject not any book is extant in our English tongue. Faithfully translated out of Latin by J. Birchensha . . . London, 1663.*

In spite of this title blurb, Playford's book, *An Introduction to the Skill of Musick,* had been in print since 1654, and new editions appeared at frequent intervals until 1730. It included a section on composing music in parts, to which, after 1683, Henry Purcell contributed. The high standing enjoyed by Playford's book in New England is attested to by the fact that when, in 1698, music came to be included in the *Bay Psalm Book,* the tunes were taken from the eleventh edition of Playford's standard work, which was one of the best books of its kind ever written.

"Vayne and triflying ballades"

"Honest John" Playford was the leading English music publisher of his time, and we can safely assume that his numerous collections of vocal and instrumental music were well known in New England. There is ample evidence that secular songs circulated widely in New England, and the fact that most of the evidence is indirect does not make it any less valid. First of all, let us take an instance that rests upon direct evidence. The Rev. John Cotton had a son who was born at sea on the voyage to America. This son, aptly named Seaborn Cotton, in due course became a student at Harvard and, while there, found time to copy out in his "commonplace book" the words of several English ballads, which were currently sung to popular tunes of the day. Among these ballads are "The Lovesick Maid, or Cordelia's Lamentation for the Absence of Her Gerhard," "The Last Lamentation of the Languishing Squire, or Love Overcomes All Things," and "The Two Faithful Lovers." It is obvious that even in seventeenth-century New England, a young man's fancy turned to thoughts of love, and

that even a divinity student at Harvard could find relaxation in sentimental "tear-jerkers." The ballad of "The Two Faithful Lovers," sung
to the tune of "Franklin Is Fled Away," is a stilted tale of woe, in
dialogue form, which tells of a lover who had to flee from England.
Refusing to be parted from him, his sweetheart dresses as a man and
goes on board; during the voyage to Venice the ship is wrecked and
the girl is drowned. Whereupon the lover laments:

> You loyal lovers all
>   that hear this ditty,
> Sigh and lament my fall,
>   let's move you to pity:
> She lies now in the deep,
> In everlasting sleep,
> And left me here to weep
>   in great distress.

This is pretty poor poetry, evidently the work of some hack, and cannot compare with the magnificent old traditional ballads that undoubtedly circulated through oral tradition in New England. Benjamin Franklin, in a letter to his brother Peter, refers to "some country
girl in the heart of Massachusetts, who has never heard any other than
psalm tunes or 'Chevy Chase,' the 'Children in the Woods,' the 'Spanish Lady,' and such old, simple ditties"—mentioning in a breath three
of the most famous English ballads. Franklin, it is true, was writing
around the middle of the eighteenth century; but his remark indicates
that ballad singing and psalm singing went hand-in-hand in New England. And if a country girl of his generation knew these ballads, we
can be sure that her parents and grandparents sang them before her,
because that is how they were handed down.

The Rev. Thomas Symmes, advocating the establishment of regular singing schools in 1720, argued that these would have "a tendency
to divert young people . . . from learning idle, foolish, yea, pernicious songs and ballads, and banish all such trash from their minds."
How often, in our own times, have the comics been denounced as
trash and all kinds of alternatives been proposed for substituting more
edifying reading matter for our youngsters. Yet the vogue of the
comics continues unabated; and so, no doubt, it was in early New
England with those "idle, foolish, yea, pernicious songs and ballads"
which Reverend Symmes was so anxious to prevent young people
from learning.

Geneva jigs and Puritan hornpipes

Although young people might naturally prefer a little more variety and spice in their vocal diet, the singing of psalms was by no means such a dull and solemn business as is generally supposed. In its heyday it was done with much verve and gusto. Shakespeare, in *The Winter's Tale*, has a character say, "But one Puritan amongst them, and he sings psalms to hornpipes." Now, the hornpipe was a lively dance, and the singing of a psalm to it would make it no less lively. Even if we are not to take Shakespeare's quip literally, the point remains that early Puritan psalm singing gave an impression of liveliness and vigor, which was turned to scorn and ridicule by the enemies of Puritanism. This is confirmed by a passage in John Cotton's treatise, *Singing of Psalms a Gospel Ordinance*, in which he answers objections to psalm singing raised by those who considered the melodies were made by "sinful men." Cotton writes:

> For neither the man of sinne . . . nor any Antichristian Church have had any hand in turning Davids Psalms into English Songs and Tunes, or are wont to make any Melody in Singing them; yea, they reject them as *Genevah Gigs;* and there be Cathedrall Priests of an Antichristian spirit, that have scoffed at Puritan-Ministers, as calling the people to sing one of *Hopkins Jigs,* and so hop into the pulpit.

Let us look more closely at some of the "Genevah Gigs," to see what truth may lie behind these gibing jests.

The Plymouth Pilgrims used a psalm book prepared especially for the Separatist congregation in Holland by Henry Ainsworth and first printed at Amsterdam in 1612 (five other editions followed, the last in 1690). This is the book that Longfellow describes in "The Courtship of Miles Standish," when he pictures Priscilla singing at home:

Open wide in her lap lay the well-worn psalm-book of Ainsworth,
Printed in Amsterdam, the words and the music together,
Rough-hewn, angular notes, like stones in the wall of a churchyard,
Darkened and overhung by the running vine of the verses.

The melodies are for one voice only, printed in the customary diamond-shaped notes of the period, and without bar lines. There are thirty-nine different tunes. Concerning the origin of the melodies, Ainsworth writes:

Tunes for the Psalms I find none set of God; so that each people is to use the most grave, decent and comfortable manner of singing that they know. . . . The singing-notes, therefore, I have most taken from our former Englished Psalms, when they will fit the measure of the verse. And for the other long verses I have also taken (for the most part) the gravest and easiest tunes of the French and Dutch Psalmes.

By "our former Englished Psalms," Ainsworth meant the Sternhold and Hopkins version, which had been completed in 1562. Several years earlier an edition of "Sternhold and Hopkins" had been printed in Geneva for the use of English Protestants who had taken refuge in Switzerland; several of the tunes in this edition were taken from the French psalter, for which the music had been composed or arranged by Louis Bourgeois. Subsequent editions of "Sternhold and Hopkins" continued these borrowings from French sources, so that Ainsworth's psalter actually contained even more tunes of French origin than he suspected. To take one example, the tune for the 100th Psalm, as it appears in both "Sternhold and Hopkins" and "Ainsworth," is derived from the French setting of the 134th Psalm. And this, in turn, bears a striking resemblance to a French secular *chanson* of the sixteenth century, "Il n'a icy celuy qui n'ait sa belle" ("There Is None Here without His Fair One"). A number of other tunes in the French psalter, which eventually found their way, more or less altered, into English psalmbooks, appear to have had a similar origin.

Musically, the *Ainsworth Psalter* is of great interest. The tunes have considerable metrical variety and rhythmic freedom. Only a few of the psalms in Ainsworth's version use the four-line ballad stanza (so-called "common meter") that later became so tiresomely prevalent in English psalmody. Stanzas of five, six, eight, and twelve lines are frequently used by Ainsworth, and he has no less than eight different rhythms for the six-syllable line alone. In the words of Waldo Selden Pratt: "This music represents the folk-song style, with its symmetrical and echoing lines, each with a definite unity and all fused into a total enveloping unity. But it is folk song that has retained great freedom of inner structure. It may be that these thirty-nine melodies illustrate more than one strain of folk-song tradition." [5] Here, then, is a document fully worthy to be the cornerstone of America's music: stem-

[5] Pratt, *The Music of the Pilgrims*.

ming from folk traditions, international in background, marked by melodic freedom and rhythmic variety—qualities that will repay a careful study of the modest little psalter that the Pilgrims brought with them to Plymouth.

Below is a verse from the 100th Psalm, in Ainsworth's translation and spelling, together with the tune as he printed it. ("Jehovah" was pronounced *Jehovay*.)

> Showt to Jehovah, al the earth;
>   Serv ye Jehovah with gladness;
> Before Him come with singing mirth;
>   Know that Jehovah He God is.

This stirring tune, sung in a lively and jubilant spirit,[6] became a favorite with the Pilgrims and Puritans in New England. Nicknamed "Old Hundredth," its popularity as a hymn tune was to continue without interruption through successive generations.[7]

Another tune from the *Ainsworth Psalter*, known as "Old 124" or "Toulon," which is still used in truncated form in modern hymnals, demonstrates the type of melody used for the psalms with five lines and ten syllables to the line, as in this version of Psalm 124:

> Our sowl is as a bird escaped free
>   From out of the intangling fowler's snare.
> The snare is broke and we escaped are.
> Our succour in Jehovah's name shal bee,
> That of the heav'ns and earth is the maker.

---

[6] Rather than "With great dignity" as directed in the 1940 Hymnal of the Protestant Episcopal Church in the United States of America.

[7] The tune of "Old Hundredth" appears with various texts in modern hymnals, but is most generally identified with Thomas Ken's Doxology for his Morning and Evening Hymns (version of 1709), "Praise God, from whom all blessings flow." The famous old tune was also adopted by the Lutheran Church from 1562.

This tune was taken from the *Geneva Psalter* of 1560, and it appears as the "proper" tune for Psalm 124 in "Sternhold and Hopkins."

The early New England settlers really believed in coming before Him "with singing mirth." With St. James they said, "If any be merry, let him sing psalms." If jigs and hornpipes could be turned to the service of God, so much the better. They enjoyed psalm singing not only because it was edifying but also because it was fun.

The *Bay Psalm Book*

The Plymouth colonists continued to use the *Ainsworth Psalter* until 1692, a year after their merger with the larger and more powerful Massachusetts Bay Colony. They apparently found it increasingly difficult to cope with the long and varied melodies of Ainsworth. The prevailing trend was toward the jog-trot ballad stanza of common meter, with alternating lines of eight and six syllables, as illustrated in this translation of the 23d Psalm from the *Bay Psalm Book:*

> The Lord to mee a shepheard is,
> 　want therefore shall not I.
> He in the folds of tender grasse,
> 　doth cause me downe to lie.

The Massachusetts Bay colonists at first used the Sternhold and Hopkins Psalter, but they became dissatisfied with the translations, as not being sufficiently faithful to the original. For this reason a group of New England divines prepared a new version, which was printed at Cambridge, Massachusetts, in 1640, as *The Whole Booke of Psalmes Faithfully Translated into English Metre.* Commonly known as the *Bay Psalm Book*, it was the first book printed in the English colonies of North America and held sway in New England for several generations (the twenty-sixth edition appeared at Boston in 1744). Numerous editions were also printed in England and Scotland. A copy of the first edition was sold at auction in New York in 1947 for $151,000, said to be the highest price ever paid for any book, including the Gutenberg Bible.[8]

No music was included in early editions of the *Bay Psalm Book*, but an "Admonition to the Reader" contained detailed instructions regarding the tunes to which psalms in various meters might be sung. For example, "The verses of these psalmes may be reduced to six kindes, the first whereof may be sung in very neere fourty common tunes; as they are collected out of our chief musicians by Thomas Ravenscroft." The reference to Ravenscroft is significant, for it shows that the New England Puritans were acquainted with the best musical publications of that time. Ravenscroft's psalter had been printed at London in 1621, with the title: *The Whole Booke of Psalmes, with the Hymnes Evangelicall and Songs Spirituall. . . . Newly corrected and enlarged by Thomas Ravenscroft, Bachelar of Musicke.* This notable collection contains four-part settings by many of the most prominent English composers of the period, including Thomas Morley, Thomas Tallis, Giles Farnaby, John Dowland, John Farmer, Michael Cavendish, Richard Allison, and Ravenscroft himself—a total of 105 compositions. Note that the compilers of the *Bay Psalm Book* take pains to mention that Ravenscroft's collection enjoyed the collaboration of "our chief musicians," which would have been a matter of indifference to them had they lacked artistic appreciation.

By the time the ninth edition of the *Bay Psalm Book* was ready to appear, the editors had decided that it should be provided with a selection of the tunes most frequently used. Thus, music was included for the first time in the revised and enlarged edition printed at Boston in 1698, under the title:

> *The Psalms, Hymns, and Spiritual Songs, of the Old and New Testament. . . . For the use, Edification and Comfort of the Saints in publick and private, especially in New-England. The Ninth Edition.*

The music, in two parts (soprano and bass), with solmization syllables, is printed in five pages near the end of the book. The tunes are those known as "Oxford," "Litchfield," "Low-Dutch," "York," "Windsor,"

[8] *The New York Times,* Jan. 29, 1947.

"Cambridge," "St. David's," "Martyrs," "Hackney," "119th Psalm Tune," "100th Psalm Tune," "115th Psalm Tune," and "148th Psalm Tune." For these tunes, the compilers of the *Bay Psalm Book* turned once more to an excellent English source, Playford's *Introduction to the Skill of Musick,* of which numerous editions had been published in London.[9] The instructions for singing the psalms, with the classification in various meters, are also taken from Playford's book. No better guide than Playford could have been chosen.

In contrast to the metrical variety displayed in the melodies of the *Ainsworth Psalter,* nearly all the tunes printed in the *Bay Psalm Book* were in common meter. This was indicative of the trend toward regularity and standardization that made itself increasingly felt in New England psalmody and hymnody during the eighteenth century. But along with this trend toward standardization, as manifested in the movement for "Regular Singing," there was a countercurrent, stemming from the folk, that opposed the imposition of regular rules and standardized procedures in singing. Thus, near the very beginning of America's musical history, we encounter one of those clashes of conflicting cultural traditions that dramatize the creation of a people's music.

[9] Irving Lowens adduces evidence for the existence of an earlier (as yet unlocated) edition of the *Bay Psalm Book* containing music, which may have been printed in England. It also appears that the tunes for the 9th edition of the *Bay Psalm Book* were taken from various editions of Playford's work, not from the 11th edition of 1687 as previously assumed. See Lowens, "The Bay Psalm Book in 17th-Century New England," in *Music and Musicians in Early America* (New York, 1964).

chapter two

New England reformers

They use many Quavers and Semiquavers, &c. And on this very account it is they are pleased with it, and so very loath to part with it.
REV. NATHANIEL CHAUNCEY, REGULAR SINGING DEFENDED, NEW LONDON, 1728.

It is important to understand the conditions under which psalmody and hymnody developed in New England during the eighteenth century and to comprehend, in particular, the nature of the divergent and conflicting cultural trends that made New England a virtual battleground between the zealous reformers who advocated and tried to impose "Regular Singing," and the common folk who preferred their own way of singing, handed down by oral tradition. The reformers, most of whom were clergymen educated at Harvard, held that "the usual way of singing" practiced by the people was an abomination and an offense against good taste. But many of the people clung tenaciously to their own way, for they thoroughly enjoyed it and were therefore "so very loath to part with it," as the Rev. Nathaniel Chauncey wrote. A typical argument of the opponents of the folk style of psalm singing is the following, which appeared in a pamphlet published by Chauncey: "It looks very unlikely to be the right way, because that young people fall in with it; they are not wont to be so forward for anything that is good." [1] This indicates, among other things, that the folk way of singing was not cherished only by die-hard oldsters, but that it also appealed to the younger generation.

The reformers referred to the style of singing to which they were opposed as "the usual way" or "the common way" of singing. The style of singing that they advocated they called "Regular Singing" or "Singing by Note." Each camp was evidently thoroughly convinced of the superior merits of its own kind of singing. There is no indica-

[1] Chauncey, *Regular Singing Defended.*

22

tion, however, that those who practiced "the common way" of singing endeavored to impose their convictions or their methods upon
others. They simply wished to be left alone to sing as they pleased.
It was the reformers, with their righteous zeal, who wanted to impose
their standards on everyone else. The title of a pamphlet written by
the Rev. Nathaniel Chauncey, of Durham, Connecticut, is revealing
in this respect: *Regular Singing Defended and proved to be the only
true way of singing the songs of the Lord. . . .* New London, 1728.
Note the self-righteous tone: this is "the *only* true way."

In his pamphlet, Chauncey employs the method of "Objection"
and "Answer." The arguments advanced in favor of "the common
way" are listed as "Objections." Each objection is followed by an answer intended to refute the argument. For example:

Objection. This way of singing we use in the country is more
solemn, and therefore much more suitable and becoming.

Answer. But suppose by solemn you mean grave and serious.
Nothing makes more against the common way; for they will readily
grant that they use many Quavers and Semiquavers, &c. And on this
very account it is they are pleased with it, and so very loath to part
with it; neither do we own or allow any of them [i.e., "quavers, semiquavers, &c."] in the songs of the Lord. Judge then which is most
solemn.

Notice that in the Objection "the common way" of singing is referred to as the way of singing used in the country, which defines it
as a rural folk tradition. As for the use of "many Quavers and Semiquavers, &c.," we shall deal with that presently when we undertake
to describe the characteristics of the two opposed styles of singing,
one upheld by the common folk, the other by the educated clergy.

The printed accounts of early New England psalm singing that
have come down to us were all written by the advocates of Regular
Singing. The common people sang but did not write. Hence the
written accounts are definitely one-sided. It is upon these one-sided
accounts, polemical and prejudiced as they are, that historians have
based their descriptions of early New England psalmody. For example, in 1721 Cotton Mather wrote: "It has been found . . . in some of
our congregations, that in length of time, their singing has degenerated into an *odd noise*, that has more of what we want a name for,

than any Regular Singing in it." [2] In the same year, Thomas Walter wrote: "I have observed in many places, one man is upon this note while another is upon the note before him, which produces something so hideous and disorderly as is beyond expression bad." Seizing upon such expressions as "an odd noise" and "hideous and disorderly," modern writers have not hesitated to make sweeping generalizations regarding the manner of singing in New England, and have been content to dismiss it as deplorable. They have repeated as objective truth the words of men who were *attacking* something they did not like, something that was contrary to their own interests and inclinations. The procedure is about the same as that of a writer who would base a biography of a public man on material contained in the campaign speeches of his political opponents.

Once we accept the premise that the advocates of Regular Singing are polemical writers, that they are prejudiced and one-sided, we are in a position to use their writings more intelligently and more fruitfully. We may begin by discounting all that comes under the heading of sheer name-calling, which includes such expressions as "an odd noise," and such adjectives as "hideous," "disorderly," and "bad." The same expressions have always been applied to music by people who do not like it.[3] Their only objective value is to indicate that the music to which such terms are applied is *different* from the kind of music to which the name-callers are accustomed or which they regard as "the right thing." These abusive terms, then, serve to confirm the existence of a type of singing that was not "regular," that was not conventional or correct according to educated opinion in early New England.

The next question that we ask is: what were the characteristics of that "common way of singing" to which the reformers were so strongly opposed? Since the writings of the reformers are the only sources of *written documentation* that we possess, we must extract our information from them. But we must look for whatever objective information may be imbedded in the polemical verbiage. Chauncey's

[2] Mather, *The Accomplished Singer*, published in 1721 and "Intended for the assistance of all that sing psalms with grace in their hearts: but more particularly to accompany the laudable endeavours of those who are learning to sing by Rule, and seeking to preserve a REGULAR SINGING in the Assemblies of the Faithful."

[3] For a thorough (and entertaining) documentation of this statement, consult the *Lexicon of Musical Invective* by Nicolas Slonimsky (New York, 1953).

statement regarding the "use of many Quavers and Semiquavers, &c." (that *etcetera* is very important) is an example of objective information that may be extracted from a polemical context. This written documentation can be supplemented by the evidence of folklore, which, being a survival of archaic practices, is a valuable adjunct to cultural history. The evidence furnished by folklore will be discussed later in this chapter.

The reformers

The leaders of the reform movement in New England's singing methods were the Rev. Thomas Symmes (1677–1725), the Rev. John Tufts (1689–1750), and the Rev. Thomas Walter (1696–1725), supported by a number of other clergymen, such as the Rev. Cotton Mather and the Rev. Nathaniel Chauncey, who preached and wrote in favor of "Regular Singing" or "Singing by Note." The Rev. John Tufts, a graduate of Harvard, published a little work called *A Very Plain and Easy Introduction to the Singing of Psalm Tunes,* which may have been issued around 1714, though no edition earlier than the fifth (Boston, 1726) has been located. This went through eleven editions up to 1744. It was a modest pamphlet of only twelve pages, containing thirty-seven tunes set in three parts, with instructions for singing adapted from Ravenscroft and Playford. Instead of musical notation, Tufts used letters to indicate the notes of the scale, according to the system of solmization then prevalent: F (fa), S (sol), L (la), M (mi). The time value of the notes was indicated by a system of punctuation. A letter standing alone was equal to a quarter note; a letter followed by a period was equal to a half note; and one followed by a colon, to a whole note. Tufts thought he had introduced an "easy method of singing by letters instead of notes," but his system was not widely adopted.

The Rev. Thomas Walter of Roxbury was also a graduate of Harvard, though during his student days he thought more of social pleasure than of application to his studies. Fortunately he had a good memory and supplemented his education by listening to the remarkable conversation of his learned uncle, Cotton Mather. In 1721, Walter brought out *The Grounds and Rules of Musick Explained, or An Introduction to the Art of Singing by Note. . . .* Boston, Printed by J. Franklin (who, by the way, was James Franklin, older brother of

Benjamin, who was then an apprentice in the shop). Walter's book went through at least eight editions, the last in 1764. It was highly regarded and exerted wide influence for upwards of forty years. It was the first music book to be printed with bar lines in the North American colonies.

The alternate title of Thomas Walter's book, *An Introduction to the Art of Singing by Note*, claims closer attention at this point. As we observed above, "singing by note" was one of the terms used by the musical reformers to designate the "correct" or "regular" way of singing that they advocated, which in effect meant singing the notes as written or printed, without alterations, additions, or embellishments, and in strict time and pitch. In his preface, Walter asserts that he was thoroughly familiar with the common or country way of singing, and speaks of himself as one "who can sing all the various Twistings of the old Way, and that too according to the *genius* of most of the Congregations." By the latter statement he meant that each congregation had its own special manner of singing within the style of the old or common way. It was only natural that Walter should be familiar with this manner of singing, since it was the way practiced by most people. But as a college graduate, and an up-to-date, progressive young clergyman, he repudiated the old, common way of singing, and denounced it in the strongest terms. He writes of tunes which

. . . are now miserably tortured, and twisted, and quavered, in some churches, into an horrid Medley of confused and disorderly Noises. . . . Our tunes are, for Want of a Standard to appeal to in all our Singing, left to the Mercy of every unskilful Throat to chop and alter, twist and change, according to their infinitely divers and no less odd Humours and Fancies. . . .

And he sadly concludes: "Our Tunes have passed through strange Metamorphoses . . . since their first introduction into the World." Metamorphosis, or change, is the fate of all folk music, and constitutes indeed one of its defining traits. So Walter is simply telling us, indirectly, that these tunes underwent what we would now call a process of folklorization. (The term "folklore," by the way, did not come into usage until after 1840.)

In defending the Regular Way of singing psalm tunes, Walter writes: "And this I am sure of, we sing them as they are prick'd down, and I am sure the Country People do not." Of course not; they never do.

The *New England Courant* for March 5, 1722, contains this significant item:

On Thursday last in the afternoon, a Lecture was held at the New Brick Church [Boston], by the Society for Promoting Regular Singing in the worship of God. The Rev. Thomas Walter of Roxbury preach'd an excellent Sermon on that Occasion, *The Sweet Psalmist of Israel*. The Singing was perform'd in Three Parts (according to Rule) by about Ninety Persons skill'd in that Science, to the great Satisfaction of a Numerous Assembly there Present.

This sermon was afterwards printed, also by J. Franklin, under the following title: *The sweet Psalmist of Israel: A Sermon Preach'd at the Lecture held in Boston, by the Society for promoting Regular and Good Singing, and for reforming the Depravations and Debasements our Psalmody labours under, In Order to introduce the proper and true Old Way of Singing. . . .* (Boston, 1722.)

Both of these citations are interesting for several reasons. The first reveals that there was a Society for Promoting Regular Singing at Boston in the early 1720s, and that there then existed large choral groups trained to sing in parts. The second defines the aims of the reform movement as the correction of the "depravations and debasements" of New England psalmody, and the introduction of "the proper and true Old Way of Singing." If the reformers stood for new methods and the correction of existing abuses, why did they speak of restoring the Old Way of Singing, and why was this the "proper and true" way? The Rev. Thomas Symmes will help us to answer these questions.

Symmes's anonymous pamphlet, *The Reasonableness of Regular Singing, or Singing by Note* (1720), is subtitled "An Essay to revive the true and ancient mode of Singing psalm-tunes according to the pattern of our New-England psalm-books." According to Symmes, singing by note was "the ancientest way" among the early New England settlers. Emphasizing this point, he writes:

There are persons now living, children and grand-children of the *first* settlers of New-England, who can very well remember that their Ancestors sung by *note*, and they learned to sing of them, and they have more than their bare words to prove that they speak the truth, for many of them can sing tunes exactly by note which they learnt of their fathers.

Symmes will also define for us Regular Singing or Singing by Note:

> Now singing by note is giving every note its proper pitch, and turning the voice in its proper place, and giving to every note its true length and sound. Whereas, the usual way varies much from this. In it, some notes are sung too high, others too low, and most too long, and many turnings or flourishings with the voice (as they call them) are made where they should not be, and some are wanting where they should have been.

This is an extremely significant passage, for it sums up the two opposing styles of singing that were contending for supremacy in New England. Regular Singing was according to the pattern of the psalm-books: giving to every note its proper pitch and true length as "prick'd" in the book, and turning the voice only as required by the melody. This, according to the reformers, was the proper and true "Old Way of Singing." How and why, then, was it abandoned and allowed to undergo "depravations and debasements," to become incrusted with what Cotton Mather called "indecencies"? Again, the obliging Mr. Symmes has an explanation:

> The declining from, and getting beside the rule, was *gradual and insensible*. Singing Schools and Singing books being laid aside, there was no way to learn; but only by hearing of tunes sung, or by taking the run of the tune, as it is phrased. The rules of singing not being taught or learnt, every one sang as best pleased himself, and every leading-singer, would take the liberty of raising any note of the tune, or lowering of it, as best pleased his ear; and add such turns and flourishes as were grateful to him; and this was done so gradually, as that but few if any took notice of it. One Clerk or Chorister would alter the tunes a little in his day, the next a little in his, and so on one after another, till in fifty or sixty years it caused a considerable alteration. If the alteration had been made designedly by any Master of Music, it is probable that the variation from our psalm-books would have been alike in all our congregations; whereas some vary much more than others, and it is hard to find two that sing exactly alike. . . . Your usual way of singing is handed down by tradition only, and whatsoever is only so conveyed

down to us, it is a thousand to one if it be not miserably corrupted, in three or four-score years' time. . . .

The Rev. Thomas Symmes is truly invaluable; what he tells us is interesting, but what he reveals between the lines is priceless. He does not explain why the singing schools and singing books should have been laid aside by the early colonists, he just assumes that they were. However, he does trace very revealingly, though with no intention of doing so, the formation of a folk tradition. Let us note some of its characteristics: it is handed down by tradition only (that is, by oral tradition, since books had been set aside); the variation from the standard norm (that is, from the tunes as printed) is not uniform, but differs from congregation to congregation, so that hardly any two sing exactly alike; the singing was not learned by rule or lesson, but by ear, and everyone sang as best pleased himself; the leading-singer would raise or lower notes at will, and add such turns and flourishes as he pleased. In short, we have here the complete description of a folk tradition in singing. We may therefore call this the Early New England Folk Style.

Some musical historians account for the "decline" of New England psalmody by pointing to the difficult conditions of frontier life, aggravated by political dissension and military strife. This explanation falls through when we realize that a similar "decline" took place in England, which was not precisely a struggling colony. In the preface to his edition of *Psalms and Hymns in solemn musick* (1671), Playford vividly describes the sad state of psalm singing in England at that time, concluding with the assertion that "this part of God's service hath been so ridiculously performed in most places, that it is now brought into scorn and derision by many people." Apparently the "decline" continued for a long time, because in 1796 a letter in the *Gentleman's Magazine*, referring to psalm singing in England, states: "In some churches one may see the Parish Clerk, after giving out a couple of staves from Sternhold and Hopkins, with two or three other poor wights, drawling them out in the most lamentable strains, with such grimaces, and in such discordant notes, as must shock every serious person, and afford mirth to the undevout." [4] We gather from these quotations that, in every generation, there was a kind of singing going on, both in old and new England, that offended the taste and

---

[4] Quoted by Curwen, *Studies in Music Worship*, p. 30.

provoked the scorn and ridicule of educated persons because it failed to conform to the culturally dominant standards of "good" singing.

Summarizing the characteristics of the Early New England Folk Style as described by contemporary writers: the singing is very slow; many grace notes, passing notes, turns, flourishes and other ornaments are used; pitch and time values are arbitrarily altered; there is a lack of synchronization among the voices; everyone sings as best pleases himself. This is not to be taken as a complete description of the style, because the reformers were interested only in pointing out what they considered some of its most prominent faults: they cover up many details with an "&c." In order to spell out that *etcetera* we must find an analogous and more fully documented tradition. It will then be within the bounds of reasonable conjecture to assume that the New England Folk Style embodied the traits of the analogous tradition.

The logical place to look for this analogous tradition is in eighteenth-century England and Scotland, whence came the early New England settlers. We may begin by glancing at the old Gaelic psalmody of Scotland. Our earliest written documentation on this tradition dates from the 1840s, but its persistence from generation to generation enables us to reconstruct the eighteenth-century practice with reasonable fidelity. John Spencer Curwen, the English authority on congregational singing who wrote at a time when Gaelic psalmody could still be heard in Highland parishes in much the same manner as it was sung a hundred years earlier, summarized the main features of this tradition as follows: "There are five tunes—*French, Martyrs, Stilt* (or *York*), *Dundee,* and *Elgin*—which are the traditional melodies used for the Psalms. These have been handed down from generation to generation, amplified by endless grace notes, and altered according to the fancy of every precentor. When used, they are sung so slowly as to be beyond recognition." And he adds: "Each parish and each precentor had differences of detail, for the variations were never written or printed, but were handed down by tradition." Now, is this not, in all essential points, an exact counterpart of the description of the "usual" New England way of psalm singing as contained in the writings of Symmes and his colleagues?

Note that the traditional repertory consisted of five tunes. Writers on early New England psalmody have continually harped on the theme that only five or six tunes seem to have been commonly used in the Puritan congregations, and they have adduced this as further evidence of the musical impoverishment of Puritan New England. When we stop to consider that in England the number of psalm tunes in common usage in the second half of the seventeenth century had dwindled down to six or eight, we realize that New England enjoyed no position of privileged inferiority in this respect. Here, again, it is necessary to look at the matter from a different point of view, and to regard this limitation of repertory as characteristic of the folk tradition with which we are dealing; in England, in Scotland, in America, the same pattern prevails. This small inherited repertory of tunes provided a firm foundation for the improvisations and embellishments of the folk style. There was a core of unity with scope for endless variety. (Compare the core of "stock" tunes used in hot jazz improvisation, as another illustration of the same principle.)

Before going on to see what we can discover in eighteenth-century England, we may pause to discuss briefly the practice of "lining-out," a prominent feature of folk psalmody in England, Scotland, and New England. The nature of lining-out is explained by the ordinances of the Westminster Assembly of 1644 which recommend the adoption of the practice in English churches: ". . . for the present, where many of the congregation cannot read, it is convenient that the minister, or some other fit person appointed by him and the other officers, do read the psalm, line by line, before the singing thereof." The Rev. John Cotton, in his treatise *Singing of Psalms a Gospel Ordinance* (Boston, 1647), granted that "where all have books and can reade, or else can say the *Psalme* by heart, it were needless then to reade each line of the Psalme beforehand in order to singing." But where this is not the case, he adds, "it will be a necessary helpe, that the lines of the Psalme, be openly read beforehand, line after line, or two lines together, that so they who want either books or skill to reade, may know what is to be sung, and joyne with the rest in the dutie of singing." The practice of lining-out became fairly widespread in New England, to judge by a passage in Cotton Mather's *Church Discipline; or Methods and Customs in the Churches in New England* (Boston, 1726):

In some [churches], the assembly being furnished with Psalm-books, they sing without the stop of reading between every line. But ordinarily the Psalm is read line after line, by him whom the Pastor desires to do that service; and the people generally sing in such grave tunes, as are the most usual in the churches of our nation.

The practice of lining-out has been deplored, condemned, and ridiculed by most writers on early American music. Once again, the important thing is to understand, not to sneer. Granted that the custom was introduced as a practical and temporary expedient, how shall we account for its persistence in circumstances where these practical considerations were not a factor? How shall we account for the tenaciousness with which the people clung to it, and their resentment of, and determined opposition to, all efforts to abolish the custom? How shall we account for the fact that it has endured, in one form or another, for more than three hundred years? John Cotton admitted—what is in any case quite obvious—that lining-out had no practical justification where the people knew the psalms by heart. Yet the custom prevailed even when the repertory of psalms was limited, orally transmitted, and learned by memory. We must, therefore, seek some other *raison d'être* for the practice of lining-out. This will be found if we can locate a tradition in which lining-out was not an expedient, but an organic element of style. For this we return momentarily to the Highlands of Scotland.

The Scottish church accepted the custom of lining-out reluctantly, under a directive from the Westminster Assembly in the middle of the seventeenth century. Yet, when attempts to abolish it were made a hundred years later, great resentment arose among the people of Scotland, and in some parishes the custom was not abandoned until well into the nineteenth century. As Curwen writes: "Lining-out, which had at first been resented as a concession to illiterate England, was clung to as a vital principle." Now, what had happened in the interval to transform lining-out from a foreign imposition to a "vital principle" of Scottish popular psalmody? The tradition of Gaelic psalmody will help us to answer this question. Dr. Joseph Mainzer published a monograph on *Gaelic Psalm-Tunes* in 1844, in which he collected vestiges of the traditional psalmody handed down through many generations. In these psalms the lining-out becomes an integral musical factor. The precentor gives out one line at a time, chanting it on the tonic or dominant, according to the key of the tune. According to Mainzer, the dominant is preferred, but if it is too high or too low for the voice, the tonic is taken. The recitative is not always on a monotone: it often touches the tone next above. The congregation then sings the line *with much elaboration of the melody.*

This shows the process by which an apparently extraneous element is incorporated into a folk tradition and becomes an organic stylistic factor. Because of this it is "clung to as a vital principle"—not because the people prefer what is "bad" in opposition to what the learned doctors from Oxford or Harvard tell them is "good." We have already seen that the Gaelic tradition of psalmody had several points of similarity with the Early New England Folk Style. We should not jump to the conclusion that the details of lining-out were identical in the two traditions. It is sufficient to have established, by analogy, that lining-out was an organic element in the folk tradition of New England psalmody. It should be pointed out, moreover, that lining-out constitutes a form of the "call-and-response" pattern that is basic in certain folk-song traditions, including the Afro-American. Lining-out still persists in the singing of some Negro congregations.

In 1724 the *New England Courant* published a curious satirical letter attacking the so-called defects of popular psalmody, written by an individual who signed himself "Jeoffrey Chanticleer" and who may have been James Franklin. Lining-out is the particular target of his attack, and in describing what he considers the evil results of this practice he sheds additional light on the Early New England Folk Style of psalmody. According to "Jeoffrey Chanticleer":

> . . . the same person who sets the Tune, and guides the Congregation in Singing, commonly reads the Psalm, which is a task so few are capable of performing well, that in Singing two or three staves the Congregation falls from a cheerful Pitch to downright *Grumbling;* and then some to relieve themselves mount an Eighth above the rest, others perhaps a Fourth or Fifth, by which means the Singing appears to be rather a confused Noise, made up of *Reading, Squeaking,* and *Grumbling,* than a decent and orderly part of God's Worship. . . .[5]

Translating this into unpolemical language, we get an aural image of a successive lowering of pitch among the main body of the congregation carrying the tune, while other voices sing above it at intervals of a fourth, a fifth, or an octave. Compare Curwen's account of "two old ladies in the North of England who were noted among their friends for their power of improvising a high part above the melody of the tune." This custom, he adds, had been common, "and it was

[5] Quoted by Foote, *Three Centuries of American Hymnody,* p. 376.

always considered a sign of musicianship to be able to sing this part."
This last remark should be emphasized, for it underlines the point we
are trying to establish throughout this chapter: that what is considered bad taste or "a confused Noise" by conventional standards may
be regarded as a sign of musicianship and a source of pride in the folk
tradition.

We must quote another brief passage from the letter of "Jeoffrey
Chanticleer": "The Words are often murder'd or metamorphos'd by
the *Tone* of the Reader. By this Means it happens in some churches,
that those who neglect to carry Psalm Books with them, only join
in Singing *like so many musical Instruments*, piping out the Tune to
the rest. . . ." (The italics are mine.) Any reader acquainted with
the history of opera will recognize the general trend of these remarks as being similar to criticisms leveled at the florid vocal style
of Italian opera and oratorio: that the words could not be understood,
and that the human voice was therefore used merely as an instrument.
Compare, for example, Benjamin Franklin's remark on the vocal style
of Handel and other contemporary composers, in which "the voice
aims to be like an instrument" (see p. 96).

In England, where organs and other instruments were used in the
established church, some observers commented adversely on what
they regarded as the abuse of ornamentation in the organ accompaniments. A certain William Riley, who in 1762 published a book
titled *Parochial Music Corrected*, complained that the parish organists
introduced tedious variations in every line, indulged in ill-timed flourishes, and insisted on putting a "shake" (trill) at the end of every
line. He quotes as an absurd example:

> The Lord's commands are righteous and (*shake*)
>   Rejoice the heart likewise;
> His precepts are most pure and do (*shake*)
>   Give light unto the eyes.

Instrumental music was, of course, forbidden in the Puritan churches
of New England, though organs were used in such Episcopalian
churches in America as King's Chapel in Boston (which acquired in
1713 an organ bequeathed by Mr. Thomas Brattle) and Bruton Parish
Church in Williamsburg, Virginia. The reason I have made reference
to organ playing in English parish churches is because of the obvious

analogy with New England psalm singing suggested by "Jeoffrey Chanticleer's" previousy quoted remark that the people "join in Singing like so many musical Instruments, piping out the Tune to the rest." We may conclude that the people of New England, deprived of musical instruments in church, did their best to supply this lack by using their voices for the production of those shakes, flourishes, and variations that so annoyed the worthy Mr. Riley no less than the sarcastic "Chanticleer."

According to Curwen, congregational singing in English parish churches during the eighteenth century "was a string of grace-notes, turns, and other embellishments." This is exactly what Symmes, Walter, Chauncey, and other contemporary writers tell us about the popular psalmody of early New England, except that their statements are surrounded with polemical verbiage, which has to be cleared away before we can get at the truth. Though Curwen wrote in the 1870s, he interviewed informants whose memory and experience reached back to the early years of the century, and who spoke of traditional practices handed down from an earlier generation. One informant stated that in his early days, when the melody leaped a third, the women invariably added the intervening note; and if it leaped more than a third, they glided up or down, portamento, giving the next note in anticipation. Another informant confirmed the common use of appoggiaturas and gliding from one note to another. Another told of men in his congregation who "sing the air through the tune until they get to the end, and then, if the melody ends low, they will scale up in falsetto to the higher octave, and thus make harmony at the end." [6] I am not prepared to state categorically that these practices prevailed in eighteenth-century New England, but there is every reason to believe that they did, for they evidently belonged to the same tradition of folk psalmody and would doubtless have contributed to conveying an impression of what learned gentlemen like Cotton Mather called "an odd Noise."

[6] Curwen's informant also told him that "in the old times the people liked the tunes pitched high; the women especially enjoyed screaming out high G. It made the psalmody more brilliant and far-sounding." It should be observed that in those days it was the men, not the women, who carried the "tune" or principal air; therefore, the screaming on high notes may have been a compensatory means of feminine self-assertion.

Thus far we have relied upon analogy, conjecture, description, and tradition for our reconstruction of the Early New England Folk Style of psalmody. These methods are legitimate; yet it would be gratifying to be able to reinforce them with an actual musical document of the eighteenth century. Such a document exists, though from a slightly later period than the one we are discussing. Once again I am indebted to the admirable Curwen for putting me on its track. Let Curwen tell the story in his own words:

Mr. John Dobson, of Richmond, has shown me an interesting publication by Matthew Camidge, organist of York Minster, bearing the date 1789. Camidge discovered in a library same psalm-tunes composed by Henry Lawes, a musician of the time of Charles I. He came to the conclusion that these tunes, if amended in accordance with modern feeling, might be revived for church uses. What did he mean by this amendment? Simply the addition of passing notes in the melody, trills, and such like devices. In order to show the reader how greatly he has improved Henry Lawes, Camidge prints the original and amended versions side by side throughout the book, and the result is ludicrous. The taste of today has returned to that of Lawes' time, but the old-fashioned tricks of vocalisation may still be heard from old people in remote country places.[7]

In other words, the once fashionable style of singing lived on as folk-lore, as an archaic survival, long after it ceased to be part of the dominant cultural pattern: a perfect example of the process of "folklorization." The result of Camidge's "improvement" of Lawes' music appeared "ludicrous" to Curwen, regarded solely from an aesthetic or artistic point of view. But from the historical point of view, Camidge's versions throw valuable light on the tradition of embellished psalmody in the eighteenth century.

Camidge's volume, entitled *Psalmody for a Single Voice*, is extremely rare. No copy exists in the United States, as far as is known, and until recently there was none in the British Museum in London. I was able to obtain a microfilm of the copy that is in the National Library of Scotland. The following musical example, a setting of Psalm 1 in the translation of George Sandys, illustrates both the original unadorned melody by Lawes and the "Variation" or embellished version of Camidge:

[7] Curwen, *op. cit.*, p. 66.

Original

Variation

That Man is tru - ly ____ blest who_scorns to

stray By false ad-vice or walk theSin-ners__ way, Or ____

deigns to_min-gle_ with the_Sons of Pride Who God con -

temn_and_ Pi - e· - ty de - ride.

Like most codified and printed versions of music that stems primarily from oral tradition, Camidge's version probably gives a schematic presentation of the actual traditional practice. Yet it is revealing as far as it goes.[8]

It remains to explain how New England psalmody, which among the original Plymouth Pilgrims and the first Puritan settlers was evidently "regular" (that is, according to the strict notes of the melody, and sung in a lively tempo), acquired the characteristics of embellished and slow-paced psalmody that we have been discussing. In the first place, the Pilgrims or Separatists, who had taken refuge in Holland, and the early Puritans, many of whom had lived in Geneva, were strongly influenced by the methods and customs of the French, Swiss, and Dutch Protestants, among whom the practice of lining-out was not used in psalm singing. My belief is that regular "singing by note" and the lively pace called for by the vigorous and varied tunes of the early psalters prevailed in New England, as in England and Scotland, until the spread of lining-out opened the door for the introduction of the florid style. The custom of lining-out in psalmody necessarily interrupted the free flow of the music and caused a slackening of the pace. To this may be added the natural tendency of some persons in an untrained and undirected group to sing more slowly than others —to take, as it were, their own time. This could have the effect of slowing up the whole group, but it could also have a more important effect in permitting the more skilled, or the more ambitious, or the bolder members of the group to indulge in the embellishments to which we have so often referred. The late G. P. Jackson aptly called this "a compensatory florid filling in." And why, it may be asked, did they indulge in these embellishments? Simply because they enjoyed it, because it was fun. The Rev. Nathaniel Chauncey is explicit on this point: "They use many Quavers and Semiquavers, &c. *And on this very account it is they are pleased with it, and so very loath to part with it.*"

When Henry W. Foote, in his history of American hymnody, writes that the old psalm tunes "which had once been sung with vigor and at reasonable speed, had become flattened with usage into weari-

[8] For other examples of the tradition of embellished psalmody and hymnody, the reader may wish to compare, in the present work, the ornamented versions of "Ah, Lovely Appearance of Death" (p. 49), "Amazing Grace" (p. 203), "I Stood Outside de Gate" (p. 250), and "Jordan's Stormy Banks" (p. 456).

some and dragging measures which had lost all their freshness and vitality," he expresses a modern opinion that actually distorts the whole situation by failing to take into account the values of the tradition which he is attempting to discuss. If the people who sang in that manner found it dull and wearisome, they would have sought some other manner of singing that pleased them better. But they did nothing of the sort. On the contrary, they clung tenaciously to their own style of singing. They liked it. And who is to say that they should have preferred something else?

It would be interesting to trace the transition from plain to embellished psalmody that took place in New England during the seventeenth century. But the available documentation scarcely permits us to trace the process in detail. We must not, in any case, assume that the process was complete and uniform; that is to say, that it occurred all at once and everywhere at the same time. Cultural processes are never as simple as that. As an illustration of this particular phase of cultural dynamics, let us take two representative dates and events. Symmes tells us that the Plymouth colonists took up the practice of lining-out at about the same time that they abandoned the *Ainsworth Psalter*, around the year 1692. And lining-out, as we have seen, prepared the way for the growth of responsorial, embellished, and improvisational psalmody. Now, only a few years later, in 1699, the practice of lining-out was abolished at the Brattle Square Church in Boston. In other words, the relatively backward and undeveloped colony at Plymouth was taking up a traditional practice which the relatively advanced and progressive city of Boston was on the point of abandoning. The sophisticated urban congregation was discarding a custom that already began to be associated with rural crudeness and backwardness. In the course of time, as urban culture tended to dominate the whole New England area, lining-out disappeared from that region and took refuge in the relatively undeveloped frontier sections.

The movement for Regular Singing led to the rise of singing schools. Reverend Symmes was one of the reformers who argued most persuasively in favor of regular musical instruction to improve the quality of singing:

Would it not greatly tend to promote singing of psalms if singing schools were promoted? Would not this be a conforming to scripture pattern? Have we not as much need of them as God's people of old? Have we any reason to expect to be inspired with the gift of singing, any more than that of reading? . . . Where would be the difficulty, or what the disadvantage, if people who want skill in singing, would procure a skillful person to instruct them, and meet two or three evenings in the week, from five or six o'clock to eight, and spend the time in learning to sing? Would not this be an innocent and profitable recreation, and would it not have a tendency, if prudently managed, to prevent the unprofitable expense of time on other occasions? . . . Are they not very unwise who plead against learning to sing by rule, when they can't learn to sing at all, unless they learn by rule? [9]

As the eighteenth century advanced, more and more people decided that it was a pleasant recreation to come together at certain times to receive instruction in Regular Singing and to sing as a group the music that they learned. Thus the singing schools prospered and became an important institution during the second half of the century. The singing schools had to be provided with instruction books and collections of tunes. Hence the thriving trade in music books compiled and issued by the successors of Tufts and Walter. The singing schools did not exclusively promote the singing of psalms. Hymns, spiritual songs, and anthems were soon added to the repertory. Then came the exciting "fuguing tunes," which in turn proved to be the center of another controversy.

The singing school, as an institution, developed in two directions. In the cities it prepared the way for the formation of choirs and choral societies, such as the celebrated Handel and Haydn Society of Boston, devoted chiefly to the performance of music imported from Europe. In the rural areas, mainly in the South and Middle West, it formed the foundation for a homespun hymnody and for a communal type of singing that kept alive many of the old New England tunes along with the later "revival spirituals" and camp-meeting songs that were a distinct product of the American frontier.

The rise of evangelical hymnody, largely under the impulse of Methodism, and the transition from psalmody to hymnody, together with the musical activities of various dissenting sects and minority groups, will form the subject matter of the next chapter.

[9] Symmes, *The Reasonableness of Regular Singing.*

chapter three

Singing dissenters

Likewise in Amerikay
Shines the glorious Gospel-day.
JOSEPH HUMPHREYS, SACRED HYMNS.

The attitude of nonconformity represented by the Separatists and other Puritans who first settled in New England continued to manifest itself in many successive or simultaneous dissenting movements and groups that spread throughout the American colonies and had, in several instances, a lasting influence after the formation of the Republic. Through the inevitable irony of history, the nonconformists of one generation became the conformists of the next. Psalmody, which had been a symbol of Protestant and Puritan dissent, came to be regarded in the eighteenth century as a sign of adherence to restricted and arbitrary forms of worship. The nonconformist English divine, Dr. Isaac Watts (1674–1748), strongly objected to the old, strict, metrical psalmody, and even protested, in the preface to his *Hymns and Spiritual Songs* (1707), against the very contents of the psalms:

> Some of 'em are almost opposite to the Spirit of the Gospel: Many of them foreign to the State of the New-Testament, and widely different from the present Circumstances of Christians. . . .

On the other hand, those who clung to the old metrical psalmody, as opposed to the new hymns, were convinced that the word of God was being impiously replaced by "man-made" concoctions. Actually, a few hymns had been included in the appendixes of the metrical psalters as early as the sixteenth century. And the first supplement to Tate and Brady's *New Version of the Psalms*, issued in 1700, included three hymns for Holy Communion, two for Easter, and the familiar Christmas hymn beginning, "While shepherds watched their flocks by night," based on a passage from Luke (2:8–14). In the early years of the eighteenth century, the hymns of Dr. Watts swept like a flood over England and soon spread to the North American colonies.

The influence of Dr. Watts in America was enormous. The first American edition of his *Hymns and Spiritual Songs* appeared in 1739, but his hymns and paraphrases of the psalms were known on this side of the ocean many years before that. As early as 1711 the Rev. Benjamin Colman of Boston wrote to Cotton Mather, saying: "Mr. Watts is a great Master in Poetry, and a burning Light and Ornament of the Age. . . . You will forgive me that I emulate, and have dared to imitate, his Muse in the Inclosed. . . ." [1]

Colman was not the only imitator of Watts in America. There were many others, among them that precocious literary ornament of New England, the famous Dr. Mather Byles, hailed by a contemporary as "Harvard's honour and New England's hope." In his early youth, Byles addressed the following admiring verses to Dr. Watts:

> What Angel strikes the trembling Strings;
> And whence the golden Sound!
> Or is it Watts—or Gabriel sings
> From yon celestial Ground?

Watts did not entirely discard the psalms. He selected those that he considered most appropriate for Christian worship and paraphrased them freely. In 1719 he brought out *The Psalms of David Imitated,* of which an American edition was printed at Philadelphia by Benjamin Franklin ten years later. The "System of Praise" of Dr. Watts continued to gain favor in America, though eventually the Revolution made it necessary to emend certain passages in which he alluded to British sovereignty and the glory of British arms. In 1784 the ingenious Mr. Joel Barlow of Connecticut was appointed to "accommodate" the psalms of Dr. Watts for American usage. Barlow, a poet of some reputation and one of the group of "Hartford Wits," aroused some opposition by making too free with Dr. Watts. For this he was censured by a fellow rhymster:

> You've proved yourself a sinful cre'tur;
> You've murdered Watts, and spoilt the metre;

[1] Cotton Mather, *Diary*, Dec. 2, 1711. Quoted by Foote, *Three Centuries of American Hymnody*, p. 65.

> You've tried the Word of God to alter,
> And for your pains deserve a halter.

But the alteration of "the word of God" had gone too far to be halted even by threats of a halter. Paraphrases of the psalms became so free that they could scarcely be distinguished from the new hymnody that soon prevailed almost everywhere in the English-speaking world. Timothy Dwight, president of Yale College, paraphrased a portion of the 137th Psalm ("If I forget thee, O Jerusalem, let my right hand forget her cunning") and produced what turned out to be a favorite hymn:

> I love thy Kingdom, Lord,
>   The house of thine abode,
> The Church our blest Redeemer saved
>   With his own precious blood.

The blood of the Redeemer was to be a recurrent theme of evangelical hymnody, and thence of the revival spirituals ("Are you washed in the blood of the Lamb?").

Later Dwight himself was commissioned to prepare another "accommodation" of Watts's version of the psalms, which he did with a characteristic combination of poetic and patriotic zeal. There is more of General Washington than of King David in Dwight's "accommodation" of Watts's paraphrase of the 18th Psalm:

> When, fir'd to rage, against our nation rose
> Chiefs of proud name, and bands of haughty foes,
> He train'd our hosts to fight, with arms array'd,
> With health invigor'd, and with bounty fed,
> Gave us his chosen chief our sons to guide,
> Heard every prayer, and every want supplied.
> He gave their armies captive to our hands,
> Or sent them frustrate to their native lands.

Such paraphrases of scripture, sometimes with local or topical allusions inserted, were frequently set to music by New England composers of the eighteenth century. But that is another chapter of our story; for the present we must return to the spread of evangelical hymnody, a movement, which, receiving its initial impulse from Isaac Watts, was given an extraordinary impetus through the work and influence of the Wesleys, John and Charles.

The Wesleys in America

In the year 1735 Governor Oglethorpe of Georgia was in England seeking ways to strengthen his recently founded colony. Realizing the importance of religion as a stabilizing factor in a frontier settlement, he invited a serious-minded young minister named John Wesley to accompany him to Georgia and preach to the colonists there. John Wesley and his younger brother Charles were then active in Oxford as members of a group of religious zealots known variously as the "Holy Club," the "Bible Moths," and the "Methodists" (because they studied methodically—a strange innovation at the university). The elder Wesley accepted Oglethorpe's invitation, and Charles decided to go along with him. Together they embarked on the ship *Simmons*, bound for Savannah.

On board the ship was a group of twenty-six Moravian missionaries, members of a persecuted German Protestant sect, under the leadership of Bishop Nitschmann and Peter Boehler. These Moravian brethren were enthusiastic hymn singers, and their hymnody made a deep impression upon the Wesleys. The English brothers remembered one occasion particularly, when, during a severe storm that terrified most of the passengers, the Moravian missionaries calmly stood on the deck singing their hymns, entirely unperturbed by the raging storm and the towering waves. John Wesley began at once to study the hymnbooks of the Moravians, as attested by an entry in his journal for October 27, 1735: "Began Gesang Buch," referring to *Das Gesang-Buch der Gemeine in Herrnhut*, the principal hymnal of the Moravian brethren in their central community at Herrnhut, Germany.

When their ship sailed into the Savannah River, John Wesley was agreeably surprised by the sight of "the pines, palms, and cedars running in rows along the shore," making "an exceedingly beautiful prospect, especially to us who did not expect to see the bloom of spring in the depths of winter." The admiration was not all one-sided, for during his sojourn in Savannah, John Wesley apparently made a considerable impression upon a young lady by the name of Sophia Hopkey, a niece of the chief magistrate of that town. The young Methodist, however, balked at matrimony, and departed from the colony a free man.

Feminine allurements notwithstanding, Wesley's chief concern in the colonies was to spread the Gospel, and also to introduce the rather radical practice of hymn singing to which he had been converted by his contact with the Moravians. It will be recalled that during this period psalmody still held sway in the colonies, though the hymns of Dr. Watts were beginning to gain favor. In 1737 John Wesley published in "Charles-Town," South Carolina, *A Collection of Psalms and Hymns*, which is highly significant as containing the first of his translations of German hymns. Half of the seventy items in this book were by Dr. Watts, and the two Samuel Wesleys each contributed five hymns. Charles, who returned to England in 1736, was not represented in this collection. It is interesting to note that on the title page John Wesley is called "Missioner of Georgia." This octavo volume of seventy-four pages, printed by L. Timothy, forms a tangible link between Methodist hymnody and the American colonies, where the former was to have such far-reaching effects.

After his return to England in 1738, John Wesley frequented the meetings of the Moravian brethren in London, whose leader was his former shipmate Peter Boehler. This association led to a crucial experience in Wesley's religious development, namely, his so-called "conversion." This occurred during a reading of Luther's Preface to the Epistle of the Romans, as described by Wesley in his journal:

> About a quarter before nine, while he was describing the change which God works in the heart through faith in Christ, I felt my heart strangely warmed. I felt I did trust in Christ, Christ alone for salvation; and an assurance was given me that He had taken away my sins, even mine, and saved me from the law of sin and death.[2]

This might be called the basic text, the gospel, as it were, for the whole movement of evangelical and revivalist hymnody. Note the emphasis on direct salvation through faith in Christ, the conviction of salvation coming as an emotional and heartwarming personal experience, and the feeling of elation resulting from the taking away of sin. This type of emotional reaction, this attitude toward conversion and salvation, and this basic imagery of sin and death, are the seeds out of which grew American folk hymnody, including the Negro spirituals.

Soon after this experience, John Wesley made a visit to the headquarters of the Moravians at Herrnhut in Germany, where he met their patron and protector, Count Zinzendorf, himself a prolific writer

[2] John Wesley, *Journal*, ed. by Curnock, vol. 1, pp. 475ff.

of hymn texts (he is credited with over 2,000). The Moravians, officially known as "Unitas Fratrem," were a Pietist sect, stemming from the reforms of John Hus in the fifteenth century. After many vicissitudes and persecutions, the church of the "Unitas Fratrem" or the Moravian Brethren was revived by Count Zinzendorf, a Saxon nobleman who had been brought up under Pietist influence, and from the late 1720s its activity spread rapidly, including the establishing of missions and settlements in the American colonies. Like the Methodist movement initiated by the Wesleys, the Moravian church represented a blend of Puritan asceticism with emotional fervor, the latter strikingly expressed in their numerous hymns.

"The great awakening"

As a result of his visit to Herrnhut, John Wesley, upon his return to England, began with renewed fervor "to declare . . . the glad tidings of salvation" among his countrymen. His voice was also heard, indirectly, in America, where others were likewise engaged in spreading the glad tidings of salvation, soon to be embodied in a fast-growing hymnody, made largely by, and wholly for, the people. It was the time of "The Great Awakening," a popular mass movement in which the folk took religion into their own hands, though the initial impulse came from the emotional preaching of such powerful orators as John Wesley, George Whitefield, and Jonathan Edwards of New England, whose sermon on "The Reality of Spiritual Light" (1734) touched off the rather sensational Northampton revival of 1735. Shortly thereafter, George Whitefield, leader of the Calvinist Methodists, made the first of his several journeys to America and aroused tremendous enthusiasm by his preaching. Some idea of his eloquence and emotional appeal may be gained from the fact that when speaking in Philadelphia he cast such a spell upon the thrifty and prudent Franklin that the latter, intending at first to give only a few coppers to the collection, ended by pouring out all the money he had with him.

It will not be necessary to consider in detail the doctrinal difference and the multiple sectarianism that characterized the religious movements in England and America during the eighteenth century. Suffice it to say, in the words of Thomas C. Hall, that the gospel of the Wesleys and of Whitefield was in essence "the intensely individualistic proclamation of a way of escape for the soul from eternal damnation. The test of conversion was an emotional reaction rather than an intellectual acceptance of a creedal statement." If we bear in mind this double concept of individual salvation and emotional acceptance, it will provide us with the main thread for following the course of musical revivalism in America. We may further note that this individualism, through what might be called a process of collective individualism, proliferated into a great number of religious sects, offshoots of the main dissenting or reforming branches. Not all the evangelical reformers were dissenters. Wesley himself, for example, always remained nominally within the Church of England. John Wesley wished to reform the Church, not to break with it. But because his strongest appeal was to the masses, the working people, the downtrodden and economically distressed, the movement that he inspired drew further and further away from the established Church, nearer and nearer to the spirit and form of Dissent, with which eventually it became fully identified. It was characteristic of the religious ferment of that period that dissenting groups were continually breaking off from the main dissenting or reforming bodies and forming new sects.

Among the principal dissenting groups were the Quakers, the Moravians, the Baptists, the Presbyterians, and the Congregationalists. The Baptists split into "New Lights," "Free Willers," and "Separates." There were also the "Shakers," the "Shaking Quakers," and the "Dancing Baptists." The Presbyterians split into "Old Side" and "New Side," the latter going in strongly for enthusiastic revivalism. Dissenters were bitterly attacked, though here and there they had a sturdy champion, of whom the most notable was perhaps the Rev. Samuel Davies, a staunch upholder of religious toleration and very important in his day as a writer of hymns. Some idea of the prevailing acrimony may be gathered from the following passage in Davies's *Impartial Trial Impartially Tried:*

Tho' the pulpits around me, I am told, ring with exclamatory harangues, accusations, arguments, railings, warnings, etc., etc., etc., against New-Lights, Methodists, Enthusiasts, Deceivers, Itinerants, Pretenders, etc., etc., etc., yet I never design to prostitute mine to such mean purpose.[3]

[3] Bost, *Samuel Davies*, p. 185.

And Reverend Davies adds: "Satires, etc., are published in the *Gazette*, to alarm the world of these dangerous animals." Strange as it may seem, among all these dissenting sects there was actually one who called themselves simply "Christians"—and it was founded by two men named Smith and Jones!

Before attempting to follow the singing dissenters along what one writer has called "the broad road of revivalism," it would be well to take a closer look at the development of Wesleyan hymnody in England, the indispensable background for musical revivalism in America.

Rise of the evangelical hymn

John Wesley found that the singing of hymns by his congregations was one of the most effective means for spreading the glad tidings of salvation. He and his brother Charles wrote the words of a great many hymns that were published in various collections. The first of these to include musical notation was *A Collection of Hymns . . . as they are commonly sung at the Foundry* (1742), generally known as "The Foundry Collection." Wesley and his followers had acquired for their meetings a building formerly used by the government for casting cannon, hence called "The Foundry." This collection was followed in 1746 by *Hymns on the Great Festivals and Other Occasions*, containing twenty-four tunes by a German bassoonist, resident in London, named John Frederick Lampe. In *Hymns on the Great Festivals* we have a fundamental document for the study of the antecedents of American popular hymnody, as regards both text and music. It contains hymns that have become part of America's folklore and that oral tradition has kept alive to the present day. The best-known of these hymns is probably the one that begins with the line "Ah, lovely Appearance of Death" (Hymn XXII) and is entitled "Over the Corpse of a Believer." Versions of this are widespread in American folk tradition.[4]

Musically, the tunes of John Frederick Lampe are remarkably interesting for their demonstration of the florid style in evangelical

---

[4] John A. and Alan Lomax, in *Our Singing Country*, p. 38, print a version of this hymn as sung for them by a deacon and a deaconess of the Hard-Shell Baptists in Clay County, Kentucky, in 1937. The Lomaxes refer to it as "George Whitefield's funeral hymn," and in their head-note they write: "Reverend George Whitefield . . . ten years before his death wrote this song to be sung at his own funeral." Whitefield died in 1770. He could not have written "this song" ten

hymnody. All the tunes are profusely ornamented, with grace notes, turns, trills, appoggiaturas, etc. Thus we can observe in this collection the extent to which embellished hymnody had gained ground in England through the spread of Wesleyan Methodism. Herewith is Lampe's setting of the hymn, "Ah, Lovely Appearance of Death." [5]

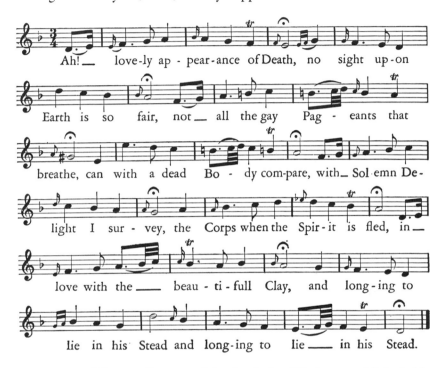

In 1753 Thomas Butts, a friend of the Wesleys, published his *Harmonia Sacra*, containing a large number of hymns with both words and tunes, many of the latter in florid style. This collection proved popular but did not entirely meet with the approval of John Wesley, who evidently felt that the trend toward embellished hymnody was getting out of hand. It was not long before Wesley expressly forbade the use of "vain repetitions" in congregational singing. He also condemned florid singing and fuguing tunes as being no better than

years before his death, because it was published in London in 1746. That this hymn may have been sung at Whitefield's funeral is possible, and there is evidently a tradition that links it with that event. See Billings, *The New-England Psalm-Singer* (1770), p. 109 (verso): "An HYMN, compos'd by the Rev. Mr. Whitefield, with design to be sung at his own funeral . . . ."

[5] From *Hymns on the Great Festivals and Other Occasions*, p. 56. Courtesy of the Library of Congress.

"Lancashire hornpipes"—a condemnation curiously reminiscent of the attacks made on Puritan psalm tunes as "Geneva Jigs"! [6] In opposing the popular trend toward florid singing of hymns, John Wesley, paradoxically, allied himself with the conservative and "respectable" elements who advocated a decorous and dignified type of congregational singing and would not tolerate any liberties taken with the tunes.

In an effort to impose his own standards of hymnody, John Wesley in 1761 brought out *Select Hymns for the Use of Christians*, with a selection of tunes and directions for singing. He gives seven rules or precepts for the singing of hymns: (1) Learn these tunes before any others, (2) Sing them exactly as printed, (3) Sing all of them, (4) Sing lustily, (5) Sing modestly, (6) Sing in tune, (7) Above all, sing spiritually, with an eye to God in every word. Of these precepts, the most significant is the second, urging that the tunes be sung as printed: a clear indication that in practice the people tended to do just the opposite. The printing of plain tunes was not enough to ensure plain singing, which obviously did not appeal to the people as much as did the florid style.

Thus, in Wesleyan hymnody, as in New England psalmody, we witness what is essentially another manifestation of the perennial conflict between "conservative" and "liberal" elements. John Wesley, at first considered "radical" because of his leaning toward evangelical hymnody of the German Pietist type, becomes the upholder, within his own Methodist movement, of an "authorized" body of hymnody and an "authorized" style of singing which he seeks to impose upon his followers but which is rejected or freely altered by the more radical or less conventional proponents of personal salvation and revivalism. We shall see, very shortly, the results of this conflict on the American frontier, but for the moment, we must turn our attention to two other significant figures in English evangelical hymnody: John Cennick (1718–1755) and John Newton (1725–1807).

John Cennick was a Quaker who became a follower of John Wesley and later (in 1745) joined the Moravian Brethren. His first collection of hymns was *Hymns for the Children of God* (second edition, London, 1741), and his second, *Sacred Hymns for the Use of Religious Societies, Generally Composed in Dialogues* (Bristol, 1743). The importance of Cennick is, in the words of G. P. Jackson, that he

[6] Benson, *The English Hymn*, p. 239.

"was destined to become the real founder of folksy religious song in the rebellious eighteenth century movement." Typical of his style is the hymn "Jesus My All to Heaven is Gone," which, again quoting the same authority, "was to become one of the most widely sung religious lyrics among the country folk of America during the entire 200 years which have elapsed since it appeared." [7] This is the highly characteristic final stanza:

> I'll tell to all poor sinners round
> What a dear Saviour I have found;
> I'll point to thy redeeming blood
> And say, behold the way to God.

The "dialogues" mentioned in the title of Cennick's second collection were pieces sung antiphonally by men and women who, at this time and for about a hundred years thereafter, sat on opposite sides of the meetinghouse (sometimes they used a "double-deck" meetinghouse, with the women below and the men above).

John Newton was a rather wild character who went to sea at the age of eleven, was flogged as a deserter from the Royal Navy, became servant to a slave dealer in Africa, and before long was in the slaving trade himself. While acting as captain of a slaving ship he was converted by reading Thomas a Kempis, and soon afterward he came under the influence of John Wesley and Whitefield, leading to his ordination as curate of Olney in 1764. Together with his friend, the unfortunate poet William Cowper, Newton undertook a remarkable collection of hymns, which was published in three books in 1779 as *Olney Hymns*. Cowper, stricken by insanity in 1773, wrote only 68 of the 280 hymns in the collection; the rest were by John Newton. This "old African blasphemer," as he called himself, drew largely upon his own experience in wrestling with sin and being snatched from damnation into eternal salvation. His hymns, like those of Cowper, are marked by what the critics call "excessive emotionalism" (as though emotion should be meted out by measure), by "morbidity" (that is, preoccupation with blood, sacrifice, and death), and by a perpetual swing from gloom to exultation, corresponding to the basic antithesis of sin and salvation. Cennick and Newton represent what might be called the "leftist" or radical tendency in evangelical hymn-

[7] Jackson, *White and Negro Spirituals*, p. 20.

ody, as compared with the relative conservatism of the Wesleys, and still more as compared with the "middle-of-the-road" hymnody of Watts.

This struggle between Wesleyan authority and the popular mass movement of religious dissent, including complete unrestraint in religious singing, continued in America, where it found, indeed, its most dramatic battleground. At a Methodist conference held in Virginia and in Baltimore in 1784, the fourteenth query on the agenda was: "How shall we reform our singing?" And the answer was: "Let all our preachers who have any knowledge in the notes, improve it by learning to sing true themselves, and keeping close to Mr. Wesley's tunes and hymns." This is essentially a repetition, or rather a continuation, of the same fundamental conflict that we found in New England psalm singing fifty or sixty years earlier: the conflict between Regular Singing and the free style of the folk. The situation has been aptly summarized by Benson:

> The entire course of Methodist Episcopal Hymnody may be viewed as a continuous effort to keep the Church on a level sufficiently described as Wesleyan, and a failure to cooperate therein on the part of a considerable section of the people who preferred the plane of the Revival Hymn and the popular Spiritual Song.[8]

That, of course, is written from a conservative and institutional point of view. The masses of people who preferred the lively revival hymns and the popular spiritual songs that sprang up in the American camp meetings after 1799 did not merely manifest a lack of cooperation with religious institutionalism: they were all out for freedom of song, freedom of expression to the utmost limits of the human spirit and body. And we shall see in a later chapter what were the results of this wild freedom of emotional expression that produced the "singing ecstasy" of the great revivals.

The Shakers

In some ways the most remarkable of all the dissenting sects were the Shakers, who established themselves in America about the time of the Revolution and grew from a mere handful to a large and flourishing organization with many communities scattered from Maine to

[8] Benson, *op. cit.*, p. 285.

Kentucky. The sect originated in England as an offshoot of the Quakers, and its adherents were at first popularly known as "Shaking Quakers." Their official designation was United Society of Believers in Christ's Second Coming. In England the society split into two groups, one of which came under the leadership of a young woman of humble origin and forceful character named Ann Lee, soon to be known to the faithful as "Mother Ann." Ann Lee was illiterate, had worked in a cotton factory in Lancashire, and had suffered from an unhappy marriage followed by the death of her four children. It is no wonder that she looked upon sexual relationships as the root of all evil, and imposed the rule of celibacy upon her followers. Mother Ann had the power of being spiritually "possessed" and of seeing visions. In one of these manifestations she had a vision of America. "I saw a large tree, every leaf of which shone with such brightness as made it appear like a burning torch. . . . I knew that God had a chosen people in America; I saw some of them in a vision and when I met with them in America I knew them. . . ."

To America, accordingly, Mother Ann went, accompanied by eight of her followers, in the year 1774. It was scarcely a propitious moment to arrive in America, especially from England. After some time, Mother Ann's band found their way to a small settlement near Albany, then called Niskeyuna (later Watervliet), where they suffered much persecution, including imprisonment on a charge of treason. After their release they settled in New Lebanon, New York, where they built their first meetinghouse. They recruited new members from the Baptists, who in 1780 were in the midst of a fervent revival. In 1784, Mother Ann died, but her work was continued by James Whitaker and Joseph Meacham, and, from 1796, by another remarkable woman, Lucy Wright. The Shakers believed in equality of the sexes and proved it in their leadership. By this time the society had some dozen communities, in New York, Connecticut, Massachusetts, New Hampshire, and Maine. Around 1805 communities were established in Kentucky and Ohio.

The spirit of Mother Ann continued to exert a strong influence on the Shakers. They followed her advice: "Put your hands to work and your hearts to God." They developed handicrafts; they were thrifty and practical and, as they grew stronger, resisted persecution and condemnation with vigor and determination. Music was important in their culture, not as sensuous delectation but as a means of expressing their faith. From Mother Ann they received a number of songs that had been revealed to her in visions.[9]

Mother Ann is also supposed to have revealed by inspiration the system of musical notation used by the Shakers. This consisted of designating the notes of the scale by the first seven letters of the alphabet, beginning with "a" for middle C. Differences in note values were indicated by different types of letters: roman letters for quarter notes, italics for eighth notes, and so forth. This was but one of many systems devised for using letters instead of notes, with some of which we have already become acquainted.

Singing, dancing, shaking, running, leaping—all these were means whereby the Shakers expressed the joy of their religious faith and their victory over the flesh and the devil. Mother Ann believed firmly in the reality of the devil. "The devil is a real being," she said, "as real as a bear. I know, for I have seen him and fought with him." This belief in the corporeal reality of the devil, this expression of faith and spiritual victory through song and the violence of bodily motion, found their full manifestation in the nineteenth-century revivals, where we shall again meet the Shakers and their songs and dances.

Music among minority sects

In addition to the predominantly Anglo-Saxon movements of dissent that made themselves felt in eighteenth-century America, there were a number of religious sects from continental Europe which established settlements in the New World and which gave varying degrees of importance to music in their worship and recreation. Though they remained relatively self-contained and isolated from the popular mass movement of religious dissent, their musical activities are part of the American experience and deserve, therefore, a place in our narrative.

According to chronological priority, we may mention first the Mennonites, followers of Menno Simon, who came from Switzerland and the German Palatinate and who emigrated to the American colonies from 1683 to 1748. The first small group of Mennonites came to Pennsylvania via Rotterdam and London in 1683 and settled in Germantown, near Philadelphia, where in 1708 they built a meeting-house. Their first pastor in America was Willem Rittinghuysen, great-grandfather of the celebrated astronomer and mathematician

[9] For examples of Shaker songs, see Chapter 11.

David Rittenhouse (the name having become thus anglicized). In 1770 they built a new stone church, which is still in use. The Mennonites used a hymnbook which had originally been printed at Schaffhausen in 1583 and which was reprinted at Germantown in 1742, under the title *Der Ausbund: Das ist Etliche Schöne Christliche Lieder* (later editions in 1751, 1767, and 1785). With regard to religious beliefs, the Mennonites were related to the Dunkers or German Baptists, but they practiced baptism by affusion rather than by immersion. They were opposed to instrumental music in church worship and their hymnody was not particularly important.

In 1694 a group of German Pietists under the leadership of Johannes Kelpius came to Pennsylvania and after a brief sojourn in Germantown settled on the banks of the Wissahickon, not far from Philadelphia. These Pietists became known as the Hermits or the Mystics of the Wissahickon. Their leader Kelpius, besides being a dabbler in Oriental lore and cabbalistic philosophy, was somewhat of a musician and hymn writer. He was only twenty-one when he sailed for America in 1694 with about forty other German Pietists, among whom there were evidently several musicians. This we gather from a sentence in Kelpius's own account of the voyage: "We had also prayer meetings and sang hymns of praise and joy, several of us accompanying on instruments that we brought from London." It is believed the instruments mentioned by Kelpius may have been those used at the ordination of Justus Falckner in Gloria Dei Church on November 23, 1703. For this occasion the Mystics of the Wissahickon provided music with viols, hautboys, trumpets, and kettledrums. The church already had an organ, which had been sent from Germany in response to a plea from Justus Falckner, written shortly after his arrival in Pennsylvania in 1700. The text of this letter is worth quoting, in part, for it shows the importance that Falckner attached to music and gives us an insight into the reactions of the Indians when exposed to European music. Speaking of the desired organ, he writes:

It would not only attract and civilize the wild Indian, but it would do much good in spreading the Gospel truths among the sects and others by attracting them. . . . Thus a well sounding organ would prove of great profit, to say nothing of the fact that the Indians would come running from far and near to listen to such unknown melody, and upon that account might be willing to accept our language and teaching and remain with people who had such agreeable things: for they are said to come ever so far to listen to one who plays even upon a reed pipe; such an extraordinary love have they for any melodious and ringing sound.

The Gloria Dei Church in Philadelphia, of which Falckner became pastor, was built by Swedish Lutherans, who had first settled on the Delaware River in 1638. Falckner himself was a German Lutheran, a native of Saxony, educated at the universities of Leipzig and Halle. He wrote several hymns, of which the best known is "Rise, Ye Children of Salvation," sung to the tune of "Meine Hoffnung."

Magister Johannes Kelpius, leader of the Wissahickon Hermits, has been put forward by some writers as the first Pennsylvanian composer, a claim based on his supposed authorship of some hymn tunes contained in a manuscript collection entitled *The Lamenting Voice of the Hidden Love, at the time when She lay in Misery & forsaken; and oprest by the multitude of Her Enemies. Composed by one in Kumber. . . . Pennsylvania in America 1705.*[10] "Kumber" or "cumber" is an obsolete English word for "distress." There is a possibility that Kelpius may have written the text in this manuscript (which is not in his handwriting), but there is no valid evidence that might substantiate a claim for him to be regarded as the composer of the music, most of which is taken from identifiable German sources. The words of the hymns are in German, with English translations that have been attributed to Dr. Christopher Witt, an Englishman who emigrated to America in 1704 and joined the Mystics of the Wissahickon. He seems to have been a musician, a portrait painter, and an amateur organ builder, for he is believed to have built the pipe organ that he owned —said to be the first private organ in the North American colonies. As for *The Lamenting Voice of the Hidden Love*, it has an antiquarian interest as containing, in the words of Albert Hess, "the earliest known practical example of a *continuo* realization in mensural notation." This realization of the figured bass or *basso continuo* is found in the hymn titled "Colloquium of the Soul with Itself." [11] The realization reveals lack of technical skill, and is characterized by the prevalence of three-part harmony.

[10] A facsimile reproduction of this manuscript will be found in *Church Music and Musical Life in Pennsylvania*, vol. 1, pp. 21–165.

[11] A transcription of this hymn, made by Hess, was printed in the *Journal of the American Musicological Society*, vol. 3, p. 221.

Francis Daniel Pastorius, who became the leader of a German Pietist colony in Germantown, Pennsylvania, was a friend of William Penn, whose liberal laws encouraged so many minority sects to settle in his colony. The Quakers themselves were generally opposed to church music, but it is curious to note that George Fox, after attending a Quaker meeting in 1655, wrote that those present "were much exercised by ye power of ye Lorde in Songes and Hymns & made melody and rejoiced." So apparently not all Quakers were antimusical. Pastorius wrote the words of a love song, "Come, Corinna, let me kiss thee," which has been given a modern musical setting for male quartet by Arthur L. Church. John Greenleaf Whittier's poem "The Pennsylvania Pilgrim" was written around the life and character of Pastorius.

We turn now to one of the most original of the Pennsylvania religious sects, the Ephrata Cloister or the Community of the Solitary, who under the leadership of Conrad Beissel and Peter Miller settled on the Cocalico River in 1720, in what is now Lancaster County. They were Seventh-day Baptists who believed strongly in music as an aid to worship. But instead of drawing upon established musical traditions, they used their own homespun music, based on principles set forth by Beissel in his curiously quaint *Dissertation on Harmony*. Beissel himself not only composed the hymns for the community, he also sang and played several instruments, including the violin, and organized the musical life of the Ephrata Cloister down to the most minute details. He established choirs and singing schools, and even prescribed special diets for different types of singers—one diet for altos, another for basses, and so forth. The singing of the Ephrata Cloister was usually in four parts, and their repertoire consisted of nearly a thousand selections. A visitor to the Ephrata Cloister in 1735 wrote "many of the younger sisters are just now constantly employed in copying musical note books for themselves and the brethren." These hand-copied songbooks were beautifully illuminated. In addition, the Ephrata Cloister used printed hymnbooks, of which several were printed by Benjamin Franklin in the 1730s. The main body of Ephrata hymnody was contained in a work entitled *Song of the Lonely and Forsaken Turtle Dove, the Christian Church*, more conveniently known as the *Turtel-Taube*, a manuscript volume with some 750 hymns, compiled in 1746. This unique book was at one time in the possession of Benjamin Franklin, who took it with him to England

and loaned it to the Lord Mayor of London in 1775. Eventually it was acquired by the Library of Congress. Beissel's last collection of hymns, the *Paradisiacal Wonder Music*, dating from 1754, was partly hand-written and partly printed.

Beissel's musical system was crude but doubtless effective for his purpose. There is no question that he made the Ephrata Cloister a community of musical enthusiasts, of whom many were amateur composers and nearly all singers. Beissel divided the notes of the scale into "masters" and "servants." The notes belonging to the common chord were the "masters," the others the "servants." In his metrical system he simply followed the rhythm of the words, the accented syllables having the longer notes and the unaccented ones the shorter notes. In setting the texts to music, he provided that the accent should always fall on a "master" note, while the "servants" took care of the unaccented syllables. With the help of chord tables for all the keys, compiled by Beissel, the art of musical composition became an easy exercise for the brethren of the Ephrata Cloister. The method thus evolved had no repercussions in the outside world and did not shake the foundations of established musical theory; but it did produce a remarkable example of "primitive" art that deserves a special niche among the curiosities of musical Americana.

Music of the Catholic Church

The Catholic Church welcomed the aid of music, both vocal and instrumental, in its religious worship. The less wealthy Catholic churches in the English colonies could not match the musical ceremony in the churches of the Spanish colonies, especially those in the viceregal cities of Mexico and Lima. But the seduction of music in the Catholic Church, even in North America during the eighteenth century, is attested by several entries in the diary of John Adams. On October 9, 1774, Adams wrote: "Went in the afternoon, to the Romish Chapel [in Philadelphia]. The scenery and the music are so calculated to take in mankind that I wonder the Reformation ever succeeded . . . the chanting is exquisitely soft and sweet." On July 4, 1779, the French Ambassador Gerard arranged for a celebration of the anniversary of the signing of the Declaration of Independence with a ceremony in St. Mary's Church, Philadelphia, which was attended by members of the Congress and other important personages, and where "the great event was celebrated by a well-adapted discourse, pronounced by the Minister's chaplain, and a *Te Deum* solemnly sung by a number of very good voices, accompanied by the organ and other kinds of music."

The first hymnbook published for the use of Catholics in the United States was *A Compilation of the Litanies and Vesper Hymns and Anthems as They are Sung in the Catholic Church, Adapted to the Voice or Organ by John Aitken* (Philadelphia, 1787). The music was in two parts (treble and bass); in later editions a third part was added. Perhaps the most interesting selection in this book is "The Holy Mass of the Blessed Trinity," with the plainsong harmonized and with instrumental interludes (called "symphonies") in typical eighteenth-century style, including the standard Alberti bass.

Meanwhile the influence of the Catholic Church, with music always prominent in its missionary program, was spreading to other parts of North America then under Spanish domination but later destined to be incorporated in the territory of the United States. The Spanish missionary Cristóbal de Quiñones, for example, entered New Mexico between 1598 and 1604 and was therefore probably "the first music teacher who worked within the confines of the present United States" (L. M. Spell).[12] Fray Alonso de Benavides, whose *Memorial* was written in 1630, states that in New Mexico there existed "schools of reading and writing, singing, and playing of all instruments."[13] Fray Antonio Margil de Jesús went into Texas in 1716 and taught the Indians there to sing the *Alabados* and *Alabanzas*, simple songs of religious praise that remained in the musical folklore of the Southwest long after the end of Spanish control. The Spanish missionaries also introduced the *autos sacramentales* or religious plays with music, which likewise have survived in the folklore of the region, notably in the Christmas play *Los Pastores*, performed annually or at less frequent intervals in some communities of Texas and New Mexico.

The founding of the famous California missions, from 1769 to 1823, represented another phase of the cultural penetration of Spain and of Catholic church music within the area that was eventually to become part of the United States. Music was a very important feature in the educational, recreational, and religious regime of the missions. The Indians of the region, most of whom proved docile, were soon

[12] "Music Teaching in New Mexico in the 17th Century." In *New Mexico Historical Review*, II, 1 (Jan. 1927).

[13] *The Memorial of Fray Alonso de Benavides,* translated by Ayer, Chicago, 1916.

taught the rudiments of European music, after which they were formed into choirs and small orchestras. The latter usually consisted of violins, violas, violoncellos, bass viols, flutes, trumpets, horns, *bandolas* (a kind of lute), guitars, drums, and triangles. The orchestra of the Mission of San Luis Rey consisted of forty players. Many of the instruments were made by the Indians themselves in the mission workshops.

The most notable musician among the Franciscan missionaries in California was Padre Narciso Durán, choirmaster at the Mission of San José, where in 1813 he compiled a choir book that constitutes one of our chief sources for the study of Spanish mission music in this area. Padre Durán is believed to be the composer of a Mass, *La Misa Catalana*, the manuscript of which was discovered at the Mission of San Juan Capistrano.

Music of the Moravians

For the quality and abundance of their musical production, and for continuous activity in both composition and performance, the most important of the minority religious sects in America was undoubtedly that of the Moravian Church, or the Unitas Fratrum, about whom something has already been said in connection with their influence on John Wesley and Methodist hymnody. They produced several generations of noteworthy composers, in both vocal and instrumental, sacred and secular, forms.

After the failure of their first colony in Georgia, the Moravian brethren in America moved northward to Pennsylvania, and in 1741 established a settlement on the Lehigh River which they called Bethlehem. There, under the personal leadership of Count Zinzendorf, their bishop, they organized a communal society in which all worked for the common good and were provided for from a common store. Private property, however, was not abolished, and the colonists were free to withdraw if they so wished. Soon joined by other Moravian brethren from Europe, the colony prospered (though it was never very large), and other settlements were established in Pennsylvania.

Shortly after the founding of Bethlehem, a group of Moravians went to North Carolina, where they made several settlements, of which the most important was at Salem (now Winston-Salem). There they built churches with organs, formed trombone choirs, and continued their characteristic interest in both vocal and instrumental music. Typi-

cal of their experiences and customs is this passage from the diary
of a Moravian settler in North Carolina, dated November 17, 1753:

> We drove three miles further on the new road, then turned
> to the left and cut a road for 2½ miles to the little house that the
> Brethren found yesterday. . . . We at once made preparations for
> a little Lovefeast, and rejoiced with one another. Brother Gottlob
> began singing, with the little verse:
>
> > We hold arrival Lovefeast here
> >   In Carolina land,
> > A company of Brethren true,
> >   A little Pilgrim band.[14]

The Moravians were interested in carrying on missionary work
among the Negroes and the Indians, and in 1763 they published a
collection of hymns in the language of the Delaware Indians. In 1803
the Rev. David Zeisberger brought out *A Collection of Hymns for
the Use of the Christian Indians of the Mission of the United Brethren
in North America.* The Moravians were also a highly international
group. On September 4, 1745, there took place in Bethlehem a remarkable example of polyglot singing, when the hymn "In Dulci Jubilo"
was sung in thirteen languages simultaneously: Bohemian, Dutch, English, French, German, Greek, Irish, Latin, Mohawk, Mohican, Swedish,
Welsh, and Wendish. A Dane, a Pole, and a Hungarian were also
present but did not join in the singing. Here, surely, is a preview
of the American melting pot.

The Moravians were partial to trombones, which they organized
in "choirs" (soprano, alto, tenor, and bass), and which they used both
on festive occasions and for the sad duty of announcing the death
of a member of the community. On such occasions it was customary
for the trombone players to station themselves on the roof of one
of the buildings, so that they could be heard far and wide. There
is a tradition that during the French and Indian War a band of Indians
was planning to attack the settlement and for this purpose lay in
wait on Calypso Island until the coming of darkness. Just then the
trombones sounded for the death of one of the brethren, and the
Indians, thinking this strange noise from above must be the voice of
the Great Spirit warning them away, decided to give up the attack.

[14] *Records of the Moravians in North Carolina.* Publications of the North
Carolina Historical Commission. Raleigh, N.C., 1922, p. 79.

The story is also told that a certain Christian Ettwein, player on the bass trombone, on one Easter morn drank seventeen mugs of mulled wine. The effect this had on his performance has not been recorded.

What distinguishes the Moravians from other minority sects in America is that, in addition to cultivating the performance of the finest European music of that time with persistent devotion, they also developed a "school" of composers, extending through several generations, who were worthy emulators of their European models. The earliest of these composers was Jeremias Dencke (1725–1795), followed by Johannes Herbst (1735–1812), John Antes (1740–1811), Simon Peter (1743–1819), Johann Friedrich (John Frederick) Peter (1746–1813), David Moritz Michael (1751–1827), Georg Gottfried Müller (1762–1821), Johann Christian Bechler (1784–1857), Peter Wolle (1792–1871), Francis F. Hagen (1815–1907), and Edward W. Leinbach (1823–1901), whose last name was more commonly written as Lineback.

The most important composer of the group was John Frederick Peter; born in Holland of German parents, he came to America in 1770 and joined the Moravian colony in Bethlehem, Pennsylvania. There he became organist of the church, director of music, and secretary of the Brethren's House. He brought to America manuscript copies that he had made in Germany of music by C. F. Abel, Johann Christoph Friedrich Bach, Johann Stamitz, and other prominent (as well as many obscure) European composers. Later he copied a number of works by Franz Josef Haydn, who strongly influenced his own style of composition. Peter was active at several Moravian settlements, but his most important work, musically, was done at Bethlehem and at Salem (North Carolina), whither he went in 1780, remaining there for the next ten years. He gave a strong impetus to the musical movement at Salem, which resulted in the creation, in 1786, of the *Collegium musicum der Gemeine* in Salem. The repertoire of this collegium musicum, of which Peter was the musical director, embraced some 500 compositions, including chamber works, symphonies, anthems, and oratorios. Most of the music belonged to the early classical period, from about 1760 to 1780; Haydn and Mozart are represented by some chamber works and several symphonies.

It was during his stay in Salem, in 1789, that John Frederick Peter composed the six *Quintetti à Due Violini, Due Viole e Violoncello*, upon which his reputation as an instrumental composer chiefly rests.

All but one of these string quintets are in three movements. There is a curious discrepancy between the degree of virtuosity required by the violin and first viola parts, and the lack of technical difficulty in the second viola and cello parts.[15] This was doubtless an example of making the music fit the skills of the available performers (of whom Peter himself was evidently one). Following the classical pattern that he had so thoroughly assimilated, the quintets of Peter nevertheless show considerable harmonic freedom and boldness in modulation, and one may agree with Dr. Hans T. David that at times they are even brilliant in execution. Certainly they can still be heard with aesthetic pleasure and performed with satisfaction; by no means are they to be regarded merely as musical antiques. Their historical interest resides in the fact that they are the first examples of chamber music written by an American composer.

In the realm of sacred music, Peter wrote more than a hundred anthems and arias, mostly with instrumental accompaniment. Typical of his work in these forms are the anthem "It Is a Precious Thing," for soprano, baritone, mixed chorus and string orchestra (1772); and the aria "The Lord Is in His Holy Temple," for baritone (or soprano) and string orchestra (1786). The latter was written in Salem, North Carolina, presumably for that community's leading soprano, Catherine Leinbach, who became the composer's wife and accompanied him when he returned to Bethlehem in 1790. It was there that Peter died, on July 19, 1813. He was the teacher of John C. Till and Peter Wolle, who in turned handed down the fine musical tradition of Bethlehem to future generations. The celebrated Bach Choir of Bethlehem was an outgrowth of this tradition.

John Antes, like Peter, wrote both sacred vocal music and instrumental chamber music. He was the first native-born American among the eighteenth-century Moravian composers. Although he was born and raised in Pennsylvania, his adult life was spent in Germany, in Egypt, and in England. He was sent to Egypt as a missionary in 1769, after being ordained a minister in the Moravian Church; there he suffered hardship, peril, and cruel punishment. From 1781 he lived in England, where, in the midst of various occupations, he found time to compose sacred arias, anthems, and chorales, as well as *Three Trios*

[15] This was pointed out by Hans T. David, in "Musical Life in the Pennsylvania Settlements of the Unitas Fratrum" (*Transactions of the Moravian Historical Society*, Nazareth, 1942), p. 40.

for 2 Violins and Violoncello, which rank with the best music of
the early Moravians. Antes always regarded himself as an amateur
or *dilettante* in music; but he was a good musician and a talented
composer. His sacred music includes the aria for soprano "Go, Congregation, Go!," and the anthem for mixed chorus and string orchestra
"Surely He Has Borne Our Griefs" (Isaiah 53:4,5).

In the mid-twentieth century there was a revival of early American
Moravian music. In 1956 the Moravian Church in America chartered
the Moravian Music Foundation, Inc., with headquarters in Winston-
Salem, North Carolina, for the purpose of advancing the knowledge
and appreciation of this musical heritage through performance, publication, and propaganda. Under the auspices of the Foundation, the
musical archives of the various Moravian communities were catalogued,
and some of the music was edited for church and concert performance.
Festivals of Moravian music were organized and recordings issued,
notably of chamber music by Antes and Peter, and of *Arias, Anthems,
and Chorales of the American Moravians* (1760–1860), performed by
the Moravian Festival Chorus and Orchestra under the direction of
Thor Johnson.

Interesting as American Moravian music may be from an antiquarian—and even an artistic—point of view, its historical significance is
limited by the fact that "very little of this enormous quantity of music
ever entered the stream of musical life in America."[16]

---

[16] Donald M. McCorkle, *The Moravian Contribution to American Music*
(Moravian Music Foundation Publications, No. 1, 1958), p. 9. The full quotation
is as follows: "Unfortunately for the history of American music, very little
of this enormous quantity of music ever entered the stream of musical life
in America."

chapter four

African exiles

Jove fix'd it certain, that whatever day
Makes man a slave, takes half his worth away.
HOMER, THE ODYSSEY XVII, 233 (QUOTED BY JEFFERSON, NOTES ON VIRGINIA).

Dutch ships landed a few African slaves in Virginia as early as 1619. A century later the American slave trade was in full swing. By 1727 there were 75,000 Negroes in the North American colonies, and by 1790 there were more than ten times that number. Ten years later, in 1800, there were over a million Negroes in the United States, of whom more than 100,000 were free—a significant fact to bear in mind. At that time the Negroes formed nearly 19 per cent of the population of this country. Such was the rapid growth of a socioeconomic system that resulted in the transplanting of a large measure of African culture on the continents of the New World.

What did enlightened Americans think of the institution of slavery? Patrick Henry, in a letter to a friend, expressed his views on the subject: "Every thinking honest man rejects it in Speculation, how few in practice. Would anyone believe that I am Master of slaves of my own purchase? I am drawn along by ye general Inconvenience of living without them; I will not, I cannot justify it. . . ." Henry's sister Elizabeth freed her slaves with the declaration that "it is both sinful and unjust, as they are by nature equally free as myself, to continue them in slavery." It was Thomas Jefferson who, in 1782, was instrumental in getting the Virginia legislature to pass an act making it lawful for any person "by last will and testament or other instrument in writing sealed and witnessed, to emancipate and set free his slaves." In his *Notes on Virginia*, Jefferson elaborated a scheme for gradually emancipating all slaves in Virginia and sending them to be "colonized to such places as the circumstances of the time should render most

65

proper." Jefferson treated his own slaves kindly, but did not hesitate to sell them on the open market when the need arose.

Jefferson makes an unfavorable comparison between the Negro and the Indian, claiming that the latter was superior in imagination and artistic skill. Yet on one point he grants the superiority of the blacks, not only over the Indians, but over the white man also: "In music they are more generally gifted than the whites, with accurate ears for tune and time, and they have been found capable of imagining a small catch. Whether they will be equal to the composition of a more extensive run of melody, or of complicated harmony, is yet to be proved." This, and a footnote on the "banjar" (which will be quoted later), is all that Jefferson wrote about the Negroes and music in his *Notes on Virginia*. It is just enough to be tantalizing, not enough to be really enlightening. It corroborates what we already know: that even in slavery the Negroes cultivated their precious gift of music, and this with a skill that impressed even such a connoisseur as Jefferson.

Certain it is that the Negroes came from Africa singing, dancing, and drumming. This in spite of the horrible and cruel conditions under which they were transported in the slave ships. Harsh as were the methods of the slaver, it was not to his interest to let his human cargo pine and die. Music and dancing were used to keep up the morale of the miserable captives. In 1700 Thomas Starks of London directed the captain of the *Africa* to take on a cargo of 450 slaves, and included the typical admonition: "Make your Negroes cheerful and pleasant makeing them dance at the Beating of your Drum, etc." When weather permitted, it was customary to drive the slaves on deck for exercise. What better exercise than dancing, which of course had to be accompanied by drumming (tin pans would do if nothing else) and usually by singing also? It is said that "slave captains preferred happy tunes and frequently would resort to whips to exact their preference." Evidence from a later period, but surely typical of the whole slaving era, is found in a work titled *Captain Canot, or Twenty Years on an African Slaver* (*1827–1847*): "During afternoons of serene weather, men, women, girls and boys are allowed while on deck to unite in African melodies, which they always enhance by an extemporaneous tom-tom on the bottom of a tub or tin kettle."

When no other instruments were at hand, a tub or tin kettle would do: this is characteristic of the Negro's knack for improvised percussion. He also had a knack for making musical instruments in a simple manner out of easily available materials. Writing of the Negroes and music in his *Notes on Virginia*, Jefferson says, "The instrument proper to them is the Banjar, which they brought hither from Africa, and which is the original of the guitar, its chords [i.e., strings] being precisely the four lower chords of the guitar." This is the instrument which came to be known as the banjo. Jefferson is not historically accurate when he says that it was "the original of the guitar," for there is evidence to indicate the contrary: namely, that the West African *bania* (as it was called) was a modification of the Arabian guitar (from which the European guitar is derived). The main point of interest, however, is that the African slaves brought to America a musical instrument that subsequently became so important in our folklore.

It is a pity that Jefferson did not describe the construction of the "banjar" as it existed in his time. Very likely it was made in the same primitive fashion followed by later generations of Negroes. The seeds were scooped out of a large gourd, and the bowl cut away so as to be level with the handle attached to it. Over the bowl of the gourd a tanned coonskin was tightly stretched, forming a drumhead. Four strings were passed over a bridge placed near the center of the drum and attached to the neck or handle of the instrument. The strings were made of any suitable material at hand.

The slaves at work and play

The Negroes were brought from Africa to America for the purpose of working. That truism is stated in order to remind the reader of an equally obvious fact; namely, that the desire to sing while working was the prime impulse for the growth of Afro-American folksong. The emphasis placed upon the "spirituals" has tended to overstress the religious factor in the origins of American Negro music. It is true, as we shall soon observe, that exposure to white psalmody and hymnody had a direct influence on the course of Afro-American folksong and determined one direction that it was to take. But this was a gradual and relatively late development, which did not attain significant proportions until the latter part of the eighteenth century. The Rev. Samuel Davies estimated that in 1750, out of about 120,000 Negroes in Virginia, only 1,000 had been converted and baptized. The

Virginia House of Burgesses, toward the end of the seventeenth century, declared that religious progress among the Negroes was impossible because of the "Gros Barbarity and Rudeness of their manners, the variety and strangeness of their languages, and the weakness and shallowness of their minds. . . ." No wonder that Du Bois speaks of "the spread of witchcraft and persistence of heathen rites among Negro slaves."

We know that the Negroes in Africa sang at their work; there was nothing to prevent them from doing the same in America. Neither the plantation owner nor the overseer cared whether the slaves sang, as long as they did their work. If anything, singing might be regarded with favor, since it tended to lighten the burden and tedium of labor, and thus might make the slaves more docile and contented; which is to say, from the owner's point of view, less troublesome. If slave-ship captains encouraged the Negroes to sing on shipboard, plantation overseers would have at least as much reason for doing likewise.

It was difficult enough to get the slaves to do a real day's work under any circumstances. No sooner was the overseer's back turned, than a slowdown would begin, and not even the most energetic overseer could be everywhere at once. An American slaveowner stated that "his Negroes never worked so hard as to tire themselves—always were lively, and ready to go off on a frolic at night. . . . They could not be made to work hard: they never would lay out their strength freely, and it was impossible to make them do it. . . ." [1]

In general, the slaveowner's attitude toward the singing and other pastimes of the Negroes was tolerant so long as these did not interfere with his own peace and comfort. The making of drums was discouraged, when not positively forbidden, because drums could be used as signals for uprisings, of which there was constant fear in the South. But makeshift drums could be improvised out of boxes, kegs, or kettles; and simple instruments of one kind or another, like the "banjar," could be readily made out of available materials. Then the clapping of hands, the stamping or tapping of feet, and every sort of rhythmic bodily movement, together with the voice used both melodically and rhythmically, could reinforce the primitive music-making of the first Africans who found themselves in a new world not of their choosing.

Although Jefferson recognized the superior musical gifts of the

[1] Quoted in Herskovits, *The Myth of the Negro Past*, p. 102.

Negroes, he remarked on their alleged inferiority to the Indians in arts and crafts. In this connection he wrote, "It would be unfair to follow them to Africa for this investigation." Today our approach is different. We believe it is both fair and necessary to follow the trail of the Negro's past into Africa, to learn what we can of his traditional values and ancestral folkways. We do not look upon the Negro as "a man without a past." His past is in Africa; it is an ancient past, and one not without deep influence upon European, and thence American, culture. Jefferson would have been surprised, for example, if he could have foreseen the effect of African sculpture upon modern art. Our next step, therefore, must be to glance at the African backgrounds of Negro culture in general and of music in particular.

African backgrounds

Although some slaves were taken from East Africa (Mozambique), from Angola, and from the region of the Congo, the majority of those shipped to the New World came from the coastal area of West Africa, along the Gulf of Guinea. The heart of the slave territory lay in Nigeria, Dahomey, western Congo, and the Gold Coast. This region is still inhabited, as it was in the time of the slave trade, by the Ashanti, the Congo, the Dahomeans, the Yoruba, and the Bini. Most of the African survivals found in the Americas can be traced to these main cultural-linguistic groups.

Music, dance, and religious beliefs and practices seem to be the phases of African culture that have left strongest traces in the New World. Music and dance, indeed, are often closely allied with African religion; hence an outline of the latter is pertinent to our subject. Persons not disposed to regard such matters objectively have dismissed African religions as gross superstition, a crude mixture of magic and idolatry. It is true that magic does play a very important part in West African beliefs, but it is only one aspect of a complex supernatural system that implies a definite world view, a profound conception of man's relation to Fate, and a highly organized relationship between human beings and the spiritual powers who are conceived as gods or deities. There is a hierarchy of gods, and the great gods, in the words of Herskovits, "are grouped in pantheons, which follow the organization of the social units among men, each member having spe-

cific names, titles, functions, and worshipers. The cult groups are organized in honor of these deities, and the outstanding religious festivals
are held for them."

The spirits of ancestors are also worshiped, and those who were
most powerful in life are believed to have retained that power—either
for good or evil—after death. This leads to elaborate funeral rites, for
it is necessary to appease the spirits of the departed and assure their
good will by these observances. The cult of ancestor-spirit worship,
in determining the attitude toward the dead and in setting the pattern for burial customs, has had a marked influence on Negro customs in the New World.

Something must be said about the fetish in connection with West
African beliefs. Outwardly the fetish is represented by a charm worn
around the neck, or elsewhere on the body, or hung up within a
dwelling. Certain powers and taboos are associated with this charm.
Fetishism is the belief that possession of the charm, and observance of
the rituals and taboos associated with it, can procure the help and
protection of the spirit that it represents. The charm itself, as a material object, is simply the symbol of a supernatural power. The fetish
charm, in addition to doing good for its wearer or owner, can also
work harm upon the latter's enemy. Hence it becomes an instrument
of so-called black magic.

The cult of Fate or Destiny is extremely important in relation to
the African world view. Fate rules the universe. Everything is pre-
determined, nothing happens by chance or accident. Nevertheless, the
individual is believed to have a fighting chance to alter the course of
destiny in his own case, provided he can be forewarned in time to
invoke the supernatural intercession of some deity whom he has duly
propitiated. If one is a faithful worshiper and observes all the rites of
the cult, one may perhaps obtain a better deal from Fate. Because of
this belief, the art of divining, or foretelling the future, is of the utmost importance. Knowing what lies in store, one can take steps to
meet the situation.

Such, very briefly, are some of the beliefs that determined the
world view, the attitude toward life and death, of those Africans who
were forcibly brought to America as slaves, and which they used to
cope with the new problems of fate and destiny that beset them in a
strange environment. In the course of time we shall see some of these

ancestral patterns reflected in their folklore and their music. For the moment, let us glance at the background of music in African life.

Music of West Africa

Song is the characteristic musical expression of Africa. There are songs for every occasion: for marriages and funerals, for ceremonies and festivals, for love and for war, for work and for worship. The African expresses all his feelings in song. He taunts his enemies or rivals with songs of derision. He propitiates or implores his deities with an infinite number of sacred melodies. The African sings while he works: at his labor in the fields, on the rivers, in his household, and in the communal tasks. The dances of Africa are usually accompanied by singing; the sounds of the ubiquitous African drums most often blend with human voices, providing a strong and complex rhythmical foundation for song.

The alternation between solo and chorus is a fundamental trait of West African singing. This is the "call-and-response" or antiphonal type of song that has been carried over into Afro-American folk music. Richard Waterman makes some highly interesting comments on the overlapping call-and-response patterns of African song:

> While antiphonal song-patterning, whereby a leader sings phrases which alternate with phrases sung by a chorus, is known all over the world, nowhere else is this form so important as in Africa, where almost all songs are constructed in this manner. A peculiarity of the African call-and-response pattern, found but infrequently elsewhere, is that the chorus phrase regularly commences while the soloist is still singing; the leader, on his part, begins his phrase before the chorus has finished. This phenomenon is quite simply explained in terms of the African musical tradition of the primacy of rhythm. The entrance of the solo or the chorus part on the proper beat of the measure is the important thing, not the effects attained through antiphony or polyphony. Examples of call-and-response music in which the solo part, for one reason or another, drops out for a time, indicate clearly that the chorus part, rhythmical and repetitive, is the mainstay of the songs and the one really inexorable component of their rhythmic structure. The leader, receiving solid rhythmic support from the metrically accurate, rolling repetition of phrases by the chorus, is free to embroider as he will.[2]

[2] Waterman, *African Influence on the Music of the Americas*, p. 214.

Contrary to a widespread notion, harmony is not unknown in African music, although there is no modulation from one key to another, and the feeling for harmony is less developed than in European music. Apart from the accidental harmony that may result from the overlapping song patterns described above, singing in parallel thirds, fourths, sixths, and octaves is common in West African music. The Babira of the Belgian Congo have been known to use *parallel seconds* in their choral singing! Of course, not all African music is uniform. Practices differ among the various tribes. In Dahomey, use of harmony is relatively rare, but two-, three-, and four-part harmony is frequent in the music of the Ashanti of the Gold Coast.

We are apt to think of African music as "weird." This is largely owing to peculiarities of intonation and to melodic practices to which we are unaccustomed. W. E. Ward writes illuminatingly on this point:

> The "weird" intervals are most noticeable at the beginning and end of the tune or of a phrase. Now it is at these places that the African, instead of endeavoring to end or begin with his phrase on a pure note as any European singer would, allows himself to slide on to the note or down from it. It seems to be left to the individual to decide the range of the slide, and whether to approach the note from above or below. A final note is always quitted in a downward glide.[3]

Notice the similarity between this procedure and the "dirty" notes of American jazz music.

Rejecting the hypothesis of an "African" scale of fractional or microtonal intervals,[4] Ward believes that "African melodies are essentially diatonic in structure, modified by a liberal, and unregulated, use of *portamento*" (i.e., sliding from one note to another). Waterman also asserts the diatonic character of the African scale, a fact which now seems beyond dispute; and he remarks that "the tendency toward variable intonation of the third and seventh of the scale has occasionally been noted in West African music." The diatonic scale with ambiguous intonation of the third and seventh degrees—usually somewhat flattened—is the so-called "blues" scale of American popular music.

[3] Ward, *Music of the Gold Coast.*
[4] Nicholas Ballanta-Taylor put forth the theory of an African scale based on a division of the octave into sixteen intervals.

The African conception of rhythm is more complex than the European. In European music different rhythms, as a rule, may be employed successively but not simultaneously; but in African music several rhythms go on simultaneously. Every piece of African music has at least two or three rhythms, sometimes four or five. A frequent combination is to have two percussion parts, one of which may be the clapping of hands, and one vocal part with its own metrical pattern. Often there are several metrical patterns in the percussion, played by drums of different sizes. Confusion is avoided by the presence of a fundamental underlying beat that never varies. If there are several drums, this regular beat is played by the largest drum. The diverse rhythms of all the other instruments must coincide on the first beat of the fundamental rhythm. Rhythm in African music, therefore, is conceived as a combination of time patterns that must coincide at a given moment.

In a recording of Gold Coast drums with gong, the following combination of rhythms appear, with the basic beat of the drum in 3/4 and that of the gong in 6/8 (in the background a second drum is heard in another rhythm, with what Waterman describes as "a fluttering beat in 12/8 time"—a rhythmic pattern frequently found in African music): [5]

The following example of an African song with accompaniment of hand clapping will serve to illustrate further some of the varied rhythmical patterns of this music: [6]

[5] In Alberts (ed.), *Tribal, Folk and Cafe Music of West Africa*, p. 7.

[6] From Ballanta-Taylor, *St. Helena Island Spirituals*, p. 19. Quoted by permission of Penn Community Services, Inc., Frogmore, S.C.

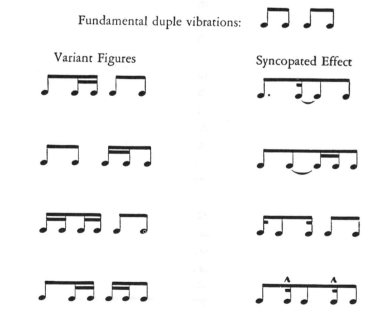

Commenting on this example, Nicholas Ballanta-Taylor remarks that the pattern ♩. ♪♪♪ is a rhythmic figure popular among the Africans, its duple character being suited to their usual dance steps. It is one of numerous metrical patterns derived from the basic duple pulse (♩ ♩). Some of the more common patterns, together with their corresponding syncopated effects, are as follows: [7]

[7] Ballanta-Taylor, *loc. cit.*

These syncopated effects are frequently met with in Afro-American music.

The "metronome sense" is cited by Waterman as crucial for the understanding of African music; and, we may add, for the appreciation of Afro-American music also. In view of its importance, Waterman's explanation is given herewith:

> From the point of view of the listener, it entails habits of conceiving any music as structured along a theoretical framework of beats regularly spaced in time and of co-operating in terms of overt or inhibited motor behavior with the pulses of this metric pattern whether or not the beats are expressed in actual melodic or percussion tones. Essentially, this simply means that African music, with few exceptions, is to be regarded as music for the dance, although the "dance" involved may be entirely a mental one. Since this metronome sense is of such basic importance, it is obvious that the music is conceived and executed in terms of it; it is assumed without question or consideration to be part of the conceptual equipment of both musicians and listeners and is, in the most complete way, taken for granted. When the beat is actually sounded, it serves as a confirmation of this subjective beat.[8]

A grasp of this fundamental concept underlying the traditional values of African music enables us to understand readily how and why the Afro-American influence has had such a tremendous impact on the dance music of the Western world.

Notwithstanding the differences in the concept of rhythm that have been pointed out, there is a basis of unity between European and African music. The diatonic scale is common to both systems and forms, indeed, the strongest link between them, as well as the mark that distinguishes them from all other systems. Then there is the basic concept of harmony that they share. Though the harmonic sense may be less developed in African music, it exists as a concrete factor.

These considerations lead us to conclude, with Kolinski and Waterman, that African and European music have enough basic factors in common to facilitate the process of musical "syncretism" or blending when they are brought into contact with each other over a period of time, as occurred in America. This explains, as Kolinski observes, the homogeneous character of the American Negro spirituals and of

[8] Waterman, *African Influence on the Music of the Americas,* p. 211.

Afro-American music as a whole. We shall now observe some phases, secular and religious, of this process of musical syncretism.

Negro fiddlers and dances

With that remarkable musical aptitude that Jefferson observed, the Negroes in America soon learned to play various European musical instruments. It must be remembered that conditions in which Negroes lived in the American colonies and the early United States differed greatly according to circumstances, and accordingly provided different kinds and degrees of opportunity for the acquisition and display of musical skills. In some cases slaves employed as household servants were encouraged to develop musical skills that might contribute to the pleasure or social prestige of their masters. In 1753 the *Virginia Gazette* carried an advertisement for "an orderly Negro or mulatto who can play well the violin." The same paper also printed an advertisement offering for sale "A young healthy Negro fellow . . . who [plays] extremely well on the French horn." Another announcement requested the return of a runaway slave "who took his fiddle with him." Captain Richard Bailey, of Accomac County, Virginia, is reported to have had a Negro servant who fiddled for the whole neighborhood.

An aristocrat among Negro musicians was Sy Gilliat, body servant to Lord Botecourt, who was the official fiddler at state balls in Williamsburg. He wore an embroidered silk coat and vest of faded lilac, silk stockings, and shoes with large buckles. He also wore a powdered brown wig, and his manners were said to be "as courtly as his dress." Another Negro musician, known as "London Brigs," who became Gilliat's assistant after the capital was moved from Williamsburg to Richmond, was reputed to be equally skillful on the flute and the clarinet. According to Samuel Mordecai, "To the music of Gilliat's fiddle and 'London Brigs' flute all sorts of capers were cut. . . . Sometimes a 'congo' was danced and when the music grew fast and furious, a jig would wind up the evening." This mention of the congo as a social dance in colonial Richmond arouses a curiosity that the historian finds difficult to satisfy. Unfortunately this is not a contemporary reference, for Mordecai's book was published in 1860, and his sources are vague. Nevertheless, the fact that he does mention the congo provides a clue that may some day lead to interesting data regarding the influence that Negro music and dancing may have had upon the American upper classes in the eighteenth century.

The congo has been well documented as a Negro dance of the Antilles, found also in Louisiana (it is not to be confused with the Cuban *conga*, of later origin). Lafcadio Hearn, in 1885, described the congo as he saw it danced by Negroes in New Orleans. He said it was "as lascivious as is possible." The women "do not take their feet off the ground," while the men "dance very differently, like savages leaping in the air." We are not to assume that the ladies and gentlemen of old Virginia carried on in this uninhibited manner. But the history of social dancing is full of instances in which a dance existed simultaneously on two levels, assuming a decorous form in polite society and manifesting a licentious character among the populace. It is quite possible that the congo, a primitive Negro dance of African origin, flourished in the slave quarters of the plantations, while at the same time a dance of the same name, though certainly not with the identical choreography, was admitted to the ballrooms of the ruling class.

In considering the plausibility of this hypothesis, it is important to bear in mind that in many cases the musicians who played for these society balls were Negroes. And if the music they played "grew fast and furious," cannot we suppose that it reverted to some wild and primitive strain, however modified and restrained by imposed conventions? We know that in Latin America many dances adopted by polite society had their origin in Negro dances which would be regarded as objectionable by the standards of this same society. Albert Friedenthal, a musician who traveled widely in Latin America during the nineteenth century, has some interesting comments to make on the influence that the music and dancing of the Negroes exerted upon their white masters:

Every day in their hours of rest they [the whites] had opportunities to see the partly sensual, partly grotesque and wild dances of their black slaves, and to hear their peculiar songs. . . . Added to this the strange instruments of percussion which, while marking the rhythm, exerted an almost uncanny effect.[9]

Although the slaves in Latin America, on the whole, had wider opportunities to express themselves musically than those of North America, the conditions described by Friedenthal are largely applicable

[9] Friedenthal, *Musik, Tanz und Dichtung bei den Kreolen Amerikas*, p. 95.

also to the United States. The songs and dances of the plantation Negroes provided first a source of amusement for the landowners and their families; and later, imitated by white entertainers with their faces blackened, the "coon songs," "plantation melodies," and "cakewalks" provided amusement for the whole country through the immensely popular minstrel shows. Ragtime, blues, and jazz were other and still later manifestations of the fascination and influence that Negro music exerted upon the white population. In another chapter we shall observe the influx of Latin American songs and dance rhythms from the Caribbean area, dominated by African influences, into the region of Louisiana and New Orleans in particular. There, in the nineteenth century, the Negro folk music of the American South and the Afro-Hispanic music of the Caribbean were to converge in the creation of jazz.

After this glimpse into the future, we must return to the Atlantic seaboard and the plantations of the South in the eighteenth century to trace the spread of Christianity and of evangelical hymnody among the Negroes, which provide the background for the development of that important body of American folk song known as the Negro spirituals.

The Negroes and the Gospel

In 1675 John Eliott, the Puritan "apostle of the Indians," speaking of the slave trade, said, "to sell souls for money seemeth to me a dangerous enterprise." He meant, of course, dangerous for one's spiritual welfare. But the majority of slaveowners were untroubled by such scruples. A writer in the *Athenian Oracle* of London, in 1705, expressed what was probably a prevalent attitude:

> Talk to a planter of the soul of a Negro, and he'll be apt to tell you (or at least his actions speak loudly), that the Body of one of them may be worth twenty Pounds, but the Souls of an hundred of them would not yield him one farthing.

A plantation owner of Barbados voiced the opinion that one "might as well baptize puppies as Negroes." The vested interests of colonial society, as represented by their official bodies, clothed similar sentiments in the more pretentious verbiage of moral self-justification.

Samuel Davies, the eighteenth-century evangelist and champion of religious tolerance, deplored "the almost universal neglect of the many thousands of slaves . . . who generally continue Heathens in a Christian country." In the course of time these conditions were to change gradually, thanks to the efforts of many zealous missionaries and to a more enlightened attitude on the part of the slaveowners.

It is true that some masters insisted upon having their slaves attend religious services and that special galleries were set apart for this purpose in colonial churches, such as the one in Bruton Parish, Williamsburg, where several hundred Negroes were baptized. Yet the formality of an established religion like the Episcopalian could exert no strong appeal, nor affirm a deep hold, upon the emotions of the Negro slaves. Much more effective was the fervor and freedom, the ecstasy and exuberance, of revivalism as represented by the dissenting sects and the evangelical denominations. The Methodists and the Baptists, to say nothing of the numerous minor sects, far outdid in popular appeal the Episcopalians, the Presbyterians, and the Catholics.

The Rev. John Davies of Virginia was one of the most active preachers of the gospel among the Negroes. John Wesley, the famous founder of Methodism, tells in his journal of receiving a letter "sent from a gentleman in Virginia," who was probably Davies, since he is mentioned later as the writer of a similar letter which Wesley quotes at length. As these letters are among the very few firsthand accounts we have of Christianization among the slaves, and as they contain significant references to music, I quote extensive passages from them. The first letter runs, in part, as follows:

> The poor Negro slaves here never heard of Jesus or his religion till they arrived at the land of their slavery in America, whom their masters generally neglect, as though immortality was not the privilege of their souls, in common with their own. These poor Africans are the principal objects of my compassion, and, I think, the most proper subject of your charity. . . .
>
> The number of these [Negroes] who attend on my ministry is uncertain; but I think there are about 300 who give a stated attendance. And never have I been so much struck with the appearance of an assembly, as when I have glanced on one part of the house, adorned (so it appeared to me) with so many black countenances, eagerly attentive to every word they heard, and some of them covered with tears. . . . As they are not sufficiently polished to dissemble with a good grace, they express the sensations of their hearts so much in

the language of simple nature, and with such genuine indications of artless sincerity, that it is impossible to suspect their professions. . . .

I have supplied them to the utmost of my ability [with books]. They are exceedingly delighted with Watt's [*sic*] Songs. And I cannot but observe, that the Negroes, above all of the human species I ever knew, have the nicest ear for music. They have a kind of ecstatic delight in psalmody; nor are there any books they so soon learn, or take so much pleasure in, as those used in that heavenly part of divine worship.[10]

This emphatic corroboration of the Negro's musical aptitude is impressive; and it seems to me that these paragraphs from the pen of an eyewitness tell us more about the genesis of the Negro spirituals than any amount of *a posteriori* theorizing. Our imaginations can easily reconstruct the atmosphere of emotionalism and fervor, the tears, the heartfelt outpourings in simple language not devoid of striking imagery, the delight in the *Hymns and Spiritual Songs* of Dr. Watts with their direct appeal to the common feelings of plain people, the ecstatic pleasure in the surge of communal song, and the sense of spiritual and physical satisfaction at expressing themselves freely through an innate talent that not even the conditions of slavery could repress.

Further details of the picture may be filled in from another letter quoted in John Wesley's journal, which he specifically states is "from the Rev. Mr. Davies, in Virginia":

When the books arrived, I gave public notice after sermon, and desired such Negroes as could read, and such white people as would make good use of them . . . to come to my house. For some time after, the poor slaves, whenever they could get an hour's leisure, hurried away to me, and received them with all the genuine indication of passionate gratitude. All the books were very acceptable, but none more so, than the Psalms and Hymns, which enabled them to gratify their peculiar taste for psalmody. Sundry of them lodged all night in my kitchen; and sometimes when I have awaked at two or three in the morning, a torrent of sacred psalmody has poured into my chamber. In this exercise some of them spend the whole night.[11]

Extremely illuminating, and bearing even richer stuff for the imagination to work on, is this vivid picture of Negroes spending the whole

---

[10] *The Journal of the Rev. John Wesley, A.M.*, vol. 2, p. 303.
[11] *Ibid.*, p. 320.

night in the singing of psalms and hymns, producing a veritable "torrent" of sacred song. Lacking a direct detailed description of this "torrent of psalmody," we must draw upon analogy and inference. At this point it will be helpful if the reader goes back to Chapter 2 and rereads the description of the Early New England Folk Style of psalmody, noting that its main characteristics are singing by ear rather than by note or "rule"; the raising or lowering of notes at will; the adding of grace notes, turns, and other embellishments; the "sliding" from one note to another; the adding of parts at the intervals of a fourth, a fifth, and an octave; and the practice of "lining-out," with the leader reading or chanting the verses of the psalm, one or two lines at a time, and the congregation singing them afterward. Now compare the description of African singing earlier in the present chapter, and ask whether the two styles do not possess sufficient elements in common to produce a natural fusion or syncretism. Compare, again, the following description of the singing of a so-called "long meter" hymn (also significantly known as "Doctor Watt") as heard among Southern Negroes some years ago by George Pullen Jackson:

A deacon or the elder "lines out" a couplet of the text in a sing-song voice and at a fair speaking pace ending on a definite tone. This "tones" the tune. The deacon then starts singing, and by the time he has sung through the elaborately ornamented first syllable the whole congregation has joined in on the second syllable with a volume of florid sound which ebbs and flows slowly, powerfully and at times majestically in successive surges until the lined-out words have been sung. Without pause the deacon sing-songs the next couplet, and the second half of the four-line tune is sung in the same manner. No instrument is ever used. No harmony is indulged in excepting here and there a bit, hit upon by accident as it would seem, and sometimes a one-singer attempt at bass. The women and the men sing, with these exceptions, the same notes an octave apart.[12]

As this type of singing corresponds in its essential aspects to a well-established popular tradition of eighteenth-century psalmody, I venture the hypothesis that something of this sort assailed the ears of the Rev. Mr. Davies when he awoke in the small hours of the morning and heard "a torrent of sacred psalmody" pouring from the throats of the Negroes assembled in his kitchen.

[12] Jackson, *White and Negro Spirituals*, p. 248.

In the same letter to John Wesley from which we quoted above, John Davies wrote: "There are thousands of Negroes in this Colony [Virginia], who still continue in the grossest ignorance, and are as rank Pagans now, as they were in the wilds of Africa." In other words, while a certain percentage of Negroes was exposed to the doctrines of Christianity, and some of them were converted and baptized, the large majority continued to live, spiritually, as though they were still "in the wilds of Africa," which in the eyes of the missionaries meant they were "rank Pagans" clinging to barbarous beliefs.

It is important to keep these proportions in mind as we trace the growth of Afro-American music, observing that there was no uniform development, no general conformity of conditions, but rather a variety of social and cultural conditions, ranging from the comparative sophistication of urbanized Negroes to the primitive plantation life of the Georgia Sea Islands, where slaves living in relative isolation retained definite Africanisms of speech and customs for generation after generation. If we look at Afro-American music as it exists today, we can see that it contains elements derived from these various levels of culture and experience and what the sociologists call "acculturation" (the results of continuous firsthand contact between different cultural groups): there are the highly self-conscious and artistically "correct" arrangements of spirituals, closely conforming to traditional standards of European art music; there are the relatively primitive work songs, shouts, hollers, and blues, strongly marked by African retentions; there are the "Dr. Watt" hymns and "surge songs," survivals of eighteenth-century psalmody and hymnody; and there is jazz and its derivative styles, stemming from the Negro's contact, in urban environments, with the dances and instruments of the dominant white culture fused with the ancestral African heritage. Even within the frame of American musical culture as a whole, Afro-American music is in itself a complex whose diverse strands need to be traced individually as well as in their mutual interaction.

Our minds tend to reject all complexes in favor of simplified stereotypes. It is thus that there emerges the image of the "plantation darkie" as a stock figure of our stage and popular-song literature, leading to a whole musico-theatrical production ranging from the grotesque to the sentimental. From the eighteenth-century sentimental songs about the poor Negro boy, to the "Mammy" songs of twentieth-century tin-pan alley, there is a continuous popular tradition. We shall in due course trace this tradition and its tenuous connection with the actual life of the plantation Negroes. For the moment we simply point to it as one of the phases of America's music that stemmed from the backgrounds of Negro slavery in the United States.

All generalities tend to be misleading through oversimplification. But if we must carry in our minds a composite picture of plantation life in the early days of slavery, then let it be one drawn by a master hand, the informal but authoritative sketch of a great scholar in this field, Ulrich B. Phillips:

> The plantation was a pageant and a variety show in alternation. The procession of plowmen at evening, slouched crosswise on their mules; the dance in the new sugarhouse, preceded by prayer; the bonfire in the quarter with contests in clogs, cakewalks and Charlestons whose fascinations were as yet undiscovered by the great world; the work songs in solo and refrain, with not too fast a rhythm; the baptizing in the creek, with lively demonstrations from the "sisters" as they came dripping out; the torchlight pursuit of 'possum and 'coon, with full-voiced halloo to baying houn' dawg and yelping cur; the rabbit hunt, the log-rolling, the house-raising, the husking-bee, the quilting party, the wedding, the cock fight, the crap game, the children's play, all punctuated plantation life—and most of them were highly vocal. A funeral now and then of some prominent slave would bring festive sorrowing, or the death of a beloved master an outburst of emotion.[13]

And intertwined with the frolic and the fun, the sorrow and the mourning, the work and the prayer, there was always music, not music of one kind, but of many kinds, changing and taking to itself melodies and harmonies and rhythms from here and there, but always based on the bedrock of the black man's intense love and great gift for the solace and beauty and excitement of music.

It is only natural that Thomas Jefferson should have been the first prominent American to recognize and to proclaim publicly the exceptional musicality of the Negro. For Jefferson was not only one of the most perceptive and enlightened men of his time, he was also a keen and discriminating music lover. In the next chapter we shall learn something about the musical tastes of Jefferson, as well as about the interests and activities of other American gentlemen of the eighteenth century who cultivated music as amateurs.

[13] Phillips, *Life and Labor in the Old South*, pp. 202–203.

chapter five

Gentlemen amateurs

They would talk of nothing but high life, and high-lived company; with other fashionable topics, such as pictures, taste, Shakespeare and the musical glasses.
OLIVER GOLDSMITH, THE VICAR OF WAKEFIELD.

On October 11, 1760, the *South Carolina Gazette* carried the announcement of "A Concert of Vocal and Instrumental Music" to be given in Charleston with the assistance of "the Gentlemen who are the best performers, both in Town and Country." In the eighteenth century professional musicians were not considered gentlemen. Hence this announcement, like many others of similar tenor that appeared in newspapers throughout the colonies, refers to the participation of those "gentlemen amateurs" who practiced music because they loved it and who played in public because there were not in those days enough professional musicians in any American community to make up a "full band." As a rule they played in semiprivate subscription concerts such as those sponsored by the St. Cecilia Society of Charleston, but when a worthy member of the musical profession gave a public "benefit" concert—that is, according to the custom of those times, a concert for his own benefit—then the Gentlemen from Town and Country rallied gallantly to his assistance with their fiddles, flutes, and hautboys. French horns, clarinets, and even an occasional bassoon, were not unknown; but these were not regarded as particularly genteel instruments.

That the gentlemen amateurs had no prejudice against performing in the theater is indicated by the following announcement in the *Pennsylvania Gazette* of Philadelphia for November 30, 1769: "The Orchestra, on Opera Nights, will be assisted by some musical Persons, who as they have no View but to contribute to the Entertainment of the Public, certainly claim a Protection from any Manner

84

of Insult." This implies that the professionals, being paid for their pains, had no recourse save to suffer the abuse of the public if their efforts failed to please, while the amateurs claimed immunity from criticism by virtue of their voluntary service. Besides, *they* were Gentlemen.

As a typical gentleman amateur of colonial America, let me introduce Councillor Robert Carter of Nomini Hall in Virginia. Philip Vickers Fithian, a tutor in his household, wrote of him: "He has a good ear for Music, a vastly delicate Taste and keeps good instruments; he has here at Home a Harpsichord, Forte Piano, Harmonica, Guitar & German Flute, and at Williamsburg has a good Organ; he himself also is indefatigable in the Practice." [1] Lest the mention of "Harmonica" evoke an unseemly image of Mr. Carter playing the mouth organ, let me explain that this was, according to a description in the Councillor's own notebook, an instrument invented by Mr. B. Franklin of Philadelphia, "being the musical glasses without water, framed into a complete instrument capable of thorough bass and never out of tune." We shall hear more presently about this wonderful invention. For the moment simply pause to contemplate the edifying spectacle of a country squire who keeps good instruments as one might keep good horses, and who is as familiar with a thorough bass as with a thoroughbred. He, moreover, is reputed to have "a vastly delicate Taste"— than which there could be no higher compliment to a gentleman of the eighteenth century. Good taste was the touchstone of the age.

We take for granted the good taste of our colonial ancestors in architecture and interior decoration because we are familiar with the incontestable beauty of the homes, churches, and public buildings of that period. But we are sadly ignorant concerning the musical taste of our eighteenth-century forebears because it is attested only by musty newspaper files, library inventories, and documental archives. Recently, however, the Williamsburg Festival Concerts have revived the musical elegance and sophistication of that colonial capital, which knew the music of the best European composers, such as Handel, Hasse, Vivaldi, Corelli, Galuppi, Pugnani, Boccherini, Rameau, Arne, Stamitz, the "London" Bach, and many others.

Young Thomas Jefferson, while studying law at the College of William and Mary in Williamsburg, belonged to the intimate circle of Governor Francis Fauquier, of whom he later wrote: "The Gov-

[1] Fithian, *Journal and Letters*, p. 77.

ernor was musical also, being a good performer, and associated me
with two or three other amateurs in his weekly concerts." Jefferson
himself played the violin; he and Patrick Henry often played duets
together. Do not imagine that this sort of thing pertained exclusively
to the Cavalier tradition of the South. While there may have been
more gentlemen of leisure in the Southern colonies, there were musical
amateurs everywhere. Take, for example, Lieutenant Governor John
Penn of Pennsylvania, a keen music lover and a good violinist who
gave private chamber-music concerts at his home in Philadelphia every
Sunday evening during the season, and who, together with his friend
Francis Hopkinson, was one of the chief promoters of musical activity
in the Quaker City. In all our cities, from Charleston in the South
to Boston in the North, the gentlemen of high degree were paying
their respects to the heavenly Muse.

The sage of Monticello

Among the devotees of music none was more ardent in his devotion than Thomas Jefferson. Consequently none felt more keenly
than he the deterioration in American musical activity that took
place during the Revolutionary War. Patriot though he was, he must
have looked back wistfully on those halcyon days when, as a crony
of Francis Fauquier, he joined in the governor's chamber-music concerts. We know by his own confession that he gazed with intense
longing upon the greener pastures of European musical life. In 1778
he wrote to a friend whose name we do not know, probably a
Frenchman, saying: "If there is a gratification which I envy any people
in this world, it is your country its music." Years later, when his
diplomatic mission to France had enabled him to savor this gratification at firsthand, he repeated the same thought in a letter to Charles
Bellini, a professor at the College of William and Mary, dated Paris,
September 30, 1785: "Were I to proceed to tell you how much I
enjoy their architecture, sculpture, painting, music, I should want
words. It is in these arts they shine. The last of them, particularly, is
an enjoyment, the deprivation of which, with us, cannot be calculated.
I am about ready to say it is the only thing which from my heart I
envy them, and which in spite of all the authority of the Decalogue,
I do covet."

Can this passage be reconciled with the thesis that early musical life in America was not as crude and primitive as it has generally been depicted? I think it can. The concert programs so painstakingly unearthed and assembled by Sonneck prove that the music of the best European composers of that time was known and performed in America. But it would be absurd to pretend that the performances were on a par with the best that could be heard in Europe. Jefferson was thinking of Europe's finest: the Paris Opéra, the "Concert Spirituel," the English oratorio performances. Only the best, and a great deal of it, would satisfy his passion for music. Moreover, after the Revolution the Northern cities took the lead in our musical life, while the South, where Jefferson lived, lagged behind.

Had Jefferson been able to carry out a cherished idea, he would have created a small musical world of his own at Monticello. In the letter of 1778 from which I have already quoted, he outlined an in-genious scheme for providing himself with a private musical establishment somewhat after the manner of the European nobility:

> The bounds of an American fortune will not admit the indulgence of a domestic band of musicians, yet I have thought that a passion for music might be reconciled with that economy which we are obliged to observe. I retain, for instance, among my domestic servants a gardener, a weaver, a cabinet maker and a stone cutter, to which I would add a *vigneron*. In a country where like yours music is cultivated and practised by every class I suppose there might be found persons of those trades who could perform on the French horn, clarinet or hautboy & bassoon, so that one might have a band of two French horns, two clarinets & hautboys and a bassoon, without enlarging their domestic expenses.[2]

Nothing seems to have come of the scheme, but the letter leaves no doubt that Jefferson knew what he wanted. He was not exaggerating when, in this same letter, he referred to music as "this favorite passion of my soul." The truth is that the father of American democracy was an aristocrat in his musical tastes. He courted the Muse like a *grand seigneur*.

The eminent Dr. Franklin

Among Jefferson's letters from Paris there is one to Francis Hopkinson of Philadelphia, dated July 6, 1785, which casts a curious side-

[2] Quoted in *The Writings of Thomas Jefferson*, ed. by P. L. Ford (New York, 1892–1899), vol. 2, p. 159.

light on the musical inclinations of another famous Philadelphian: "I communicated to Doctr. Franklin your idea of Mesmerising the Harpsichord. He has not tried it, probably because his affairs have been long packed & packing; as I do not play on that instrument I cannot try it myself. The Doctr. carries with him a pretty little instrument. It is the sticcado, with glass bars instead of wooden ones, and with keys applied to it. It's principle [*sic*] defect is the want of extent, having but three octaves. I wish you would exercise your ingenuity to give it an upper and lower octave. . . ." [3] These men of the eighteenth century were always exercising their ingenuity on something or other! The reference in the first sentence is to Hopkinson's improved method for quilling the harpsichord, a very ingenious device. As for the "pretty little instrument" that Dr. Franklin carried about with him, it was a sort of glass dulcimer, usually called the "Sticcado-Pastorale." James Woodforde, in his *Diary of a Country Parson*, said that it looked, "when covered, like a working box for ladies." So, what Dr. Franklin carried around in Paris was not necessarily a dispatch box full of state papers.

Benjamin Franklin's musical accomplishments were by no means limited to playing the Sticcado-Pastorale. He played the guitar and the harp, both fashionable instruments at that time. While living in London he offered his services as guitar teacher to the mother of Leigh Hunt, the English poet and essayist. And Franklin was also somewhat of a virtuoso on the instrument that he himself invented, the so-called "Glass Harmonica." He was fond of singing in congenial company and was especially partial to Scotch songs. He tells us of one called "The Old Man's Wish" that he sang "a thousand times in his singing days." In his seventieth year he wrote to the Abbé de la Roche recalling "a little drinking song which I wrote thirty years ago" and quoted from it the following verse and chorus:

SINGER: Fair Venus calls: Her voice obey.
          In beauty's arms spend night and day.
          The joys of love all joys excell
          And loving's certainly doing well.

CHORUS: Oh! No!
          Not so!
          For honest souls know
          Friends and a bottle still bear the bell.

[3] Sonneck, *Francis Hopkinson and James Lyon*, p. 67.

Some biographers have conjectured that Franklin composed music for this and other songs, but it is more probable that he simply set the verses to well-known tunes, as was the custom in those days. The evidence that he might have tried his hand at composing rests chiefly on a passage in a letter from Mme. Brillon, addressed to Franklin, in which she mentions receiving "your music engraved in America." This may refer to music engraved, rather than composed, by Franklin. A manuscript recently discovered in the library of the Paris Conservatory and published in 1946 bears the inscription: *Quartetto a 3 violini con violoncello del Sigre* [Signore] *Benjamin Francklin* (*sic*). This is a kind of suite consisting of five short movements, each bearing a conventional title (*Menuetto, Siciliano,* etc.). The music is written for the open strings only and employs an unusual type of tuning known as *scordatura*. The manuscript is not in Franklin's hand, nor is there any further evidence to substantiate his authorship of this string quartet, which has been called "a mathematical tour de force."

The celebrated Glassychord

It was primarily as a musical inventor that Benjamin Franklin made the greatest impression on musical circles both in Europe and America. According to the *Musikalischer Almanach für Deutschland* for the year 1782, "Of all musical inventions, the one of Mr. Franklin of Philadelphia has created perhaps the greatest excitement." By this time the instrument in question had been enjoying a widespread vogue for some twenty years, as indicated by the following news item from the *Bristol Gazette,* dated January 12, 1762:

The celebrated Glassy-chord, invented by Mr. Franklin of Philadelphia; who has greatly improved the Musical Glasses, and formed them into a compleat Instrument to accompany the voice. . . . Miss Davies, from London, was to perform in the Month of January, several favorite Airs, English, Scotch and Italian, on the Glassychord (being the only one of the kind that has yet been produced) accompanied occasionally with the Voice and German Flute.

From this it appears that Franklin invented his improved version of the musical glasses in 1761 and that the novel instrument was originally called Glassychord (hyphen apparently optional!), a rather clumsy appellation soon dropped in favor of "Armonica," the name that

Franklin himself gave it, in honor, as he said, of the musical Italian language. With the addition of a superfluous but persistent aspirate, it became generally anglicized as Harmonica.

The use of musical glasses was known to the Persians and Arabs at least as early as the fourteenth century and may possibly have spread to Europe from the Near East. A work published at Nuremberg in 1677 mentions "making a cheerful wine-music" by stroking the rims of partially filled glasses with a moistened finger. The same volume also describes a musical experiment with four glasses, filled with brandy, wine, water, and salt water or oil.

No less a personage than the Chevalier Gluck, already crowned with the laurels of operatic success, performed on the musical glasses in London in 1746 and claimed them to be, with some exaggeration, "a new instrument of his own Invention." Gluck's claim could not be taken too seriously, for an Irish adventurer named Richard Pockrich had been giving concerts on the musical glasses since 1743 and continued to win popular acclaim as a performer until both he and his "angelick organ," as he called it, perished in a fire at London in 1759. Something of Pockrich's reputation can be gathered from these verses from "The Pockreiad," an epic poem by Brockhill Newburgh:

> Old Pock no more, still lives in deathless fame,
> He blazed when young, when old expired in flame. . .
> Be silent, dumb, ye late harmonious glasses:
> Free from surprise securely sleep ye lasses.

The musical glasses did not long remain dumb, for one E. H. Delaval made a set modeled after Pockrich's and played on it in London, where among his enraptured listeners was Benjamin Franklin. In his letter to Padre Beccaria describing the Armonica (written from London under date of July 1, 1762),[4] Franklin states that Delaval's instrument was "the first I saw or heard." And he continues: "Being charmed by the sweetness of its tones, and the music he produced from it, I wished only to see the glasses disposed in a more convenient form, and brought together in a narrower compass, so as to admit of a greater number of tones, and all within reach of hand to a person sitting before the instrument. . . ." This, then, was the origin of Dr. Franklin's celebrated Glassychord or Armonica.

[4] This letter is printed in *The Complete Works of Benjamin Franklin*, ed. by Bigelow, vol. 3, pp. 198–204; also in Sonneck, *Suum Cuique*, pp. 60–62.

Instead of having the glasses filled with varying quantities of water to obtain variety of pitch, Franklin had the glasses made of different sizes and used only the bowls, without the stems. He placed the glasses on a horizontal rod or spindle which was rotated by foot action, like a spinning wheel. The instrument, wrote Franklin, "is played upon, by sitting before the middle of the set of glasses as before the keys of a harpsichord, turning them with the foot, and wetting them now and then with a sponge and clean water."

This simple yet ingenious mechanism made the musical glasses infinitely more practical and led to their immediate and widespread success both as a domestic and a concert instrument. Miss Marianne Davies—the young lady mentioned in the item from the *Bristol Gazette* —undertook an extensive concert tour of the Continent in 1768, together with her sister Cecilia, a well-known singer. Paris, Florence, Turin, Milan, and Vienna acclaimed the charming Misses Davies and the novel instrument with the celestial tones *"inventato dal celebre dottore Franklin."* Marianne Davies was especially appreciated in Vienna. The court poet Metastasio wrote an "Ode" which was set to music (for soprano and harmonica) by the fashionable operatic composer Johann Adolph Hasse and performed by the Misses Davies at the wedding of the Archduchess of Austria to the Duke of Parma. Leopold Mozart and his brilliant young son, Wolfgang, were well acquainted with Miss Davies and her harmonica. In the summer of 1773 Leopold wrote from Vienna: "Do you know that Herr von Mesmer plays Miss Davies's harmonica unusually well? He is the only person in Vienna who has learned it and he possesses a much finer instrument than Miss Davies does. Wolfgang too has played upon it. How I should love to have one!"

The Herr von Mesmer mentioned in this letter was Franz Anton Mesmer, the exponent of "animal magnetism" or hypnotism. According to A. Hyatt King, "there seems little doubt that Mesmer used his mastery of the highly emotional tones of the harmonica to induce a receptive state in his patients." The harmonica seems to have had an extraordinary physiological effect. Its tones could unnerve the strongest man and cause women to faint. Most of those who played it frequently, including Marianne Davies, ended by having their nerves shattered. Franklin himself was an exception: he must have had nerves of iron.

In 1791, the year following Franklin's death and the last year of his own life, Mozart, inspired by the playing of a blind girl named Marianne Kirchgässner, composed a remarkable piece of music for the instrument that had so delighted him and his father when he was a boy. This was the lovely Quintet (Adagio and Rondo) for harmonica, flute, oboe, viola, and cello (Köchel 617). Mozart also composed an Adagio for harmonica solo (K. 356). Other more or less celebrated European composers who wrote music for the harmonica were Hasse, Martini, Jommelli, Galuppi, J. G. Naumann, K. L. Röllig, W. L. Tomaschek, and Beethoven. The unearthly tone quality of the harmonica appealed strongly to the Romantic imagination, and inspired the enthusiastic praise of such poets as Goethe, Schiller, Wieland, and Jean Paul Richter. Robert Schumann also succumbed to its spell.

As a musical inventor Benjamin Franklin was not without honor in his own country. To show what impression the harmonica made on his countrymen, let us return to Nomini Hall, the home of Councillor Robert Carter in Virginia, and read Philip Vickers Fithian's description of a certain winter evening in that gentleman's household, in the year 1773: "Evening. Mr. Carter spent in playing on the Harmonica; it is the first time I have heard the Instrument. The Music is charming! The notes are clear and inexpressibly soft, they swell, and are inexpressibly grand; and either it is because the sounds are new, and therefore pleased me, or it is the most captivating Instrument I have ever heard."

Franklin as music critic

Franklin, though many-sided, was no mere dabbler. His interest in music was neither casual nor superficial. Proof of his profound and original thinking on musical subjects is afforded by two of his letters, one to the philosopher Lord Kames of Edinburgh, the other to his brother Peter Franklin, both written from London in 1765. These documents speak for themselves, and in view of their remarkable contents I make no apology for quoting from them at length. In his letter to Lord Kames, Franklin writes as follows:

In my passage to America I read your excellent work, "The Elements of Criticism," in which I found great entertainment. I only wish that you had examined more carefully the subject of music, and demonstrated that the pleasure artists feel in hearing much of that composed in the modern taste is not the natural pleasure arising from melody or harmony of sounds, but of the same kind with the pleasure we feel on seeing the surprising feats of tumblers and rope-dancers, who execute difficult things. For my part, I take this really to be the case, and suppose it to be the reason why those who are unpracticed in music, and therefore unacquainted with those difficulties, have little or no pleasure in hearing this music. I have sometimes, at a concert, attended by a common audience, placed myself so as to see all their faces, and observed no signs of pleasure in them during the performance of a great part that was admired by the performers themselves; while a plain old Scotch tune, which they disdained, and could scarcely be prevailed upon to play, gave manifest and general delight.

Give me leave, on this occasion, to extend a little the sense of your position, that "melody and harmony are separately agreeable and in union delightful," and to give it as my opinion that the reason why the Scotch tunes have lived so long, and will probably live forever (if they escape being stifled in modern affected ornament), is merely this, that they are really compositions of melody and harmony united, or rather that their melody is harmony. I mean the simple tunes sung by a single voice. As this will appear paradoxical, I must explain my meaning.

In common acceptation, indeed, only an agreeable *succession* of sounds is called *melody*, and only the *coexistence* of agreeable sounds *harmony*. But, since the memory is capable of retaining for some moments a perfect idea of the pitch of a past sound, so as to compare it with the pitch of a succeeding sound, and judge truly of their agreement or disagreement, there may be and does arise from thence a sense of harmony between the present and past sounds equally pleasing with that between two present sounds.

Now, the construction of the old Scotch tunes is this, that almost every succeeding emphatical note is a third, a fifth, an octave, or, in short, some note that is in concord with the preceding note. Thirds are chiefly used, which are very pleasing concords. I used the word *emphatical* to distinguish those notes which have a stress laid on them in singing the tune, from the lighter connecting notes that serve merely, like grammar articles in common speech, to tack the whole thing together.

[Franklin here puts forth several arguments to demonstrate that the mind can retain "a most perfect idea of sound just passed."]

Farther, when we consider by whom these ancient tunes were composed and how they were first performed, we shall see that such harmonical succession of sounds were natural, and even necessary, in their construction. They were composed by the minstrels of those days to be played on the harp, accompanied by the voice. The harp was strung with wire, which gives a sound of long continuance, and had no contrivance like that in the modern harpsichord, by which the sound of the preceding could be stopped the moment a succeeding note began. To avoid actual discord it was therefore necessary that the succeeding emphatical note should be a chord with the preceding, as their sounds must exist at the same time. Hence arose that beauty in those tunes that has so long pleased, and will please forever, though men scarce know why. That they were originally composed for the harp, and of the most simple kind, I mean a harp without any half notes but those in the natural scale and with no more than two octaves of strings, from C to C, I conjecture from another circumstance, which is, that not one of those tunes, really ancient, has a single artificial half note in it, and that in tunes where it was most convenient for the voice to use the middle notes of the harp and place the key in F, then the B, which, if used, should be a B flat, is always omitted by passing over it with a third. The connoisseurs in modern music will say I have no taste, but I cannot help adding that I believe our ancestors, in hearing a good song, distinctly articulated, sung to one of those tunes and accompanied by the harp, felt more real pleasure that is communicated by the generality of modern operas, exclusive of that arising from the scenery and dancing. Most tunes of late composition, not having this natural harmony united with their melody, have recourse to the artificial harmony of a bass and other accompanying parts. This support, in my opinion, the old tunes do not need, and are rather confused than aided by it. Whoever has heard James Oswald play these on his violoncello will be less inclined to dispute this with me. I have more than once seen tears of pleasure in the eyes of his auditors; and yet, I think, even *his* playing those tunes would please more, if he gave them less modern ornament.[5]

Notice that Franklin, in standing up for his convictions, has the supreme courage to risk being regarded as a person of no taste by "the connoisseurs in modern music."

Now here is the letter to Peter Franklin, which tells something

[6] *Ibid.*

about Benjamin Franklin's own attitude to that "modern music" whose artificialities he deplored and attacked. He writes:

Dear Brother: I like your ballad, and I think it well adapted for your purpose of discountenancing expensive foppery and encouraging industry and frugality. If you can get it generally sung in your country, it may probably have a good deal of the effect you hope and expect from it. But as you aimed at making it general, I wonder you chose so uncommon a measure in poetry that none of the tunes in common use will suit it. Had you fitted it to an old one, well known, it must have spread much faster than I doubt it will do from the best new tune we can get composed for it. I think, too, that if you had given it to some country girl in the heart of Massachusetts, who has never heard any other than psalm tunes or "Chevy Chase," the "Children in the Woods," the "Spanish Lady," and such old, simple ditties, but has naturally a good ear, she might more probably have made a pleasing popular tune for you than any of our masters here, and more proper to the purpose, which would best be answered if every word could, as it is sung, be understood by all that hear it, and if the emphasis you intend for particular words could be given by the singer as well as by the reader; much of the force and impression of the song depending on those circumstances. I will, however, get it as well done for you as I can.

Do not imagine that I mean to depreciate the skill of our composers of music here; they are admirable at pleasing practiced ears and know how to delight one another, but in composing for songs the reigning taste seems to be quite out of nature, or rather the reverse of nature, and yet, like a torrent, hurries them all away with it; one or two, perhaps, only excepted.

You, in the spirit of some ancient legislators, would influence the manners of your country by the united powers of poetry and music. By what I can learn of their songs, the music was simple, conformed itself to the usual pronunciation of words, as to measure, cadence or emphasis, etc., never disguised and confounded the language by making a long syllable short, or a short one long, when sung; their singing was only a more pleasing because a melodious manner of speaking, it was capable of all the graces of prose oratory, while it added the pleasure of harmony. A modern song, on the contrary, neglects all the proprieties and beauties of common speech, and in their place introduces its *defects* and *absurdities* as so many graces. I am afraid you will hardly take my word for this, and therefore I must endeavour to support it by proof. Here is the first song I lay my hand on. It happens to be a composition of one of our greatest masters, the ever famous Handel. It is not one of his juvenile performances, before his taste could be improved and formed; it appeared when his reputation was at the highest, is greatly admired by all his admirers, and is really excellent in its kind. It is called, "The additional favorite Song in Judas Maccabeus." Now I reckon among the defects and improprieties of common speech the following, viz.:

1. *Wrong placing the accent or emphasis* by laying it on words of no importance or on wrong syllables.

2. *Drawling;* or extending the sound of words or syllables beyond their natural length.

3. *Stuttering;* or making many syllables of one.

4. *Unintelligibleness;* the result of the three foregoing united.

5. *Tautology;* and

6. *Screaming* without cause.

Franklin, like an exact and conscientious critic, then quotes musical examples from Handel's song to illustrate each one of these defects. In a postscript he adds that he might have mentioned *inarticulation* among the defects in common speech that are assumed as beauties in modern singing. And he concludes with these two trenchant sentences: "If ever it was the ambition of musicians to make instruments that should imitate the human voice, that ambition seems now reversed, the voice aiming to be like an instrument. Thus wigs were first made to imitate a good natural head of hair; but when they became fashionable, though in unnatural forms, we have seen natural hair dressed to look like wigs."

Though it undoubtedly belongs among the London letters of 1765, this extraordinary document was first published in the *Massachusetts Magazine* for July, 1790, with the title "Criticism on Musick." [6] And excellent musical criticism it is, too, for it reveals wit, exactness, originality, sound judgment, and independence of thought. Franklin is not cowed by the enormous reputation of a composer like Handel; at the same time, he recognizes Handel's greatness and admits his music "is really excellent in its kind."

Franklin was one of the first to recognize the beauty, the power, and the integrity of folk tunes in their pristine state. His contention

[6] *Ibid.*

that these melodies should not be cluttered with new-fangled accompaniments and incongruous harmonizations anticipates the modern aesthetic position derived from the scientific study of folklore, which began fifty years after his death. In his musical ideas, as in everything else, Franklin was the most modern American of his times, the man who, in the words of Ibsen, was "most closely in league with the future."

In a letter to Mary Stevenson written from Philadelphia in 1763, Franklin wrote: "After the first cares of the necessaries of life are over, we shall come to think of the embellishments. Already some of our young geniuses begin to lisp attempts at painting, poetry and music." We shall now meet one of these "young geniuses" who lisped elegantly in all three arts.

"The sacred flame"

In the month of September, 1766, a young lawyer from Philadelphia named Francis Hopkinson, on a visit to relatives in England, attended a performance of Handel's *Messiah* at Gloucester. He had the misfortune of being afflicted by a large and painful boil, which just then was at the height of tension and inflammation. Listening to the music, he no longer felt any pain. The boil even broke while he was at the concert, without his perceiving it. Yet, as he told his friend Thomas Jefferson long afterward, had he been alone in his chamber he "should have cried out with Anguish." And, in a characteristic speculative vein, he added: "May not the Firmness of Martyrs be accounted for on the same principle?"

Whatever Francis Hopkinson may have thought about the Firmness of Martyrs, there can be no question about his belief in the Power of Music, for he repeatedly proved it both by word and deed. Some seven years before his English journey he had written a "Prologue in Praise of Music," in which these lines occur:

> Such pow'r hath music o'er the human soul,
> Music the fiercest passions can controul,
> Touch the nice springs that sway a feeling heart,
> Sooth ev'ry grief, and joy to joy impart.
> Sure virtue's friends and music are the same,
> And blest that person is that owns the sacred flame.

If "the sacred flame" be taken to symbolize devotion to music rather than creative genius, then Francis Hopkinson was abundantly blessed with that gift. At the age of seventeen, when he began to take up the study of the harpsichord, he wrote an "Ode to Music" that fully reveals his enthusiasm for the divine art:

> Hark! Hark! the sweet vibrating lyre
> Sets my attentive soul on fire;
> Thro' all my frame what pleasures thrill,
> Whilst the loud treble warbles shrill,
> And the more slow and solemn bass,
> Adds charms to charm and grace to grace.

And so on for four more stanzas, rising to a grand pæan of praise for "th' admir'd celestial art." To demonstrate Hopkinson's fidelity to the Muse, we need only quote the concluding lines of his poem titled "Description of a Church," in which he describes the effect made upon his sensibilities by the sound of the organ:

> Hail heav'n born music! by thy pow'r we raise
> Th' uplifted soul to arts of highest praise:
> Oh! I would die with music melting round,
> And float to bliss upon a sea of sound.

The final couplet almost matches the emotional mysticism of Fray Luis de León—and this from the pen of an eighteenth-century American lawyer, businessman, and public official!

This was the Age of Reason and of Good Taste, but it was also the Age of Sentiment and of Enthusiasm. A "rational" man like Francis Hopkinson could indulge his sensibilities to the full while keeping a firm hand on practical matters. Although as a poet he wrote about music like an enthusiast (which in eighteenth-century parlance meant a "crackpot"), he could also class it with "reading, walking, riding, drawing &ca." as agreeable pastimes that "season the Hours with calm and rational Pleasure."⁷ If Hopkinson let himself go in his feelings toward music, it was precisely because he considered it a "calm and rational pleasure" that even in its most ecstatic moments would not lead him from the path of Virtue and Reason. It thus contrasted with those moral dangers that he mentions in a letter to his mother from London: "You can have no Idea of the many Powerful Tempta-

---

⁷ Letter to Benjamin Franklin from Hartlebury Castle, England, 1767.

tions, that are continually thrown out here to decoy unwary Youth into Extravagance and Immorality."

Being by this time fairly well acquainted with the habits of the gentleman amateur, the reader will not be too surprised at finding a Philadelphia lawyer playing the harpsichord and dabbling in verse, or even trying his hand at painting, which was Hopkinson's third avocation. Born in Philadelphia on September 21, 1737, son of a distinguished father and a pious mother, Francis Hopkinson graduated from the College of Philadelphia, was admitted to the bar, and became prominent in the political, religious, educational, and artistic life of his native city. A staunch patriot, he cast his fortune and the power of his pen with the cause of the American Revolution, was a delegate to the Continental Congress and a signer of the Declaration of Independence. In 1779 he was appointed Judge of the Admiralty from Pennsylvania, and he took an active part in the Constitutional Convention of 1787, influencing its decisions with a humorous political pamphlet titled "The History of a New Roof." During the war he wrote his famous satirical poem, "The Battle of the Kegs," which became immensely popular. It was set to music and widely sung.

John Adams met Hopkinson in the studio of the artist Charles Willson Peale at Philadelphia in 1776 and wrote about the meeting to his wife: "He is one of your pretty, little, curious, ingenious men. His head is not bigger than a large apple. . . . I have not met with anything in natural history more amusing and entertaining than his personal appearance; yet he is genteel and well-bred, and is very social." Adams envied the leisure and tranquillity of mind that enabled Hopkinson to "amuse" himself with "those elegant and ingenious arts of painting, sculpture, statuary, architecture, and music."

Hopkinson as composer

Besides playing the harpsichord and the organ, which many other gentlemen amateurs also did, Francis Hopkinson composed a number of songs, which was a less common accomplishment. That Hopkinson himself was fully aware of the distinction to be derived from this achievement is indicated by the dedication (to George Washington) of his *Seven Songs for the Harpsichord* (1788), in which he says: "However small the Reputation may be that I shall derive from this Work I cannot, I believe, be refused the Credit of being the first

Native of the United States who has produced a Musical Composition." Let us see on what grounds he rested his claim to be regarded as America's first native-born composer.

It is not known for certain whether Hopkinson was self-taught in composition or whether he took lessons from one of the professional musicians who were active in Philadelphia. There is a strong probability that he studied with the English organist James Bremner, with whom he long maintained ties of friendship and upon whose death he wrote a touchingly sincere elegy. During his college days, young Hopkinson had already distinguished himself as a poet, as a performer, and, it would seem, as a composer. In the winter of 1756–1757 the students at the College of Philadelphia produced an adaptation of *The Masque of Alfred the Great* which, according to a newspaper report, included "an excellent Piece of new Music by one of the performers." The piece of music in question was a song, "Alfred, Father of the State," and in all likelihood Francis Hopkinson was its composer.

In 1759 Hopkinson began to copy out in a large book, in his neat and methodical manner, a collection of songs, operatic airs, cantatas, anthems, hymns, and duets, by various celebrated European composers, including Handel, Pergolesi, Purcell, and Arne. The completed collection contained over a hundred pieces in a volume of more than two hundred pages, and scattered among them were six songs signed with the initials "F. H." The first of these is "My Days Have Been So Wondrous Free" (a setting of Thomas Parnell's "Love and Innocence"), which has attained a somewhat unwarranted notoriety as the first known secular song composed by an American. The others are "The Garland," "Oh! Come to Mason Borough's Grove," "With Pleasures Have I Past [sic] My Days," "The Twenty-Third Psalm," and "An Anthem from the 114th Psalm." All of them are written in two parts—the ubiquitous eighteenth-century "treble and bass." The common procedure was for the accompanist to fill in the harmony at the harpsichord. It is curious to notice that the anthem includes a figured bass, a rarity in early American music.

The inclusion of the psalm and anthem in this collection points to Hopkinson's lifelong interest in church music. There is strong evidence to indicate that he was the compiler of *A Collection of Psalm Tunes, with a few Anthems and Hymns* . . . published at Philadelphia in 1763 for the United Churches of Christ Church and St.

Peter's Church. Hopkinson served as organist at Christ Church during the absence of James Bremner, and he also instructed the children of the two churches in "the art of psalmody." In 1786 he wrote *A Letter to the Rev. Dr. White on the Conduct of a Church Organ*, which contains some interesting observations on "the application of instrumental music to purposes of piety." Arguing for the dignity of church music, he writes: "It is as offensive to hear lilts and jigs from a church organ, as it would be to see a venerable matron frisking through the public street with all the fantastic airs of a *Columbine*."

During the 1780s, pro-French sentiment was at its height in Philadelphia. Hence we are not surprised to find the following notice in the *Freeman's Journal* for December 19, 1781:

> On Tuesday evening of the 11th inst. his Excellency the Minister of France, who embraces every opportunity to manifest his respect to the worthies of America, and politeness to its inhabitants, entertained his Excellency General Washington, and his lady, the lady of General Greene, and a very polite circle of gentlemen and ladies, with an elegant Concert, in which the following ORATORIO, composed and set to music by a gentleman whose taste in the polite arts is well known, was introduced and afforded the most sensible pleasure. The Temple of Minerva: An ORATORICAL ENTERTAINMENT.

The gentleman whose taste in the polite arts was so well known was, of course, our friend Francis Hopkinson.

A few weeks after this performance, the *Royal Gazette* of New York published the libretto of *The Temple of Minerva*, together with a grossly indecent parody by a Philadelphia correspondent, titled *The Temple of Cloacina*. Hopkinson's reply, published in the *Pennsylvania Gazette*, described the circumstances under which he first saw the parody, in thoroughly Rabelaisian terms. Such was the obverse of eighteenth-century elegance and taste!

On October 25, 1788, Hopkinson wrote to his friend Thomas Jefferson:

> I have amused myself with composing Six easy & simple Songs for the Harpsichord—Words & Music all my own. The Music is now engraving. When finished, I will do myself the Pleasure of sending a Copy to Miss Jefferson. The best of them is that they are so easy that any Person who can play at all may perform them with-

out much Trouble, & I have endeavour'd to make the Melodies pleasing to the untutored Ear.[8]

The work was published before the end of the year and was advertised as follows in the *Pennsylvania Packet:* "These songs are composed in an easy, familiar style, intended for young Practioners on the Harpsichord or Forte-Piano, and is the first work of this kind attempted in the United States."

The letter to Jefferson mentions six songs, the title of the book is *Seven Songs,* and the collection actually contains eight, with the last song bearing a note to the effect that it was added after the title page was engraved. Here is the complete contents, which consists of first lines:

Come, fair Rosina, come away
My Love is gone to the sea
Beneath a weeping willow's shade
Enraptur'd I gaze when my Delia is by
See down Maria's blushing cheek
O'er the hills far away, at the birth of the morn
My gen'rous heart disdains
The traveller benighted and lost

Hopkinson dedicated the volume to George Washington in a letter from which we quoted the passage in which he claims credit for being the first native American composer. He expresses the hope that "others may be encouraged to venture on a path, yet untrodden in America, and the Arts in succession will take root and flourish amongst us." Washington, who was fond of music though he played no instrument, replied in an amiable and humorous letter in which he laments his inability to do anything in support of the music, for "I can neither sing one of the songs, nor raise a single note on any instrument to convince the unbelieving." [9]

There is no point in attempting a detailed analysis and critique of Hopkinson's music. His songs are typical of hundreds written during the eighteenth century and show no creative individuality whatever. However quaint and innocuous they seem to us now, we must not

[8] Quoted in Hastings, *Life and Works of Francis Hopkinson,* pp. 436–437.
[9] The complete dedication and Washington's reply are printed in Hastings, *op. cit.,* pp. 441–444.

assume that they were without emotional effect either for Hopkinson or his listeners. Writing to Jefferson about the collection, Hopkinson said: "The last Song, if play'd very slow, and sung with Expression, is forcibly Pathetic—at least in my Fancy. Both Words & Music were the Work of an hour in the Height of a Storm. But the Imagination of an Author who composes from his Heart, rather than his Head, is always more heated than he can expect his Readers to be."

That at least one listener found this song "forcibly Pathetic" is indicated by Jefferson's reply: "Accept my thanks . . . and my daughter's for the book of songs. I will not tell you how much they have pleased us, nor how well the last of them merits praise for its pathos, but relate a fact only, which is that while my elder daughter was playing it on the harpsichord, I happened to look toward the fire, & saw the younger one all in tears. I asked her if she was sick? She said 'no; but the tune was so mournful.'" So that the reader may compare his or her own reactions with those of Jefferson and his daughter, we quote a portion of this song, *The Traveller Benighted and Lost.*

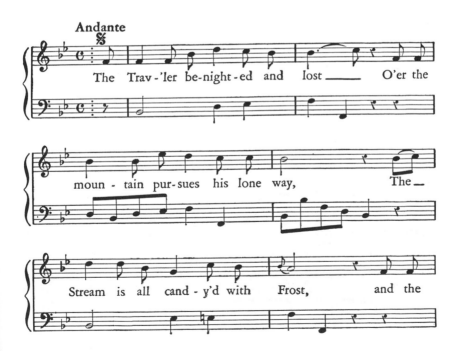

Hopkinson composed only one more song before his death in 1791. Titled "A New Song," it was a gay love lyric in which the poet asks, "What's life without the Joys of Love?"

Francis Hopkinson was correct in assuming that his historical priority would secure him a permanent place in the annals of America's music. It is not so much for his music that we value him, as for his attitude toward music. He represented the Golden Age of American culture, in which men of affairs, successful in business and in the conduct of government, thought it no shame not only to love music and practice it in private, but also to make public their love of the "Divine Art." Men like Jefferson, Franklin, and Hopkinson, in helping to create a nation that recognized man's inalienable right to the pursuit of happiness, did not overlook the aid and comfort that music can give in this unceasing quest.

Each of these three great American music lovers might be taken as a representative figure. Jefferson is the prototype of the patron of music, who, if he had been wealthy enough, would have endowed orchestras and formed rare collections of manuscripts and printed scores. Such patrons, backed by the wealth of the country's industrial development, were eventually to play an important role in the growth of our musical institutions. Franklin was the practical man with a strong inclination toward philosophical speculation: our first music critic, and one of the rare individuals of the eighteenth century who appreciated the strength and character of the musical vernacular. Hopkinson was the ancestor of a long line of amateur composers in the United States, from William Henry Fry in the nineteenth century to John Alden Carpenter in the twentieth. After all, most of our early American composers were amateurs, though few enjoyed such social and political prominence as Hopkinson. Our first professional musicians were those who came from Europe, and it is to these professional emigrants that we turn in the next chapter.

chapter six

Professional emigrants

The promptness of this young country in those sciences which were once thought peculiar only to a riper age, has already brought upon her the eyes of the world.
WILLIAM SELBY, ADVERTISEMENT FOR THE NEW MINSTREL (1782).

On the last Sunday of August in the year 1757, a tall, thin man, about sixty years of age, mounted on a small, white horse, rode rapidly along a road in Westmoreland County, Virginia. A glance inside his saddlebags would have revealed an assortment of musical instruments, including a violin, a German flute, an oboe, and a bassoon. A glimpse into his mind would have revealed that his chief concerns were, first, to place as much distance as possible between himself and Stratford, the home of Philipp Ludwell Lee, Esquire; and secondly, to reach a town whose inhabitants would appreciate the talents of a versatile fellow like himself, skilled in the polite arts of music, fencing, and dancing.

Meanwhile, the master of Stratford was fuming in anger over the loss of his prized bassoon. To relieve his feelings, he sat down and wrote an advertisement to appear in the leading colonial newspapers: "Runaway from the subscriber, at Stratford, in Westmoreland County . . . Charles Love . . . he professes Musick, Dancing, Fencing, and plays exceedingly well on the Violin and all Wind Instruments; he stole when he went away, a very good Bassoon, made by Schuchart, which he carried with him. . . . It is supposed he will make towards Charlestown in South Carolina." This, together with a description of the said Love, and the offer of a generous reward for his apprehension, drew public attention to Mr. Lee's loss.

The interesting point about all this is not that Charles Love stole a bassoon, but that, among the tidewater estates of colonial Virginia, there was a bassoon for him to steal, and a very good one, "made by Schuchart."

Apart from his larcenous propensities, which we may regard as a personal idiosyncrasy, Charles Love was in many ways typical of the professional musician who emigrated to the American colonies: a symbol of those hundreds of obscure musicians, more adventurous than their stay-at-home colleagues, who took their luck, for better or worse, in the New World. Versatile and resourceful they had to be in order to survive in a pioneer society in which the "polite arts" had yet to win a secure place. Few of them could earn a living solely by music, even with dancing and fencing as more remunerative side-lines. Some of them were obliged to become Jacks-of-all-trades. Herman Zedwitz, "violin teacher just from Europe," ran a chimney-sweeping business in New York. Giovanni Gualdo of Philadelphia was wine merchant as well as music teacher, concert manager, composer, and performer. William Selby, the organist and composer, sold groceries and liquor in Boston during the Revolution. Many of them found it difficult to keep one step ahead of their creditors. The English flutist and composer William Young, who settled in Philadelphia, was made so desperate by mounting debts that in a fit of rage he killed the constable sent by his creditors to arrest him.

In spite of all hazards and uncertainties, musical emigrants kept coming to America in steadily growing numbers. Before the Revolution, Charleston, South Carolina, was the chief point of attraction for professional musicians. This was because Charleston, in the words of Edmund Burke, "approached more nearly to the social refinement of a great European capital" than any other American city. And music was, of course, an indispensable ingredient of this "social refinement."

French horns and macaronis

The oldest musical society in the United States, the St. Cecilia Society, was founded at Charleston in 1762. It combined private subscription concerts with the most elegant and exclusive social amenities. The activities of the Society are mentioned in the journal of Josiah Quincy of Boston, who visited the Southern metropolis in 1772. Describing a dinner with the Sons of St. Patrick, Quincy writes:

"While at dinner six violins, two hautboys, etc. After dinner, six French horns in concert:—most surpassing music. Two solos on the French horn, by one who is said to blow the finest horn in the world. He has fifty guineas for the season from the St. Cecilia Society." This was considered a handsome remuneration.

To Josiah Quincy's journal we turn again for a priceless vignette of eighteenth-century music and manners. He recounts his impressions of a concert in Charleston:

> The music was good—the two base viols and French horns were grand. One Abercrombie, a Frenchman just arrived, played the first violin, and a solo incomparably better than any one I ever heard. He cannot speak a word of English, and has a salary of five hundred guineas a year from the St. Cecilia Society. There were upwards of two hundred and fifty ladies present, and it was called no great number. In loftiness of headdress, these ladies stoop to the daughters of the north,—in richness of dress, surpass them,—in health and floridity of countenance, vail to them. In taciturnity during the performance, greatly before our ladies; in noise and flirtation after the music is over, pretty much on a par. The gentlemen, many of them dressed with richness and elegance, uncommon with us: many with swords on. We had two macaronis present, just arrived from London.

As a revelation of the colonial mind, the key to this passage is in the final sentence, and especially the last phrase. Why should a serious and sensible man like Josiah Quincy bother to mention a couple of mincing fops—the two "macaronis"—in his description of a concert? Simply because they had "just arrived from London" and therefore set the ultimate note of fashionable bon ton upon the event he was describing. They brought the latest gossip from the Pall Mall coffee houses, reports of the latest hit at the Drury Lane Theatre, news of the latest Court scandal—just as Monsieur Abercrombie (queer name for a Frenchman!) brought the latest musical fashions from Paris. It was all part of the general pattern of eighteenth-century American urban culture (which the Revolution did not destroy): the imitation of European standards of taste. Though it could be carried to foolish extremes, the tendency at bottom sprang from a desire to get the "best" of everything, from fiddlers to fops. No cultivated American was naïve enough to believe that his youthful country could produce overnight musicians to equal the best of Europe. Yet their partiality to the sons of Bach, to Haydn, Stamitz, and other European celebrities, did not blind them to the merits of local talent. In the liberal-minded eighteenth-century attitude there was room for all: famous masters and local lights, professionals and amateurs, immigrants and native-born. The important thing was to have music, a lot of it, and the best that could be had. The fact that they preferred music by living composers is an amiable eccentricity, difficult for the twentieth-century music lover to understand, since for us the only "great" composers are the dead ones.

To get back to colonial Charleston, concerts had been given there long before the founding of the St. Cecilia Society. In 1737 a concert was announced "for the Benefit of Mr. Theodore Pachelbel," with the following significant notice: "N.B. As this is the first time the said Mr. Pachelbel has attempted anything of this kind in a publick manner in this Province, he thinks it proper to give Notice that there will be sung a Cantata suitable to the occasion." No further details are given regarding this cantata, but it is quite possible that it may have been composed by Pachelbel himself. There exists an admirable Magnificat of his, for eight voices with organ accompaniment, which reveals him as a well-schooled composer of superior ability.[1] This is not surprising in view of his background.

Charles Theodore Pachelbel was the son of the famous Nuremberg organist and composer Johann Pachelbel, one of the notable masters of the South German organ school and a precursor of J. S. Bach. Born in 1690, he migrated to America at the age of forty-three and became organist at Trinity Church in Newport, Rhode Island. In January, 1736, Pachelbel gave the first concert in New York of which a definite record exists. The following year he was in Charleston, where he died in 1750. His career indicates that even in the early decades of the eighteenth century America was attracting distinguished musicians from the Old World.

After the Revolution, musicians began to drift away from Charleston, to New York, Boston, and Philadelphia. The trend of musical progress swung northward. Philadelphia, in particular, became the leading cultural center of the young Republic and the chief center of musical activity.

[1] Published in the New York Public Library Music Series, ed. by H. T. David.

The general attends a benefit

A French observer, Moreau de Saint-Mery, declared that there were more beautiful women in Philadelphia than anywhere else in the world. This feminine pulchritude was matched by an impressive array of professional talent: the city was full of teachers, lawyers, physicians, scientists, philosophers, authors, and artists. In spite of the Quakers, the city was gay. A few cranks tried to clamp down on theatrical amusements but were eventually overridden by the more liberal majority. The pleasure-loving ranks received strong support from the example of General Washington, who never missed an opportunity to attend a play or a concert.

In June, 1787, the General was in Philadelphia as a delegate to the Constitutional Convention. His diary reveals that on June 12 he attended a concert for the benefit of a certain Mr. Alexander Reinagle, a musician from England who had recently established himself in Philadelphia. The program began with an Overture by Johann Christian (the "London") Bach, and ended with two compositions by Reinagle: a Sonata for the Pianoforte, and a new Overture (in which is introduced a Scotch strathspey). Whatever Washington thought of the music—and he probably enjoyed it, for his taste was good—he must have been impressed by Reinagle's skill and commanding presence at the pianoforte.

Alexander Reinagle was then about thirty years old, a handsome and vigorous man with firm features and the air of being a gentleman as well as a musician (a difficult combination to achieve in those days). Regarding his distinctive style of playing the pianoforte, a contemporary wrote: "He never aimed at excessive execution, but there was a sweetness of manner—nay, in the way he touched the instrument I might add, there was a sweetness of tone which, combined with exquisite taste and neatness, produced unusual feelings of delight." [2] The fact is that on this occasion George Washington, whether he knew it or not, was hearing the finest piano playing and the finest piano music produced in America up to that time. That Washington had high regard for Reinagle is indicated by his having engaged the latter to give music lessons to his adopted daughter, Nellie Custis. These two men, the soldier and the musician, had much in common, for each was

---

[2] John R. Parker, in *The Euterpeiad.*

a leader in his own field, a man of character and integrity who commanded respect from all. Reinagle before his orchestra was a counterpart of Washington before his army. And sometimes an eighteenth-century theater could be almost as dangerous as a battle field.

When General Washington, as President of the United States, attended the theater in Philadelphia (which was the nation's capital from 1790 to 1800), some measure of decorum was preserved by a special military guard, with a soldier posted at each door and four in the gallery—where trouble was most likely to break out. That part of the house was always crowded, and the rowdy element found safety in numbers. The "gods" of the galleries, as they were called, would hurl bottles and glasses, as well as apples, nuts, and vegetables, onto the stage and into the orchestra. No one obeyed the no-smoking signs, hence sensitive nostrils were continually assailed by the stench of cigars. In spite of regulations to the contrary, liquor was brought into the house and freely imbibed during the performance. The gay ladies of the town used the best boxes in the theater as their professional headquarters, until, in 1795, the managers decreed that "no persons of notorious ill fame will be suffered to occupy any seat in a box where places are already taken." When political feeling ran high, riots sometimes broke out in the theater.

As musical director of the New Theatre in Chestnut Street, Alexander Reinagle reigned over this unruly mob like a monarch over his court. This is the picture we get of him from a contemporary historian of the theater:

Who that only once saw old manager Reinagle in his official capacity, could ever forget his dignified *personne*. He presided at the pianoforte, looking the very personification of the patriarch of music—investing the science of harmonic sounds, as well as the dramatic school, with a moral influence reflecting and adorning its salutary uses with high respectability and polished manners. His appearance was of the reverend and impressive kind, which at once inspired the universal respect of the audience. Such was Reinagle's imposing appearance that it awed the disorderly of the galleries, or the fop of annoying propensities and impertinent criticism of the box lobby, into decorum. . . . It was truly inspiring to behold the polished Reinagle saluting from his seat (before the grand square pianoforte in the orchestra) the highest respectability of the city, as it entered into the boxes to take seats. It was a scene before the curtain that suggested a picture of the master of private ceremonies receiving his invited guests at the fashionable drawing-room. Mr. Reinagle was a gentleman and a musician.[3]

The admirable Mr. Reinagle

If Reinagle was not a "gentleman" in the strict meaning of the term as understood in the eighteenth century, he undoubtedly had qualities and accomplishments that led his contemporaries to bestow this title upon him *honoris causa*. The only false note we can detect in the description quoted above is that Reinagle was not actually "old" at the time. He was in his forties, and the fact is that he died at the age of fifty-three. He spent slightly less than half of his life in America, and he was among the most gifted and the most distinguished of the professional musicians who emigrated to this country before 1800.

Alexander Reinagle was born in the busy English seaport and naval base of Portsmouth, in April, 1756—just a few months after the birth of Mozart. His father was an Austrian musician, a fine trumpet player, who had settled in England. When Alexander was in his late teens, the family moved to Edinburgh, where the youngster seems to have received some lessons from the organist and composer Raynor Taylor, who later followed him to America. Young Reinagle became an excellent pianist as well as a violinist of considerable skill. He plunged into the brilliant and cosmopolitan musical life of London and came under the spell of the man who dominated the English musical scene between the death of Handel and the coming of Haydn—the clever and fashionable Johann Christian Bach, "Music Master in the Queen's Household" and chief arbiter of musical taste. The "London" Bach specialized in composing keyboard pieces "such as ladies can execute with little trouble," and in graceful sonatas for piano or harpsichord with violin accompaniment. Reinagle commenced his career as a composer along both of these lines, publishing first two collections of "short and easy pieces" for the pianoforte, followed by Six Sonatas for the Pianoforte or Harpsichord, with an accompaniment for Violin.

In the autumn of 1784 Reinagle went to Lisbon together with his younger brother Hugh, a cellist. They gave a concert there and also played for the Royal Family. Hugh was ill of consumption and died

[3] Durang, *History of the Stage in Philadelphia.*

during their sojourn in Lisbon. It was probably about this time that Reinagle paid a visit to Carl Philipp Emanuel Bach in Hamburg, who wrote him a cordial letter dated February 25, 1785, in which such a visit is mentioned. The "great" Bach expressed a desire to have a portrait of Reinagle to place in his cabinet or gallery of celebrities. The younger man no doubt fully appreciated the honor of such a request, coming from a master who was recognized as the greatest organist of the age. Bach's art and personality made a deep and lasting impression on Reinagle. Like all his contemporaries, Reinagle knew nothing of the art of Johann Sebastian Bach, for the old Cantor of Leipzig had enjoyed only a local reputation and his "difficult" style of composition was entirely out of fashion. The sons of Johann Sebastian were the men of the day.

In the spring of 1785 Alexander Reinagle found himself back in Portsmouth, saddened by the death of his brother. He was nearing thirty and must have felt that he stood at a turning point in his life. He was a member of the Society of Musicians of London and enjoyed good professional standing. Yet he did not take up again the old round of music-making in London. Instead he turned his thoughts to the New World. Was it the sight of the ships in Portsmouth harbor that directed his thoughts to America? Whatever the impulse that drove him, within a year he found himself sailing across the ocean, bound for the port of New York, facing an uncertain future in an unknown land.

Shortly after his arrival in the summer of 1786, Reinagle gave a concert in New York. He also announced that he was prepared to give lessons on the pianoforte, harpsichord, and violin. The response was far from encouraging, for New York, thriving commercially, had yet to develop a demand for musical culture. Hearing about the more favorable prospects offered by Philadelphia, Reinagle soon betook himself there. In Philadelphia he found three of his ex-European colleagues—Henry Capron, William Brown, and John Bentley—engaged in a professional quarrel, as a result of which the "City Concerts" had been discontinued. Reinagle immediately took the situation in hand. Effecting a reconciliation between Capron and Brown (Bentley conveniently left for New York), he revived the City Concerts with himself as principal manager and featured performer. His superior ability was at once apparent, and he forthwith assumed a decisive role in the musical affairs of the Quaker City.

Reinagle as composer

When the actor Thomas Wignell, in 1792, formed a new theatrical company in Philadelphia, Reinagle was appointed musical manager of the enterprise. His first task, however, was to supervise the building of the New Theatre in Chestnut Street, a large and handsome structure that came to be regarded as one of the seven wonders of America, while Wignell went abroad to recruit a company of actors and singers. In those days it was customary for theatrical companies to include musical works—chiefly "ballad operas" like *The Beggar's Opera*—as well as spoken drama in their repertoire. After a long delay caused by the terrible epidemic of yellow fever that ravaged Philadelphia, the New Theatre was formally opened on February 17, 1794, with a performance of Samuel Arnold's opera *The Castle of Andalusia*.

Wignell and Reinagle aimed to give equal importance to music and drama in their repertoire. Hence Reinagle was kept busy arranging and adapting musical works for the theater, and composing the music for several so-called "operas" and pantomimes. We qualify the term "opera" because most of these works were simply plays with incidental music and vocal numbers interspersed at suitable intervals. Among the plays for which Reinagle composed music were *Columbus, or The Discovery of America; Pizarro, or The Spaniards in Peru* (in collaboration with Raynor Taylor); *Slaves in Algiers, or A Struggle for Freedom* (described as "a play, interspersed with songs"); the *Savoyard, or The Repentant Seducer* ("musical farce"); and *The Volunteers*, "comic opera in two acts." This list gives a good idea of the sort of musical fare served up by American theaters in the eighteenth century, ranging from an historical tragedy in five acts (*Pizarro*) to a frothy two-act farce.

Very little of Reinagle's music for the theater has been preserved. The music for *Columbus*, arranged for piano, was copyrighted at Philadelphia in 1799, but no copy has been located. There are, however, two known copies of an *Indian March* "of the much admired play called *Columbus*," which may very likely be one of the numbers composed by Reinagle. The Library of Congress has a score of *The Volunteers*, the text of which was written by Mrs. Susanna Rowson, author of one of the earliest American novels (*Charlotte Temple,* 1791). The comic opera is mildly satirical and rather trite; the music, we may hope, does not represent Reinagle at his best.

Reinagle earned a living and exerted wide influence through his theatrical activities, but as a composer he makes his strongest appeal to us in a more intimate type of music, namely, his sonatas for piano. Some time after his arrival in Philadelphia, Reinagle composed four sonatas for piano, which were never published during his lifetime. (A modern edition was published in 1966, edited by Frederick Freedman from the original manuscript.) We have already seen that Reinagle's early sonatas and piano pieces, published in London, were written under the influence of Johann Christian Bach. Those early works reveal no marked individuality, for Reinagle had not yet fully found himself as a composer. Evidently his meeting with another and greater Bach—Carl Philipp Emanuel of Hamburg—shortly before his departure for America, was the beginning of a new phase in Reinagle's creative development, which found its complete fruition in the four Philadelphia sonatas. While the double influence of C. P. E. Bach and Haydn—where could he have found better models?—is apparent in these works, they are by no means mere imitations. They reveal a fresh and lively invention, resourcefulness in development and figuration, a fine feeling for structure and proportion, and a capacity for sustained lyrical expression in the Adagios.

All but the first of these sonatas are in three movements (fast-slow-fast), following the pattern established by Emanuel Bach. In the first sonata the slow movement is missing. Bound together with it in the manuscript, however, are two pieces, both in the form of theme with variations. The second of these, an Andante in A major, is particularly attractive and might well serve as a middle movement for this sonata.

During his last years, which he spent in Baltimore, Reinagle worked enthusiastically on composing a kind of secular oratorio based on selections from Milton's *Paradise Lost.* The original feature of the work was that spoken narrative replaced the usual recitatives. We can only guess at its musical contents, for the manuscript—left incomplete at his death—has disappeared.

One of the musicians associated with Reinagle in the City Concerts of Philadelphia was the organist, pianist, and composer John Christopher Moller (*d.* 1803). Arriving in Philadelphia in 1791, Moller became organist of Zion Church and two years later opened a music store together with Henri Capron; to this enterprise a music school was added. In 1795 Moller went to New York, where he succeeded Peter A. Van Hagen as manager of the Old City Concerts. He frequently appeared as a performer on Franklin's glass harmonica. He composed a quantity of instrumental music, including a Sinfonia and a String Quartet.

A rare character

Frequently associated with Reinagle as a composer for the New Theatre was his older friend, colleague, and former teacher, Raynor Taylor, who outlived him by many years. Trained in the King's singing school as one of the boys of the Chapel Royal, Taylor was for a time musical director of the Sadler's Wells Theatre in London He came to America in 1792 and appeared in Baltimore as "music professor, organist and teacher of music in general." He also appeared in the less dignified role of theatrical entertainer, specializing in a type of musical skit called "olio," very similar to a modern vaudeville sketch. Moving to Philadelphia soon afterward, he became organist at St. Peter's Church, without renouncing his theatrical high jinks— which is further proof of the eighteenth century's tolerant attitude toward such matters.

Raynor Taylor seems to have been a rare blend of erudition and clownishness. He had the reputation of being the finest organist in America, famous for his masterly improvisations. Reinagle declared that he considered Taylor's extemporizing on the organ "to be equal to the skill and powers of Bach himself"—by whom, of course, he meant C. P. E. Bach of Hamburg. John R. Parker, who often heard him play, wrote of his "never failing strain of harmony and science. . . . His ideas flowed with wonderful freedom in all the varieties of plain chant, imitation and fugue." The same writer mentions the composer's "shelves groaning under manuscript files of overtures, operas, anthems, glees, &c." In spite of his extraordinary skill and industry, Raynor Taylor achieved no other material recompense than "the drudgery of teaching and a scanty organ salary."

But lack of the world's goods did not dampen Taylor's sense of humor. His hilarious parodies of Italian opera were highly appreciated by a select circle. Let Parker, an eyewitness, be once again our chronicler: "Sometimes among particular friends he would in perfect playfulness sit down to the pianoforte and extemporise an Italian opera. . . . The overtures, recitatives, songs and dialogue, by singing alternately in the natural and falsetto voice, were all the thought of the moment, as well as the words, which were nothing but a sort of gibberish with Italian terminations. Thus would he often in sportive mood throw away ideas sufficient to establish a musical fame."[4]

Many of Taylor's compositions have been preserved, but they are mostly comic skits, light songs, and incidental pieces that give little idea of his real stature as a composer. Yet, bearing in mind the importance that the "olio" was to acquire in the minstrel show of the mid-nineteenth century, we may look upon Raynor Taylor, the erudite church organist, as a significant precursor of the popular American lyric theater. He has also another claim to fame, for before his death in 1825 he was active in founding the Musical Fund Society of Philadelphia, one of the most important musical organizations in America.

The versatile Mr. Carr

Associated with Raynor Taylor in founding the Musical Fund Society was Benjamin Carr (1768–1831), one of the most versatile, most energetic, and most successful of the post-Revolutionary musical emigrants. Arriving at New York in 1793, he was soon followed by his brother Thomas, and his father, Joseph Carr. The three of them became very successful as music publishers and dealers, with stores in Philadelphia, Baltimore, and New York. Benjamin Carr made his American debut as a singer and quickly won popular favor in ballad operas. But his most important contributions to America's musical life were made as composer, arranger, organist, pianist, and, above all, as publisher and editor. He edited the *Musical Journal* founded by his father and published *Carr's Musical Miscellany in Occasional Numbers*.

The Carrs imported the best vocal and instrumental music from Europe, but did not neglect local talent. The first issue of *The Gentleman's Amusement*, a periodical musical collection published by Carr in Philadelphia, contained *The President's March* by Philip Phile. This is of special interest to us because later this march was used for the tune of "Hail Columbia," the famous patriotic song written by Joseph Hopkinson, son of our friend Francis Hopkinson. Hopkinson wrote the words of this song at the request of the actor Gilbert Fox, who

[4] Parker, *Musical Biography*.

sang it for the first time with immense success at the New Theatre on the night of April 25, 1798. Two days later, Carr brought out the old tune in a new edition, advertising it as "the very favorite New Federal Song." And as "Hail Columbia" it soon became established as one of our first national songs.

Also published in *The Gentleman's Amusement* was Carr's *Federal Overture*, arranged as a "duetto for two German flutes," consisting of a medley of patriotic airs, including the highly popular "Yankee Doodle"—this being the first time that this famous tune was printed in America, though it had been widely known since pre-Revolutionary days.

In launching his weekly *Musical Journal* (1800), Carr announced that for his selections of vocal and instrumental music he would draw on "a regular supply of new music from Europe and the assistance of Men of Genius in the Country" (that is, in the United States). This sums up Carr's sound and constructive policy of striking a fair balance between foreign importations and native products. And he recognizes that there are already "Men of Genius" in the country. Of course, the eighteenth century did not attach exactly the same meaning to "genius" that we do: it meant talent and skill rather than supreme inspiration.

That Benjamin Carr was a musician of exceptional talent, if not precisely a "genius," is proved by his extant compositions, including some of the music of his opera, *The Archers; or, the Mountaineers of Switzerland*, produced at New York in 1796. The libretto deals with the story of William Tell. The only two musical numbers from this opera that have been preserved are a graceful Rondo from the overture and the song, "Why, Huntress, Why?" which Carr published in his *Musical Journal*.[5]

New York and Boston

Among the musicians who came to America before the Revolution were William Tuckey (1708–1781) and William Selby (1738–1798), both organists from England. The former settled in New York (around 1753), the latter in Boston (around 1771). Tuckey became organist and choirmaster of Trinity Church, taught music in the affiliated Free

[5] Julian Mates, in his book *The American Musical Stage before 1800* (1962), is concerned almost exclusively with Benjamin Carr's *The Archers*, which he regards as a forerunner of the American musical play.

School, and organized concerts. In 1770 he presented, for the first time in America, excerpts from Handel's *Messiah* (the Overture and sixteen numbers). He composed anthems, psalm tunes, and odes, which were printed in various American collections. In 1760 his *Thanksgiving Anthem* was performed at Trinity Church "before his Excellency General Amherst on his return to New York from the Conquest of Canada."

Selby was appointed organist at King's Chapel shortly after his arrival in Boston, but during the lean years of the Revolution he earned a living by keeping a grocery store. He composed Ten Voluntaries for the organ or harpsichord (*ca.* 1767), anthems, odes, songs, and instrumental pieces. His "Ode for the New Year" (January 1, 1790) was printed in *The Massachusetts Magazine* (Boston, 1789).[6] In 1782 he issued proposals for the publication of a musical collection in monthly installments, to be titled *The New Minstrel*. Selby's advertisement (printed in the *Boston Evening Post*, February 2, 1782) reflects the self-confidence and the cultural aspiration of the new Republic:

At this age of civilization, at this area [sic] of the acquaintance with a nation far gone in politeness and fine arts—even the stern patriot and lover of his country's glory, might be addressed on the present subject with not less propriety than the man of elegance and taste.

The promptness of this young country in those sciences which were once thought peculiar only to riper age, has already brought upon her the eyes of the world.

And shall those arts which make her happy, be less courted than those arts which have made her great? Why may she not be "In song unequall'd as unmatched in war"?

While it was doubtless an exaggeration to claim that the eyes of the world were fixed with admiration on the arts in America, it is a fact that after Independence, artists and musicians were increasingly attracted to "this young country." After 1790, New York and Boston began to assume greater importance as musical centers: the trend of musical activity flowed northward.

In 1789 the leading musician in New York was Peter Albrecht Van Hagen (*ca.* 1750–1803), lately "organist and director of the City's Concert in Rotterdam," who had come from Charleston, South Carolina, with his musically gifted family—wife, daughter, and son, Peter

[6] Reprinted in the anthology *Music in America*, by Marrocco and Gleason.

Albrecht, Jr. In New York Van Hagen advertised himself as prepared to give instruction on the "violin, harpsichord, tenor [viola], violoncello, German flute, clarinet, bassoon, and singing." He organized subscription concerts in which he appeared as violinist while his son reaped applause as a child prodigy on the piano (later Junior also took up the violin).

In 1796 the Van Hagen family moved to Boston,[7] where the father was appointed conductor at the Haymarket Theater. (Boston by this time had two theaters—the other was the Federal Theater.) Van Hagen Senior wrote the music for at least two "musical dramas" performed at the Haymarket Theater: *The Adopted Child* (1797) and *Columbus* (1800). In 1798, father and son established a "Musical Magazine and Warehouse" for the sale of music and instruments, but their main activity was as teachers. Between them they covered not only Boston but many of the neighboring towns, such as Salem, Dedham, Dorchester, Newton, Cambridge, and Waltham. After the elder Van Hagen's death in 1803, the family's influence declined, and Peter Albrecht, Jr. (1781–1837), died in obscurity.

Perhaps one of the reasons why the Van Hagens moved to Boston was that after 1792 they faced strong competition from a group of professional musicians who had been active at the opera house (Hanover Square) in London and in "Professional Concerts under the direction of Haydn, Pleyel, etc." Among them were the English violinist and composer James Hewitt (1770–1827), the ill-fated flutist William Young, and the Belgian violinist Jean Gehot. Their first concert in New York included Gehot's Overture in twelve movements, expressive of a voyage from England to America, and Hewitt's Overture in nine movements, expressive of a battle. The former had the advantage—if such it was—of being based on personal experience, while the latter catered to a fad of the day, the musical battle-piece, of which Kotzwara's *Battle of Prague* (introduced to America by Benjamin Carr) was a notorious example.

The music of these overtures has disappeared; but another battle-piece by Hewitt has survived: *The Battle of Trenton*, a sonata for pianoforte published in 1797 and dedicated to General Washington. The composer undertook to depict musically such episodes as "The Army in Motion"—"Attack-Cannons-Bombs"—"Flight of the Hessians" —"General Confusion"—"Articles of Capitulation Signed"—"Trumpets

---

[7] After moving to Boston, the Van Hagens changed the prefix of their name to "Von."

of Victory"—"General Rejoicing." In order to prevent unnecessary confusion, the descriptive captions were printed with the score. The appearance of "Yankee Doodle" attested to the popularity of this tune. Hewitt also wrote some non-descriptive Sonatas for piano, which are more elegant but less entertaining.

Hewitt's position in New York was comparable to that of Reinagle in Philadelphia: he organized subscription concerts, appeared as performer, and was the principal composer and arranger for the Old American Company. In addition, he bought the New York branch of Benjamin Carr's store and embarked upon the business of selling and publishing music. In this enterprise he was less successful; the business only prospered after it had been taken over by his son, John Hill Hewitt (who will reappear later as an important composer).

James Hewitt's opera *Tammany* was performed in 1794 under the auspices of the Tammany Society of New York, then a center of anti-Federalist feeling. This sponsorship made him the target of political animosity: the Federalist faction decried his opera as "a wretched thing" and "a mélange of bombast." Since the music is lost, no calm judgment of its merit is now possible. In the same year, Hewitt composed another opera, *The Patriot, or Liberty Asserted,* based on the story of the Swiss patriot William Tell. This score has also disappeared, so that Hewitt's reputation as a composer for the theater rests solely on hearsay.

In 1810, Hewitt decided to move with his family to Boston. There he continued to give concerts, but his rivals were so firmly entrenched that he did not become the dominant figure he had been in New York. In his last years, separated from his second wife, he returned to New York, where he died—anxious to the last about the precious manuscripts he had left with his wife in Boston.

Associated with Hewitt in New York as composer and arranger for the Old American Company was the French musician Victor Pelissier, who wrote or arranged the music for some twenty operas or musical plays. Some of these he adapted from works by well-known composers of the time, such as Samuel Arnold, Charles Dibdin, William Shield, and Stephen Storace. Pelissier's opera *Edwin and Angelina* (1796) was based on a novel by Oliver Goldsmith. He also composed a patriotic song, "Washington and Independence."

The Italian composer Filippo Trajetta, or Philip Traetta (1777–1854), a native of Venice and a pupil of Piccini, was active in Boston, New York (1808–1817), and Charleston before settling at

Philadelphia in 1822. His cantata *Peace* (Jubilate), written to celebrate peace with England after the War of 1812, was performed by the Handelian Society of New York in 1815. He also wrote the oratorios *Jerusalem in Affliction* and *The Daughters of Zion;* an opera, *The Venetian Maskers;* cantatas, marches, piano pieces, and songs. One of his topical pieces was *Commodore Decatur's Turkish March* (1817).

During his sojourn in Boston, Traetta joined forces with the French musician François Mallet (1750–1834) and the German musician Gottlieb Graupner (1767–1836) in founding a musical academy (1801), which at first was very successful. The triple partnership soon broke up, however, and Traetta departed for Charleston, leaving Graupner to carry on the enterprise. This he did with remarkable success, especially in the music-printing branch of the business, which he established in 1802. For the next twenty years or more, Graupner was to be the leading music publisher in Boston, as well as the most successful teacher.

Johann Christian Gottlieb Graupner was the son of a professional oboist in Hanover, Germany, where he was born. Trained as an oboist, he went to England, where he played in the orchestra conducted by Josef Haydn. In 1795 he emigrated to America, establishing himself in Charleston, South Carolina. There he married the English singer Catherine Comerford Hillier (or Hellyer), who was enjoying a very successful career in America. After touring together for a while, they settled in Boston in 1797 and quickly became the musical luminaries of that city, in the theater and the concert hall. In 1810 the Boston *Gazette* informed its readers that Mrs. Graupner's benefits were "annually attended by the most brilliant and respectable circles of the community." That was the year in which Graupner and some associates founded the Philharmonic Society, which continued its activities until 1824. He was also one of the founders, in 1815, of the famous Handel and Haydn Society. His *Rudiments of the art of playing on the piano forte. . . .* appeared in 1806 and was reissued in 1819, 1825, and 1827. We can agree with the historian of music in Boston who wrote that, "For twenty-five years, or the first quarter of the century, Graupner remained the unquestioned leader of all musical forces, and the most esteemed musical scholar of the town."[8]

[8] H. Earle Johnson, *Musical Interludes in Boston*, p. 191. This work includes a "Catalogue of Graupner Publications," which lists 420 items by some 120 composers.

chapter seven

Native pioneers

Our Country is made up of the small fry. Give me a Seine of small meshes.
MASON L. ("PARSON") WEEMS, LETTER TO MATHEW CAREY (MARCH 25, 1809).

The native-born American musician in the eighteenth century occupied a sort of no man's land between the privileged security of the gentleman amateur and the acknowledged competence of the professional emigrant. Salaried positions in church or theater were almost invariably filled by the foreign musicians. Our native musical pioneers, being self-taught empiricists with more zeal than skill, could not at this early stage hope to compete with the imported professionals on their own ground. Nevertheless, by their energy and enthusiasm, and the frequent success of a good hymn tune, they managed to stake out an area for themselves which, if it seldom provided them with a living, yet enabled them to supply with considerable effectiveness a large portion of the country's rapidly growing musical needs. Being mostly "small fry" themselves, they knew how to make a seine of small meshes to catch their own kind. They could not boast of having performed before the crowned heads of Europe, but they knew what the farmers and artisans and tradesmen of America wanted. Being of the people, they made music for the people.

As Balzac remarked in a conversation, "To live in a material way one must work—one must be a sower, a reaper, a spinner, a weaver, a carpenter, a mason, a blacksmith, a wheelright. . . . The rest is luxury—luxury of the mind, of genius, of reason." True enough; yet even a mason or a blacksmith may aspire to a taste of that luxury of mind or spirit. The question is, if touched by "the sacred flame," how far shall he let it carry him from the material realities of life—to what heights, or to what depths? Take the case of Jacob Kimball, a blacksmith of Topsfield, Massachusetts. Old Jake had some musical ability; no doubt he sang at his forge; and surely it was a proud day for him when he was "chosen to set ye psalms, and to sit in ye elder's seat" in the local church. Thus on the Sabbath and on meeting days he enjoyed the mild luxury of setting ye psalms—but the rest of the time he stuck to his smithy. Now, the blacksmith of Topsfield had a son, Jacob Kimball, Jr., who was fortunate enough to attend Harvard College, where he prepared himself for the practice of law. What an opportunity, in this democratic land, for the second generation to advance in wealth and social prestige! But what had been a mild infection in the father became virulent in the son. On December 7, 1795, the Rev. William Bentley of Salem wrote in his diary: "Found Mr. Kimball, the celebrated musician, at his father's. It is his purpose to establish himself in the law in Maine." So Jacob Junior, promising young lawyer, is already known as a "celebrated musician." He had, in fact, compiled and published in 1793 *The Rural Harmony*, containing original compositions by himself "for the use of singing schools and singing assemblies." Whatever intention he may have had of establishing himself in the law was soon abandoned in favor of music. Kimball went about teaching singing schools in New England and promoting his own collections of psalms and hymns. He finally died at the almshouse in Topsfield.

Let us glance for a moment at the career of the most popular American composer of his generation, William Billings. He gave up the trade of tanner to devote himself entirely to music. He published many collections, and his music was known and sung all over the country. He managed to buy a house in Boston, but at his death he left his family in poverty. They could not even afford to buy a tombstone for his grave in Boston Common. In the official record of his decease his occupation was given as "tanner." For the American pioneer, music had not yet become either a trade or a profession.

Let us call the roll of these native musical pioneers, for names convey something of the character and background and even perhaps the history of the men who bear them. Here they are: Supply Belcher, Asahel Benham, William Billings, Bartholomew Brown, Amos Bull, Amos Doolittle, Josiah Flagg, Ezekiel Goodale, Oliver Holden, Jeremiah Ingalls, Stephen Jenks, Thomas Loud, Justin Morgan, Daniel Read, Timothy Swan, Abraham Wood. These are not all, but they are enough to give the feel of the breed: solid yeoman names, smacking of the humbler trades and occupations. The records confirm this: Belcher was a tavernkeeper; Billings a tanner; Bull a storekeeper; Doolittle a silversmith; Holden a carpenter; Ingalls a cooper; Morgan a horse breeder; Read a combmaker; Swan a hatter; Wood a fuller, or dresser, of cloth.

Not all of them remained poor and humble. Being Americans in a free society, they were entitled to climb as high on the social and economic ladder as their enterprise and energy could take them. While none of them attained to remarkable wealth or eminence, several became substantial and influential citizens in their communities. Oliver Holden, starting as a carpenter in Charlestown, Massachusetts, became a large-scale real-estate operator and a member of the Massachusetts House of Representatives. Daniel Read set himself up as a manufacturer of ivory combs, and also established a business as publisher and bookseller. Supply Belcher settled in Farmington, Maine, where he became a justice of the peace and a representative in the legislature. These were typical figures in our early musical life, men in close touch with the little people of our country. It will be the purpose of this chapter to relate something of their lives, their achievements, and their lasting influence in shaping America's music.

Almost our first composer

Although the New England group of composers and compilers of sacred music dominates this period, it so happens that the first American book of psalmody to appear after the publications of Tufts and Walter in the 1720s was a work entitled *Urania*, printed at Philadelphia in 1762. Its author was James Lyon (1735–1794), a native of Newark, New Jersey, where his father was "yeoman of the town." Orphaned at an early age, Lyon was sent by his guardians to the College of New Jersey, which until 1756 was located in Newark. In that year the College (later Princeton University) was moved to Princeton, where Lyon received his Bachelor of Arts degree in 1759. The commencement exercises for that year included the singing of an Ode "set to music by Mr. James Lyon, one of the students." Thus we find him already appearing as a composer, without knowing when or how he acquired a musical education. The music of Lyon's commencement ode has not been preserved.

It will be recalled that Francis Hopkinson's earliest extant song dates from 1759, the same year in which Lyon's Ode was sung at Princeton. How, then, does Hopkinson claim precedence over Lyon as "America's first native-born composer"? The fact is that the assignment of such a title to Hopkinson is rather arbitrary and meaningless, because in all probability there were earlier amateur composers active in the Colonies. There is, indeed, evidence that Rev. John Tufts of Massachusetts may have composed some psalm tunes in the early eighteenth century. Hopkinson is simply the first American composer whose identified works have been preserved. Though Lyon's collection of psalms and hymns was not published until 1762, it is probable that some of his compositions included in that volume were composed somewhat earlier.

Curiously enough, Hopkinson and Lyon shared the musical honors at a public commencement program given by the College of Pennsylvania in Philadelphia on May 23, 1761. According to a notice in the *Pennsylvania Gazette* the event took place "before a vast Concourse of People of all Ranks," and "there was performed in the Forenoon an elegant *Anthem* composed by James LYON, of New Jersey College, and in the Afternoon an *Ode* . . . written and set to music in a very grand and masterly Taste by Francis Hopkinson, Esq. A.M. of the College of this City." Note that Hopkinson, a "favorite son," is given abundant praise, while Lyon, an outsider who had only recently come to Philadelphia, has to be satisfied with the trite adjective "elegant." Anyway, Lyon's music was publicly performed in the cultured stronghold of Brotherly Love, and this was an important steppingstone to fame.

Shortly after his arrival in Philadelphia in 1760, Lyon issued proposals for the publication by subscription of a collection of psalms, hymns, and anthems, which appeared two years later with the following title:

URANIA, or a choice Collection of Psalm-Tunes, Anthems and Hymns from the most approved Authors, with some entirely new; in two, three and four Parts, the whole adapted to the Use of Churches and Private Families; to which are prefixed the plainest and most necessary Rules of Psalmody.

A new edition was published at Philadelphia in 1767, and another in 1773, indicating the continued demand for Lyon's collection. The author's avowed purpose was "to spread the art of Psalmody, in its perfection, thro' our American colonies." The work was liberally dedicated to "the Clergy of every Denomination in America."

Lyon himself was ordained to the Presbyterian ministry in 1764 (he had taken his M.A. at Princeton in 1762), and the following year was sent to Nova Scotia, where he had a hard struggle to support himself and his family. In 1771 he became pastor in the newly settled town of Machias, Maine, remaining there, except for two brief intervals, until his death. During the Revolution he was an ardent supporter of the American cause, and in 1775 he wrote a long letter to George Washington outlining a plan for conquering Nova Scotia, which he proposed to carry out himself. Washington replied politely, but nothing came of the scheme.

These practical interests and activities apparently did not prevent Lyon from continuing to compose music, judging by an entry in the diary of Philip Vickers Fithian, whom we met previously as a tutor in the home of Councillor Carter of Virginia. In 1774 Fithian spent his vacation at Cohansie, New Jersey, where Lyon also happened to be visiting at the time. Under date of Friday, April 22, 1774, Fithian wrote:

Rode to the Stage early for the Papers thence I went to Mr. Hunters where I met with that great master of music, Mr. Lyon.— He sung at my request, & sings with his usual softness and accuracy —He is about publishing a new Book of Tunes which are to be chiefly of his own Composition. . . .[1]

Besides confirming Lyon's reputation as a composer, this passage offers our only clue to the possible existence of another book by him. No trace of this "new Book of Tunes" has been found, and for all we know it may never have been published. In the 1930s an old hymn-book with the title page missing was found in a barn in Newburyport, Massachusetts. The first composition in this book is an *Anthem on Friendship* by James Lyon. This has led to the conjecture that the unidentified Newburyport volume might be Lyon's "new Book of Tunes." [2]

The collection titled *Urania* contains six compositions by Lyon: settings of the 8th, the 18th, the 23d and the 95th Psalms; an Anthem taken from the 150th Psalm; and the 104th Psalm "imitated" by Dr. Watts. Other compositions by Lyon appeared in various collections: *A Marriage Hymn* in Daniel Bayley's *New Universal Harmony* (1775), the 17th Psalm in *The Chorister's Companion* (1788) compiled by Simeon Jocelyn, the 19th Psalm in the fourth edition of Andrew Law's *The Rudiments of Music* (1792). The *Anthem on Friendship*, already mentioned, was published in Stickney's *Gentlemen's and Ladies' Musical Companion* (1774) and, as late as 1807, in

[1] Fithian, *Journal and Letters*, p. 101.
[2] See *Notes* of the Music Library Association, IV, 3, p. 293.

Elias Mann's *Massachusetts Collection of Sacred Harmony*. This makes a total of ten compositions that can definitely be ascribed to James Lyon.

Today we can discover little intrinsic merit in Lyon's music, but we should note his considerable reputation among his contemporaries, who obviously considered his music worthy of praise, publication, and public performance. At one of Andrew Adgate's "Uranian Concerts" at Philadelphia in 1786, an anthem by Lyon was performed on the same program with music by Handel—an indication that our ancestors managed to combine recognition of native talent with admiration for the great European masters. Lacking such encouragement and recognition, the path of our musical pioneers would have been drear and difficult indeed.

Billings of Boston

William Billings was born in Boston on October 7, 1746. As a youth he was apprenticed to learn the tanner's trade, and as far as the official records are concerned, a tanner he remained to the end of his days. But, like so many others around him, he caught the contagion of music, and before long he was devoting all of his remarkable energy and promotional ability to teaching, conducting, composing, and publishing music. Unlike his colleagues, he engaged in no business side lines, but devoted himself completely, recklessly, tirelessly, to the art that he loved above all else. "Great art thou O Music!"—he exclaimed in one of his frequent outbursts of enthusiasm—"and with thee there is no competitor. . . ."

His natural gifts, his energy and industry, and his force of character, all concentrated without deviation on his life's one ambition—the composition, performance, and promotion of music—gave Billings a unique position among his fellow Americans. Great must have been his force of character, for his personal appearance, to judge by the account of a contemporary, was not prepossessing. The Rev. William Bentley of Salem wrote of him just after his death: "He was a singular man, of moderate size, short of one leg, with one eye, without any address, and with an uncommon negligence of person. Still he spake and sang and thought as a man above the common abilities." Billings knew his own worth.

Billings probably received no formal schooling after the age of fourteen, when his father, a shopkeeper, died. He is said to have received some music lessons from a local choirmaster, and he evidently studied Tans'ur's *Musical Grammar*. He was only twenty-four when he published his first book, *The New England Psalm Singer, or American Chorister* (Boston, 1770), containing psalm tunes, anthems, and canons of his own composition. His other collections were: *The Singing Master's Assistant* (1778; popularly known as "Billing's Best"); *Music in Miniature* (1779); *The Psalm Singer's Amusement* (1781); *The Suffolk Harmony* (1786); and *The Continental Harmony* (1794). He died in Boston on September 26, 1800.

Billings was not in the least disconcerted by his lack of scientific knowledge. On the contrary, he gloried in his musical independence. In *The New England Psalm Singer* he aired his views in words that may be taken as his own musical credo:

Perhaps it may be expected by some, that I should say something concerning Rules for Composition; to these I answer that Nature is the best Dictator, for all the hard, dry, studied rules that ever was prescribed, will not enable any person to form an air. . . . It must be Nature, Nature must lay the Foundation, Nature must inspire the Thought. . . . For my own Part, as I don't think myself confin'd to any Rules for composition, laid down by any that went before me, neither should I think (were I to pretend to lay down Rules) that any one who came after me were any ways obligated to adhere to them, any further than they should think proper; so in fact, I think it best for every *Composer* to be his own *Carver*.

In justice to Billings, it must be pointed out that he sought to strike a happy balance between nature and art. In the same essay from which we have just quoted, he writes:

But perhaps some may think I mean and intend to throw Art entirely out of the Question. I answer by no Means, for the more Art is displayed, the more Nature is decorated. And in some forms of Composition, there is dry Study required, and Art very requisite. For instance, in a *Fuge* [*sic*], where the parts come in after each other, with the same notes; but even there, Art is subservient to Genius, for Fancy goes first, and strikes out the Work roughly, and Art comes after, and polishes it over.

By the term "Fuge," Billings did not, of course, mean what we understand by the term "fugue," in the sense of a formal composition in contrapuntal texture. His "fuges" were brief imitative passages in which, as he says, "the parts come after each other, with the same notes." Although he did not create the "fuging tune," which was known in England and had earlier antecedents in the old psalm tunes called "Rapports," Billings's name is popularly associated with this type of composition because of his success in exploiting it.

In his *Thoughts on Music*, Billings tells us something about the way in which he thinks his music should be sung:

> Suppose a Company of Forty People, Twenty of them should sing the Bass, the other Twenty should be divided according to the discretion of the Company into the upper Parts, six or seven of the deepest voices should sing the Ground Bass . . . which if well sung together with the upper Parts, is most Majestic; and so exceeding Grand as to cause the floor to tremble, as I myself have often experienced. . . . Much caution should be used in singing a Solo, in my opinion Two or Three at most are enough to sing it well, it should be sung as soft as an echo, in order to keep the Hearers in an agreeable suspense till all the parts join together in a full chorus, as smart and strong as possible.

This reveals the effects at which Billings aimed, and his manner of achieving them. He wanted to produce a strong, powerful, majestic impression, with startling contrasts between the soft "solo" passages and the full chorus. We cannot measure the effect his music had upon his first hearers unless we hear it sung that way, by large groups of powerful voices, and the floor trembling with the reverberation of the booming basses.

In *The New England Psalm Singer*, Billings printed a poem by the Rev. Mather Byles of Boston, which gives us an idea of the impression that the "fuging tunes" made upon listeners and singers of that time:

On Music

Down steers the Bass with grave Majestic Air,
And up the Treble mounts with shrill Career;
With softer Sounds, in mild Melodious Maze,
Warbling between the *Tenor* gently Plays:
But if th' aspiring *Altus* joins its Force,
See, like the Lark, it Wings its tow'ring Course;
Thro Harmony's sublimest Sphere it flies,
And to Angelic Accents seems to rise;
From the bold Height it hails the echoing Bass,

> Which swells to meet, and mix in close Embrace.
> Tho' diff'rent Systems all the Parts divide,
> With Music's Chords the distant Notes are ty'd;
> And Sympathetic Strains enchanting winde
> Their restless Race, till all the Parts are join'd:
> Then rolls the Rapture thro' the Air around
> In the full Magic Melody of Sound.

Incidentally, according to the pronunciation of that time, "winde" and "join'd" formed a perfect rhyme. There can be no question that those who sang or heard Billings's music, especially under his dynamic direction, experienced "the full Magic Melody of Sound."

The continued effectiveness of Billings's famous hymn tune "Majesty" is attested by a passage in one of the stories of Harriet Beecher Stowe, who was born in 1811 and as a girl in Litchfield, Connecticut, frequently heard the old fuguing tunes sung by the village choir. The story is called *Poganuc People* and deals with New England life in the early years of the nineteenth century. This is the passage:

> . . . there was a grand, wild freedom, an energy of motion in the old 'fuging tunes' of that day that well expressed the heart of the people courageous in combat and unshaken in endurance. . . . Whatever the trained musician might say of such a tune as old Majesty, no person of imagination or sensibility could hear it well rendered by a large choir without deep emotion. And when back and forth from every side of the church came the different parts shouting—
>
> > On cherubim and seraphim
> >   Full royally He rode,
> > And on the wings of mighty winds
> >   Came flying all abroad,
>
> there went a stir and thrill through many a stern and hard nature, until the tempest cleared off in the words—
>
> > He sat serene upon the floods
> >   Their fury to restrain,
> > And He as Soverign Lord and King
> >   For evermore shall reign.

Mrs. Stowe's reference to the singing coming from "every side of the church" would seem to indicate the practice of having a "dispersed choir," with the various sections located in different parts of the church and "answering" one another, which of course would increase the effectiveness of the fuguing tunes. The words to which "Majesty" was sung were from the Sternhold and Hopkins version of the 18th Psalm, beginning, "The Lord descended from above." Billings's setting first appeared in *The Singing Master's Assistant.*

To take the measure of the man, let us run through some of his compositions. Observe how he always identifies himself completely with the subject or the mood that his music portrays. Is the subject Creation? Then Billings strikes the note of grandeur and—as in the hymn of Dr. Watts beginning "When I with pleasing wonder stand"—when he reaches the last line, "Strange that a harp of a thousand strings should keep in tune so long," he brings in his "Fuge" *con spirito*, first the basses, then the tenors, next the altos and sopranos, and so they go flying along fortissimo, one after the other, until they meet in the broad, impressive climax of the final phrase.

Now it is Jesus weeping, and our composer gives us a beautiful, tender melody, cast in the form of a canon or round for four voices, a melody that for sheer inspiration marks the culminating point of American musical primitivism (the term "primitive" is used stylistically, with no connotation of inferiority). Here it is, "When Jesus Wept," from Billings's first book, *The New England Psalm Singer:*

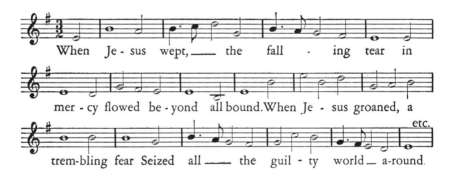

Now it is an old English Christmas carol, "A Virgin Unspotted" ("Judea"), to which Billings has provided one of his most delightful and spirited tunes. When he comes to the refrain, "Then let us be merry, put sorrow away, Our Saviour Christ Jesus was born on this day," his tune becomes as lively as a jig—which no doubt offended the Doctors of Divinity no less than it pleased the people for whom Billings wrote.

We turn next to the Easter anthem, "The Lord Is Risen Indeed," in which a strong, surging rhythm contributes to the general effect of jubilant exultation, heightened by the recurrent ejaculation, "Hallelujah." Rhetorically, the anthem employs the device of interrogation and affirmation. One after another the sections of the choir fling forth the interrogation, "And did He rise?" And the full choir peals out affirmatively, "Hear ye, O ye nations, Hear it, O ye dead, He rose, He rose, He rose, He burst the bars of death." Then it is the risen Christ who speaks, affirming His Ascension, and when we reach the lines, "Then first humanity triumphant past [passed] the crystal ports of light," Billings achieves one of his most striking, most original, and most apt effects, using a succession of fourteen open fifths and sixths that convey the image of "the crystal ports of light" with surprising vividness.

Turning to the Old Testament, we have Billings's version of David's lamentation, which reveals his powers of pathos achieved through stark, simple means. When David laments, "Would to God I had died for thee, O Absalom, my son!" the music compels us to share his grief, as Billings himself undoubtedly felt it and partook of it, and embodied it in the austere yet deeply expressive texture of his composition. The "incorrect" consecutive octaves and fifths in this passage are precisely what is needed to achieve the desired result. This lament has the strength and simplicity of the ancient ballads, and indeed Billings at his best was a bard of the folk.

And so we might go on and on, to savor the joy of "The Shepherd's Carol," the quaint charm of "The Bird," the lyrical sensuousness of "The Rose of Sharon," the stirring tunefulness of "Chester" (which became an American Revolutionary tune), the grandiose drama of the anthem "Be Glad Then America"—and everywhere we would find the vitality, the originality, the variety, and the inspiration of a natural genius, a true primitive of musical art.

Since we have mentioned two anthems by Billings, we should remark that the anthem was the most important musical form cultivated by the early New England composers, because it allowed greater freedom for variety, contrast, and sectional development. Billings himself composed about forty-five anthems; his contemporaries and successors followed suit. The anthem was characterized by brief solo passages for any or all of the four voices (treble, counter, tenor, bass) alternating with the full chorus.

Some Yankee music makers

When Francis Hopkinson, in one of his letters, was describing some of the differences in American and European ways of living, he remarked that in Europe one could get any kind of work done by a specialist, but the average American, in those days, was accustomed to doing everything for himself, from building a house to pulling a tooth. Music was no exception to this rule. Our early music makers belonged to that self-reliant breed of men who built our first towns, established farms, schools, banks, and stores, and yet who believed that music was no less essential than the more mundane needs of life.

Now we meet another of this sturdy breed, Supply Belcher of Stoughton and points north, robust, prolific, sire of ten offspring, hailed by his contemporaries as "the Handel of Maine." For several years Belcher kept a tavern in his native town, where the singing-school movement flourished, but his pioneer spirit urged him on to the northern frontier. He moved with his wife and family to Maine, settling first in Hallowell and later in Farmington, where he remained until his death in 1836 at the age of eighty-five. He taught the first school in Farmington, became choir leader, justice of the peace, and representative in the Massachusetts legislature (Maine was a part of Massachusetts until 1820). In his leisure time he composed music that he hoped would "be ornamental to civilization."

Supply Belcher published *The Harmony of Maine* at Boston in 1794, containing psalms, hymns, fuguing pieces, and anthems of his own composition. He was partial to the "fuging tunes" that Billings had made popular, and aimed at a lively, expressive style of writing. He alternated between extreme simplicity and an elaborate imitative texture. Sometimes the transition from simple to complex texture was made in the same composition, as in his setting of the Christmas hymn, "While shepherds watch'd," which begins in a homophonic style and then repeats the last line in extended imitative passages which Belcher's contemporaries called "fuging" (probably pronounced "fudging").

Elaborations of this type doubtless caused Belcher to be dubbed the Handel of Maine, but he perhaps appeals more to us in his simpler moments, and if our minds run to comparisons we would be inclined to regard him as a precursor of Stephen Foster. Like Foster, he had the gift to be simple and close to the folk; he could be tenderly lyrical or contagiously vivacious. The fact that some of his liveliest tunes were written for hymns need not cause us to deny that they would be equally suitable for a minstrel show. Imagine what a lift the farmers and villagers of the rural singing schools must have got in singing a hymn to Belcher's sprightly tune "Omega":

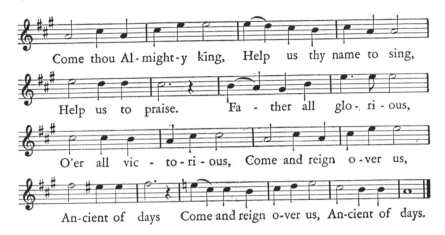

Come thou Al-might-y king, Help us thy name to sing, Help us to praise. Fa - ther all glo-ri-ous, O'er all vic - to-ri-ous, Come and reign o-ver us, An-cient of days Come and reign o-ver us, An-cient of days.

Scarcely less lively is the skipping and leaping tune, known as "York," that Belcher wrote for the hynm "So let our lips and lives express." Here we have the forerunner of the gospel hymn of later days. That Belcher could also write in a more dignified style of hymnody is proved by his fine setting of Isaac Watt's "He reigns! the Lord, the Saviour reigns!" for which he composed the tune called "Cumberland."

There is charm, freshness, and expressiveness in Belcher's three-part setting of "Invitation" ("Child of the summer, charming rose"). The same qualities are also evident in the four-part "Spring," of which we quote the beginning of the air (placed, according to the old custom, in the tenor part):

The scatt - 'red clouds are fled_ at _ last, The rain _ is gone, the win - ter's past, The love-ly ver - nal flow'rs ap - pear, The feath-er'd choir, de-light our ear.

Both for his music and his personality, Supply Belcher is one of the most engaging figures among the primitives of American music.

The 1936 edition of the *Original Sacred Harp*, the modern shape-note songbook of our rural singing societies, contains at least eight tunes that bear the name of Daniel Read as composer, including that fine fuguing tune, "Sherburne." Now, Daniel Read was born in the town of Rehoboth, Massachusetts, in the year 1757, and died at New Haven in 1836. Thus his music has had continuous appeal to thousands of Americans throughout many generations.

After brief periods of service in the Continental Army, Read settled in New Haven, where, in partnership with Amos Doolittle, he entered business as a bookseller and publisher. He courted Jerusha Sherman of New Haven, whose father, wrote Read, "would not consent to her marriage with me, because I was guilty of the unpardonable crime of poverty." Nevertheless, Daniel wed his Jerusha, four offspring were born—one of them christened George Frederick Handel—and the *pater familias* proceeded to overcome the crime of poverty. He became a manufacturer of ivory combs, a stockholder in one of the New Haven banks, and a director of the library—also a composer, compiler, and publisher of sacred music.

Read published *The American Singing Book* in 1785, *An Introduction to Psalmody* in 1790, and *The Columbian Harmonist* in 1793 (fourth edition, 1810). In 1786 he began to publish, as a monthly periodical, *The American Musical Magazine*, "intended to contain a great variety of approved music carefully selected from the works of the best American and European masters." Note that Read takes for granted the presence of "American masters" worthy to be included side by side with "the best . . . European masters." The American inferiority complex in music was a later development. The men of Read's generation proceeded with sublime self-assurance and confidence in America's musical destiny.

As we become acquainted with these early American composers, we find ourselves wondering what made them take to music, what opportunities they had for acquiring musical knowledge, and by what steps they established a reputation as composers. Something of a pattern has already emerged from the lives touched on thus far: the generally humble beginnings, the versatility, the determination, the enthusiasm. The case of Timothy Swan will fill in further details of the picture. He was born in 1758 at Worcester, Massachusetts, the eighth of thirteen children. Upon the death of his father, he was apprenticed to a merchant, and at sixteen went to live with a brother in Groton. There he attended a singing school, and it was this that awakened his musical interest. It also provided him with his meager musical education and started him on the road to composing. Apprenticed to a hatter in Northfield, he began to jot down tunes at odd moments, writing a few notes at a time. Thus while still very young he composed several hymn tunes that at first circulated in manuscript. He was an enthusiastic admirer of Billings—twelve years his senior—to whom he doubtless looked up as an "American master."

Swan married the daughter of a pastor in Suffield, where he lived for nearly thirty years. In 1807 he moved to Northfield, and died there on his eighty-fourth birthday. It is difficult to understand how he made a living, and it is reported that his neighbors said he was "Poor, proud, and indolent." He was fond of poetry, trees, and birds. He read widely, and wrote verse as well as music.

Like Read, Swan cultivated the fuguing style. His major compilation was *The New England Harmony* (Suffield, 1801). Another collection, *The Songster's Assistant*, published about a year earlier, contained a number of secular songs by Swan. His last publication, *The Songster's Museum*, which likewise reflected Swan's dual interest as singer and poet, appeared in 1803.

It was said of Timothy Swan that, "Melody was ever the great object with him." This gift for melody he manifested early in life: at the age of eighteen he had composed several hymn tunes that came into wide use, including "Poland." Other standard hymn tunes written by Swan are "China," "London," "Ocean," "Montague," "Quincy," and "Spring." One of his finest fuguing tunes is "Rainbow," used for a setting of Watts's Psalm 65, "'Tis by thy strength the mountains stand," which appeared in the second edition of *The Worcester Collection* (Worcester, 1788). The fuguing section begins with the second verse, "The sea grows calm at thy command."

Justin Morgan (1747–1798) of West Springfield, Massachusetts, earned a living by teaching school, keeping a tavern, and breeding horses. Among his stallions, by which he bred the "Morgan horse," were Sportsman, Diamond, and True Briton (this was in 1783!). In 1788 Morgan moved with his family to Randolph, Vermont, where he became town clerk. Much of his time was given to teaching singing schools, to which he used to ride on "the original Morgan horse."

Unlike most of his fellow singing teachers, Morgan did not publish any collections of music, though he left such a book in manuscript. Among his more ambitious compositions is a "Judgment Anthem," but his best-known tune is "Montgomery," a fuguing piece that has remained popular with American rural hymn singers up to the present day. Yet the historian Frank J. Metcalf wrote in 1925 that the music of Justin Morgan "has now passed entirely out of use, and is of interest only to the historian." Such statements, all too frequent in our historical writing, can be made only by persons acquainted with but a small segment of America's musical culture. Besides, a good tune never passes entirely out of use; it simply passes into a different cultural environment. We shall see this process at work in a later section of this book, when we deal with the rural singing tradition of the fasola folk in the South and West.

Jeremiah Ingalls (1764–1828) was another native of Massachusetts (he was born in Andover) who moved to Vermont, though he did this when he was much younger than Morgan. Ingalls was in his early twenties when he settled in Newbury, Vermont, where in 1800 he built a house that he kept as a tavern for about ten years. In 1819 he moved to Rochester, Vermont, and later to Hancock, where he died. In addition to keeping a tavern, being deacon of the Congregational Church, leading the choir, teaching singing school, composing and compiling music, Ingalls worked also, at various times, as a farmer and as a cooper.

Jeremiah Ingalls was married to Mary Bigelow in 1791, and they had several children. The following anecdote, quoted by Metcalf without indication of source, depicts music in the Ingalls's family circle:

His children were musical and his sons could play clarinet, bassoon, flute, and violin, and they would often practice for hours, the old man leading the band with his bass viol. One Sunday they were having an excellent time performing anthems, and after a while the youngsters started a secular piece, the father with composure joining in. From that they went on until they found themselves furiously engaged in a boisterous march, in the midst of which the old gentleman stopped short, exclaiming, "Boys, this won't do. Put away these corrupt things and take your Bibles."[3]

This anecdote is pointed up by the fact that Ingalls's collection, *The Christian Harmony; or, Songster's Companion*, printed at Exeter, New

[3] Metcalf, *American Writers and Compilers of Sacred Music*, p. 123.

Hampshire, in 1805, contains a large number of very lively tunes, obviously taken from secular songs or dances, as settings for sacred texts. Ingalls may have objected to his boys getting overboisterous on Sunday, but he certainly had no objections to making use of good tunes wherever he found them. One of the songs in *The Christian Harmony*, titled "Innocent Sounds," is a plea for the use of secular tunes for religious purposes:

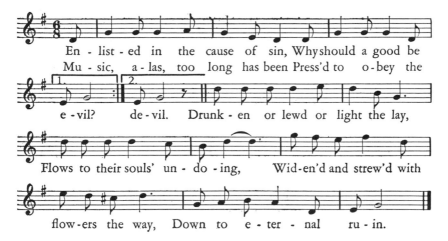

En - list - ed in the cause of sin, Why should a good be
Mu - sic, a - las, too long has been Press'd to o - bey the

e - vil? de - vil. Drunk - en or lewd or light the lay,

Flows to their souls' un - do - ing, Wid - en'd and strew'd with

flow - ers the way, Down to e - ter - nal ru - in.

The second stanza goes on to develop the idea of recovering the "innocent sounds" that have been misused for carnal pleasures:

> Who, on the part of God, will rise,
> Innocent sounds recover;
> Fly on the prey and seize the prize,
> Plunder the carnal lover;
> Strip him of every moving strain,
> Of every melting measure;
> Music in virtue's cause retain,
> Risk the holy pleasure.

Ingalls himself did a rather effective job of "plundering the carnal lover," judging by the large number of tunes in *The Christian Harmony* that are strongly reminiscent of English, Scottish, and Irish popular tunes. A typical example is the anonymous "Redeeming Love." Other tunes in *The Christian Harmony* that have a marked secular character, recalling British dance tunes, are "Angels' Song," "Clamanda," "Mecklinburg," "Rose Tree," and "Separation." Ingalls evidently was very close to the folk hymnody of his day. As we shall see later, he was the first compiler to include in his collection the revival camp-meeting songs that began to be so popular from around 1800.

Ingalls's most popular tune is "Northfield," a fuguing piece that has remained a favorite with the rural hymn singers down to our own times. Frederic P. Wells recounts the following anecdote about the origin of "Northfield":

> Returning from fishing one day, he [Ingalls] laid [*sic*] down before the fire to get dry and, impatient at the slow progress of dinner, began to sing a parody to a well-known hymn [by Dr. Watts]:
>
> > How long, my people, Oh! how long
> > Shall dinner hour delay?
> > Fly swifter round, ye idle maids,
> > And bring a dish of tea.
>
> "Why, Jerry," said his wife, "that's a grand tune."
> "So it is," replied the man of song: "I'll write it down." And dinner waited the completion of "Northfield."[4]

Jeremiah Ingalls's famous fuguing piece passed from *The Christian Harmony* to one songbook after another, including the 1854 edition of *The Southern Harmony* and the 1936 revision of *The Original Sacred Harp*. A recording of it, as sung by the Sacred Harp Singers of Alabama, has been issued by the Library of Congress. So that Jerry Ingalls and his music are still very much alive today, and not merely of "antiquarian interest."

The trend toward "progressive improvement"

A number of the better-educated American musical pioneers were dissatisfied with the kind of music that was being disseminated by Billings, Belcher, Ingalls, and other unsophisticated singing-school masters and self-made tune-smiths. They regarded this music as technically crude, and as lacking in dignity and decorum, especially for the uses of religious worship. Prominent among these advocates of "improvement" in American musical composition were Andrew Law, Oliver

---

[4] The music of "Northfield," as well as of "Innocent Sounds," will be found in the anthology *Music in America* (1964), edited by Marrocco and Gleason. This also contains music by most of the other composers mentioned in the present chapter, from Francis Hopkinson to Oliver Shaw.

Holden, Samuel Holyoke, and Oliver Shaw. They represent the transition from the eighteenth to the nineteenth century, which was to be dominated, culturally, by the widespread doctrine of "progressive improvement."

When *The Psalms of David, imitated in the language of the New Testament*, by Dr. Isaac Watts, was issued in one of several American editions at Philadelphia in 1781, the volume contained an appendix of sixteen pages with "A select number of plain tunes adapted to congregational worship. By Andrew Law, A.B." Law had first published his *A Select Number of Plain Tunes* at Boston in 1777, and this went through four editions up to 1785. Andrew Law (1749–1821) stood somewhat higher in the social scale than most of his fellow pioneers in American music. A grandson of Governor Law of Connecticut, he received a master's degree from Brown University, studied divinity privately, began preaching in 1777, and was ordained to the ministry ten years later at Hartford. According to his obituary notice, he was for forty years "an assiduous cultivator and teacher of sacred music." That he was also a musician who prided himself on his good taste, is attested by a sentence in a newspaper article that appeared after his death: "To his correct taste and scientific improvements may be ascribed much of that decent, solemn and chaste style of singing so noticeable in so many of the American churches." He was, in effect, a staunch upholder of the genteel tradition and one of the first advocates of the "better music" movement that was soon to dominate American hymnody through the influence of Lowell Mason. From the vantage point of his superior education and "correct taste," Andrew Law looked down with disdain upon the antics of the musical small fry that were overrunning our land. In the preface to *The Musical Primer* he deplored the frivolity of the singing in many churches, which resembled more the singing of "songs" than of dignified hymns, and castigated the creative efforts of the American musical pioneers:

. . . hence the dignity and the ever varying productions of Handel, or Madan,[5] and of others, alike meritorious, are, in a great measure, supplanted by the pitiful productions of numerous composuists,

[5] The Rev. Martin Madan, founder and chaplain of Lock Hospital in London, was one of the prime movers in the development of Anglican hymnody. In 1760 he published a *Collection of Psalms and Hymns*, known as the *Lock Hospital Collection*, which had considerable influence in America (it was reprinted in Boston). He composed the tune "Denmark," used for the setting of "Before Jehovah's awful throne."

whom it would be doing too much honor to name. Let any one acquainted with the sublime and beautiful compositions of the great Masters of Music, but look round within the circle of his own acquaintance, and he will find abundant reason for these remarks.

From Law's quotation we extract that curious word "composuist," doubtless derived from the obsolete use of "composure" to mean "composition." But Law obviously uses it with disdain—and it *does* have a certain contemptuous ring. It is, in any case, a useful word to have at hand; for there are "composuists" in every age. Whether we call them composers or composuists, Law's remarks make it clear that persons addicted to the writing of music abounded in eighteenth-century America.

Law's second publication was *The Select Harmony* (New Haven, 1778), containing, "in a plain and concise manner, the rules of singing." In 1793 appeared *The Musical Primer*, also printed at New Haven. It was apparently in the fourth edition of this work, issued at Cambridge, Massachusetts, in 1803, that Law introduced what he termed "a new plan of printing music." This innovation consisted of using, in place of the customary round notes, characters of four different shapes: diamond, square, round, and triangular. No staff lines were employed, the pitch of the notes being indicated by the relative position of the "shape-note" characters. As Law described this method, the characters "are situated between the single bars that divide the time, in the same manner as if they were on lines, and in every instance where two characters of the same figure occur their situations mark perfectly the height and distance of their sounds." Below is the hymn tune "America" as it appears in *The Musical Primer* in Andrew Law's shape-note system (the music is in four parts, of which only the highest is here reproduced):

Cheerful.

Behold the morning sun   Begins his glorious

way;   His beams through all the nations run, And life and light convey.

Law energetically promoted his "new plan" of musical notation and prevailed on several prominent persons, including John Hubbard of Dartmouth, to endorse it. To the objection that the system was new and not in general use, he replied that if this argument were accepted there would be an end to all improvement in the arts.

The strange and baffling aspect of all this is that a similar method of notation, with identical shape notes, had appeared in the United States two years earlier—so that Law's "new plan" was actually not new. The earlier work, compiled by two American singing-school teachers named William Smith and William Little, titled *The Easy Instructor* or *A New Method of Teaching Sacred Harmony*, was published at Philadelphia in 1801. It was evidently assured of success from the beginning, because in advance of publication the authors had gathered more than 3,000 subscribers.[6] Smith and Little had entered their work for copyright as early as 1798; but no edition earlier than that of 1801 is extant, and there is reason to doubt that any really appeared before that date. In any case, the priority of Smith and Little in the introduction of shape notes is indisputable; and it was their system, rather than Law's, that was adopted when shape-note singing books became so widely used throughout the South and West (as described in Chapter 10, The fasola folk). The only difference between the two systems was that Smith and Little reversed the order of the shape notes and kept the staff lines—the latter retention doubtless contributing to the success of their method.

Although Andrew Law remained an important and influential figure in his own sphere, he cannot claim credit for the innovation that was to make history in the grass-roots movement of American rural hymnody for the next century and a half. History has also divested Law of another claim to distinction: although the hymn tunes "Archdale" and "Bunker Hill" are traditionally attributed to him, the most recent research indicates that there is no valid evidence for attributing these to him.[7]

Oliver Holden (1765–1844) is remembered chiefly as the composer of the tune "Coronation," used for Edward Perronet's hymn "All Hail the Power of Jesus' Name." Born in Charlestown, Massachusetts, he was trained as a carpenter but rose to be a real-estate operator, a

[6] Irving Lowens, *Music and Musicians in Early America*, p. 125. Lowens discusses in detail the extremely complicated bibliographical history of *The Easy Instructor*.

[7] Richard Crawford, *Andrew Law (1749–1812): The Career of an American Musician* (Dissertation, University of Michigan, 1965).

preacher, a prominent Mason, and a member of the state legislature. His musical activities comprised choir-directing, teaching singing-school, running a music store, and composing, compiling, and publishing sacred music. His first book, *The American Harmony* (Boston, 1792), was a small compilation of 32 pages; but his second work, *The Union Harmony* (Boston, 1793), ran to some 300 pages and came out in two volumes. It was followed by *The Massachusetts Compiler* (Boston, 1795), in which Holden collaborated with Samuel Holyoke (1762–1820) and Hans Gram, the latter a professional musician of Danish origin active in Boston. It is perhaps because of Gram's influence that this work has been described as "the first American theory manual to espouse 'modern' European principles."[8] The term "modern," in this context, I take to mean simply "not archaic."

Holden was also responsible for editing the sixth, seventh, and eighth editions of *The Worcester Collection of Sacred Harmony* (Boston, 1797, 1800, 1803), one of the most widely used tune books of that period. In 1803 he brought out *The Charlestown Collection of Sacred Songs*. Thus, although not very successful as a composer ("Coronation" was a lucky hit), he was widely influential as a compiler and publisher of sacred music. His aim, in his own words, was to compose "music in a style suited to the solemnity of sacred devotion." In the preface to the eighth edition of *The Worcester Collection*, he wrote: "It is to be lamented that among so many American authors so little can be found well written or well adapted to sacred purposes, but it is disingenuous and impolitic to throw that little away while our country is in a state of progressive improvement." He was therefore one of the first to proclaim the doctrine of "progressive improvement" as a guiding principle. But the presence of his hymn tune "Concord" in recent editions of *The Sacred Harp* proves that some of his own music could survive several generations of progressive improvement.

Samuel Holyoke (1762–1820), a native of Boxford, Massachusetts, and a graduate of Harvard, published the *Harmonia Americana* at Boston in 1791, with the endorsement of the "Singing Club of the University." It contained the hymn tune "Sturbridge," by which he is best known. Like Holden and Law, he advocated a dignified style of church music and catered to the conservative elements in the com-

[8] Alan C. Buechner, in notes for *The New England Harmony*, A Folkways Recording of Early American Choral Music, p. 31.

munity. While living in Salem he compiled a large collection titled *The Columbian Repository of Sacred Music* (Exeter, 1802), containing music for all of Dr. Watts's psalms and hymns.

Holyoke was also interested in instrumental music (he played the clarinet) and while in Salem he directed the efforts of an amateur group called "The Instrumental Club." This activity led to the publication of *The Instrumental Assistant*, issued at Exeter in two volumes (1800, 1807)—"the first comprehensive instruction manual and collection of traditional music for band instruments published in America."[9]

The trend toward instrumental music also received an impulse from the work of Uri K. Hill (1780–1844), a native of Vermont who was active in Northampton, Boston, New York, and Philadelphia (from 1822 until his death). He compiled *The Vermont Harmony* (Northampton, 1801), *The Sacred Minstrel* (Boston, 1806), *The Handelian Repository* (New York, 1814), and *Solfeggio Americano* (New York, 1820). His instrumental compositions include a number of marches, among them *Governor Sullivan's March*, scored for two clarinets, bassoon, and "tenoroon." His patriotic song for the War of 1812, "The Heroes of the Ocean," had an accompaniment for piano and violin. Himself a violinist, Hill wrote several duets for violin.

Hill's almost exact contemporary, the blind organist and composer Oliver Shaw (1779–1848), was likewise partial to instrumental music. His first compilation was titled *A Favorite Selection of Music; adapted to the piano forte, consisting of the newest and most fashionable songs, airs, marches, etc.* (Dedham, 1806). Shaw, a native of Middleboro, Massachusetts, lost one eye through an accident while at school, and a later illness rendered him totally blind. Music being his main hope for a useful life, he went to study at Newport, Rhode Island, with the organist John L. Berkenhead, who was also blind. His next teacher was Gottlieb Graupner in Boston, with whom he studied various instruments, including the piano. Perhaps because of his contact with Graupner, Shaw was imbued with the idea of going to Europe for further study. But before he could put this plan into effect he was offered a position as organist and teacher in Providence, Rhode Island, which he felt bound to accept because of its importance to his career (this was in 1807).

Thereafter Shaw was industrious in compiling collections of music: *The Columbian Sacred Harmonist* (1808), *The Providence Selection*

[9] Buechner, *loc. cit.*, p. 27.

of Psalm and Hymn Tunes (1815), *Melodia Sacra, or Providence Selection of Sacred Music* (1823), *Social Sacred Melodies* (1835). Especially revealing of the new trend in American music is a compilation that Shaw published at Providence in 1818: *Sacred Melodies, Selected from Handel, Haydn, Mozart, Beethoven, and others, with several original compositions, arranged with an accompaniment for the pianoforte or organ.* Some of the accompaniments are actually for small orchestra. Thus, we have here a confluence of two currents that were rapidly gathering momentum: one bringing a predominance of European art-music, the other a growing emphasis on instrumental accompaniment for vocal music (as well as on independent instrumental expression).

Shaw composed many military marches, several of which he included in the publication titled *For the Gentlemen: A Favorite Selection of Instrumental Music . . . consisting principally of marches, airs, minuets, etc. Written chiefly in four parts, viz. 2 clarionettes [sic], flute and bassoon, or 2 violins, flute, and violincello [sic]. . . .* (Dedham, 1807.) Other pieces were included in *A Plain Introduction to the Art of Playing the Piano Forte; to which is added a selection of progressive airs, songs, etc.* (Dedham, 1811; the "selection" was also published separately). Among Shaw's marches are *The Battle of the Nile, Bonaparte's Grand March, General Abercrombie's March,* and *General Bates' Quick March.* In 1824 (probably) he published *Welcome the Nation's Guest. A Military Divertissement for the piano forte. Composed and respectfully dedicated to General La Fayette on his visit to Providence. . . .*

In 1816, together with T. S. Webb and other associates, Shaw founded the Psallonian Society "for the purpose of improving themselves in the knowledge and practice of sacred music and inculcating a more correct taste in the choice and performance of it." The Society flourished for sixteen years, with Shaw serving as president and conducting most of its concerts, which brought to the public sacred music by eminent European composers from Handel to Mendelssohn.

two

The frontier is the line of most rapid and effective Americanization.

FREDERICK J. TURNER, THE FRONTIER IN AMERICAN LIFE.

chapter eight

Progress and profit

A line of demarcation between the Musical Art and that other and more worldly pursuit known as the Musical Business . . . is difficult to trace.
PAUL S. CARPENTER, MUSIC, AN ART AND A BUSINESS.

We have seen how the combined efforts of gentlemen amateurs and professionally trained musical emigrants, reinforced by the energy and enthusiasm of some native pioneers, led to the establishment during the eighteenth century of orchestral concerts, operatic performances, choral societies, and similar types of organized musical activity requiring group participation and public support. This organized musical activity at first inevitably concentrated in the cities that formed a sort of fringe along the Atlantic seaboard, from Boston in the North to Charleston in the South. As the nineteenth century advanced, these cities, particularly those of the North, grew in wealth and size due to the effects of a steadily expanding commerce and a rapidly increasing rate of immigration. Thus there were gradually created the three conditions propitious for the regular consumption of art: population, wealth, and leisure. When these three factors assume large proportions in any given society, the consumption of art tends to increase, and may indeed become itself a major economic enterprise.[1]

It was during the first half of the nineteenth century that this pattern of music as big business began to take shape in the United States. For the first time, musicians began to make real money from their art. They profited from American methods of mass production and distribution. They were among the first to use high-pressure pro-

[1] For two recent studies of this phase of music in America, the reader may consult *Music, An Art and a Business,* by Paul S. Carpenter (Norman, Oklahoma, 1950), and *Worlds of Music,* by Cecil Smith (Philadelphia, 1952).

149

motion and sensational advertising. When the ex-blacksmith Isaac Baker Woodbury wanted to tell the public about his collection of sacred music called *The Dulcimer*, he, or his advertising manager, ran an advertisement in Dwight's *Journal of Music* which screamingly proclaimed:

125,000 Copies in Two Seasons!

Live Music Book!

The Dulcimer

The sacred-music collections of Lowell Mason topped them all. His *Carmina Sacra*, in various editions, sold 500,000 copies between 1841 and 1858. Another of Mason's collections, *The Hallelujah*, sold 150,000 copies in five years! This may not seem impressive in comparison with sales of popular sheet music in later times, but remember that this was "sacred" music, that the unit cost was greater, and that the music industry was still in its infancy. To our early struggling musical pioneers, such as Billings, Lyon, and Kimball, who were likely to end in the poorhouse or a pauper's grave, the idea of making $100,000 from a collection of sacred music, as Mason did, would surely have appeared fantastic.

In the musical activity of the United States during the first half of the nineteenth century, it seems to me that two things stand out as most typical of the age. One is that the leading musical impresario of that period was also the creator of the American circus, the great master of ballyhoo, the exploiter of Tom Thumb and Joice Heth—that incomparable and sensational showman, Phineas Taylor Barnum. The other symbolically significant phenomenon is that the leading musical figure of that mid-century period, Lowell Mason, was in his career and his character the prototype of the self-made, successful American business magnate. The one succeeded by appealing to the frivolity of the public. The other succeeded by "uplifting" the public. The common meeting point is that both were excellent promoters and both were highly successful in a practical and tangible way.

Here are some impressions of Lowell Mason by various persons who knew him. He was very handsome and finely dignified in appearance. He had a "commanding personality." He had "a remarkable degree of personal magnetism." He was "a manager of men, an organizer of movements. . . ." He had "huge industry," "great ability, penetrating foresight, splendid ideas." He was "a clear-sighted, practical man, just the leader the American people could then understand,

and be willing to follow." He was shrewd and successful in business. He was "a man of strong and impressive individuality, a virile nature in which an iron will was coupled with a gentle and tender heart." Discounting the tender heart as sheer sentimentality, would not these characterizations convey the impression that the man in question was one of America's "empire builders," a railroad baron, a real-estate operator, or a shipping magnate? And in effect, Lowell Mason *was* an "empire builder": he opened up vast new areas for musical exploitation, and he did it through industry, energy, determination, and organization. Of all musicians active in the United States during the nineteenth century, Lowell Mason has left the strongest, the widest, and the most lasting impress on our musical culture. This is not a tribute of praise: it is merely an objective statement of fact. Let us examine the record.

The rise of Lowell Mason

Lowell Mason was born in Medfield, Massachusetts, on January 8, 1792. His father was town treasurer and a member of the state legislature; he also sang in the church choir and played several musical instruments. His grandfather, Barachias Mason, had been a singing-school teacher as well as a schoolmaster. Lowell Mason, therefore, inherited a traditional New England musical background. As a boy he attended for a time the singing school of Amos Albee, compiler of *The Norfolk Collection of Sacred Harmony*, and later received musical instruction from Oliver Shaw, a prominent musician of Dedham. He learned to play the organ, the piano, the flute, the clarinet, and various other instruments. In 1812 he accompanied the Medford organ builder George Whitefield Adams to Savannah, where he took a job as clerk in a bank. In Savannah, Mason met a recently arrived German musician named F. L. Abel, from whom he received competent musical instruction. This Abel was the forerunner of many professional German musical immigrants who were to exert a far-reaching influence on America's musical development as the nineteenth century progressed.

Mason became organist and choirmaster of the Independent Presbyterian Church in Savannah, began to compose hymns and anthems, and in 1817 married Abigail Gregory of Westboro, Massachusetts. Though not yet intent on making music his career, Mason, like many of his predecessors and contemporaries, decided to compile and publish a collection of sacred music. In it he included some of his own tunes, as well as melodies from instrumental compositions by Handel, Mozart, Beethoven, and other European masters, adapted to familiar hymns and arranged "for three and four voices with a figured base [sic] for the organ or pianoforte." Completing this work in 1819–1820, Mason sought a publisher in Philadelphia and other large cities, but without success. Then he met Dr. George K. Jackson, organist of the Handel and Haydn Society of Boston, who took an interest in the compilation and recommended that the Society sponsor its publication—with several of his compositions incorporated in it. Dr. Jackson, whose opinion carried much prestige, endorsed it as "much the best book of the kind I have seen published in this country." Thus was born the famous *Boston Handel and Haydn Society Collection of Church Music*, which went to press in 1821 and was copyrighted the following year. Lowell Mason's name did not appear as editor, though he was mentioned in the preface. In later years, Mason gave this explanation for the omission of his name: "I was then a bank officer in Savannah and did not wish to be known as a musical man, and I had not the least thought of making music my profession." [2] The success of this collection soon caused Mason to change his mind. The book went through twenty-two editions and brought handsome profits both to its compiler and to the Handel and Haydn Society, to which it gave financial stability and permanent security.

Mason returned to Savannah after the publication of his collection, but in 1826 he was in Boston to deliver a lecture on church music (later printed), and in July, 1827, he was persuaded to settle in Boston as choirmaster of Dr. Lyman Beecher's church on Hanover Street. [3] Being a prudent man, for a while he also took a position as teller in a bank: he was not yet fully convinced that music could be made to pay. In 1827 he was elected president of the Handel and Haydn Society, holding this office until 1832. One of the reasons for his resignation was that he wished to devote more time to teaching music and singing to children, a line of activity that he had begun in Savannah and that was to occupy his attention increasingly as time went on. In 1829 Mason brought out his *Juvenile Psalmist, or The Child's Intro-*

[2] Quoted by Rich, *Lowell Mason*, p. 9.

[3] This church was burned down shortly after Mason's arrival in Boston, and a new one was built on Bowdoin Street, where he continued to conduct the choir.

duction to Sacred Music, followed in 1830–1831 by the *Juvenile Lyre,* which he claimed was "the first school song book published in this country." Mason's work in public-school music is so important that it will be advisable to treat this subject separately in another section of this chapter. Meanwhile, let us briefly summarize the rest of his career.

In 1832, together with George J. Webb and other Boston musicians, Mason founded the Boston Academy of Music for the purpose of applying the Pestalozzian method to the teaching of music to children. The Academy, which had as many as 1,500 pupils in its first year, continued in existence until 1847. The instruction was "free to all children, no other condition being required of the pupils than that they be over seven years of age, and engaged to continue in the school one year." Classes for adults were also given. The Academy was apparently responsible for the beginnings of "music appreciation" in this country, for it sponsored a translation of Fétis's *Music Explained to the World; or, How to Understand Music and Enjoy its Performance.* This work has long been obsolete, but the title still has a familiar ring!

In the summer of 1837, Mason went to Europe to study the Pestalozzian methods of instruction in Switzerland and Germany. At the end of 1851 he again sailed for Europe, this time remaining there fifteen months and spending much of his time in England. After his return to America in 1853, Mason made his headquarters in New York. He died at his home in Orange, New Jersey, on August 11, 1872, at the age of eighty. Of his four sons, the youngest, William, became an influential pianist and teacher. Lowell, junior, with his brother Henry, founded the firm of Mason & Hamlin, manufacturers first of organs and later of pianos. A grandson, Daniel Gregory Mason, was to become a prominent composer.

The age of progress

As the eighteenth century stood for improvement through reason, so the nineteenth century stood for progress through science. One still heard the words "good taste" and "correctness" used occasionally, but they were generally coupled with the words "science" and "progress," and gradually one heard less and less of good taste and more and more of progress. Nowhere was this belief in improvement through progress more firmly entrenched than in the United States. It runs through the thought and the career of Lowell Mason like a leading motive, marking him once again as a highly typical American of his time.

In order to succeed in his ventures, Mason had to strike a balance between lack of novelty and an excess of innovation. The public was conservative in its tastes, strongly attached to the accustomed and the familiar. Yet a certain amount of novelty, if skillfully administered and prepared, could prove attractive, especially if associated with the notion of being "up to date," of keeping up with the times. The manner in which Lowell Mason handled this delicate problem is illustrated in the various editions of *The Boston Handel and Haydn Society Collection of Church Music,* in which the older hymns and psalm tunes were gradually supplanted, in large part, by more "modern" compositions from the pen of celebrated European composers, and of course from the pen of Mason himself. Let us take, for example, the tenth edition of this famous collection, published in 1831. The following passages from the preface are illuminating:

> The several later editions of this work have presented an almost uniform appearance. . . . It is obvious, however, from the progressive nature of science and taste, in respect to music as well as other subjects, that this uniformity cannot be, and ought not to be perpetual. Within the last few years, much attention has been directed to the subject, and, as was to be expected, great improvement has been made, not only in the manner of performing psalm and hymn tunes, but also in their composition.
>
> Is it to be supposed that in psalmody, science and taste have accomplished all that they can accomplish? and is it desirable that all attempts at improvement should be checked? This is impracticable if it were desirable. . . .
>
> Unless, therefore, it be maintained that the present psalm and hymn tunes cannot be improved, and that no better can be substituted in their stead, or else, that bad tunes are as valuable as good ones, there may be as valid reasons, founded in public utility, for introducing alterations into text books of psalmody, as for introducing alterations into text books on arithmetic or grammar. [Another good reason: new editions promote sales].

All this, and considerably more to the same effect, is by way of justifying a "thorough revision" of the *Handel and Haydn Collection.* Mason gives some indication of what he means by "bad" tunes, when he states that he has reduced the number of "imitative and fugueing [*sic*] pieces," kept down the proportion of "light music" in the collection in deference to "the good sense and improved taste of the public." Certainly the public that would show its good sense and improved taste by preferring Mason to Billings would be thoroughly in line with "scientific progress"! In reviewing this collection, the New Haven *Chronicle* wrote: "A book so valuable must become the standard of music in our churches, since its harmony and style are fixed on the immovable basis of science and correct taste." Here the drive toward standardization is clearly manifested. The assumption is that earlier tune writers, not having benefited by "the immovable basis of science" (happily a nineteenth-century discovery) could only write inferior music that needed improvement, correction, or complete elimination by the products of modern science. According to this criterion, Mason's "From Greenland's Icy Mountains" is inevitably a better hymn than Madan's "Before Jehovah's Awful Throne." People who persisted in singing the old-fashioned anthems could be made to feel that they were failing to take advantage of modern improvements, and not many Americans liked to admit that they were behind the times. Hence the sweeping success of the "better music" movement led by Lowell Mason.

As a typical product of this movement, let us glance at a collection of church music edited by Mason entitled *The New Carmina Sacra*, published "under the sanction of the Boston Academy of Music" in 1853. According to the customarily elaborate descriptive title, this collection comprised "the most popular Psalm and Hymn Tunes in General Use, together with a great variety of New Tunes, Chants, Sentences, Motetts, and Anthems; *principally by distinguished European Composers* . . ." (the italics are mine). Once again, "made in Europe" was being stressed as the trade-mark of distinction in music for American consumption, as it had been in the days of the thirteen colonies. Looking through the table of contents of this collection, we come across the names of Arne, Beethoven, Cherubini, Giardini, Handel, Josef and Michael Haydn, Mozart, Palestrina, Pleyel, J. J. Rousseau, Schubert, Vogler, Weber—certainly an impressive and eclectic choice of "distinguished European composers." Perhaps the first question that strikes the reader is, "What are these composers doing in a collection of American church music?" The answer is: "They were providing tunes." The procedure of plundering secular music for making hymn tunes was not, as we have seen in earlier chapters, something new. The Wesleys, among others, had done it. The main difference is that Lowell Mason and his associates did it more systematically and more successfully than any of their predecessors. And as their movement coincided with the era of mass production and standardization, its effects were more widely felt.

At this point the reader should begin to perceive that the emphasis on church music in America during the mid-portion of the nineteenth century was by no means as "churchly" as might appear at first sight. The trend toward secularization was accelerated by two factors. One was the increasing use of tunes from secular compositions: in fact, any tune that appealed to the taste of the day, whatever its origin, was likely to be adapted for a hymn. The second factor was the increasing emphasis on quality of performance: *how* one sang was becoming almost more important than *what* one sang. Here, too, Lowell Mason was an influential leader. He zealously trained his choir at Dr. Lyman Beecher's Bowdoin Street Church in Boston to such a point of excellence that it drew nationwide attention and admiration. According to T. F. Seward:

> Pilgrimages were made from all parts of the land to hear the wonderful singing. Clergymen who attended ministerial gatherings in Boston carried home with them oftentimes quite as much musical as spiritual inspiration. . . .[4]

With the general shift from religious to secular emphasis that took place in American life during the latter part of the nineteenth century, this striving for technical virtuosity and impressive perfection in choral singing was transferred to the schools, resulting eventually in the wonderfully trained public-school choirs that dot the land today.

Returning for a moment to the *New Carmina Sacra*, it should be observed that this collection made a bow to the older traditions of psalmody by including some of the most famous tunes of Tallis, Playford, Tans'ur, and Aaron Williams. Even a few native American pioneers were included: Daniel Read, Isaac Tucker, Oliver Holden. Mason could not afford to alienate completely that portion of the public that clung somewhat stubbornly to its old-fashioned tastes.

One of the most curious features of Mason's musical arrangements

4 Quoted by Rich, *Lowell Mason*, p. 12.

is the introduction of what might be called "ejaculatory codas." In his Preface to the *New Carmina Sacra*, Mason writes:

The Codas added to many of the tunes form quite a new feature in a book of this kind, and it is hoped they may add interest to the performance of psalmody. Although they are called codas, yet they are not designed for the close, merely, but may be introduced before the first stanza, or between the stanzas of a hymn as may be appropriate. In the singing schools and choir meetings, they may be always sung, but in public worship the propriety of singing them must depend upon the circumstances of the occasion, hymn, &c. The hymns in which these Hallelujahs may with propriety be introduced, are more numerous than may at first be supposed; for under what circumstances does not the devout heart say, "Praise the Lord?"

Herewith is an example of Mason's "coda," showing only the rhythmic pattern:

Hal - le - lu - jah!   Hal - le - lu - jah!

Mason says that these "codas" constitute "quite a new feature" in collections of sacred music. That such ejaculations were not in themselves a new feature of hymn singing, will be apparent from the account of the beginning of revival hymnody given in Chapter 11. The interjection of "Hallelujah!" sometimes after each line, sometimes after each stanza, was a characteristic of popular hymnody. Sometimes the "Hallelujah" was inserted before the first stanza, which, as Mason suggests, may be done in his collection. Mason claimed this as a novelty which he hoped might "add interest to the performance of psalmody" (here this word is evidently used as synonymous with hymnody). Yet it was a practice that had been prevalent among certain sections of the populace for some fifty years before the publication of Mason's collection. Many examples of the "Hallelujah" refrain and its variants can be found in popular collections of hymns and "spiritual songs" printed before 1850. The evidence seems to indicate that Mason borrowed a feature from popular hymnody in the hope that it would add spice to his collection and perhaps also with the thought that it might keep his followers from straying into the camp of the revivalists. It would never do to let his competitors have a monopoly of the more obvious joys in hymn singing. Let it be noted, in passing, that one of Mason's most successful collections was called *The Hallelujah*.

Mason and the schools

Mason believed and preached that all school children should be taught to sing, just as they were taught to read. He advocated this policy as early as 1826, and after settling in Boston he directed a major portion of his activities toward the introduction and development of music teaching in the public schools of that city. The achievement of this goal was a long and difficult process because the idea was new and had to overcome both inertia and opposition. Finally, in 1838, the Boston School Committee authorized the introduction of music as a branch of instruction in the city schools. Lowell Mason was given charge of this musical instruction, becoming the first Superintendent of Music in an American public-school system. He continued in this post until 1845, when he was forced out by some political intrigue, though the official reason given was "the principle of rotation in office."

In 1851, referring to the Boston school program of music instruction, the first to be officially established in this country, Mason wrote:

> The result already is, that a multitude of young persons have been raised up who . . . are much better able to appreciate and to perform music than were their fathers; and experience proves that large classes of young persons, capable of reading music with much accuracy, may be easily gathered in almost any part of the New-England, or indeed of the United States.[5]

Moreover, Mason pointed out that an increasing number of persons who had received their first musical instruction in the public schools were devoting themselves to the profession of music, particularly as choral conductors, church musicians, and organists.

Mason stressed vocal instruction as the basis of the musical education in the schools. His course of instruction consisted of four main phases: (1) rote singing, (2) the song approach to note reading, (3) note reading, (4) part singing and choral singing. Mason's theory and practice of education were based on the methods of the Swiss reformer Pestalozzi, which in turn were influenced by the theories of Jean Jacques Rousseau. As Mason summed it up: "The teacher in pur-

[5] Mason, *An Address on Church Music*, p. 16.

suance of the right method, is guided by nature; he looks . . . to the intuitions, instincts, and opening faculties or active powers of his pupils. . . ." He stated that music "should be cultivated and taught . . . as a sure means of improving the affections, and of ennobling, purifying and elevating the whole man." Hence, he declared, "the chief value of music . . . in schools or families, will be social and moral." His method of music instruction is embodied in the *Manual of the Boston Academy of Music, for Instruction in the Elements of Vocal Music, on the System of Pestalozzi* (Boston, 1834), and in *The Pestalozzian Music Teacher* (New York, 1871).

Mason was also a pioneer in the teacher-training movement in America. In 1834 he established at the Boston Academy of Music an annual summer class for music teachers. Out of this was formed, in 1836, a Convention "for the discussion of questions relating to the general subject of Musical Education, Church Music, and Musical Performances. . . ." In 1840 the teachers organized themselves into a National Music Convention, which later was reorganized as the American Musical Convention. The idea of holding musical conventions spread rapidly to other cities throughout the country, and, in the words of A. L. Rich, "they were a power in American musical life and musical education," though "often dominated by commercial interests." The latter feature was perhaps inevitable, for music education in America was fast becoming "big business." Today the national music conventions are mammoth affairs involving many thousands of persons, many thousands of dollars, and an impressive array of commercial exhibits ranging from band instruments to television sets. All this has grown from the seeds sown by Lowell Mason.

Among the numerous collections of music compiled by Mason were: *Choral Harmony* (1830), *Spiritual Songs for Social Worship* (with Thomas Hastings, 1831), *Lyra Sacra* (1832), *The Choir; or Union Collection of Church Music* ("including many beautiful subjects from the works of Haydn, Mozart, Cherubini, Naumann, Marcello, Méhul, Himmel, Winter, Weber, Rossini, and other eminent composers, harmonized and arranged expressly for this work," 1832; seven more editions by 1839), *Manual of Christian Psalmody* (with David Greene, 1832), *Sacred Melodies* (with G. J. Webb, 1833), *Sabbath School Songs* (1833), *The Boston Academy's Collection of Church Music* (1835), *The Sacred Harp or Eclectic Harmony* (with Timothy Mason, 1835), *The Boston Academy's Collection of*

Choruses (1836), *The Odeon: a collection of secular melodies, arranged and harmonized for four voices* (with G. J. Webb, 1837), *The Boston Glee Book* (1838), *The Boston Anthem Book* (1839), *The Modern Psalmist* (1839), *Carmina Sacra* (1841; twelve more editions by 1860), *The Psaltery* (with G. J. Webb, 1845), *The Choralist* (1847), *The National Psalmist* (1848, with G. J. Webb), *Mason's Handbook of Psalmody* (1852), *The Hallelujah* (1854), *The People's Tune Book* (1860), *Carmina Sacra Enlarged: The American Tune Book* (1869).

This list, by no means complete, will serve to give an idea, not only of Mason's industry but also of the demand that existed in the United States for vocal music of every kind. When we bear in mind that Mason and his Boston associates, such as Webb (his chief collaborator in the work of the Boston Academy of Music), were not the only ones compiling and publishing collections of music for the American public, we begin to realize that the songbooks of the early American pioneers were producing an enormous progeny. And this, as we shall see later, is only part of the picture. In addition to the urban songbook production dominated by European importations and imitations, the rural and frontier songbook production flourished simultaneously and independently (it will be discussed fully in a later chapter).

As a composer, Lowell Mason wrote mostly hymns, anthems, and school songs. His best-known tune is "Missionary Hymn," used as a setting for "From Greenland's Icy Mountains," written between 1824 and 1827, when Mason was a bank clerk in Savannah. Scarcely less familiar are the tunes for "Nearer My God to Thee" and "My Faith Looks Up to Thee." He attempted some more ambitious anthems, without rising above mediocrity. It is not as a composer but as an organizer, a musical empire builder, that Lowell Mason claims our attention. He exerted a decisive and lasting influence on the course of musical activity in the United States. On the negative side, he was instrumental in thrusting the native American musical tradition, as represented by our early New England music makers, into the background, while opening the gates for a flood of colorless imitations of the "European masters." On the positive side, he brought systematic musical education into our public schools, raised the standards of choral performance, and paved the way for professional music schools. And he was the first American musician to make a fortune out of music. That in itself was no mean accomplishment. He believed in "scientific improvement," and he made progress pay.

Lowell Mason collected a large and valuable musical library, which after his death was presented by his family to Yale University. When the library of Professor Dehn of Berlin was placed on sale, Mason sent an agent to purchase it. According to Metcalf, "It is said that he was unable to read one of the books that were thus acquired, but he wanted them to add value to his growing collection." [6]

The eminent Dr. Hastings and others

Outdoing Lowell Mason in longevity, rivaling him in productivity, success, influence, and mediocrity, was his older contemporary and colleague Thomas Hastings (1784–1872). Metcalf, usually a reliable writer, credits Hastings with having written six hundred hymns, composed over one thousand hymn tunes, published fifty volumes of music, and "many articles on his favorite subject." Out of this huge production, what remains musically alive are about four hymn tunes, of which the most familiar is "Toplady," sung to the words, "Rock of Ages, cleft for me." Other tunes frequently used are "Ortonville," "Retreat," and "Zion."

Thomas Hastings was the son of a country physician and farmer of Washington, Connecticut. When he was twelve years old, the family moved to Clinton, New York, where at eighteen young Hastings became choir leader. In 1828 he settled in Utica, New York, where he edited a religious paper, *The Western Recorder*, in which he aired his musical opinions. From 1832 he was choirmaster at various churches in New York, including the Bleecker Street Presbyterian Church. In 1858, New York University conferred upon him the honorary degree of Doctor of Music. He died in New York City.

One of Hastings's most popular collections was *Musica Sacra*, first issued in 1816 and subsequently republished in numerous editions up to 1836. (For an account of the use of this publication in a Connecticut singing school, see Chapter 10.) Other collections were *The Juvenile Psalmody* (1827), *The Manhattan Collection* (1837), *The Sacred Lyre* (1840), *The Selah* (1856), and *The Songs of the Church* (1862). The *Mendelssohn Collection* of 1849—clearly indicating in its title the Europeanizing trend of the "better music" school—he edited

---

[6] Metcalf, *American Writers and Compilers of Sacred Music*, p. 215.

in collaboration with William B. Bradbury, the third member of this triumvirate of sacred music in the United States.

William Batchelder Bradbury turned out an average of more than two music books a year from 1841 to 1867. One of his most popular collections was *The Jubilee*, which sold over 250,000 copies. Another collection, *The Golden Chain* (1861), was so successful that it drew severe attacks from his competitors, who claimed that it was full of errors. Doctored up by Bradbury's friend Doctor Hastings, *The Golden Chain* went on selling and brought its compiler a golden harvest. It is estimated that over two million copies of Bradbury's music books were sold.

Bradbury was born in York, Maine, in 1816, and inherited his musical talent from his parents, who were good singers. As a young man he lived in the home of a Boston musician, Sumner Hill, from whom he received lessons in harmony. He entered the Boston Academy of Music, becoming associated with Webb and Lowell Mason. The latter recommended him to teach singing school in Machias, Maine, where James Lyon, the eighteenth-century American composer, had been active for twenty-three years. After a few years, Bradbury went to New York as church organist and choir leader. In 1847 he went to Europe, remaining two years in Germany, where he studied music at Leipzig. He was thus one of the first American musicians to study in Germany, a trend that was soon to become general.

Together with Lowell Mason, Thomas Hastings, and George F. Root, Bradbury taught in the recently established Normal Institutes—a scientifically improved version of the old singing schools—that were organized in the Northeastern states for the training of music teachers. Not satisfied with manufacturing music books, Bradbury entered the piano business with his brother, manufacturing and selling pianos and other musical supplies. He died in 1868. As a composer of hymns, Bradbury is remembered chiefly for "He Leadeth Me" and "Sweet Hour of Prayer."

Another composer of this group who managed to study in Europe for a year was Isaac Baker Woodbury (1819–1858), a native of Beverly, Massachusetts. He began the study of music in Boston at the age of thirteen, learning to play the violin. After a sojourn in London and Paris, he taught music in Boston for six years and later traveled throughout New England with the Bay State Glee Club. He organized the New Hampshire and Vermont Musical Association and became its conductor. Later he went to New York as choirmaster and was also editor of the *New York Musical Review*. Plagued by ill-health, he went to Europe again, hoping to recuperate, and while there gathered music for publication in his magazine. In 1858 he left New York to spend the winter in the South and got as far as Columbia, South Carolina, where he fell mortally ill and died after three days, leaving a wife and six small children.

Among Woodbury's most successful collections were *The Dulcimer* (1850), *The Cytherea* (1854), and *The Lute of Zion* (1856). He also brought out *Woodbury's Self-Instructor in Musical Composition and Thorough Bass*, catering to the American appetite for self-instruction. It is interesting to note that he attempted to gain a following in the South by publishing two collections especially designed for Southern use, *The Harp of the South* (1853) and *The Casket* (1855), the latter sponsored by the Southern Baptist Society and published in Charleston, South Carolina. Woodbury's secular songs, extremely popular in their day, are now forgotten.

In the next chapter we shall discuss the music of another member of this group, George Frederick Root, compiler of *The Young Ladies' Choir* and other church collections, but whose reputation rests more firmly upon his secular songs.

chapter nine

The genteel tradition

I would ask if there are not words in the Anglo-Saxon language that can be associated so as to express what is, in the supreme affectation of fashionable parlance, termed "soirée musicale"?
JOHN HILL HEWITT, SHADOWS ON THE WALL (1877).

Nothing could be more elegant than to refer to a public concert as a *soirée musicale*. These two words were fragrant with the aristocratic aroma of a Paris salon, redolent of an elite society in which artistic celebrities mingled with the representatives of rank and wealth. They disguised the crude fact that the performing musicians were professional entertainers who hoped to make money from their public appearances. Could such a distinguished personage as the Baron Rudolph de Fleur, pianist to His Majesty the Emperor of Russia, be concerned with vulgar pecuniary considerations when, in the year 1839, he gave a recital that attracted the elite of New York society? Or could one place on a mere level of commercial entertainment the elegant series of *soirées musicales* given in New York on alternate Thursdays during February and March of the same year by the eminent maestro Charles Edward Horn and his accomplished wife? The programs offered by Mr. and Mrs. Horn featured vocal selections by the most celebrated European composers of the day, among whom Mr. Horn might be justified in including himself, for he had achieved some success both as composer and singer in England before coming to the United States in 1833, at the age of forty-seven. Moreover, some of these *soirées* were graced by the participation of two of the most successful English ballad composers and singers of that time, Mr. Joseph Knight and Mr. Henry Russell, both of whom were then intent upon elevating the musical taste of the American people.

These gentlemen were not alone in this endeavor. Two distinguished opera singers from England, Anna and Arthur Seguin, who had come to the United States in 1838, offered New York music lovers a series of ten recitals featuring selections from Italian opera. Those who favored this truly fashionable type of musical entertainment were also regaled with Italian operatic selections by such visiting artistes as Madame Albini, Madame Vellani, Signora Maroncelli, and Signor Rapetti.

About this time the Irish composer William Vincent Wallace, author of the opera *Maritana*, was also in New York. It was Wallace who, some years later, made a gallant musical offering to the ladies of America in the form of *Six Valses Elegantes*—six elegant waltzes for piano—further described and pictorially represented on the cover as a bouquet of *"Fleurs Musicales, Offertes aux Dames d'Amérique."* The elegance of the French language, the exquisite gallantry of the gesture, the beautiful bouquet of flowers on the cover, the polite banality of the music—everything about this musical offering bespoke the influence of the genteel tradition that was being imposed like a veneer on American society.

To savor fully the tone and character of the genteel tradition, one should see the elaborately illustrated sheet-music editions published in the United States during the mid-portion of the nineteenth century, in which sentimental songs and elegant piano pieces are adorned with ornate covers depicting fashionable ladies in refined or poetic attitudes, in domestic or pastoral settings untouched by sordid reality. In 1868, William A. Pond & Co. of New York issued a piece titled *The Grecian Bend*, described as "The Latest Sensation in the Fashionable World." On the cover is shown a young lady of fashion, carrying a ridiculously small parasol and bending over in what is presumably an authentic demonstration of "the Grecian bend." Figuratively speaking, large sections of American society were engaged in doing the Grecian bend, preferably with a Parisian dip and an Italian twist.

The genteel tradition is characterized by the cult of the fashionable, the worship of the conventional, the emulation of the elegant, the cultivation of the trite and artificial, the indulgence of sentimentality, and the predominance of superficiality. Its musical manifestations are found chiefly in a flood of vocal literature that presumably drew tears or sobs from its original listeners or filled them with chills and thrills in its more dramatic moments, but that in the cold light of the twentieth century seem to us more silly than pathetic, more ludicrous than impressive. Nevertheless, we cannot afford to neglect these songs in the chronicle of America's music: some of them continue to appeal to the sentimental streak that is in all of us, and even those that are forgotten once appealed to millions of people and struck deep into the heart of our musical consciousness.

Henry Russell, who composed the music for "Woodman, Spare That Tree," tells an anecdote that is revealing in this respect. He writes:

> A very dear friend of mine, now well-known as a public man . . . has often told me that he dates the birth of his sentimental nature to the fact that an old nurse used to sing *Woodman, Spare That Tree,* at his bedside, and that scores of times as a child he cried himself to sleep over the simple song.

Well, this is not the worst of the sentimental ballads; but it is not really a "simple" song: it is an artificial song, a concocted song, inflated with a synthetic sentimentality; it does not have the genuine emotion, the organic vitality, the timeless and impersonal quality of, for example, the old folk ballads. There is no point in comparing unlike elements, and this contrast is made simply to emphasize the vitiating effect of pseudosimple, artificially sentimental songs in forming adult musical tastes through childhood experiences.

During the nineteenth century the people of the United States as a whole were in this state of aesthetic immaturity. Hence the success of any music that made a blatant appeal to the feelings of the listeners, and the success of musical performers who stressed the elements of exhibitionism and showmanship, like the pianist who played while balancing a glass of water on his head. Aesthetic appreciation—that is, the quality that permits an artistic experience to be received and enjoyed as such—was almost entirely lacking. People were continually crossing the line that separates art from reality; indeed, most of them were not aware that such a dividing line existed. Henry Russell, in his memoirs, tells several anecdotes regarding the reactions of his listeners that illustrate this attitude. One of them concerns the song "Woodman, Spare That Tree," with which Russell never failed to work on the emotions of his audience. One night when he had sung this number at a concert, a dignified gentleman in the audience stood up, and in a very excited voice called out, "Was the tree spared, sir?"

To which Russell replied, "It was." With a sigh of heartfelt relief, the man said: "Thank God for that."

Because he spent nine years in the United States, because he was a shrewd and sympathetic observer of the American scene—"I doubt whether I am not a little more than half American in thought and sentiment," he wrote of himself—because he exerted considerable influence on American musical taste, and because he is such a typical representative of the genteel tradition, Henry Russell deserves more than casual mention in these pages. He began his musical career as a boy singer in England, then went to Italy for further study at Bologna and Milan, becoming acquainted there with Rossini, Donizetti, and Bellini. From Bellini he received some lessons in composition and orchestration. He then went to Paris, where he met Meyerbeer and other celebrities. He thus received the double accolade of Italy and Paris, indispensable for admission to the ranks of fashionable gentility.

Back in England, Russell found no immediate means of turning his fashionable assets into concrete financial returns. He decided to try his fortune in a less crowded portion of the world. Going first to Canada, he was disappointed in that dominion's potentiality for cultural exploitation. A friend persuaded him to visit Rochester, New York, whither he traveled by cart. In Rochester he was offered the position of organist and choirmaster at the Presbyterian church, which he accepted. And it was in Rochester that he began his career as a composer of songs.

According to Russell's own account, "the orator Clay was the direct cause of my taking to the composition of descriptive songs." It seems that Henry Clay delivered a speech in Rochester and made a deep impression on Russell by the musical quality of his voice. "Why," Russell asked himself, "if Henry Clay could create such an impression by his distinct enunciation of every word, should it not be possible for me to make music the vehicle of grand thoughts and noble sentiments, to speak to the world through the power of poetry and song!" Why not, indeed! Then and there Henry Russell set to music a poem by his friend Charles Mackay, "Wind of the Winter Night, Whence Comest Thou?" In the composer's own words, which have a vaguely familiar ring, "Success followed success." The songs "which leapt quickest into popularity" were "Woodman, Spare That Tree," "A Life on the Ocean Wave," "The Gambler's Wife," and "The Maniac."

When Russell went on to New York, he met there his old London friends, the Seguins, and the composer Vincent Wallace. Uniting their forces, they gave "six concerts at New York, Brooklyn, Jersey City, and several other towns in the United States." This proves that even at that time Brooklyn was avid for culture. These concerts, according to Russell, "proved an immense success, both financially and artistically." Thereafter Russell at various times toured all over the United States, singing his own songs and accompanying himself on the piano. Dwight called him a "charlatan" but this did not interfere with his success. After all, Dwight had only five hundred readers for his *Journal*, whereas the songs of Henry Russell sold in the hundreds of thousands.

But it was not through the sale of his songs that Russell made money. As he wrote in his memoirs:

I have composed and published in my life over eight hundred songs, but it was by singing these songs and not by the sale of the copyrights that I made money. There was no such thing as a royalty in those days, and when a song was sold it was sold outright. My songs brought me an average price of ten shillings each . . . though they have made the fortune of several publishers. Had it not been that I sang my songs myself . . . the payment for their composition would have meant simple starvation.[1]

This bears out my theory that the only way Stephen Foster could have been assured of a lucrative living would have been to appear in public as the interpreter of his own songs, if he could have trained his voice sufficiently for that purpose. Later we shall see that Russell's contemporary, John H. Hewitt, most popular American ballad composer of this period, also found it impossible to make money from his songs and turned to various other occupations for a living.

One of Russell's most dramatic songs was "The Ship on Fire," text by Charles Mackay. It has an elaborate piano accompaniment, full of runs, tremolos, octaves, and arpeggios. The piano begins with a two-page introduction, opening quietly, sweeping up and down in a tremendous run in sixths, crescendo, followed by tremolo chords and crashing octaves. Then the voice enters, *Quasi ad lib: ma Largamento:*

The storm o'er the ocean flew furious and fast,
And the waves rose in foam at the voice of the blast,
And heavily labour'd the gale-beaten Ship. . . .

[1] Russell, *Cheer! Boys, Cheer!*, p. 198.

After further description of the ship, the poet paints this pathetic picture:

> A young mother knelt in the cabin below,
> And pressing her babe to her bosom of snow,
> She pray'd to her God 'mid the hurricane wild,
> Oh Father have mercy, look down on my child.

The storm passes away and terror is succeeded by joy; the mother sings a sweet song to her babe as she rocks it to rest; the husband sits beside her, and they dream of the cottage where they will live when their roaming is finished.

> Ah, gently the ship glided over the sea. . . .

(here the music fades to a pianissimo cadence). But now thunderous octaves strike an ominous warning of impending disaster. "Hark! what was that—Hark, hark to the shout,—FIRE!" The young wife is shaken with terror:

> She flew to her husband, she clung to his side,
> Oh there was her refuge what e'er might betide.

Fire! Fire! Raging above and below. The smoke, in thick wreaths, mounts higher and higher (furious octave runs in the piano accompaniment, fortissimo). There's no remedy save to lower the boat.

> Cold, cold was the night as they drifted away,
> And mistily dawn'd o'er the pathway the day.

Then suddenly, oh joy!

> Ho, a sail, ho! a sail! cried the man on the lee.

The chords of the accompaniment take on a solemn and joyous grandiosity. "Thank God, thank God, we're sav'd."

This is the genteel tradition's equivalent of purging the spirit through pity and terror, running the gamut from bombast to bathos. There are eleven pages to this opus—far too much to quote in full. And it is the sort of thing one has to enjoy *in toto* or not at all (there *are* ways of enjoying such a masterpiece of banality). The reader whose curiosity has been irresistibly whetted by the above résumé may find the complete song, music and words, in the collection titled

Songs of Yesterday, edited by Jordan and Kessler (see bibliography for this chapter).

It is a curious fact, and one that needs to be considered in appraising the "social significance" of the vocal literature of this period, that Henry Russell did not regard himself solely as an artist or an entertainer, but also as a social reformer. Toward the end of his life Russell wrote: "Slavery was one of the evils I helped to abolish through the medium of my songs." Developing this theme, he goes on to give himself credit for promoting other social reforms:

When I commenced my Anti-Slavery Crusade, I did not stop at seeking to relieve the distresses of the unfortunate coloured race, but, to a certain extent, I happened to forestall the good work that is being done by "The Early Closing Association," by the publication of a song, written in the interests of the overworked shop assistants, and entitled: TIME IS A BLESSING. . . . The private lunatic asylum, another sore in our social system, was attacked . . . by my song, "The Maniac," which was written with the object of exposing the horrors of the iniquitous system.

One may be permitted to wonder whether "The Maniac" was not actually composed for the purpose of making an effect on paying audiences rather than in the interests of social reform. Nevertheless, the fact remains that the espousal of "Causes" was characteristic of this period, and that the trend is amply illustrated in the song literature, as well as in the writings and activities of leading singers, such as Russell and the Hutchinson Family, whom we shall meet presently. In addition to Abolition, a favorite cause was Temperance. Russell did his bit for this cause with his song "Let's Be Gay," which begins:

Let's be gay, let's be gay, let's be gay, boys,
We'll quaff, we'll quaff from this cup, ha, ha!

And ends with this anticlimax, followed by two solid lines of "ha, ha" that must indeed have rung out gaily around the flowing bowl:

But let the draught, but let the draught, be water, water!

Perhaps the most astonishing aspect of Henry Russell's connection with American music is his claim to have composed virtually all of the most popular Negro minstrel or blackface "Ethiopian" songs, from

"Coal Black Rose" to "Old Dan Tucker." No less surprising is his account of the manner in which he composed these songs:

One hot summer afternoon, when I was playing the organ at the Presbyterian Church, Rochester, I made a discovery. It was that sacred music played quickly makes the best kind of secular music. It was quite by accident that playing the "Old Hundredth" very fast, I produced the air of "get out o' de way, Old Dan Tucker." This was the first of a good many minstrel songs that I composed or rather adopted, from hymn tunes played quickly. Among them are "Lucy Long," "Ober de Mountain" and "Buffalo Girls." . . . Afterwards, when giving my entertainments about the country, I would occasionally illustrate this principle to my audiences by playing slowly and pathetically the "Vesper Hymn," and then repeat it, gradually quickening the time till it became a humerous plantation song, "Oh! take your time, Miss Lucy," or "Coal Black Rose." [2]

Although Russell's claim to these songs cannot be substantiated, his description of the "speed up" method of producing popular tunes out of hymns has fascinating implications. He seems to be describing a sort of rudimentary method for "jazzing the classics"; although this actually requires more than a speed-up in tempo. A few off-beat accents and syncopations would help to produce the desired effect. The reader might find it instructive and amusing to put Russell's formula to the test.

In New York, Henry Russell formed a friendship with a man who played an important role in the genteel tradition. This was George Pope Morris (1802-1864), journalist and poet, founder of the *New York Mirror and Ladies' Literary Gazette*, to which the leading contributors were William Cullen Bryant, Nathaniel Parker Willis, Fitz-Greene Halleck, and Morris himself. A contemporary satirist referred to Morris as,

> A household poet, whose domestic muse
> Is soft as milk, and sage as Mother Goose.

It was Morris who wrote the text of the first published song of Stephen Foster, "Open Thy Lattice, Love." He wrote the words of "Woodman, Spare That Tree" and of "On the Lake, Where Droop'd

[2] Russell, *Cheer! Boys, Cheer!*, p. 68.

the Willow," the latter set to music by his friend Charles Edward Horn, who simply lifted the tune from a popular minstrel song, "Long Time Ago." This is the first stanza of Morris's poem, with the melody as arranged by Horn:

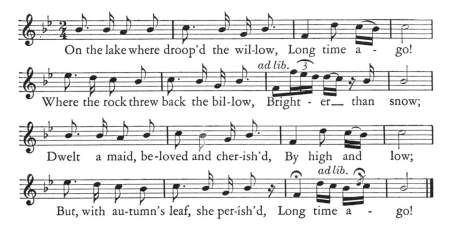

On the lake where droop'd the wil-low, Long time a - go!

Where the rock threw back the bil-low, Bright - er— than snow;

Dwelt a maid, be-loved and cher-ish'd, By high and low;

But, with au-tumn's leaf, she per-ish'd, Long time a - go!

In later editions the title was changed to "Near the Lake," perhaps to counteract the impression that the heroine was a mermaid or a water sprite. This song, completely typical of the genteel tradition, enjoyed a great vogue in its time.

Morris wrote the libretto of an opera in three acts, *The Maid of Saxony*, which was set to music by C. E. Horn and in 1842 had a run of about two weeks in New York City. Charles Edward Horn (1786–1849), the son of a German musician who had settled in London, was active in New York from 1833 to 1843. After four years in England he went to Boston as conductor of the Handel and Haydn Society, and died in that city. Together with two other foreign-born musicians, Henry Christian Timm (1811–1892) and William Scharfenberg (1819–1895), and the "Connecticut Yankee" Ureli Corelli Hill (1802–1875), Horn participated in the founding of the New York Philharmonic Society in 1842. He also established a music-publishing business. As a composer he is interesting to us chiefly for his attempts to inject local color into his musical settings of a cycle of poems by G. P. Morris, published collectively as *National Melodies of America*. Besides "On the Lake" the series included a song called "Meeta," "adapted from a negro air," and "Northern Refrain," based on the "carol of the sweeps of the city of New York."

The singing Hutchinsons

It was not only in New York that the year 1839 proved eventful in the annals of American music. On Thanksgiving Day of that year, in the town of Milford, New Hampshire, the eleven sons and two daughters of the Hutchinson family ("the tribe of Jesse") gave a vocal concert in the Baptist meetinghouse. The building was packed with sympathetic listeners who applauded the program of hymns, anthems, and glees. The Hutchinsons felt that they had started something with their first public concert. And they were right. They gave another concert in Lynn and then decided that they needed more scope. Said John Hutchinson to his brothers, "We need more discipline and more culture." So they went to Boston in search of culture. Instinct or fore-knowledge guided them straight to the fountainhead of musical culture in the City of Culture: the office of Professor Lowell Mason. Humbly they requested his advice. The eminent musical magnate gave them impeccable advice: he recommended that they acquire and use his latest singing book.

The Hutchinson brothers (only four of them had gone to Boston) thereupon betook themselves to that other eminent apostle of musical culture in Boston, Professor George James Webb, president of the Handel and Haydn Society, composer of such genteel ballads as "Art Thou Happy, Lovely Lady?" "I'll Meet Thee, Sweet Maid," "When I Seek my Pillow," and of the tune used as a setting for the hymn "Stand Up, Stand Up for Jesus." Professor Webb received the Hutchinson brothers most courteously—and invited them to join the Handel and Haydn Society.

At this point the New Hampshire lads probably decided that what they really needed was less culture and more discipline. Renting a room, they settled down to systematic practice. John Hutchinson spent his last dollar to acquire a copy of Henry Russell's cantata, "The Maniac." It was an investment that paid off, for they made a tremendous hit with this number on their concert tours, singing it even more effectively than Russell himself. John was the star performer in this number. While his brothers played a prelude on the violin and the cello, John would sit in a chair behind them, raising the hair on his head with the fingers of each hand. Then he would rise, suitably disheveled, "with the expression of vacancy inseparable from mania," and proceed with the gruesome performance, to the horror and delight of the audience. We shall spare the reader further details of this excruciating opus, though it might still be good for a few laughs.

By 1843, after several successful concerts in Boston and elsewhere, the Hutchinsons were able to have several of the songs in their repertoire published by Oliver Ditson of Boston. These were "The Snow Storm," "Jamie's on the Stormy Sea," "The Grave of Bonaparte," and a temperance song, "King Alcohol." The music for the first of these songs was written by Lyman Heath, a composer and singer of Nashua, New Hampshire; the words by Seba Smith. "The Snow Storm," with its pathetic portrayal of a young mother struggling through the snow drifts, carrying her little babe, is indeed a classic of the genteel tradition.

Armed with a New England reputation and such sure-fire numbers as the above, the Singing Hutchinsons ventured to New York in May, 1843. They were delighted with the metropolis on the Hudson. In his diary Asa Hutchinson wrote:

> O! New York is all that I have had it represented to be; Boston does not compare with it for life and business. The Splendid Street "Broad Way" is the most splendid street that I ever saw, and then the Grand Park, and the splendid water works where the water is thrown into the air to the height of 25 or 30 feet and then falls into the Pool again in the most majestic style.

At their concert in the Broadway Tabernacle, the Hutchinsons were introduced by the celebrated Dr. Lyman Beecher. They sang four of their favorite numbers: "King Alcohol," "We Are Happy and Free," "We Have Come From the Mountains," and their theme song, "The Old Granite State," for which they used the tune of that rousing revival song, "The Old Churchyard." The program was announced as one that had pleased "fashionable audiences in Boston." Though they were country boys themselves, the Hutchinsons aspired to receive the accolade of fashion and of gentility, and they succeeded. In New York they met George P. Morris, who became "their dear friend" and several of whose poems they set to music and featured in their programs. Among these was "My Mother's Bible," thoroughly typical of the Morris output:

This book is all that's left me now,
   Tears will unbidden start;
With faltering lip and throbbing brow,
   I press it to my heart.

Through Morris, the Hutchinsons met Henry Russell, who said to them: "I think you are the best singers in America." With such friends and admirers, the New Hampshire lads—and their sister Abby, who formed part of the concert group—were definitely established in the genteel tradition. Russell's song "The Gambler's Wife" gave Abby Hutchinson a chance to shine as soloist and wring tears from the audience with her description of the poor, lonely, deserted wife.

The Hutchinsons made a four-part vocal setting of Longfellow's "Excelsior" and then called on the poet to request a few words of explanation of the poem's meaning, which they might append to the sheet music. The poet obligingly complied, and the Hutchinsons had another feather in their cap as well as another successful number in their repertoire. This musical setting of "Excelsior," too long to quote here, will be found in the collection *Songs of Yesterday*.

In 1845 the Singing Hutchinsons made a tour of England and Ireland. Returning to America, they toured widely in this country, not only entertaining large audiences but also espousing such causes as Temperance, Women's Suffrage, and especially Abolition, to which they were enthusiastically devoted. It would be plausible to claim that the Hutchinsons were concerned with bringing music to ordinary people, to "the masses" rather than "the classes," and that therefore they did not really represent the genteel tradition. My view is that they allied themselves with the genteel tradition as far as repertoire is concerned and in their desire to obtain the approval of fashionable urban audiences. Compared with the repertoire of Italian opera, that appealed only to the initiated or the snobbish, their programs were popular and designed for mass appeal. They therefore represented what might be called the "left wing" of the genteel tradition, approaching the popular tradition while retaining the prestige of elegance and refinement associated with such names as Morris and Longfellow and with the accolade of urban culture acquired in Boston and New York. They had, it is true, some humorous songs in their repertoire; but these avoided vulgarity. To the raucous banjo and bones of minstrelsy they opposed the gentle tones of the violin and violoncello, and in dress and manner they emulated a discreet and genteel respectability.

There were numerous other singing families in America, of which the most prominent, after the Hutchinsons, were the Bakers of New Hampshire. Their repertoire included such numbers as "The Happiest Time Is Now," "Where Can the Soul Find Rest?," "The Inebriate's Lament," and "The Burman Lover," all composed by the leader of the group, John C. Baker.

Poet and composer

When Edgar Allan Poe formulated his famous dictum that the most poetic subject was the death of a beautiful young woman, he voiced an aesthetic principle that was a fundamental tenet of the genteel tradition. The maid who dwelt on the lake, or near the lake, and who perish'd with the autumn's leaf, was first cousin to Poe's rare and radiant maiden whom the angels named Lenore. To the same family, and more popular though not so *distinguée,* belonged sweet Lilly Dale, immortalized in verse and music by H. S. Thompson, in a song copyrighted in 1852, which in turn inspired many other musical mementos for the departed maiden, including Sigmund Thalberg's *Lilly Dale, Air Américain varié pour le Piano*—one of the numerous variations on favorite airs with which pianists of that period regaled the public. In Thompson's song the vocal solo is followed by a chorus for four mixed voices.

Poe himself, notwithstanding his superior genius, exhibited at times a surprising indulgence toward the productions of the genteel tradition. Many are the now forgotten female poets upon whom he bestowed flattering praise. Of George Pope Morris's poems, "Woodman, Spare That Tree" and "Near the Lake," he wrote in the *Southern Literary Messenger* (April, 1849) that they were "compositions of which any poet, living or dead, might justly be proud."

While composers such as Henry Russell and Charles E. Horn turned to successful poetasters such as Morris and Mackay for the texts of their songs, the American musician John Hill Hewitt (1801–1890) enjoyed the advantage, if such it was, of being both poet and composer. His accomplishments as a poet, in fact, gained him quite a reputation in his day. In 1833 Hewitt submitted his poem "The

Song of the Wind" in a poetry contest sponsored by the publisher of the Baltimore *Saturday Visitor*, of which Hewitt himself was at that time editor. Among the contestants was Edgar Allan Poe, whose poem "The Coliseum" vied for the first prize with Hewitt's entry. The prize for the best short story, under the same sponsorship, had just been awarded to Poe's *A Manuscript Found in a Bottle*. According to Hewitt, the judges hesitated to bestow the poetry prize upon the author who had also carried off the honors, and the cash, for prose. Hence the first prize for poetry—fifty dollars in cash—was awarded to Hewitt. "This decision," wrote Hewitt, "did not please Poe, hence the 'little unpleasantness' between us."

Poetry and journalism were, together with music, the chief but not the only activities to which John H. Hewitt turned in his varied career. He was a son of the English musician James Hewitt who had emigrated to America in 1792 and had become a prominent leader in the musical life of New York and Boston. John was born in New York, but in 1812 the family moved to Boston, where he attended public school. Hewitt *père* did not favor a musical career for his son. After leaving school the boy was apprenticed to a sign painter, an arrangement not at all to his liking. He ran away and led an adventurous existence for the next few years. In 1818 he received an appointment to the military academy at West Point. During his four years there he studied music with the band leader, and when he was not permitted to graduate with his class because of deficiency in his studies, he decided to take up a musical career.

Joining a theatrical troupe directed by his father, young Hewitt traveled to the South and soon found himself stranded in Augusta, Georgia, when the company failed. He spent the ensuing years in Georgia and South Carolina, reading for the law, publishing a newspaper, and also composing and teaching music. His first song, "The Minstrel's Return from the War," was written at this period and proved widely successful; but as it was not copyrighted, it brought him no money. He fared somewhat better, financially, with his next song, "The Knight of the Raven Black Plume."

The death of his father in 1827 brought Hewitt north to Boston, but a year later he was in Baltimore, which he regarded henceforth as his home city, though he continued to be rather restless. In Baltimore he was active as editor and publisher, and for a time was a political supporter of Henry Clay in Washington. In 1861 he was living in Richmond, and at the outbreak of the Civil War offered his services to the Confederacy. He was assigned the dreary task of drilling recruits. Two years later he was active in Augusta as manager of a theater troupe for which he wrote or adapted numerous plays and operettas. His song "All Quiet Along the Potomac To-Night" was one of the hit tunes of the Civil War.

In the 1870s Hewitt returned to Baltimore and remained there till his death at an advanced age. He had been twice married. By his first wife he had seven children, and four by his second. He composed over three hundred songs, which earned him the title of "Father of the American Ballad," a considerable number of stage works with music, and some oratorios, of which the best known is *Jephtha*, performed in New York, Washington, Baltimore, and Norfolk. In spite of the wide popularity of his songs, Hewitt found that music as a profession did not pay. "The publisher pockets all," he wrote, "and gets rich on the brains of the poor fool who is chasing that *ignis fatuus*, reputation." In his volume of recollections, *Shadows on the Wall*, he summed up his attitude toward music:

Music has always been, and still is, my frailty. Since my earliest youth I have sought its gentle influence . . . and it finally became my profession, though my parents were solicitous that I should adopt any other honorable calling but that. I studied it as an art and a science; but only for the sake of the accomplishment, never thinking that I should use it as the means of support. . . . Whenever I failed in any enterprise I fell back on music; it was my sheet-anchor.[3]

It is curious that Hewitt's father, a musician himself, should not have wished his son to adopt music as a profession. But his mother, the elder Hewitt's second wife, was the daughter of Sir John King of the British Army, and it is probable that social prejudice, as well as economic motives, may have been behind their desire to have their son adopt "any other honorable calling" but music. Hewitt himself was resentful of being regarded as a professional musician. When he was invited to the homes of wealthy or prominent persons, he wished to be received as an equal, to converse on intellectual or political matters like the other gentlemen, and not to be kept in reserve as an entertainer when the company requested some music. Although he was an outstanding representative of the genteel tradition, he resented

[3] Hewitt, *Shadows on the Wall*, pp. 65–66.

and ridiculed the mania for foreign fashions that was a hallmark of
that tradition. He particularly detested the affectation which caused
people in society to admire, or pretend to admire, Italian vocal music.
His resentment may have been due in large part to his dislike of the
foreign musicians—Italian, French, and German—who were becoming
increasingly prominent in the musical life of the United States, and
whose success hindered the acceptance of native-born musicians like
himself. It may be conceded that Hewitt was not an important composer, but he was certainly a representative figure in this transitional
period of America's music.

Some Civil War songs

George Frederick Root (1825–1895) was so many-sided in his musical activities that his work might well be distributed among several
chapters. He was associated with Mason, Webb, and Bradbury in the
"better music" movement radiating from Boston, and wrote hymns
that were suitably sentimental, such as "The Shining Shore" ("My
days are gliding swiftly by"). Born in Sheffield, Massachusetts, he had
from childhood the ambition to be a musician. In Boston he became a
pupil of Benjamin Franklin Baker and later assisted Lowell Mason at
the Academy of Music. Around 1845 he went to New York, assuming the position of music teacher at Abbot's Institute for Young
Ladies. In 1850 a trip to Europe for further musical study gave him
the foreign finish needed to uphold the genteel tradition with distinction. Three years later he collaborated with Mason in organizing the
Normal Institute for music teachers in New York. One of the interesting aspects of Root's career, however, is that he did not remain in the
cultural strongholds of the East, but followed the westward trend
of expansion. His brother had opened a music store in Chicago with
C. M. Cady as partner, under the firm name of Root & Cady, which
became an important publishing house. Root joined his brother in
1859, making Chicago his headquarters henceforth. The business was
ruined by the fire of 1871, but recovered rapidly. In 1872 Root attained to the peak of eminent respectability by receiving the degree
of Doctor of Music from the University of Chicago.

Root definitely belongs to the genteel tradition through his sentimental ballads. The words for some of these were written by his
former pupil, the blind poetess Fanny Crosby, who provided the verses

for "Hazel Dell," "There's Music in the Air," and "Rosalie the Prairie Flower." Rosalie proved to be a popular girl, bringing the composer $3,000 in royalties. During the Civil War, Root turned out some of the most successful songs associated with that struggle: "Just Before the Battle, Mother," "The Vacant Chair," "The Battle Cry of Freedom," and "Tramp! Tramp! Tramp!" or "The Prisoner's Hope." It was through these war songs that Root achieved his most lasting reputation. "The Battle Cry of Freedom" was included in the repertoire of the Hutchinson Family and stirred audiences throughout the Northern states. Root also composed several cantatas that are now forgotten.

Henry Clay Work (1832–1884) is best known for his Civil War songs—"Kingdom Coming," "Babylon is Falling," "Marching Through Georgia"—and he was also associated with American minstrelsy through such songs as "We're Coming, Sister Mary" (which he sold to E. P. Christy) and "Wake, Nicodemus," which many people know without being aware that Work composed it. Work was a native of Connecticut but spent part of his boyhood in Illinois, where his father, an ardent abolitionist, had migrated. In 1845 the family returned to Connecticut. At the age of twenty-three, Work, who had learned the printer's trade, went to Chicago and combined the occupations of printer and composer. Like his father, he was an active abolitionist. He also championed the cause of temperance and produced that classic of temperance songs, "Come Home, Father." Work belongs to the genteel tradition through such songs as "The Lost Letter," "The Ship that Never Returned," "Phantom Footsteps," and "Grandfather's Clock."

Expansion and transition

The period that marked the rise of the genteel tradition was also the period of westward expansion. Though most of the songs associated with the genteel tradition deal with romantic or sentimental subjects, there was also a certain type of song written by "armchair pioneers"—musicians and writers who lived comfortably in large cities while turning out jolly songs urging the delights of life on the ocean waves or the allurements of existence on the wild open prairie. Henry Russell actually prided himself on having promoted the westward movement of population through some of his songs. An American song of this type was written and composed by Ossian E. Dodge, voicing the theme of "manifest destiny." The song is titled "Ho, Westward, Ho!" and lauds the virtues of the West as a glorious source of health and wealth.[4] The refrain, "Ho, Westward, Ho!" occurs after each line, following a familiar pattern of revival songs and of Negro work songs, such as the one quoted in Chapter 13, with the refrain, "Ho, meleety, ho!" The song continues for six stanzas on the same theme, like a singing commercial for a real-estate development project.

It seems to me that we can get a rather good perspective on musical life in the United States during this era of transition and expansion by listening to the conversation of two foreign musicians, each of whom had contrasting experiences in this country in the antebellum period. One of these musicians is our friend Henry Russell, the other is the Norwegian violinist Ole Bull (1810–1880), who made five visits to America, the first in 1843, and who eventually married an American woman. The scene is New Orleans, and the conversation is reported by Russell in his autobiography. The English musician had gone to pay a professional visit of courtesy to his Norwegian colleague.

B.–I have heard a great deal of you, Mr. Russell,–I am glad to see you; pray sit down. You have been some considerable time in this country; how do you like it?

R.–Very much, but I fear the reception accorded to you has not been worthy of your great talent.

B.–I regret to say that is so. I have encountered, since I have been there nothing but jealousy and rivalry, with but little sympathy from those I most expected it from.

R.–You must not lose sight of the fact that, until the beginning of this century, musical culture was a thing practically unknown outside such towns as New York, Philadelphia, and Boston. It is only now the denizens of the smaller towns are beginning to take an interest in things musical, therefore do not be downhearted. I need hardly say that those people who know anything whatever of music, are charmed with your exquisite playing. Tell me, sir, how do you like New Orleans?

B.–Not a great deal. The people here prefer the nigger's violin to mine. I have travelled from New York to play to people who do not understand me.

[4] This song will be found in *Songs of Yesterday*, edited by Jordan and Kessler.

R.–Yes, the generality of the nation are young in scientific music; their idea of fine music consists of simple song. My dear Mr. Bull, you must have patience. It is only time and perseverance that will teach the uneducated to appreciate your marvellous performance.[5]

Henry Russell was right; in time America would learn to appreciate the playing not only of Ole Bull, but of every other visiting virtuoso with a foreign accent and a European reputation. The Age of Innocence, the Era of Simple Song, would soon be over. Enter then the Age of Scientific Music, the Triumph of Progress, the Era of Big Business. But before we reach those dizzy heights of progress and appreciation, of standardized production and mass consumption, there are other phases of the Era of Simple Song to be explored.

[5] Russell, *op. cit.*, pp. 146–148.

chapter ten

The fasola folk

'Ask for the old paths and walk therein.'
BENJAMIN FRANKLIN WHITE, PREFACE TO 1869 EDITION OF THE SACRED HARP.

In the year 1848 a certain Miss Augusta Brown wrote an article which appeared in *The Musician and Intelligencer* of Cincinnati. Pointing to the musical superiority of Europe, Miss Brown voiced her opinion as to the causes of America's inferiority in this field:

The most mortifying feature and grand cause of the low estate of scientific music among us, is the presence of common Yankee singing schools, so called. We of course can have no allusion to the educated professors of vocal music, from New England, but to the genuine Yankee singing masters, who profess to make an accomplished amateur in one month, and a regular professor of music (not in seven years, but) in one quarter, and at the expense, to the initiated person, usually one dollar. Hundreds of country idlers, too lazy or too stupid for farmers or mechanics, "go to singing school for a spell," get diplomas from others scarcely better qualified than themselves, and then with their brethren, the far famed "Yankee Peddlars," itinerate to all parts of the land, to corrupt the taste and pervert the judgment of the unfortunate people who, for want of better, have to put up with them.

This outburst of snobbishness, so typical of the genteel tradition, not only confirms the widespread influence and popularity of the singing schools but also reveals the radiating influence of New England's pioneer folk tradition throughout the expanding frontier country. The "genuine Yankee singing masters" were keeping alive throughout the land the spirit of old Bill Billings of Boston. After 1800 many singing-school teachers and compilers of songbooks sprang up in the South and in what was then the West: Kentucky and Tennessee and the valley of the Mississippi. This chapter is the story of these frontier singing folk, their songbooks, and their tunes, which are so vital a part of America's music.

In the eighteenth century the singing school was an urban as well as a rural institution. It was patronized by city idlers as well as country idlers, by ladies and gentlemen as well as country yokels. This is made clear in an advertisement that appeared in the *Pennsylvania Gazette* of 1760:

> Notice is hereby given that the Singing-School, lately kept in the Rooms over Mr. William's School in Second Street [Philadelphia], will again be opened on Monday Evening, the 3d of November next, at the same Place; where the ART OF PSALMODY will be taught, as usual, in the best Manner, on Monday and Friday Evenings, from Six to Eight. And that, if any Number of Ladies and Gentlemen incline to make up an exclusive Set, to Sing on two other Nights, they may be gratified by making Application in time.

So that, if Miss Augusta Brown had lived a couple of generations earlier, she might have joined a singing school in Boston or Philadelphia in the company of an exclusive Set of Ladies and Gentlemen. But under the impact of the "progressive improvement" described in the previous chapter, the singing schools, considered old-fashioned and backward because they failed to adopt the latest European musical fashions, were driven out from the cities to the hinterlands, and the vast new territories opened up for musical cultivation by the expanding frontier. For a while the singing schools lingered as an anachronism in small towns of New England. The most complete description of a singing school in the genuine Yankee tradition was written by the Rev. E. Wentworth in his old age, referring to a period sixty years earlier, probably around 1820, when he attended his first singing school as a lad. His account contains so many curious details that it is worth quoting almost in full:

> Time, sixty years ago; place, south-eastern Connecticut; locality, a suburban school-house; *personelle*, the choir of a Congregational church, and two dozen young aspirants, thirsting for musical knowledge; teacher, a peripatetic Faw-sol-law-sol, who went from town to town during the winter months, holding two schools a week in each place; wages, two dollars a night and board for himself and horse, distributed from house to house among his patrons, according to hospitality or ability; instrument, none but pitch-pipe or tuning-fork; qualifications of teacher, a knowledge of plain psalmody,

ability to lead an old style "set piece" or anthem, a light, sweet, tenor voice, and a winning manner. . . .

For beginners, the first ordeal was trial of voice. The master made the circuit of the room, and sounded a note or two for each separate neophyte to imitate. The youth who failed in ability to "sound the notes" was banished to the back benches to play listener, and go home with the girls when school was out. The book put into our hands was Thomas Hastings' *Musica Sacra*, published in Utica in 1819, in shape like a modern hymnal. There were four pages of elements and two hundred tunes, half of them written in three parts, wanting the alto or confounding it with the tenor. The elements were given out as a lesson to be memorized, studied by question and answer for a couple of evenings or so, and then we were supposed to be initiated into all the mysteries of staff, signature, clef, flats, sharps, and naturals, notes, rests, scales, and, above all, ability to find the place of the "mi." Only four notes were in use—faw, sol, law, mi; and the scale ran faw, sol, law, faw, sol, law, mi, faw. The table for the "mi" had to be recited as glibly as the catechism, and was about as intelligible as some of its theology:—

The natural place for mi is B;
If B be flat, the mi is in E;
If B and E, the mi is in A and C;
If F be sharp, the mi is in G;
If F and C, the mi is in C and C.

The Continental scale, do, re, mi, had not yet been imported. The key-note was called the "pitch," and preliminary to singing, even in church, was taking the key from the leader, and sounding the "pitch" of the respective parts, bass, tenor, and treble, in the notes of the common chord. A few simple elements mastered, or supposed to be, the school plunged at once into the heart of the book, and began to psalmodize by note in the second week of the brief term. . . .

The rest of the winter's work comprehended "Barby," "St. Ann's," "St. Martin's," "Colchester," "Portugal," "Tallis," "Winchester," "Shirland," "Silver Street," "Easter Hymn," "Amsterdam," and many others now forgotten. The favorite fugues [i.e., fuguing tunes] of the preceding century had passed out of fashion, and the leading church airs of this were not yet. A few anthems of the simpler sort we tackled, such as "Denmark," "Dying Christian," and "Lord of all Power and Might." . . . That, reader, was sixty years ago. Germany and Italy have since been transported to America, and, musically, we live in a new earth and a new heaven. Yet the simple strains of those days were as perfectly adapted to those who made them as Wagner, Liszt, Mendelssohn, and Chopin are to us today![1]

What a tremendous segment of America's musical history is enclosed in that passage! The last stand of a popular musical institution against the rising tide of urban domination, the lingering anachronism of the fa-sol-la system of solmization, brought to America by the early English colonists; the falling out of fashion of the fuguing tunes in the urbanized communities of the Eastern seaboard; the oblivion into which many of the old hymns fell among educated music lovers brought up on the latest European importations, "Germany and Italy . . . transported to America." But this shows only one half of the picture. For Reverend Wentworth and other educated city dwellers, the old order may have passed away, but it was not dead. It may have been thrust out of sight and hearing by "progressive improvement," but it was thriving and flourishing, and becoming more American all the time, under the influence of the frontier and of the rural South, where folks preferred to go their own way rather than to take up newfangled notions and "scientific" innovations.

Take, for example, the fa-sol-la system, mentioned by Reverend Wentworth as not yet having been superseded by the imported Continental do-re-mi scale. If the fa-sol-la system was good enough for the first American settlers, it was good enough for the rural singing-school teachers and singing folk of the South and West. So they kept the four-syllable solmization, used it in their singing schools, singing conventions, and songbooks, for generation after generation. That is why we call them the "fasola folk," for the old-time syllables are a symbol of the folkways of a large body of rural singers who have kept alive the tunes and the traditions of the American pioneers.

Along with the fa-sol-la system, the rural singing folk clung to another device that was considered backward and unprogressive by the advocates of scientific improvement. This was the device of having each of the four notes represented by a character of different shape. In an earlier chapter we mentioned that two singing-school teachers, William Smith and William Little, had introduced the shape notes in their book *The Easy Instructor* (Philadelphia, 1801), subtitled *A New Method of Teaching Harmony*. In this system, *fa* (or *faw*) is repre-

---

[1] From Curwen, *Studies in Music Worship*, pp. 115ff.

sented by a right-angled triangle, *sol* by a circle or round note, *la* (or *law*) by a square, and *mi* by a diamond shape, each with a stem appended to it, thus:

$$\vdash \ \mathsf{P} \ \mathsf{P} \ \Diamond$$

A second edition of *The Easy Instructor* was printed at New York in 1802, and thereafter numerous editions were printed in rapid succession at Albany, attesting to the work's immediate popularity. The last edition appeared in 1831.[2]

One of the reasons why *The Easy Instructor* is so important in the history of American music—apart from the shape-note innovation— is that it gave predominance to compositions by native American composers at a time when the tendency was to include a greater number of European compositions in collections of this kind.

In the 1830s Timothy Mason, brother of Lowell Mason, went to Cincinnati and prepared for publication a work called *The Ohio Sacred Harp*. The Masons attempted to do away with the fasola singing and the shape notes (also called "patent" or "buckwheat" notes), and wrote a preface to the above collection in which they attacked the use of these old-fashioned methods. "By pursuing the common method of only *four* syllables," they wrote, "singers are almost always superficial. It is therefore recommended to all who wish to be thorough, to pursue the system of seven syllables, disregarding the different forms of the notes." Perhaps they would have been more successful in their campaign if they had used the homely argument of William Walker, when the latter decided to switch to the seven-character system in 1866: "Would any parent having seven children, ever think of calling them by only four names?" As it was, the publishers of *The Ohio Sacred Harp* were the first to disregard the Masons' advice, for they issued the collection with shape notes, explaining that this was done "under the belief that it will prove much more acceptable to a majority of singers in the West and South."

Thus the two sets of syllables, fa-sol-la and do-re-mi, came to represent two conflicting cultural trends. The do-re-mi system, with

[2] See "A History and Bibliography of the First Shape Note Book," by Irving Lowens and Allen P. Britton, *Journal of Research in Music Education*, I, 1 (1953), pp. 31–55.

all that it implied in the way of "scientific improvement," was victorious in the cities and those areas, chiefly of the Eastern seaboard, dominated by urban culture. But the fasola folk held their own in the hinterland.

Fasola leaders and songbooks

The main path of the singing-school movement appears to have been from New England to Pennsylvania, thence southward and westward. Frédéric Ritter, writing of Andrew Law in his book *Music in America*, says: "He did good pioneer work in the New England States and in the South." Since this statement is unconfirmed by documentary evidence, the extent of Law's activity and influence in the South must remain a matter of conjecture. There was, however, another advocate of the shape-note system, a New Englander by the name of John Wyeth (1770–1858), who settled in Harrisburg, Pennsylvania, and who published there in 1810 a collection titled *Repository of Sacred Music*, which went through seven editions up to 1834 and had an extremely wide circulation for those times. In this collection, Wyeth used the shape-note system of Little and Smith.

John Wyeth was born in Cambridge, Massachusetts, learned the printer's trade, and at twenty-one went to Santo Domingo to superintend a printing establishment in that island, from which he was soon afterward driven away by the Negro insurrection, escaping with great difficulty and danger, disguised as a sailor. He reached Philadelphia, worked there as a printer, and in 1792 moved to Harrisburg, where he purchased a newspaper, established a bookstore and a publishing house. President Washington appointed him postmaster of Harrisburg in 1793. The hymn tune "Nettleton" ("Come, Thou Fount of Every Blessing") is attributed to Wyeth.

The *Repository of Sacred Music* contains numerous pieces by the early New England composers, such as Billings, Holyoke, Read, and Swan, whose music was falling into neglect in the North but was to continue flourishing in the songbooks and singing conventions of the South and West. In 1813 Wyeth issued a supplement to the *Repository*, as Part II, intended particularly for Methodists, which includes the hymn "Come, Thou Fount of Every Blessing" followed by the refrain, "Hallelujah, Hallelujah, We are on our journey home." This is a typical camp-meeting chorus, of which more will be said in the next chapter.

Here it is necessary to emphasize the importance of Wyeth's *Repository of Sacred Music, Part Second,* as a primary source of American folk hymnody. It was intended especially for use at revivals and camp meetings and, as such, contained a large proportion of tunes that may properly be classified as "folk hymns," that is, basically "a secular folk tune which happens to be sung to a religious text." [3] Most of the southern tune-book compilers of the early nineteenth century, beginning with Ananias Davisson, borrowed extensively from *Part Second* of Wyeth's collection (which in spite of the misleading title, was entirely different in character from the original *Repository of Sacred Music*).

According to Irving Lowens, the "musical brains" behind Wyeth's influential tunebook was the Rev. Elkanah Kelsay Dare (1782–1826), author of a theoretical work on music (which seems never to have been published: Wyeth quotes from it as a "Manuscript work"), who is named as the composer of thirteen tunes in this collection. Reverend Dare must therefore take his place as one of the initiators of the important Southern folk-hymn movement.

After 1815 we find the chief concentration of the fasola movement in the South and Midwest. Ohio, Virginia, North and South Carolina, Kentucky, Tennessee, Alabama, and Georgia, were the homegrounds of several generations of rural singing-school teachers and songbook compilers who carried on the tradition of the native New England pioneers. Let us make the acquaintance of some of these fasola leaders.

Not much is known of Ananias Davisson (1780–1857), except that he was an elder of the Presbyterian Church, that he was active in northwestern Virginia, and that he acquired "a practical knowledge as a teacher of sacred Music." His most important compilation, the *Kentucky Harmony* was published in 1816, with four later editions up to 1826. This collection contains 144 tunes in four-part harmony, the parts being bass, tenor, counter, and treble. In his instructions on singing, Davisson writes: "The bass stave is assigned to the gravest voices of men, and the tenor to the highest. The counter to the lowest voices of the Ladies, and the treble to the highest of Ladies' voices." What this means is that the principal melody or "air" was

---

[3] The definition is by Irving Lowens; see his *Music and Musicians in Early America,* p. 138. But the definition raises more questions than it answers. In the absence of a definite secular counterpart, for instance, how does one actually recognize a folk hymn?

carried by high male voices in the tenor part, while the women sang subordinate parts. This practice of having men sing the melody was another heritage from colonial times and was opposed to the "improved" urban practice of having the women sing the melody in the soprano. The custom of the tenor melody continued to prevail in the fasola tradition, although it should be pointed out that the arrangers of these tunes tried to make each voice melodically interesting and independent. Their conception of voice-leading was "horizontal" rather than "vertical": they aimed at real part singing rather than at harmonized melody.

The reader must not suppose, however, that the voice-leading and the resultant harmonies were "correct" according to the academic tradition. On the contrary, the violation of conventional "rules" was so persistent, and generally so consistent, as to constitute a well-defined style. In the first place, it should be pointed out that in the most authentic fasola tradition the vocal settings were for three voices rather than four. Although Davisson arranged his tunes for four voices in the *Kentucky Harmony*, many other tune books, including the *Harp of Columbia*, the *Southern Harmony*, the *Missouri Harmony*, and the *Sacred Harp*, employed the more characteristic three-part arrangement (with the "tune" in the middle part). Charles Seeger, who has made the most thorough study of the contrapuntal style of these three-voiced shape-note hymns, found that they systematically violated most of the established rules, such as those forbidding parallel fifths, octaves, and unisons; parallel fourths between outer voices or between upper voices without a third in the bass; unprepared and unresolved dissonances; and crossing of voices.[4] It is not *because* the rules are violated that this type of authentic American music is interesting to us, but rather because, in seeking their own style of expression, these early composers created a kind of choral writing that has a "rigorous, spare, disciplined beauty" of its own. And it is also interesting to observe that a similar rigorous and spare quality, avoiding harmonic lushness and padding, has characterized some of the most significant "new" music of our own times. It is no wonder that modern composers like Cowell and Thomson have drawn inspiration from the texture and the spirit of the American folk hymns. But let us return now to Ananias Davisson and his companions of the shape-note tradition.

In compiling the *Kentucky Harmony*, Davisson drew on the col-

---

[4] For musical examples of the three-voiced shape-note style, see the article by Charles Seeger listed in the bibliography for this chapter.

lections of Billings, Holyoke, Andrew Adgate, Smith and Little, Wyeth, and others. Among the New England composers represented are Billings, Justin Morgan, and Timothy Swan. Fifteen tunes were claimed as his own by Davisson. Of these, the best-known is "Idumea," a pentatonic melody, used with a text by Charles Wesley:

And am I ___ born to ___ die? To lay this ___ bod - y down? And must my trem-bling spir- it fly, In - to a ___ world un - known?

In 1820 Davisson brought out the *Supplement to the Kentucky Harmony*, proudly placing after his name the initials A. K. H.—"Author of Kentucky Harmony." Davisson claimed authorship of eleven tunes in this collection, besides six written in collaboration with others. It is difficult to say with certainty whether any of the tunes in these collections were actually composed by the musicians whose names are affixed to them. In some cases the compilers frankly acknowledged that they had merely harmonized or arranged the tunes, and therefore considered them as their own. In other cases they expressly state that some of the tunes were taken from oral tradition. And in some instances the same tune was claimed by several different "composers." The whole question of individual authorship is not of prime importance in the fasola singing-school tradition. These self-taught rural musicians were not composers in any academic sense of the term. They inherited a large body of traditional music, derived mainly from the British Isles. This, together with the techniques and rules of the early New England music teachers and compilers, was their musical stock-in-trade. Sometimes they took over these tunes in their natural state; sometimes they altered them, or constructed new tunes with the same melodic elements. They were craftsmen rather then creators. The tradition was more important than the individual.

Whatever hand Davisson may have had, therefore, in the composition of the twenty-six tunes that he claimed as his own, the real significance of his work lies in his having compiled and published three tune books that served as a reservoir of American rural hymnody, upon which later compilers drew freely. Through his work we can observe the beginnings of a widespread regional movement in America's music, the true homespun music of the American people.

About 1826, Davisson published his last compilation, *A Small Collection of Sacred Music*, which apparently had only one edition. Davisson's chief rivals were Wheeler Gillet (*The Virginia Sacred Minstrel*, 1817), James M. Boyd (*The Virginia Sacred Music Repository*, 1818), and the Rev. James P. Carrell.

The Rev. James P. Carrell (or Carroll) of Lebanon, Virginia, was the compiler of *Songs of Zion* (1821) and *Virginia Harmony* (1831). Born in 1787, Carrell become a Methodist minister, clerk of the county court, and a substantial citizen, owning farmlands and slaves. Perhaps his comparatively elevated social status accounts for the fact that he endeavored to make his song collections as dignified and correct as possible. The preface of the *Virginia Harmony* states that the editors "have passed by many of the light airs to be found in several of the recent publications . . . and have confined themselves to the plain psalmody of the most eminent composers." This means, for example, that he snubbed his colleague Ananias Davisson, using only two of the latter's tunes. It is curious to observe these nuances of caste and decorum in the popular tradition. Lowell Mason would have looked down his nose at Carrell as a rustic singing teacher, but Carrell in turn deprecated the "light airs" composed or arranged by his less dignified associates. Yet Carrell was entirely loyal to the fasola system itself, extolling in his *Rudiments* the advantages of the four-shape notes, which he calls "patent" notes, "on account of their author's having obtained a patent for the invention."

Carrell affixed his name as composer to seventeen tunes in the *Virginia Harmony*. In spite of his ministerial dignity, he was very close to the folk tradition in his music. This is demonstrated, for instance, in his "Dying Penitent," a characteristic specimen of the American religious ballad stemming directly from British folk music:

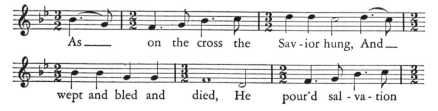

on a wretch, That lan-guish'd at_his_ side. His
crimes with in - ward grief_ and shame, The
pen - i - tent con - fess'd; Then turn'd his dy-ing_
eyes on_Christ, And thus his prayer ad - dress'd.

Eight other religious songs signed by Carrell were reprinted in later
collections by other compilers, indicating that he continued to enjoy
some regional reputation as a composer. Carrell died in 1854.

In 1825 William Moore, of Wilson County, Tennessee, brought
out his *Columbian Harmony*, printed in Cincinnati. In his "General
Observations" Moore gives some rather amusing admonitions to singers: "Nothing is more disgusting in singers than affected quirks and
ostentatious parade, endeavoring to overpower other voices by the
strength of their own, or officiously assisting other parts while theirs
is silent." Much of his material is taken from Ananias Davisson, thirteen of whose songs are included in Moore's collection.

Moore himself claimed authorship of eighteen songs in the *Columbian Harmony*. One of these songs, "Sweet Rivers," is interesting as
containing one of the early examples of the "crossing over Jordan"
theme that is so frequent in American folk hymnody. The tune also
is typical of this tradition.

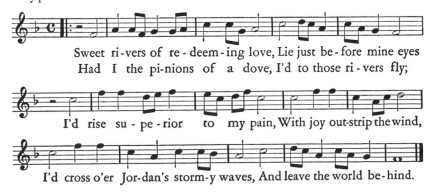

Sweet ri-vers of re - deem-ing love, Lie just be-fore mine eyes
Had I the pi-nions of a dove, I'd to those ri - vers fly;
I'd rise su - pe - rior to my pain, With joy out-strip the wind,
I'd cross o'er Jor-dan's storm-y waves, And leave the world be-hind.

Another Tennessee collection is William Caldwell's *Union Harmony*, printed at Maryville in 1837. Caldwell ascribed to himself forty-two of the songs in this collection. He admits, however, that many of these are not entirely original, but that, as he has harmonized the tunes, he claims them as his own. He furthermore states that "many of the airs which the authors has reduced to system and harmonized, have been selected from the unwritten music in general use in the Methodist Church, others from the Baptist and many more from the Presbyterian taste." This is an extremely interesting statement, for it confirms the existence of a body of "unwritten music"—that is, folk music transmitted by oral tradition—among the Methodists and other denominations, and through William Caldwell's enterprise actual specimens of this early American folk music have been preserved on the printed page.

"A wonderful book"

Passing over John B. Jackson's *Knoxville Harmony*, printed at Madisonville, Tennessee, in 1838, we turn to a book of exceptional interest and importance: William Walker's *Southern Harmony*. "Singin' Billy" Walker, as he was familiarly called, was the son of poor parents who settled near Spartanburg, South Carolina, when he was eighteen years old (he was born in 1809). He received only a rudimentary education, but early in life was filled with the ambition "to perfect the vocal modes of praise." According to a quaint account in Landrum's *History of Spartanburg County* (Atlanta, 1900):

From the deep minstrels of his own bosom he gathered and arranged into meter and melody a wonderful book suitably adapted to the praise and glory of God. . . . Notwithstanding some depreciation by the press, he adhered to his original system [i.e., shape notes], and his reputation for attainments in his science soon spread all through the South and Southwest. Everywhere his popularity as a music teacher went and his work received a most popular indorsement.

The "wonderful book" was Walker's *Southern Harmony*, first published in 1835 (printed for the author in New Haven, Connecticut), with seven later editions, the last in 1854. Walker stated that 600,000 copies of *Southern Harmony* were sold. In the 1960s Walker's book was still being used by fasola singers in the South—more than a hundred years after the publication of the last edition!

The original edition of *Southern Harmony* contained 209 songs, of which twenty-five were claimed by Walker as composer. In later editions he ascribed other songs to himself, making a total of forty songs to which he claimed authorship. Before me is a reproduction of the 1854 edition of *Southern Harmony*, which carries us right into the heart of the fasola singing movement. The title page is worth reproducing in full, for in itself it tells us much about this aspect of America's musical culture:

THE

SOUTHERN HARMONY, AND MUSICAL COMPANION:

CONTAINING A CHOICE COLLECTION OF

TUNES, HYMNS, PSALMS, ODES, AND ANTHEMS:

SELECTED FROM THE MOST EMINENT AUTHORS IN THE UNITED STATES:

TOGETHER WITH

NEARLY ONE HUNDRED NEW TUNES, WHICH HAVE NEVER BEFORE BEEN PUBLISHED:

SUITED TO MOST OF THE METRES CONTAINED IN WATTS'S HYMNS AND PSALMS, MERCER'S CLUSTER, DOSSEY'S CHOICE, DOVER SELECTION, METHODIST HYMN BOOK, AND BAPTIST HARMONY:

And Well Adapted To

CHRISTIAN CHURCHES OF EVERY DENOMINATION, SINGING SCHOOLS, AND PRIVATE SOCIETIES: ALSO, AN EASY INTRODUCTION TO THE GROUNDS OF MUSIC, THE RUDIMENTS OF MUSIC, AND PLAIN RULES FOR BEGINNERS

BY WILLIAM WALKER

Sing unto God, ye kingdoms of the earth; O sing praises unto the Lord.—DAVID Speaking to yourselves in psalms, and hymns, and spiritual songs and making melody in your hearts to the Lord.—PAUL

NEW EDITION, THOROUGHLY REVISED AND MUCH ENLARGED

PHILADELPHIA:

PUBLISHED BY E. W. MILLER, 1102 and 1104 SANSOM STREET

and for sale by

J. B. LIPPINCOTT & CO., AND BOOKSELLERS, GENERALLY, THROUGHOUT THE UNITED STATES

Outwardly, this title page, which is typical of other shape-note collections, is not much different from the title pages of collections published by Lowell Mason and his associates. And, in effect, we actually find in Walker's collection a tune "arranged from Handel," taken from Mason's *Carmina Sacra*, as well as a few tunes by Mason himself, just as we find in Mason's collections a few tunes by the old New England pioneer school. The urban and the rural traditions had certain points of contact, but the *emphasis* was entirely different. What was occasional and peripheral in one was predominant in the other. The fasola books gave much place to fuguing pieces, to pentatonic and other "gapped scale" melodies of folk character, and to revival "spiritual songs" used at camp meetings. In spite of an occasional bow to progress and elegance, folk hymns, religious ballads, revival spirituals, and fuguing pieces formed the bulk of the fasola repertory.

Another important collection is the *Sacred Harp* (1844), compiled by B. F. White and E. J. King, both active in Georgia. Not much is known of King, but Benjamin Franklin White (1800–1879) was one of the most prominent figures in the fasola movement. White was born in Spartanburg, South Carolina, the youngest of fourteen children. He attended school for a few months only, but inherited a musical inclination from his father. Like most of these singing-school teachers, he was self-taught in music. Around 1840, White moved to Harris County, Georgia, where he published a newspaper called *The Organ*, in which many of his sacred songs first appeared. He was also clerk of the superior court of Harris County. The teaching of singing he considered his life's work, but, says his biographer Joe James, "he never used his talent as a musician to make money." He gave instruction free to those who could not afford to pay for it, and lodged many of his pupils in his home without charge. "He was gentle in his nature, lovable in disposition and treated everyone with universal kindness." In religious matters he was remarkably liberal, for while himself a Missionary Baptist, he worshipped also in the churches of other denominations: the Primitive Baptist, Presbyterian, Lutheran, Methodist, Christian, etc. He had fourteen children, of whom nine lived to adulthood. Several of them carried on the family's musical tradition.

White became president of the Southern Musical Convention, organized in 1845, which, together with the Chattahoochee Musical Convention, founded in 1852, was the chief center of *Sacred Harp* activity and influence. These conventions brought fasola singers together for annual "singings" lasting several days—a custom still kept up in some sections of the Deep South, notably Georgia, Alabama, and Texas. The *Sacred Harp* has had the longest continuous history of any of the shape-note singing books, for in various editions and revisions, it has been in print and in use from 1844 to the present day (1965). Revised editions appeared in 1850, 1859, 1869, 1911, 1936, 1949 (Cooper Revision), and 1960 (Denson Revision).

The Rev. William Hauser, M.D.—he was doctor, preacher, editor, teacher, composer, and singer—was one of the most remarkable figures in the Southern fasola movement, and indeed in all the annals of American music. Born in Forsyth County, North Carolina, in 1812, the youngest son of eleven children, he lost his father when he was two years old, and his mother was able to provide him with only a meager education. But Hauser had a strong thirst for knowledge, plus the determination and perseverance to acquire it. Joining the Methodist Church in 1827, he was licensed to preach seven years later. He then traveled a circuit for two years, "preaching, praying, and singing wherever he went." In 1837 he married, and in 1839 went to Emory and Henry College, Virginia, to study Greek and Latin. In 1841 he settled in Richmond County, Georgia, where he taught school and began the study of medicine, which he commenced to practice in 1843, becoming a highly successful and respected member of the profession. He was appointed professor of physiology and pathology in the Oglethorpe Medical College, Savannah (1859–1860) and was assistant editor of the *Oglethorpe Medical Journal.*

It is interesting to note that Hauser was of Moravian stock, his grandfather, Martin Hauser, having emigrated to North Carolina about the year 1750. As we mentioned in an earlier chapter, the Moravians gave exceptional importance to music not only in their religious observances but also in their community life. It will be recalled also that Winston-Salem, North Carolina, was the center of a Moravian settlement in that state.

Such was the man, versatile, hard-working, practical, with a genius for self-improvement and a strong, simple, religious faith, who in 1848 brought out the work that has been called "the rural South's biggest and best song book," the *Hesperian Harp*, printed in Philadelphia, filled with over 550 pages of music ranging from "standard" hymns of urban or European provenience to pure folk melodies recorded from oral tradition. Hauser's name stands as composer of thirty-six songs in this colossal collection, and as arranger of numerous others. Well represented are his Southern colleagues: Ananias Davisson, William Walker, and William Caldwell.

As a "composer" William Hauser was very close to the folk tradition. Let this pentatonic tune, "Hope Hull," taken from Hauser's *Hesperian Harp*, serve to confirm the foregoing statement:

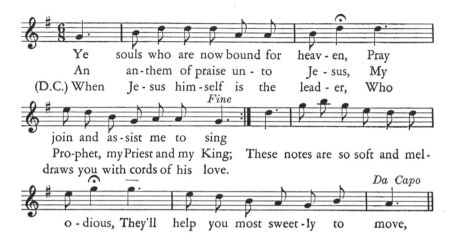

Like their New England predecessors, these Southern singing leaders and music makers were practical, hard-working men, taking a full part in the tasks and the affairs of daily life, closely identified with the people for whom they made their music. John Gordon McCurry (1821–1886), of Hart County, Georgia, was a farmer and a tailor as well as a singing-school teacher. He was also a Missionary Baptist and a Royal Arch Mason. He compiled the *Social Harp* (Philadelphia, 1859), which is exceptionally rich in songs of indigenous flavor, including "revival spirituals" (which will be discussed in a later chapter). Forty-nine songs in this collection were claimed by McCurry as composer. One of these is "John Adkins' Farewell," typical of the religious or moral ballad in which a repentant wrongdoer bids other people to take warning by his example and avoid the pitfalls of sin and crime. John Adkins, it seems, was a drunkard who killed his wife and was hanged for it. This is his farewell message, which consists of nine doleful stanzas, culminating in a final plea for the mercy "That pardons poor drunkards, and crowns them above."

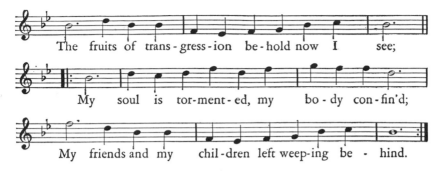

The fruits of trans-gress-ion be-hold now I see;

My soul is tor-ment-ed, my bo-dy con-fin'd;

My friends and my chil-dren left weep-ing be - hind.

Dr. George Pullen Jackson has pointed out that this tune is similar to that of the folk song "When Boys Go A-Courting," recorded in the Appalachians by Cecil Sharp. There is a Negro version of the tune adapted to the ballad of the fabulous race horse "Noble Skew-ball."

As a "composer" McCurry was partial to lively tunes. Among the songs which he ascribed to himself, many will be found of the kind that was anathema to the "better music" boys. Thoroughly typical of this trend is the camp-meeting song "Few Days," with its syncopations that savor more of minstrelsy than of hymnody. As a matter of fact, a song embodying the same idea ("I am going home") and the identical refrain, appeared in the *Negro Singer's Own Book* (1846), though without any tune. A variant of McCurry's tune and text, with the interpolation of two lines about Jonah and the whale, has been recorded among the mountain whites of Tennessee sometime in the 1920s. It is clear, therefore, that this song, like many others of its kind, has had a long life in America's music; how long, we cannot exactly tell, for it may have existed in oral tradition before McCurry caught it up and put his name to it. A song with such a history, and so characteristic of the American popular tradition, deserves quotation. Here is "Few Days," from McCurry's *Social Harp*, dated 1855:

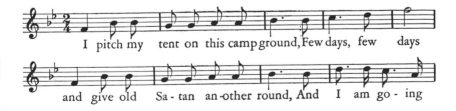

I pitch my tent on this camp ground, Few days, few days

and give old Sa-tan an-other round, And I am go-ing

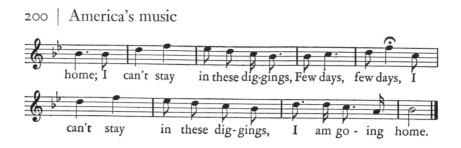

home; I can't stay in these dig-gings, Few days, few days, I
can't stay in these dig-gings, I am go-ing home.

Seven-shape songsters

We have seen that the fasola folk used only four syllables in sing-ing the notes of the scale: fa-sol-la-fa-sol-la-mi. We also remarked that the newer European system of solmization, using a different syllable for each note (do-re-mi-fa-sol-la-si) was rapidly gaining ground in America during the first half of the nineteenth century and soon be-came firmly entrenched in the urban and urban-dominated singing tradition as exemplified by Lowell Mason and his followers. From 1832 attempts were made to combine the do-re-mi system with the shape notes or patent notes to which the vast majority of rural sing-ers were stubbornly attached. The most successful manipulator of this combined system was Jesse B. Aikin of Philadelphia, whose collection, the *Christian Minstrel* (Philadelphia, 1846), went into many editions by 1873. Aiken simply added three more shape notes to the four that had been in general use, so that his complete scale appeared as follows:

At least six other seven-shape systems were introduced by various com-pilers up to 1866, but Aiken's was the one that proved most popular and that was accepted as standard by the numerous seven-shape song-book publishers of the South.

William Walker, in the introduction to the 1854 edition of his *Southern Harmony*, devoted a page to discussing "The Different Plans of Notation." He says there are seven plans of notation used in vari-ous parts of the world, including one that employs numerals, used "in Germany (among the peasants) and in some parts of the United States." Regarding what he calls the Italian "doe, rae, me" system, he has this to say:

Some contend that no one can learn to sing correctly without using the seven syllables. Although I have no objections to the seven syllable plan, I differ a little with such in opinion, for I have taught the four syllable patent notes, the Italian seven syllables, and the numerals also, and in twenty-five years' experience, have always found my patent note pupils to learn as fast, and sing as correct [sic] as any.

Nevertheless, William Walker was wavering. The seven-shape practitioners seemed to be aligned with progress. Walker decided to switch to the Italian system. When he published his *Christian Harmony*, printed at Philadelphia in 1866, it appeared with a seven-shape system of his own invention. Now he was convinced that the "seven-syllable character-note singing" was "the quickest and most desirable method known."

A certain aspiration toward "scientific improvement" accompanied the spread of the seven-shape do-re-mi system. Its principal champion, Jesse Aiken, expressed the hope that his *Christian Minstrel* would supplant the "trashy publications" so widely used in the South and West. Even "Singin' Billy" Walker endeavored to include in his *Christian Harmony* "more music suitable to church use," and in the edition of 1873 he incorporated "the most beautiful and desirable of modern tunes." The editors of another important seven-shape book, the *New Harp of Columbia* (1867), stated that many tunes originally published in the first edition of their collection (1848) had been discarded "and their places filled by others of superior merit." This is the language of Lowell Mason and progressive improvement.

The transition from four to seven shapes can also be observed in the widely used and influential publications of Joseph Funk (1777–1862), who was active in the Shenandoah Valley of Virginia. His first compilation, *Choral-Music* (1816), was in German, for he himself was of German origin.[5] Sixteen years later he brought out his first English collection, *A Compilation of Genuine Church Music* (1832), which continued to use the four shapes through its next three editions (1835, 1842, 1847). The title page announced that it contained "a copious elucidation of the science of vocal music." Then, in 1851, Funk shifted to the seven-shape notation and at the same time changed the title of his book to *Harmonia Sacra*. This important collection

---

[5] See "Joseph Funk's *Choral-Music* (1816)," by Harry Eskew, in *Report of the Society for the History of the Germans in Maryland* (1965).

went into six editions up to 1860, easily outrunning such rivals as John W. Steffy's *The Valley Harmonist* (1836), George Hendrickson's *The Union Harmony* (1848), and Levi C. Myers's *Manual of Sacred Music* (1853). Funk's work was continued by his sons, with whom he published a periodical, *The Musical Advocate and Singer's Friend* (4 vols., 1859–1868). The long and continuous history of Funk's major compilation is attested by the republication in 1959 of *The New Harmonia Sacra, a Compilation of Genuine Church Music* (Harrisonburg, Virginia, H. A. Brunk).

While tune books proliferated in the Shenandoah Valley, the chief center of "progressive improvement" in Southern church music was Richmond, the capital of Virginia. There the leaders of the "better music" movement were two brothers, L. C. Everett (1818–1867) and A. B. Everett (1828–1875), both of whom received a superior musical education, including a period of European study. Indicative of their aims was the title of a compilation they brought out in 1855: *The Progressive Church Vocalist;* this was published for them in New York by Mason Brothers—a further link with the Lowell Mason school. A year later, at Richmond, the Everett brothers published *The New Thesaurus Musicus; or United States Collection of Church Music*—the pretentious Latinized title proclaiming their highbrow aspirations. The "Everett Method" of church music was propagated through the South by such an active proponent as Rigdon McCoy McIntosh (1836–1899) of Tennessee and Georgia, whose *Tabor: or, The Richmond Collection of Sacred Music* was published at New York in 1866. McIntosh achieved the pinnacle of respectability when the firm of Oliver Ditson of Boston, in 1881, published his *Light and Life: A Collection of New Hymns and Tunes for Sunday-schools, prayer meetings, praise meetings, and revival meetings.* Thus, sixty years after Lowell Mason published the *Boston Handel and Haydn Collection of Church Music,* the movement that he had started was still strong and influential over wide areas of the nation.

Religious ballads and folk hymns

Since the fuguing tune is essentially an eighteenth-century product, and as the revival songs will be discussed in the next chapter, it will be appropriate now to give one or two more examples of the religious ballad and folk hymn. From a song literature so abundant and so rich in traditional values, it is difficult to make such a limited selection. Perhaps a good example of the religious ballad would be "Weeping Mary," of which the earliest printed version appeared in Ingalls's *Christian Harmony* of 1805. The version reproduced here is from William Walker's *Southern and Western Pocket Harmonist*, published in 1846. The tune belongs to a large family of English secular folk songs.

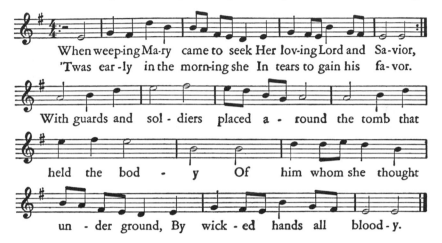

For an example of the folk hymn, we may take one that has had a long history in the American oral tradition, "Amazing Grace," with text by the English evangelist John Newton, whose colorful career was described in an earlier chapter. The tune, under various names, is found in numerous fasola songbooks without any composer's name affixed to it. Numerous versions have also been recorded from oral tradition by modern folk-song collectors. In William Walker's *Southern Harmony* it appears under the title "New Britain." The melody is pentatonic. It is this version (from the edition of 1854) which we quote here:

Dr. George Pullen Jackson recorded in 1936 an ornamented version of this tune, sung very slowly and with numerous grace notes, which he describes as "an excellent illustration of the widespread southern folk-manner in the singing of hymns of this sort." Thus we have here a continuation of the tradition of ornamented psalmody that flourished in the eighteenth century and that caused such consternation and condemnation among the New England divines. This is the ornamented version as printed by Dr. Jackson in *Spiritual Folk-Songs of Early America:*

The fasola singing leaders and compilers did not, of course, think of their songs according to the classifications mentioned above. We need to bear in mind the cultural law that "folklore does not exist for the folk." These people did not regard themselves as quaint or backward or as followers of an archaic tradition. Conservative they were, yes; and believers in the tried-and-true values of their ancestors. When a revision of the *Sacred Harp* was being discussed in 1879, and the question of adopting the seven-shape notation was raised, Benjamin Franklin White held out firmly for the old four-shape system. "The four-note scheme," he declared, "has had the sanction of the musical world for more than four hundred years [!]; and we scarcely think that we can do better than to abide by the advice . . . 'Ask for the old paths and walk therein.'" Preserve the past, yes; but as something alive and useful for the present. The fasola leaders considered themselves as supplying the musical needs of their communities according to methods and values that they thought were suitable and acceptable to the people around them.

When Ananias Davisson published his *Kentucky Harmony* in 1816 he divided the contents into two main classifications: (1) "Plain and easy tunes commonly used in time of divine worship" and (2) "More lengthy and elegant pieces, commonly used at concerts, or singing societies." The same classification was adopted by other fasola compilers. William Walker, in his *Southern Harmony*, for instance, includes in Part II the more dignified or elaborate hymns, the fuguing pieces, and anthems. One of the hymns in this section, taken probably from the *Supplement to the Kentucky Harmony*, is titled "Mississippi," the composer's name being given as "Bradshaw." In spite of the composer's name and the imposingly grandiose text, the melody bears all the earmarks of an eighteenth-century English popular tune. It was used by Shield in his ballad opera *The Lock and Key*, and for a patriotic song called "Bold Nelson's Praise." Here we have simply another case of a hymn tune borrowed from secular sources. This is the religious version of this tune, "Mississippi," as it appears in *Southern Harmony:*

When __ Ga-briel's aw-ful trump shall sound And rend the rocks, con-vulse the __ ground, And __ give to time her ut-most __ bound, Ye __ dead, a-rise to __ judg-ment; See light-nings flash and thun-ders roll, See earth wrapt up like __ parch-ment scroll; Co-mets blaze, Sin-ners __ raise, Dread a-maze, Hor-rors seize The __ guilt-y __ sons of A-dam's __ race, Un-saved from sin by __ Je-sus.

William Walker included in his *Southern Harmony*, with no indication of the author or composer, another tune that has an exceptionally curious history. This is "Long Time Ago," obviously borrowed from an old Negro song that was already widely known by the time the first edition of *Southern Harmony* appeared in 1835. According to the editors of *Slave Songs of the United States* (1867), the original Negro melody was sung to words beginning, "Way down in Raccoon Hollow." An arrangement by William Clifton, beginning, "O I was born down ole Varginee," was published in 1836 and described as "A Favorite Comic Song and Chorus" (see musical example on page 279). As we have seen, a "refined" version, in the high-flown sentimental fashion of the genteel tradition, was made by the composer Charles E. Horn with words by George P. Morris (see musical example on page 172). This is a striking illustration of the borrowing of material among different cultural traditions. Although the original Negro version has not been located, we can assume that it existed; thus we have four different traditions represented in the various versions of this song: (1) Negro folk tradition, (2) urban popular tradition (blackface minstrelsy), (3) white rural folk tradition, (4) urban cultivated tradition. The religious version of "Long Time Ago," as printed by William Walker, is given below:

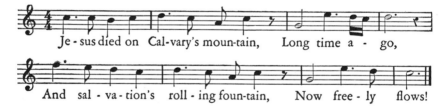

Je-sus died on Cal-vary's moun-tain, Long time a - go,

And sal - va - tion's roll - ing foun-tain, Now free - ly flows!

While these rural fasola singing teachers, compilers, arrangers, and composers were keeping alive the pioneer musical tradition, other forces were at work on the frontier that contributed to shape the vernacular idioms of America's music.

chapter eleven

Revivals and camp meetings

Shout, shout, we're gaining ground,
  Halle, hallelujah!
Satan's kingdom is tumbling down,
  Glory hallelujah!
REVIVAL HYMNS (BOSTON, 1842).

It has been said that "to the American frontier Methodism gave the circuit rider and to Methodism the frontier gave the camp meeting." The circuit rider was an itinerant preacher who traveled up and down the countryside on horseback, preaching, praying, singing, and bringing the gospel to the widely scattered rural population. Francis Asbury, the first American circuit rider, is credited with having ridden a total of 275,000 miles. But no matter how many miles the preacher on horseback traveled, he could bring the gospel only to as many people as were gathered together within reach of his voice at a single time. Hence it was a natural development for the people of a certain territory to come together at a specified time and place to hear the itinerant preacher, whose arrival had been announced in advance; and since these rural people often had to travel long distances to the meeting ground, they came prepared to stay several days. This was the origin of the American camp meetings, of which the first was held in Logan County, Kentucky, near the Gaspar River Church, in July of the year 1800.

The immediate instigator of the camp-meeting movement appears to have been the Rev. James McGready, a Presbyterian minister. Hence the movement was not exclusively Methodist. In fact, it was customary for preachers of several denominations to get together and arrange for a camp meeting jointly. The crowds were so large, ranging anywhere from two thousand to twenty thousand, that several preachers were needed to conduct the activities. If the Methodists soon gained the ascendancy in the camp meetings that quickly spread from Kentucky to the rest of the United States, it was partly because they had a large stock of popular hymnody that could readily be thrown into the emotionally boiling caldron out of which was to emerge the revival spiritual. Speaking of the Methodist invasion of the early camp meetings, a historian of the Presbyterian Church writes:

> They succeeded in introducing their own stirring hymns, familiarly, though incorrectly, entitled "Wesley's Hymns"; and as books were scarce, the few that were attainable were cut up, and the leaves distributed, so that all in turn might learn them by heart.[1]

The book so roughly handled at these first camp meetings was probably *The Pocket Hymn Book* (Philadelphia, 1797), which was rapidly going through one edition after another in response to the eager demand for revival hymns. This book, like many others published in the next few decades to supply the revivalist movement, contained only the words of the hymns or spiritual songs, not the music. The tunes were either familiar ones that everybody already knew, or of such a simple and catchy nature that they could quickly be picked up from the singing of the preacher, who was also the song leader. As Benson remarks, "Of the tunes to which the Camp Meeting Hymns were sung the leaders demanded nothing more than contagiousness and effectiveness."[2]

In a previous chapter, tracing the development of evangelical hymnody in England under the influence of the Wesleys and their followers, with particular reference to the intensely emotional and folksy hymns of Cennick and Newton, we described the background out of which grew the popular religious songs of the American camp meetings. We should recall the use of the term "spiritual songs" in many of the collections of evangelical hymnody, including the *Hymns and Spiritual Songs* of Isaac Watts in 1709. This term was taken over in American collections, such as Joshua Smith's *Divine Hymns or Spiritual Songs* (Portsmouth, New Hampshire, 1794), Henry Alline's *Hymns and Spiritual Songs* (Stoningtonport, Connecticut, 1802), David Mintz's *Spiritual Song Book* (Halifax, North Carolina, 1805), and John C. Totten's *A Collection of the most admired hymns and spiritual songs, with the choruses affixed as usually sung at camp-meet-*

---

[1] Davidson, *History of the Presbyterian Church in Kentucky*, p. 134.
[2] Benson, *The English Hymn*, p. 294.

ings (New York, 1809). Many such books (a total of over fifty) were published up to the time of the Civil War. Totten's collection is particularly interesting as making specific mention of camp meetings and of the choruses that, as we shall presently see, constituted the most striking feature of revival hymnody.

Since the compilers speak of hymns *and* spiritual songs, it is obvious that some distinction between the two categories was intended. For our purpose it will be convenient to treat of revival hymnody as a whole, in relation to the camp-meeting movement; but we shall place the emphasis on those songs that were most specifically and organically a product of the revivalist fervor, and it is to these that the term "spiritual songs" may be especially applied. In its shortened form, "spirituals," the term has come to be generally associated in America with the religious songs of the Negroes. But the term is clearly of English evangelical origin, and in this chapter we shall refer to the camp-meeting songs either as "revival spirituals" or as "spirituals." Since both Negroes and whites attended the same camp meetings and sang the same songs, there is no need, at this stage at least, to make any kind of racial distinction. Amid the sometimes unedifying features of the revivalist frenzy, we have to put down in the credit column that the camp meetings broke through rigid denominational barriers and encouraged both religious and racial tolerance.

Traveling the circuit

Perhaps the best way to share the spirit of the camp meetings is to travel the circuit with one of the Methodist riders who was most fervently engaged in the revivalist movement. Lorenzo Dow (1777–1834) of Connecticut early in life felt the call to preach, and in spite of much opposition and many difficulties, caused in part by his eccentric and extravagant character, he succeeded in carrying the gospel throughout most of the United States, and even brought the camp-meeting movement to England, where he aroused large crowds with his fervor and enthusiasm. He married a person as enthusiastic and eccentric as himself, Peggy Dow, who in 1816 brought out *A Collection of Camp-meeting Hymns*, printed in Philadelphia (words only). Dow left a voluminous journal of his travels and experiences in America and the British Isles.

According to a footnote in Dow's journal, "Camp meetings *began* in Kentucky—next N. Carolina—attended them in Georgia—introduced them in the centre of Virginia, N. York, Connecticut, Massachusetts and Mississippi Territory!—1803–4–5." Thus within five years the camp-meeting craze had spread all over the United States, from North to South, and westward to the frontier territory. In 1804, Lorenzo Dow attended a camp meeting at Liberty, Tennessee, and wrote in his journal:

> Friday 19th. Camp-meeting commenced at Liberty: here I saw the *jerks;* and some danced: a strange exercise indeed; however it is involuntary, yet requires the consent of the will: i.e., the people are taken *jerking* irresistibly, and if they strive to resist it, it worries them much, yet is attended with no bodily pain, and those who are exercised to dance (which in the pious seems an antidote to the jerks) if they resist, it brings deadness and barrenness over the mind; but when they yield to it they feel happy, although it is a great cross, there is a heavenly smile and solemnity on the counte-nance, which carries great conviction to the minds of the beholders; their eyes when dancing seem to be fixed upwards as if upon an in-visible object, and they lost to all below.[3]

The question of dancing, so closely related to the jerks, was evi-dently a matter of some theological concern. On Sunday the 21st, writes Dow,

> I heard Doctor Tooley, a man of liberal education, preach on the subject of the *jerks* and the *dancing exercise:* He brought ten pas-sages of scripture to prove that dancing was once a religious exer-cise, but corrupted at Aaron's calf, and from thence young people got it for amusement. I believe the congregation and preachers were generally satisfied with his remarks.

Lorenzo Dow found that the jerks had no respect for denomina-tions. In Tennessee he met some Quakers who said, "the Methodists and Presbyterians have the *jerks* because they *sing* and *pray* so much, but we are still a peaceable people, wherefore we do not have them." But later, at a meeting, he found that about a dozen Quakers "had the *jerks* as keen and as powerful as any I have ever seen, so as to occa-sion a kind of grunt or groan when they would jerk." Summing it all up, Lorenzo wrote:

[3] Dow, *Journal,* p. 213.

I have seen Presbyterians, Methodists, Quakers, Baptists, Church
of England, and Independents, exercised with the *jerks;* Gentleman
and Lady, black and white, the aged and the youth, rich and poor,
without exception. . . .[4]

So much for the universal democracy of the jerks.

Back in his native Connecticut, Lorenzo gives us a brief picture of
the general atmosphere of a camp meeting:

About three thousand people appeared on the ground, and the rejoicing of old saints, the shouts of young converts, and the cries of
the distressed for mercy, caused the meeting to continue all night.[5]

It was at night that the revival frenzy reached its greatest intensity. As the campfires blazed around the grounds, preachers went
through the crowds exhorting the sinners to repent and be saved
from the fires of Hell. The volume of song rose to a mighty roar, the
sound of shouting shook the earth; men and women jerked, leaped, or
rolled on the ground until they swooned and had to be carried away.
Amid sobs and groans and shouts, men and women shook hands all
around and released all their frustrations and emotions in great bursts
of song that culminated in "the singing ecstasy."

> Jesus, grant us all a blessing,
> Shouting, singing, send it down;
> Lord, above may we go praying,
> And rejoicing in Thy love.
> Shout, O Glory! sing glory, hallelujah!
> I'm going where pleasure never dies.

The typical revivalist is a pilgrim traveling through the wilderness,
burdened with the sins of the world but rejoicing in the vision of the
promised land, which is in sight just on the other side of Jordan, and
when he gets there he'll be able to lay his burdens down, his troubles
will be over.

A well-known hymn by the English dissenting divine, Samuel
Stennett,

> On Jordan's stormy banks I stand, and cast a wishful eye
> To Canaan's happy land, where my possessions lie,

[4] *Ibid.,* p. 184.
[5] *Ibid.,* p. 187.

was taken up by the revivalists and appears with a variety of typical camp-meeting choruses appended to it. Here is one, first printed in the *Southern Harmony* of 1835, that is thoroughly typical:

I am bound for the prom-ised land ___ I'm bound for the prom-ised land, Oh ___ who will ___ come and go with me? I am bound for the prom-ised land.

Here on earth life is full of woe and trouble, of trials and tribulations; but just ahead lies the prospect of the promised land—O, glory, hallelujah!

We have ___ our ___ tri-als here ___ be-low, O glo-ry, hal·le-lu-jah! We have ___ our ___ tri-als here ___ be-low, O glo-ry hal-le-lu-jah! There's a bet-ter day a-com-ing, Hal-le-lu-jah! There's a bet-ter day a-com-ing, Hal-le-lu-jah!

This revival spiritual is also from William Walker's *Southern Harmony*, where it is entitled "Christian Prospect." It belongs to the pattern that has a refrain interpolated after each line. This was a very popular pattern in revival singing, because it was easy to "compose" a song in this manner on the spot, and because it gave an effective opportunity for mass participation and all-out shouting.

One of the earliest recorded songs of this type is "Satan's Kingdom Is Tumbling Down," which was printed in *Revival Hymns*, compiled by H. W. Day (Boston, 1842). In a headnote to this spiritual song, the compiler writes:

> This hymn and the original melody, *which have been so useful in revival seasons, for more than half a century*, and which, it is believed, have never before been published together, were lately procured after considerable search, from the diary of an aged servant of Christ, bearing the date 1810.

I have italicized the passage above simply to emphasize that many of these spirituals had circulated in oral tradition long before they were published in books; this applied particularly to the music, for it was not until after 1840 that the music of the camp-meeting spirituals began to be included to any extent in the songbooks with notation, and then they found a place chiefly in the shape-note books described in the preceding chapter.

Another interesting feature of "Satan's Kingdom" is that the text is pieced together by an accumulation of "wandering verses" that formed the stock-in-trade of revivalism. It was by having a large reserve of such material, usually in the form of rhymed couplets, to draw upon that the camp-meetings spiritual could proliferate so rapidly and so abundantly. "Satan's Kingdom" has the refrain after each line of the quatrain, and this in turn is followed by a typical camp-meeting chorus of four lines:

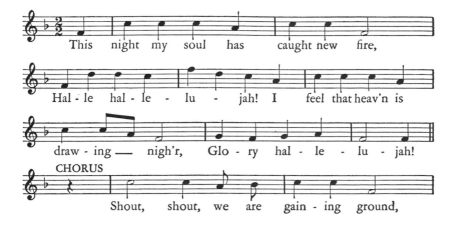

Hal - le hal - le - lu - jah! Sa - tan's king-dom is
tum - bling— down, Glo - ry hal - le - lu - jah!

By inserting a familiar tag line after each verse, and singing the whole to a rollicking tune, it was easy to transform a Wesleyan hymn into a camp-meeting spiritual. This is what happened to Charles Wesley's hymn, "He comes, he comes, the Judge severe." The revivalists tacked on the refrain, "Roll, Jordan, roll," after each line, and added a characteristic "I want to go to heaven" chorus.

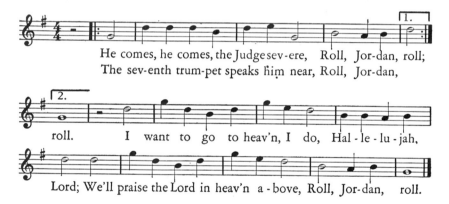

He comes, he comes, the Judge sev-ere, Roll, Jor-dan, roll;
The sev-enth trum-pet speaks him near, Roll, Jor-dan,
roll. I want to go to heav'n, I do, Hal - le - lu - jah,
Lord; We'll praise the Lord in heav'n a - bove, Roll, Jor-dan, roll.

Perhaps Charles Wesley's hymn deserved this treatment, for he is said to have written it as a parody on a popular song celebrating the return to England of Admiral Vernon (after whom Washington's Mount Vernon was named) following the capture of Portobello in 1739. As for the tune, it belongs to a type that has enjoyed wide circulation in America's music, from the folk hymns of the fasola singers to the minstrel songs of Stephen Foster.

Often the camp-meeting choruses bore little or no relation to the words of the hymns to which they were appended. An illustration is the hymn by Robert Robinson, "Come, thou fount of ev'ry blessing," to which the revivalists appended the following chorus, as recorded in McCurry's *Social Harp* and dated 1849:

And I hope to gain the prom-is'd land, O hal-le, hal-le-lu-jah; And I hope to gain the prom-is'd land, yes I do; Glo-ry, glo-ry, How I love my Sav-ior, Glo-ry, glo-ry, yes I do.

Also included in McCurry's *Social Harp* (1855) is a version of John Cennick's popular hymn, "Jesus, my all, to heaven is gone," with a "Jordan" chorus added to it, and the refrain "Happy, O happy" after each line. The chorus goes like this:

> We'll cross the river of Jordan
> Happy, O happy,
> We'll cross the river of Jordan,
> Happy, in the Lord.

Another one of Cennick's hymns, "Children of the heavenly King," was printed in the *Social Harp* with McCurry's name as composer and with the following "happy" chorus of camp-meeting origin:

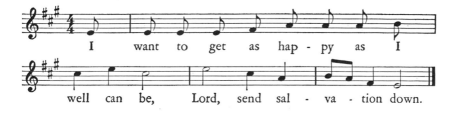

I want to get as hap-py as I well can be, Lord, send sal-va-tion down.

In the following revival spiritual from William Hauser's *Hesperian Harp* (1848), the Jordan theme is combined with the highly popular and widespread theme of the "Old Ship of Zion," of which numerous versions are found in various songbooks. In Hauser's version the Ship of Zion does not make its appearance until the second stanza.

Then the second stanza:

>What ship is this that will take us all home?
> O glory hallelujah!
>'Tis the old ship of Zion,
> O glory hallelujah!

And in the fifth stanza we find another familiar theme of the revival spirituals:

>If you get there before I do,
>You may tell them that I'm coming.

It is part of the larger "traveling to Canaan" theme that recurs in so many spirituals. As the revivalist preacher passed through the crowds on the meeting ground, clapping his hands, he would sing out at the top of his voice:

>O brethren, will you meet me,
>In Canaan's happy land?

And hundreds of voices would reply in a mighty burst of song:

>By the grace of God, we'll meet you,
> In Canaan's happy land.

Another time the preacher would sing out:

>I feel the work reviving, I feel the work reviving,
> Reviving in my soul.

And the camp-meeting crowd would respond:

> We'll shout and give him glory,
> We'll shout and give him glory,
> We'll shout and give him glory,
>   For glory is his own.

It was possible to keep a song going almost indefinitely, merely by changing one word in the stanza. For instance, in the line "O brothers will you meet me," the word "brothers" could be replaced in subsequent repetitions by "sisters," "mourners," "sinners," and so on. In the same manner, "We have fathers in the promised land" could be followed by "We have brothers, sisters, mothers, etc."

We do not know exactly how the early revival spirituals were sung because when the music appeared in the songbooks it was modified by harmonized arrangements that followed the singing-school tradition, with three or four voice parts blending together in more or less correct harmony. From the patterns of the song texts, and from descriptive accounts left by some witnesses and participants in the camp meetings, such as Lucius Bellinger of South Carolina, active as a revivalist from around 1825, we can be fairly certain that many of the songs, though not all, were sung according to the leader and chorus pattern indicated above. This is, in any case, a common practice in mass group singing, where the crowd is always ready to come in on a familiar chorus.

Then there were the "dialogue songs," in which one phrase was sung by men and another by women. An example of this is the "Mariner's Hymn," from the *Millennial Harp* (1843):

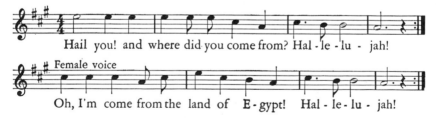

Hail you! and where did you come from? Hal-le-lu-jah!

Female voice

Oh, I'm come from the land of E-gypt! Hal-le-lu-jah!

The dialogue continues:

> Hail you! and where are you bound for?
>   Hallelujah!
> Oh, I'm bound for the land of Canaan,
>   Hallelujah!

Hail you! and what is your cargo?
 Hallelujah!
Oh, religion is my cargo.
 Hallelujah!

And so on, for several more stanzas. Dr. Guy B. Johnson believes that the pentatonic tune of this revival spiritual came from some sailor song, and points to its similarity to the hoisting chantey "Blow, Boys, Blow."

The idea of gaining ground against sin is another basic theme of the revival spirituals. We find it in a camp-meeting chorus affixed to the eighteenth-century hymn "I know that my Redeemer lives," in the following song which appeared originally in the *Social Harp* (1855), attributed to F. C. Wood of Georgia, and which is here reproduced from the Denson Revision of the *Original Sacred Harp:*

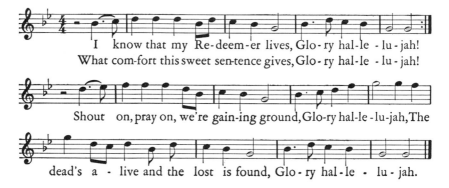

I know that my Re-deem-er lives, Glo-ry hal-le-lu-jah!
What com-fort this sweet sen-tence gives, Glo-ry hal-le-lu-jah!

Shout on, pray on, we're gain-ing ground, Glo-ry hal-le-lu-jah, The

dead's a-live and the lost is found, Glo-ry hal-le-lu-jah.

The same theme of conflict and victory is embodied in a revival spiritual called "The Good Old Way," of which the words were printed in *Zion's Songster* (1832) and the music in William Walker's *Southern Harmony* (1835). In the example below, the words of the fourth stanza are quoted with the music, as being most clearly indicative of the battle against Satan:

Though Sa-tan may his power em-ploy, O
Our peace and com-fort to de-stroy, O

hal - le, hal - le - lu - jah, Yet
hal - le, hal - le - lu - jah.

nev - er fear, we'll gain the day,— O hal - le, hal - le -
lu - jah; And — tri - umph in — the good old
way, O hal - le, hal le - lu jah.

A characteristic example of the way in which a text by Dr. Watts could be made to serve as the nucleus of a camp-meeting spiritual is "Sweet Canaan," in which the refrain "I am bound for the land of Canaan" is inserted after each line. The tune, of unknown origin, though attributed by the editors of the *Original Sacred Harp* to "Rev. John Moffitt, 1829," is probably traditional and bears a resemblance to some of Stephen Foster's minstrel songs.

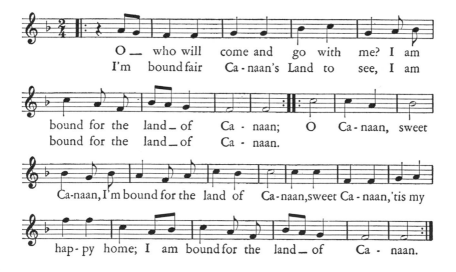

O — who will come and go with me? I am
I'm bound fair Ca - naan's Land to see, I am
bound for the land— of Ca - naan; O Ca - naan, sweet
bound for the land— of Ca - naan.
Ca-naan, I'm bound for the land of Ca-naan, sweet Ca - naan, 'tis my
hap- py home; I am bound for the land— of Ca - naan.

A well-known hymn by Dr. Watts, beginning "When I can read my title clear to mansions in the skies," was given the revival treatment and emerged as "I Want to Go" in McCurry's *Social Harp*, where it is dated 1851. McCurry ascribed it to himself as composer, but in all probability he merely arranged or harmonized a tune that had circulated in oral tradition. The chorus goes like this:

> I want to go, I want to go,
> I want to go to glory;
> There's so many trials here below,
> They say there's none in glory.

The revival movement reached its peak in the 1830s and 1840s, owing largely to the preaching of a Vermont farmer by the name of William Miller (1782–1849), who predicted that the end of the world would come in the spring of the year 1843:

> In eighteen hundred forty-three
> Will be the Year of Jubilee.

Obtaining a Baptist license to preach, Miller traveled around the country carrying his message of the coming Day of Wrath, distributing tracts, hymnbooks, and printed propaganda of every kind. His message of impending doom was reinforced by the portents of Nature. In 1833 there was a meteoric shower of "falling stars." Halley's comet appeared in 1835, and in 1843 the Great Comet appeared, seemingly in cooperation with Miller's schedule. The universe, however, did not fully cooperate. The spring of 1843 passed and the world did not come to an end. Miller announced that he had made a slight miscalculation. The Day of Judgment was definitely reset for October 22, 1844.

"Miller Madness" seized large sections of the population, driving some to suicide, some to insanity, and many others simply to becoming "Millerites," for by 1843 Miller had become the leader of his own sect, known as the Millennialists and later as the Seventh-Day Adventists. Miller's chief lieutenant in the Millennial movement was Joshua V. Himes, pastor of the First Christian Church in Boston, who in 1843 compiled and published a songbook called *The Millennial Harp* containing over two hundred songs, mostly in the tradition of revival spirituals, written or adapted especially for conveying the message of the Second Advent. Himes took, for example, a popular and widely used revival chorus, "I will be in this band, hallelujah!" and adapted it to the Millerite message by adding "In the Second Advent Band, hallelujah!" Appropriate stanzas were also added, such as:

O bless the Lord, we need not fear,
For Daniel says he'll come this year.

Here is the first stanza and chorus of "Christian Band," with the music, as published in the *Millennial Harp:*

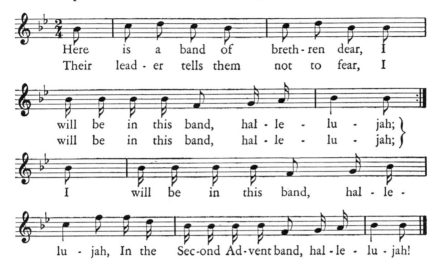

Here is a band of breth-ren dear, I
Their lead - er tells them not to fear, I
will be in this band, hal - le - lu - jah;
will be in this band, hal - le - lu - jah;
I will be in this band, hal - le -
lu - jah, In the Sec-ond Ad-vent band, hal - le - lu - jah!

Another Millennial song, evidently prepared especially for the "tarrying season" that began in the spring of 1844, had the following text:

Now we feel the Advent Glory
While the Savior seems to tarry,
We will comfort one another
And be trusting in his name.
Are your lamps all burning?
Are your vessels filled with oil?

By some unaccountable obstinacy of Nature, the world survived the fateful day of October 22, 1844. Miller himself survived his disappointment by five years, dying in 1849; his followers did not lose faith, for a few years later they were singing:

O praise the Lord, we do not fear
To tell the world he'll come next year.
In eighteen hundred fifty-four
The saints will shout their suff'rings o'er.
(*Pilgrim's Songster*, 1853)

One of the most stirring songs in the *Millennial Harp* was "Old Churchyard," sung especially at meetings in the cemeteries, for many of the Millerites "sought the graveyards where friends were buried, so as to join them as they arose from their earthly resting places and ascend with them." The tune has been widely used in American folk music. As we observed in an earlier chapter, it was the tune to which the Hutchinson Family sang their famous theme song, "The Old Granite State." Here is the song as it appeared in *Millennial Harp:*

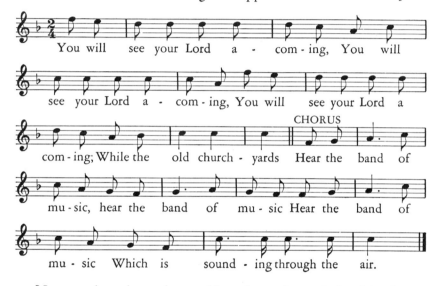

You will see your Lord a - com - ing, You will see your Lord a - com - ing, You will see your Lord a com - ing; While the old church - yards Hear the band of mu - sic, hear the band of mu - sic Hear the band of mu - sic Which is sound - ing through the air.

Now we have learned something about the revival spirit, the atmosphere of the camp meetings, and various types of revival spirituals and camp-meeting hymns. The question remains—and it is an important one—how did the singing sound? Unfortunately, those who witnessed the early camp meetings have left us more detailed accounts of the sensational manifestations of religious hysteria than of the exact nature of the singing that went on. We have to pick up clues here and there, and then rely largely on our imagination to project the old-time tunes as they were actually sung at camp meetings. The Southern revivalist Lucius Bellinger has some references to revival singing strewn among his autobiographical *Stray Leaves from the Portfolio of a Local Methodist Preacher* (1870). Writing of a preacher who led the singing: "He was a man with a sharp, strong, piercing voice. We now have old-time singing—clear, loud, and ringing." All accounts agree that the singing was loud.

Samuel E. Asbury, a descendant of the Rev. Francis Asbury who was America's pioneer circuit rider, recalling the old-time revival singing of his youth, said: "The immediate din was tremendous; at a hundred yards it was beautiful; and at a distance of a half mile it was magnificent." No musical instruments at all were used, not even a tuning fork. Some brass-lunged male pitched the tune. A lot of other brass-lunged males took it up and carried it along. It was the men, not the women, who sang the "tune." The women sang their subordinate part an octave higher, often, says Mr. Asbury, "singing around high C with perfect unconcern because they didn't realize their feat." They may have enjoyed themselves, but they were not singing for the sake of singing. "What they were there for was to hammer on the sinner's heart and bring him to the mourner's bench." There was no thought of art; the singing was like a force of nature, an uncontrollable torrent of sound.

But the tunes were beautiful and stirring. To hear them sung at the height of the revival fervor must have been a thrilling experience. Bearing in mind the remarks quoted above—the clear, loud, ringing voices, the high male voices carrying the tune, the basses below, and the female voices soaring above—let the reader give full scope to his or her imagination in recreating the sonorous texture of this wonderful revival spiritual, one of the glories of America's music: "Morning Trumpet," words by John Leland, music attributed to Benjamin Franklin White, compiler of the *Sacred Harp* (1844):

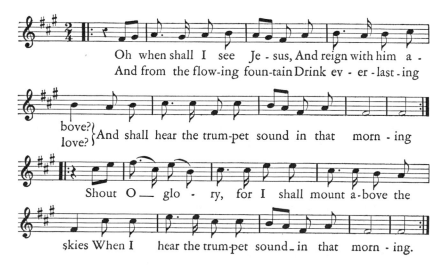

There is one aspect of revival singing that cannot be reconstructed from the printed music and that can be but inadequately described with words. That is the practice of taking familiar, conventional hymns and ornamenting the melodies with what Mr. Asbury calls "numberless little slurs and melodic variations." He mentions "Jesus, Lover of My Soul" and "How Firm a Foundation" as hymns that were sung in this manner. References to this ornamented style of folk singing were made in the second chapter of this book and also in Chapter 10, where an example was given of "Amazing Grace" with melodic ornamentation. The best way to become acquainted with this style, which was not limited to revival meetings but is widespread in folk tradition, is to listen to some of the recordings of Southern folk singers issued by the Library of Congress. Though these were recorded comparatively recently, the old tradition remains essentially unchanged, because conservatism, in its literal sense of preserving the values of the past, is the very essence of folklore.

Shakers defy the devil

When the Shakers—officially the United Society of Believers in Christ's Second Appearing—spread their activities westward in the early years of the nineteenth century, they swelled their ranks with converts from various schismatic sects that had been prominent in promoting the spirit of revivalism. Under the influence of frontier revivalism in Kentucky and Ohio, the Shakers began to develop a large body of song that, while having certain original traits of style and form stemming from the peculiarities of Shaker rituals and beliefs, was closely related to the general corpus of revivalist spiritual songs that we have been describing. Like other schismatic revivalists, the Shakers made no bones about plundering "carnal" tunes. A hymn in one of their books, *Millennial Praises* (1813), vigorously justifies this procedure:

> Let justice seize old Adam's crew,
> And all the whore's production;
> We'll take the choicest of their songs,
> Which to the Church of God belongs,
> And recompense them for their wrongs,
> In singing their destruction.

Since the Shakers' religion brought them joy and holy mirth, they saw no reason for avoiding gay and lively tunes:

> We love to sing and dance we will
> Because we surely, *surely* feel
> It does our thankful spirits fill
> With heavenly joy and pleasure.

In 1807 the Shaker community at Watervliet, New York, produced a song called "The Happy Journey," of which one line might easily be misconstrued by the evil-minded as indicating that the Shakers went in for nudism:

> O the happy journey that we are pursuing,
> Come brethren and sisters let's all strip to run.

While the act of stripping to run was no doubt symbolic, in many instances the Shakers interpreted literally and realistically the actions described in their songs. When they sang of their faithful brethren,

> I love to see them *stamp* and *grin*,
> And curse the flesh, the seat of sin,

they actually stamped and grimaced.

In warring against the flesh and the devil, the Shakers found a perpetual source of excitement and of realistic ritual:

> The act of chasing or shooting the devil was a revival ritual. In one account, as some one spies the devil coming into the meeting, he gives the alarm, whereupon every true believer "opens the battery at once." This was done "by drawing the right knee nearly to the chin, placing the arm in the position of a sportsman, then straightening themselves out with a jerk, and a stamp of the foot, accompanied by a quick bursting yelp, in imitation of a gun. . . ." As the devil starts to flee, cries arise: "See him dart!" "Shoot him!" "Kill him!" All rush for spiritual weapons from the "spiritual Arsenal." The fight then commences.[6]

As "Old Ugly" was driven away, the victory of the faithful might be celebrated with a song: [7]

[6] Andrews, *The Gift to Be Simple.*
[7] The Shaker songs in this chapter are quoted from *The Gift to Be Simple,* by permission of the author, Edward D. Andrews.

Be joy-ful, be joy-ful, be joy-ful, be joy-
ful, For Old Ug-ly is go - ing.

Even though "Old Ugly" did not always appear in person, it was necessary to wage continual battle against the flesh. The process of "shaking" was a powerful weapon in this fight, as described in the following song, "Shake Off the Flesh":

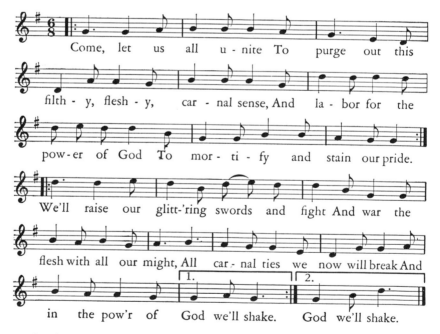

Good rid-dance, good rid-dance, good rid-dance we say,
And don't you nev-er come here a - gain.

Come, let us all u-nite To purge out this
filth-y, flesh-y, car-nal sense, And la-bor for the
pow-er of God To mor-ti-fy and stain our pride.
We'll raise our glitt-'ring swords and fight And war the
flesh with all our might, All car-nal ties we now will break And
in the pow'r of God we'll shake. God we'll shake.

In the autumn of 1837 the Shakers experienced a great revival that lasted for more than ten years and that produced a large quantity of songs. Many of these were "gift" or "vision" songs, revealed to the faithful in dreams or visions, sometimes by the spirit of Mother Ann, sometimes by angels, and other times by the spirits of famous persons whose relation to the Shaker religion is not readily explicable: Alexander the Great, Queen Elizabeth, George Washington, William Penn, Christopher Columbus, Thomas Jefferson, Napoleon, and many others. "Native" songs were received from the spirits of American Indians, Eskimos, Chinese, Hottentots, and other heathen races. When the Shakers were possessed by the spirits of Indians, they behaved like Indians themselves. An eyewitness described a "dancing night" at which "eight or nine of the Sisters became possessed of the Spirits of Indian Squaws and about six of the Brothers became Indians: then ensued a regular 'Pow Wow,' with whooping, yelling, and strange antics. . . ." Here is an example of an Indian "vision song" received in 1838:

One of the Shaker exercises consisted of a sort of lively whirling dance, "during which the worshippers constantly turned or whirled" (Andrews), at the same time singing an appropriate song. Many of the Shaker songs were "action songs," that is, songs that described an action which was performed during the singing. They had, for instance, "bowing songs," such as the following:

I will bow and be simple
I will bow and be free
I will bow and be humble
Yea bow like the willow tree.

Then there was a "hopping and jumping" song which is quite graphic in its description of movement:

Hop up and jump up and whirl round, whirl round,
Gather love, here it is, all round, all round.
Here is love flowing round, catch it as you whirl round,
Reach up and reach down, here it is all round.

In a ritual song of mortification, the faithful "scour and scrub" to take away the stains of sin:

Bow down low, bow down low,
Wash, wash, clean, clean, clean, clean.
Scour and scrub, scour and scrub
From this floor the stains of sin.

Another time the ritual might be that of sweeping the floor clean:

Sweep, sweep and cleanse your floor,
Mother's standing at the door,
She'll give us good and precious wheat,
With which there is no chaff nor cheat.

The imaginary drinking of "spiritual wine" was another Shaker ritual that had its appropriate songs. "The Gift of spiritual wine," wrote Isaac N. Youngs, "carried a great evidence of its reality, by the paroxysms of intoxication which it produced, causing those who drank it to stagger and reel like drunken people." This realistic imitation of drunkenness is reflected in such drinking songs as the following:

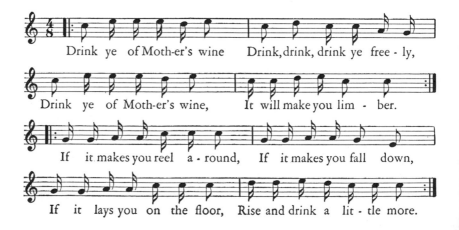

Drink ye of Mother's wine Drink, drink, drink ye free-ly,
Drink ye of Mother's wine, It will make you lim-ber.
If it makes you reel a-round, If it makes you fall down,
If it lays you on the floor, Rise and drink a lit-tle more.

It is easy to laugh at the antics of the Shakers and to ridicule the crude and naïve manifestations of their religious fervor. But they contributed something vital and genuine to American folkways, both in their songs and in their dances. They had what one of their most famous songs describes as "the gift to be simple." In their best songs and rituals there is a spirit of play, a sense of the dramatic, and a feeling for plastic movement that can readily be transferred to the aesthetic realm of choreographic art, as Martha Graham has done in the ballet *Appalachian Spring*, with music by Aaron Copland based partly on traditional Shaker tunes.

No song more fully embodies the Shaker spirit than does the one titled "Simple Gifts," a favorite among all Shaker communities in the United States. It is said to have been composed in 1848. The tempo is allegro:

'Tis the gift to be sim - ple, 'tis the
gift to be free, 'Tis the gift to come down
where we ought to be, And when we find our-selves in the
place just right, 'Twill be in the val - ley of
love and de - light. When true sim - pli - ci - ty is gain'd, To
bow and to bend we shan't be a-sham'd, To turn, turn will
be our de - light till by turn-ing, turn - ing we come round right.

When fully under control, the exercises of the Shakers, including elaborate marching formations and ritual dances of various kinds. were well ordered and disciplined. But under the effect of revival frenzy, decorum was often destroyed and unrestrained freedom prevailed in the expression of religious emotion through song and dance. A meeting at West Union, Indiana, in 1851, was thus described by an eye-witness:

The Sound is like mighty thunderings, Some a Stamping with all their might and Roaring out against the nasty stinking beast. . . . Others turning with great Power and warring against the flesh, and at the same time a number Speaking with new tongues with such Majestic Signs and motions that it makes the powers of Darkness tremble. . . .

Another eyewitness account, by A. J. Macdonald, describes a meeting in the grip of extreme revival frenzy:

As the singing and dancing progress, the Worshippers become more zealous, then frantic with excitement—until nothing but what the "World" would call disorder and confusion reigns. As the excitement increases, all order is forgotten, all unison of parts repudiated, each sings his own tune, each dances his own dance, or leaps, shouts, and exults with exceeding great joy—The more gifted of the Females engage in a kind of whirling motion, which they perform with seemingly incredible velocity their arms being extended horizontally and their dresses blown out like a Balloon all around their persons by the centrifugal force occasioned by the rapidity of their motion. After performing from Fifty to One Thousand revolutions each, they either swoon away and fall into the arms of their Friends, or suddenly come to a stand, with apparently little or no dizziness produced. Sometimes the Worshippers engage in a race round the Room, with a sweeping motion of the Hands and Arms, intended to present the act of sweeping the Devil out of the Room.

While the details might differ, the general symptoms are the same as those manifested in the revival meetings of other separatist sects. We may recall, for instance, that at the great Cane Ridge revival in Kentucky in the summer of 1801, three thousand persons fell helpless to the ground after swooning from religious ecstasy, and had to be carried to the nearby meetinghouse until they recovered.

In this chapter we have tried to give representative examples of the songs that came out of the great revivals and camp meetings that swept the country from about 1800 to the eve of the Civil War, reaching their apogee in the 1830s and 1840s. The music, as we have observed, came from many sources and could not, in its constituent elements, be regarded as a product of American revivalism. But the songs as a whole were shaped by the environment and emerged remade as manifestations of the American frontier.

If anyone doubts that these revival songs are woven deep in the fabric of America's music, deep in the strands of our national culture, let him recall a song that all Americans know, that they have sung for generations, and that each rising generation inherits anew—the song that we know as "The Battle Hymn of the Republic," but that, years before Julia Ward Howe wrote the words beginning "Mine eyes have seen the glory of the coming of the Lord," was a rousing camp-meeting spiritual, with a typical repetitive stanza and a swinging hallelujah chorus.

While the revivalist movement and the camp-meeting tradition were developing this large body of popular hymnody, a closely related but distinctive body of religious folk song was taking shape among the Negroes of the United States. The growth of the Negro spirituals, and their "discovery" by the country at large at the time of the Civil War, will be the subject of the next chapter.

chapter twelve

The Negro spirituals

Ole Satan is a busy ole man,
He roll stones in my way;
Mass' Jesus is my bosom friend,
He roll 'em out o' my way.
NEGRO SPIRITUAL.

There are very few accounts of the singing of the Negroes on South-ern plantations previous to the Civil War. One of the earliest and most detailed accounts is that of Frances Anne (Fanny) Kemble, the Eng-lish actress and writer who was married to Pierce Butler and spent some time on his plantations on the coast of Georgia. In her *Journal of a Residence on a Georgia Plantation in 1838–1839*, Fanny Kemble writes of a Negro funeral that she attended in the evening, by torch-light: "Presently the whole congregation uplifted their voices in a hymn, the first high wailing notes of which—sung all in unison . . . — sent a thrill through all my nerves." Here is Mrs. Kemble's description of the singing of the Negroes who rowed to St. Simon's, one of the Georgia Sea Islands at the entrance of the Altamaha on which her husband's rice and cotton plantations were located: [1]

. . . As the boat pushed off, and the steersman took her into the stream, the men at the oars set up a chorus, which they continued to chant in unison with each other, and in time with their stroke, till their voices were heard no more from the distance. I believe I have mentioned . . . the peculiar characteristics of this veritable negro minstrelsy—how they all sing in unison, having never, it appears, at-tempted or heard anything like part-singing. Their voices seem oftener tenor than any other quality, and the tune and time they

[1] Kemble, *Journal of a Residence on a Georgia Plantation in 1838–1839*, pp. 128–129.

keep something quite wonderful; such truth of intonation and accent would make almost any music agreeable. That which I have
heard these people sing is often plaintive and pretty, but almost always has some resemblance to tunes with which they must have become acquainted through the instrumentality of white men; their
overseers or masters whistling Scotch or Irish airs, of which they
have produced by ear these *rifacciamenti*. The note for note reproduction of "Ah! vous dirai-je, maman?" in one of the most popular
of the so-called negro melodies with which all America and England are familiar, is an example of this very transparent plagiarism;
and the tune with which Mr. ——'s rowers started him down the
Altamaha, as I stood at the steps to see him off, was a very distinct
descendant of "Coming Through the Rye." The words, however,
were astonishingly primitive, especially the first line, which, when
it bursts from their eight throats in high unison, sent me into fits of
laughter:

> Jenny shake her toe at me,
>   Jenny gone away.
> (*bis*)
> Hurrah! Miss Susy, oh!
>   Jenny gone away.
> (*bis*)

Elsewhere Mrs. Kemble speaks of "an extremely pretty, plaintive,
and original air," to which "there was but one line, which was repeated with a sort of wailing chorus—'Oh! my massa told me, there's
no grass in Georgia.' Upon inquiring the meaning of which, I was
told it was supposed to be the lamentation of a slave from one of the
more northerly states, Virginia or Carolina, where the labor of hoeing
the weeds, or grass as they call it, is not nearly so severe as here, in
the rice and cotton lands of Georgia."

Later in her journal, Mrs. Kemble confesses that in her daily voy-
ages up and down the river she has encountered a number of Negro
songs that seemed to her "extraordinarily wild and unaccountable," and
for which she could recall no counterpart in any European melodies
familiar to her. Of these songs she writes: "The way in which the
chorus strikes in with the burden, between each phrase of the melody
chanted by a single voice, is very curious and effective. . . ." What
she describes here is the leader-and-chorus or call-and-response pattern
that we have noted as characteristic of African singing.

Mrs. Kemble refers repeatedly to the "strangeness" of the words of the Negro songs, most of which made no sense to her. She was struck by the oddness of one song whose burden was the line "God made man, and man makes money!" Truly, as she remarks, "a peculiar poetical proposition." She mentions "another ditty . . . they call Caesar's song: it is an extremely spirited war-song, beginning, 'The trumpets blow, the bugles blow—Oh, stand your ground!'" It would be strange indeed to hear the slaves sing a "war-song," and there is a strong suspicion that this may be an early example of a Negro spiritual.

Apparently no sharp distinction was made, either in the occasion or the manner, between the singing of purely secular songs and those having some sacred or spiritual import. Sir Charles Lyell, writing about a visit to a Southern plantation in 1849, remarks of some Negro boatmen: "Occasionally they struck up a hymn, taught them by the Methodists, in which the most sacred subjects were handled with a strange familiarity." [2] Just such a rowing song as Lyell describes, from the Port Royal Islands of South Carolina, is included in the first collection of Negro spirituals to be published, *Slave Songs of the United States* (1867). In it the Archangel Michael is made to row the boat ashore:

1. Mi-chael row de boat a-shore, Hal-le-lu-jah!

2. Mi-chael boat a gos-pel boat, Hal-le-lu-jah!

Each line of this spiritual that was used as a rowing song is followed by the refrain, "Hallelujah!" Additional verses of this song, "Michael Row the Boat Ashore," are quoted below to illustrate the making of a Negro spiritual:

> On de rock gwine home in Jesus' name.
> Gabriel blow de trumpet horn.
> Jordan stream is wide and deep.
> Jesus stand on t'oder side.
> O de Lord he plant his garden deh.
> He raise de fruit for you to eat.

[2] Lyell, *A Second Visit to the United States of North America*, New York, 1849, p. 244.

> He dat eat shall neber die.
> Sinner row to save your soul.

In addition to the repeated hallelujah refrain, the reader will recognize in these verses some of the basic themes or tag lines of the revival hymns discussed in the previous chapter. What is distinctive about the Negro song, besides the manner of singing, is the adaptation of the imagery and vocabulary of evangelical hymnody to concrete situations related to his own environment and experience. For instance, in the last verse the idea of the sinner saving his soul is fused with the necessity of performing a given task (rowing) and attaining a practical objective (the shore). The crossing over Jordan is identified with the immediate task of rowing across a body of water. The line "Michael boat a music boat" probably an improvised variant on the line "Michael boat a gospel boat," takes one by surprise; yet it leads naturally to the mention of Gabriel's trumpet in the next line. This in turn suggests the Last Judgment and the need to care for one's soul:

> O you mind your boastin' talk.
> Boastin' talk will sink your soul.

There the soul, like the boat, is in possible danger of *sinking*—a bold and appropriate metaphor. The danger incurred by the sinner is assimilated into the prospect of danger that could beset the boat in landing if overtaken by darkness and rising waters:

> When de ribber overflo,
> O poor sinner, how you land?
> Ribber run and darkness comin'.
> Sinner row to save your soul.

The more one lingers over this Negro spiritual, the more one becomes aware of how beautifully its seemingly disparate elements are bound together by an imaginative fusion of themes and images.

The English musician Henry Russell, who was in the United States from 1833 to 1841, writes in his memoirs about a Negro service that he attended:

I had long taken a deep interest in negro life, and I often wondered whether it was possible that negroes could originate melody. I was desirous of testing this, and I made up my mind to visit many negro meetings throughout several of the States. On my entering the chapel at Vicksburg [then a slave town] there was a restlessness about the little congregation—whether it emanated from one or two white people being present I cannot say. There was one peculiarity that struck me very forcibly. When the minister gave out his own version of the Psalm, the choir commenced singing so rapidly that the original tune absolutely ceased to exist—in fact, the fine old psalm tune became thoroughly transformed into a kind of negro melody; and so sudden was the transformation, by accelerating the time, that, for a moment, I fancied that not only the choir but the little congregation intended to get up a dance as part of the service.[3]

Russell was not far wrong in this last supposition. Had white persons not been present it is very likely that the Negroes at that service would have taken up that peculiar type of religious dancing and singing known as "shout," which will be described later in this chapter. It should be remarked that when Russell speaks of "negro melody" he means that of blackface minstrelsy, the only kind with which he was familiar. We may assume therefore that the old psalm tune which he heard was not only greatly accelerated but also strongly syncopated, in the manner of most minstrel melodies.

It is important to observe that hymns and spirituals were sung not only in church and at religious meetings but also as accompaniment to all kinds of labor. The singing of spirituals by rowers among the Georgia Sea Islands has already been noted. In an account written by William Cullen Bryant, who visited a tobacco factory in Richmond, Virginia, in 1843, we learn of Negroes singing while performing sedentary work. The owner of the factory, noticing that Bryant's attention was caught by the singing, offered some comments on it:

What is remarkable [he continued], their tunes are all psalm tunes and the words are from hymn books; their taste is exclusively for sacred music; they will sing nothing else. Almost all these persons are church members; we have not a dozen about the factory who are not so. Most of them are of the Baptist persuasion; a few are Methodists.[4]

If we compare this with the description of Negro singing given by Samuel Davies in 1755 (see p. 80), we are at once impressed by the

[3] Henry Russell, *Cheer! Boys, Cheer!*, pp. 84–85.
[4] Bryant, quoted in *DeBow's Review*, n.s., I (1850), p. 326. Cited by Johnson, *Folk Culture on St. Helena Island*, p. 85.

similarity, for Davies wrote that the Negroes "are exceedingly delighted with Watts' Song" and "they have a kind of ecstatic delight in psalmody." Behind the Negro spirituals, then, was a century-long tradition "of ecstatic delight in psalmody." And what, indeed, is more characteristic of the spirituals than that quality of ecstatic delight in the glories of Heaven, the visions of the Promised Land, the mercy of Jesus, and the salvation of the sinner?

Although the religious instruction of the Negroes left much to be desired, they had ample opportunity to become familiar with English hymnody. In 1833 the Rev. Samuel J. Bryan of Savannah issued *A Plain and Easy Catechism: designed for the benefit of colored children, with several verses and hymns.* Charles C. Jones, in his work *The Religious Instruction of the Negroes*, published in 1842, states that the period from 1820 to 1842 was "a period of revival of religion in respect to this particular duty, throughout the Southern states; more especially between the years 1829 and 1835. This revival came silently, extensively, and powerfully; affecting masters, mistresses, ministers, members of the church, and ecclesiastical bodies of all the different evangelical denominations." [5] The author's statement that the revival "came silently" is not, we suppose, to be taken literally; for it gave a further impetus to the singing of hymns among the colored population.

The spread of religious instruction among the Negroes coincided with the rise of the camp-meeting movement. As we know from the journals of Lorenzo Dow and other contemporary sources, Negroes as well as whites took part in the early camp meetings. How long this practice continued is uncertain, but in any case there is no doubt that the same songs were sung by both races. In a book published in 1860 there is an account of revival singing that implies a sort of rivalry in this respect: ". . . the loudest and most fervent camp-meeting singers amongst the whites are constrained to surrender to the darkeys in *The Old Ship of Zion* or *I Want to go to Glory*." [6] The Southern evangelist Lucius Bellinger wrote of one of his camp meetings: "The negroes are out in great crowds, and sing with voices that make the woods ring." [7]

Some early writers are struck by the "wildness" of the Negroes'

---

[5] Jones, *The Religious Instruction of the Negroes*, pp. 96–97.

[6] Dr. R. Hundley, *Social Relations in Our Southern States.* New York, 1860, p. 348. Cited by Johnson, *loc. cit.*

[7] Bellinger, *Stray Leaves*, p. 17.

singing, others are impressed by its musicality and "correctness." An English journalist, William Howard Russell, writing in 1863, speaks of "those wild Baptist chants about the Jordan in which they delight."[8] Another Englishman, the Rev. William W. Malet, writing about the same time (1862), has this to say about the Negroes' singing:

> Just before bed-time more solemn sounds are heard: the negro is demonstrative in his religion, and loud and musical were heard every evening the hymns. . . . Remarkable for correctness are their songs, and both men's and women's voices mingled in soft though far-sounding harmony. Some old church tunes I recognized.[9]

It is a question as to whether Reverend Malet is using the term "harmony" in its literal or in a figurative sense. If the former, it would mean that the singing was in parts, something which no other account mentions. It is likely that the writer refers simply to the blending of voices of different *tessitura*, especially as he mentions the blending of men's and women's voices. In any case, the manner of Negro singing cannot be accurately described in terms either of "unison" or "harmony." It is more complex than that, a style *sui generis*. A clue to the style is contained in Emily Hallowell's remark that the "harmonies seem to arise from each [singer] holding to their own version of the melodies or from limitation of compass." A fairly comprehensive description is given by William Francis Allen in his preface to *Slave Songs of the United States,* based on singing heard in the Port Royal Islands (South Carolina) in the early 1860s:

> There is no singing in *parts,* as we understand it, and yet no two appear to be singing the same thing; the leading singer starts the words of each verse, often improvising, and the others, who "base" him, as it is called, strike in with the refrain, or even join in the solo when the words are familiar. When the "base" begins the leader often stops, leaving the rest of the words to be guessed at, or it may be they are taken up by one of the other singers. And the "basers" themselves seem to follow their own whims, beginning when they please and leaving off when they please, striking an octave above or below (in case they have pitched the tune too high), or hitting some other note that "chords," so as to produce the

---

[8] W. H. Russell, *My Diary, North and South,* Boston, 1863, p. 143.
[9] Malet, *An Errand to the South in the Summer of 1862,* p. 49. Cited by Johnson, *loc. cit.*

effect of a marvellous complication and variety and yet with the most perfect time and rarely with any discord. And what makes it all the harder to unravel a thread of melody out of this strange network is that, like birds, they seem not infrequently to strike sounds that cannot be precisely represented by the gamut and abound in "slides from one note to another and turns and cadences not in articulated notes."

Surely the reader who still bears in mind the account of early New England popular psalmody cannot fail to recognize the analogies between that style and the manner of singing described above: "no two appear to be singing the same thing" . . . "seem to follow their own whims" . . . "striking an octave above or below" . . . "hard to unravel a thread of melody" . . . abounding in "slides from one note to another and turns and cadences not in articulated notes." There is practically the whole catalogue of indictments drawn up against the followers of the folk tradition by the New England reformers. That Negro singing in America developed as the result of the blending of several cultural traditions is certain; and it seems equally certain that one of these traditions was the folk style of early New England psalmody and hymnody, carried southward in the late eighteenth and early nineteenth centuries.

From Allen's description of Negro singing, apart from the specific details, it is important to retain the impression of "a marvellous complication and variety," for it is this complication and variety, fused together by a powerful musical impulse (basically rhythmic), that gives to the spirituals, and to other types of American Negro song, their original and fascinating quality, most of which has been distorted or destroyed in the standardized arrangements made to conform with conventional European musical practice.

Discovery of the spirituals

As we have seen, the singing of the Negroes attracted the attention of an isolated writer here and there in the period before the Civil War. But it was only during and after the war that the songs of the Negro, and the spirituals in particular, began to arouse widespread interest and to receive general attention. The impulse to the "discovery" of the spirituals came, as might be expected, from the North. The immediate occasion was the sending of an educational mission to the

Port Royal Islands in 1861. In the words of the editors of *Slave Songs of the United States:*

> The agents of the mission were not long in discovering the rich vein of music that existed in these half-barbarous people, and when visitors from the North were on the islands, there was nothing that seemed better worth their while than to see a "shout" or hear the people sing their "sperichils."

Listed as "established favorites" in those days were "Roll, Jordan, Roll," "I Hear from Heaven Today," "Blow Your Trumpet, Gabriel," "Praise, Member," "Wrestle On, Jacob," "The Lonesome Valley."

The first American Negro spiritual to appear in print with its music is believed to be "Roll, Jordan, Roll," published by Miss Lucy McKim of Philadelphia in 1862. The second spiritual to be printed was probably "Done Wid Driber's Dribin," which appeared in an article by H. G. Spaulding titled "Under the Palmetto," published in *The Continental Monthly* for August, 1863. This song has the familiar revival refrain, "Roll, Jordan, Roll":

The verses continue with "Done wid Massa's hollerin' " and "Done wid Missus' scoldin'." This is one of the very few spirituals that make direct reference to emancipation.

Another emancipation song was published by Colonel Thomas Wentworth Higginson in his interesting essay, "Negro Spirituals," in *The Atlantic Monthly* for June, 1867. This was "No More Peck o' Corn for Me," also known, from its refrain, as "Many Thousands Go." Other verses are: "No more driver's lash for me,"—"No more pint o' salt for me,"—"No more hundred lash for me," etc. According to Higginson, the peck of corn and pint of salt were slavery's rations. It is said to have been first sung when Beauregard took the slaves to the islands to build the fortifications at Hilton Head and Bay Point:

No more peck o' corn for me, No more, no more;

No more peck o' corn for me, Man - y tou - sand go.

Colonel Higginson speculated on the origin of the spirituals and recounted an incident that enabled him actually to witness the "birth" of one of these songs. This occurred when he was being rowed across from Beaufort to Ladies' Island:

> One of the oarsmen, a brisk young fellow . . . on being asked for his theory of the matter, dropped out a coy confession. "Some good sperituals," he said, "are start jest out o' curiosity. I bin a-raise a sing myself once." . . . I implored him to proceed.
>
> "Once we boys went for tote some rice, and de nigger driver, he keep a-callin' on us: and I say, "O, de ole nigger driver!" Den anudder said, "Fust t'ing my mammy tole me was not'in so bad as a nigger driver." Den I made a sing, just puttin' a word and den anudder word."
>
> Then he began singing and the men, after listening a moment, joined in the chorus as if it were an old acquaintance, though they evidently had never heard it before. I saw how easily a new "sing" took root among them.

> O' de ole nigger driver!
>   O, gwine away!
> Fust t'ing my mammy tell me.
>   O, gwine away!
> Tell me 'bout de nigger driver,
>   O, gwine away!
> Nigger driver second devil,
>   O, gwine away!
> Best t'ing for do he driver,
>   O, gwine away!
> Knock he down and spoil he labor—
>   O, gwine away!

One reason, of course, that the Negroes could so readily improvise a song was that the metrical pattern was pretty well established beforehand. The above arrangement conforms to the general pattern of Negro songs with which the reader is already familiar. In the same manner, a poet can readily turn out a sonnet, because the form has already been determined for him.

In an address delivered in Philadelphia on July 9, 1862, J. Miller McKim told of a somewhat similar experience, except that he was given only an explanation, not a specimen of the product:

> I asked one of these blacks, one of the most intelligent of them, where they got these songs.
> "Dey make 'em, sah."
> "How do they make them?"
> After a pause, evidently casting about for an explanation, he said:
> "I'll tell you; it's dis way: My master call me up an' order me a short peck of corn and a hundred lash. My friends see it and is sorry for me. When dey come to de praise meeting dat night dey sing about it. Some's very good singers and know how; and dey work it in, work it in, you know, till dey get it right; and dat's de way." [10]

Although this anecdote savors of abolitionist propaganda, we may accept the hypothesis that many of the spirituals (and other songs too, for that matter) were "made" in this spontaneous manner, while reiterating the proviso that they were made largely out of pre-existing elements, both as regards the words and the music. That the factor of invention, as well as of accretion and transformation, entered into the process, is not to be denied. But it was probably invention of detail rather than of a whole: some felicitous phrase or contagious tag line thought up and caught up on the spur of the moment and incorporated into the ever-changing content of a traditionally established form. We have already observed something of this "spontaneous generation" of song in connection with the revival hymns, and the principle underlying the creation of the Negro spirituals is the same; as it is, indeed, for all folk music.

This seems an appropriate place to quote the definition of a spiritual —rather ironic, but realistic—attributed by R. W. Gordon to "a learned colleague":

> A Spiritual is nothing but a tune—never twice the same—accompanied by not over two standard verses—not the same—followed by

[10] Quoted in *Slave Songs of the United States*, p. xviii.

as many other verses from different songs as the singer happens to
remember.[11]

It is salutary to quote this definition here because it will serve to warn
the reader against assuming that there is ever one and only one version
of a Negro spiritual. There is, for example, no fixed, definite, and un-
varying musicopoetic entity known as "Nobody Knows the Trouble
I See." Any particular printed version or arrangement is arbitrary and
artificially static. The spiritual itself is a composite and infinitely varied
creation that exists with its own genuine being only in that moment
of time during which it is actually sung. Captured on a phonograph
recording, that experience can be repeated at will, but the song itself
goes on having its own independent existence, so that another recording made a year later will not be exactly the same song. We may be
able to record a hundred different versions of a song to which we give
the same title; but we cannot say that any *one* of these versions is
the song. The song is all of them together and none of them individually.

The first collection of Negro spirituals

As a result of the activities of the United States Educational Mission to the Port Royal Islands, the first collection of American Negro
spirituals was published in 1867 under the title, *Slave Songs of the
United States*, edited by William Francis Allen, Charles Pickard Ware,
and Lucy McKim Garrison. Though this collection contains many
errors and bears slight evidence of musical scholarship, it yet retains
its importance as a primary source. Only the words and the tunes are
printed, without harmonization. Some representative spirituals from
this collection will be quoted. The editors were at least aware of the
difficulties of their undertaking. They had heard these spirituals sung
in their pristine state by the Negroes on these isolated rice and cotton
plantations: they knew it was different from any other kind of singing with which they were familiar, and they made it clear in their
prefatory remarks that their notations could only approximate, not
accurately reproduce, the characteristic traits of the music in actual
performance:

[11] Gordon, "The Negro Spiritual," in *The Carolina Low Country*, p. 193.

It is difficult to express the entire character of these negro ballads by mere musical notes and signs. The odd turns made in the throat and the curious rhythmic effect produced by single voices chiming in at different irregular intervals seem almost as impossible to place on the score as the singing of birds or the tones of an aeolian harp.

Only the advent of the phonograph could solve this problem of reproducing folk music as it actually sounds.

Most of the early writers refer to the spirituals as being in the "minor," probably because the unusual intervals and the manner of singing gave in many cases an impression of "melancholy" or "plaintiveness." In spite of this impression, it has been established that the majority of spirituals are in the major mode. Of 527 Negro songs examined by H. E. Krehbiel, 331 were found to be in the major mode. In addition, 111 songs were pentatonic. Furthermore, according to Krehbiel's data:

Of the 331 major songs twenty . . . have a flat seventh; seventy-eight—that is, one fourth—have no seventh, and forty-five, or nearly one-seventh, have no fourth. Fourth and seventh are the tones which are lacking in the pentatonic scale, and the songs without one or the other of them approach the pentatonic songs in what may be called their psychological effect.

On the whole, Krehbiel interprets the musical data "as emphasizing the essentially energetic and contented character of Afro-American music, notwithstanding that it is the fruit of slavery." [12]

One of the most characteristic spirituals, both musically and poetically, that appeared in this pioneer collection, is the one called "O'er the Crossing," concerning which the editors printed the following note: "This 'infinitely quaint description of the length of the heavenly road,' as Col. Higginson styles it, is one of the most peculiar and widespread of the spirituals. It was sung as given [here] in Caroline Co., Virginia, and probably spread southward from this state variously modified in different localities." What is especially to be remarked in this song is the rhythmic pattern of the melody at the phrase beginning, "Keep prayin'." This rhythmic figure, ♪♪♩, is characteristic

[12] Krehbiel, *Afro-American Folk Songs*, p. 70. Copyright 1914 by G. Schirmer, Inc.

of all types of Afro-American music, from spirituals to ragtime. Here is the song:

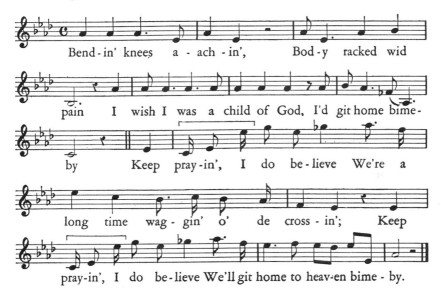

Bend-in' knees a - ach - in', Bod-y racked wid pain I wish I was a child of God, I'd git home bime-by Keep pray-in', I do be-lieve We're a long time wag-gin' o' de cross-in'; Keep pray-in', I do be-lieve We'll git home to heav-en bime-by.

It is not clear what is meant by the line "We're a long time waggin' o' de crossin'." It has been suggested that "waggin'" may be a corruption of "lagging." Another possibility is "Waggoning o'er de crossin'," which would relate to a familiar experience in fording rivers. The fourth stanza of this spiritual contains some striking imagery:

> O see dat forked lightnin'
>   A-jump from cloud to cloud,
> A-pickin' up God's chil'n;
>   Dey'll git home bime-by.
> Pray, mourner, I do believe, etc.

The use of spirituals as working songs has already been mentioned. Of the spirituals included in *Slaves Songs of the United States*, twelve were most commonly used for rowing. One of the editors, Charles P. Ware, writes as follows about these songs:

As I have written these tunes, two measures are to be sung to each stroke, the first measure being accented by the beginning of the stroke, the second by the rattle of the oars in the rowlocks. On the passenger boat at the [Beaufort] ferry they rowed from sixteen to thirty strokes a minute; twenty-four was the average. Of the tunes I heard I should say that the most lively were "Heaven bell a-ring," "Jine 'em," "Rain fall," "No man," "Bell da ring" and "Can't stay behin'"; and that "Lay this body down," "Religion so sweet" and "Michael, row," were used when the load was heavy or the tide was against.

Accounts such as the above confirm the lively, vigorous, strongly rhythmic character of the Negro spirituals.

We have already examined the spiritual "Michael, Row the Boat Ashore," and now we may glance at another spiritual mentioned above as one of the songs used for the slower and heavier tasks of rowing, "Lay This Body Down":

This may have been the same song that W. H. Russell heard when he was being rowed from Pocotaligo to Barnwell Island by some Negro boatmen at midnight:

> The oarsmen, as they bent to their task, beguiled the way singing in unison a real negro melody, which was unlike the works of the Ethiopian Serenaders as anything in song could be unlike another. It was a barbaric sort of madrigal, in which one singer beginning was followed by the others in unison, repeating the refrain in chorus, and full of quaint expression and melancholy:—

> Oh your soul! oh my soul! I'm going to the churchyard
>   To lay this body down;
> Oh my soul! oh your soul! We're going to the churchyard
>   To lay this nigger down.

And then some appeal to the difficulty of passing the "Jawdam" constituted the whole of the song, which continued with unabated energy during the whole of the little voyage. To me it was a strange scene. The stream, dark as Lethe, flowing between the silent, houseless, rugged banks, lighted up near the landing by the fire in the woods, which reddened the sky—the wild strain, and the unearthly adjurations to the singers' souls, as though they were palpable, put me in mind of the fancied voyage across the Styx.[13]

Apart from its picturesque quality, this account from a book published in 1863 confirms the description given by Mrs. Kemble of the manner in which the spirituals were sung: the singing in unison, the beginning of each verse by the leader alone, the repeating of the refrain in chorus, and a certain wild and barbaric effect that these writers are able to feel but not to define.

Russell states that the Negro melodies he heard in the Port Royal Islands were completely unlike those of the "Ethiopian Serenaders," that is, the blackface minstrels. H. G. Spaulding, in the article previously cited, wrote that the melodies of the Negro spirituals "bear as little resemblance to the popular Ethiopian melodies of the day as twilight to noonday." Both writers are contradicted by the musical facts. Doubtless they received an impression of hearing something completely different because of the manner of singing and the circumstances under which they heard the spirituals. But the tunes themselves in many cases reveal a close kinship with those made familiar by the blackface minstrels. The editors of *Slave Songs of the United States* were sometimes aware of these similarities. Regarding the spiritual "Gwine Follow," William Allen observes: "The second part of this tune is evidently 'Buffalo' (variously known also as 'Charleston' or 'Baltimore') 'Gals.' "—

Tit - ty Ma - ry, you know I gwine fol-low, I gwine fol-low, gwine fol-low, Brud-der Wil-liam, you know I gwine to fol-low, For to do my Fa-der will. 'Tis well and good I'm a-

[13] W. H. Russell, *op. cit.*, chap. 18.

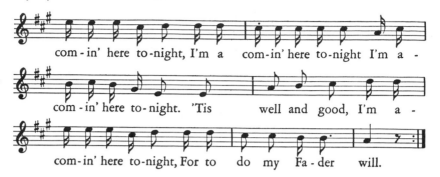

com-in' here to-night, I'm a com-in' here to-night I'm a-
com-in' here to-night. 'Tis well and good, I'm a-
com-in' here to-night, For to do my Fa-der will.

Additional similarities were noted by H. E. Krehbiel in his work, *Afro-American Folk Songs*. He observed particularly "a palpable likeness" between "Lord, Remember Me" and "Camptown Races," the latter composed by Stephen Foster in 1850. He believes that the tune was invented by Foster and borrowed by the Negroes for their spiritual. This is entirely plausible; yet the possibility of a common ancestor for both should not be discounted. The exact process of tune borrowing, conscious and unconscious, that went on during this period will in all probability never be fully known nor completely traced. What matters most, perhaps, is to recognize, in addition to definite borrowings (whatever their direction), a general family resemblance in the basic melodic materials of the three main popular traditions of vocal music that developed in the United States during the first half of the nineteenth century: the revival hymns of the whites, the Negro spirituals and work songs, and the so-called "plantation" or "Ethiopian" melodies. What gave to each current or branch its peculiar character was the "working over" of the material, the transformation of basic elements through the shaping spirit and the prevailing trend of each tradition, each with its concomitant cultural factors, ranging from ancestral African patterns to vulgarized commercial entertainment. None of these traditions was particular about the kind of materials it used, provided these could be made effective for the purpose at hand. And the force of the tradition, in each case, generally brought about the transformation required for its needs. There are examples of old British ballads, for instance, so "worked over" by the tradition of Negro folk singing that they are scarcely recognizable.

Regarding the spiritual "Oh, Freedom Over Me," Krehbiel remarks that it "challenges no interest for its musical contents, since it is a compound of two white men's tunes—"Lily Dale," a sentimental ditty, and "The Battle Cry of Freedom," a patriotic song composed by George F. Root. . . ." [14] The challenge, however, would lie in hearing what the Negroes might do with this composite, borrowed tune after they had worked it over for a generation or two. Folk music is made, not born.

As a final selection from *Slave Songs of the United States*, we quote the spiritual "Good-bye, Brother," which thoroughly resembles a typical "Ethiopian" melody, or, if you prefer, a Stephen Foster tune:

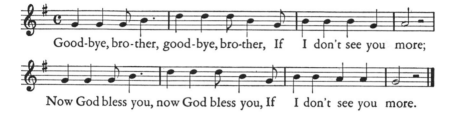

Good-bye, bro-ther, good-bye, bro-ther, If   I don't see you more;

Now God bless you, now God bless you, If   I don't see you more.

The folk tradition of the spirituals

Mention has previously been made of the survival of lining-out among the Negroes. This practice is found in connection with the slow-paced and embellished singing of old hymns, undoubtedly derived from the eighteenth-century tradition. Since this procedure conforms perfectly to the leader-and-chorus or call-and-response pattern of African song, its adoption by the Negroes in America is a natural instance of musical syncretism or blending. Mary Allen Grissom, in *The Negro Sings a New Heaven*, recorded some examples of Negro hymns sung and chanted with lining-out by the leader. Regarding these she writes:

This type of singing is used particularly at funerals and very solemn occasions. It is rarely heard now. It probably had its origin in the old type of hymn-singing, used in the early church, in which the hymn was "lined" by a leader. When given with the Negro's peculiar style of chanting and sliding to and from the main melody note, it is distinctly a thing apart. The example given here is purely Negro both in tune and words, but frequently one hears a well-known

[14] Krehbiel, *op. cit.*, p. 17.

hymn chanted. The entire congregation sings in unison with each line of the verse chanted by the leader.[15]

FULL CHORUS
Very slowly

I ___ stood out - side ___ thay ___ gate They___
would __ not __ let ___ me ___ in ___ me ___
CHANT (LEADER)
in. I prayed to my good lawd. I ___ prayed __ to ___
CHANT
my ___ good ___ Lawd to cleanse me from all sin To ___
cleanse __ me ___ from ___ all ___ sin uh all ___ sin.

We have now brought the history of the religious songs of the American Negro—including the African backgrounds discussed in an earlier chapter—up to the time of their general "discovery" and initial diffusion through the printed page shortly after the close of the Civil War. It would be well at this point to summarize the data that we have been able to assemble from the various contemporary accounts to which reference has been made.

1. The spirituals were sung with a freedom, independence, and individuality in the vocal lines that conveyed the effect of a sort of unconventional polyphony, attaining to "a marvellous complication and variety."

2. There was a prevalence of the leader-and-chorus (or call-and-response) pattern, the melody sung or chanted by a single voice, the chorus joining in with the refrain.

3. Spirituals were used as working songs, e.g., for rowing and for field tasks, as well as at religious meetings.

4. Some of the melodies resembled familiar European tunes, while others were "extraordinarily wild and unaccountable."

[15] Descriptive note and musical example used by permission of the publisher, The University of North Carolina Press.

5. There was much singing of standard hymns, especialy Methodist and Baptist, among the Negro population of the South.

6. The Negroes participated in camp-meetings and often sang the same revival songs as the whites did.

7. At some Negro services, psalms and long-meter hymns were sung according to the old practice of lining-out (which could be readily assimilated into the call-and-response pattern).

8. The singing of the Negroes was characterized by peculiar vocal effects, difficult if not impossible to indicate by regular notation.

In the remainder of this chapter an attempt will be made to throw further light on these aspects of Negro song, with a view to establishing its true nature and its present status.

It is necessary to recognize the existence of two main currents in the history of the Negro spiritual after the Civil War. One current tended to assimilate the spirituals into the forms and techniques of European art music. The other tended to conserve their traditional folk character with retention of primitive and archaic survivals. The first spread rapidly and widely through the publication of harmonized arrangements, the tours of trained Negro choirs at home and abroad, concert performances by celebrated artists, the vogue of choral arrangements used by choirs and glee clubs everywhere, and instrumental transcriptions or stylizations of every sort. The second followed a kind of undercover existence, somewhat as the original Negro spirituals did during the ante-bellum period; that is, cultivated by the folk, chiefly in rural areas or small communities, and attracting little attention from outsiders. It is to this second current that we shall direct our attention, not because we deprecate the pleasure that may be derived from listening to artistic arrangements of Negro spirituals beautifully sung by trained artists but because it seems more important, from the standpoint of cultural history, to try to know and understand a musical tradition in its unique and essential nature rather than in its secondary derivations. The spirituals are a folk product, and their true character must therefore be sought in a folk tradition.

The folklorist should be our guide in any folk tradition. It is to the folklorists of the twentieth century that we owe the "rediscovery" of the Negro spirituals, and indeed of virtually the whole body of Negro folk music, including the remarkable wealth of secular songs of which very little was known previously. In several current collections of American folk music, there can now be found numerous Negro songs carefully and faithfully notated with the most scrupulous regard for authenticity and accuracy. Better still, in recordings issued by Ethnic Folkways Records and by the Library of Congress, the singing itself can be heard in all the "marvellous complication and variety" that astonished and delighted the first Northern visitors to the Port Royal Islands.

One of the earliest and most detailed descriptions of authentic Negro folk singing was given by Jeannette R. Murphy in an article published in *Popular Science Monthly* for September, 1899. Speaking of the difficulty that a white person has in singing Negro spirituals, she points out that "he must break every law of musical phrasing and notation." Furthermore:

> . . . around every prominent note he must place a variety of small notes, called "trimmings," and he must sing tones not found in our scale; he must on no account leave one note until he has the next one well under control. . . . He must often drop from a high note to a very low one; he must be very careful to divide many of his monosyllabic words in two syllables, placing a forcible accent on the last one, so that "dead" will be "da-*ade*," "back" becomes "ba-*ack*," "chain" becomes "cha-*ain*."

To illustrate some of these points, Mrs. Murphy printed her notation of a spiritual, which is of exceptional interest both textually and musically: [16]

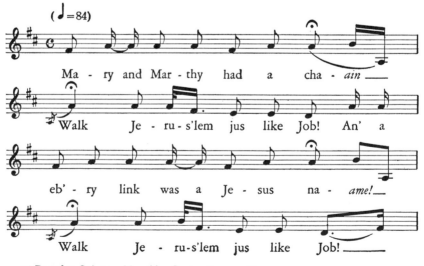

[16] *Popular Science Monthly*, Sept. 1899, p. 665.

REFRAIN

When I comes ter die _____ I want ter be _____ read - y When I comes ter die _____ gwine ter walk Je - ru - s'lem jus like Job!

It should be added that the difficulties mentioned above apply chiefly to persons accustomed to standard or conventional musical practice; there are white folk singers who sing spirituals in this same style, with "trimmings" and all the other characteristics of the tradition.

Natalie Curtis Burlin, in an article titled "Negro Music at Birth," published in 1919, caught the mood of Negro singing with real sympathy and understanding; she is describing a group of Negroes in a meeting at the Calhoun Industrial School in Alabama:

Seated in rows, reverent and silent, they waited for something to happen. And as they sat, patient in the early warmth of the April sun, suddenly a rhythmic tremor seemed to sway over the group . . . there arose a vibration, an almost inaudible hum . . . and then the sound seemed to mold itself into form, rhythmic, melodic, taking shape in the air . . . till soon the entire gathering was rocking in time to one of the old plantation melodies. Men, women and children sang, and the whole group swung to and fro, from side to side, with the rhythm of the song, while many of the older people snapped their fingers in emphasis like the sharp click of an African gourd rattle. . . .

And as usual with Negroes, this was extemporaneous part-singing—women making up alto, men improvising tenor or bass, the music as a whole possessed so completely by them all (or so utterly possessing them!) that they were free to abandon themselves to the inspiration of their creative instinct.[17]

[17] *Musical Quarterly*, V, 1 (Jan. 1919), 87–88.

Elsewhere in the same article, the author tells of hearing a group of Negro workers in a tobacco factory and of being impressed by "their brilliant unmodulated grouping of diatonic chords, their sudden interlocking of unrelated majors and minors, and their unconscious defiance of all man-made laws of 'voice progressions.'"

The transition from unison to part singing in the Negro spirituals evidently took place in the decades following the Civil War and was probably due to increased contact with white persons and to the influence of the schools in particular. The educated Negro grew to be ashamed of the "barbaric" elements in his music. Institutions for the education of Negroes, such as Fisk University, and the Hampton and Tuskegee Institutes, attempted to "improve" the musical quality of Negro singing by making it conform to the standards of "refined" practice. "Wrong" notes and "incorrect" harmonies had to be changed in the name of "progress." Nevertheless, the folk tradition persisted, as we have remarked, with its own style of singing, its own harmonies and progressions.

The question remains: what were the sources of this tradition? Did it originate with the Negro or did he adopt it from the white man? In recent years much controversy has surrounded this question. Some investigators, notably George Pullen Jackson, Guy B. Johnson, and Newman White, maintain that the Negro spirituals were copied from the white spirituals, that is, the religious folk songs of the rural Southern white population. Guy B. Johnson found pentatonic scales, flat sevenths, and "neutral" thirds in the folk songs of the whites as well as the Negroes, and concluded from this evidence that the songs of the latter were imitations of the former. The melodic and textual analogies between white and Negro spirituals compiled by G. P. Jackson are intended to support the same conclusion. What these investigators have done is to establish an incontrovertible correspondence or analogy between the white and Negro spirituals, but they have proved nothing as regards the *direction* of the influences. The fact that the white spirituals were *printed* before the Negro spirituals is not proof that they existed earlier in the oral tradition.

The opposite theory, upheld by Krehbiel, by Kolinski, by Herzog, and by Waterman, is that the Negro spirituals, and all Afro-American music in general, embody traits that are fundamentally of African origin, though blended with Anglo-American elements. Waterman stresses the concept of "hot" rhythm as the essential characteristic of African and Afro-American music, and states:

The religious songs the Negroes learned from the missionaries were soon given the "hot" treatment. Known today as "Spirituals," they are found, in their folk setting . . . to employ hand-clapping and foot-stamping in lieu of drumming, and to make consistent use of off-beat phrasing in a manner directly in line with African musical thought-patterns. The concept of "hot" religious music had been communicated to Southern whites by the close of the revivalistic period, during which heavily rhythmic hymns were useful in inducing camp-meeting "possession." [18]

More will be said regarding the concept of "hot" rhythm and its influence on American music in the chapter dealing with the rise of jazz. Waterman's thesis that Negro "hot" rhythm, as exemplified in the spirituals, may have influenced the camp-meeting hymns of Southern whites, is plausible and extremely interesting.

The musicologist M. Kolinski made a comparative study of Negro spirituals and West African songs, which has not been published, but which Waterman summarizes as follows: [19] Thirty-six spirituals are either identical or closely related in tonal structure (scale and mode) to West African songs. The spiritual "Cyan' Ride" has an almost exact counterpart in a Nigerian song, and "No More Auction Block" is clearly the same as one of the Ashanti songs. Certain features of melodic progressions such as "pendular thirds," sequences of at least three intervals of a third moving in the same direction, and both linear and pendular combinations of fourths, are common in both the spirituals and the West African songs. Duple or binary meters are predominant in both groups of songs. Syncopated and rubato figures, triplets, off-beat phrases, and sequences of several notes of equal time value, appear in the same forms in both bodies of music. The beginning rhythms of thirty-four spirituals are almost exactly like those of several songs of Dahomey and the Gold Coast. Regarding the leader-chorus pattern, generally admitted to be an African survival in the spirituals, Kolinski found that in many cases the overlapping of parts produced identical polyphonic patterns in the two types of songs.

---

[18] Waterman, *Journal of the American Musicological Society*, I, 1 (1948), 30.
[19] See bibliography for Chapter 4.

Fifty spirituals were discovered, in this respect, to have the identical formal structure of certain West African songs.

Kolinski concludes, according to Waterman, that while many of the spirituals are evidently patterned after European tunes, some without *apparent* distortion, they are all either altered so as to conform, or selected for adoption because they already did conform, to West African musical patterns. It is in this connection that he indicates the role of a "common musical base" of European and West African music, which facilitated this musical syncretism.

The theory of musical syncretism of West African and European elements in the American Negro spiritual—whether or not the hypothesis of a "common musical base" be accepted—seems the soundest conclusion that can be reached in the light of the available evidence.

There remains to speak of a highly important custom in connection with Negro religious practice, one having a direct and vital bearing on the preservation of the spirituals in their traditional form. We refer to the "shout" or "holy dance" of the Negroes. This ceremony was described in *The Nation* of May 30, 1867, by a writer who had witnessed it on a Southern plantation:

. . . The true "shout" takes place on Sundays, or on "praise" nights through the week, and either in the praise-house or in some cabin in which a regular religious meeting has been held. Very likely more than half the population of a plantation is gathered together. . . . The benches are pushed back to the wall when the formal meeting is over, and old and young, men and women . . . all stand up in the middle of the floor, and when the "sperichil" is struck up begin first walking and by and by shuffling around, one after another, in a ring. The foot is hardly taken from the floor, and the progression is mainly due to a jerking, hitching motion which agitates the entire shouter and soon brings out streams of perspiration. Sometimes they dance silently, sometimes as they shuffle they sing the chorus of the spiritual, and sometimes the song itself is also sung by the dancers. But more frequently a band, composed of some of the best singers and of tired shouters, stand at the side of the room to "base" the others, singing the body of the song and clapping their hands together or on the knees. Song and dance are alike extremely energetic, and often, when the shout lasts into the middle of the night, the monotonous thud, thud of the feet prevents sleep within half a mile of the praise-house.[20]

[20] Quoted in *Slave Songs of the United States*, pp. xiii–xiv.

It is above all through the rhythmic ecstasy of the shout that the "hot" element in the spirituals has been kept alive.

The association of the shout or holy dance with the spiritual seems natural indeed, for in the words of Robert W. Gordon, "Anyone who has heard the spiritual properly sung has found it practically impossible to keep still while listening. The rhythm demands bodily movement. The feet insist on tapping, the body sways in time, or the hands pat. There is an almost uncontrollable desire to rise and throw the whole body into the rhythm." [21]

The sentence, "The rhythm demands bodily movement," links the spirituals and shouts to the tradition of African music on the one hand, and on the other to some of the most distinctive manifestations of America's music from blackface minstrelsy to ragtime and jazz. We have seen that Henry Russell, when he attended the Negro church service in Vicksburg, momentarily expected the congregation "to get up and dance." Had they done so, Russell would doubtless have found the spectacle "quaint," or "barbaric," or "amusing." These were the terms most often applied by white observers to Negro singing and dancing. The dancing, in particular, was always regarded as amusing by white people. It exerted a peculiar and powerful fascination, whether in the plantation "walk-arounds" or in the "ring shouts." The division of secular or secular usage made little difference as far as the basic facts are concerned. The prancing walk-arounds and the shuffling shouts were motivated by an identical impulse and resulted from the same traditional concept of "hot" rhythm in the indissoluble union of song and dance.

The Northern abolitionists and educational uplifters who "discovered" and publicized the Negro spirituals during and after the Civil War were intent upon dignifying the Negro and emphasizing what they considered to be his higher, spiritual qualities. Hence they stressed the Negro's religious songs and neglected his secular songs, though they could not in many instances fail to recognize that there was a close connection between the two. The members of the educational mission to the Port Royal Islands prided themselves that they "were not long in discovering the rich vein of music that existed in these half-barbarous people"; but actually this was no discovery at all. At least forty years earlier white musicians and entertainers had

[21] Gordon, "The Negro Spiritual," *op. cit.*, p. 192.

begun to discover "the rich vein of music" that existed among the Negroes. From the early 1820s they began tentatively to exploit that vein, and by the 1840s the exploitation was in full swing. This exploitation of the rich vein of Negro music in the realm of popular entertainment came to be known as the "Ethiopian business," or "Negro minstrelsy," or simply "American minstrelsy." It brought to the whole of America, and to much of the rest of the world, a new type of humor and a new note of pathos that could have come only from the background of American plantation life.

chapter thirteen

The Ethiopian business

The source of Negro minstrelsy is to be found in the soil of the Southland.
CARL WITTKE, TAMBO AND BONES.

One evening in February of the year 1843, four grotesque figures in blackface, wearing white trousers, striped calico shirts, and blue calico coats with long swallowtails, appeared on the stage of the Bowery Amphitheatre in New York City. They proceeded to entertain the delighted audience with a combination of singing, dancing, Negro dialect patter, and instrumental music played on the banjo, violin, bone castanets, and tambourine. Their performance concluded with a "walk-around" and "breakdown" (grotesque plantation dance).

This was the historic debut of "the novel, grotesque, original and surpassingly melodious Ethiopian Band, entitled, the Virginia Minstrels," as advertised in the New York papers. The Virginia Minstrels had been recently organized in New York City by four friends who possessed a measure of musical and comic talent, and some theatrical experience. These four friends were Daniel Decatur Emmett [1] (violin), Billy Whitlock (banjo), Frank Brower ("bones"), and Dick Pelham (tambourine). All of them were to leave their mark in the American popular theater, and one of them—"Old Dan" Emmett—was to win great and lasting fame as the composer of "Dixie." They advertised their show as "an exclusively minstrel entertainment . . . entirely exempt from the vulgarities and other objectionable features which have hitherto characterized Negro extravaganzas."

From this it appears that "Negro extravaganzas"—blackface entertainment by white performers who blackened their faces with burnt cork—had been familiar to the American public for some time. American entertainers, such as George Washington Dixon and "Daddy"

[1] In his early years on the minstrel stage, he was known as "Old Dan Emmit."

259

Rice, had been giving blackface performances since the 1820s. How, then, could the Virginia Minstrels claim that their "Ethiopian Band" was a novel and original type of entertainment? The novel feature of the Virginia Minstrels was the association of four entertainers in a coordinated team, dressed in distinctive costumes, each assigned a specific role in the ensemble, each playing a characteristic instrument, and putting on a complete, self-contained show. This four-man team was the classic type of American minstrel show that sprang into enormous popularity in the two decades preceding the Civil War.

The "Ethiopian business" prospered tremendously, much to the chagrin of the upholders of the genteel tradition. As one writer lamented: "How frequently the most eminent in tragedy or comedy, have toiled through the choicest efforts, to scanty listeners; while upon the same evenings, fantazias upon the bones, or banjo, have called forth the plaudits of admiring thousands." It should perhaps be added that among those "admiring thousands" were some of "the most eminent in tragedy or comedy," who by no means disdained the novelty, the exuberant nonsense, the genuine pathos, and even the underlying implications of tragedy, that characterized the best of American minstrelsy. Thackeray was deeply moved by Negro minstrel melodies; the great actor Forrest declared that "he knew no finer piece of tragic acting than the impersonation of Dan Bryant as the hungry Negro in *Old Time Rocks*." (Dan Bryant, like Emmett and E. P. Christy, was one of the famous pioneer figures of minstrelsy.)

The vogue of minstrelsy spread rapidly and far. It reached California with the forty-niners during the gold rush. One minstrel troupe, headed by Henry Whitby, brought the "plantation melodies" to South America when it appeared at Santiago de Chile in 1848, en route to California around Cape Horn. American minstrel troupes went to England in the 1840s and 1850s, achieved resounding acclaim, and succeeded in amusing Queen Victoria. Blackface minstrelsy was a unique and novel type of entertainment, completely a product of the American scene. Often crude, sometimes mawkish, at its best it had an exuberant vitality and an exotic fascination. It brought to birth and kept alive a vast body of American popular song; it remained the mainstay of American popular entertainment for over half a century; and before it expired it ushered in one of the most typical and influential forms of American popular music: ragtime.

The antecedents of American minstrelsy are therefore worth looking into. Without discussing isolated eighteenth-century examples,[2] we may begin with what might be called "the pre-minstrel-show period," with such early nineteenth-century blackface entertainers as G. W. Dixon, George Nichols, Bob Farrell, and "Jim Crow" Rice. George Nichols, for many years a clown in "Purdy Brown's Theatre and Circus of the South and West" (there was a close connection between the circus and minstrelsy), is said to have got the idea of singing in Negro make-up "from a French darky banjo player, known throughout the Mississippi Valley as Picayune Butler, a peripatetic performer who passed the hat and sang, 'Picayune Butler is Going Away.'" The reference to "a French darky"—probably a Louisiana Negro from Saint Domingue or Martinique—is interesting. Nichols was one of those who claimed authorship of that popular minstrel song, "Zip Coon"—a claim disputed by both Dixon and Farrell. According to Wittke, Nichols was the first to sing in public another old-time favorite that enjoyed immense popularity, "Clare de Kitchen," which "he had adapted from a melody which he had heard sung by Negro firemen on the Mississippi River." One frequently comes across statements that this or that minstrel song was adapted from a Negro melody; but since the original source is never given, such statements cannot be corroborated. Whatever may have been the origin of "Clare de Kitchen," it was first copyrighted in 1832 by George Willig, Jr., the Baltimore music publisher, and it was widely popularized (in a somewhat altered version) by "Jim Crow" Rice.

George Washington Dixon was one of the most successful of the early blackface entertainers. He was doing Negro songs in character at Albany as early as 1827, and two years later he appeared at the Bowery Theatre in New York, where he introduced one of the favorite numbers in his repertoire, "Coal Black Rose," which Foster Damon describes as "the first burnt-cork song of comic love." Edward L. Rice, in *Monarchs of Minstrelsy*, states that the tune was "appropriated from an old ballad," which he does not identify. An edition of 1829 attributes the authorship of "Coal Black Rose" to White Snyder. Because of its early date and wide popularity—it was sung at all the theaters from 1829 on—a sample of the words and melody is given

[2] It should nevertheless be mentioned that eighteenth-century English stage impersonations of Negroes had considerable influence on early American minstrelsy, particularly as regards the use of dialect and the type of melody used in certain so-called "plantation melodies."

here, from a sheet-music edition published by Firth & Hall of New York.

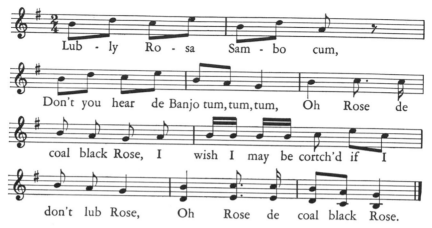

Lub - ly Ro - sa Sam - bo cum, Don't you hear de Banjo tum, tum, tum, Oh Rose de coal black Rose, I wish I may be cortch'd if I don't lub Rose, Oh Rose de coal black Rose.

The edition from which this music was quoted has a crude sketch of "Lubly Rosa" and of "Sambo," each playing on the primitive Negro gourd banjo, also known as the "bonja" or "banga." The reader may recall that Thomas Jefferson, in his *Notes on Virginia*, called it the "banjar." This brings to mind one of the earliest of the blackface songs, the "Bonja Song," published in a sheet-music edition sometime between 1818 and 1821. The words, written by R. C. Dallas, show the stilted, artificial style of pseudo-Negro diction.

Since we have mentioned the "bonja" here, we may jump ahead chronologically for a moment to trace its transformation into the "banjo." The man credited with this development is Joel Walker Sweeney (1813–1860), who played the banjo and sang with various minstrel shows and circuses. According to Foster Damon: "Dissatisfied with the four-stringed gourd, he cut an old cheese-box in half, covered it with skin, and strung it with five strings, thus inventing the modern banjo. He is credited with doing this as early as 1830; by 1840 his reputation was secure." In the absence of concrete evidence, one is inclined to regard Mr. Sweeney's "invention" of the five-stringed banjo as rather mythical, like the invention of the lyre by Apollo. In any case, it is the instrument with four strings, not five, that is depicted on the cover of "The celebrated Banjo Song" titled "Whar Did You Cum From?" or "Knock a Nigger Down," advertised as "Sung with great Applause at Broadway Circus by Mr. J. W. Sweeney" (New York, Firth & Hall, 1840). The transition to the five-stringed banjo probably took place around 1845, and there is no proof that Sweeney was responsible for it.

Minstrel music for banjo is an extremely interesting phase of early American popular music that has not yet been sufficiently studied. On this subject Dr. Hans Nathan writes:

> Some of it is fashioned after Irish-Scotch tunes; other tunes are banjo variants of well-known minstrel songs (using typical banjo figuration); and there are original tunes. The latter kind are so primitive (constant repetition of brief motives of small range, with downward trend of the motives, etc.) that these tunes no doubt include many elements of the early plantation music. In many minstrel banjo tunes (though less frequently in those related to the fiddle music of the Old World) there are distinct and tricky syncopations.[3]

The following is an example of such a syncopated banjo tune, taken from one of Emmett's manuscripts but *not* composed by him:

Returning to George Washington Dixon— He claimed the authorship of another early and highly popular minstrel song, "Long Tail Blue," which he featured in his performances from 1827. Other blackface entertainers, such as Barney Burns and William Pennington, helped to popularize this song, which became a standard minstrel number for the next fifty years. The character is that of a Negro dandy out strolling on Sunday dressed in his elegant blue swallowtail coat. As one of the earliest and most successful of the burntcork melodies, "Long Tail Blue" deserves quotation; here are the words and tune of the chorus:

Oh! for the long tail blue. Oh! for the long tail blue.

I'll — sing a song not ver - y long a - bout my long tail blue.

[3] In a letter to the author, dated Feb. 26, 1954. Dr. Nathan was kind enough to supply the banjo tune quoted here.

As Foster Damon observes, "Long Tail Blue" was the first comic song of the Negro dandy, a character that was to reappear frequently in our popular entertainment. The "dandy" stood as a contrast to that other stock type of blackface minstrelsy, the ragged "plantation darky."

"The father of minstrelsy"

We come now to the man who has been called "the father of American minstrelsy," known to his contemporaries as "Daddy" or "Jim Crow" Rice, but whose full name was Thomas Dartmouth Rice (1808–1860). He was born of poor parents in New York City and was trained to be a wood carver. Lured by the stage, he obtained occasional jobs as a supernumerary at the Park Theatre, and soon took to the road as an itinerant player, heading for the frontier settlements of the Ohio Valley. He got a job as general handyman in Ludlow and Smith's Southern Theatre in Louisville, Kentucky, and later joined a stock company at the Louisville Theatre, where he played bit parts. This was in 1828. One of the parts he played was that of a Negro field hand in a local drama titled *The Rifle*. As was customary in those days, Rice interpolated a Negro song between the acts of this play (this was done in all theaters, whether the play was a serious drama or a comedy). The song was "Jim Crow." It made Rice famous and became the first great international song hit of American popular music.

According to the generally accepted tradition, Rice saw an old, deformed Negro cleaning the horses in a stable near the Louisville Theatre, singing an odd melody and doing a curious sort of shuffling dance. Every time he reached the chorus of his song, he gave a little jump that set his "heel a-ricken." His right shoulder was drawn up high and his left leg was crooked at the knee and stiff with rheumatism, so that he walked with a limp. Rice decided to imitate this old Negro on the stage, and to copy his song, making up additional stanzas of his own. His impersonation, his shuffling step and jump, and his song, all caught the fancy of the public: in Louisville, in Cincinnati, in Pittsburgh, in Philadelphia, in Baltimore, in Washington, in New York (1832), and finally in London, where "Jim Crow" Rice achieved a sensational success in 1836.

In Pittsburgh, Rice got his friend W. C. Peters (who afterward published Stephen Foster's first minstrel songs) to write down the music of "Jim Crow." Peters opened a music store in Louisville in 1829, and it may have been at that time that Rice became friendly with him. By the end of 1830, however, Peters was back in Pittsburgh, where he went into partnership with Smith and Mellor. Within a short time many editions of "Jim Crow" were published, some of them making no mention at all of Rice. Both words and melody varied considerably in different editions. Here is the tune of "Jim Crow" as it appears in an edition published in Baltimore by George Willig, Jr., with no date, but probably issued around 1828 (the introductory measures and the piano accompaniment are omitted in the example quoted below).

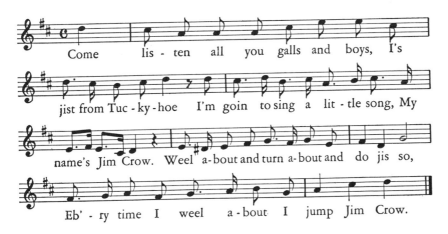

In the innumerable stanzas of "Jim Crow" that accumulated as the song was put through the paces of minstrelsy, we find echoes from topical events ranging from politics ("I put de veto on de boot/ An nullefy de shoe") to the playing of the celebrated violin virtuoso Paganini:

> I'm a rorer on de fiddle,
>   An down in ole Virginny
> Dey say I play de skientific
>   Like massa Pagganninny.

Verses such as this show clearly the accretion of commercialized theatrical jargon in some of the more obviously concocted "plantation melodies." One may contrast this type of "darky" song with the verses of a genuine Negro song as given by a Southern plantation owner and printed in *Putnam's Monthly*, January, 1855:

> De ladies in de parlor,
>   Hey, come a rollin' down—
> A drinking tea and coffee;
>   Good morning, ladies all.
>
> De genmen in de kitchen,
>   Hey, come a rollin' down—
> A drinking brandy toddy;
>   Good morning, ladies all.

This is evidently the same song that Fanny Kemble mentions in *A Journal of a Residence on a Georgia Plantation, 1838–1839* (p. 127). She says that the tune was "pretty and pathetic." It is quite possible that the early minstrel performers, such as Dixon, Nichols, and Rice, may have derived their inspiration from hearing Negroes sing such songs as this; but as American "Negro" minstrelsy developed, it was largely a white man's production. Nevertheless, American minstrelsy could not have developed without the background of Negro tradition. The songs, the humor, the dances, and the instruments of the plantation darkies formed the nucleus out of which grew the first distinctly American type of theatrical entertainment. Granted that the minstrel-show "darky" was a caricature of the Negro; yet the caricature could not have been created without the original model, however great the subsequent distortion. After all, the theater, especially the comic stage, has always created standard "types" that everyone recognizes as caricatures. And the early minstrel performers managed to convey a great deal of pathos and emotion in their presentation of the more serious songs. Once, after attending a minstrel performance, Thackeray wrote: ". . . a vagabond with a corked face and a banjo sings a little song, strikes a wild note, which sets the heart thrilling with happy pity." Something genuine did come through.

Rise of the minstrel show

Wittke, in his book *Tambo and Bones*, states that one of Rice's better-known renditions "contained the idiotic line, 'Kitty-co-dink-a-ho-dink! oh, oh, roley-boley-Good morning, ladies all!'" Now, the line probably is nonsense; or, at least, we have lost the clue to its original meaning, as happens in the case of many of the old Negro songs; but the last four words are identical with the last line of the song quoted above as representing a "genuine" Negro plantation melody. The question is: did Rice copy the song from the Negroes, or did the latter copy it from him? As far as the dates and the documentary evidence are concerned, it could have happened either way.

"Daddy" Rice was not merely an impersonator and singer of blackface songs: he was the creator of numerous farces and burlesques, full of crude, often vulgar, humor, into which he wove his "plantation melodies." Among these farces, which for a time were known as "Ethiopian Operas," may be mentioned *Long Island Juba*, *The Black Cupid*, and *Bone Squash Diavolo*. He also concocted a burlesque of *Othello*. These blackface extravaganzas were the forerunners of the variety acts that were incorporated into the "second part" of the minstrel show after the latter became fully organized. Rice himself was primarily identified with the preminstrel show period. In later life he played the role of Uncle Tom in the dramatization of Harriet Beecher Stowe's antislavery novel. He suffered a stroke of paralysis around 1850, recovered, but was again stricken, fatally, in September, 1860. At the time of his death he was poor and alone, for he had squandered the fortune that his popularity had brought him.

We have seen how Dan Emmett and his associates launched the first organized minstrel show in New York in 1843. There is some controversy as to whether this really was the first minstrel company organized in this country. Claims have been made that E. P. Christy organized the first minstrel troupe in Buffalo in 1842. We need not concern ourselves overmuch with these rival claims. What seems fairly well established is that the Virginia Minstrels set the pattern of the minstrel show in its conventional form: the division into two parts, and the semicircular arrangement of the performers, with a middleman or interlocutor in the center and two endmen, known respectively as "Tambo" and "Bones" because one played the tambourine and the other the bone castanets. Christy organized the routine of songs, jokes, and repartee which made of the first part a lively, continuous, coordinated program. The second part, called an "olio," consisted, as has been said, of variety acts, a farce or burlesque opera, closing with a singing and dancing number for the entire cast.

E. P. Christy was born in Philadelphia in 1815. After organizing the Christy Minstrels in Buffalo, he toured through the West and the South, and in 1846 appeared at Palmo's Opera House in New York. In 1847 Christy leased Mechanics' Hall on Broadway, where his troupe played for almost ten years, In 1854 Christy retired with a fortune, and the company was taken over by his brother, George Christy. The victim of attacks of melancholia, E. P. Christy died in 1862 as the result of jumping from a second-story window of his home in New York.

Many other minstrel troupes sprang up in the two decades from 1850 to 1870, which was the heyday of American Negro minstrelsy.[4] The blackface minstrel show became an American institution and enjoyed an international vogue, for several companies toured in the British Isles with great success. This is not the place for an account of minstrel companies as such, because our main concern is with the music of minstrelsy, and in particular the songs of its two outstanding composers, Daniel Decatur Emmett and Stephen Collins Foster. Just as Foster's beginnings in minstrelsy are associated with E. P. Christy, so the first notable musical success of Emmett as a composer is associated with Bryant's Minstrels. Dan Bryant (*recte* Daniel Webster O'Brien) was an enterprising Irishman who, after playing with various minstrel troupes, formed his own company in New York in 1857. Among those who joined Bryant's Minstrels in that year was Dan Emmett, who remained with the company until 1865. He was engaged both as performer and composer, it being his task to provide songs for the show.

"Old Dan" Emmett

Daniel Decatur Emmett was born in Mt. Vernon, Ohio, on October 29, 1815, of an Irish-American pioneer family that had followed the path of westward migration from Virginia, first across the Blue Ridge Mountains, then beyond the Alleghenies, and finally to the frontier country of Ohio. The first of four children, he received scant

[4] This refers to the rise of Negro minstrelsy as a widespread type of commercialized popular entertainment. The most authentic or "classical" period of minstrelsy was from 1830 to 1850. After 1870 the minstrel shows became more lavish and spectacular, and in the 1880s it was customary to have as many as 100 performers in a troupe. These shows were designated by such adjectives as "Gigantean," "Mammoth," and "Gargantuan." Thereafter their decline was rapid. By 1896 there were only ten minstrel companies on the road.

schooling, but somehow learned to read and write while helping in his father's blacksmith shop. At thirteen he began to work in a printing office, and at seventeen he joined the Army as a fifer. Emmett's own account of his army experience is worth quoting:

> At the early age of 17, I enlisted in the U.S. Army as a fifer, and was stationed at Newport Barracks, Ky., the then school of practice for the western department. For one year, or more, I practiced the drum incessantly under the tuition of the renowned John J. Clark (better known as "Juba"), and made myself master of the "Duty" and every known "side beat" then in use. Being transferred to the 6th U.S. Infantry, then stationed at Jefferson Barracks, Mo., I was retained as "leading fifer" until discharged. In the meantime I continued my drum practice, which was then taught according to the *School of Ashworth*. In after years I travelled as Small Drummer with the celebrated Edward Kendall while he was leader of Spalding and Rogers' Circus Band.[5]

Whoever "the renowned John J. Clark" may have been, it is interesting to note that he was nicknamed "Juba," for this is the name of a familiar Negro dance song frequently encountered in the folklore of the South.[6] In addition to his competence on the fife and drum, Emmett learned to play other instruments, excelling particularly on the violin and the flute. He was also a good singer. In the summer of 1835 he was discharged from the Army "on account of minority," and it was then that he entered show business via the circus, traveling through the West and South before organizing his own minstrel troupe in New York.

If army and circus bands provided a major portion of Emmett's musical training on the instrumental side, his musical talent and his earliest musical repertoire, were inherited from his mother, who had a nice voice and sang to him often when he was a child. In later years Emmett said:

> As far back almost as I can remember, I took great interest in music. I hummed familiar tunes, arranged words to sing to them and made up tunes to suit words of my own. I paid no especial attention to the poetry and thought little about the literary merit of

[5] Cited by Galbreath, *Daniel Decatur Emmett*.
[6] It is also found as a Negro name in the West Indies as early as the eighteenth century.

what I wrote. I composed *Old Dan Tucker* in 1830 or 1831, when I was fifteen or sixteen years old, before I left Mt. Vernon.[7]

Whenever it may have been written, "Old Dan Tucker" was not published until 1843. An edition copyrighted in that year and published by Millet's Music Saloon, New York, describes it as "A Favorite Original Negro Melody . . . By Dan. Tucker, Jr." As often happened with minstrel songs, the authorship of "Old Dan Tucker" has been disputed. Perhaps the most curious claim is that of the English singer and composer Henry Russell, mentioned in an earlier chapter, who asserted that he composed the tune at Rochester, New York, in 1835, and in the following strange manner: "It was quite by accident that, playing 'Old Hundredth' very fast, I produced the air of 'Get Out o' de Way, Old Dan Tucker.' "

Musically, the most interesting feature of "Old Dan Tucker" is the syncopation in the chorus, at the words, "Get out de way!":

Old Dan Tuck-er's come to town, so get out de way! Get out de way!

Dan Emmett himself was convinced that his "walk-arounds" faithfully reflected the character and the traditions of the Southern plantation Negro. In some preliminary remarks for a manuscript collection of his minstrel "walk-arounds," he wrote:

In the composition of a "Walk 'Round" (by this I mean the style of music and character of the words), I have always strictly confined myself to the habits and crude ideas of the slaves of the South. Their knowledge of the world at large was very limited, often not extending beyond the bounds of the next plantation; they could sing of nothing but everyday life or occurrences, and the scenes by which they were surrounded. This being the undeniable fact, to be true to the Negro peculiarities of song, I have written in accordance.[8]

The whole question of the relationship between the tradition of Negro minstrelsy and the reality of Southern Negro life and character is a

[7] Regarding this passage, Dr. Nathan comments: "Emmett said all kinds of things when he was old. The *tune* of 'Old Dan Tucker' is definitely *not* by him."

[8] Cited by Galbreath, *op. cit.*

complex sociocultural problem that needs to be studied carefully by anyone wishing to get at the truth. The subject has been very ably treated in *The Southern Plantation* by Francis Pendleton Gaines, described as "A Study in the Development and the Accuracy of a Tradition." The interested reader should consult in particular Chapter V, A, "The Plantation in Minstrelsy," and Chapter VIII, "Plantation Characters" (The Conception Compared with the Actual).

Most writers agree that in its beginnings American minstrelsy, in the words of Brander Matthews, "endeavoured to reproduce the life of the plantation darkey. The songs sung by the Ethiopian serenaders were reminiscences of the songs heard where the Negro was at work, on the river steamboat, in the sugar field, or at the camp-meeting. . . ." It is likely that the steamboats of the Mississippi and the Ohio, as well as the Southern plantations, were the direct source of many Negro tunes and songs that found their way into the repertoire of the earliest blackface entertainers, such as Dixon, Rice, and Emmett. The river was a great carrier of songs, and many Negroes worked on the river.

One of Dan Emmett's best songs, "De Boatman's Dance," copyrighted and published in 1843, is a direct reflection of life on the river.[9] Here are a couple of typical stanzas of this song:

> When you go to de boatman's ball,
> Dance wid my wife, or don't dance at all;
> Sky blue jacket and tarpaulin hat,
> Look out my boys for de nine tail cat.

> De boatman is a thrifty man,
> Dars none can do as de boatman can;
> I neber see a putty gal in my life
> But dat she was a boatman's wife.

As far as we can judge, from internal and external evidence, "De Boatman's Dance" seems to belong in the group of early minstrel songs

[9] The chorus of this song appears to have been sung by Ohio River boatmen one or two decades before the publication of Emmett's version (cf. *The Pioneers of the West*, by W. P. Strickland, New York, 1856, p. 198). According to Nathan, the words of this song, except for the chorus, are by Emmett, and the tune is probably his also, though this is by no means certain. "Boatman's Dance" appears with the remark "Words by old Dan Emmit" in *Songs of the Virginia Minstrels: A Correct Edition of the Celebrated Songs of the Virginia Minstrels . . .* Boston, 1843. (Information from Nathan's bibliography of Emmett's songs.)

that reflect with comparative fidelity the music that the Negro may have actually used. Be that as it may, the song has outlived its vogue on the minstrel stage and passed into the tradition of American folklore. Here, then, are the tune and the words of the first stanza as printed in a sheet-music edition of 1843:

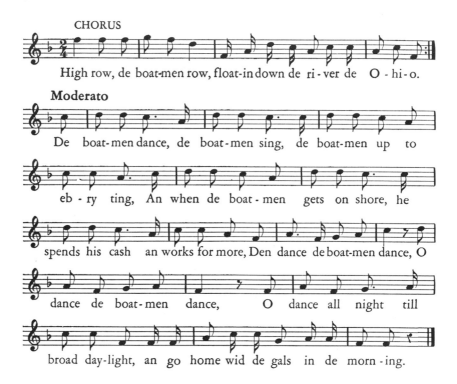

High row, de boat-men row, float-in down de ri-ver de O - hi-o.

De boat-men dance, de boat-men sing, de boat-men up to

eb-ry ting, An when de boat-men gets on shore, he

spends his cash an works for more, Den dance de boat-men dance, O

dance de boat-men dance, O dance all night till

broad day-light, an go home wid de gals in de morn-ing.

Another song by Emmett, also copyrighted in 1843, is "My Old Aunt Sally." The words are of the stilted, artificial pseudo-darky type that soon became prevalent in minstrelsy; but the tune is of interest as containing examples of the "flattened seventh" (in this case F natural) which is characteristic of much American Negro music.

"In Dixie Land . . ."

To most people Emmett is known, if he is known at all, as the composer of "Dixie," a song which has become more famous than the man who wrote it. This was one of the walk-arounds that Emmett wrote for Bryant's Minstrels in 1859. To give an idea of his output in this field, we print below the list of the walk-arounds composed by Emmett (words and music) from 1859 to 1868, as set forth by his biographer Galbreath: [10]

1859

I ain't got time to tarry
Nigger in de tent
John come down de holler
Road to Georgia
Flat foot Jake
Billy Patterson
Hai, Johnny Roach
Loozyanna low grounds
I wish I was in Dixie's Land
Johnny Gouler
Chaw roast beef
What o'dat?
Turkey in de straw

1860

Darrow Arrow
Old K.Y., Ky.
De Contrack

1862

De Back-log
Bress old Andy Jackson
Mr. Per Coon
Black Brigade

1863

High Daddy
Here we are, or cross ober Jordan
Greenbacks
Goose and Gander
Ober in Jarsey

1864

Foot-falls on de karpet
U.S.G.

1865

Whar ye been so long?
Old times rocks

1868

Burr Grass
Pan-cake Joe
Want any shad?
Sugar in de ground
Whoa, Bally!
Yes or no
Abner Isham Still
I am free

From the foregoing it will be seen that when Emmett joined Bryant's Minstrels in the fall of 1858, he entered upon an extremely productive period as a writer of minstrel melodies. He now had a job that required the full exercise of his talents as a musician and a black-face entertainer. Unlike Stephen Foster, whose association with minstrelsy was marginal, Dan Emmett was thoroughly immersed in the "Ethiopian business"; hence his songs, and the walk-arounds in particular, are an epitome of the minstrel tradition in its heyday. This heyday coincided with the growing tension over the slavery issue, and it is important to realize that political factors, however disguised by humor or sentiment, were increasingly reflected in the minstrel

[10] The list is not complete; it does not, for instance, include variants.

songs of the decade preceding the outbreak of the Civil War. When war came, Dan Emmett's "Dixie" was claimed by both sides; but it was the Confederacy that decisively took it over and made it virtually into a national anthem. The war gave an unforeseen significance to the lines of the carefree chorus: "In Dixie Land I'll take my stand, To lib and die in Dixie."

Emmett's song "Johnny Roach," performed in March 1859 and published in New York the following year, tells of a Negro slave bound for Canada by "de railroad underground," but who wishes "he was back agin." Then he tells why he wishes to be back in the South again:

> Gib me de place called "Dixie's Land,"
> Wid hoe and shubble in my hand;
> Whar fiddles ring an' banjos play,
> I'll dance all night an' work all day.

According to Hans Nathan, who has made the most thorough study to date of Emmett's life and work, this is "the very first occurrence in print of the word 'Dixie' as another name for the South—the black one, to be exact."

There has been much discussion as to the origin of the word "Dixie." A common assumption is that it was derived from the name Dixon and referred to the South as the part of the country below the Mason and Dixon's line. Another theory is that the name was taken from the French bank notes issued in New Orleans, said to be called "dixies"—from the French word "*dix*," meaning "ten." A third version has it that Dixie was the name of a man who kept slaves on Manhattan Island, New York, until the hostility of the abolitionists obliged him to move to the South, taking his slaves with him. The latter allegedly kept wishing they were back in "Dixie's Land." This last version is absurd and has no foundation whatever. The other two theories are more plausible but are unsupported by any valid evidence. Emmett himself, in later life, stated that the phrase "I wish I was in Dixie's Land" was a common expression referring to the South used by people in the entertainment business. The available evidence indicates that the term "Dixie," in any case, was of Northern origin. The earliest use of the name that Nathan was able to discover occurred in 1850 in a Northern minstrel play titled *United States Mail and Dixie in Difficulties*. Here the name "Dixie" is given to a stupid

Negro postboy. Nathan is probably right when he suggests that the name may have been invented by white showmen as an occasional nickname for a Negro character, by phonetic analogy with such Negro stage-types as "Pompey" and "Cuffee."

The whole vexing matter of the origin and significance of the term Dixie has been authoritatively summarized by Dr. Nathan:

> Since "Dixie" meant the Negro, "Dixie's Land" was obviously the land of the Negro—that is, according to the consensus of the mid-nineteenth century, the black South. When Emmett in his famous song abbreviated the phrase to "Dixie Land" and finally to "Dixie," the original name appeared again, though not referring to a person but to a locale. Thus "Dixie" had five connotations: it was first a synonym for the Negro; as a simplified version of "Dixie's Land" and "Dixie Land," it became a synonym for the Negro's South; next it became the South pure and simple; and finally it became a synonym for the South as seen by the Confederates. Parallel to this, "Dixie" was the popular title by which Emmett's song was known.[11]

Emmett's famous song was originally billed as "Dixie's Land" when it was first performed by Bryant's Minstrels at Mechanics' Hall, New York City, on April 4, 1859. It was announced as a "Plantation Song and Dance . . . Introducing the whole Troupe in the Festival Dance." On that occasion it did not conclude the program, but was next to the last number. According to the custom prevailing in minstrel walk-arounds, "Dixie's Land" was sung in a manner reminiscent of the call-and-response pattern of Afro-American music. The first part of the song (it is divided into two sections of sixteen measures each) was sung alternately by a soloist and by a small chorus in unison which came in at the end of every other line with a brief interjection, "Look away! Look away! Dixie Land!" As performed on the minstrel stage, "Dixie," like other walk-arounds, also had an instrumental section of eight measures, during which the members of the troupe would do a grotesque dance.

"Dixie" became an immediate popular success, and several publishers clashed over the copyright. Emmett gave the song to Firth,

[11] Nathan, *Dan Emmett and the Rise of Early Negro Minstrelsy*, p. 266. Quoted by permission of the publisher, University of Oklahoma Press.

Pond & Co. of New York, who brought it out in June, 1860. In the same year several other editions appeared, without credit to Emmett. One of these editions was published by P. P. Werlein of New Orleans, with the composition accredited to J. C. Viereck! This matter was eventually straightened out, and in subsequent editions Viereck's name appeared as "arranger." Then, in February, 1861, Emmett sold all his rights in the song to Firth, Pond & Co. for the sum of $300. Werlein, on his side, took advantage of the outbreak of hostilities to bring out another edition of "Dixie" in which Emmett's name was omitted as composer and Viereck's restored. The writ of Northern publishers and composers did not run in the Confederacy. Soon there were many unauthorized Southern editions of "Dixie." It was sweeping the South, both as a song (often with words written especially for the war) and as a march arranged for military band. A Confederate band played "Dixie" at the inauguration of President Jefferson Davis, and many Southern regiments marched in quickstep to its enlivening rhythm and jaunty tune. Emmett himself, whose sympathies were with the North, is reported to have said, "If I had known to what use they were going to put my song, I'll be damned if I'd have written it."

The North, for its part, was anxious to claim "Dixie" as its own. During the first year of the war, "Dixie," in spite of its adoption by the Confederacy, was at the peak of its popularity in the North, especially in New York, the city of its origin. The words, of course, were not considered appropriate for Northern usage, but that could easily be remedied. Many "Northern" versions of the song began to appear, among them "Dixie for the Union" and "Dixie Unionized." A "Unionized" text was published in *John Brown and the Union Right or Wrong Songster* (San Francisco, 1863).

At the end of the Civil War—in fact, the day after the surrender of General Lee's army at Appomattox—President Lincoln took steps to restore "Dixie" to the Union. A crowd had assembled at the White House to serenade him with a band. The President made a very brief speech, and then requested the band to play "Dixie," which he said was one of the best tunes he ever heard. Alluding to its quasi-official status as a Confederate song, he remarked dryly: "I had heard that our adversaries over the way had attempted to appropriate it. I insisted yesterday that we had fairly captured it . . . I presented the question to the Attorney-General, and he gave his opinion that it is our lawful prize. . . . I ask the Band to give us a good turn upon it." In this manner "Dixie" was "officially" restored to the North; but since the South never relinquished its claim upon the song, it belongs now to both North and South—it is a truly national song, probably the most genuinely "American" song that we possess.

According to Marius Schneider, "The popularity of a melody is the result of its degree of simplicity and of its conformity to the melodic type current in a given culture." Melodically and harmonically, the music of "Dixie" is simplicity itself. In style it closely resembles other tunes by Emmett, and it has a family kinship with a wide range of popular tunes current in America, stemming from Irish-Scotch sources. "Dixie" is in duple time, in the major mode, does not modulate, and employs syncopation.[12] These traits are common to a vast body of American vernacular music that has been put to various usages, from revival meetings to minstrel shows. Yet "Dixie" itself is unique, for it possesses high individuality within its conformity to type. In spite of its simplicity it is a well-constructed song, both unified and varied.

In 1888 Dan Emmett retired to a small country home near his native town of Mt. Vernon, Ohio. There he was discovered by A. G. Field, who persuaded him to take to the road again with Field's Minstrels.[13] This was in the year 1895. "Old Dan's" tour was triumphant, especially in the South (he never aired his antisecessionist views publicly). On April 11, 1896, he bade farewell to the public for the last time and returned to his rural homestead once more. There he lived on a pension from the Actors' Fund of New York until his death on June 28, 1904, at the age of eighty-eight.

Minstrel medley

Among the hundreds of songs associated with American minstrelsy, let us glance more closely at some that, for one reason or another, seem to merit special attention.

Recalling Jefferson's proposal for the establishment of a Negro "haven" abroad, and remembering that in the 1830s the Negro Republic of Haiti appeared to offer just such a haven, we turn to a blackface song published at Boston in 1833 as "Sambo's Address to He' Bred'rin" and also known as "Ching a Ring Chaw," in which the "bred'rin" are urged to emigrate to "Hettee," where each one will be

---

[12] The syncopation in "Dixie" is slight but effective. It is used twice in the chorus with a peculiarly characteristic effect.

[13] Apparently all that he did in the performance was to sing "Dixie."

received "gran' as Lafayette," where all will "lib so fine wid our coach and horse," where "we smoke de best segar, fetch from Havanna," where "our wibes be gran', an in dimons shine," and "dar dance at nite jig, what white man call cotillion, in hall so mity big it hole haff a million." In contrast with this life of ease and luxury, the song depicts the hard lot of the Negro in the United States, forced to perform all the menial and unpleasant tasks. Although this is obviously a white man's concoction, and was treated as a comic number, it shows what might be called the "social significance" aspect of Negro minstrelsy.

One of the most widely successful of the early blackface songs was "Jim Along Josey," written and introduced on the stage by Edward Harper around 1838. The tune uses only the five notes of the pentatonic scale. The song itself is followed by a lively "Dance" in which the comic actor had a chance to "do his stuff." The popularity of the song was doubtless due in large measure to the catchy tune of the chorus:

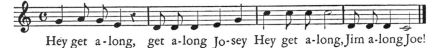

Hey get a-long, get a-long Jo-sey Hey get a-long, Jim a-long Joe!

Apart from its popularity on the minstrel stage, "Jim Along Josey" became widely used as a "Play Party Song" in the Middle West, and, as Foster Damon observes, was admitted as a game even among those stricter sects that prohibited dancing, "although to uncritical eyes the players seemed to be doing something easily mistaken for a Virginia Reel." There are many examples of songs and tunes passing from the minstrel stage into the realm of folklore.

To complete the cycle of borrowings, we should reiterate that many minstrel songs have their origin in anonymous folk tunes, so that they have passed from the domain of folklore and back to it again after the usual process of being modified or "reworked." A case in point is "Zip Coon," one of the most successful of the early minstrel songs, which has persisted in American folklore in numerous versions. As "Turkey in the Straw" it became a favorite fiddle tune for country dances. Bob Farrell, who sang "Zip Coon" in New York in 1834, claimed authorship of the song. His claim was disputed by George Washington Dixon. There is no reason to believe that either of these men actually "composed" the song—certainly not the music (one of them may have written the words). There is strong evidence to indicate that this is one of the many American minstrel songs of Scotch-Irish descent. Hans Nathan has found a Scotch reel that is very similar to parts of "Zip Coon." And Francis O'Neill writes that there is "convincing evidence of its Irish antecedents." [14]

Another old favorite is "Clare de Kitchen," popularized by "Daddy" Rice in the early 1830s, which has the "Old Virginny never tire" refrain. The text of the song is closer to the tradition of Negro humor than are the later minstrel songs. In a succession of nonsense verses we meet various animals: an old blind horse, a jaybird sitting on a hickory limb, a bull frog dressed in soldier's clothes, and "a little Whip poor will" whose sad fate it is to be eaten. In the last stanza of one version, the line occurs, "I wish I was back in old Kentuck"—the first of the "I wish I was . . ." tag lines that became a stock item in the nostalgic type of minstrel song.

Another song popularized by "Daddy" Rice and later by William Clifton, who arranged a version printed in 1836, was "Long Time Ago," in which the refrain is sung at the end of each line. Of interest is the syncopation on the words "Varginee" and "free." The whole structure of this song, in relation to Negro music, is worth noting (my reference is to Clifton's version, copyrighted 1836). The structure of the song is as simple as possible: the verse consists of two lines, each repeated, with an identical metrical pattern in the melody. Letting "C" stand for the chorus, the scheme may be expressed thus: A-C, A-C, B-C, B-C. The music example below is printed so as to show this parallel arrangement:

O I was born—down ole Var-gin-ee Long time a - go.

O I was born—down ole Var-gin-ee Long time a - go.

O Mas-sa die____ an make me fre-e Long time a - go.

O Mas-sa die an make me fre-e Long time a - go.

[14] *The Dance Music of Ireland*, Chicago, 1907.

Compare this pattern with that of the following corn-shucking song published in *Putnam's Monthly*, 1855, as an example of a genuine Negro plantation song:

> Cow boy on middle 'e island—
>   Ho, meleety, ho!
> Cow boy on middle 'e island—
>   Ho, meleety, ho!

Mrs. Kemble, in *A Journal of a Residence on a Georgia Plantation, 1838–1839*, quotes the words of a "rowing chant" with an identical pattern:

> Jenny shake her toe at me
> Jenny gone away
> Jenny shake her toe at me
> Jenny gone away.

The editors of *Slave Songs of the United States* (1867) state in a footnote in their preface that " 'Long Time Ago' . . . was borrowed from the negroes, by whom it was sung to words beginning 'Way down in Raccoon Hollow.' " This still does not prove that the plantation Negroes originated the melody, which was very likely picked up from a white man's song. A version of "Long Time Ago," published by John Cole of Baltimore in 1833, has the following words:

> As I was gwoin down shinbone alley,
>   Long time ago! (chorus)
> To buy a bonnet for Miss Sally,
>   Long time ago! (chorus)

The alternation of solo and chorus is of course characteristic of Negro singing, and doubtless we have here, once again, an example of a song that passed back and forth among Negroes and whites, becoming in the process a thoroughly hybridized product.

The song "Ole Tare River" (1840) deserves mention for its combination of the "Way down in . . ." tag line with other catch phrases that reappear in Stephen Foster's songs, such as:

> I go from dar to Alabama
> For to see my ole Aunt Hannah.

and

> Now Miss Dinah I'm going to leave you
> And when I'm gone don't let it grieve you.

One thinks also of "Way down upon the Swanee River," and one observes that both melodies are based on the pentatonic scale. Old Aunt Hannah seems to be a close relative of Miss Susanna. Herewith is a portion of "Ole Tare River," omitting the instrumental interludes:

The song "Lubly Fan" (Will You Come Out To Night?), written and copyrighted by Cool White in 1844, has had a varied history. A few years later it was brought out by the Christy Minstrels as "Bowery Gals," and in 1848 it was featured by the Ethiopian Serenaders as "Buffalo Gals." It is with this last title that the song has circulated most widely in the oral tradition, although in the South it was often heard as "Charleston Gals." The tune is so well known that direct quotation may be spared.

These old minstrel songs are so much a part of the American tradition, and have in many cases such wide ramifications in our folklore, that one is tempted to linger over them indefinitely, discussing and quoting one after another. Enough has been given, at least, to show the roots of the tradition and to trace some of its most characteristic manifestations and developments. If we have dwelt almost exclusively on the early period of minstrelsy, from the appearance of the first blackface entertainers to the rise of the original minstrel troupes in the 1840s, it is because this period produced the songs that were most deeply rooted in America's music, and which in turn branched out most widely into the oral tradition of the folk, both black and white. Moreover, we shall have more to say of Negro minstrelsy and its influence on America's music when we discuss the life and work of Stephen Collins Foster.

chapter fourteen

America's minstrel

I have concluded . . . to pursue the Ethiopian business without fear or shame and . . . to establish my name as the best Ethiopian songwriter.
STEPHEN C. FOSTER, LETTER TO E. P. CHRISTY, MAY 25, 1852.

In the spring of 1853 the pious, respectable, and prolific Mr. Thomas Hastings, composer of over a thousand hymn tunes, most of which have been forgotten by almost everybody, took his pen in hand to indite an indignant epistle to the editor of the *Musical Review and Choral Advocate*. The editor of that chaste periodical had recently commented on the deplorable fact that certain "Ethiopian melodies" were being adapted for use in Sunday schools. Mr. Hastings, while carefully protecting his respectability by stating that he was "not very conversant with Ethiopian minstrelsy," disclosed that he had actually discovered a Sunday-school superintendent endeavoring to foist the melody of "Old Folks at Home" on a large class of innocent "infant scholars." The superintendent thought the children would not recognize the tune. So the teacher sang a line or two—with suitably pious words, of course—and then asked, " 'Children, have you ever heard anything like that before?'—*Old Folks at Home! Old Folks at Home!*' shouted the little urchins with such merry glances and gesticulations as showed them upon the very point of 'cutting up,' when the experiment ended and the piece was abandoned."

Mr. Hastings, in his letter, went on to castigate those responsible for perverting the taste of children by "fishing up something from the lowest dregs of music" by which their minds "are filled with poisonous trash, to forget which in after life would be to them a blessing." The practice he describes, he says, is nothing new. "It is an old trick, which many seem determined to 'play off' every time they have an opportunity." Mr. Hastings fears these abuses will not yet be abandoned, in spite of the fact that there are, he says, plenty of good hymn tunes in circulation. But "Christy has more melodies; and then *Yankee Doodle, Frog and Mouse,* and *Jim Crow,* I believe, have not yet been appropriated." Thus the eminent Mr. Thomas Hastings, soon to receive the degree of Doctor of Music from New York University, vented his sarcasm and his scorn upon "the lowest dregs of music," including the "Ethiopian melodies" of Stephen Collins Foster.[1]

Perhaps the perpetrator of "Old Folks at Home," before his tragic death at the age of thirty-seven, had an opportunity to redeem himself in the eyes—or the ears—of Mr. Hastings and other advocates of the "better music" movement. In 1863, the last year of his life, when he had sunk to his lowest level of physical and spiritual vitality, Foster turned out what his granddaughter calls "about a dozen uninspired expressions of religious hack-writing" that surely were respectable and mediocre enough to satisfy even Mr. Hastings. The latter lived to be eighty-eight; when he finally went to his reward, perhaps his soul had been edified by hearing such masterpieces of bathos as Stephen Foster's "Little Ella's an Angel in the Skies" or "Willie's Gone to Heaven, Praise the Lord." Sad as was the physical and social deterioration of Stephen Foster in the last years of his life, it is still sadder to observe his deterioration as an artist, his surrender to mediocrity. But in his short life, with its unhappy ending, Stephen Foster, in spite of some vacillations and an eventual succumbing to adverse circumstances, succeeded surprisingly well in producing the kind of songs that earned the disapproval of the "better music" advocates.

The pontifical John S. Dwight, in his *Journal of Music,* had to admit—this was in the year 1853—that such tunes as "Old Folks at Home" were whistled and sung by everybody; but he asserted that they had not really taken a deep hold of the popular mind; that their charm was only *skin-deep;* and that such melodies "are not popular in the sense of musically inspiring, but that such and such a melody *breaks out* every now and then, like a morbid irritation of the skin."[2]

The battle lines were clearly drawn, and the worst of it is that Stephen Foster often had to fight the same battle in his own mind. As a member of a solid and highly respectable middle-class family, he did not grow up naturally into show business and the world of popular entertainment as did the poor country lad Dan Emmett. In his circle,

[1] Morneweck, *Chronicles of Stephen Foster's Family,* vol. 2, p. 467.
[2] Quoted by J. T. Howard, *Our American Music,* p. 185.

music was not considered a suitable profession. If one did take up music, it should be of the most respectable kind. Stephen Foster aspired to be a writer of sentimental ballads and elegant songs "rendered" by sentimental and elegant young ladies in the most polite society. In his younger days he omitted his name on the title pages of his Ethiopian melodies because he feared the association would injure his reputation as a composer of refined music—he does not actually use the word "refined" but that is the implication of his meaning when he writes that the prejudice against Ethiopian songs might injure his reputation "as a writer of another style of music." Yet in May, 1852, a few months after the publication of "Old Folks at Home," he writes to E. P. Christy saying that he had decided "to pursue the Ethiopian business without fear or shame." That was Stephen Foster's first and greatest spiritual victory: to overcome the fear of not appearing respectable, to fight off the feeling of shame associated with writing the kind of music that everybody liked and sang and whistled and remembered forever.

Yet the fight went on. The forces of respectability would not let him be himself. He had to be continually tilting against the genteel tradition. The *Musical World and Times* of New York, on January 29, 1853, deplored the talented Mr. Foster's propensity for Ethiopian melodies and expressed the hope that he would turn his attention to a higher type of music. More: it informed the public that Mr. Foster had personally given his assurance to the editor that henceforth he intended to devote himself to composing "white men's music." Here, apparently, we have a bit of race prejudice thrown in to enrich the theme of respectability. When Foster made the statement reported above, "My Old Kentucky Home" had just been published. It was to be followed by "Massa's in de Cold Ground," in July, 1852, and by "The Glendy Burk," "Old Black Joe," and "Down Among the Cane Brakes," the last three all published in the same year, 1860. No, fortunately for us and for America's music, Stephen Foster did not abandon the writing of Ethiopian melodies. He turned out a few more glorious songs before succumbing to drink and the genteel tradition.

Early life in Pittsburgh

Stephen Collins Foster was born on July 4, 1826, in "The White Cottage" on his father's farm overlooking the village of Lawrenceville, near Pittsburgh, Pennsylvania. His father, Colonel William Barclay Foster, had moved from eastern Pennsylvania to Pittsburgh when the latter place was little more than a frontier trading post. He became associated with a firm of local merchants and took charge of their river trade, which obliged him to journey down the Ohio and Mississippi Rivers about twice a year. While on a business trip to Philadelphia, Colonel Foster met Eliza Tomlinson, member of a substantial Eastern family, whom he married in 1807. They had ten children, of whom two died in infancy. Stephen grew up with three sisters—one of whom, Charlotte Susanna, died young—and five brothers—one of whom (William) was an adopted child. Stephen himself was next to the youngest in the family.

Colonel William B. Foster became wealthy, but later suffered financial reverses, which in 1826 led to the loss of his property by foreclosure. The family lived for a while in the village of Harmony, and in the autumn of 1832 moved into a new home in the town of Allegheny. Music in the Foster family was encouraged as a form of recreation and as a polite accomplishment for young ladies. Mrs. Foster, who had been raised in Baltimore and was filled with ideas of gentility, was eager to have her daughters receive the benefits of a "polite education," including the accomplishment of playing the piano and singing sentimental ballads. Opportunities for acquiring the "polite arts" were not lacking in Pittsburgh. Charlotte Foster's music teacher was one Williams Evens, who in 1826 issued the following advertisement: [3]

> Wm. Evens, teacher of the French Horn,
> Trumpet, Bugle, Serpent, Bassoon, Clarionet,
> German Flute, Hautboy, Violin,
> Violoncello, and Tenor Viol—
> at Six Dollars per quarter.
> W. E. professes the Andante stile. Those
> who wish to play Concerto's or become
> Prestissimo Players need not apply.
> Tempo Gusto. [*sic*]

Here, indeed, was every guarantee of sedate respectability, even to the exclusion of *tempo rubato!*

This William Evens was a plane maker by trade, but in 1817 he opened a singing school in his shop, and afterward was very active as

---

[3] Quoted by Morneweck, *op. cit.*, vol. 1, p. 30.

a choir leader and teacher in Pittsburgh. He formed a manuscript collection of the works of Bach, Haydn, Handel, and Beethoven, copying them out meticulously by hand and employing in the process, we
are told, gallons of homemade black ink. To his pupils he offered instruction in the music of "the most celebrated modern composers." It
is not true, as some writers have stated, that Stephen Foster grew up
in a musical wilderness. Pianos were by no means unknown in Pittsburgh. Some were transported from the East, some were manufactured
to order, right in the town, by Charles Rosenbaum, as early as 1815.
The Fosters had a piano in their home by 1818; they had to give it up
in 1821, but Brother William, hard-working and prosperous, presented
the family with a new piano in 1828, two years after Stephen's birth.
As his granddaughter writes, "From early childhood, Stephen Foster
was always accustomed to music in the home of his parents and their
friends." The question, of course, is: what kind of music? The answer,
I think, is: many kinds. Popular ballads of the day (that is, currently
popular songs, chiefly of a sentimental type) probably held first place.
Evelyn Foster Morneweck, in her excellent and valuable *Chronicles
of Stephen Foster's Family*, evokes a picture of the little boy Stephen
leaning against the piano "whilst his sisters charmed their admiring
family circle with 'Come Rest in This Bosom'; 'Go, My Love, Like
the Gloom of Night Retiring'; 'Flow on, Thou Shining River'; 'I Have
Loved Thee, Mary'; 'Home, Sweet Home'; 'I'd Be a Butterfly,' and
'Susan in the Valley.' " Among the more than two hundred songs that
Foster was to compose, there were many of this type, and most of
them have been forgotten as completely as most of the songs mentioned above. Undoubtedly, an inescapable portion of Foster's musical
heritage was the genteel tradition of his own family circle. But it was
not the whole heritage. The children used to be delighted by their
father's singing of some jolly old songs, in particular "Good Old
Colony Times," with its tale of three rogues: a miller, a weaver, and
a little tailor.

The Fosters had a colored servant named Olivia Pise, called "Lieve,"
said to be the mulatto daughter of a French dancing master from the
West Indies. As a boy Stephen loved to attend the services in the
Negro church with Lieve and to hear the "shouting" of the people.
Later in life, Stephen told his brother Morrison that two of his songs,
"Oh! Boys, Carry Me 'Long" and "Hard Times Come Again No
More," were based on snatches of Negro melodies that he heard while

attending Negro services as a boy with Olivia Pise. Many other snatches of melody may have remained in his memory and been used unconsciously in his plantation melodies. It is also tempting to speculate on the possibility that Lieve may have sung to him some West Indian songs, like those that the French Negroes brought to Louisiana from Martinique and Saint Domingue.

According to Morrison Foster, when Stephen was two years old, he would lay his sister's guitar on the parlor floor and pick out harmonies on the strings of the instruments. When he was about six, he took up a flageolet—an instrument that he had never before handled—in Smith & Mellor's Music Store, and in a few minutes was playing "Hail, Columbia" with perfect correctness. Soon afterward, his mother bought him a clarinet. There was no question of providing systematic music instruction for the boy: music was not a serious occupation for boys or men in the Foster household. Foster's granddaughter believes that all he knew of musical theory was acquired from an older friend and professional musician of German origin named Henry Kleber, from whom he received some lessons. However, Stephen's earliest composition, *The Tioga Waltz*, written at the age of fourteen when he was attending a school at Athens, near Towanda, was apparently produced before he received any instruction from Kleber. Nor does Stephen appear to have taken advantage of the musical instruction that was offered at Athens Academy. He did not like school, and preferred to follow his own inclinations both in study and in music. There must have been a general feeling in the family that Stephen was devoting too much time to music, for once he wrote to his brother William saying "I will also promise not to pay any attention to my music untill after eight Oclock in the evening." He was lonesome and homesick at Athens and in 1841 returned home, somewhat to the distress of his father, who wrote: "He is a very good boy, but I cannot get him to stick at school. He reads a good deal, and writes some in the office with me." William B. Foster was then mayor of Allegheny.

Sometime in 1843, probably after passing his sixteenth birthday, Stephen set to music a poem by George Pope Morris titled "Open Thy Lattice, Love," which was published in the following year by George Willig of Philadelphia. This was his first published song. It was as pretty and polite as anyone could wish. On the back of the original manuscript of this song, Stephen wrote a little waltz for piano, "Dedicated to Miss Maria Bach"—we do not know who she was.

Foster and Negro minstrelsy

But neither the pretty song nor the conventional waltz were indicative of the main road that Stephen Foster was to take as a composer. For an indication of this we must go back to another aspect of his boyhood. Stephen Foster had a keen feeling for fun, a talent for comedy, and a love for lively, zestful song. He and his brothers, together with neighborhood youngsters, formed a "Thespian Company" for the performance of plantation melodies, the popular blackface songs of the 1830s mentioned in the previous chapter: "Coal Black Rose," "Long Tail Blue," "Jim Crow," and "Zip Coon." Stephen was the star performer of the company; his brother writes that his performance was so inimitable and true to nature that he was greeted with uproarious applause and called back again and again. Later the boys made the acquaintance of the celebrated clown Dan Rice, who in 1843 wrote to Morrison Foster: "I am making money pretty fast. . . . A Bout twenty five dollors A Weeke. I am clowning an also my nigero singing an Dancing is drawing good houses." [4] Stephen doubtless thought Rice's spelling was pretty bad, but he was probably intrigued by the "nigero singing." The reader will recall that this was the year, 1843, in which the first organized minstrels shows made their appearance. The result was to be decisive for the budding songwriter Stephen Foster.

About this time Stephen obtained a position in a Pittsburgh warehouse, checking cotton bales as they were rolled up from the steamboat wharf to the building. The work was done by Negro roustabouts who sang cheerfully at their task. We may be sure that Stephen kept his ears open. It may be that the river, and the men who worked on it, were his best music teachers. Echoes not only of his churchgoing experiences with Lieve, but also of the singing of the Negro roustabouts, mingled with the currently popular plantation melodies, must have been in Stephen's mind when, in the year 1845, he began to compose his first Ethiopian songs. In Morrison Foster's biography of his brother, the origin of these songs is described as follows:

In 1845, a club of young men, friends of his, met twice a week at our house to practice songs in harmony under his leadership. . . . At that time, Negro melodies were very popular. After we had sung over

[4] Morneweck, *op. cit.*, vol. 1, p. 265.

and over again all the songs then in favor, he proposed that he would try and make some for us himself. His first effort was called *The Louisiana Belle*. A week after this, he produced the famous song of *Old Uncle Ned*. . . . At the time he wrote "His fingers were long like de cane in de brake," he had never seen a canebrake, nor even been below the mouth of the Ohio river, but the appropriateness of the simile instantly strikes everyone who has travelled down the Mississippi.

In these songs Stephen followed his usual practice of writing both the words and the melody himself.

Around 1845 Stephen's brother Dunning established himself in business in Cincinnati under the firm name of Irwin & Foster. Either late in 1846 or early the following year Stephen went to Cincinnati to work as a bookkeeper in his brother's office, which was near the largest steamboat landing in the city. He frequented the music store of Peters & Field, of which one of the partners was William C. Peters of Pittsburgh, who published some of Stephen's earliest songs. He met William Roarke, member of a minstrel troupe known as the Sable Harmonists, who introduced his song "Old Uncle Ned" in one of their programs. This was probably Stephen's first professional contact with the minstrel stage.

In September, 1847, the proprietors of The Eagle Saloon in Pittsburgh organized a musical contest for the best Ethiopian melody. Stephen submitted a lively little song called "Away Down Souf," which has a curious geographical juxtaposition in the chorus:

> No use talkin' when de darky wants to go
> Whar de corntop blossom and de canebrake grow;
> Den come along to Cuba, and we'll dance de polka-juba,
>   Way down souf, whar de corn grow.

Stephen's song "Away Down Souf" did not win the silver Prize Cup. But Nelson Kneass, musical director of The Eagle Saloon, wrote it down and tried to copyright it under his own name the next day! This Kneass, incidentally, was the author of "Ben Bolt," one of those moribund songs that refuses to die. On September 11, 1847, The Eagle Saloon announced a Grand Gala Concert which featured:

SUSANNA—A new song, never before given to the public.

Once "given to the public"—and, one might say, given to the publishers, because Stephen got only a hundred dollars for it—"Susanna" took the country by storm. Before long, the "forty-niners" had carried it all the way to California. Stephen sold the song to Peters, who had it copyrighted on December 30, 1848. Meanwhile, a pirated edition was issued in New York and copyrighted in February of the same year. Such piratings and copyright imbroglios were not uncommon in those days. Small as was the sum he received, Stephen was pleased at getting paid for his work. He wrote to Robert Nevin:

> Imagine my delight in receiving one hundred dollars in cash! Though this song was not successful, yet the two fifty-dollar bills I received for it had the effect of starting me on my present vocation of song-writer.

Stephen was wrong about the success of his song: Peters made more than ten thousand dollars from it and from "Old Uncle Ned." Within a year both songs were being featured by minstrel troupes throughout the country. Another song of this period, featured by the Sable Harmonists, titled "Way Down South in Alabama," was recently discovered to have been composed by Foster, though the published version was arranged by Frank Spencer.

In spite of the success of these plantation melodies, Stephen felt that he should be composing music of a more genteel character, suitable for the parlor rather than the stage. He turned out a piano piece called *Santa Anna's Retreat from Buena Vista*, full of elegant pianistic effects. Immediately afterward he wrote "Nelly Was a Lady," one of his delightfully simple and effective plantation melodies, with much of that plaintive quality that was to endear his songs to millions of people. Yet Stephen was ashamed of it, called it a "miserable thing," told his brother to take "10$, 5$ or even 1$ for it," and ended by giving all the rights to Firth, Pond & Co., in return for fifty copies of the printed music. He did the same thing with another "darky" song, "My Brudder Gum," and the only benefit he received from this transaction was that it led to signing a contract, in the autumn of 1849, with Firth, Pond & Co., leading music publishers of New York, who brought out most of his songs for the next ten years. The signing of this contract was doubtless one of the major factors that caused Stephen to abandon bookkeeping in favor of a musical career. He was encouraged to believe that he could earn a living as a writer of songs.

Returning to his family's home in Pittsburgh, Stephen began to court Jane McDowell, the daughter of a prominent neighbor, with whom he had fallen in love while she was visiting in Cincinnati. On June 22, 1850, Stephen and Jane were married. His financial assets as a married man had been augmented by the writing and publication of "Dolcy Jones," "Summer Longings," "Oh! Lemuel!", "Mary Loves the Flowers," "Soiree Polka," "Camptown Races," "Dolly Day," "Angelina Baker," "Ah! May the Red Rose Live Alway," "Way Down in Cairo," "Molly! Do You Love Me?", and "The Voice of Bygone Days." Of these, the one that turned out to be most successful was "Camptown Races"—at least from the standpoint of fame and popularity. Financially it did not prove to be a best seller, for in seven years it brought Foster only $101.25 in royalties, representing a sale of some 5,000 copies over that period. This was a bonanza, however, in comparison with "Angelina Baker," which in the same seven-year period earned for the composer a total of $16.87!

Let it be noticed that of the songs listed above, half were plantation melodies. Stephen was determined to use the minstrel stage to forward his career as a songwriter. On February 23, 1850, he wrote to E. P. Christy, leader of the famed Christy Minstrels, sending him copies of "Camptown Races" and "Dolly Day," and saying, "I wish to unite with you in every effort to encourage a taste for this style of music so cried down by opera mongers." Stephen was now composing at a great rate. In July, 1851, he rented an office, where he could work without interruption, and installed a piano in it. By this time he had a baby girl, as well as a wife, to support. He was trying to be as businesslike as possible.

It was in the summer of 1851 that Stephen composed the most famous of all his songs, "Old Folks at Home." According to his brother Morrison's account, Stephen asked him, "What is a good name of two syllables for a southern river? I want to use it in this new song, *Old Folks at Home*." With a laugh, Morrison answered, "How would Yazoo do?" referring to a current comic song called "Down on the Old Yazoo." Stephen replied, "Oh, that's been used before," and they both started looking for a suitable river in an atlas that Morrison had on his desk. They hit on Suwannee, a river flowing from Georgia through Florida to the Gulf of Mexico. Stephen, delighted, crossed out the name "Pedee," which he had originally written, and substituted the more euphonious "Suwannee," merely simplifying it to "Swanee"—thus producing the familiar opening line of his song, "Way down upon the Swanee River."

Foster made an arrangement with Christy whereby the latter would have "first performance" rights on his new songs, in advance of publication, in return for a payment of ten dollars on each song. In the case of "Old Folks at Home" this payment was increased to fifteen dollars. Moreover, Stephen agreed to let Christy's name appear on the title page as the composer of this song. It was a foolish thing to do, and Stephen soon realized his mistake, for on May 25, 1852, he wrote a significant letter to Christy, parts of which have already been quoted in this chapter, and which is important enough to reproduce in full: [5]

E. P. Christy, Esq.
Dear Sir:

As I once intimated to you, I had the intention of omitting my name on my Ethiopian songs, owing to a prejudice against them by some, which might injure my reputation as a writer of another style of music, but I find that by my efforts I have done a great deal to build up a taste for the Ethiopian songs among refined people by making the words suitable to their taste, instead of the trashy and really offensive words which belong to some songs of that order. Therefore I have concluded to reinstate my name on my songs and to pursue the Ethiopian business without fear or shame and lend all my energies to making the business *live*, at the same time that I will wish to establish my name as the best Ethiopian song-writer. But I am not encouraged in undertaking this so long as "The Old Folks at Home" stares me in the face with another's name on it. As it was at my own solicitation that you allowed your name to be placed on the song, I hope that the above reasons will be sufficient explanation for my desire to place my own name on it as author and composer, while at the same time I wish to leave the name of your band on the title page. This is a little matter of pride in myself which it will certainly be to your interest to encourage. On the receipt of your free consent to this proposition, I will if you wish, willingly refund you the money which you paid me on that song, though it may have been sent me for other considerations than the one in question, and I promise in addition to write you an opening chorus in my best style, free of charge, and in any other way in my power to advance your interests

[5] Morneweck, *op. cit.*, vol. 2, pp. 395ff.

hereafter. I find I cannot write at all unless I write for public appro-
bation and get credit for what I write. As we may probably have a
good deal of business with each other in our lives, it is best to proceed on a sure basis of confidence and good understanding, therefore
I hope you will appreciate an author's feelings in the case and deal
with me with your usual fairness. Please answer immediately.

Very respectfully yours,

Stephen C. Foster

According to Morrison Foster, who must have had the information
from Stephen himself, Christy paid $500 for the privilege of placing
his name as author on the title page of "Old Folks at Home." Christy
refused to accede to Foster's request. In fact, on the back of Stephen's
letter the celebrated minstrel performer wrote down his opinion of the
composer as "a vacillating skunk"! Royalties on the song were paid
to Stephen, but for the rest of his life he suffered the humiliation of
seeing his most famous song appear with the name of another man
as author and composer. Not until the copyright was renewed in 1879
did Stephen C. Foster's name appear as the composer of "Old Folks
at Home."

In February, 1852, Stephen and Jane and a party of friends took a
trip to New Orleans on the steamboat *James Milligan*, of which
Stephen's brother Dunning was captain. They were away for a month.
This was Stephen's only trip to the deep South.

In that year, 1852, Stephen wrote two of his best-known plantation
melodies, "Massa's in de Cold Ground" and "My Old Kentucky Home,
Good Night." There is a legend, without foundation in fact, that the
latter song was written at Federal Hill, the home of the Rowan family
in Bardstown, Kentucky. Stephen wrote the first draft of his song as
"Poor Uncle Tom, Good Night," evidently influenced by the vogue of
Harriet Beecher Stowe's *Uncle Tom's Cabin*, published in 1851–1852.
Later he changed it to its present form, doubtless thinking that there
were enough Uncle Toms on the market already. It is also interesting
to note that in the first draft, the Uncle Tom version, Stephen used
Negro dialect, as he had in his other "darky" songs; but in the revised
version he dropped the dialect, and "My Old Kentucky Home" is
written in ordinary English. Stephen's taste guided him wisely in this,
for the absence of dialect doubtless adds to the universal appeal of the
song. He followed the same practice in "Old Black Joe," the last of his
great plantation melodies, written in 1860.

The last years

Stephen's marriage was not running smoothly. Quarrels grew more frequent, and in May, 1853, Jane left Stephen, taking baby Marion with her. Stephen went off to New York, but within the year he and Jane were reconciled and began living together again. Their troubles, however, were not over. Stephen's financial situation was not flourishing. John Tasker Howard has calculated that from 1849 to 1857 his average yearly income from royalties was $1425.84, enough for the small family to live on with careful management. But Stephen was not a good manager. He was in debt and overdrawn at his publishers. In 1857, therefore, he sold out all his future rights in the songs published by Firth, Pond & Co., for the sum of $1872.28. He also sold the complete rights to sixteen other songs (including "Camptown Races") to F. D. Benteen for $200. He thus raised immediate cash, but forfeited the future income from royalties, upon which he depended for a living. This, in turn, put him under the necessity of continuing to produce at a rapid rate, regardless of quality or inspiration, in order always to have something to sell. If Stephen Foster had been a good showman and self-promoter like Henry Russell, if he had gone on the stage and presented his own songs in person, surrounded with unlimited ballyhoo, he doubtless would have made money. But as a mere writer of songs he was doomed to an unequal struggle and a losing battle. The performers and the publishers were the ones who made the money.

In 1860 Stephen moved to New York with his wife and daughter. By this time he had practically ceased to write the plantation melodies that were his true vein. "Old Black Joe," "The Glendy Burk," and "Down Among the Cane Brakes" were published in 1860, but these were the last of their kind. Of far different character were the other songs that Foster submitted to his publishers in that year: "Poor Drooping Maiden," "None Shall Weep a Tear for Me," "The Wife; or He'll Come Home," and "Under the Willow She's Weeping." In spite of potboilers, he continued to be seriously overdrawn at Firth, Pond & Co., and was trying to make contracts with other publishers in a desperate effort to improve his situation.

Stephen by this time was drinking heavily. Jane left him in the summer of 1861, though she visited him that September and continued to be anxious about his welfare. They were together again in 1862, but the following year found Jane working as a telegraph operator at Greensburgh, Pennsylvania. Meanwhile, Stephen's relations with Firth, Pond & Co. had deteriorated. His latest songs were not making money. Firth, Pond, refused to take his song, "Our Bright, Bright Summer Days are Gone"; so Stephen gave it to his friend John Mahon, told him to submit it to another publisher, "and take what he will give you." Stephen Foster was reduced to a mere peddler.

After 1862 Stephen Foster was a defeated man. America's greatest songwriter was transformed into a slovenly alcoholic, an ailing and penurious hack. He turned out potboilers at a furious rate: forty-six songs in one year! And only once did any of these songs reveal a gleam of inspiration: "Beautiful Dreamer, Wake Unto Me," composed in 1863. Incidentally, this was not, as William Pond claimed, the "last song" written by Foster before his death.

In New York Stephen lived at the New England Hotel, on the corner of Bayard Street and the Bowery. There, on January 9, 1864, he went to bed ill and weak with fever. The next morning, when he tried to get a drink of water, he fell against the washbowl and cut a severe gash in his face and neck. When his friend George Cooper arrived in response to an emergency call, Stephen gasped, "I'm done for." Cooper took him to Bellevue Hospital and sent a telegram to Henry Foster telling him that his brother Stephen was very sick and wished to see him. He also wrote a letter to Morrison Foster with the same message, adding, "He desires me to ask you to send him some pecuniary assistance as his means are very low."

For a while Stephen seemed to rally, but on Wednesday afternoon he fainted and did not regain consciousness. He died at half past two o'clock on the afternoon of January 13, 1864. No friend or relative was at his bedside. The next day George Cooper telegraphed to Henry and Morrison: "Stephen is dead. Come on."

On January 21, 1864, while an orchestra played "Come Where My Love Lies Dreaming," the remains of Stephen Collins Foster were interred in Allegheny Cemetery, Pittsburgh. His grave is marked by a simple marble tombstone. In Pittsburgh's Highland Park a statue was erected to his memory. There are two figures in the sculptured group: one is that of the composer, seated and writing down a song; the other is that of a Negro strumming a banjo.

A summing-up

Stephen Foster's music may be described as a product of the urbanized frontier. Had he been raised in Boston, New York, or Philadelphia, he would have grown up hearing concerts of music "by the
most celebrated European composers"; he would have heard operas,
oratorios, symphonies, concertos, and he might have been tempted to
try to become a composer in the grand style. He would, in any case,
have been entirely an urban, that is to say, a thoroughly Europeanized
product, completely cut off from the frontier. In Pittsburgh, and in
Cincinnati, he had contact with the frontier, he became a part of the
process of Americanization achieved by the frontier. Yet his environment was that of the *urbanized* frontier, which was rapidly ceasing to
be a frontier at all as the cities of the then West became more and
more Europeanized, aspiring to cultivate the "polite arts" in the same
degree as the older cities of the Atlantic seaboard. Stephen Foster's
wide appeal lies largely in this cultural dualism of his background,
through which he was able to combine the vitality of the frontier and a
certain element of primitive simplicity with the genteel tradition of
the urban fringe, dominated by sentimentality, conventionalism, and
propriety.

To appreciate Stephen Foster's musical output in relation to the
cultural context in which it was produced, one needs to go through
all of his more than two hundred songs in their original or at least contemporary sheet-music editions, or in nineteenth-century songbooks
like *The Love and Sentimental Songster* or *The American Dime Song
Book,* to see their illustrated covers with portraits of sentimental maid-
ens and lovers in stilted romantic attitudes, and to realize the overwhelming proportion of merely "pretty" songs that he turned out for
the genteel trade. Stephen Foster's preeminence as an American song-
writer rests upon some dozen songs, to which may be added another
dozen of lesser fame but of evident superiority to the rest of his output or to that of his contemporaries. The "big four" among Foster's
songs, the pillars of his universal fame, are "Old Folks at Home," "My
Old Kentucky Home," "Massa's in de Cold Ground," and "Old Black
Joe." Now, these are not the songs that are closest either to the roots
of Negro folksong or to the prevailing style of blackface minstrelsy.
Neither are they the closest to the genteel tradition of the European-

ized urban fringe. In terms of Foster's songs, they stand midway between "Oh! Susanna" or "Camptown Races" and "Come Where My Love Lies Dreaming" or "Wilt Thou Be Gone, Love?" In three of the "big four," the Negro dialect has been eliminated, and in the fourth, "Massa's in de Cold Ground" it is somewhat attenuated. Foster himself stated that he intended to make the minstrel melodies or Ethiopian songs palatable to refined tastes, and this is part of the cleaning-up process. Musically, these four songs are in slow tempo: *Moderato con espressione, Poco adagio, Poco lento*, and again *Poco adagio* for "Old Black Joe." Above all, *"con espressione"!*—that is an indispensable requirement of the genteel tradition. Compare, for example, such an old-time minstrel song as "Long Time Ago" with "Old Folks at Home." The former is really rooted in popular tradition: it is marked Allegro, and the minstrels have their way with it as a comic song. As we saw in the previous chapter, Morris and Horn made a sentimental song out of "Long Time Ago." Their concoction strikes us as ludicrous now because it leans so obviously on a faded tradition. Foster wrote plenty of sentimental songs that seem equally ludicrous—one need only mention "Willie We Have Missed You" as an example. But he was not, like Charles Horn, a hopeless victim of the genteel tradition. Like the Ohio and the Missouri flowing into the Mississippi, two traditions converged in the broad stream of Stephen Foster's best music. It is this that gives him his unique position and significance in American music. How thoroughly he was master of both traditions is proved by the fact that he excelled in the pure minstrel song, he excelled in the sentimental ballad, and he excelled in the combination of both types: the blending of simplicity and pathos with expression and refinement that marks his most famous and most beloved songs.

Stephen Foster's songs may be divided into two broad categories: minstrel songs and nonminstrel songs. Under the latter there are some minor subdivisions, such as religious songs and war songs, which have slight value if any. The best of Foster's Civil War songs is probably "We Are Coming Father Abraham, 300,000 More," published in 1862. As for the "Ethiopian" productions, they fall into two groups: the comic songs and the sentimental songs, the latter represented chiefly by the "big four" already mentioned. Let us glance more closely at a song in each of these groups.

"Oh! Susanna" is a typical example of the comic or nonsense minstrel song. The music consists of four nearly identical periods, each divided into two phrases to correspond with the eight lines of the verse. The same period is used for the last two lines of the chorus, so that the only new material occurs in the first portion of the chorus, which also contains the one instance of syncopation, on the word "Susanna." Having said that the melodic periods are nearly identical, it remains merely to remark that the only difference lies in a slight melodic variation of the second phrase. The first period leads to a semicadence on the dominant, the second to a full cadence. The second phrase of the chorus, "do not cry for me," has exactly the same melodic and metrical pattern as the last phrase of the first line. This unity through repetition, with only slight but effective contrasts, is characteristic of Foster's songs. Harold Vincent Milligan, remarking on this trait, wrote: "The repetitiousness of Foster's melodies is such that one cannot fail to wonder that they exert such an influence upon the listener as they do." [6] But, being such good tunes to begin with, it is precisely through this repetitiousness that they make their unfailing effect. And this, in turn, makes the variation doubly effective when it does occur.

"Old Folks at Home" may be taken as an example of the sentimental plantation melody constructed on the same simple basis. As in the case of "Oh! Susanna," the first introduction of new melodic material occurs in the first two lines of the chorus, and again this is followed by a repetition of the main melody. Again we have four successive repetitions of the principal melody, ending twice on a semicadence and twice on a full cadence. Very characteristic is the rhythmical "snap" which dislocates the accent on words having normally a feminine ending, such as "ribber," "ebber," "plantation," and "weary." Except for the first part of the chorus, the melody of "Old Folks at Home" uses only the five tones of the pentatonic scale.

While recognizing the element of repetition in Foster's melodies, we should nevertheless bear in mind that slight metrical variations in the melody were, in some cases, introduced for different stanzas, as shown by the original editions. For instance, in the original edition of "Old Folks at Home," published by Firth, Pond & Co. in 1851, the following metrical variants occur for the second and third stanzas of the song:

[6] Milligan, *Stephen Collins Foster*, p. 113.

As regards harmony, Foster stays pretty close to the tonic, dominant, and subdominant. A rare example of the use of secondary chords
is to be found in the song "Ah! May the Red Rose Live Alway."
Modulations are very scarce and confined chiefly to the dominant key,
as in "My Old Kentucky Home" and "Old Black Joe."

Among Foster's nonminstrel songs, the best known is, of course,
"Jeanie with the Light Brown Hair." It seems that in his original
manuscript book Foster wrote the name as "Jennie," definitely indicating that he had his wife Jane in mind, for she was often affection-
ately addressed as Jennie. But the publishers preferred "Jeanie" and
brought the song out with this name. "Jeanie" has not always been
so popular. After the composer's death, when the copyright was renewed for the benefit of his widow and daughter, they received, for
a nineteen-year period, accumulated royalties of 75 cents! Only fifteen copies had been sold.

We have already observed, according to the dictum of Marius
Schneider, that the popularity of a melody depends partly on its
degree of simplicity and partly on its conformity "to the melodic
type current in a given culture." The melodies of Stephen Foster ful-
fill these conditions in the highest degree. Simplicity is the essence
of his music. His songs conform to melodic types widely current in
American folklore. These melodic types and their basic harmonic patterns, in turn, are deeply rooted in age-old folk traditions inherited
from Anglo-Celtic civilization transplanted to America. These factors
contribute to make Stephen Collins Foster the most beloved composer
whom America has produced.

chapter fifteen

The exotic periphery

Existence in a tropical wilderness, in the midst of a voluptuous and half-civilized race, bears no resemblance to that of a London cockney, a Parisian lounger, or an American Quaker.

L. M. GOTTSCHALK, NOTES OF A PIANIST.

In the 1820s, somewhat more than two decades after the Louisiana Purchase, there arrived in the turbulent and colorful city of New Orleans a young Englishman from London named Edward Gottschalk. He had studied medicine at Leipzig, but after emigrating to America in his twenty-fifth year he became a successful broker. Handsome, cultured, and affluent, he was admitted to the best Creole society—that is, the old French and Spanish families—of New Orleans, and in this aristocratic milieu he met, and fell in love with, a young girl of exceptional charm and beauty, Aimée Marie de Bruslé. Her grandfather had been governor of the northern province of the French colony of Saint-Domingue, one of the wealthiest and most luxurious colonies of the New World until its prosperity was shattered by war and civil strife. In that troubled period, Mlle. de Bruslé's father, an army officer, fled to Jamaica, where he married a lady of French and Spanish noble birth. Soon afterward, like many other refugees from the West Indies, they settled in New Orleans, a city congenial to them because of its gay social life and its mixed heritage of French and Spanish culture.

Founded by the Sieur de Bienville in 1718, New Orleans soon became a city of strong contrasts, ranging from the most refined elegance to the most unbridled depravity. While the French royal governor, the Marquis de Vaudreuil, busied himself with creating a little Versailles on the Mississippi and organizing grand balls with court dress *de rigueur*, he at the same time fostered gross corruption and nepotism, while his official laxity made the provincial capital an open

301

city for thieves, prostitutes, gamblers, and lawless adventurers of every description. Negro slaves were brought from Africa in considerable numbers (later they came mostly from the West Indies) and in 1724 the original "Black Code" was promulgated for the regulation of Negroes in Louisiana. It prohibited any mingling of the races, black and white, either through marriage or concubinage, regardless of whether the Negroes were free or slave. To manumitted slaves it granted "the same rights, privileges, and immunities which are enjoyed by free-born persons." This was the basis of the code adopted by the Louisiana legislature after the territory became a part of the United States.

In 1762, by a secret treaty, France ceded Louisiana to Spain, whose colonial empire already included vast sections of what is now the United States, from Florida to California. Not until 1769 did Don Alexander O'Reilly arrive in New Orleans to take possession of the city and the province in the name of the Spanish King. New Orleans then became a Spanish colonial city, with its *cabildo*, its *regidores*, its *alcaldes*. In spite of two disastrous fires, the city grew and prospered under the Spanish regime; in fact, the fires may have done some good, for as a result the Spaniards rebuilt most of the city, thus giving rise to the local saying that they found "a town of hovels and left it a city of palaces."

In 1800 Spain retroceded Louisiana to France, but before the French authorities could take effective possession, the territory was purchased by the United States, and in 1803 New Orleans became officially an American city. Essentially it remained an exotic city within the borders of the United States. The son born to Edward Gottschalk and his Creole wife on May 8, 1829, an American citizen by reason of the Louisiana Purchase, was to become and remain an exotic personality within his native country; and, like the city of his birth, he acted as a link between the progressive, practical civilization of the expanding United States, and the seductive, colorful civilization of Latin America. Louis Moreau Gottschalk—he was named after his mother's uncle, Moreau de l'Islet—whether he lived in Paris or New York, never forgot that he was a child of the tropics; and what we value in his music today is not the glitter of the concert hall or the sophistication of the salon, but the alluring charm of his Caribbean rhythms and melodies.

"Caribbean" is perhaps the best word to describe the musical atmosphere of New Orleans in which Louis Moreau Gottschalk spent his boyhood. I do not, of course, refer to the world of French opera as performed at the Théâtre d'Orléans, attended by fashionable audiences in full dress. Gottschalk knew this world of "cultivated" music, both at home and during his years of study in Europe. What I refer to is that exotic, unconventional, hybrid, exciting blend of musical elements, the product of complex racial and cultural factors in a new society evolving under strange conditions, which finds its most characteristic expression in the Caribbean area. There was an influx of population from the islands of the Caribbean to New Orleans. Negro slaves were brought from the West Indies, but many other persons, both white and colored, came to the city on the Mississippi as refugees from the terrors of revolution in Haiti, or to escape the international strife that afflicted the Caribbean area. In 1809 and 1810, more than ten thousand refugees from the West Indies arrived in New Orleans, most of them originally from Saint-Domingue (or Haiti, as the former French colony was called after it became independent in 1804). Of these, about three thousand were free Negroes, or rather "persons of color," for their racial composition varied greatly. In order to understand the racial background of this emigration, it will be helpful to glance at a breakdown of the population in the French colony of Saint-Domingue in the year 1789:

White 30,826   Free Negroes and Mulattoes 27,548   Slaves 465,429

To be noted in particular are (1) the overwhelming majority of Negro slaves, and (2) the large proportion of free "persons of color." It was the coming of the latter class to New Orleans that gave the city, in large part, its peculiar social structure. The mulatto women—called quadroons or octoroons, according to the proportion of white blood in their veins—were famous for their seductive beauty, as well as for their gay and attractive dress. The gentlemen of Louisiana flocked to the celebrated Quadroon Balls not merely to dance and admire but also to select the mistress of their choice. The free men of color could gain admittance to these balls only in the capacity of musician, to fiddle for the dancers. Thus it was that the "f.m.c."—free male of color—frequently turned to music as a profession; if such it could be called, for the dance musician was little more than a menial.

The persons of color, *gens de couleur*, having even a single drop of white blood, were a class apart from the blacks, the Negroes. Even within the *gens de couleur* there were rigid caste distinctions, according to the proportion of white blood. It might be unnecessary to dwell on this subject, were it not for the importance of the caste-and-color system in New Orleans for the future development of American music, particularly with relation to the origin and growth of jazz. Furthermore, these distinctions have led to a curious confusion in the use of the term "Creole." This word is the French equivalent of the Spanish *criollo*, which was used from early colonial times to designate a person of European parentage born in America. It was during the Spanish regime that this term came into usage in Louisiana. As a noun the term was always applied to white persons of European ancestry, born in the New World. But as an adjective, it was applied also to Negroes born in the New World, as opposed to those brought from Africa. It was also applied to the dialect, or patois, spoken by these Negroes, which was a strongly corrupted variety of French. Hence in popular speech the term "Creole" became associated with Louisiana Negro dialect, songs, customs, and dances. Later the octoroons of New Orleans began to be called Creoles, which added to the confusion. In short, the term "Creole" has become so laden with conflicting connotations that it can be used only when hedged around with definitions.

New Orleans had three colorful, exotic dance rituals that all visitors wanted to see: the Quadroon Balls, the voodoo ceremonial dances, and the dances of the Negroes in Place Congo, or Congo Square. The cult of voodoo (more correctly, *vodoun*) is a form of African religion involving ritualistic drumming and dancing to induce "possession" by the *loa* or supernatural spirits. Because one of the leading deities of the cult is Damballa, the serpent god, voodooism is popularly associated with snake worship. Voodoo probably existed in Louisiana from the earliest colonial period, but it received a marked impetus from the influx of West Indian refugees from 1809 to 1810, for the cult flourished primarily among the free "persons of color." Although basically African in origin, voodoo became mixed with Roman Catholic elements, and therefore, like most Caribbean cultural manifestations, was a hybrid product. In New Orleans the principal public voodoo ceremonies took place on St. John's Eve (June 23) and attracted a multitude of spectators. But there were also secret ceremonies that few if any outsiders ever witnessed. George W. Cable described voodoo dances in New Orleans with a great show of moral indignation and the vividness of an eyewitness:

. . . the voodoo dance begins. The postulant dances frantically in the middle of the ring, only pausing, from time to time, to receive heavy alcoholic draughts in great haste and return more wildly to his leapings and writhings until he falls in convulsions. He is lifted, restored, and presently conducted to the altar, takes his oath, and by a ceremonial stroke from one of the sovereigns is admitted a full participant. . . . But the dance goes on about the snake. The contortions of the upper part of the body, especially of the neck and shoulders, are such as to threaten to dislocate them. The queen shakes the box and tinkles the bells, the rum bottle gurgles, the chant alternates between king and chorus:

> Eh! Eh! Bomba hon, honc!
> Canga bafio tay,
> Canga moon day lay,
> Canga do keelah,
> Canga li!

There are swoonings and ravings, nervous tremblings beyond control, incessant writhings and turnings, tearing of garments, even biting of the flesh—every imaginable invention of the devil.[1]

That gifted writer Lafcadio Hearn, whose book on the West Indies might well serve as background for this chapter, became interested in the music of the Louisiana Negroes, and at one time conceived the idea of writing a book on the subject in collaboration with the music critic H. E. Krehbiel. According to the latter, Hearn proposed to relate the migrations of African music through the ages: "Then I would touch upon the transplantation of Negro melody to the Antilles and the two Americas, where its strangest black flowers are gathered by the alchemists of musical science and the perfume thereof extracted by magicians like Gottschalk." [2]

Dancing in Congo Square

But in Gottschalk's time "the alchemists of musical science" (today more prosaically called comparative musicologists) were not yet busy gathering the "strange black flowers" of Negro music; so Gottschalk had to gather the flowers himself as well as extract the per-

[1] Cable, *The Century Magazine*, Apr. 1886.
[2] Krehbiel, *Afro-American Folksongs*, p. 39.

fume thereof. The question is, under what circumstances did he do it? In his entertaining book on the New Orleans underworld, *The French Quarter*, Herbert Asbury asserts in a footnote: "Louis Moreau Gottschalk . . . based one of his best known compositions, *La Bamboula*, on what he heard and saw in Congo Square as a boy." Now, it is true that the bamboula was one of the Negro dances that could be seen and heard (it was also a song) in Congo Square when Gottschalk was a boy in New Orleans. Whether the boy Moreau—as his family called him—was ever taken to see the dances in Congo Square is a matter of conjecture. But before we attempt to bring him to this exciting spectacle, let us first bring him out of the cradle, where we left him some time ago.

Louis Moreau Gottschalk took only three years to progress from the cradle to the piano. Such, at least, is the family tradition. According to his sister, when Moreau was three years old, one day everyone in the family was startled by a faint but most exquisite melody on the piano. "The tone and touch were perfect." When Mamma rushed into the drawing room, "she found little Moreau standing on a high stool, playing the melody she had sung to him in the morning." After that, Papa lost no time arranging for his small son to take music lessons. He studied both piano and violin, but the piano was his instrument. At the age of eight he gave his first public concert, a benefit for his violin teacher Miolan. Shortly before his twelfth birthday, his father decided to send him to Europe for further study. In May, 1842, after giving a farewell concert, young Moreau sailed for France and was placed in a private school in Paris. Three years later, while convalescing from an attack of typhoid fever in the French provinces, he composed the piano piece that was to become so popular everywhere, *La Bamboula.*

If Gottschalk based that composition on "what he heard and saw in Congo Square," then it is obvious that he must have been taken to see the dancing there before his departure for Europe. Assuming that the sheltered child was taken there, perhaps by a Negro nurse if not by his parents, what would he have seen and heard? Firsthand accounts are lacking, but George W. Cable, in his article *The Dance in Place Congo,* published in 1886, seems to have reconstructed the scene with considerable authenticity. The following is extracted from his article.

The booming of African drums and blast of huge wooden horns called to the gathering. . . . The drums were very long, hollowed, often from a single piece of wood, open at one end and having a sheep or goat skin stretched across the other. . . . The smaller drum was often made from a joint or two of very large bamboo . . . and this is said to be the origin of its name; for it was called the Bamboula.

The drummers bestrode the drums; the other musicians sat about them in an arc, cross-legged on the ground. One important instrument was a gourd partly filled with pebbles or grains of corn, flourished violently at the end of a stout staff with one hand and beaten upon the palm of the other. Other performers rang triangles, and others twanged from jew's-harps an astonishing amount of sound. Another instrument was the jawbone of some ox, horse or mule, and a key rattled rhythmically along its weatherbeaten teeth. . . . But the grand instrument at last, was the banjo. It had but four strings, not six. . . .

And then there was that long-drawn human cry of tremendous volume, richness, and resound, to which no instruments within their reach could make the faintest approach:

Eh! pou' la belle Layotte ma mourri 'nocent,
    Oui 'nocent ma mourri!

All the instruments silent while it rises and swells with mighty energy and dies away distantly, "yea-a-a-a-a!"—and then the crash of savage drums, horns, and rattles.

Cable then goes on to describe the dancing of the bamboula:

The singers almost at the first note are many. At the end of the first line every voice is lifted up. The strain is given the second time with growing spirit. Yonder glistening black Hercules, who plants one foot forward, lifts his head and bare, shining chest, rolls out the song from a mouth and throat like a cavern. . . . See his play of restrained enthusiasm catch from one bystander to another. They swing and bow to right and left, in slow time to the piercing treble of the Congo women. . . . Hear that bare foot slap the ground! one sudden stroke only. . . . The musicians warm up at the sound.

A smiting of breasts with open hands begins very softly and becomes vigorous. The women's voices rise to a tremulous intensity. . . . The women clap their hands in time, or standing with arms akimbo receive with faint courtesies and head-liftings the low bows of the men, who deliver them swinging this way and that.

See! Yonder brisk and sinewy fellow has taken one short, nervy step into the ring, chanting with rising energy. . . . He moves off to the farther edge of the circle, still singing, takes the prompt hand of an unsmiling Congo girl, leads her into the ring, and leaving the chant to the throng, stands before her for the dance. . . . A sudden frenzy seizes the musicians. The measure quickens, the swaying, attitudinizing crowd starts into extra activity, the female voices grow sharp and staccato, and suddenly the dance is the furious Bamboula.

Now for the frantic leaps! Now for frenzy! Another pair are in the ring. The man wears a belt of little bells, or, as a substitute, little tin vials of shot, "bram-bram sonnette!" And still another couple enter the circle. What wild—what terrible delight! The ecstasy rises to madness; one—two—three of the dancers fall—*bloucoutoum! boum!*—with foam on their lips and are dragged out by arms and legs from under tumultuous feet of crowding new-comers. The musicians know no fatigue; still the dance rages on:

Quand patate la cuite na va mangé li!
("When that 'tater's cooked don't you eat it up!")

Quand pa - tate la cuite na va man - gé
li, na va man - gé na va man - gé li!
Fine

For Cable, the bamboula represented "a frightful triumph of body over the mind," and he adds: "Only the music deserved to survive, and does survive. . . . The one just given, Gottschalk first drew from oblivion." The second musical example quoted above is one of several tunes included in a supplement to Cable's article. It is titled *The Bamboula,* the arrangement is credited to Miss M. L. Bartlett, but no source for the music is given. Actually this tune bears little resemblance to a West Indian dance; so it is not surprising to find Cable remarking, "I have never heard another to know it as a bamboula."

But he goes on to remark that in *Slave Songs of the United States* there is a bamboula from Louisiana, "whose characteristics resemble the bamboula reclaimed by Gottschalk in so many points that here is the best place for it." He then quotes the music of this song, under the title "Miché Banjo," in an arrangement by H. E. Krehbiel (who, incidentally, calls attention to what he describes as "the particularly propulsive effect of the African 'snap' at the beginning"). I quote the music as it appears on page 113 of *Slave Songs of the United States* (New York, 1867), where it is titled "Musieu Bainjo": the song is about a mulatto who puts on airs, with his hat on one side, his cane, and his new boots that creak. The spice of the text is in the double meaning between *mulet* (mule) and *mulatre* (mulatto).

Creole songs and dances: the background

The editors of the collection from which this song was taken, state that, along with six others in the same volume, it was obtained from a lady who heard them sung, before the Civil War, on the Good Hope plantation, St. Charles Parish, Louisiana. According to them, it represents "the attempt of some enterprising Negro to write a French song." There is perhaps no need to take this information literally, but they were undoubtedly correct in recognizing this song as the product of French music plus Negro "enterprise." Its West Indian character is unmistakable. When the French *contredanse* was transplanted to Haiti in the eighteenth century, it began to undergo rhythmic modifications under Negro influence, particularly by the introduction of the "habanera rhythm" in the bass. This rhythm became the basis of the *contradanza* of the Antilles, as well as of the habanera, the tango, and numerous other Latin American dances. Further modifications occurred when Negro musicians altered this fundamental rhythm by transferring the accent to a weak beat. This may be seen in the bass of a *contradanza* titled *Los Merengazos:* [3]

The alert reader will at once notice that this metrical pattern corresponds exactly to that of the first and third measures of "Musieu Bainjo." It is, moreover, identical with the so-called "cakewalk" figure that forms the rhythmic basis of American ragtime music.

Let us now seek a Caribbean counterpart for the metrical pattern of the second and sixth measures of "Musieu Bainjo." Among many examples that could be quoted, we shall choose a Cuban *contradanza* from the early nineteenth century, which also shows the habanera rhythm in the bass.[4] The metrical pattern that concerns us particularly is marked with a bracket.

The foregoing, among numerous other illustrations that might be cited, should serve to indicate concretely the extremely close relationship between the music of the "Creole" Negroes of Louisiana and the music of the Caribbean islands, with its mixture of Spanish, French, and African elements. It is worth noting that the editors of *Slave Songs of the United States* speak of these tunes as "peculiar . . . difficult to write down, or to sing correctly." Their notation is probably only an approximation of what the Louisiana Negroes actually played and sang when they made their music "hot" for Place Congo.

The supposition that Gottschalk "lifted" his *Bamboula* from Congo Square seems farfetched. A more likely explanation is that, like the anonymous lady who supplied the Creole tunes for *Slave Songs of the United States*, he heard this, and other similar tunes, sung by Negroes in his household or on nearby plantations. Cable is correct

[3] From Carpentier, *La Música en Cuba*, p. 119.
[4] *Ibid.*, p. 112.

in remarking the traits that Gottschalk's *Bamboula* has in common with "Miché Banjo" (or "Musieu Bainjo"). The points of resemblance have to do chiefly with the use of two characteristic rhythmic figures: that of the habanera and that of the cakewalk. Gottschalk uses the former in the treble over a heavily accented first beat in the bass: [5]

The cakewalk figure appears in the following measures in combination with a typical pattern of the *contradanza*:

Elsewhere in this piece, he uses the *contradanza* rhythm with the characteristic accent on the weak beats.

In his Cuban dance titled *Ojos Criollos*, there is an interesting juxtaposition of the cakewalk and the habanera rhythms, with syncopation in the bass. In another Cuban dance, *Dí que si* (also known by its French title, *Réponds-moi*), the cakewalk figure appears systematically over a bass that repeatedly stresses the weak beat of the measure (in 2/4 time).

Although Gottschalk adapted his Creole and Caribbean compositions to the prevailing style of mid-nineteenth-century piano writing in the virtuoso manner, he was highly sensitive to the nuances of local color and extremely perceptive of the rhythmic intricacies of this New World music.

[5] This and the following example copyrighted in 1908 by G. Schirmer.

Among other dances of the Louisiana Negroes, all reported by various writers as found in the West Indies also, were the *babouille*, the *cata* (or *chacta*), the *counjaille* (or *counjai*), the *voudou*, the *calinda*, and the *congo*. According to Cable, the congo ("to describe which would not be pleasant") was known as the *chica* in Santo Domingo, and in the Windward Islands was confused under one name with the calinda. It is indeed difficult to unravel the nomenclature of these dances. Probably the most widespread of all was the calinda, which Cable says was the favorite dance all the way from New Orleans to Trinidad.

The editors of *Slave Songs of the United States* wrote that the calinda "was a sort of contra-dance." They quote the description of a French writer, Bescherelle, who mentions the two lines of dancers as "advancing and retreating in cadence, and making very strange contortions and highly lascivious gestures." [6] They were right in characterizing the calinda as an adaptation of the French *contredanse*, which as brought to the West Indies by the French colonists was a polite and circumspect social dance. But, as Curt Sachs has pointed out,[7] dances in which men and women line up in two rows facing each other and advance and retreat, were not unknown in Africa. So the Negroes found in the *contredanse* a natural point of departure for a new type of hybrid dance combining European and African elements. This applies to the choreography. What about the music? In *Slave Songs of the United States*, the following song (No. 134) is given as an example of the calinda:

Mi - ché Pré - val li don - nin gran bal, Li fait
naig pa - yé pou sau - té in - pé Dan - sé ca - lin - da, bou - doum, bou - doum, Dan - sé . ca - lin - da, bou - doum, bou - doum.

[6] I have been unable to identify the work from which this quotation is taken. Compare, however, the quotation from Père Labat given on p. 314. It would not be surprising if this were the source of the description attributed to Bescherelle.

[7] Sachs, *World History of the Dance.*

The first thing that strikes one about this tune is its completely European character; it is clearly a tune of French origin, which has undergone little or no modification by the Caribbean milieu. In this connection we observe also that of seven Creole tunes included in the collection, this is the only one in 6/8 meter. Of the others, four are in 2/4 and two in common time. This distinction is significant, for, although 6/8 meter is not foreign to Caribbean music, the 2/4 meter is by far the more prevalent, not only in Caribbean music, but in Afro-American music as a whole. In short, this calinda is obviously a tune that has scarcely been "worked over" at all by the Negroes, and one cannot but be struck by the incongruity between this pleasant little tune and the wild orgies which Cable describes as taking place in the Congo Square. Of course, it no doubt sounded wilder when the Negroes played and sang it to the accompaniment of drums, gourd rattles, triangles, jew's-harps, jawbone and key, quils (Pan's pipe made of three cane reeds), and banjos.

The songs of the calinda are satirical and often personally abusive. The calinda quoted above is about a certain Monsieur Préval who gave a ball in New Orleans, using a stable as the ballroom—much to the astonishment of the horses, says the song—and neglecting to obtain the necessary license. Krehbiel, in his book *Afro-American Folksongs*, gives a composite text for this song, in which he includes several stanzas that he says were supplied to him by Lafcadio Hearn. One of these is particularly interesting: "Black and white both danced the bamboula; never again will you see such a fine time." Two points are significant here: one, that the bamboula was a ballroom dance; two, that it may have been danced by both blacks and whites. Let the reader return for a moment to what was said in Chapter 4 of this book, where mention was made of the congo as a ballroom dance in Colonial Virginia. Cable and other writers describe the congo and the bamboula as wild, lascivious, primitive dances. Yet it is likely that they also existed as more or less restrained social dances, performed to such European instruments as the violin and the clarinet.

Mention of the calinda as a favorite dance of the Antilles goes back as far as the early part of the eighteenth century. Père Labat, in *Nouveau Voyage* . . . (The Hague, 1724), mentions it as an "African" dance, which he saw in Santo Domingo around the year 1698. According to this author, the Spaniards learned the "calenda," as he calls it, from the Negroes, who brought it over from the Coast of Guinea in Africa. His description follows:

> The calenda is danced to the sound of instruments and of voices. The participants are arranged in two lines, one in front of the other, the men facing the women. The spectators form a circle around the dancers and the musicians. One of the participants sings a song, of which the refrain is repeated by the spectators, with clapping of hands. All the dancers then hold their arms half-raised, leap, turn, make contortions with their posteriors, approach within two feet of each other, and retreat in cadence, until the sound of an instrument or the tone of the voices, signals them to approach again. Then they strike their bellies together two or three times in succession, after which they separate and pirouette, to begin the same movement again, with highly lascivious gestures, as many times as the instrument or the voice gives the signal. From time to time they go arm in arm, and circle around two or three times, while continuing to strike their bellies together and exchanging kisses, but without losing the cadence.

This description, which was copied (without acknowledgment) by several later writers, supplies the realistic details omitted by Cable in his account of the dance in Place Congo. It would not be at all surprising to find that this passage was also one of the major sources for Cable's article. Cable was born in 1844, a year after the dancing in Place Congo was suppressed; he had to reconstruct the scene from earlier accounts of writers who had actually witnessed the West Indian dances that were transplanted to New Orleans. As for the music, he took most of the tunes from the Creole songs included in *Slave Songs of the United States*. These songs evidently circulated widely in Louisiana, and Gottschalk must have had ample opportunity to hear them elsewhere than in Congo Square.

Gottschalk in Europe

There is sufficient evidence that Moreau Gottschalk carried with him to Europe, deeply impressed in his mind, the Creole songs of his native Louisiana. Besides his *Bamboula*, there is his Ballade Creole (Opus 3 *de la Louisiane*) titled *La Savane*, dating from his first years in Europe, in which he uses the theme of a song called "Lolotte" (No. 135 in *Slave Songs of the United States*):

Gottschalk used only a portion of the original melody, which is one of the most attractive of the Creole songs. Poor Lolotte, says the song, has only a heartache, while Calalou has an embroidered petticoat and a Madras kerchief. Pointing out that *calalou* was originally the term for a West Indian dish, a noted ragout, Cable thinks that in this song "Calalou" is a derisive nickname "intended to apply here to the quadroon women who swarmed into New Orleans in 1809 as refugees from Cuba, Guadeloupe, and other islands. . . ." A composite version of "Pov' piti Lolotte," with the music arranged by H. T. Burleigh, is given in Krehbiel's *Afro-American Folksongs*.

One more remark may be made about this song, and that is the strong resemblance it bears to the familiar American play-party song, "Skip to my Lou." Numerous versions of this old play-party song are available in collections of American folk music, so that the reader can easily verify this similarity—if indeed the familiar tune be not remembered from one's own childhood. Are the two songs related? Do the words "Skip to my Lou" indicate some connection with Louisiana? Is the play-party song derived from the Creole song? I do not know the answers.

La Savane was among the pieces that Gottschalk composed while he was in France, at the age of fifteen or sixteen. *La Bamboula*, as previously stated, was another; and a third was *Le Bananier* ("The Banana Tree"), subtitled "*Chanson nègre*." These youthful compositions might be called a Louisiana trilogy and were to become and remain favorites with the public, along with that other characteristic and brilliant showpiece, *The Banjo*, subtitled "*Fantaisie grotesque*" and probably composed in Spain in 1851. (According to Gottschalk's Cuban biographer Fors, there was an earlier version of *The Banjo*, published by Espadero; but I have not located a copy of it.)

Gottschalk's first piano teacher in Paris was Charles Hallé, with whom he worked for six months. He then studied piano with Camille Stamaty and harmony with Maledan. Through his mother's family connections he was received and feted in the *salons* of the French nobility. In April, 1845, just after his sixteenth birthday, he gave his first public concert in the Salle Pleyel and attracted the attention of Chopin, who saluted him as a future "king of pianists." He became the pupil and friend of Hector Berlioz, with whom he gave a series of concerts at the Théâtre des Italiens during the season of 1846–1847. Concerning Gottschalk as a pianist, Berlioz wrote (in the *Journal des Débats* of April 3, 1851):

Gottschalk is one of the very small number who possess all the different elements of a consummate pianist–all the faculties which surround him with an irresistible prestige, and give him a sovereign power. He is an accomplished musician–he knows just how far fancy may be indulged in expression. . . . There is an exquisite grace in his manner of phrasing sweet melodies and throwing light touches from the higher keys. The boldness, the brilliancy, and the originality of his playing at once dazzles and astonishes. . . .

In 1850 Gottschalk made a concert tour of the French provinces, Savoy, and Switzerland. The following year he went to Spain, where his success was enormous. The Queen entertained him in the royal palace and bestowed upon him the diamond cross of the Order of Isabel la Católica. He remained in Spain nearly two years, concert-izing, composing, and basking in adulation. Among the compositions that recall his Spanish sojourn are *Midnight in Seville, Manchega (Etude de Concert), The Siege of Saragossa,* and *Jota Aragonesa.*

In the autumn of 1852 Gottschalk returned to Paris, where he took leave of his mother and his sisters, who had been living there since the end of 1847. He then embarked for New York, where he was met by his father and where his formal American debut as a mature pianist took place on February 11, 1853, in the ballroom of Niblo's Garden. The success of the concert may be judged by the fact that P. T. Barnum immediately offered him a contract for $20,000, plus expenses, for a concert tour of one year. Gottschalk refused, on the advice, it is said, of his father, whose dignity was doubtless offended at the thought of having his son exhibited in public like a side show. Nevertheless, under the management of Max Strakosch, Gottschalk embarked on a tremendously successful concert career. In the winter of 1855–1856 he gave eighty concerts in New York alone, and in 1862–1863 he gave more than eleven hundred concerts in the United States and Canada. In the intervening years he was far otherwise engaged: the lure of the tropics, the spell of the Caribbean, held him in thrall.

Caribbean vagabondage

Gottschalk seems to have visited Cuba for the first time in 1853. In his *Notes of a Pianist* he wrote:

> I shall never forget the two months which I passed at Caymito, in the interior of Cuba. The house which I inhabited was at an hour's distance from the first cabins of Caymito. . . . Unfortunately, the only company of my Eden was a very ugly negress, who, every evening, after having roasted the coffee, bruised her corn in a hollow piece of wood, and recited the Ave Maria before an old coloured image of the Virgin, came and squatted down at my feet on the veranda, and there, in the darkness, sung to me with a piercing and wild voice, but full of strange charm, the *canciones* of the country. I would light my cigar, extend myself in my *butaca*, and plunge, surrounded by this silent and primitive nature, into a contemplative reverie, which those in the midst of the everyday world can never understand. The moon rose over the Sierra de Anafe. . . . The distant noises of the savanna, borne softly by the breeze, struck on my ear in drawn-out murmurs. The cadenced chant of some negroes belated in the fields added one more attraction to all this poesy, which no one can ever imagine.

What a pity that Gottschalk did not write down for us the notation of these Afro-Cuban songs and chants. He did, however, try to capture some of this atmosphere in his own music. Meanwhile, the atmosphere of the tropics captured him. In 1856 he returned to Havana and then began a period of vagabondage in the Caribbean that lasted nearly six years: ". . . six years madly squandered, scattered to the winds"—so he wrote of this period afterward. About these irresponsible years he tells us in his *Notes of a Pianist:*

> I have wandered at random, yielding myself up indolently to the caprice of Fortune, giving a concert wherever I happened to find a piano, sleeping wherever night overtook me,—on the green grass of the savanna, or under the palm-leaf roof of a *veguero* [caretaker of a tobacco plantation], who shared with me his corn-tortilla, coffee, and bananas. . . . And when, at last, I became weary of the same horizon, I crossed an arm of the sea, and landed on some neighbor-

ing isle, or on the Spanish Main. Thus, in succession, I have visited all the Antilles,—Spanish, French, English, Dutch, Swedish, and Danish; the Guianas, and the coasts of Pará [Brazil]. At times, having become the idol of some obscure *pueblo*, whose untutored ears I had charmed with its own simple ballads, I would pitch my tent for five, six, eight months, deferring my departure from day to day, until finally I began seriously to entertain the idea of remaining there for evermore. Abandoning myself to such influences, I lived without care, as the bird sings, as the flower expands, as the brook flows; oblivious of the past, reckless of the future, and sowed both my heart and my purse with the ardor of a husbandman who hopes to reap a hundred ears for every grain he confides to the earth. But, alas! . . . the result of my prodigality was, that, one fine morning, I found myself a bankrupt in heart, with my purse at ebb-tide. Suddenly disgusted with the world and myself, weary, discouraged, mistrusting men (ay, and women too), I fled to a desert on the extinct volcano of M—— [in Guadeloupe], where, for several months, I lived the life of a cenobite. . . .

My hut, perched on the verge of the crater, at the very summit of the mountain, commanded a view of all the surrounding country. . . . Every evening I rolled my piano out upon the terrace; and there, facing the most incomparably beautiful landscape, all bathed in the soft and limpid atmosphere of the tropics, I poured forth on the instrument, and for myself alone, the thoughts with which the scene inspired me. . . .

Amid such scenes I composed "Réponds-moi," "La Marche des Gibaros," "Polonia," "Columbia," "Pastorella e Cavaliere," "Jeunesse," and many other unpublished works. . . . My despair was soothed; and soon the sun of the tropics . . . restored me with new confidence and vigor to my wanderings.

I relapsed into the manners and life of these primitive countries: if not strictly virtuous, they are, at all events, terribly attractive. . . . The mere thought of re-appearing before a polished audience struck me as superlatively absurd. . . . It was at this period that Strakosch wrote to me, offering an engagement for a tour of concerts through the United States. . . .

Gottschalk hesitated, breathed a sigh of regret—and accepted. He felt morally rescued: ". . . but who could say, if, in the rescue, youth and poetry had not perished?" Meanwhile, thousands of America's youth were perishing in the Civil War; but this did not diminish the brilliant success of Gottschalk's concert tour. Actually, Gottschalk did not remain indifferent to the issues of the Civil War. His sympathies were with the North, perhaps in part because—as John Kirkpatrick surmises—he was conscious of his musical debt to the Negroes. In 1862 or 1863 he composed a piece called *The Union*, an allegory prophesying the rescue of the Union by the Northern armies.

From his sojourn in Cuba, Gottschalk drew material for a number of his most effective piano pieces. These include *Souvenir de la Havane* (Opus 39), *Souvenir de Cuba* (Mazurka), *Dí que sí* (*Répondsmoi!*), *Suis-moi!*, *Ojos Criollos*, and *La Gallina* ("The Hen"). John Kirkpatrick, the pianist who frequently features Gottschalk's pieces on his programs of American music, tells me that he thinks the piece titled *Suis-moi!* ("Follow Me!") shows the composer "at his very best." Kirkpatrick has made a two-piano arrangement of Gottschalk's symphony in two movements, *La Noche de los Trópicos* ("The Night of the Tropics"). Another large work inspired by tropical atmosphere is the *Escenas Campestres Cubanas* ("Cuban Country Scenes") for vocal soloists (soprano, tenor, baritone, and bass) and orchestra.

In all his travels Gottschalk never forgot that he was an American. Whenever the occasion arose, he was ready to talk on American subjects, and in his concerts he also recalled his native land. At a concert in Havana in 1854, he performed a fantasia for piano on "Old Folks at Home," which he titled *Recuerdos de mi Patria* ("Memories of my Homeland"). Wherever he went in Latin America, he was highly esteemed and honored, both as a person and as an artist.

It is ironic that American musicians had to wait until 1893 for Antonin Dvořák to tell them about the possibilities of utilizing American Negro music to achieve "local color," when Gottschalk began doing just that as early as 1845.

South American triumphs

In April, 1865, Gottschalk sailed for California, where he spent the summer concertizing. Then he embarked for Panama, beginning what was to be his life's last journey. Continuing to Peru, he remained there long enough to give about sixty concerts and to receive "a gold, diamond, and pearl decoration." Gottschalk was always ready to place his talent at the disposal of charity and other worthy causes. Hence it is not surprising that in Valparaiso, Chile, the board of public schools, the common council, the board of visitors of the hospitals, and the municipality each presented him with a gold medal.

Gottschalk sailed around Cape Horn to the River Plate, disembarking at Montevideo in July, 1867. There he gave several concerts at the Teatro Solís, including a gala benefit for the Society of the Friends of Education. In a letter to the Society, he expressed himself eloquently and with evident conviction on the subject of democracy and education in the United States. He pointed out that "The popular system of education in the United States . . . which, of a child, makes successively a man, and later a citizen, has, for its principal object, to prepare him for the use of liberty. . . ."

Crossing the river to Buenos Aires, Gottschalk gave his first concert there at the Coliseum on November 5, 1867, using two Chickering pianos shipped from Boston. The following April he gave a gala concert at the famous Teatro Colón, at which he performed his *Grand Caprice on the Argentine National Anthem*. Shuttling between the two capitals, in October of 1868 he organized a large "festival" at the Teatro Solís in Montevideo, with over three hundred participants. The program included his own *Marche Solennelle* and *Montevideo* (a descriptive symphony). In the spring of 1869, Gottschalk went on to Rio de Janeiro, where his triumphs exceeded anything previously experienced. Brazil was then ruled by the Emperor Dom Pedro II, a benevolent and liberal monarch. Gottschalk's success in Brazil is best described in his own words, from a letter to a friend in Boston:

My Dear Old Friend,–My concerts here are a perfect *furore*. All my houses are sold eight days in advance. . . . The emperor, imperial family, and court never missed yet one of my entertainments.

His Majesty received me frequently at palace. . . . The *Grand Orient* of the masonry of Brazil gave me a solemn reception. . . .

The enthusiasm with which I have been received here is indescribable. At the last concert, I was crowned on the stage by the artists of Rio. . . .

The emperor is very fond of my compositions, especially "Printemps d'Amour" and "Ossian."

My "Morte" (she is dead!) has had here, the same as in the Rio de la Plata, *un succès de larmes*, as several of my fair listeners wept at listening to that rather sad and disconsolate of my last effusions, which is my favorite now, and which I consider as being neither better nor worse than old "Last Hope."

My fantaisie on the national anthem of Brazil, of course, pleased the emperor, and tickled the national pride of my public. Every time I appear I must play it.

In great haste, yours as ever,
GOTTSCHALK

Of the compositions mentioned in this letter, *Ossian* was one of his earliest piano pieces, written for his mother's birthday when he was a young student in Paris (from the same period dates his *Danse Ossianique*, originally called *Danse des Ombres*). The piece titled *Morte* is mentioned again in a letter to the music publishers Hall & Son of New York, dated Rio, October 24, 1869:

Herewith I send you a new piece ("Morte,"—"She is Dead"),— a lamentation. I do not know whether it will be successful or not, but I believe it to be my best effort for years. Ever since I have played it, it has been encored; and a great many women have hysterics and weep over it—maybe owing to the romantic title. . . .

For once, Gottschalk appears to have been too modest. If anything could make women weep and swoon, it was his own playing and the romantic aura of his personality. And if *Morte* did not become as famous as his earlier sentimental effusions, *The Last Hope* and *The Dying Poet,* it was probably because Gottschalk did not live long enough to play it himself for the American public in his own inimitable manner.

On July 24, 1869, Gottschalk wrote to his Boston friend F. G. Hill, saying, among other things: "On the 30th, the emperor gives a grand fête at the palace, at which I am to play. I see his Majesty very often. He is a very kind and liberal-minded man. He is fond of inquiring about the States; and we have long talks together, alone in his private apartments." Soon after this, Gottschalk was stricken with yellow fever. On August 5 he was so low that the physicians gave him up. Yet by the latter part of September he had recovered sufficiently to resume his concerts. He was preparing "three grand festivals, with eight hundred performers, at which I will produce my symphonies, and the grand 'Marche Triomphale' I dedicated to the emperor. He is very anxious to have those festivals organized, and has offered me the means to muster in Rio all the musicians that can be had within the province." In another letter he exclaimed: "Just think of eight hundred performers and eighty drums to lead!" There speaks the disciple of Berlioz. Gottschalk burned up all his energy, expended the last ounce of his depleted strength, to organize and conduct this mammoth festival, scheduled to take place on November 24 and 26, 1869, at the Opera House of Rio de Janeiro.

The *Marche Triomphale*, which closed the first program, and into which the composer had woven the strains of the Brazilian national anthem, aroused tremendous enthusiasm, the excited audience rising to its feet and cheering. Gottschalk was called to the stage again and again to receive the ovations of the public. It was his last triumph. The next day he felt very weak, drove to the Opera House in his carriage, but was unable to conduct the orchestra in the second program of the festival. About two weeks later he was taken to the suburb of Tijuca, where, after much suffering, he died at four o'clock on the morning of December 18, 1869. The next day his embalmed body was exposed in state in the hall of the Philharmonic Society of Rio de Janeiro, and there the orchestra of the society played Gottschalk's *Morte* before the coffin was removed to the cemetery of St. John the Baptist, several miles outside the city. The newspapers of Brazil printed glowing eulogies of the dead musician. The following year Gottschalk's remains were taken to New York and placed in Greenwood Cemetery (October, 1870).

While admitting that he was no more than a *petit maître*, it seems to me that Gottschalk is a significant figure in America's music, not merely a historical effigy. Apart from the fact that his best music still has power to delight and charm the listener, his significance lies in his capacity for fully absorbing the atmosphere of the New World in some of its most characteristic aspects. As far as most American composers of the nineteenth century were concerned, Columbus might just as well have never discovered the New World. Our national folkloristic movement in music did not acquire definite momentum until the arrival of Dvořák, half a century after Gottschalk had composed his characteristic Creole pieces. Under more favorable circumstances, Gottschalk might have been the Glinka of America's music, the initiator of an impulse toward exploring and exploiting a new world of musical impressions. As it was, he remains an isolated, exotic figure, his music marked by a curious ambivalence. On the one hand he produced elegant *salon* pieces that stand as slightly tarnished gems of the genteel tradition. And on the other hand he ventured into exotic realms of personal and musical experience, projecting, however tentatively and incompletely, something of that untrammeled eclecticism, that reaching out for, and eager acceptance of, unprecedented sensations and impressions, that should characterize the artist who feels himself privileged to be born in a new world.

chapter sixteen

Europe versus America

Shun the lures of Europe.
TIMOTHY DWIGHT, GREENFIELD HILL (1794).

Americans of the eighteenth century were as confident of America's artistic glory as they were of her political, military, and material success. This confidence extended to all the arts, including music. Billings was hailed as a man of extraordinary genius, whom Nature had made "just such a musician, as she made Shakespeare a poet." Supply Belcher was called "the Handel of Maine." There was a general belief that the American, "the new man" saluted by Crèvecœur as one "who acts upon new principles," would manifest his freedom and his newness in powerful and individual works of the imagination, whether in literature, painting, or music. Yet, in 1838, Emerson had to admit: "This country has not fulfilled what seemed the reasonable expectation of mankind." In his address at Dartmouth, he went on to say:

> Men looked, when all feudal straps and bandages were snapped asunder, that nature, too long the mother of dwarfs, should reimburse itself by a brood of Titans, who should laugh and leap in the continent, and run up the mountains of the West with the errand of genius and of love. But the mark of American merit in painting, in sculpture, in poetry, in fiction, in eloquence, seems to be a certain grace without grandeur, and is itself not new, but derivative, a vase of fair outline, but empty. . . .[1]

Emerson might have included music in his catalogue, had he deigned to consider music seriously as an art. In any event, his remarks apply to American art music of the nineteenth century, and continued to

[1] "Literary Ethics, An Oration Delivered before the Literary Societies of Dartmouth College," July 24, 1838.

324

apply long after they ceased to be applicable to literature, since American music had to wait much longer for the equivalent of a Melville or a Walt Whitman.

The post-Revolutionary self-confidence was succeeded by an attitude of condescension toward American culture. In their obsession with good taste, with elegance, with gentility, cultivated Americans sought, like the colonial gentry, to imitate or import the products of European culture. While folk and popular music (also derived in the main from Europe) became gradually transformed by the American environment, fine art music, on the contrary, developed for several generations with scarcely any organic relationship to that environment.

It was inevitable that European musicians, both immigrants and those who came to America temporarily, should endeavor to exploit the American musical market. True, an American showman, P. T. Barnum, did the same thing, but he did it with European talent. And an American musician, Lowell Mason, made a fortune out of selling hymn books, but these, too, offered a thinly disguised European product. What actually happened was that European musical culture, with much of its apparatus and its standard repertoire, was transported to the United States and superimposed upon our social structure. In a sense, however, it is incorrect to say that European *culture* was brought to America, because culture, strictly speaking, is inseparable from its environment. It would be more accurate to say that the products, the techniques, and the carriers of European musical culture were transported to America.

And it was precisely because these products, these techniques, and these carriers had no organic—that is, no true cultural—relationship to the structure of American society, that they proved sterile, that they failed to provide the American composer with "a usable past," an operative tradition. Not until the end of the nineteenth century did a composer in the larger forms arise who carried within him the living tradition of "a usable past" in America's music. Most of the nineteenth century is merely an extended parenthesis in the history of American art music. Take it out and nothing vital is lost in the cultural continuity. (I am speaking, be it understood, of the cultivated fine-art tradition, not of our popular composers such as Emmett and Foster.) Nevertheless, in the discourse of history, we cannot ignore that long parenthesis, since history imposes itself upon us not only by its significance but also by its existence as preterit fact. We cannot change what has happened, however strongly we may be convinced that it should have happened differently.

A champion of American music

The musician who may be taken as the typical professional composer of art music in the United States during the nineteenth century was the son of an English organist—a circumstance that may not be pleasing to everyone. On the other hand, he was born in Brooklyn, which entitles him to some sort of consideration as a native son. George Frederick Bristow was born in Brooklyn, New York, on December 19, 1825. His life spanned nearly the whole of the remaining three-quarters of the century, for he died in 1898. If we view the American musical scene through his eyes, we will encounter most of the major developments in the panorama of musical art in the United States during the nineteenth century. He was the first American composer to handle successfully the traditional forms of European art music, including opera and symphony. Not that his treatment of these forms was in any way remarkable, but he did display sufficient competence and industry to establish his reputation as a professional composer and to get his works publicly performed during a period of some fifty years. He showed an interest in American subjects for his stage works, he endeavored to be inspired by the natural wonders of America (viz., in the symphony *Niagara*, his last work), and he showed himself to be properly patriotic in his symphonic ode, *The Great Republic*. Moreover, he championed the "cause" of the American composer.

Apparently there was no question about Bristow's taking up a musical career. He learned the violin and at the age of eleven played in the orchestra of the Olympic Theatre in New York. He studied theory and composition with Henry Christian Timm, a native of Hamburg, Germany, who had settled in New York in 1835, and who later was one of the founders of the New York Philharmonic Society and its president from 1847 to 1864. Bristow also had some lessons from the English composer G. A. MacFarren. When the New York Philharmonic was founded in 1842, Bristow joined the violin section of the orchestra, an activity which he continued for some forty years. One of his earliest compositions, a Concert Overture (Opus 3), was performed by the New York Philharmonic in November, 1847. Two years earlier Bristow had composed his First Symphony, in E flat. His cantata *Eleutheria* was written in 1849. In 1851 he became conductor of the Harmonic Society of New York, a choral association, holding this position until 1862.

In 1850, when P. T. Barnum brought Jenny Lind, "the Swedish Nightingale," to the United States for her first sensational concert tour —he offered her a guarantee of $150,000 plus expenses—Bristow was in the orchestra that played for her opening concert in New York's Castle Garden. Three years later Bristow was among the sixty American musicians engaged by the no less sensational French conductor Jullien to augment the band of forty players he had brought from Europe. Jullien was a Frenchman who specialized in giving popular concerts heralded by high-powered publicity and presented with elaborate showmanship. He boasted of having twelve hundred pieces in his repertoire, including an *American Quadrille* "which will contain all the NATIONAL AIRS and embrace no less than TWENTY SOLOS AND VARIATIONS." The New York *Courier and Enquirer* declared roundly that "Monsieur Jullien is a humbug," but admitted that "the discipline of his orchestra is marvellous" and concluded that both the humbug and the music were magnificent. Along with his quadrilles, polkas, schottisches, galops, and so forth, Jullien occasionally played some "classical" music—a movement from a symphony by Mozart, Beethoven, or Mendelssohn—and, what is more to the point, he included in his programs the music of American composers.

This matter of performing the works of native American composers was one upon which Bristow felt strongly. When the New York Philharmonic Society was founded, a clause in its constitution formulated the policy in regard to the performance of American works:

> If any grand orchestral compositions such as overtures, or symphonies, shall be presented to the society, they being composed in this country, the society shall perform one every season, provided a committee of five appointed by the government shall have approved and recommended the composition.

Actually, the phrase "composed in this country" left the door wide open for visiting musicians or recent immigrants, so that the native-born American composer was really given no special consideration at all. The attitude of the New York Philharmonic toward American music was made into a public issue in 1853 by a letter written by William Henry Fry and published in the *Musical World*, in which he declared that ". . . the Philharmonic Society of this city is an incubus on Art, never having asked for or performed a single American composition during the eleven years of its existence."

Henry C. Timm, president of the Philharmonic Society, published an answer to Fry's letter in which he said that the society had performed "several American compositions by either native or adopted citizens of this country." However, of the ten works mentioned, only three were by native Americans: a Duetto for two cornets by Dodworth, a Serenade by William Mason, and an Overture by George F. Bristow.

At this point Bristow himself jumped into the controversy. In a letter to the *Musical World* he wrote:

As it is possible to miss a needle in a hay-stack, I am not surprised that Mr. Fry has missed the fact, that during the eleven years the Philharmonic Society has been in operation in this city, it played once, either by mistake or accident, one single American composition, an overture of mine. As one exception makes a rule stronger, so this single stray fact shows that the Philharmonic Society has been as anti-American as if it had been located in London during the Revolutionary War, and composed of native-born British tories. . . .

It appears the society's eleven years of promoting American art have embraced one whole performance of one whole American overture, one whole rehearsal of one whole American symphony, and the performance of an overture by an Englishman stopping here. . . .[2]

The "American symphony" to which Bristow refers was his own First Symphony which, according to Timm, had been "performed twice at public rehearsal." Bristow evidently chose to overlook the two small pieces by Dodworth and Mason. Under the circumstances, it is not surprising that Bristow's resignation from the Philharmonic Society was announced two weeks later.

Yet the breach was not permanent. Bristow soon returned to his desk at the Philharmonic, and on March 1, 1856, the Society per-

[2] Quoted in Howard, *Our American Music*, p. 247.

formed his Second Symphony, in D minor. This was followed, on March 26, 1859, by a performance of his Third Symphony, in F sharp minor. Finally, to complete the tale, Bristow's Fourth (*Arcadian*) Symphony, in E minor, was played by the Philharmonic Society on February 14, 1874. Perhaps his letter had done some good, after all! The Overture to Bristow's unfinished opera, *Columbus*, was performed at the first concert given by the Philharmonic Society in Steinway Hall (then located at Fourteenth Street), November 17, 1866.

In March, 1861, the New York Harmonic Society, the choral group of which Bristow was director, performed his oratorio *Praise to God*. Another oratorio, *Daniel*, was performed by the Mendelssohn Union on December 30, 1867. As conductor of the Harmonic Society, Bristow made it a policy to perform the works of American composers—when he could find them.

"American" grand opera

"Sebastopol has fallen, and a new American opera has succeeded in New York!"—thus began an article by the critic Richard Storrs Willis published in the New York *Musical World* in the autumn of 1855. The opera was *Rip Van Winkle*, the composer was George F. Bristow, and the première took place at Niblo's Theatre on September 27, 1855. It ran for four weeks. The box-office receipts compared favorably with those of other New York attractions. They were better, for example, than those of the Italian opera at the Academy of Music.

Rip Van Winkle was the second grand opera composed by a native American (the first was Fry's *Leonora*). In adapting Washington Irving's tale for the operatic stage, Bristow's librettist introduced a love affair between Rip's daughter Alice and a British officer, which provided opportunity for the indispensable love duets.

Richard S. Willis found something to praise in Bristow's work, though not without reservations:

The opera of Rip Van Winkle exhibits an easy flow of melody. This melody is free from effort and spontaneous—an important quality in a dramatic composer. But in none of the arias of Mr. Bristow do we meet with large conception or rich development of ideas; none of them is shaped after a large pattern. The same re-mark will apply to the choruses. . . .

Willis criticized most severely the instrumentation of the opera: "The orchestra of Rip Van Winkle is in general inanimate and life-less, and devoid of that brilliancy which we must meet with in modern opera."

In spite of these shortcomings, *Rip Van Winkle* showed some vitality, for in 1870 it was revived. Today it stands on the shelf of musical antiques as the first specimen of American grand opera dealing with a "native" subject, a subject taken from American legend and literature. Before taking leave of Bristow we should remark that from 1854 until the year of his death he was a supervisor of music in the public schools of New York. Thus, as composer, as executant, as conductor, as church organist, as educator, and as champion of Ameri-can music, his career reflected virtually every phase of organized musical activity in the United States during the second half of the nineteenth century.

We mentioned William Henry Fry as the man who protested publicly about the New York Philharmonic Society's neglect of the American composer. Fry was born in Philadelphia in 1815, the son of a newspaper publisher, and received a good education, with the empha-sis on literature rather than music. He learned to play the piano, com-posed an overture at the age of fourteen, and then studied theory and composition with Leopold Meignen, a graduate of the Paris Conserva-tory who had settled in Philadelphia. Fry turned out three more overtures before he was twenty, and one of them was locally per-formed. But it was not his intention to take up music as a profession. He embarked on a journalistic career by entering his father's office in 1839, became editor of the Philadelphia *Public Ledger* in 1844, and from 1846 to 1852 was in Europe as correspondent for this and other newspapers, including the New York *Tribune*, for which he served as music editor after returning to the United States. In 1861 he re-ceived a diplomatic appointment at Turin, but his health was poor, and in 1864 he died of tuberculosis at Santa Cruz, in the West Indies.

Like his Russian contemporary Glinka, Fry was an amateur, and like Glinka he tried his hand at opera. But unlike the Russian com-poser, Fry did not draw upon his country's folk music for his mate-rial, or upon its history and legend for his subject matter. The libretto of Fry's opera *Leonora* was adapted from Bulwer-Lytton's novel *The Lady of Lyons*. It was "grand opera" according to the most approved Italian recipe, complete with coloratura arias, recitatives, choruses, and ensemble numbers. The initial production, at the Chestnut Street Theatre in Philadelphia, on June 4, 1845, was given by the Seguin opera troupe, and paid for by the composer. The opera was sung in English and ran for twelve nights.

During his sojourn in Europe, Fry tried unsuccessfully to have *Leonora* produced in Paris, at his own expense. According to Fry's account, the director of the Paris Opera told him: "In Europe we look upon America as an industrial country—excellent for electric telegraphs, but not for art . . . they would think me crazy to produce an opera by an American."

After his return to America, Fry succeeded in having his opera performed by an Italian company at the Academy of Music in New York (1858), this time sung in Italian. The New York critics were not impressed by *Leonora*. The critic of the *Express* wrote:

> The opera seems to us a study in the school of Bellini. It is full of delicious, sweet music, but constantly recalls the Sonnambula and Norma. It is marked by skill in instrumentation. . . . It has many flowing melodies, many pretty effects, much that should encourage its author to renewed efforts. . . . The peculiarities which most strongly distinguish his production are sweetness of melody and lack of dramatic characterization.

The *Times* praised the fertility of melodic invention but pointed out that some of the melodies carried the memory "to past pleasures afforded by other composers." The *Musical Review and Gazette* was condemnatory: "Almost everything is poorly shaped and put together, and what is still worse, worked closely after the most common pattern."

In May, 1929, a concert of excerpts from *Leonora* was presented by the Pro Musica Society in New York, with the metropolitan music critics present. Oscar Thompson of the *Post* made a good point when he wrote: ". . . at least one tenor-soprano duet in mellifluous thirds would not have been laughed at, it is fair to assume, if it had been heard in a performance of Norma, Puritani or Sonnambula at the opera." If Fry, as Herbert Peyser said, "played the sedulous ape to Bellini, Donizetti, and Auber," he seems to have done it rather well.

However, one can scarcely blame the American public for preferring the genuine article, imported from Italy, to an American imitation made in Philadelphia. There is no suggestion that Fry *improved* on Rossini, Bellini, or Donizetti.

The ambitious Mr. Fry also tried his hand at writing symphonies. He composed four, each with an appropriate title indicating the programmatic content: *Childe Harold*, *A Day in the Country*, *The Breaking Heart*, and *Santa Claus*. These concoctions were actually performed, thanks to the enterprising Monsieur Jullien, who thought they would be effective "novelties" on his American programs. Willis, writing in the *Musical World*, refused to take the *Santa Claus Symphony* seriously as a work of art. He called it "a kind of extravaganza which moves the audience to laughter, entertaining them seasonably with imitated snow-storms, trotting horses, sleighbells, cracking whips, etc." This made Fry furious. He dashed off a spirited reply to Willis, saying among other things: "I think that the American who writes for the mere dignity of musical art, as I understand it, without recompense, deserves better treatment at the hands of his countrymen at least." It was in this letter that Fry made his attack on the New York Philharmonic Society, previously quoted.

One of Fry's most ambitious undertakings was a series of lectures on the forms and history of musical art, illustrated with selections performed by a chorus and orchestra of eighty players. The series started on November 30, 1852, in the Metropolitan Hall, New York. We are told that the second part of the first lecture opened with some specimens of Chinese music. "This was followed by the overture to *Der Freyschutz* [*sic*] which marked all the advance of Christian upon Pagan civilization."

In the last lecture of his series, Fry voiced his opinions on musical art in the United States. He called for a Declaration of Independence in Art on the part of American composers. Let them cease to bow down to a Handel, a Mozart, or a Beethoven. Let them strike out into untrodden realms, guided only by nature and their own inspirations. Let them discard their European liveries and found an American school of composition. Only then shall we cease to be provincial in Art. Brave words, yet strange from the lips of one who "played the sedulous ape" to Bellini and Donizetti, who cultivated the form of "grand opera" which lies entirely outside the tradition of American culture. It is not the last time that we shall encounter this strange dichotomy in American music: the case of the composer who pleads for artistic independence while (perhaps unconsciously?) imitating European models in his own work.

The true worshipers

Fry's plea for nonworship of European composers did not meet with much response. In the same year that he gave his New York lectures, an item in Dwight's *Journal of Music,* sent in by a correspondent from Newport, Rhode Island, expressed the prevailing atmosphere of musical incense burning:

> The lover of music has great privileges here. . . . In Mr. Scharfenberg's little cozy parlor, Beethoven, Chopin and Mendelssohn, Spohr, and other worthy associates, are daily worshipped by a few of the true worshippers. . . .

In this atmosphere, most American musicians found it advisable to become "true worshippers" themselves, in the hope that at least a little of the incense might eventually be wafted in their direction.

Take, for example, the case of William Mason (1829–1908), son of the eminent Doctor Lowell Mason of Boston. After preliminary study with Henry Schmidt in Boston, young Mason sailed for Europe in 1849. There he studied with Moscheles and Hauptmann in Leipzig, with Dreyschock in Prague, and with Liszt in Weimar. To Liszt, Mason dedicated one of his first piano pieces, elegantly titled *Les Perles de Rosée.* After five years of soaking up this superrefined musical atmosphere, Mason returned to America to spread the gospel of good music. On one occasion, when giving a piano recital on tour, he was asked by a member of the audience to improvise by playing "Old Hundred" with one hand and "Yankee Doodle" with the other. By offering to improvise on any themes that might be suggested, he had placed himself in the position of a showman bound to please the public. Later Mason became more austere. He formed a string quartet with which he appeared as pianist in concerts of chamber music, not precisely a popular form of entertainment. Much of Mason's time was devoted to teaching the piano, a field in which he was extremely successful and influential.

We mention William Mason chiefly because he and his family are so typical of the prevailing trend in American musical life. His great-grandfather, Barachias Mason, conducted singing schools in his spare time. His grandfather, Johnson Mason, found time, among more important civic duties, to play the cello and sing in the parish choir. His father, Lowell Mason, as we know, passed from the banking business to a full-time, lucrative career in music. But Lowell Mason was still partly bound by the tradition of hymnody and the singing-school movement. He did not fully penetrate the inner circle of those who worshiped at the shrine of Liszt, Mendelssohn, and Brahms. To his son William was vouchsafed the privilege of entering this arcanum: the culmination of four generations of progressive improvement. The fruits: some piano pieces, such as *Les Perles de Rosée* and *Amitié pour Amitié*. The latter, we are told, was a favorite with Liszt. *Summum bonum!*

We turn now to two American musicians who were born in the same year, 1839, and whose life span extended into the first decade of the twentieth century. Each was highly successful and widely honored in his lifetime. (We must go far to find that mythical creature, the "neglected American composer.") Their names were Dudley Buck and John Knowles Paine, and both were New Englanders. Dudley Buck's background is interesting as showing the transition from mercantile to artistic interests in an American family of the upper middle class. His father was a shipping merchant of Hartford, Connecticut, and the son was intended for a commercial career. Not until he was sixteen did he begin to receive music lessons. His progress was then so impressive that Buck senior gave his consent to a musical career and decided that the youngster should have the best musical education that money could buy. This meant, of course, packing him off to Germany. In Leipzig, Buck became a pupil of Hauptmann, Moscheles, Plaidy, and Richter. He studied the organ in Dresden and then spent a year in Paris before returning to the United States in 1862. He had been abroad four years.

After holding positions as church organist in Hartford, Chicago, and Boston, Buck in 1875 settled in New York in a similar capacity. As a composer he devoted himself chiefly to choral works, including a series of short cantatas for church use. Among his more ambitious works are the *Centennial Meditation of Columbus* (1876, with words by Sidney Lanier), *Scenes from the Golden Legend* (1880, after Longfellow), *King Olaf's Christmas* (1881, also after Longfellow), *The*

Light of Asia (dramatic cantata), and *The Voyage of Columbus* (another dramatic cantata, adapted from Irving's *Life of Columbus*).

Some remarks on *The Golden Legend* will serve to illustrate Buck's style. The legend tells of Prince Henry of Hoheneck, who is afflicted with an incurable malady that can be cured only by the blood of a maiden who will freely consent to die for his sake. He finds such a maiden, but refuses to let her make the supreme sacrifice. Instead, the prince is miraculously healed and marries the willing maiden. The music employs the Wagnerian device of the leitmotiv—melodic themes to identify characters, emotions, and the forces of Nature. Here, for example, is one of the storm motives:

There is a suitably sentimental solo for "Elsie's Prayer," a Pilgrims' Chorus, a Bacchanalian Monks' Song, a scene of Revel, a Drinking Song, an orchestral Barcarolle, a Chorus of Sailors, a solemn Cathedral motive (with Gregorian reminiscences), and a grand finale with a Hymn of Praise by full chorus and orchestra. In short, there is all the conventional paraphernalia of pseudo-Wagnerian claptrap, chords of the diminished seventh included.

Buck enjoyed some reputation abroad. His cantatas were performed in England and Germany. At home he wrote for the taste of the day and for a ready market. He supplied the demand for church music that was mellifluous and not difficult to perform. He died in 1909.

The composer as professor

John Knowles Paine (1839–1906) was born in Portland, Maine, of a musical family. His grandfather had built the first organ in Maine. In Portland young Paine studied with a local musician, Hermann Kotzschmar, and in 1857 went to Germany, becoming a pupil of Haupt in Berlin. He concentrated on the organ and gave numerous recitals in Germany before returning to America in 1861. The following year he was appointed director of music at Harvard College, where he remained until a year before his death. Beginning as an instructor, he attained full professorship in 1875, not without opposition from those who felt that music was not a subject to be taken seriously in the college curriculum. It seems that Francis Parkman, the historian, was one of the most stubborn opponents of music at Harvard. As a member of the Corporation, he is said to have ended every meeting of that body with the words "musica delenda est." [3] Whenever the question of raising funds came up, Parkman was ready with a motion to abolish the music department in the interests of economy.

In 1867 Paine revisited Germany, where his Mass was performed under his direction at the Berlin Singakademie. At home he lacked neither recognition nor public performance. In 1873 he conducted the first performance of his oratorio *St. Peter* in his native city, Portland. In 1876 Theodore Thomas conducted the première of Paine's First Symphony in Boston. In the same year Paine set to music Whittier's "Hymn" for the Centennial Exposition at Philadelphia. The first performance of his Second Symphony, a programmatic work titled *Im Frühling* ("In the Spring"), given at Boston in 1880, was received with unprecedented enthusiasm. According to contemporary accounts, ladies waved handkerchiefs, men shouted their approval, and the dignified John S. Dwight, arbiter of musical taste in Boston, "stood in his seat, frantically opening and shutting his umbrella as an expression of uncontrollable enthusiasm." [4] This was the same man who dismissed Stephen Foster's songs as cheap trash.

As we look at Paine's *Spring Symphony*, we may well wonder what all the shouting was about. The first movement portrays the departure of winter and the awakening of Nature. Here is the winter theme, given out by the cellos:

[3] "Music must be abolished," a paraphrase of the Latin sentence that embodied Rome's undying enmity against Carthage.

[4] Richard Aldrich in *Dictionary of American Biography*, vol. 14.

The second movement, "May-night Fantasy," is a scherzo. Then comes the slow movement, "A Romance of Springtime" (Adagio), which is in the form of a rondo. The final movement, Allegro giocoso, depicts "The Glory of Nature" and is in sonata form. The musical idiom is that of academic postromanticism, stemming from the school of Raff. It is a coincidence that Raff composed a *Spring Symphony* in 1878, the year before Paine's symphony was completed. The plan of both symphonies is remarkably similar. No doubt it was mere coincidence, but a coincidence that serves to emphasize to what an extent American composers were simply echoing the current clichés of German postromanticism.

Paine wrote what is probably his best and most enduring music for a performance of Sophocles' *Oedipus Tyrannus* given at Cambridge, Massachusetts, in 1881. The music consists of a Prelude, six Choruses, and a Postlude. This is one of the few examples of Paine's music with which the listener of today may become acquainted, for the Prelude has been recorded under the direction of Howard Hanson in the album "American Music for Orchestra." A comment made by Rupert Hughes on the opening chorus is worth noting. After remarking that the second strophe has a few good moments, he adds "but soon [it] falls back into what is impudent enough to be actually catchy!" Fortunately for his reputation as our leading academic composer, Paine seldom succumbed to the temptation of writing catchy tunes.

Among other compositions of Paine are the *Columbus March and Hymn* for the Chicago World's Fair, *Hymn to the West* for the St. Louis World's Fair, several symphonic poems (*The Tempest, Poseidon and Aphrodite, Island Fantasy*), and an opera, *Azara*, based on the medieval story of Aucassin and Nicolette, for which Paine himself wrote the libretto and which never had a stage performance (it was performed twice in concert form, in 1903 and 1907). From this score he extracted three *Moorish Dances* and some ballet music, which were frequently performed—as was, indeed, nearly all of Paine's music during his lifetime.

Paine's music has some qualities of workmanship and invention that raise it above work previously attempted by American composers in the symphonic field. Nevertheless, it remains primarily of historical interest. Paine has a place as our first notable academic composer in the larger forms, and as the teacher of others who were to carry on the academic tradition with some distinction. Among his pupils were

Arthur Foote, Frederick S. Converse, Daniel Gregory Mason, and John Alden Carpenter.

Gilchrist and Gleason

Two composers born in the 1840s may be mentioned as having attained a considerable reputation in their time. They were William Wallace Gilchrist (1846–1916) and Frederick Grant Gleason (1848–1903). The latter was born in Middletown, Connecticut, where his father was a banker. Like many another well-to-do gentleman, Gleason senior was an amateur flutist. He considered music a pleasant pastime but not a serious occupation. He wanted his son to enter the ministry—a good old New England tradition. But the son insisted on becoming a composer, and the father yielded. Young Gleason studied with another Connecticut Yankee who had gone musical: Dudley Buck. He then made the inevitable pilgrimage to Europe, studying with a long list of musicians in Germany. After six years in Europe he returned to America, and in 1877 went to Chicago, where he was active as a teacher and music critic. In 1897 he became president of an organization titled the "American Patriotic Musical League" (!).

Gleason's compositions include a *Processional of the Holy Grail* written for the Chicago World's Fair; a symphonic poem, *Edris*, based on a novel by Marie Corelli; the tone poem *Song of Life;* a Piano Concerto; a cantata with orchestra, *The Culprit Fay;* and two operas: *Otho Visconti* and *Montezuma*. The former was produced at Chicago in 1907. He left other scores in manuscript, with instructions that they were not to be publicly performed until fifty years after his death. W. S. B. Mathews describes Gleason's operatic style as an attempt "to combine the melodic element of Italian opera with the richness of harmonization characteristic of the modern German school and the leit-motif idea of Richard Wagner." [5] At least, in fifty years American grand opera had "progressed" from Bellini to Wagner.

Gleason applied the leitmotiv principle to his setting for solos, chorus, and orchestra of Joseph Rodman Drake's poem *The Culprit Fay*, described as "A Fairy Cantata." The poem is a coyly romantic concoction that tells about a "fay" (a river sprite) who "has loved an earthly maid" and who in punishment therefor is assigned the accom-

[5] Mathews, *The Great in Music* (1900), p. 188.

plishment of two difficult tasks, one of which is to catch a drop of brine from the brow of a leaping sturgeon on the shore of elfin land, the other to follow a shooting star and light the elfin lamp from a spark of its burning train. Gleason's music is developed from the following themes: summer-night motive, mystery motive, gathering of the fays, fairy life, the fay's love, penalty motive, night on the Hudson, water sprites' motive, task motive, and sylphid queen's love motive. A quotation of the motive of the fay's love will serve to illustrate Gleason's style. The theme is begun by the clarinets, taken up by the oboes, and continued by the flutes.

Gleason's contemporary William Wallace Gilchrist was born in Jersey City in 1846 and at the age of eleven moved with his family to Philadelphia, where he studied music with H. A. Clarke. His father's business having been ruined during the Civil War, young Gilchrist turned to the law and to business for his own living, but finally decided to take up music as a career. With the exception of a short period in Cincinnati (1871–1872), he lived in Philadelphia, where he was active as church organist, teacher, and leader of musical clubs. He founded the Mendelssohn Club of Philadelphia.

In 1882 Gilchrist won the Cincinnati Festival Prize for his setting of the 46th Psalm, for soprano solo, chorus, and orchestra. Among his other choral works are *Ode to the Sun, Journey of Life, The Uplifted Gates,* and *Legend of the Bended Bow.* He composed two nonprogrammatic symphonies, and some chamber music, including a nonet for piano, strings, flute, clarinet, and horn.

Although Gilchrist was one of the very few American composers of this period who did not study in Europe, his style is no less imitative and conventional than that of his Europeanized colleagues.

The self-made man in music

No account of American music in the nineteenth century would be complete without an example of that typically American product, the self-made man. A perfect specimen of the type is to be found in the person of Silas Gamaliel Pratt (1846–1916), a native of Vermont whose family moved to Illinois while he was still a boy. His father's business failed and he was obliged to start working at the age of twelve. His liking for music induced him to get employment as clerk in several Chicago music stores. Determined to take up a musical career, he saved enough money to go to Europe (i.e., Germany) in 1868, remaining there three years while studying piano and composition. An injury to his wrist from overstrenuous practice prevented him from becoming a concert pianist. Returning to Chicago in 1871, he had his First Symphony performed there. But he felt the need for another touch of Germany, whither he returned in 1875 for further study with Liszt and Heinrich Dorn. It was in Germany that he composed his *Centennial Overture*, performed in Berlin on July 4, 1876, and later played in the Crystal Palace, London, in the presence of General Grant, to whom the piece was dedicated. In 1885, Pratt visited London again for a performance of his Second Symphony (*The Prodigal Son*) at the Crystal Palace. Meanwhile his opera *Zenobia* had been produced in Chicago and New York (1883). Another opera, *Lucille* (originally called *Antonio*), was performed in Chicago in 1887. From 1888 to 1902 Pratt taught at the Metropolitan School of Music in New York, and in 1906 he founded the Pratt Institute of Music and Art in Pittsburgh.

Pratt aspired to be the great national composer of the United States, a sort of grand exalted tonal commentator on national events, past and present. His dramatic cantata, *The Triumph of Columbus* (1892), celebrated the discovery of America. The list of his symphonic works includes *Paul Revere's Ride*, a *Fantasy* depicting the struggle between the North and the South, a *Lincoln* Symphony, *The Battle of Manila*, and *A Tragedy of the Deep* (on the sinking of the *Titanic*).

The remarks on Pratt's career made by F. L. Gwinner Cole in the *Dictionary of American Biography* deserve to be quoted not only as a comment on this composer's life but also as a priceless recipe for success from which all aspiring composers may profit:

Throughout his life he had been industrious and persevering and had succeeded in bringing his name before the public as a composer of rank. In this he was greatly aided by his exaggerated opinion of the worth of his own compositions.

In contrast to these practical men who succeeded in becoming known as composers by dint of application and imitation, the man to whom we shall now dedicate a page or two was a stifled genius, perhaps the most magnificent and tragic failure in the annals of American music. He was born in 1842 and died in 1881. His name was Sidney Lanier.

Poet-Musician of the South

One of Lanier's best biographers, Edwin Mims, remarked: "It is unfortunate that he left no compositions to indicate a musical power sufficient to give him a place in the history of American music." True, Sidney Lanier, dying of tuberculosis at the age of thirty-nine, did not live to complete the larger musical compositions that he was planning: a *Choral Symphony* for chorus and orchestra (being a setting of his "Psalm of the West"), and a *Symphony of the Plantation* ("being the old and the new life of the negro, in music"). It may be doubted whether, if he had lived to finish these works, he could have risen above the limitations of his training and his background. The tragedy of Sidney Lanier as a creative musician depends not so much on his premature death as on his premature existence. He was born too soon, too early in America's cultural development.

Sidney Lanier's father was a lawyer in Macon, Georgia, his mother the daughter of a Virginia planter. From early childhood the boy could play any musical instrument on which he happened to lay hands; his favorites were the violin and the flute. Music as recreation was a good old Southern tradition, but music as a profession was not to be considered by a gentleman or the son of a gentleman. Yet Lanier was fully conscious of his musical capacities and inclinations. In a notebook written while he was at college, probably before the age of eighteen, he inquired earnestly of himself regarding "God's will" for his future life:

I am more than all perplexed by this fact, that the prime inclination, that is, natural bent (which I have checked, though) of my nature is to music; and for that I have the greatest talent; indeed, not boasting, for God gave it me, I have an extraordinary musical talent, and feel it within me plainly that I could rise as high as any composer. But I cannot bring myself to believe that I was intended for a musician, because it seems so small a business in comparison with other things which, it seems to me, I might do. Question here, What is the province of music in the economy of the world?[6]

In later years Lanier was to answer that last question to his own satisfaction and on a lofty mystical plane: "Music is Love in search of a word." Whether he could have persuaded his father to let him study composition professionally is a moot question. Had he been a New Englander, things might have been different. Well-to-do New England parents encouraged their sons to enter the ministry or take up business; but if the sons insisted on music the fathers usually yielded and sent the sons to Boston or to Europe for musical training. In New England there was a practical (economic) rather than a social (aristocratic) prejudice against music as a profession. In the South the conviction prevailed that music was not a fit profession for a gentleman. Although young Lanier felt himself to be endowed with remarkable musical powers, sufficient to carry him to the pinnacle of creative music, he hesitated to take the plunge, to commit himself fully to the hazard of art.

Whatever his plans at the moment may have been, they were interrupted by the outbreak of the Civil War, into which Lanier threw himself with high spirit and confidence. He believed that "the new Confederacy was to enter upon an era of prosperity such as no other nation, ancient or modern, had ever enjoyed," and that "the city of Macon, his birthplace and home, was to become a great art-centre." And perhaps he dreamed that in this great art center he, Sidney Lanier, might become the great composer of a new nation. The impact of reality was harsh and bitter. After serving in the Confederate Army for four years he was captured and imprisoned at Point Lookout, Maryland. Released at the end of the war, he made his way painfully on foot to his home city and fell dangerously ill for two months. Thereafter it was a struggle for existence, for mere survival. He clerked in a hotel, he worked in his father's law office, he did some teaching. In 1867 he married and soon there was the burden of a family to support. During these years poetry as well as music had attracted his

[6] Quoted in Mims, *Sidney Lanier*.

latent creative talents. His father wanted him to settle in Macon and share his law practice, with a comfortable assured income. But Lanier was now ready to commit himself to art, to his twin stars of music and poetry. From Baltimore, where he had moved with his family, he wrote to his father, in 1873, a letter from which I quote the following passages:

> Then, as to business, why should I, nay, how *can* I, settle myself down to be a third-rate struggling lawyer for the balance of my life, as long as there is a certainty almost absolute that I can do some other things so much better? . . . My dear father, think how, for twenty years, through poverty, through pain, through weariness, through sickness, through the uncongenial atmosphere of a farcical college and of a bare army and then of an exacting business life . . . I say, think how, in spite of all these depressing circumstances, and of a thousand more which I could enumerate, these two figures of music and of poetry have steadily kept in my heart so that I could not banish them. Does it not seem to you as to me, that I begin to have the right to enroll myself among the devotees of these two sublime arts, after having followed them so long and so humbly, and through so much bitterness?

The father was won over by this plea, and thenceforth did what he could to help his son. But Lanier's great enemy now was tuberculosis. He went to San Antonio, Texas, for his health, and while there composed a piece for flute, *Field-larks and Blackbirds*. It was about this time that he wrote in a letter, "I am now pumping myself full of music and poetry, with which I propose to water the dry world. . . . God has cut me off inexorably from any other life than this. . . . So St. Cecilia to the rescue! and I hope *God* will like my music."

Mere mortals, in any case, liked Lanier's music, and praised it enthusiastically. In Baltimore he played his *Field-larks and Blackbirds* for the conductor Asger Hamerik, who was in the process of organizing the Peabody Symphony Orchestra. Hamerik "declared the composition to be that of an artist, and the playing to be almost perfect." Lanier was engaged as first flutist of the Peabody Symphony: he was now a professional musician. He kept on studying and practicing, striving always to perfect himself in his art. His playing had an extraordinary effect on those who heard him. The opinion of Hamerik, a highly competent professional musician, is worth quoting:

In his hands the flute no longer remained a mere material instrument, but was transformed into a voice that set heavenly harmonies into vibration. Its tones developed colors, warmth, and a low sweetness of unspeakable poetry. . . . His playing appealed alike to the musically learned and to the unlearned—for he would magnetize the listener: but the artist felt in his performance the superiority of the momentary living inspiration to all the rules and shifts of mere technical scholarship. His art was not only the art of art, but an art above art.

Miss Alice Fletcher indulged in feminine hyperbole when she declared that Lanier "was not only the founder of a school of music, but the founder of American music." [7] What I would venture to say is that Sidney Lanier was the truest artist among American musicians of the nineteenth century, the only one to whom the term "genius" might be applied.

Lanier's known compositions are the following: *Sacred Melodies* for flute solo (performed in Macon, July, 1868); *Field-larks and Blackbirds*, for flute solo (composed in 1873); *Swamp Robin*, flute solo (same year); *Danse des Moucherons*, for flute and piano (probably composed in December, 1873; three manuscripts are at The Johns Hopkins University); *Longing*, flute solo (composed early in 1874); *Wind-song*, flute solo (1874); songs for voice with piano: *The Song of Love and Death* (Tennyson, "Lancelot and Elaine"), *Love That Hath Us in the Net* (Tennyson, "The Miller's Daughter"), *Little Ella* ("A Beautiful Ballad"; words and music by Sidney Lanier; composed in 1866; published in 1888), and *My Life Is Like a Summer Rose* (poem by Richard Henry Wilde). He left unfinished a Choral Symphony, Symphony of Life, and Symphony of the Plantation.

This is, of course, a pitifully slight output with which to impress posterity, and it is overbalanced by the weight of Lanier's literary reputation and his poetic production. Nevertheless, the music he left is the work of a gifted musician and a true artist. It has been my privilege to hear Lanier's *Wind-song* admirably played by that modern "gentleman amateur" of American musicians, Carleton Sprague Smith, and the piece is certainly worthy of being included in the permanent repertoire of American music for flute. Perhaps Sidney Lanier was right when he felt in his soul that he could become a great com-

[7] Quoted by Starke, *Musical Quarterly*, XX, 4 (1934), p. 389.

poser. The fact that circumstances did not permit him to develop his creative genius to the full is one of the major tragedies of America's music.

Lanier's ideas on music, his system of prosody based on the identity of music and poetry, his remarkable poem titled "The Symphony"— these and other aspects of his work and thought might well claim our attention, did space permit. Here we must content ourselves with giving to Sidney Lanier, the musician, the place that he deserves as a precursor in the long struggle for the recognition and encouragement of native musical talent in the United States. The light of his tragic glory illumines the fulfillment of America's music that he did not live to see.

Very different was the fate of the American composer whose life and work will be discussed in the next chapter. Though Edward MacDowell was struck down by illness at the height of his powers, his musical talents were carefully nurtured from an early age, and he had full opportunity to develop his natural talents and to receive the proud acclaim of his country during his lifetime.

chapter seventeen

A romantic bard

Music . . . is a language, but a language of the intangible, a kind of soul-language.
EDWARD MACDOWELL, CRITICAL AND HISTORICAL ESSAYS.

In a book published in 1900,[1] Rupert Hughes wrote of Edward Mac-Dowell that "an almost unanimous vote would grant him the rank of the greatest of American composers." One is mildly surprised at the intrusion of the qualifying adverb "almost." Who was there to cast a dissenting vote? Perhaps some admirer of John Knowles Paine or of Ethelbert Nevin. The opposition, indeed, was not strong. Now, half a century later, if such a hypothetical plebiscite were held among American music lovers, it would be rash to predict that MacDowell would be kept in top place by an electoral landslide. To the present generation his name is more familiar than his music. We have more or less agreed to let the handsome effigy of Edward MacDowell stand on the pedestal where our admiring parents placed him, to gaze respectfully on the statue labeled "America's greatest composer," and to write *tacet* over most of his musical scores. Amateur pianists doubtless continue to delight in the smaller piano pieces, but the larger works —the sonatas, the concertos, the orchestral suites—are heard infrequently in our concert halls.

No such neglect afflicted the composer during his lifetime. Mac-Dowell was fully, even fulsomely, appreciated by his contemporaries; his music was played, published, applauded, and praised without stint. Americans of the *fin de siècle* were so pleased at finding an authentic composer in their midst that they heaped superlatives upon him. When MacDowell was offered the professorship of music at Columbia Uni-

[1] Hughes, *Famous American Composers*, p. 34.

346

versity, the nominating committee cited him as "the greatest musical genius America has produced." For Rupert Hughes, the piano sonatas of MacDowell were "far the best since Beethoven."

MacDowell found his most eloquent panegyrist in the person of the critic Lawrence Gilman, who, in 1905, three years before the composer's death, contributed an enthusiastically appreciative volume to the "Living Masters of Music" series; a volume which he later brought out, revised and enlarged, as *Edward MacDowell: A Study* (1908). Gilman, who became music critic of the New York *Herald Tribune*, and the author of many other books, may have lived to regret some of his more unabashed outbursts, such as the statement that Mac-Dowell's name "is the one name in our music which . . . one would venture to pair with that of Whitman in poetry." This is Gilman's summing up of the American composer's art:

He was one of the most individual writers who ever made music—as individual as Chopin, or Debussy, or Brahms, or Grieg. His manner of speech was utterly untrammelled, and wholly his own. Vitality—an abounding freshness, a perpetual youthfulness—was one of his prime traits; nobility—nobility of style and impulse—was another. The morning freshness, the welling spontaneity of his music, even in moments of exalted or passionate utterance, was continually surprising: it was music not unworthy of the golden ages of the world.

Twenty years later, Paul Rosenfeld, adventurous "voyager among the arts," impressionistic critic of music, art, and literature, wrote in *An Hour With American Music* (1929):

The music of Edward MacDowell . . . amounts more to an assimilation of European motives, figures and ideas than to an original expression. In any case, the original elements are small and of minor importance. . . . The ideas of the main romantic composers, particularly Wagner, continued to haunt MacDowell even in his later, more personal phase. . . . He was badly equipped in polyphonic technique; and where . . . he attempted canonic imitation, we find him essaying it clumsily, and with all the obsessive rapture of a child in possession of a new and dazzling toy. . . . Even where he is most individual, even in the personal, characteristically dainty and tender little piano pieces, he frequently appears fixed and rigid in invention.

It might be wise to steer a middle course between these poles of affirmation and negation; to put aside the issue of MacDowell's greatness, to avoid adulation and deprecation, and to regard him, sympathetically but objectively, in his historical role as one of the first Americans to acquire fame as a composer of "serious" music.

The lure of Europe

Edward Alexander MacDowell (he dropped the middle name in later life) was born in New York City on December 18, 1861, of Irish-Scotch descent. His father was a prosperous businessman with artistic inclinations which had been thwarted by Quaker parents. There is no mention of a musical heritage in the family, but Edward early manifested musical aptitude and around the age of eight began to receive piano lessons from a family friend, a Colombian by the name of Juan Buitrago. His next piano teacher was a professional musician, Paul Desvernine, with whom he studied until the age of fifteen. It was then decided that Edward should go abroad for further study. Accompanied by his mother, he sailed for Europe in April, 1877, and in the following autumn was admitted to the Paris Conservatory as a pupil of Marmontel (piano) and of Savard (theory).

The methods and atmosphere of the Conservatory appear to have been uncongenial for the young American student. After hearing Nicholas Rubinstein play in the summer of 1878—the year of the Paris Exposition—Edward exclaimed to his mother, "I can never learn to play like that if I stay here." His ambition then was to become a pianist rather than a composer. Leaving Paris, mother and son went first to Stuttgart, which proved to be even more unsatisfactory, and then to Wiesbaden, where Edward took some lessons in theory and composition from Louis Ehlert, whose informal approach "rather staggered" the American because, as he said later, his idea in leaving Paris "was to get a severe and regenerating overhauling." Edward worked hard all winter and heard lots of new music, which, he tells us, "was like manna in the desert after my long French famine." This is an early example of MacDowell's persistent Francophobia. The primary purpose in coming to Wiesbaden was to meet the pianist Karl Heyman, who was visiting there at the time. Heyman taught at the Frankfort Conservatory, and it was there that MacDowell decided to go in the autumn of 1879, his mother having meanwhile returned to America.

The director of the Frankfort Conservatory was Joachim Raff (1822–1882), whom Alfred Einstein characterizes as a composer of "mostly Romantic routine works, none of which have shown lasting vitality," and whose music Adolfo Salazar describes as being "of a Mendelssohnian and picturesque Romanticism and of weak pulsation." When Raff was told that MacDowell had studied for several years the "French school" of composition, he flared up and declared that there was no such thing nowadays as "schools"—that if some French writers wrote flimsy music it arose simply from flimsy attainments, and such stuff could never form a "school." [2] This was the man with whom MacDowell studied composition, and in whom, according to Gilman, he encountered "an influence at once potent and engrossing—a force which was to direct the currents of his own temperament into definite artistic channels."

MacDowell felt thoroughly at home in Germany. "His keen and very blue eyes, his pink and white skin, reddish mustache and imperial and jet black hair, brushed straight up in the prevalent German fashion, caused him to be known as 'the handsome American.' " MacDowell had now been five years in Europe, but apparently he had no intention of returning to his native land. His studies were finished and he had embarked on his professional career as pianist, teacher, and composer. In 1881 he applied for, and obtained, the position of head piano teacher at the nearby Darmstadt Conservatory. He commuted between Frankfort and Darmstadt, composing on the train. He also read a great deal, especially Goethe, Heine, Byron, Shelley, and—his favorite—Tennyson.

After a year the Darmstadt duties proved burdensome, and MacDowell resigned. In the spring of 1882 he went to visit Liszt at Weimar, taking with him the score of his First Piano Concerto, which Liszt heard and praised. It was upon Liszt's recommendation that MacDowell's Second Modern Suite, Opus 14, was published at Leipzig by Breitkopf & Härtel. Meanwhile, in the summer of 1882, Joachim Raff died. His death was felt as a deep personal loss by MacDowell.

It was Raff who had persuaded MacDowell that his real path lay in composition, and during the next two years he gave an increasing amount of time to composing. In June, 1884, MacDowell returned to America to marry his former pupil, Marian Nevins. A few days after

[2] Cited by Gilman, *Edward MacDowell: A Study*, p. 9.

the wedding the couple sailed for Europe, going first to England and then to Frankfort, which by this time must have seemed like home to MacDowell. He applied, unsuccessfully, for a position at the Würzburg Conservatory (as he had done previously at the Frankfort Conservatory). During this period he wrote the two-part symphonic poem, *Hamlet and Ophelia*. In 1885 he applied, again unsuccessfully, for the position of examiner at the Royal Academy of Music in Edinburgh. The following winter was spent in Wiesbaden, and in the summer of 1886 the MacDowells visited London again. Returning to Wiesbaden, they made their home in a small cottage in the woods, where MacDowell worked at his composition. But, according to Gilman, "Musicians from America began coming to the little Wiesbaden retreat to visit the composer and his wife, and he was repeatedly urged to return to America and assume his share in the development of the musical art of his country."

The Boston years

In September, 1888, MacDowell and his wife sailed for the United States. It would be incorrect to say that he left Germany behind, because actually he brought it along with him. Furthermore, Boston, where the MacDowells settled, was musically a sort of German province. With the exception of the brief trip in 1884, MacDowell had lived in Europe from his fifteenth to his twenty-seventh year. Most of these twelve years were spent in Germany, warming his hands in the embers of a dying Romanticism.

In Boston, before his arrival, MacDowell was already known as a successful composer—that is, one who had received the accolade of European performance and publication. The celebrated pianist Teresa Carreño had included some of his pieces on her programs. In April, 1888, MacDowell's First Piano Concerto was performed in Boston, and, wrote W. F. Apthorp in the *Transcript*, "The effect upon all present was simply electric." After his return to America, MacDowell further consolidated his position both as composer and executant. His first great success was when he played his Second Piano Concerto in New York in March, 1889; a success repeated soon afterward in Boston. In the summer of that year he appeared as soloist in this concerto at a concert of American music conducted by Van der Stucken in Paris (July 12, 1889). Other composers represented on this historic program were Dudley Buck, George W. Chadwick, Arthur Foote, Henry Holden Huss, Margaret Ruthven Lang, John K. Paine, and Frank Van der Stucken.

In Boston, where he remained for eight years, MacDowell taught privately and composed industriously. The more important works composed during this period include the Concert Study for piano (Opus 36), the Twelve Studies for piano (Opus 39), the Six Love Songs (Opus 40), the Sonata *Tragica* (Opus 45), the twelve Virtuoso Studies (Opus 46), the Eight Songs (Opus 47), the Second (*Indian*) Suite for orchestra, the Sonata *Eroica* (Opus 50), and the *Woodland Sketches* (Opus 51). This last collection contained some of his best-known pieces, such as *To a Wild Rose, From an Indian Lodge,* and *To a Water Lily.* Several of his larger works—the symphonic poem *Lancelot and Elaine,* the Orchestral Suite in A Minor, *The Saracens* and *The Lovely Alda* (episodes from *The Song of Roland*), *Hamlet and Ophelia*—were performed by the Boston Symphony Orchestra. The public applauded, the critics praised him. James Huneker wrote of the D minor Piano Concerto that "it easily ranks with any modern work in this form." W. J. Henderson called the same work "a strong, wholesome, beautiful work of art, vital with imagination, and made with masterly skill."

Teaching at Columbia

In May, 1896, the trustees of Columbia University in New York offered MacDowell the newly created professorship of music at that institution. After some hesitation, he accepted. He seems to have been fired by the vision of accomplishing great things in music education. This was his program of instruction: "First, to teach music scientifically and technically, with a view to training musicians who shall be competent to teach and to compose. Second, to treat music historically and aesthetically as an element of liberal culture."[3] This program was to be carried out in five courses of study. For the first two years MacDowell bore the entire burden of teaching by himself, after which an assistant was appointed. As a teacher, MacDowell worked hard and conscientiously, shirking none of the drudgery associated with this

[3] W. J. Batzell, in Preface to MacDowell's *Critical and Historical Essays.*

task. He was an inspiration to his students and his courses were well attended. His lectures ranged over the entire field of musical history, from the ancient Greeks and Romans, and included a survey of Oriental and primitive music. He was outspoken in his opinions, independent in his ideas, and repeatedly urged his students to think for themselves rather than to accept ready-made judgments from others. As a lecturer he was fluent, dynamic, and, on occasion, humorous.

During the academic year 1902–1903, MacDowell took his sabbatical vacation, making first an extended concert tour in the United States and then spending the spring and summer in Europe. It was in 1902 that Nicholas Murray Butler succeeded Seth Low as president of Columbia University, and while MacDowell was absent Butler undertook to reorganize the teaching of the fine arts at the university. Now, this was a subject very near to MacDowell's heart; he had definite ideas on the scope and nature of a department of fine arts that would embrace music, painting, sculpture, architecture, and belles-lettres. These ideas, according to MacDowell, were rejected as impractical by President Butler. Feeling dissatisfied with the situation, MacDowell, early in January of 1904, presented his resignation. Indiscreetly, he talked to two student reporters who came to interview him, and the next day the story of his resignation was featured in the New York papers, with such tendentious headlines as "No Idealism Left in Columbia." Thus "the MacDowell affair" became overnight a *cause célèbre* in the annals of America's music. Butler issued a statement to the press in which he stated that MacDowell's resignation had been prompted by the latter's wish to devote all his time and strength to composition. MacDowell countered with another statement for the press, in which he said:

> President Butler has evidently misunderstood my interview with him when he affirms that my sole object in resigning from Columbia was to have more time to write: he failed to explain the circumstances which led to my resignation. . . . There is certainly individual idealism in all universities, but the general tendency of modern education is toward materialism.

Thus, for MacDowell the fundamental issue was one between idealism and materialism. In his report to the trustees he made his position fully clear. He was opposed to Butler's plan for a Division of Fine Arts with "the inclusion of Belles Lettres and Music, including kindergarten, etc., at Teachers College. . . . The Division of Fine Arts thus acquires somewhat the nature of a co-educational department store, and tends toward materialism rather than idealism. . . . For seven years I have put all my energy and enthusiasm in the cause of art at Columbia, and now at last, recognizing the futility of my efforts, I have resigned the chair of music in order to resume my own belated vocation."

There is no point in attempting to follow further the details of the controversy. The important thing to emphasize is that in Mac-Dowell's mind it was a question of idealism versus materialism: whether art should be dispensed as in "a co-educational department store" or whether it should be considered on a high aesthetic and technical level. The issue is a vital one, and by no means dead in American higher education. The only footnote that it seems necessary to add to this affair is that the chief professorship of music at Columbia University now bears the name of the Edward MacDowell Chair of Music.

During the years at Columbia, MacDowell continued to compose and to develop as a creative artist. He wrote the admirable *Sea Pieces* (Opus 55), the Third Piano Sonata (called *Norse*, Opus 57), the *Keltic* Sonata (Opus 59), the *Fireside Tales* (Opus 61), the *New England Idyls*, and some of his best songs. In 1896 he had acquired a farmhouse and some arable and wooded land near Peterboro, New Hampshire, where he and his wife thenceforth spent their vacations. In a log cabin that he built in the woods he did most of his composing, during the summer months. It was an ideal spot for both work and relaxation, but MacDowell, after his resignation from Columbia, was not long to enjoy the satisfaction of creative work. In the spring of 1905 his health began to deteriorate. He showed signs of nervous exhaustion, but the malady proved to be malignant and incurable: it soon left him helpless and mentally impotent. Tended by his faithful wife, he dragged out his existence for many months and finally passed away in New York City on the evening of January 23, 1908. His remains were taken to Peterboro for burial. Today the artists' colony at Peterboro, established by his widow as a summer haven for creative workers in the arts, stands as a tribute to MacDowell's memory.

To understand the personality, the background, and the art of Edward MacDowell is to understand a large segment of our musical culture. To arrive at this understanding, we should consider Mac-

Dowell's attitude toward America, his relation to Europe, and his conception of the art of music.

MacDowell and America

Writing sympathetically of MacDowell in the *Dictionary of American Biography*, John Erskine remarked that "undoubtedly he missed some of the contacts with national life which are helpful to creative art." This is an understatement. The composer spent his boyhood in New York City, in the sheltered circle of an upper middle-class family. At fifteen he went to Europe and stayed there until he was twenty-seven. Upon his return he lived in Boston and New York. It was a narrowly circumscribed cultural orbit, bounded on all sides by the conventions of the urban genteel tradition. As we have pointed out, the prevailing weakness of the genteel tradition was sentimentality, and from this weakness the music of MacDowell suffered grievously. In the words of Paul Rosenfeld:

> The feelings entertained about life by him seem to have remained uncertain; and while fumbling for them he seems regularly to have succumbed to "nice" and "respectable" emotions, conventional, accepted by and welcome to, the best people. It is shocking to find how full of vague poesy he is. . . . His mind dwells fondly on old-fashioned New England gardens, old lavender, smouldering logs, sunsets, "a fairy sail with a fairy boat," little log cabins of dreams, the romance of German forests and the sexual sternness of Puritan days.[4]

Apropos of this last phrase, it is interesting to compare Gilman's remark about MacDowell's music: "It is music curiously free from the fevers of sex." And he says of the composer that "his sensuousness is never luscious." Shall we then speak of subconscious puritan inhibitions in the music of MacDowell? That is scarcely necessary; it is enough to observe the ravages of a sentimentality which turns the artist away from life into a private dreamworld, where even the erotic becomes sublimated into "vague poesy." In paying tribute to MacDowell, Philip Hale said he was one "who in his art kept himself pure and unspotted." We may connect this with Howard's statement that in his latter years MacDowell "often told his friends that he

[4] Rosenfeld, *An Hour with American Music.*

avoided hearing music, so that he would not be in danger of showing its influence." This I construe as a sort of aesthetic sterilization.

Erskine claims that MacDowell's "interest in America was genuine and deep, reaching far beyond the field of music." Even within the field of music, he concerned himself with the problem of an American "national" school. Opposing the ideas of Dvořák, he rejected the concept of musical nationalism based on folklore. His views on this subject are worth quoting in full:

> So-called Russian, Bohemian, or any other purely national music has no place in art, for its characteristics may be duplicated by anyone who takes the fancy to do so. On the other hand, the vital element in music—personality—stands alone. . . . We have here in America been offered a pattern for an "American" national musical costume by the Bohemian Dvořák—though what the Negro melodies have to do with Americanism in art still remains a mystery. Music that can be made by "recipe" is not music, but "tailoring." To be sure, this tailoring may serve to cover a beautiful thought; but— why cover it? . . . The means of "creating" a national school to which I have alluded are childish. No: before a people can find a musical writer to echo its genius it must first possess men who truly represent it—that is to say, men who, being part of the people, love the country for itself: men who put into their music what the nation has put into its life; and in the case of America it needs above all, both on the part of the public and on the part of the writer, absolute freedom from the restraint that an almost unlimited deference to European thought and prejudice has imposed upon us. Masquerading in the so-called nationalism of Negro clothes cut in Bohemia will not help us. What we must arrive at is the youthful optimistic vitality and the undaunted tenacity of spirit that characterizes the American man. That is what I hope to see echoed in American music.[5]

This passage, taken from one of his lectures at Columbia University, seems amazing, almost incredible, coming from MacDowell. Is it this bard of the Celtic twilight, this worshiper of Arthurian flummeries, who cries for the expression of "youthful optimistic vitality" in American music? Is his the prophetic voice that summons American composers to put into their music what the nation has put into its life? The phrases are there, and we can only wonder at this dichotomy of

[5] Quoted in Gilman, *op. cit.*, pp. 83–85.

word and deed, repeating the query of the apostle: "What *doth it* profit, . . . though a man say he hath faith, and have not works? . . ."

As we shall see later in this book, it was Dvořák, and not Mac-Dowell, who proved to be the man of the hour, the man who felt the historical need of the moment in American music. This does not mean that MacDowell was entirely wrong in theory and Dvořák entirely right. MacDowell was right in maintaining that folklore and nationalism are not permanent, absolute values in artistic creation. Art is the product of a personality multiplied by a cultural tradition, or by the sum of several traditions, depending on the complexity of the artist's heritage and equipment. MacDowell inherited the genteel tradition of American urban culture, which in turn was a derivation of conventional European modes. In so far as the American imitation failed to reproduce the authentic atmosphere of the European original, by that much was MacDowell a spiritual expatriate from Europe. As Erskine writes:

The deep emotions of his early manhood were bound up with Europe, with a tradition and an atmosphere not to be found on this side the ocean. Perhaps he was always looking for it here, wistfully and tragically. He gave the impression, against his will, of being a visitor in his own land, trying to establish himself in alien conditions.

Perhaps this explains his remarks on American music previously quoted: he was trying desperately, trying too hard, to say what he thought he should say as an American composer; but the lack of conviction—or, rather, the lack of an operative American tradition in his cultural heritage—prevented him from embodying a bold, independent speech in his own creative work. He was in love with Europe, and the worst of it is that, in the words of Erskine, "the Europe he loved was a dream country, suggested by the great poets and artists and by ancient monuments, by folk-lore, by enchanting forests." Even after he transferred his *décor* to New England, it was this dream country that continued to inspire him. His music was a bridge from reality to that dream.

Music as a "soul-language"

What, then, was MacDowell's conception of music, of its nature and meaning? This is what he said in one of his lectures:

The high mission of music . . . is neither to be an agent for expressing material things; nor to utter pretty sounds to amuse the ear; nor a sensuous excitant to fire the blood, or a sedative to lull the senses; it is a *language*, but a language of the intangible, a kind of soul-language. It appeals directly to the *Seelenzustände* it springs from, for it is the natural expression of it, rather than, like words, a translation of it into stereotyped symbols which may or may not be accepted for what they were intended to denote by the writer.[6]

For MacDowell, then, music is a language in which one soul speaks to another. He states plainly that "*music is not an art*, but psychological utterance" (my italics). He denies that music can be compared with architecture, painting, or poetry. "Painting is primarily an art of externals . . . for that art must touch its audience through a palpable delineation of something more or less material; whereas *music is of the stuff dreams are made of*." (Again the italics are mine.) Speaking of the type of music that "suggests," as contrasted with music that "paints," he says:

The successful recognition of this depends not only upon the susceptibility of the hearer to delicate shades of sensation, but also upon the receptivity of the hearer and his power to accept freely and unrestrictedly the mood shadowed by the composer. *Such music cannot be looked upon objectively*. To those who would analyze it in such a manner it must remain an unknown language; its potency depends entirely upon a state of willing subjectivity on the part of the hearer.[7]

This passage, particularly the sentence italicized (by me), is crucial in relation to MacDowell's own music. If we do not voluntarily place ourselves in a state of willing subjectivity to the "mood shadowed by the composer," if we do not lay aside an objective awareness of the musical substance, the sonorous structure as such, then his music remains for us "an unknown language"—that is, it does not communicate —and thereby loses its potency.

Perhaps the key to MacDowell's limitations in his attitude toward music as a medium of artistic expression has been unwittingly provided for us by Gilman in the following sentence:

[6] MacDowell, *Critical and Historical Essays*.
[7] *Ibid.*, p. 259.

His standpoint is, in the last analysis, that of the poet rather than that of the typical musician: the standpoint of the poet intent mainly upon a vivid embodiment of the quintessence of personal vision and emotion, who has elected to utter that truth and that emotion in terms of musical beauty.

What this means, in effect, is that MacDowell did not think in terms of musical expression. Therefore, if we find ourselves unable or unwilling to share a priori his moods and emotions, we are apt to find his musical expression inadequate. He will have the listener abjure "that objective state which accepts with the ears what is intended for the spirit." He considers that a higher order of music which "aims at causing the hearer to go beyond the actual sounds heard, in pursuance of a train of thought primarily suggested by this music."

In contrast to this superior type of soulful music is "mere beauty of sound," which is, in itself, "purely sensuous." Developing this thought, MacDowell writes: "It is the Chinese conception of music that *the texture of a sound is to be valued;* the long, trembling tone-tint of a bronze gong, or the high, thin streams of sound from the pipes are enjoyed for their ear-filling qualities. . . ." Thus the concept that the texture of sound is to be valued is regarded as an outlandish notion, the mark of an inferior civilization, for, says Mac-Dowell, this is "sound without music." One wonders why he does not simply advocate music without sound, since that is the surest way of eliminating the "purely sensuous" element of sonorous beauty. The following passage is extremely revealing: "If we could eliminate from our minds all thoughts of music and bring ourselves to listen only to the *texture* of sounds, we could better understand the Chinese ideal of musical art." [8] This is truly an amazing dichotomy, which draws a line between *music* and *the texture of sounds.* Further on this subject: "For instance, if in listening to the deep, slow vibrations of a large gong we ignore completely all thought of pitch, fixing our attention only upon the roundness and fullness of the sound and the way it gradually diminishes in volume without losing any of its pulsating colour we should then realize what the Chinese call music." In other words, if we listen to a musical sound with full aesthetic awareness of its properties and effects as sound, we should then realize what the Chinese call music but what is not music for MacDowell. The significance of all this, apart from its revelation of MacDowell's atti-

[8] *Ibid.,* p. 60.

tude toward music, is that many people are still prevented from appreciating, for instance, twentieth-century music, because of this concept of music as a "soul-language" divorced from consideration of the actual texture of sounds in the musical artwork. Conversely, no amount of insistence upon the "nobility" of the message contained in the "soul-language" of MacDowell's music will arouse a response in those of us who find that his sonorous texture lacks interest and structural vitality.

MacDowell spoke disparagingly of counterpoint: "*Per se*, counterpoint is a puerile juggling with themes, which may be likened to high-school mathematics. In my opinion, J. S. Bach . . . accomplished his mission, not by means of the contrapuntal fashion of his age, but in spite of it. . . . Neither pure tonal beauty, so-called 'form,' nor what is termed the intellectual side of music (the art of counterpoint, canon, and fugue), constitutes a really vital factor in music." [9]

Writing of the music of Schumann, which he admired, MacDowell said: "It represents . . . the rhapsodical reverie of a great poet to whom nothing seems strange, and who has the faculty of relating his visions, never attempting to give them coherence, until, perhaps, when awakened from his dream, he naïvely wonders what they may have meant." This passage tells us much more about MacDowell than it does about Schumann. Many of MacDowell's smaller pieces are musical reveries, or moods expressed in tone, while his larger works, particularly the four piano sonatas, tend toward the rhapsodical. Even in the sonatas, however, as Rosenfeld remarks, "we are never very far from the little old rendezvous" represented by echoes of such pieces as *At an Old Trysting-place* or *An Old Garden*. Here, for example, is a passage from the second movement of the Fourth (*Keltic*) Sonata, which is supposed to be a musical portrait of the enchanting Deirdre: [10]

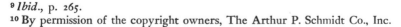

[9] *Ibid.*, p. 265.
[10] By permission of the copyright owners, The Arthur P. Schmidt Co., Inc.

The music for piano

Most of MacDowell's piano pieces may be divided into two categories: the "quaint" (sentimental) and the "frisky" (lively). In the former class belong *To a Wild Rose, At an Old Trysting-place, To a Water Lily, A Deserted Farm, Told at Sunset, An Old Garden, With Sweet Lavender, Starlight,* and *Nautilus.* The second class includes *Will o' the Wisp, In Autumn, From Uncle Remus, By a Meadow Brook, The Joy of Autumn*—to mention only pieces from *Woodland Sketches* and *New England Idyls.* There is a third category, in which the descriptive or emotional content tends toward the "dramatic," with contrasting moods of emotional emphasis and lyrical tenderness. The prototype of this category is *From Puritan Days,* in which the musical message is underlined by such directions as "pleadingly" and "despairingly." In this class also belong *In Deep Woods, To an Old White Pine, From a Log Cabin, From an Indian Lodge, A.D. MDCXX, Song* (from *Sea Pieces*), and *In Mid-Ocean.* The first of the *Sea Pieces,* titled *To the Sea,* might also be placed in this category, though it is more of a single mood, to be played throughout "with dignity and breadth."

It seems unnecessary to dwell at length on the four piano sonatas. The first, Sonata *Tragica* in G minor (Opus 45), is said to have been composed while MacDowell "was moved by the memory of his grief over the death of his master Raff." The work attempts "to heighten the darkness of tragedy by making it follow closely on the heels of triumph." As for the music, on the evidence of its facile romanticism, one can truly believe that the composer was moved by memories of Raff.

The Sonata *Eroica* in G minor (Opus 50), published in 1895, bears the motto *Flos regum Arthuris*. It has a programmatic content, as explained by the composer: "While not exactly programme music, I had in mind the Arthurian legend when writing this work. The first movement typifies the coming of Arthur. The scherzo was suggested by a picture of Doré showing a knight in the woods surrounded by elves. The third movement was suggested by my idea of Guinevere. That following represents the passing of Arthur." Gilman called this work "the noblest musical incarnation of the Arthurian legend which we have."

The Third Sonata, called *Norse* (Opus 57), published in 1900, bears the following verses at the head of the score:

> Night had fallen on a day of deeds.
> The great rafters in the red-ribbed hall
> Flashed crimson in the fitful flame
> Of smouldering logs;
> And from the stealthy shadows
> That crept 'round Harald's throne,
> Rang out a Skald's strong voice,
> With tales of battles won;
> Of Gudrun's love
> And Sigurd, Siegmund's son.

Along with the crashing chords and sweeping figurations of this music, we find such passages of chromatic tenderness as the following, marked to be played "Very dreamily, almost vague." [11]

[11] By permission of the copyright owners, The Arthur P. Schmidt Co., Inc.

The Fourth (*Keltic*) Sonata (Opus 59), was published in 1901 and, like the third, was dedicated to Edvard Grieg. Like the third also it has only three movements. Four lines of MacDowell's own verse stand at the head of the score:

> Who minds now Keltic tales of yore,
> Dark Druid rhymes that thrall,
> Deirdre's song and wizard lore
> of great Cuchullin's fall.

Hedging, as usual, on the matter of programmatic content, MacDowell wrote that "the music is more a commentary on the subject than an actual depiction of it." He wrote of this sonata that it was "more of a 'bardic' rhapsody on the subject than an attempt at actual presentation of it, although I have made use of all the suggestion of tone-painting in my power." It is as "bardic rhapsodies" that the sonatas of MacDowell, particularly the last two, may best be appreciated.

Orchestral works: *Indian Suite*

MacDowell did not compose symphonies, overtures, or string quartets. For orchestra he wrote symphonic poems, suites, and two piano concertos. The Second Piano Concerto, in D minor (Opus 23), completed in 1885, remains one of MacDowell's most viable works, probably because it purports to carry no solemn "soul message" but is simply a good, workable concerto in neo-romantic style. Of his orchestral works, the best is the Second or *Indian* Suite (Opus 48), first performed in 1896, which consists of five movements: (1) "Legend," (2) "Love Song," (3) "In War Time," (4) "Dirge," (5) "Festival." According to Henry F. Gilbert, who was at one time a pupil of MacDowell, the genesis of the *Indian Suite* was as follows:

MacDowell became somewhat interested in Indian lore and curious to see some real Indian music. He asked me to look up some for him, so I brought him Theodore Baker's book, *Die Musik der Nordamerikanischen Wilden*. "Oh, yes," he said, "I knew of this book, but had forgotten about it." From Baker's book the main themes of his Indian Suite are taken. . . . Although all the themes have been changed, more or less, the changes have always been in the direction of musical beauty, and enough of the original tune has been retained to leave no doubt as to its barbaric flavor.

The theme of the first movement ("Legend") occurs in a sacred ceremony of the Iroquois. A love song of the Iowas is used as the theme of the second movement ("Love Song"). A Kiowa tune, a chant of mourning, provides the theme for the fourth movement ("Dirge"), which is considered by many to be the most beautiful and effective orchestral music written by MacDowell. The last movement ("Festival") utilizes a women's dance and a war song of the Iroquois. Gilman quotes MacDowell as having said, in 1903: "Of all my music, the 'Dirge' in the Indian Suite pleases me most. It affects me deeply and did when I was writing it. In it an Indian woman laments the death of her son; but to me, as I wrote it, it seemed to express a world-sorrow rather than a particularized grief."

We have already seen that MacDowell frowned upon musical nationalism based on folklore. To Hamlin Garland he said: "I do not believe in 'lifting' a Navajo theme and furbishing it into some kind of musical composition and calling it American music. Our problem is not so simple as that." Certainly not. Yet there is something curiously ironic in the fact that MacDowell should have drawn from American Indian music the material and the inspiration for some of his best and most effective pages. It represents at least an attempt to get away from secondhand romanticism and genteel sentimentality. If we are now in considerable doubt as to "its barbaric flavor," and if we have no delusions regarding its significance as "American music," we at least are ready to acknowledge that it is rather good music, and to be thankful that MacDowell turned for a moment from Teutonic forests, New England nooks, and Celtic legends, to look into a book on American Indian music.

Something should be said about MacDowell's songs, though his production in this field was not large: he wrote forty-two songs for single voice with piano. He believed that "song writing should follow declamation," and that "the accompaniment should be merely a background for the words." MacDowell had literary aspirations and wrote the words for many of his own songs. He felt that much of the finest poetry, including that of Whitman, was unsuitable for musical setting. Among his more effective songs are "Fair Springtide," "Confidence," "Constancy, "The Swan Bent Low to the Lily," "A Maid Sings Light," "Long Ago," "To the Golden Rod," and "As the Gloaming Shadows Creep."

When Edward MacDowell appeared on the scene, many Americans felt that here at last was "the great American composer" awaited by the nation. But MacDowell was not a great composer. At his best he was a gifted miniaturist with an individual manner. Creatively, he looked toward the past, not toward the future. He does not mark the beginning of a new epoch in American music, but the closing of a fading era, the *fin de siècle* decline of the genteel tradition which had dominated American art music since the days of Hopkinson and Hewitt. This does not mean that the genteel tradition died with MacDowell: it survived in countless other composers of lesser reputation. But MacDowell was the last to endow it with glamour and prestige, the last important figure to live and work entirely within its orbit. After him the tradition either becomes identified with academic dignity, as in the composers of the so-called "Boston Group," or simply peters out in inconsequential drivel. Since we shall not concern ourselves with the latter, we may turn now to the group of composers sometimes called the "Boston Classicists," among whom MacDowell lived for a time and whose ideals he shared in large measure.

chapter eighteen

The Boston classicists

One truth you taught us outlived all the rest:
Music hath Brahms to soothe the savage breast.
D. G. MASON, LINES TO PERCY GOETSCHIUS, ON HIS EIGHTY-SECOND BIRTHDAY.

On Thanksgiving Day in the year 1895 a young American composer wrote in his journal: "Thank God Wagner is dead and Brahms is alive. And here's to the great classical revival of the 20th century in America." The name of this ardent young classicist—he was then only twenty-two—was Daniel Gregory Mason.[1] The reader is familiar with the name of Mason and what it stands for in American music: the transition from the pioneer singing-school tradition of early New England to the imitative provincialism of such Europeanizers as William Mason. Daniel Gregory was the nephew of William, and with him this New England musical dynasty reaches its culmination in an almost ecstatic surrender to the potent spell of the classical-romantic European tradition. In a volume of reminiscences, *Music in My Time*, Daniel Gregory Mason has described both the musical background of his boyhood in Massachusetts and his own musical credo as a mature individual. Describing the musical atmosphere of the family circle, he writes:

> The truth is, our whole view of music was based on the style of classic and romantic symphonists, beginning with Haydn and Mozart and ending with Mendelssohn and Schumann. Even Bach was rather on the edge of the music we recognized, and the rhythmic freedom or unmetricality of say, Gregorian chant, was decidedly beyond our horizon.[2]

[1] Mason died on Dec. 4, 1953, at the age of eighty. For an account of his compositions, see p. 380.
[2] Mason, *Music in My Time*, p. 14.

In speaking of rhythmic freedom and unmetricality, Mason need not have gone as far afield as Gregorian chant: he might have cited American folk music as an example; but that, of course, was also a closed book in this highly restricted musical circle. As regards his own views of musical art, Mason says:

. . . one of my deepest convictions has always been a sense of the supreme value in art of balance, restraint, proportion—in a word, of classic beauty. Hence my lifelong adoration of men like Bach, Mozart, Schubert, Beethoven, Brahms, in whom this ideal is supremely realized. Contrariwise I have always felt an instinctive antipathy toward excess, unbalance, romantic exaggeration, sensationalism, typified for me in such composers, great artists though they be, as Wagner, Tschaikowsky, Liszt, Strauss.[3]

As we shall see, Mason also felt, and expressed, "an instinctive antipathy" toward everything in American music that did not conform to this classic ideal of balance and restraint. And his antipathy crystallized around an element in American music that came to symbolize for him the "excess" and "exaggeration" that he hated. This element was the Jewish influence. But of that we shall speak later. For the moment we must attempt to define the prevailing New England attitude toward musical art, that is to say, the attitude that dominated the musical thinking of those New England composers who, in the final decades of the nineteenth century and the first of the twentieth, succeeded in forming a rather impressive school variously known as the "Boston Classicists" or the "New England Academicians." It might be denied that they formed a "school" in the strict sense of the term, but, like all New England cultural manifestations, this musical movement that centered in Boston and that flourished from about 1880 to World War I assumed rather definite characteristics, and I think it can be shown that it stemmed from a fairly homogeneous cultural and aesthetic background.

If we look at American art music as a whole during the period covered by the activity of this Boston group, we must admit that their achievement was notable. With such men as Chadwick, Foote, and Parker, American art music certainly had a group of composers who counted for something. At the same time, we may bear in mind R. H. Shryock's observation that "New England once excelled in cultural

[3] *Ibid.*, p. 101.

achievement, by the simple device of defining culture in terms of those things in which New England excelled." [4] Translated into musical terms this means, for example, that if you arbitrarily set up Brahms as the ideal of musical art, then all music reflecting Brahmsian influence must *ipso facto* be considered superior to any other type of music.

We have already dealt with John Knowles Paine, who may be regarded as the ancestor of the Boston academicians. Among his pupils was Arthur W. Foote (1853–1937). In one respect, Foote's musical education was not typical of the New England group: he did not study in Europe. Born in Salem, Massachusetts, he was allowed by his parents to take piano lessons when he was fourteen, but with no thought that he would take up music as a profession. At Harvard he became conductor of the Glee Club and studied music with Paine, yet still had a business career in sight when he graduated. It was B. J. Lang, to whom he had gone for some lessons on the organ, who persuaded young Foote that his future lay in music rather than business. So Foote became an organist and a pianist, opened a teaching studio in 1876, began to compose, and settled down to a quiet, productive existence in Boston. Like most of his contemporaries he was a Brahmsian, but, with exceptional adroitness, managed to be simultaneously a devotee of Wagner.

The Brahmsian influence is apparent chiefly in Foote's chamber music: Piano Quartet (Opus 23, 1891), String Quartet in E (1894); Quintet for piano and strings (1898), Piano Trio in B flat (1909). He followed the lead of Liszt in his ambitious symphonic poem called, after Dante, *Francesca da Rimini* (1893), in which he attempted some moderately realistic programmatic effects. He had a predilection for strings: his compositions for string orchestra include a pseudoclassical Serenade in E and Suite in D, and a rather austere Suite in E, composed in 1910. He also composed a mildly evocative *Night Piece* for flute and strings. Among his works for full orchestra are an overture, *In the Mountains* (1887), a Cello Concerto (1894), and *Four Character Pieces after Omar Khayyám* (1912).

Foote's Serenade for string orchestra, Opus 25, consists of Prelude, Air, Intermezzo, Romance, Gavotte. It was this sort of thing that Rupert Hughes had in mind when he wrote of Foote: "I know of no modern composer who has come nearer to relighting the fires that

[4] Shryock, in *The Cultural Approach to History*, ed. by Caroline F. Ware (New York, 1940), p. 267.

beam in the old gavottes and fugues and preludes." [5] This remark is quoted because it seems so typical of what the Bostonians were trying to do: relighting the fires of old forms and calling it a classical revival. Unfortunately, Hughes let the skeleton out of the closet (and also made a quick change of metaphor) when he went on to add that the gavottes of Foote "are an example of what it is to be academic without being only a rattle with dry bones." This gives us another characterization of the so-called "classical" revival: dry bones rattling in the academic closet. One could at least hope to cover the bones attractively. Or, as Louis Elson put it, "Foote uses the classical forces with most admirable ease and fluency." [6]

Foote left a large body of vocal music, both sacred and secular. His major choral works are *The Farewell of Hiawatha*, for men's voices (1886), *The Wreck of the Hesperus* (1888), and *The Skeleton in Armor*, with orchestra (1893). In these two latter works, Wagnerism is rampant, particularly in the storm scenes. A prolific composer, Foote wrote a quantity of church music, about one hundred and fifty songs (with a preference for Elizabethan lyrics), numerous piano pieces, and some thirty works for organ.

Among the adjectives that have been applied to the music of Arthur Foote by various writers are "noble," "pure," "refined," "dignified," "earnest," and "agreeable." These adjectives seem to me not only to delimit an individual production but also to epitomize an era and an aspiration that converged in Boston of the *fin de siècle*.

A Boston blend

In examining the antecedents of modern New England composers, time and again we find them emerging from a family background whose pattern repeats that of the native musical pioneers of the eighteenth century. Such is the case, for example, with George W. Chadwick, born in Lowell, Massachusetts, November 13, 1854. His father was one of those versatile, self-reliant Yankees who managed to combine the love and cultivation of music with success in practical matters. Beginning as a farmer, he became a machinist, and in 1860 established an insurance company, which prospered. Like the old New England singing-school masters, he taught a singing class in his

[5] Hughes, *Contemporary American Composers*, p. 227.
[6] Elson, *The History of American Music*, p. 479.

spare time, and organized a chorus in his community. His sons were encouraged to study music, and there were frequent musical gatherings in the family. In this scheme of things, music was not supposed to take the place of business, but to provide a wholesome and "uplifting" leisure-time occupation. So it was that George Chadwick, after learning to play the organ and the piano, entered his father's business according to the prescribed procedure. Before long, however, he decided that music was more important to him than business, left the paternal firm, and became a student at the New England Conservatory, of which many years later he was to be director. After a brief period of teaching music at Olivet College, young Chadwick decided to go to Europe to complete his musical education, to learn the art of orchestration, and to master the complexities of composing in the larger forms. It was then that he met with parental opposition: music as a full-time profession was still a heretical idea to the elder Chadwick. But it was too late for his opposition to be effective: music as a career was becoming a reality in America, and George Chadwick was moving with the times. He went to Europe.

Inevitably, for a Bostonian of that time, his destination was Germany. He first studied with Haupt in Berlin but soon went to work with the celebrated Jadassohn in Leipzig, after which he received a final polishing from Rheinberger in Munich. By 1880 he was back in Boston, thoroughly imbued with the laws of counterpoint and strict composition, a knowledge which he offered to impart to others for a moderate fee. Among his earliest pupils were three destined to achieve some prominence in American music: Horatio Parker, Sidney Homer, and Arthur Whiting. In 1882 he began teaching at the New England Conservatory and gradually ascended the pedagogic ladder until, fifteen years later, he was appointed director of that institution, holding this position until his death in 1931. Meanwhile, he had conducted choral societies, served as church organist, and composed industriously. His was indeed an exemplary musical career, pursued with tenacity and crowned with success.

Unlike some of his contemporaries, Chadwick did not have the benefit of a Harvard education, for he went to work after finishing high school. But, perhaps to compensate for his lack of a higher education, he continually turned to "high-brow" subjects, setting Latin texts to music, as in his *Phoenix Expirans* for mixed chorus

(1892), or alluding to ancient Greek legend and mythology, as in his overtures *Thalia* (the Muse of Comedy, 1883), *Melpomene* (the Muse of Tragedy, 1887), *Euterpe* (the Muse of Music, 1906), *Adonais* (1899), and the symphonic poem *Aphrodite* (1913). The programmatic content of the last-mentioned composition has been described as follows:

> The idea of the work was suggested by a beautiful head of the goddess, found on the island of Cnidos, and now in the Boston Art Museum. The composition endeavors to portray the scenes that might have taken place before such a statue when worshipped in its temple by the sea. There are festal dances; a storm at sea; the thanks of rescued mariners to their patron goddess; religious services in the temple; and other similar suggestions of suitable nature.[7]

The score itself is headed by the following verses:

> In a dim vision of the long ago
> Wandering by a far-off Grecian shore
> Where streaming moonlight shone on golden sands
> And melting stars dissolved in silver seas,
> I humbly knelt at Aphrodite's shrine
> Imploring her with many a fervid prayer
> To tell the secret of her beauty's power
> And of the depths of ocean whence she sprang.
> At last the wave-born goddess raised her hand
> And smiling said: "O mortal youth behold!"
> And all these mysteries passed before mine eyes.[8]

These quotations are given in full because they are so revealing of the cult for the past—especially a remote and legendary past that could be conceived only "in a dim vision of the long ago" and enveloped in vague reveries and fantasies—which characterized the artistic aspirations of the Boston classicists. It should also be observed that the sequence of scenes described in the program note to this symphonic poem—the feast, the dances, the storm, the shipwreck, the rescue, the thanksgiving—is of such a stereotyped pattern that it could serve for any descriptive seapiece. This indicates what is confirmed by the music itself: that the whole work is conceived on a plane of academic

[7] Hughes, *op. cit.*, p. 479.
[8] Score published by The A. P. Schmidt Co., Inc.

conventionality. It is no more than a proper Bostonian flirtation with the shade of Aphrodite.

Chadwick had a preference for descriptive music, either in the form of orchestral program pieces or of choral settings of narrative poems. His setting of *The Viking's Last Voyage* (1881) for baritone solo, male chorus, and orchestra, reminds one of Rupert Hughes's query, "What would part-song writers do if the Vikings had never been invented? Where would they get their wild choruses for men, with a prize to the singer that makes the most noise?"[9] Other choral works by Chadwick include *Dedication Ode*, *Lovely Rosabelle*, *The Pilgrims*, and *Phoenix Expirans*. Though he wrote smoothly and correctly for voices, his choral output "dates" more than his instrumental music, partly because the Victorian cantata as a genre has "dated," and partly because he was less original in his vocal writing than in his best instrumental works. Chadwick tried his hand at opera, both serious and light, without much success, his most ambitious effort being the music drama *Judith*, which achieved a concert performance in 1901. Of his numerous songs (over a hundred), the best-known is his setting of Sidney Lanier's "Ballad of Trees and the Master."

Chadwick's instrumental works include five string quartets, a piano quintet, three symphonies, the early program overtures *Rip Van Winkle* (1879) and *The Miller's Daughter* (1884); the symphonic ballad, *Tam O' Shanter* (1915); and a set of four orchestral pieces which he called *Symphonic Sketches* (1895–1907), consisting of "Jubilee," "Noël," "Hobgoblin," and "A Vagrom Ballad." It is these symphonic sketches that make of Chadwick a figure of more than historical interest in America's music. Heard today, they have a vitality, a genuineness, a human and emotional quality that takes them out of the category of museum pieces. We may not feel that "Jubilee" and "A Vagrom Ballad" are entirely successful in expressing, as Philip Hale said, "the frankness, swagger and recklessness that Europeans commonly associate with Americans"—nor do we necessarily feel that there is any particular virtue in the musical expression of these traits, assuming that we do indeed possess them. But we do feel that this music is *alive*, and that Chadwick was at least on the right track when he broke away from his pseudoclassical preoccupations and gave vent to the Yankee humor and humanity that was in him. At the head of the score of "Jubilee," the composer placed the following verses:

[9] Hughes, *op. cit.*, p. 213.

No cool gray tones for me!
  Give me the warmest red and green,
  A cornet and a tambourine,
To paint *my* jubilee!
  For when the flutes and oboes play,
    To sadness I become a prey;
    Give me the violets and the May,
But no gray skies for me!

To establish this mood, the sketch (Allegro molto vivace) opens with a jovial theme proclaimed by the whole orchestra, fortissimo, followed soon by another striking theme stated by bass clarinet, bassoons, violas, and cellos, in unison. Then the horns announce a phrase in C major, which Philip Hale describes as a "patting Juba horn call," referring to some verses from Richard Hovey's *More Songs From Vagabondia:* [10]

When the wind comes up from Cuba
And the birds are on the wing,
And our hearts are patting Juba
To the banjo of the spring . . .

After a lyrical episode for wood winds and horns, the piece ends excitingly with a coda marked presto.

Of the three remaining *Symphonic Sketches*, the one titled "A Vagrom Ballad" is probably the most effective. Its atmosphere is evoked in these lines:

A tale of tramps and railway ties,
Of old clay pipes and rum,
Of broken heads and blackened eyes
And the "thirty days" to come.

While this sort of toying with the seamy side of life is still conceived on a conventional plane—a sort of Boston blend of the pastoral and picaresque traditions—the attempt to grasp some kind of earthy reality, rather than to dwell on remote legends and misty myths, marks a wholesome departure from the mood of high-minded imaginings and dreamy escapism that dominates so much of the music produced by the Bostonians of this period.

[10] Boston, 1896.

Chadwick's earthiness and sense of humor are also manifested in his stage works, especially his two comic operas, *The Quiet Lodging* and *Tobasco*. His sense of realism and a rather surprising concern with themes and problems of his own time and place are displayed in his opera *The Padrone*, which deals with Italian immigrants to New England. The *padrone* is the political boss who exploits the newcomers to this land of opportunity—and sometimes of deception and disappointment. Although *The Padrone* has had no career on the stage, it should have its place in our musical annals as one of the earliest examples of operatic *verismo* in the United States.

An exquisite artificer

Charles Martin Loeffler was born in Alsace on January 30, 1861, and died at his farm in Medfield, Massachusetts, on May 20, 1935. A violin pupil of Joachim and Massart, he spent some time in Russia as a youth, then joined the Pasdeloup Orchestra in Paris. Had he remained in Paris, he would have become identified with the French impressionists, setting to music the poems of Baudelaire and Verlaine, indulging his taste for delicate nuances and his passion for polished workmanship. There would then have been no reason for including him in this book, or for raising the question as to whether or not he can really be considered an American composer. The late Carl Engel, in a disconcerting outburst of hyperbole, apparently settled that question to his own satisfaction by declaring that Loeffler was the greatest of American composers.[11] For a dissenting opinion, we may turn, as usual, to the iconoclastic Rosenfeld, who characterized Loeffler as a correct and inhibited New Englander (though he was only that by geographical proximity) who produced music that was sterile and stiff with the dead weight of tradition. And the truth, as usual, would seem to rest midway between these extremes. I do not think that Loeffler can be regarded as an American composer in anything but a literal sense of that term, that is, a composer who lived and worked for most of his life in America.

Loeffler came to the United States in 1881, spent about a year in New York, and then, upon the invitation of Major Higginson, joined

[11] Engel, in *The International Cyclopedia of Music and Musicians*, ed. by Oscar Thompson.

the recently founded Boston Symphony Orchestra as first violin. He continued in this capacity until 1903, when he resigned and retired to a farm that he had acquired in Medfield. He had been composing for a number of years, and the Boston Symphony had performed several of his works from manuscript, notably a Suite for violin and orchestra (after Gogol), *Les Veillées de l'Ukraine* (1891), a *Fantastic Concerto* for cello and orchestra (1894), and a Divertimento for violin and orchestra (1895). After his retirement he began to publish some large works, such as the symphonic poem *La Mort de Tintagiles* (after Maeterlinck) and a *Symphonic Fantasy* (after a poem by Rollinat), both published in 1905. In 1901 he had written a work titled *A Pagan Poem* for chamber orchestra with piano. This he later rewrote for full orchestra, with piano obbligato, in which form it was played by the Boston Symphony in 1907. It remains Loeffler's best-known work. *A Pagan Poem* is based on the eighth Eclogue of Virgil, which tells of a Thessalian girl who tries to use sorcery to win back her errant lover Daphnis, repeating the magical refrain: *Ducite ab urbe domum, mea carmina, ducite Daphnim* ("Draw from the city, my songs, draw Daphnis home"). Three trumpets obbligati, heard at first off-stage and then gradually drawing nearer, finally merging with the orchestra on-stage, suggest the incantation of the sorceress, gaining in passion and potency as she weaves her spell.

Of Loeffler's numerous compositions, only three others need be mentioned here. These are Music for Four Stringed Instruments (published in 1923), *Canticum Fratris Solis* for voice and chamber orchestra (1925), and *Evocation* for orchestra, women's chorus, and speaking voice (1931). All of these compositions display Loeffler's penchant for the archaic and the impressionistic, for the evocation of past ages and idioms. His setting of St. Francis's "Canticle of the Sun," commissioned by the Elizabeth Sprague Coolidge Foundation and first performed at the Library of Congress in 1925, is another example of his musical preciosity and technical refinement.

Loeffler's work forms a sort of parenthesis in the history of America's music. He drew nothing from the American environment and contributed nothing to it in the way of immediate influence or directions for others to follow. Unlike other musical immigrants, he did not throw himself into the main stream of America's musical life. Spiritually remote and physically isolated, he created a dreamworld of lovingly wrought sounds, capable, indeed, of affording us delight, but in the end perhaps palling by its very exquisiteness.

It will be appropriate here to mention briefly another member of the Boston group, Arthur B. Whiting (1861–1936), not because his music is important (he outlived its reputation) but because it is so highly symptomatic of the Boston coterie which we are discussing. A native of Cambridge, Massachusetts, Whiting studied composition with Chadwick at the New England Conservatory of Music, then betook himself to Germany for the customary academic polishing, exposing himself to the teachings of Abel and Rheinberger, two eminent Teutonic pedagogues, at the Munich Conservatory. He returned to Boston brimful of enthusiasm for Brahms and imbued with what his friend and admirer Mason calls "the classic spirit," sternly opposed to anything "slipshod or mawkish or inept." In this mood of idealistic austerity he proceeded to produce a series of works, including a Concert Overture, a Suite for horn and strings, some chamber music and songs, and a Fantasy for piano and orchestra (Opus 11), which drew from the irrepressible Philip Hale the following choice bit of critical sarcasm:

Mr. Whiting had, and no doubt has, high ideals. Sensuousness in music seemed to him as something intolerable, something against public morals, something that should be suppressed by the selectmen. Perhaps he never went so far as to petition for an injunction against sex in music; but rigorous intellectuality was his one aim. He might have written A Serious Call to Devout and Holy Composition, or A Practical Treatise upon Musical Perfection, to which is now added, by the same author, The Absolute Unlawfulness of the State Entertainment Fully Demonstrated.[12]

Mr. Hale obviously knew his early New England tracts. He did, however, concede that Whiting had put somewhat more of warmth and humanity into his Fantasy than he had permitted to appear in his earlier works. If there is any possibility at all of reviving interest in Whiting's music, it will probably be through this Fantasy for piano and orchestra.

Some cantatas and an opera

Horatio Parker is a composer who stands very near the top of the Boston group. Born in Auburndale, Massachusetts, on September 15, 1863, he came of a highly cultured New England family. His father

[12] Quoted by Hughes, *op. cit.*, p. 289.

was an architect and his mother an amateur organist and a lover of literature who knew Greek and Latin. Not until he was fourteen did Parker begin to take any interest in music, and then his mother became his first teacher, in piano and organ. Within two years the boy had made such progress that he was appointed church organist in Dedham and began to compose hymns and anthems, just as any of his early New England forebears might have done. When Chadwick returned from Europe in 1880 and opened a teaching studio in Boston, young Parker became one of his first pupils. The next step, of course, was for him to follow in Chadwick's footsteps and make his own pilgrimage to Germany, which he did in 1882, electing to sit at the feet of Rheinberger in Munich, from whom he absorbed with exemplary thoroughness the rules of counterpoint. While in Germany, Parker composed several large works—concert overtures, a Symphony, cantatas—some of which were performed in Munich. After three years abroad he settled in New York, as church organist, teacher at the National Conservatory, and music director at St. Paul's School, Garden City. In 1893 he transferred his activities to Boston, and a year later accepted the Battell Professorship of Music at Yale University, where he remained until his death in 1919. He was also very active as a choral conductor, which kept him busily commuting between New Haven and New York. Although his position at Yale and his choral conducting removed him physically from the Boston scene, Parker definitely belongs with the Boston group because of his background, his training, his associations, and his aesthetic tendencies.

Although he wrote nine orchestral works, some chamber music, and pieces for piano and for organ, it is as a composer of choral music that he made his reputation. His first conspicuous success came with the performance in New York in 1893 of his sacred cantata *Hora Novissima*, for mixed chorus and orchestra, a setting of 210 lines from the twelfth-century Latin poem by Bernard of Clairvaux, "De Contemptu Mundi." This was the work that established Parker's fame in England, when it was performed at the Three Choirs Festival, Worcester, in 1899. As a result, he was commissioned to write two choral works for English festivals: *Wanderer's Psalm* and *Star Song*. Another ambitious sacred cantata, dramatic in conception and Wagnerian in style, *The Legend of St. Christopher*, was performed in Bristol and led to the culmination of Parker's English fame when he received the degree of Doctor of Music from Cambridge University in 1902. An earlier cantata, *The Dream King and His Love*, had won the prize in a contest sponsored by the National Conservatory of Music in New York in 1892. Thus both abroad and at home Parker was honored and acclaimed.

Parker had a capacity for winning important prizes. When the Metropolitan Opera House of New York offered a prize of $10,000 for an opera by an American composer, Parker entered the competition and won the prize for his opera *Mona*, with a libretto by Brian Hooker. The story deals with the well-worn theme of love versus patriotism, for Mona is a princess of Britain at the time of the Roman conquest who falls in love with the son of the Roman governor and yet cannot stifle her hatred for the haughty invaders of her country. *Mona* was produced at the Metropolitan Opera House on March 14, 1912, being the third opera by an American to be performed by that institution (the other two were Converse's *Pipe of Desire* and Herbert's *Natoma*, produced, respectively, in 1910 and 1911). It received only a few performances that season and was never revived. Arguments as to the merits of the opera *Mona* seem rather futile. That it contains some well-written academic music is undeniable, but this does not establish it as a viable dramatic work for the lyric theater. As a footnote to Parker's operatic ventures, it should be remarked that in 1913 he won another $10,000 prize, this time offered by the National Federation of Music Clubs, with an opera titled *Fairyland*, also having a libretto by Brian Hooker. This opera received six performances in Los Angeles in 1915 and has not been heard since then.

The cantata *Hora Novissima* is generally acknowledged to be Parker's masterpiece. Yet even the admiring Philip Hale admitted that its most eloquent moments are "expressed in the language of Palestrina and Bach," while the enthusiastic W. J. Henderson spoke of an *a cappella* chorus that "might have been written by Hobrecht, Brumel, or even Josquin des Près." Other critics remarked on its Mendelssohnian mannerisms and Handelian repetitiousness, all of which adds up to a rather disconcerting hodgepodge of influences. Philip Hale, in what was meant to be high praise, wrote that *Hora Novissima* was a work to which "an acknowledged master of composition in Europe would gladly sign his name." The point is that several European masters could have legitimately signed their names to it. Perhaps this sort of accomplishment was important while America's music was coming of age. It meant that, judged by European standards, American music had no need to be ashamed of itself: the imitation was getting to be practically as good as the model. But what we really needed was some American music to which no European master of composition could sign his name and get away with it. This the Boston classicists were incapable of giving us.

A lady and two professors

The Boston group had a feminine representative in the person of Amy Marcy Cheney (1867–1944), who later became Mrs. H. H. A. Beach. A native of Henniker, New Hampshire, she belonged to one of those long-settled New England families who cultivated music and learning in their leisure and passed on this cultural heritage from generation to generation. She received her first musical lessons from her mother, continued with various teachers when the family moved to Boston, and at sixteen made her debut as a professional pianist. Meanwhile she had been composing since early childhood, and it was not long before she established a reputation as the most prominent American woman composer of her time. Official commissions confirmed her success as a career woman in musical composition: a *Festival Jubilate* for the dedication of the Woman's Building at the Chicago World's Fair in 1893; a *Song of Welcome* for the Trans-Mississippi Exposition at Omaha in 1898; and a *Panama Hymn* for the Panama-Pacific Exposition at San Francisco in 1915.

Of Mrs. Beach's larger works, the best-known are the *Gaelic Symphony*, based on Gaelic folk tunes, and a Piano Concerto. A quantity of church music, some chamber music, many piano pieces, and over one hundred and fifty songs—her most popular output—constitutes the bulk of the work that she produced in her long and busy life. She achieved considerable recognition, particularly in Germany, in the years immediately preceding World War I. While a place must always be reserved for her in the history of American music, the public will doubtless remember her best for such songs as "Ah, Love, But a Day" and "The Year's at the Spring."

Few composers have been more closely identified with the Boston tradition than was Edward Burlingame Hill (1872–1960), born in Cambridge of old New England ancestry, grandson of a president of Harvard University, son of a professor there, and himself on the staff of Harvard from 1908 until he retired in 1940. Inevitably he attended Harvard as a youth and was a pupil in music of John Knowles Paine. He also studied with Chadwick and Whiting in Boston, and with Widor in Paris. Where he differs most sharply from the Boston classicists is in his preference for French music, of which he made a special study. He lectured on this subject at the universities of Lyon and Strasbourg, and published a book titled *Modern French Music*.

Hill has written instrumental music almost exclusively. His orchestral works include three symphonies, several suites, the symphonic poems *Launcelot and Guinevere* and *Lilacs*, two sinfoniettas, a Concertino for piano and orchestra, a Violin Concerto, and Music for English Horn and Orchestra. His two *Stevensoniana* suites are based on poems from Stevenson's *A Child's Garden of Verses*. Hill's chamber music consists of a Sextet for wind instruments and piano, a Quintet for clarinet and strings, a String Quartet, a Sonata for flute and piano, and a Sonata for clarinet and piano.

When Hill's Symphony No. 3 in G major received its first performance by the Boston Symphony Orchestra on December 3, 1937, the composer wrote that the work had "no descriptive background, aiming merely to present musical ideas according to the traditional forms." As he said much the same thing about his First Symphony, this may be taken as a statement of his aesthetic position as an academic traditionalist. He aimed to maintain interest by deft instrumentation and skillful organization of his material in accepted forms. In this he is a precursor of Walter Piston and heralds the new generation of Boston traditionalists who adhere to the fundamental triad of form, style, and craftsmanship, as conceived and regulated by academic canons.

At the beginning of this chapter we mentioned the late Daniel Gregory Mason (1873–1953), who as a young man in Boston hailed "the great classical revival of the 20th century in America." Mason's classical ideal was defined by what he himself spoke of as "an instinctive antipathy toward excess, unbalance, romantic exaggeration, sensationalism, typified for me in such composers, great artists though they be, as Wagner, Tschaikowsky, Liszt, Strauss." Among European contemporaries he had little use for Debussy and Ravel, but felt a profound admiration for Vincent d'Indy, with whom he studied in Paris and from whom he learned the value of "the unbroken stream of tradition." Although Mason eventually left Boston for New York, it seems fitting to write of his life and work here because, stemming from a long line of New Englanders and imbued with a stern sense of what was fitting and proper in musical expression, he embodied throughout his long career both the virtues and the limitations that we associate with the Boston Classicists.

Born in Brookline, Massachusetts, Mason attended Harvard University and was for a time a pupil there of J. K. Paine, whom, however, he found unsatisfactory as a teacher. Later he studied composition with Chadwick in Boston and with Goetschius in New York. From 1910 he was a member of the music faculty at Columbia University, where he was appointed MacDowell Professor of Music in 1929. He retired from the chairmanship of the Music Department in 1940.

Among Mason's orchestral works are three symphonies, of which the Third (1936) is the *Lincoln Symphony*, a tone-portrait of the "Great Emancipator." His best-known orchestral composition is the *Chanticleer Overture* (1928), inspired by passages from Thoreau's *Walden*, as quoted in the score: "All climates agree with brave Chanticleer. He is more indigenous than the natives. His health is ever good, his lungs, his spirits never flag."

Mason's interest in Anglo-American folk material is revealed in his *Suite After English Folk Songs* for orchestra (1924) and his *Folk Song Fantasy (Fanny Blair)* for string quartet (1929). His numerous chamber-music works include an attractive String Quartet on Negro Themes, first performed in 1919. The first movement is based on the spiritual "You May Bury Me in the East," while the second movement develops the theme of "Deep River," with a contrastingly energetic theme in the middle section. The third movement uses three spirituals: "O What Do You Say, Seekers?" "Shine, Shine, I'll Meet You in the Morning," and "Oh, Holy Lord!"

Other chamber-music works by Mason are a Violin Sonata; Three Pieces for flute, harp, and string quartet; Sonata for clarinet and piano; Variations on a theme of John Powell for string quartet; *Divertimento* for five wind instruments; *Sentimental Sketches* for violin, cello, and piano; and Variations on a Quiet Theme for string quartet.

Mason thought of himself as "a musical humanist." But his humanism tended to be scholastic and restrictive, and caused him to balk at our "heterogeneous national character." For his views on this subject, the reader is referred to page 402. Here we may mention two of Mason's books, dealing with the contemporary scene in American music: *Tune In, America* and *The Dilemma of American Music*. Perhaps the most perceptive comment on Mason's music is that made by Randall Thompson, when he wrote: "A certain sinister and foreboding pessimism, a dour and bitter irony in Mason's music has not been fully appreciated." [13] It may be that this dour quality will endure longer than the lusty bravado of Chanticleer.

In summing up the achievements of the Boston Classicists we may say that they gave to the American composer a professional dignity, a social and artistic prestige, and a degree of recognition both at home and abroad, such as he had not previously enjoyed. In a sense their mission was similar to that accomplished in France by Vincent d'Indy and his associates of the Schola Cantorum: the affirmation of idealism combined with technical discipline. If they were stronger in idealism than in technique, and stronger in technique than in originality, that was partly the consequence of historical factors. They were epigoni rather than originators, and they almost succeeded in making Boston a musical suburb of Munich. They were not moving with the main stream of America's music, nor were they able to recognize and cherish their native musical heritage.

While many of the Boston group were still flourishing, a reaction took place among another group of American musicians, stimulated by a famous visitor from abroad and led by a composer from the Middle West, which resulted in greater awareness of American values, freedom from the musical hegemony of Germany, and a keen interest in the folk, popular, and primitive music of the United States, including Anglo-American folk songs and ballads, Negro spirituals, minstrel tunes, ragtime, and the tribal melodies of the Indians. In the next chapter, with which Part III of this book commences, we turn to the beginnings of what is generally known as "musical nationalism." Actually, the outlook of the composers who participated in this movement was widely international. They sought stimulation and fresh ideas from many sources; many of them were attracted by the folk music of far-off countries. But as Americans aware of their own cultural heritage they felt that America's native or popular music was worth looking at and listening to and using in their compositions. Thus, with the third part of this book, a new era begins in America's music. We become conscious of our musical heritage, we explore it in all its

[13] In *The Musical Quarterly*, XVIII, 1, p. 13.

aspects, we feel the excitement of new popular currents in the rise of ragtime and jazz, our vernacular musical theater develops, our composers achieve mastery of the larger forms, our innovators boldly break new paths, and we witness a tremendous expansion of all our musical resources and activities, both in creation and communication. Such, in brief, are the main developments that form the subject matter of the third and concluding section of this work.

three

The real America is not to be found either in the order of the long-settled communities or in the disorder of the frontier, but in that area of dynamic and expanding life which is born of the union of the two.

FLOYD STOVALL, AMERICAN IDEALISM.

chapter nineteen

Nationalism and folklore

I get a great kick out of a rip-snorting development of a good old American tune.
ARTHUR FARWELL.

In his *History of American Music,* Louis C. Elson recounts that Massenet once spoke enthusiastically to him about the inspiration that ought to come to the American composer. "Were I in America," said he, "I should be exalted by the glories of your scenery, your Niagara, your prairies; I should be inspired by the Western and Southern life; I should be intoxicated by the beauty of your American women; national surroundings always inspire national music!" [1] The last phrase might be supplemented by adding: "Especially if one is a foreigner." Until recently, for instance, the most effective "Spanish" music was written by foreigners: Glinka, Bizet, Lalo, Rimsky-Korsakoff, Ravel. Turning for a moment to poetic inspiration, one thinks of the Cuban, José María Heredia, spending two years of exile in the United States (1823–1825), gazing spellbound at Niagara Falls, and producing under this overwhelming impression one of the famous poems of the Spanish language, "Niágara."

Shortly before Heredia's sojourn in the United States another foreigner arrived in this country, an eccentric amateur musician from Bohemia named Anton Philip Heinrich (1781–1861), who became enthusiastic about creating an "American" music inspired by the natural scenery, the history, and the native Indian music of the United States. Formerly a banker in Hamburg, Heinrich came to America around 1818, was active first in Philadelphia as musical director of the Southwark Theatre and then went to Louisville, Kentucky, where he taught violin. He spent some time among the Indians in Bardstown and was

[1] Elson, *History of American Music,* p. 337.

385

fascinated by the possibility of using Indian themes in his compositions. In 1820 Heinrich published *Dawning of Music in Kentucky, or the Pleasures of Harmony in the Solitudes of Nature*, in which he declared that "no one would ever be more proud than himself, to be called an *American Musician*." This "*American production*" was recommended to the favorable notice of the public in the pages of Parker's *Euterpeiad*, which hailed the composer as "the *Beethoven* of America." Heinrich tried hard to play the role of great American composer. He turned out such works as *The Columbiad, Grand American national chivalrous symphony, Jubilee* ("a grand national song of triumph, composed and arranged for a full orchestra and a vocal chorus—in two parts, commemorative of events from the landing of the Pilgrim fathers to the consummation of American liberty"), *Yankee Doodliad, The New England Feast of Shells* ("Divertimento Pastorale Oceanico"), and numerous works "inspired" by his interest in Indian music: *Indian Carnival, Indian Fanfares, The Mastodon, Manitou Mysteries*, and *Pushmataha*.

Certainly old "Father" Heinrich, as he was called, found plenty of "inspiration" in the national surroundings of America; the only drawback was that he lacked talent and technique as a composer. But his enthusiasm for all things American, his aspiration to be known as an *American* musician, his interest in American Indian lore, were symptomatic of things to come. He tried to do, singlehanded and poorly equipped, what it took a whole generation of American musicians to accomplish, collectively and arduously, many decades after Father Heinrich had passed away from the American musical scene on which he made so slight and ephemeral an impression.

Curiously enough, it was another Bohemian—but this time a talented and trained musician—who gave a definite impetus to the formation of a "national" school of composers in the United States. His name was Antonin Dvořák, the composer of the Symphony "From the New World." Before recounting the circumstances of Dvořák's sojourn in the United States from 1892 to 1895, and its effects on the development of American music, it would be well to review briefly the rise of the movement known as "musical nationalism," of which Dvořák was one of the leading representatives.

The spirit of nationalism was rooted in romanticism, which exalted liberty and which recognized the artistic value of folklore. In some cases the use of folk music went hand in hand with a passionate patriotism. Chopin, writing his Polonaises and his Mazurkas, thought of his native land, Poland, enslaved and oppressed. Smetana and Dvořák thought of the political subjugation of Bohemia, a land rich in culture but deprived of independence. Edvard Grieg identified himself with the movement for the independence of Norway. In Russia, on the other hand, the movement was almost exclusively artistic and centered on the exploitation of Russian folk music for the creation of a distinctively "national" school of composition that would assert its independence from the musical hegemony exercised by Germany over Europe.

In the person of Mikhail Glinka (1803–1857), Russian music found its liberator, the creator of a national school with his operas *A Life for the Czar* and *Russlan and Ludmilla*. True, the Russian aristocracy sneered at Glinka for writing "coachmen's music," just as American snobs sneered at composers who used "Negro melodies." But Glinka's music appealed to the people, and what is more, a whole group of composers arose to follow in his footsteps. The group of composers known as the "Mighty Five"—Balakirev, Moussorgsky, Borodin, Cui, Rimsky-Korsakoff—formed the "new school of Russian music" in the 1860s, which soon became widely influential, challenging the supremacy of the Germanic tradition and, later in the century, stimulating the emergence of national schools in such countries as France, Spain, and England. The United States, isolated by the domination of German influence, was one of the few countries that did not feel this stimulating current of liberation and creative vigor until after the turn of the century. Nevertheless, thanks to the presence and the prestige of Antonin Dvořák, some American composers began to be aware of the value of their folk music before the nineteenth century drew to a close.

Dvořák in America

Dvořák had come to America in response to an invitation to be director of the National Conservatory of Music in New York. Among his pupils were William Arms Fisher (1861–1948), Rubin Goldmark (1872–1936), Harvey Worthington Loomis (1865–1930), and Henry Thacker Burleigh (1866–1949). Anyone disposed to minimize Dvořák's influence might point out that none of these men proved to be creative artists of exceptional stature. Fisher, known chiefly as a writer of songs, had the happy thought of adapting the melody of the Largo (slow movement) from Dvořák's *New World Symphony* to the words of "Goin' Home," thus producing a pseudo spiritual that has become widely popular. Goldmark, nephew of the Austrian composer Carl Goldmark and trained at the Vienna Conservatory before studying with Dvořák, became professor of composition at the Juilliard School of Music in New York. His musical Americanism manifested itself in several orchestral works: *Requiem* (suggested by Lincoln's Gettysburg Address), *Hiawatha Overture, Negro Rhapsody,* and *The Call of the Plains.* Loomis became particularly interested in American Indian music, which he studied carefully and arranged effectively in his *Lyrics of the Red-Man* for piano (Opus 76), published in 1903–1904. Burleigh, a Negro, made a career as singer and as arranger of Negro spirituals (his setting of "Deep River" is well known). His association with Dvořák is of special interest to us, for it was through Burleigh's singing that the Bohemian composer became acquainted with many of the Negro spirituals that were to fascinate him. Years later, in 1918, Burleigh wrote as follows regarding the genesis of the *New World Symphony:*

There is a tendency in these days to ignore the Negro elements in the "New World" Symphony, shown by the fact that many of those who were able in 1893 to find traces of Negro musical color all through the symphony, though the workmanship and treatment of the themes was and is Bohemian, now cannot find anything in the whole four movements that suggests any local or Negro influence, though there is no doubt at all that Dvořák was deeply impressed by the old Negro "spirituals" and also by Foster's songs. It was my privilege to sing repeatedly some of the old plantation songs for him at his house, and one in particular, "Swing Low, Sweet Chariot," greatly pleased him, and part of this old "spiritual" will be found in the 2nd theme of the first movement of the symphony, in G major, first given out by the flute. The similarity is so evident that it doesn't even need to be heard; the eye can see it. Dvořák saturated himself with the spirit of these old tunes and then invented his own themes. There is a subsidiary theme in G minor in the first movement, with a flat 7th, and I feel sure the composer caught this peculiarity of most of the slave songs from some that I sang to him; for he used to stop me and ask if that was the way the slaves sang.[2]

[2] Quoted by M. (Cuney) Hare, *Negro Music and Musicians,* p. 59.

There is a certain inconsistency in Burleigh's insistence on the identity of the "Swing Low, Sweet Chariot" theme and his statement that "Dvořák saturated himself with the spirit of these old tunes and then invented his own themes." The latter statement I believe to be true, and the thematic similarity merely a coincidence. This is confirmed by a declaration attributed to Dvořák regarding the program notes for the *New World Symphony:* "Omit that nonsense about my having made use of 'Indian' and 'American' motives. That is a lie. I tried only to write in the spirit of those national American melodies." Dvořák, then, did not advocate the literal use of folk tunes. In this he differed from Glinka, who said: "We the composers are only arrangers." Glinka, being only a gifted amateur, could afford such modesty, such self-effacement in favor of the collective document, the traditional tune. But Dvořák, the great composer, was angry at the thought of being considered a mere arranger. Fundamentally, these attitudes represent two significantly different points of view: that of the composer who "dresses up" folk tunes in attractive instrumental colors and that of the composer who, assimilating the elements of folk music, seeks to develop its idiosyncratic traits of idiom and expression. To the first group belong such composers as Glinka, Lalo, Rimsky-Korsakoff. Among representatives of the second group are Dvořák, Grieg, Falla, and Bartók. While these last-mentioned composers used folk tunes occasionally, their aim was not to provide attractive window dressing for folk songs, but rather to explore ways of musical thinking based on the characteristic rhythms, modalities, and melodic intervals of the folk tunes of a given culture.

Dvořák, of course, approached the subject much more superficially than did later composers such as Falla and Bartók, who made a profound study of the folk music of their respective countries (Spain and Hungary). The scientific study of folk music was in its infancy in Dvořák's day, and at the period of his sojourn in the United States almost nobody knew or cared anything about American folk music. Elson reflected the general opinion when he wrote: "It must be admitted that in this field [folk music] America is rather barren." [3] And Frederic L. Ritter asked rhetorically: "How are we to account for this utter absence of national people's music and poetry in America?" [4] The trouble was that most city-bred, Europeanized Americans were

[3] Elson, *The History of American Music*, p. 123.
[4] Ritter, *Music in America*, p. 388.

so busy keeping their noses in the air that they never thought of putting their ears to the ground. When they finally got down to earth, they heard the land shaking with music.

As we know, some Americans began to be interested in the Negro spirituals shortly after the Civil War; and the study of Indian music, begun by Catlin and Schoolcraft in the first half of the nineteenth century, was continued by specialists in the latter decades of the century. But MacDowell was asking superciliously what "the Negro melodies" had to do with "Americanism in art," and sneering at the pattern for "an 'American' national musical costume" offered by "the Bohemian Dvořák." The truth is that Dvořák was not offering a pattern. He was pointing to a potential source of inspiration. And more important than any particular source he mentioned—Negro spirituals or Indian melodies—was the attitude of mind, the spiritual message, that he conveyed to American musicians.

Dvořák, in effect, was saying to the American composer, "Look homeward" and "Cultivate your own garden." He was not simply saying, "Play around with folk tunes for a change." His message, translated into its broader and deeper significance, meant that American composers should turn their attention to the indigenous products of American culture, that they should value and cultivate—by assimilation rather than by imitation—the idiosyncratic elements of musical culture in America. The fact that Dvořák was incompletely acquainted with these elements—that he mistook the part for the whole—is of no particular consequence, for with time and increasing knowledge, American musicians obtained a wider perspective of the subject. The important fact is that he issued a challenge, a challenge which was accepted by a small but enthusiastic and determined group of American composers, with significant results for America's music.

Given the circumstances of his time and background, Dvořák can scarcely be blamed for sharing the common fallacy, expressed by Elson in the dictum that "American folk song in its true sense can only be derived from Indian or plantation life." Of these two elements, Dvořák attached more importance to the so-called "plantation melodies." In this connection it is interesting to note his high regard, mentioned by Burleigh, for the songs of Stephen Foster. This admiration is significant, for Foster, frowned upon by the devotees of the genteel tradition, did not at that time occupy the eminent place in our musical pantheon that we have since accorded to him.

In a statement issued before the New York première of the *New World Symphony* in 1893, Dvořák was quoted as having said, referring to the plantation melodies:

> These beautiful and varied themes are the product of the soil. They are American. They are the folk songs of America, and your composers must turn to them. In the Negro melodies of America I discover all that is needed for a great and noble school of music.

Philosophically and ethnographically considered, it would be easy to find fault with this statement. By this time, however, the reader knows much more about the Negro spirituals than did Dvořák; so there is no need to embark on a lengthy critique of his views. He was on safer ground, because simply expressing a personal preference based on taste, when, in an article published in the *Century Magazine* (February, 1895), he said, "The so-called plantation songs are indeed the most striking and appealing melodies that have been found on this side of the water." When we contrast this with the contemptuous attitude of such musical snobs as Hastings and Dwight—the latter died in the same year that the *New World Symphony* was first performed—we can begin to appreciate the wholesome and liberalizing effect of Dvořák's opinions.

Dvořák, who visited various sections of the United States and lived for a while in Spillville, Iowa, became so enthusiastic about this country that he wrote a Cantata to the American flag and even proposed to write a new national anthem for the United States! In addition to his famous Symphony "From the New World" (No. 5, in E minor), he also composed a String Quartet and a Quintet utilizing themes suggested by American Indian music.

Revolt against German hegemony

The significance of Dvořák's American visit does not reside exclusively in his enthusiasm for American folk songs (as far as he knew them), in his call for the formation of an American "national school" of composition, or in his writing of notable works inspired by his experiences in the New World. All these are important factors, but they are transcended by the over-all liberating influence symbolized by his visit in relation to this particular historical moment in the development of musical culture in the United States. To put it in plain language, let us recall MacDowell's contemptuous reference to the nationalistic notions of "the Bohemian Dvořák," quoted in a previous chapter. On the face of it, one might take MacDowell's epithet as signifying a foreigner, one who is not an American and who therefore has no business telling Americans how they shall create their "national" music. But the implication of MacDowell's epithet seems rather to be somewhat as follows: "Here is a composer *who is not German* and who yet presumes to establish values and directions for American music." Translated into its broader implications, this attitude represents the last stand of the German conservatories and their satellites against the "invasion of the barbarians"—that is, the rise and the spread of invigorating musical forces, coming chiefly from Russia, but also from France, from Bohemia, from the Orient, from the New World.

The German domination of American music was so complete that, in the words of Arthur Farwell, only German music sounded natural to concertgoers in the United States. A revolt against this domination was an absolute historical necessity. Dvořák prepared the way, and the movement of liberation found its American spokesman in the person of Arthur Farwell, musician of the Middle West, who in 1903 boldly proclaimed a plan of action:

> The first correction we must bring to our musical vision is to cease to see everything through German spectacles, however wonderful, however sublime those spectacles may be in themselves! The correction is to be effected by making the thorough acquaintance of Russian and French music of the present, by allowing Russia and France not the mere opportunity of occasionally getting a musical word in edgewise, but of engaging, with Germany, equal shares of our musical conversation. . . . Thus fortified, we will no longer fear that the American composer is going to the dogs when he revels in a new and unusual combination of notes; that is, one which differs from the good old German tradition.[5]

Farwell fearlessly proclaimed the heresy that "France and Russia lead the world today in musical invention, in all that makes for greater plasticity of tone as an art medium."

Was this simply advocating a change of masters? By no means. In the first place, Farwell was not proposing to discard German music, whose achievements he respected and valued. His plea was for an enlightened eclecticism, a search for originality resulting from the inter-

[5] Quoted by Waters, *The Wa-Wan Press*, pp. 222-223.

play of multiple influences. Imitation he believed to be a necessary step in acquiring artistic individuality, but let us begin by imitating *all* styles and forms. Eventually, from the factors of our environment, there would result a characteristically American manner of expression, compounded of many styles, in which would be found: "Notably, ragtime, Negro songs, Indian songs, Cowboy songs, and, of the utmost importance, new and daring expressions of our own composers, sound-speech previously unheard." [6] The last half of this statement we shall leave for later consideration in the chapter dealing with our musical experimentalists. Before commenting on the remainder of the statement, let us learn something about the man who made it.

Arthur Farwell was born in St. Paul, Minnesota, in 1872. Although he received violin lessons from the age of nine, he was not groomed for a musical career. He went east to attend the Massachusetts Institute of Technology, from which he was graduated with a degree in engineering in 1893—the year of the *New World Symphony*. It was after going to Boston that he heard a symphony orchestra for the first time. Music soon became his chief interest, and after graduating he studied composition with Norris in Boston. Following the nearly inevitable trend at that time, he went to Germany in 1897 for study with Humperdinck and Pfitzner; but he also went to Paris, where his teacher was Guilmant. Two years later he returned to the United States and became lecturer on musical history at Cornell University, at the same time taking up the study of American Indian music. After founding the Wa-Wan Press, in 1901, for the publication of American music, he undertook, from 1904, a series of transcontinental tours, lecturing on American music and playing his compositions based on Indian themes. During his travels he studied the Indian music of the Southwest and collected the folk songs of Spanish California. He was eager to embrace the entire range of musical expression in America.

From 1909 to 1917, Farwell was active in New York, as staff writer for *Musical America*, as Supervisor of Municipal Music (1910–1913), and finally as director of the Music School Settlement. For one year (1918–1919) he was on the staff of the University of California, and from 1927 to 1939 he taught at Michigan State College in East Lansing. He wrote the music for several pageants and was keenly interested in developing "Community Music Drama" along the lines of *La Prima-*

[6] Quoted by Waters, *loc. cit.*

vera, produced at Santa Barbara in 1920. Through these varied activities he was brought into firsthand association with virtually every aspect of America's musical life. Farwell died in 1951.

The Wa-Wan Press

It was through the Wa-Wan Press, and the movement that centered around it, that Farwell made his most significant contribution to the advancement of America's music. He had been unable to find a publisher for his Indian melodies, and he felt that the American composer simply had no status in his own country. He knew that he was not alone in this feeling. One night, while he was thinking about this problem, there suddenly came to him "the thought of William Blake and William Morris, with their presses, printing their own work and that of colleagues, at least in Morris' case." There, he believed, was the solution. Combining his work with that of others, he would "launch a progressive movement for American music, *including a definite acceptance of Dvořák's challenge to go after our folk music*" (my italics). He talked it over with Edgar Stillman Kelley and others, and they were all for it.

The enterprise was launched without capital and without financial backing of any kind. Farwell engaged a local printer in Newton Center, Massachusetts, borrowed a few dollars for postage, and set out to get subscribers. The music engraving and lithography were done in Boston. The plan was to bring out two books of music each quarter; later the publications were also issued separately, in sheet-music form. During one year the press did receive a modest subsidy from George Foster Peabody, but mostly it was supported by Farwell's lectures, for the subscriptions did not always cover expenses. The enterprise continued for eleven years and the catalogue was then turned over to the firm of G. Schirmer (excepting the compositions of Gilbert and Troyer).

In his preliminary announcement of the Wa-Wan Press, Farwell stated:

The Wa-Wan Press is a natural outcome of the rapid growth of true musical genius in America, and in proportion to its capacity and growth, will aim to render available hitherto unpublished compositions of the highest order, which because of circumstances which the art-life of America is rapidly outgrowing, have heretofore been denied the daylight of print.

He also declared:

We are in earnest. We shall ask of the composer, not that he submit to us work which is likely to be in demand, but that he express himself. We shall do our utmost to foster individuality. Name shall be nothing to us. We shall stand for no particular composer, but for a principle. . . . We shall avoid the trivial, the ephemeral, the merely pretty, and seek the poetic and vitally emotional, striving to produce works of genial fire and enduring worth.

To what extent did the publications of the Wa-Wan Press bear out this ambitious program? As far as catholicity of selection and artistic integrity are concerned, the record is creditable. As regards "genial fire and enduring worth"—which are rare in any place and any age—the results were somewhat less satisfactory. Of the thirty-seven composers represented in the catalogue of the Wa-Wan Press, the most important, besides Farwell himself, are Henry F. B. Gilbert, Arthur Shepherd, Edward B. Hill, Harvey W. Loomis, Frederic Ayres, and Edgar Stillman Kelley. Of these, only Farwell, Gilbert, and Shepherd may be said to have achieved a considerable degree of significance in our national music. Others, however, acquired an estimable reputation in various fields: Arthur Olaf Andersen, John P. Beach, Gena Branscombe, Natalie Curtis Burlin, Rubin Goldmark, Katherine Ruth Heyman, Carlos Troyer, Arne Oldberg, and Louis Campbell Tipton. Let us admit that this is scarcely a roster of flaming genius. Nevertheless, looking at the movement as a whole, there are positive values. One notices a remarkable variety of individual interests and backgrounds. This was not *coterie* music. This was not a *clique* of Indianists and Negrophiles. We have here a group of young artists working in the musical medium, striving to develop their creative capacities and to gain a hearing in a society that had hitherto virtually refused to acknowledge their existence, or even to recognize that, as social beings, they had any rightful relation to the *res publica*. The Wa-Wan Press was intended to establish the identity of the American composer as a free creative artist, independent of commercial interests.

In retrospect, Farwell wrote of his publishing venture: "There were two major departments of our plan. One comprised all American work showing talent or progress along any of the paths of musical tradition. The other comprised all interesting or worthwhile work done with American folk-material as a basis." Let us examine further the second department of this plan. Among those comparatively few composers who turned to folk material in publications issued by the Wa-Wan Press, the main interest centered on American Indian music. Farwell himself brought out *American Indian Melodies* (1901), *The Domain of Hurakan* (1902), *Impressions of the Wa-Wan Ceremony of the Omahas* (1906), *From Mesa and Plain* (Indian, Cowboy, and Negro Sketches, 1905), and *Dawn* (1902), based on Omaha Indian themes. All these were for piano solo. The *Navajo War Dance* (one of the pieces in *From Mesa and Plain*) and *Dawn* were also arranged for orchestra (unpublished). In addition, the catalogue included Farwell's collection, for voice with piano accompaniment, *Folk-Songs of the West and South* (Negro, Cowboy, and Spanish-California). Harvey Worthington Loomis was represented by his *Lyrics of the Red-Man*, already mentioned. Carlos Troyer (1837–1920), who made a special study of Indian music of the Southwest, contributed two series of *Traditional Songs of the Zúñis* for voice and piano (1904), *Hymn to the Sun* ("An ancient jubilee song of the sun-worshippers. With historic account of the ceremony and the derivation of music from the sun's rays"), *Ghost Dance of the Zúñis*, and *Kiowa-Apache War-Dance*.

An eclectic folklorist

In the case of Henry Franklin Belknap Gilbert (1868–1928) we find a composer whose interest in folk music ranged over the world. This interest is only slightly adumbrated in his publications for the Wa-Wan Press, though it is curious to notice the inclusion of *Two South American Gypsy Songs* ("La Montonera" and "Zambulidora" indicating that, after Gottschalk, he was one of our first composers to take an interest in Latin American music (his ethnology, however, was weak: there is no "Gypsy" music in South America). The *Negro Episode* for piano (1902) reflects another phase of Gilbert's concern with American material.

Henry Gilbert had an unorthodox background. Though he was MacDowell's first American pupil in Boston (1889–1892), he led no sheltered academic existence. While studying composition he earned a living playing the violin for dances and in theater orchestras. Later he took up miscellaneous occupations: real-estate agent, factory foreman, silkworm grower, and bread- and pie-cutter in a restaurant at the Chicago World's Fair of 1893. Eager to hear the first performance of Charpentier's opera *Louise* in Paris, he went to Europe on a cattle boat. Soon after the founding of the Wa-Wan Press he and Farwell became close friends, drawn together by a common interest in folklore and in promoting a national musical movement. Gilbert was an eclectic by choice: his nationalism was not narrow. This is how he explained his attitude toward music:

> It has been my ideal not to allow any composer or school of music to influence me to the point of imitating them. I have striven to express my own individuality regardless whether it was good, bad, or indifferent. I prefer my own hat to a borrowed crown. Of course, I have had many admirations and have absorbed musical nutriment from many sources. . . . More than the music of any individual composer; more than the music of any particular school, the folk tunes of the world, of all nationalities, races, and peoples, have been to me a never-failing source of delight, wonder, and inspiration. In them I can hear the spirit of all great music. Through them I can feel the very heart-beat of humanity. Simple as these folk melodies are in structure, they yet speak to me so poignantly, and with such a deep sincerity of expression, as to be (for myself, at least) more pregnant with inspirational suggestion than the music of any *one* composer.[7]

It is important to note that Gilbert's concern with "native" American music went hand in hand with an enthusiasm for music of the folk everywhere, of all nationalities and all races throughout the world. This is a significant point, to which we shall return later. It prepares the way for that eclecticism which I take to be the essence of America's music.

In a foreword printed with the score of his symphonic poem *The Dance in Place Congo*, Gilbert described the basis of his musical nationalism:

> It has been for a long time an ideal of mine to write some music which should be in its inspiration native to America. The efforts of my compatriots, though frequently very fine technically, failed to

[7] Quoted by Farwell, *Music in America*, p. 408.

satisfy me. To my mind they leaned far too heavily upon the tradition of Europe, and seemed to me to ignore too completely the very genuine touches of inspiration which exist in *our* history, *our* temperament, and *our* national life. I was, therefore, moved to strike out boldly on a different course. . . .

Gilbert furthermore tells us that in casting about for an American subject upon which to base a symphonic poem he was much attracted by the picturesque quality of the life in New Orleans during the antebellum days. Notice that what attracts him is the *picturesque*, and that he is drawn to what I have called "The Exotic Periphery" in America's musical culture. He came across the article by George W. Cable in the *Century Magazine* describing the dancing in Place Congo and decided to use this as a background for a symphonic poem, taking his themes from the tunes published by Cable (quoted in Chapter 15). The first episode is developed from the melody that Cable calls a "bamboula" (see musical example on page 308). Gilbert saw in this material "a strong and romantic picture . . . full of dramatic and colorful suggestion," and he treated it Romantically, that is, descriptively and dramatically. The subject, indeed, struck him as "so picturesque and so full of dramatic possibility" that he decided, after completing the score, to write a scenario for it, thus transforming the work into a ballet-pantomime which was performed at the Metropolitan Opera House, New York, on March 23, 1918. Later it was performed by the Boston Symphony Orchestra as a symphonic poem.

The same orchestra had performed, in 1911, Gilbert's *Comedy Overture on Negro Themes,* the first work that brought him national recognition. It was originally planned as an overture for an opera (never completed) based on the Uncle Remus stories. The overture is based on two short (four-measure) melodies taken from the collection *Bahama Songs and Stories* by Charles L. Edwards, a highly interesting work published in 1895, on part of a Mississippi boat song, "I'se gwine to Alabammy, oh," and on the first four measures of the spiritual "Old Ship of Zion," used as the subject of a fugue.

In his *Negro Rhapsody* (1913) Gilbert attempted to contrast the "barbaric" and the "spiritual" elements in Afro-American culture. Ten years earlier he had turned to tunes of the blackface minstrel tradition —"Zip Coon," "Dearest May," and "Don't Be Foolish, Joe"—in his *Americanesque* for orchestra. A set of three *American Dances in Ragtime Rhythm* was another incursion in the field of musical Americana.

With his five *Indian Scenes* for piano, Gilbert delved into Indian lore. He roamed further afield with his *Celtic Studies* for voice and piano (1905), and various piano pieces, including *The Island of the Fay* (after Poe) and *Two Verlaine Moods* (1903). *Salammbô's Invocation to Tanith* (1902), originally for voice with piano, was subsequently orchestrated. The *Fish Wharf Rhapsody* (1909) for voice with piano, is an experiment in musical realism. Finally, we should mention the Symphonic Prelude to Synge's drama, *Riders to the Sea*, originally written for small orchestra (1904), later expanded for full orchestra.

Though Gilbert's music "dates" perceptibly and is often derivative, he deserves to be honored as a forward-looking pioneer. His place in American music has been aptly summed up by Arthur Farwell: "Often rough in technique, though greatly resourceful, and rich in orchestral imagination, it is to the spirit of the time and nation that Gilbert makes his contribution and his appeal." [8]

Of Farwell himself, as a composer, something more must be said, for the reader should not be left with the impression that he was merely an arranger of Indian music. His orchestral works include *Symbolistic Study No. 3* (after Walt Whitman, 1922), *The Gods of the Mountain* (suite, 1927), *Symbolistic Study No. 6: Mountain Vision* (piano concerto in one movement, 1931), *Prelude to a Spiritual Drama* (1932), and *Rudolph Gott Symphony* (1934). His *Mountain Song* (1931) is a symphonic work in five movements with incidental songs by mixed chorus. His chamber music includes a String Quartet (*The Hako*), a Piano Quintet, and a Sonata for Violin and piano. In his later works he experimented with the use of Oriental scales. Farwell was the prototype of the eclectic composer in America.

Other "Indianist" composers

Among other composers who have utilized American Indian material, Charles Wakefield Cadman (1881–1947) achieved wide popularity with his song "The Land of the Sky Blue Water," in which the indigenous elements are so thickly sugar-coated as to be almost imperceptible. Cadman composed two operas dealing with the relation of the Indians to the civilization of the whites. The first of these, *Shanewis*, was produced at the Metropolitan Opera House in 1918;

[8] Farwell, *loc. cit.*

the second, *The Sunset Trail*, received its première at Denver in 1925. His *Thunderbird Suite* for piano (also orchestrated) is based on Omaha themes. After 1925 Cadman began to be less interested in Indian music, and turning to other aspects of Americana, composed the two-act opera *A Witch of Salem* (1926), *Dark Dancers of the Mardi Gras* for piano and orchestra (1933), *American Suite* (1937), and the overture *Huck Finn* (1945). His "abstract" compositions include a Symphony and some chamber music. He was a minor figure in the development of musical nationalism in America; his style is facile and undistinctive.

Charles Sanford Skilton (1868–1941), in spite of his New England background, his education at Yale University, and his musical training in Berlin, became strongly attracted to Indian music after he went to teach at the State University of Kansas in 1915. Like Cadman, he composed "Indian" operas: *Kalopin* (three acts, 1927) and *The Sun Bride* (one act, 1930). For orchestra he wrote *Two Indian Dances* (*Deer Dance, War Dance*), *Suite Primeval*, *American Indian Fantasie* (with cello solo), and *Sioux Flute Serenade* (chamber orchestra). Widely performed in its day, his Indianizing music, superficial and conventional, has for us now solely the interest of a period piece, demonstrating the "picture postcard" school of "native" music.

Arthur Nevin (1871–1943), brother of Ethelbert Nevin, composed the opera *Poia*, based on the traditional lore of the Blackfeet Indians of Montana. Curiously enough, this work was produced not in America but at the Royal Opera House in Berlin (1909). Two foreign-born musicians who settled in the United States, Alberto Bimboni and Carl Busch, became, like "Father" Heinrich, enamored of American Indian music. Bimboni composed the opera *Winona* (1926), using Indian themes, with the chorus singing in unison. Busch wrote the symphonic poem *Minnehaha's Vision, Four Indian Tribal Melodies* for string orchestra, and *A Chant from the Great Plains* for military band.

The "Indianist" movement in American music may now be recognized as a transitory phase. It attracted a number of composers who were looking for something indigenous, something that could immediately and unmistakably be identified as "American." But the fallacy of attempting to create representative American music out of Indian material soon became apparent. Indian tribal music was not part of the main stream of American culture. It was an interesting but essentially exotic branch that one could follow for a time as a digression, a diversion from the European heritage. But if followed to its source it led to a primitive culture that had nothing in common with prevailing norms and trends of American civilization. It is perhaps fair to say that nowadays we are more interested in the study of Indian tribal music for its own sake, as a manifestation of primitive cultural patterns, than for its possible influence on American art music and its hypothetical contributions to musical "nationalism." Indeed, musical nationalism as it was understood at the beginning of this century appears to have run its course in the United States, and with its decline as a main issue, the interest of our composers in utilizing Indian material rapidly waned. The momentum of the Indianist movement ceased about twenty-five years ago, and it is not likely to be revived.

The Anglo-American heritage

In addition to those American composers who turned to Afro-American and Indian tribal material, there were some who held that the real roots of American national music lay in the tradition of Anglo-American folk song. A leading representative of this school was John Powell (1882–1963), of Richmond, Virginia. A pupil of Leschetizky in Vienna, he appeared frequently as a pianist, often in performances of his own works, such as the *Negro Rhapsody* for piano and orchestra (1918) and *Sonata Virginianesque* for violin and piano (1919). Although Powell used highly stylized Negro material in the two works just mentioned—both of which have programmatic connotations—his abiding concern has been with the cultivation of Anglo-American folk music, of which there exists a rich heritage in his native state of Virginia.

Among Powell's compositions utilizing Anglo-American folk music are the overture *In Old Virginia* (1921); *Natchez on the Hill* (1932) and *A Set of Three* (1935), both for orchestra; *At the Fair*, suite for chamber orchestra (1925); *The Babe of Bethlehem*, folk carol for mixed chorus *a cappella; Soldier, Soldier*, folk song for chorus *a cappella* with soprano and baritone solos; *Five Virginia Folk Songs* for baritone and piano; *Twelve Folk Hymns;* and the Symphony in A, commissioned by the National Federation of Music Clubs and first performed by the Detroit Symphony Orchestra on April 26, 1947. This symphony is a noble, sincere, and ambitious effort to apply the neo-romantic symphonic technique to the development of Anglo-

American folk themes. It comes out of a lifetime of devotion to, and close study of, this aspect of America's music. Yet, impressive though it may be, the Symphony in A leaves one with the suspicion that its aesthetic premise and its technical apparatus are outmoded. It is a grand monument, but one feels that the folk songs from which it derives possess more vitality and a more enduring quality.

John Powell is definitely a composer of the South, one of the few distinctly regional composers of any stature that the United States has produced. For Daniel Gregory Mason, a New England colleague who believes in the absolute and representative value of the Anglo-American tradition in America's music, the significance of Powell's contribution is more than regional. Holding to the conviction that the characteristic musical expression of America must be based on what he calls "Anglo-Saxon reticence," Mason cites Powell's overture *In Old Virginia* as an example of this reticence. According to Mason: "This Anglo-Saxon element in our heterogeneous national character, however quantitatively in the minority nowadays, is qualitatively of crucial significance in determining what we call the American temper." [9] It is difficult to see how the national temper or character can be determined by an element that is quantitatively in the minority. It seems more reasonable to hold that "our heterogeneous national character" itself determines what is "the American temper"—all-embracing, receptive, and expansive. That is why we really have no "national" school in American music.

[9] Mason, *Tune In, America*, p. 160. This book, incidentally, offers a striking instance of musical anti-Semitism. The author quotes himself in an earlier magazine article, as follows: "The insidiousness of the Jewish menace to our artistic integrity . . . is due to the speciousness, the superficial charm and persuasiveness of Hebrew art, its violently juxtaposed extremes of passion, its poignant eroticism and pessimism." There is much more to this effect; I quote it merely as a curiosity in our musical literature.

chapter twenty

Composer from Connecticut

The future of music may not lie with music itself, but rather . . . in the way it makes itself a part with the finer things that humanity does and dreams of.

CHARLES E. IVES, MUSIC AND ITS FUTURE.

In the year 1894 Antonin Dvořák, distinguished composer from Bohemia, was teaching in New York and urging the creation of an American "national" movement in music based on the use of Negro and Indian melodies. Edward MacDowell, "a glorious young figure" (so Hamlin Garland saw him), wearing a derby hat and a curled mustache, walked in Boston Common musing upon Arthurian legends and Celtic lore. Horatio Parker, erudite, fastidious, Munich-trained, fresh from the triumph of his cantata *Hora Novissima*, had just assumed his duties as professor of music at Yale University. A twenty-year-old student from Danbury went up to New Haven and matriculated in the class of '98 at Yale. His name was Charles Edward Ives.

Young Ives was a musician, the son of a band master and music teacher in Danbury, Connecticut, where he was born on October 20, 1874. The senior Ives had an inquiring mind and an open ear. He brought up his children mainly on Bach and Stephen Foster. Conventional listening habits were not encouraged in the Ives household. When Charles was ten, his father had him sing "Swanee River" in the key of E flat major and play the accompaniment in the key of C major, in order, he said, "to stretch our ears." George Ives, the father, was a true spiritual descendant of Billings and of Benjamin Franklin: self-reliant, independent, inventive, and ingenious. He engaged in various acoustical experiments, including the investigation of quarter tones, for which purpose he constructed a device consisting of twenty-four violin strings stretched over a wooden frame.

Receiving music lessons from his father beginning at the age of five, Charles Ives learned to play several instruments, including the organ, and from the age of twelve was employed as organist in a local church. From his father he also learned harmony, counterpoint, and fugue. He began to compose at an early age, and when he was fifteen the town band performed a piece of his "suggesting a Steve Foster tune, while over it the old farmers fiddled a barn dance with all its jigs, gallops and reels." At twenty he composed a *Song for Harvest Season*, for voice, cornet, trombone, and organ pedal—*each in a different key!*

This was the musical "baggage" that Charles Ives brought to Yale in 1894. At that time not even the most advanced European composers had begun to experiment with polytonality (the simultaneous use of different tonalities, as in Stravinsky's famous bitonal chord—C major and F sharp major—in *Petrouchka*, dating from 1911). No wonder that Parker, with whom Ives studied composition at Yale, was disconcerted and annoyed. "Ives," he testily asked, "must you hog all the keys?" Thenceforth the daring young man from Danbury kept his musical heresies to himself and satisfied his teacher by turning out an impressive batch of "correct" compositions. Perhaps the discipline was good for him. At any rate, no one could claim, later, that he did not know how to write music; that is, music "according to the rules."

After graduating from Yale, Ives had to decide whether to make music a career or an avocation. It was clear to him that he had no interest in writing the conventional music that found ready acceptance with publishers and performers and public. If he depended on music as a profession he would undoubtedly face a rough road, beset by frustration. In order to be creatively independent he decided to make himself financially independent. He entered the world of business, specializing in the field of insurance. After working in this field for several years, he organized in 1909 the firm of Ives & Myrick, which became very successful. He remained with this firm until 1930, when ill-health forced his retirement. His death occurred on May 19, 1954.

Ives did his composing in the evenings, on week ends, on holidays and vacations, often working until two or three in the morning. His wife— Harmony Twitchell, whom he married in 1908—gladly renounced an active social life so that her husband could devote all his leisure to his chosen avocation.

Toward a "substantial" art

Ives himself never felt that his business career was a handicap to him as an artist. On the contrary, he felt that it was of positive value to him in every way, and not merely a matter of "expediency" (a word that he detests). It is extremely revealing, both of the man and his music, to hear what he had to say on this subject, as told to his friend Henry Bellamann:

My business experience revealed life to me in many aspects that I might otherwise have missed. In it one sees tragedy, nobility, meanness, high aims, low aims, brave hopes, faint hopes, great ideals, no ideals, and one is able to watch these work inevitable destiny. And it has seemed to me that the finer sides of these traits were not only in the majority but in the ascendancy. I have seen men fight honorably and to a finish, solely for a matter of conviction or of principle—and where expediency, probable loss of business, prestige, or position had no part and threats no effect. It is my impression that there is more open-mindedness and willingness to examine carefully the premises underlying a new or unfamiliar thing, before condemning it, in the world of business than in the world of music. It is not even uncommon in business intercourse to sense a reflection of a philosophy—a depth of something fine—akin to a strong beauty in art. To assume that business is a material process, and only that, is to undervalue the average mind and heart. To an insurance man there *is* an "average man" and he is humanity. I have experienced a great fullness of life in business. The fabric of existence weaves itself whole. You cannot set an art off in the corner and hope for it to have vitality, reality and substance. There can be nothing *"exclusive"* about a substantial art. It comes directly out of the heart of experience of life and thinking about life and living life. My work in music helped my business and my work in business helped my music.[1]

This declaration of faith reveals, among other things, that Ives has pursued the ideal of a *nonexclusive* and *substantial* art, possessing vitality, reality, and substance. In his artistic philosophy, Ives opposes

[1] *Musical Quarterly*, XIX, 1 (Jan. 1933), 47.

"substance" to "manner," and gives a higher value to the former. He equates substance with reality, quality, spirit, as against "the lower value of form, quantity, or manner." And he continues:

Of these terms, "substance" seems to us the most cogent and comprehensive for the higher, and "manner" for the under-value. Substance in a human-art-quality suggests the body of a conviction which has its birth in the spiritual consciousness, whose youth is nourished in the moral consciousness, and whose maturity as a result of all this growth is then represented in a mental image.[2]

As an illustration of his thesis, Ives uses a comparison between Emerson and Poe. The former, he says, seems to be almost wholly "substance" and the latter "manner."

The measure in artistic satisfaction of Poe's "manner" is equal to the measure of spiritual satisfaction in Emerson's "substance." The total value of each man is high, but Emerson's is higher than Poe's because "substance" is higher than "manner"—because "substance" leans toward optimism, and "manner" pessimism.

Ives takes his stand with Emerson: that is an important fact to remember about him.

Ives has written a great deal about the philosophy of art, the nature of beauty, the problems of musical expression. He evidently enjoys being a homespun philosopher. By a sort of spiritual anachronism, he has preserved much of the soaring speculativeness of the Concord Transcendentalists. But as a shrewd Connecticut Yankee he keeps at least one foot on the earth. He admits that "if one tries to reduce art to philosophy" one inevitably ends by going around in a circle. And then he adds—this is a typical Ivesian touch—"But personally, we prefer to go around in a circle than around in a parallelepipedon, for it seems cleaner and perhaps freer from mathematics. . . ." It is important also to remember that Ives has a sense of humor.

It is not our purpose to expound in detail the artistic philosophy of Ives. A few pointers toward the spiritual "climate" of his music are all that we propose to extract. We have learned something of what he means by "substance," and that he considers "substance" more important than "manner." That is because he believes substance is related to character while manner is not. On the subject of expression,

[2] From *Essays before a Sonata.*

he has this to say: "The humblest composer will not find true humility in aiming low—he must never be timid or afraid of trying to express that which he feels is far above his power to express. . . ." Ives himself has often stretched the limits of musical expression to the utmost; and it is the listener who needs to be bold and adventurous in attempting to follow him. For, as Ives writes: "Beauty in music is too often confused with something that lets the ears lie back in an easy chair. Many sounds that we are used to, do not bother us, and for that reason, we are inclined to call them beautiful." Ives remarks that familiar sounds, like drugs, can be habit-forming.

The historical perspective

Today, in the second half of the twentieth century, many sounds that might have bothered us or our parents thirty or forty years ago, no longer annoy us, or annoy us less, because the ear gradually becomes accustomed to unusual combinations of sound. We have become fully accustomed to polytonal music, and more or less accustomed to atonal music. It takes a tremendous dissonance to startle us now. This chronological factor is central to our discussion of Ives's music, especially when we attempt to place it in its historical sequence. Ives, as we have seen, was far ahead of his time in that he employed tonal, harmonic, and rhythmic combinations that did not come into general use until much later. Had his music been performed immediately or soon after it was composed, it would have appeared, in most cases, as something startlingly "new" and would presumably have created as much of a furore as did the music of Schoenberg and Stravinsky in Europe. But the music of Ives did not synchronize with the musical development of the United States. When we were finally ready for his music, he was an old man, and many of his innovations were "old hat." It is a tribute to his vitality and originality, to the "substantial" quality of his music, that so much of it appeared as new as it did, after such a disconcerting time lag in its performance. Let us glance at the record.

Ives's Second Symphony, completed in 1902, did not receive its first performance until 1951, when it was played by the New York Philharmonic-Symphony under the direction of Leonard Bernstein. His Third Symphony, completed in 1911, was performed for the first time by the New York Little Symphony, Lou Harrison conducting, on April 5, 1945. The Fourth Symphony, composed between 1910 and 1916, received its first complete performance on April 26, 1965, under the direction of Leopold Stokowski. (The first two movements of this symphony were played at a concert of the Pro Musica Society in New York on January 29, 1927, under the direction of Eugene Goossens.) The second Piano Sonata, begun in 1904 and finished in 1915, received its first complete public performance when John Kirkpatrick played it in Town Hall, New York City, on January 20, 1939. Not until 1947, when he was awarded a Pulitzer Prize for his Third Symphony, did Charles Ives approach the status of a well-known figure in American music. In 1945 Ives was elected a member of the National Institute of Arts and Letters. He was then seventy-one years old and had never heard any of his compositions performed by a full orchestra.

It might be claimed that Ives made this long neglect inevitable when he cut himself off from active participation in the musical life of the country, as well as when he wrote music that was mostly too "difficult" for the musicians and the hearers of his time. It could be argued that he chose isolation instead of having it thrust upon him. The matter might be settled by saying that he was following his destiny. However we look at it, the most significant fact is that the music of Charles Ives has entered, albeit belatedly, the main stream of America's music. Charged with vitality and substance, it flows along in the stream of enduring things that move toward the future.

However modern it may be in "manner," the "substance" of Ives's music has its sources in the past—not so much the past as history but the past as a continuing tradition, the past surviving in the present, as it does, for instance, in folklore. We can take almost the whole body of American folk and popular music, as we have traced it from the early psalmody and hymnody of New England, through the camp-meeting songs and revival spirituals, the blackface minstrel tunes, the melodies of Stephen Foster, the fiddle tunes and barn dances, the village church choirs, the patriotic songs and ragtime—and we can feel that all this has been made into the substance of Ives's music, not imitated but assimilated, used as a musical heritage belonging to him by birthright. Thanks to his early background, to the decisive influences of his formative years, and to his utter independence of conventional musical standards, Charles Ives, first and alone among American composers, was able to discern and to utilize the truly idiosyncratic and germinal elements of our folk and popular music.

This music, as we know, possesses intrinsic traits—melodic, harmonic, and rhythmic—that do not conform to the norms of European art music. These include such features as "incorrect" harmonic progressions, irregular rhythms, asymmetrical melodies, improvised embellishments, and deviations from standard pitch. Most composers and arrangers altered or discarded these traits in order to make the music conform to the academic tradition in which they had been trained; thus they destroyed or distorted all that was most vital and characteristic in the folk and popular traditions. Ives, on the contrary, by seizing precisely on the most unconventional features of folk and popular music—unconventional, that is, by academic standards—was able to create an entirely new and powerful medium of musical expression, which is at once personal and more than personal. It is personal because only he could have created it; and it is more than personal because it incorporates a vital tradition that is the cultural expression of a human collectivity through numerous generations.

Formative experiences

While his contemporaries in Boston were absorbing Brahms and Wagner, Ives was absorbing the musical experiences provided by the New England village in which he grew to manhood: the concerts of the village band, the singing of the village choir, the barn dances, the camp meetings, the circus parades. The musical impressions he received were lasting and fecund. In after years he recalled the unusual effects obtained when the village band was divided into several groups placed in and around the main square:

> The main group in the bandstand at the center usually played the main themes, while the others, from the neighboring roofs and verandahs, played the variations, refrains, and so forth. The piece remembered was a kind of paraphrase of *Jerusalem the Golden*, a rather elaborate tone-poem for those days. The bandmaster told of a man who, living near the variations, insisted that they were the real music and [that] it was more beautiful to hear the hymn come sifting through them than the other way around. Others, walking around the square, were surprised at the different and interesting effects they got as they changed position. It was said also that many

thought the music lost in effect when the piece was played by the band all together, though, I think, the town vote was about even. The writer remembers, as a deep impression, the echo parts from the roofs played by a chorus of violins and voices.[3]

Ives had always been keenly sensitive to the qualities of sound, and to the variables that affect this quality, such as the factor of *distance*. As he points out: "A brass band playing *pianissimo* across the street is a different-sounding thing from the same band, playing the same piece *forte*, a block or so away." The *volume* of sound that the listener hears will be approximately the same, but the quality will be different. The sound of distant church bells had fascinated Ives, as it did Thoreau, who loved to listen to the Concord church bell over Walden Pond. "A horn over a lake," writes Ives, "gives a quality of sound and feeling that it is hard to produce in any other way." For the understanding of Ives's music, it is valuable to retain this reference to "sound *and* feeling," for Ives is equally interested in both. Few composers have ever attached more significance to the sheer quality of sound in music, but this does not imply a doctrine of "sound for sound's sake." Sound as a medium of expression is what Ives seeks.

It would be misleading to think of Ives as belonging to the "folk-lore" school of composers. He stands as far from Dvořák as he does from MacDowell. There is nothing to indicate, either in his music or in his writings, that he had any particular interest in folklore as such; in the sense, let us say, that John Powell and Vaughan Williams were interested in folklore. Folk music is for him simply one source, among many others, of material that can be utilized to create an expressive musical language. It is also a means, when creatively utilized, of reno-vating the idiom of art music and injecting into it new vigor. In his search for vigor and vitality, Ives does not shun vulgarity. A circus band is as valid for him as a church organ. A gospel hymn may be as inspiring as a symphony. He does not limit himself. He does not exclude. What is of value to him in the tradition of European art music he takes—and fuses it with American folk and popular traditions. He assimilates and transforms disparate elements; his art is heterogeneous, and only his creative genius gives it unity.

Ives employs polytonality, multiple cross-rhythms of great complexity, extreme dissonance, tone-clusters (chords made up of minor

[3] "Music and Its Future," *New Music Quarterly*.

and major seconds), quarter tones and other fractional intervals, wide
melodic skips, asymmetrical rhythmic patterns, off-beat rhythms emphasized by dissonance, jazz effects, and other devices and procedures
that were new when he used them though later incorporated into
much of modern music. He arrived at these procedures independently,
because he was not familiar with the "advanced" European music of
his time. Besides, as already stated, some of his innovations preceded
those of Schoenberg and Stravinsky in Europe. If it is true, as Stravinsky claims, that the composer's task is to "invent" music, then Ives
will go down in musical history as one of the most inventive composers of modern times. But it is also necessary to observe that Ives,
when it suits his expressive needs, can write with the utmost simplicity. Coming to his music so late, as we do, we sometimes have to
make more allowance for his simplicity than for his complexity.

The symphonies of Ives

The Second Symphony, for example, evokes, as Burrill Phillips remarks, "in gentle and mostly lyrical language, a world long vanished.
It is a world in which leisure and individuality and strength of mind
had not become boisterous and shrill and psychotic. . . . The harmonic language throughout is of course dominated by the 19th century, but it is in the style of the parlor organ and the 19th-century
park bandstand, not the European concert hall or opera house." This
"aesthetic of the commonplace" kept Ives from uttering pretentious
banalities, as did so many of his American contemporaries.

Ives composed the Second Symphony between 1897 and 1901, except for part of the last movement, which dates from 1889. The composer describes this part as "suggesting a Steve Foster tune, while over
it the old farmers fiddled a barn dance with all its jigs, gallops, and
reels." This symphony is in five movements: Andante moderato, Allegro, Adagio cantabile, Lento maestoso, Allegro molto vivace. It is
scored for large orchestra and takes about thirty-five minutes to perform. The juxtaposition of two slow movements is characteristic of
Ives; actually, because of the proportion and balance between these
two movements, there is no trace of formal incongruity. It is also
characteristic that Ives makes no marked attempt to exploit orchestral
color in this work: he is more interested in texture than in color. In
the first movement the scoring is almost entirely for strings, with only

brief passages for horns and bassoons; and near the end an embellished restatement of the main theme is given to the oboe: [4]

quasi recitativo

In the last movement Ives introduces snatches of familiar American songs—"Camptown Races," "Turkey in the Straw," "Columbia, the Gem of the Ocean"—a procedure that he has followed in other scores also. His frequent use of traditional tunes is based on a complete assimilation of this material.

In the same year (1901) that he completed his Second Symphony, Ives began to compose his Third Symphony, which he finished in 1904 except for some revision in 1911. The Third Symphony is considerably shorter than the Second (it requires about seventeen minutes to perform) and is scored for a small orchestra: flute, oboe, clarinet in B flat, bassoon, two horns in F, trombone, strings, and bells (ad libitum). It is in three movements: Andante maestoso, Allegro, Largo. Concluding with a slow movement is typical of Ives. The bells (or chimes) are heard in the last two measures of the work, "as distant church bells," marked with a *decrescendo* sign from *ppp* to *ppppp* —an example of Ives's insistence on dynamic nuances that verge on the impossible. The bells are heard as triads of B minor and G sharp minor, floating above the chords of B flat major and F major in the strings. This is the only touch of polytonality in the symphony.

The first and third movements are devotional in character, utilizing material originally written for the Presbyterian church service, as well as themes from familiar hymns. In the first movement there is a section, marked Adagio cantabile, based on the hymn tune "O, What a Friend We Have in Jesus." There is also a reminiscence of that old-time revival hymn, "There is a Fountain Filled With Blood." Another well-known hymn, "Just As I Am Without One Plea," figures prominently as a main theme in the third movement, treated contrapuntally with a subject derived from material in the first movement.

The contrasting middle movement, in binary form (A-B-A), has

[4] Charles E. Ives, Second Symphony, used by permission of the copyright owners. Copyright 1951 by Southern Music Publishing Company, Inc., New York.

for its principal theme an attractive and rhythmically flexible melody of folklike flavor. The middle section of this movement consists of one of those marching rhythms that are perhaps associated with memories of the band led by the composer's father.

Though its texture is fairly complex, and there are some rapidly shifting rhythms in the last movement, the Third Symphony presents no untoward difficulty for the listener. It is a work of quiet charm, mostly meditative in mood, devoid of sensational effects, appealing by its integrity and restrained eloquence, by its "substance" rather than its "manner." It sums up in symphonic form the deep-rooted tradition of American hymnody, from which our major musical impulse sprang for upwards of three centuries; and it stands as a classic "in the American grain."

Ives himself has given us a clue to the meaning of the Fourth Symphony: "The aesthetic program of the work is that of the searching questions of What? and Why? which the spirit of man asks of life. This is particularly the sense of the prelude. The three succeeding movements are the diverse answers in which existence replies."

The prelude (Maestoso adagio) is essentially a setting of the hymn "Watchman, Tell Us of the Night," with references also to "Nearer, My God, to Thee" and "In the Sweet Bye and Bye." It was written in 1910–1911. The second movement, Allegretto, is the most complex and the most thoroughly Ivesian. The composer tells us that it is not a scherzo in the accepted sense of the word, "but rather a comedy—in which an exciting, easy, and worldly progress through life is contrasted with the trials of the Pilgrims in their journey through the swamps and rough country. . . . The dream, or fantasy, ends with an interruption of reality—the Fourth of July in Concord—brass bands, drum corps, etc." Much of the material is derived from the "Hawthorne" movement of the Second Piano Sonata. Prominent among the many tunes quoted in this movement are "Marching through Georgia," "In the Sweet Bye and Bye," and "Columbia, the Gem of the Ocean." The third movement, a double fugue (Andante con moto), is an orchestral transcription of the first movement of the First String Quartet (*A Revival Meeting*), based on two hymn tunes, "From Greenland's Icy Mountains" and "All Hail the Power of Jesus' Name." The last movement (Very slowly, Largo maestoso) is derived from Ives's *Memorial Slow March* for organ (1901).

New England regionalist

Regionalism in American music has never been adequately studied, as regional literature and painting have been. Were such a study to be undertaken, Ives would provide a very strong case for musical regionalism in New England. Almost everything he ever wrote has its roots either in his own memories of growing up in a New England town or in that historical extension of memory and experience that comes with a deep affinity for traditions and values of the past. The New England culture of the mid-nineteenth century, especially the Transcendentalism of Concord, was as familiar to Ives as the background of his own boyhood in Danbury. Again and again, in his writings, he harks back to boyhood experiences and impressions. The First Piano Sonata, for instance, is described as "in a way a kind of impression, remembrance, and reflection of the country life in some of the Connecticut villages in the 1880s and 1890s." It evokes such home-town scenes as the school baseball game, the farmer's barn dance on a winter's night, the "quicksteps" played by the town band, a touch of ragtime, and echoes of old hymn tunes. Examples could be multiplied: in *A Symphony: Holidays* (1904–1913), described as "Recollections of a boy's holidays in a Connecticut country town" (the holidays are "Washington's Birthday," "Decoration Day," "Fourth of July," "Thanksgiving"); in the Sonata No. 2 for violin and piano ("Autumn," "In the Barn," "The Revival," composed 1903–1910); in the Orchestral Set No. 2 (1912–1915), consisting of "An Elegy for Our Forefathers," "The Rock-strewn Hills Join in the People's Outdoor Meeting," and "From Hanover Square North at the End of a Tragic Day"; in the Sonata No. 4 for violin and piano, subtitled "Children's Day at the Camp Meeting"; in the Second Sonata for Piano ("Concord, Mass., in the 1840's"); and in the Orchestral Set No. 1: *Three Places in New England* (1903–1914), which is also called "A New England Symphony."

The "Three Places" are (1) "Boston Common" ("The monument to Colonel Shaw and his colored regiment by St. Gaudens," with a prefatory poem by Ives), (2) "Putnam's Camp" ("A Revolutionary Memorial Park near Redding Center, Connecticut . . . A Fourth of July picnic piece"); and (3) "The Housatonic at Stockbridge," concerning which Mrs. Ives wrote: "This grand old river . . . has been an inspiring friend to Mr. Ives from his boyhood days." Together with the "Concord" Sonata, this work marks the culmination of Ives's regionalism. Here he is at once musical historian (evoking the Revolution and the Civil War), New England impressionist (evoking "the moving river, its landscapes and elm trees . . ."), and a marvelous innovator in the simultaneous projection of independent musical events that reaches its climax in the extraordinary vitality and complexity of *Putnam's Camp*. In this piece the marching tune "British Grenadiers," which was adopted by the Americans in 1779, appears as a recurrent theme.

The "transcendental" regionalism of the "Concord" Sonata will be described later in this chapter. Admitting that Ives's cosmic scope cannot be circumscribed by New England or any other region, the fact remains that his regional roots are profoundly imbedded in the spiritual soil as well as in the natural, social, and historical environment of New England.

Miscellaneous works and songs

Ives's manuscripts were given by Mrs. Ives to the Library of the Yale School of Music in 1955, and since then have been avidly studied by musical scholars, among them John Kirkpatrick, who compiled a *Catalogue of the Music Manuscripts of Ives* with all kinds of useful appendices. The most fascinating of these is undoubtedly the "Index of Tunes" quoted by Ives in his music. This includes over fifty hymns, more than twenty patriotic songs and military tunes, some thirty-five popular songs, about a dozen popular tunes (primarily instrumental), and the same number of college songs, besides "other music" (quotations from Handel, Haydn, Beethoven, Brahms, Tchaikovsky, Debussy—and his own father). The assimilation of these tunes in Ives's compositions, the creative manner in which he uses them, is an amazing process.

The Second String Quartet (1911–1913) has so many quotations that it has been called "a modern *quodlibet*" (from the Latin, "what you please"). Ives himself described this work as "String Quartet for four men—who converse, discuss, argue (politics), fight, shake hands, shut-up, then walk up the mountainside to view the firmament." Its three movements are titled "Discussions," "Arguments," and "The Call of the Mountains." Most of the quotations occur in the first and second movements. One hears snatches of "Columbia, the Gem of the Ocean," "Marching through Georgia," "Dixie," and other Civil War tunes. Later there are bits of familiar hymns, like "Nearer, My God, to Thee," and quotations from symphonies by Beethoven, Brahms, and Tchaikovsky.

From the catalogue of Ives's compositions, a few representative works will be cited to indicate the scope and character of his music. The *Variations on a National Hymn* ("America") for organ (1891), has bitonal interludes which were added later, but before 1894, which makes this "the earliest surviving piece using polytonality" (Cowell). *From the Steeples* (1901), for two sets of chimes, trumpet, and trombone, shows Ives experimenting with novel effects of timbre, anticipating the kind of instrumental juxtapositions to be found in music half a century later; the Three-Page Sonata for piano (1905) is a burlesque of sonata form; *Central Park in the Dark* (1898–1907), for chamber orchestra (described by Ives as "a cartoon or take-off"), *Hallowe'en* (1911) for string quartet and piano, and *Over the Pond* (1906), for chamber orchestra, were grouped together for publication as *Three Outdoor Scenes* and contain some of Ives's most original writing for small ensembles. Another piece that might have been included with this group is *Over the Pavements* (1906–1913), described as a "scherzo," for a chamber orchestra that includes a saxophone and three trombones ad lib. From the same period is *The Unanswered Question* (1908), described as "a cosmic landscape," for trumpet and four flutes, string quartet or string orchestra—the most original and beautiful of all Ives's works for small ensembles, combining extremes of consonance and dissonance in a hauntingly expressive manner, at once mysterious and dramatic. *Three Harvest Home Chorales* (1898–1912), for mixed chorus, brass choir, string bass, and organ, together with *Psalm 67*, contain some of Ives's most original writing for voices and instruments; the harmonic and rhythmic treatment is bold, entirely free from conventional bonds, using dissonances and cross-rhythms in a tremendously effective manner.

One of the most remarkable of Ives's vocal-instrumental works is *General William Booth Enters into Heaven* (1914), intended by the composer for chorus or solo voice with brass band, arranged for chamber orchestra by John J. Becker in 1934, and most often performed with solo voice and piano. The text is by Vachel Lindsay, and the music is based on the Salvation Army hymn "Are You Washed in the Blood of the Lamb?" It is one of the most dramatic songs ever written, and reveals the compassionate and realistic side of Ives's music.

A striking work for voices and orchestra is the setting of Edwin Markham's poem, *Lincoln the Great Commoner* (1912), which the composer has divided into three sections: Maestoso, andante; Agitando, con furore; Adagio maestoso. The voices can be either of men or women, or both; much of the writing for voices is in unison, but there are also some difficult dissonant passages, as at the *Agitando, con furore* ("step of earthquake shook the house, wrenching rafters from their ancient hold"), which includes ascending and descending scale clusters.

In 1922 Ives published a book of *114 Songs* in a privately printed edition, with a preface saying, among other things, "I have not written a book at all—I have merely cleaned house." Most of the songs were composed in the period between 1895 and 1901, but the earliest dates from 1888, and the latest from 1921. As indicated by the composer's quip about cleaning house, there is no attempt at selectivity or orderly arrangement in this volume. Anything goes. The songs range in mood from sentimentality to satire, from bathos to burlesque, from nostalgia to caricature. The best of them are art songs of marked originality and expressivity, each of which creates and projects a definite mood or emotion in a musical idiom that is unmistakably individual. In them we find many anticipations of modern musical devices, such as poly-tonality ("The Children's Hour," 1901), atonality produced by chords of fourths and fifths ("The Cage," 1906), extreme dissonance ("A Song to German Words," 1899), off-rhythms ("Walking Song," 1902), and ragtime effects ("The Circus Band," 1894).

It is necessary to stress the immense variety of mood and style in the songs of Ives. Tenderness prevails in such lyrics as "Two Little Flowers" and "Cradle Song." In "Charlie Rutledge" we have a rough-hewn Western ballad of rousing dramatic effect. "The Greatest Man," in which a boy gets to thinking about his "pa," is good, homespun human stuff. And for sustained poetic expression we turn to a song like "The White Gulls," with typical Ivesian harmonic texture.

Later collections of Ives's songs made selected items from the 1922 volume more readily available; and smaller collections of new songs, the latest composed in 1927, were also brought out by various publishers. An album of recorded songs released by Folkways in 1966 contains a representative selection from 1894 to 1925. The songs of

Charles Ives are a vital and enduring contribution to art song in America.

The "Concord" Sonata

In the years 1909 and 1910 Ives composed the greater portion of one of his most important works, the Second Pianoforte Sonata, subtitled *Concord, Mass., 1840–1860*. The last movement was completed in 1915. The sonata consists of four movements: "Emerson," "Hawthorne," "The Alcotts," "Thoreau." John Kirkpatrick, the American pianist who first overcame the tremendous difficulties of this work, has called it "an immense four-movement impressionist symphony for piano." It is indeed of symphonic proportions, and we are not surprised to learn that the first movement is based on an uncompleted score of a concerto for piano and orchestra, while the third movement uses material taken from an orchestral overture titled *Orchard House*. The first edition of the *Concord Sonata* was privately printed in the fall of 1919 and appeared together with six *Essays before a Sonata* written by the composer. The volume bore the following dedication: "These prefatory essays were written by the composer for those who can't stand his music—and the music for those who can't stand his essays; to those who can't stand either, the whole is respectfully dedicated." Summarizing the intent of the sonata, Ives wrote:

> The whole is an attempt to present one person's impression of the spirit of transcendentalism that is associated in the minds of many with Concord, Mass., of over half a century ago. This is undertaken in impressionistic pictures of Emerson and Thoreau, a sketch of the Alcotts, and a Scherzo supposed to reflect the lighter quality which is often found in the fantastic side of Hawthorne. The first and last movements do not aim to give any programs of the life or of any particular work of either Emerson or Thoreau but rather composite pictures or impressions.[5]

In the foregoing passage, Ives appears as a self-proclaimed impressionist.

---

[5] This and other quotations from Ives in the remainder of this chapter are from *Essays before a Sonata* and from the composer's notes for the Second Pianoforte Sonata (2d ed.). Copyright 1947 by Arrow Music Press, Inc., New York. Used by permission of the copyright owner.

Ives sees Emerson as "America's deepest explorer of the spiritual immensities." From the prefatory essay on Emerson, the following excerpt may serve to establish the spiritual climate of the sonata's first movement:

We see him standing on a summit, at the door of the infinite where many men do not dare to climb, peering into the mysteries of life, contemplating the eternities, hurling back whatever he discovers there—now thunderbolts, for us to grasp, if we can, and translate, now placing quietly, even tenderly, in our hands, things that we may see without effort. . . .

In addition to the prefatory essays, Ives includes numerous notes on the interpretation of the sonata, which reveal much about the composer as well as the music. In his first note on the Emerson movement, Ives applies his theory of "musical relativism," based on variable subjective factors:

Throughout this movement, and to some extent in the others, there are many passages not to be too evenly played and in which the tempo is not precise or static; it varies usually with the mood of the day, as well as that of Emerson, the other Concord bards, and the player. A metronome cannot measure Emerson's mind and over-soul, any more than the old Concord Steeple Bell could. . . . The same essay or poem of Emerson may bring a slightly different feeling when read at sunrise than when read at sunset.

While refusing to identify the music with any specific passages in Emerson's writings, the composer does indicate that certain sections of the music are associated with the poetry and others with the prose. At one point the entrance of an abrupt dissonance, marked fortissimo, is described as depicting "one of Emerson's sudden calls for a Transcendental Journey." Three pages later the performer is instructed to hit a certain formidable chord "in as strong and hard a way as possible, almost as though the Mountains of the Universe were shouting, as all of humanity rises to behold the 'Massive Eternities' and the 'Spiritual Immensities.' " Here is this passage:[6]

[6] Quotations from the Second Pianoforte Sonata are used by permission of the copyright owners, Arrow Music Press, Inc.

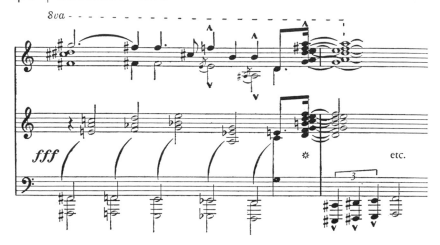

After the dramatic climax of this call to a "Transcendental Journey," there follows a meditative section leading to a mystical ending in which the upper notes in the treble clef (played by the left hand, pianissimo) are supposed "to reflect the overtones of the soul of humanity and as they rise away almost inaudibly to the Ultimate Destiny."

Concerning the second movement, a Scherzo, the composer tells us that the music makes no attempt to reflect the darker side of Hawthorne's genius, obsessed by the relentlessness of guilt:

This fundamental part of Hawthorne is not attempted in our music . . . which is but an "extended fragment" trying to suggest some of his wilder, fantastical adventures into the half-childlike, half-fairylike phantasmal realms. It may have something to do with the children's excitement on that "frosty Berkshire morning, and the frost on the enchanted hall window" or something to do with "Feathertop," the "Scarecrow," and his "Looking Glass" and the little demons dancing around his pipe bowl; or something to do with the old hymn tune that haunts the old church and sings only to those in the churchyard, to protect them from secular noises, as when the circus parade comes down Main Street; or something to do with the concert at the Stamford camp meeting, or the "Slave's Shuffle"; or something to do with the Concord he-nymph, or the "Seven Vagabonds" or "Circe's Palace," or something else in the wonderbook—not something that happens, but the way something happens; or something personal, which tries to be "national" suddenly at twilight, and universal suddenly at midnight; or something about the ghost of a man who never lived, or about something that never will happen, or something else that is not.

Here we meet several of the favorite Ivesian themes: the old hymn tune, the camp meeting, the circus parade. In treating the "phantasmal" aspects of Hawthorne's world, Ives avoids the merely quaint or fanciful. When he evokes a circus parade it is a real one, with all its gaudy vulgarity. His brass band blares in competition with the local Drum Corps marching along Main Street, and at one point in the score (the composer tells us), the Drum Corps "gets the best of the Band—for a moment." Another realistic touch is when certain notes "are hit hard by the left hand, as a trombone would sometimes call the Old Cornet Band to march."

There are other pure Ivesian touches in this Scherzo. When the old hymn tune is first heard it follows a furious arpeggio passage culminating in a chord marked *ffff*. The composer directs that "The first chord in the Hymn (*ppp*) is to be played before the *ffff* chord held with the right foot pedal is stopped—as a Hymn is sometimes heard over a distant hill just after a heavy storm." A little later he remarks: "Here the Hymn for a moment is slightly held up by a Friendly Ghost in the Church Yard."

The Scherzo is marked to be played "Very fast." Toward the end there is the direction, "From here on, as fast as possible," then "Rush it," and finally, "Faster if possible"! The final section Ives refers to as the "call of the cloud breakers." The hymn tune appears, very softly and slowly, as an echo, just before the final, up-rushing chord that brings the Scherzo to a close.

In connection with the third movement of the *Concord Sonata*, "The Alcotts," the composer has written about the spirit and aspect of Concord village, and about Orchard House, the family home where Louisa May Alcott wrote *Little Women* and where her father philosophized:

Concord village, itself, reminds one of that common virtue lying at the height and root of the Concord divinities. As one walks down the broad-arched street, passing the white house of Emerson—ascetic guard of a former prophetic beauty—he comes presently beneath the old elms overspreading the Alcott house. It seems to stand as a kind of homely but beautiful witness of Concord's common virtue—it seems to bear a consciousness that its past *is living*, that the "mosses of the Old Manse" and the hickories of Walden are not far away. Here is the home of the "Marches"—all pervaded with the trials and happiness of the family and telling, in a simple way, the story of "the richness of not having." . . . And there is the little old spinet-piano Sophia Thoreau gave to the Alcott children, on which Beth played old Scotch airs and played at the *Fifth Symphony*. . . .

We dare not attempt to follow the philosophic raptures of Bronson Alcott. . . . And so we won't try to reconcile the music sketch of the Alcotts with much besides the memory of that home under the elms—the Scotch songs and the family hymns that were sung at the end of each day—though there may be an attempt to catch something of that common sentiment . . . a strength of hope that never gives way to despair—a conviction in the power of the common soul which, when all is said and done, may be as typical as any theme of Concord and its transcendentalists.

"The Alcotts" is the shortest and the least difficult of the four movements of the *Concord Sonata*. The composer has provided all the clues that are needed for its understanding: the simplicity of the old home, the family hymns, the Scotch songs, and the reminiscences of Beethoven's Fifth Symphony. Remember, however, that the latter transcend the amateurish attempts of Beth Alcott at the spinet-piano, and are transmuted into the image of the Concord bards "pounding away at the immensities with a Beethoven-like sublimity."

For the final movement of his sonata, "Thoreau," the composer has given us a more detailed "program" than for the other movements. This section might have been subtitled "A Day at Walden." In his synopsis Ives does not specifically correlate the verbal description with the corresponding passages in the score. In giving the composer's synopsis below, I have taken the liberty of inserting musical illustrations that correspond to the scenes or moods described in the commentary.

And if there shall be a program let it follow his [Thoreau's] thought on an autumn day of Indian summer at Walden—a shadow of a thought at first, colored by the mist and haze over the pond:

> Low anchored cloud,
> Fountain head and
> Source of rivers . . .
> Dew cloth, dream drapery—
> Drifting meadow of the air . . .

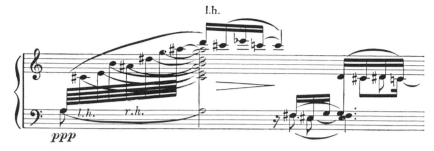

but this is momentary; the beauty of the day moves him to a certain restlessness—to aspirations more specific—an eagerness for outward action, but through it all he is conscious that it is not in keeping with the mood for this "Day." As the mists rise, there comes a clearer thought more traditional than the first, a meditation more calm.[7]

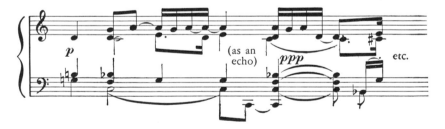

As he stands on the side of the pleasant hill of pines and hickories in front of his cabin, he is still disturbed by a restlessness and goes down the white-pebbled and sandy eastern shore, but it seems not to lead him where the thought suggests—he climbs along the "bolder northern" and "western shore, with deep bays indented," and now along the railroad track, "where the Aeolian harp plays." But his eagerness throws him into the lithe, springy step of the specie hunter

[7] Copyright 1947 by Arrow Music Press, Inc. Used by permission of the copyright owner.

—the naturalist—he is still aware of a restlessness; with these faster steps his rhythm is of a shorter span—it is still not the tempo of Nature, it does not bear the mood that the genius of the day calls for, it is too specific, its nature is too external, the introspection too buoyant, and he knows now that he must let Nature flow through *him* and slowly; he releases his more personal desires to her broader rhythm, conscious that this blends more and more with the harmony of her solitude; it tells him that his search for freedom on that day, at least, lies in his submission to her, for Nature is as relentless as she is benignant. He remains in this mood and while outwardly still, he seems to move with the slow, almost monotonous swaying beat of this autumnal day.[8]

He is more contented with a "homely burden," and is more assured of "the broad margin of his life; he sits in his sunny doorway . . . rapt in revery . . . amidst goldenrod, sandcherry, and sumach . . . in undisturbed solitude." At times the more definite personal strivings for the ideal freedom, the former more active speculations come over him, as if he would trace a certain intensity even in his submission. "He grew in those seasons like corn in the night and they were better than any works of the hands. They were not time subtracted from his life but so much over and above the usual allow-

[8] Copyright 1947 by Arrow Music Press, Inc. Used by permission.

ance." He realized "what the Orientals meant by contemplation and forsaking of works." . . . "The evening train has gone by," and "all the restless world with it. The fishes in the pond no longer feel its rumbling and he is more alone than ever. . . ." His meditations are interrupted only by the faint sound of the Concord bell—'tis prayer-meeting night in the village—"a melody, as it were, imported into the wilderness. . . . At a distance over the woods the sound acquires a certain vibratory hum as if the pine needles in the horizon were the strings of a harp which it swept. . . . A vibration of the universal lyre." . . . Part of the echo may be "The voice of the wood; the same trivial words and notes sung by the wood nymph." It is darker, the poet's flute is heard out over the pond and Walden hears the swan song of that "Day" and faintly echoes.[9]

[In these final pages, Ives has written out a part for the flute; but if no flute is used, he directs that the piano shall play the melody given in the small notes. He adds, however, that "Thoreau much prefers to hear the flute over Walden."]

Is it a transcendental tune of Concord? 'Tis an evening when the "whole body is one sense." . . . and before ending his day he looks out over the clear, crystalline water of the pond and catches a glimpse of the shadow-thought he saw in the morning's mist and haze—he knows that by his final submission, he possesses the "Freedom of the Night." He goes up the "pleasant hillside of pines, hickories," and moonlight, to his cabin, "with a strange liberty in Nature, a part of herself." [10]

Throughout this movement there are no key signatures, no time signatures, and no bar lines. But this does not mean that Ives subscribes to a principle of musical "anarchy," or that his musical discourse is merely "rhapsodic," lacking in formal cohesion. Obviously, he does not adhere to *conventional* form, but that is only one kind of form. In this connection it is well to remember that Ives called this work a "sonata" only because he could not think of a better name for it. He did not propose to write a composition in conventional sonata form. The *Concord Sonata* has *organic* form, based on thematic unity, structural parallelism, motival development, repetition, and variation. It also has *psychological* form: it follows the curves of emotion and feeling, rising to climaxes and falling to quieter moods, according to a controlled design.

In the "Emerson" and "Hawthorne" movements, Ives occasionally

[10] Copyright 1947 by Arrow Music Press, Inc. Used by permission.

uses time signatures, and therefore bar lines. In "The Alcotts" he uses a key signature in some sections, as well as time signatures. Ives is not a doctrinaire iconoclast. His object is musical expression. He will use conventional devices and commonplace materials when they suit his expressive purpose, and he will discard them when they hamper that purpose. Whatever material he employs, and whatever devices he uses, whether conventional or unconventional, we may be certain that a genuinely creative mind is at work. In the "Hawthorne" movement of the *Concord Sonata*, certain clusters of notes have to be played by using a strip of board about fifteen inches long, "heavy enough to press the keys down without striking." This is the effect that Ives felt he needed to suggest Hawthorne's "Celestial Railroad," and he adopted the only practical means to obtain that effect. Such a device is the result not of modernistic eccentricity but of Yankee ingenuity.

Past and present in the music of Ives

When Henry Bellamann wrote that "Ives is wholly of the bone and flesh of Colonial America" he overstated his case. Ives, one of the most independent artists who ever lived, cannot be circumscribed by colonialism. It is true—and this is the important thing—that Ives does have his spiritual roots deep in America's past, including all that was most "uncolonial," all that was most self-sufficient and new-seeking, in the period preceding our nationhood. But he is equally akin to the pioneer, self-made composers and singing-school masters of the late eighteenth and early nineteenth centuries; and one pictures him, in his self-reliance, his enthusiasm, his belief in the strength of Nature, and his philosophizing on the powers and properties of music, as a modern Billings. He belongs also to the great age of New England culture, blood brother to the Concord bards, achieving in music, more than half a century later, what they achieved in literature and thought. He belongs, finally, to the whole tradition of New England folkways, which he absorbed and transmuted in his music.

There is much truth in Burrill Phillips's statement that Ives "might be fairly called a historian-composer," in the sense that he evokes a past that has presumably vanished. But let us recall what Ives said of Orchard House in Concord, that "it seems to bear a consciousness that its past *is living*." The same may be said of Ives's music: that in it the past is living. And it lives in his music because it lived for him and in him. Ives did not deliberately seek to re-create the past or to be a musical historian. He embraced the past, as well as the present, simply by identifying himself completely with the traditional culture of his environment. And the deeper he immersed himself in this tradition, the more boldly he was able to reach out toward the future. The paradox is similar to that expressed by Van Wyck Brooks in *The Flowering of New England:* "Ironically enough, it was Boston and Cambridge that grew to be provincial, while the local and even parochial Concord mind, which had always been universal, proved to be also national." Ives's outlook was local but never provincial. Like the ever-widening circles that appear when a stone is thrown into a pool of water, his music proceeds from the local to the regional, thence to the national, and finally to the universal.

From 1911 to 1916 Ives worked on a projected *Universe Symphony,* intended as "a presentation and contemplation in tones, rather than in music (as such), of the mysterious creation of the earth and firmament, the evolution of all life in nature, in humanity to the divine." He completed only the prelude to this symphony and left part of one movement unfinished. The attempted distinction between "tones" and "music" *as such*—perhaps akin to the distinction between substance and manner?—indicates a tendency toward mysticism in Ives, a tendency that has always been present in his work, though counterbalanced by his sense of humor (witness the "cosmic comedy" in the second movement of the Fourth Symphony) and his feeling for reality (he himself spoke of "an interruption of reality" in that same cosmic movement). It is perhaps in one of his most original and extraordinary compositions, *The Unanswered Question,* described as "A Cosmic Landscape," that Ives's mysticism finds its most concentrated expression. To the reiterated atonal questionings of the trumpet, the scurrying dissonant flutes can find no answer, while in the background the motionless consonant strings represent the Eternal Silence. An unfinished Symphony of the Universe, an eternally Unanswered Question: these are the consummation of Ives's effort to transcend the limitation of music and to attain through tones the realm of pure contemplation.

chapter twenty-one

The rise of ragtime

I can shake the earth's foundation wid de Maple Leaf Rag!
SIDNEY BROWN, "MAPLE LEAF RAG SONG" (1903).

During the Gay Nineties, ragtime music swept the country and even made a considerable impression on Europe. It rose rapidly to an immense popularity—became, indeed, a sort of craze—was taken over for commercial exploitation by tin-pan alley, degenerated into unimaginative manipulation of clichés, and fizzled out like a wet firecracker about the time the United States went into World War I.

In the 1940s there was a revival of interest in ragtime. Looking at it in the perspective of time, one discovers that it was no ephemeral fad, but an important phase of America's music, deeply rooted in our folk and popular traditions; not a mere novelty but something strongly original; not wholly a meretricious commercialized output but a movement genuinely creative at the core that produced a permanent body of music and that exerted an enduring influence.

The convergence of ragtime and blues in classic New Orleans jazz, which occurred during the last decades of the nineteenth century, is one of the fundamental developments in the history of American music. Although these three currents of American popular music—ragtime, blues, and jazz—are closely related, it will be convenient, for the sake of clarity, to trace separately the course of each. Ragtime and blues may be considered as important tributaries of jazz, the Mississippi River of American music. These tributaries are of interest for their own sake as well as for what they contribute to the main stream of jazz.

There are direct links between ragtime and American minstrelsy. Two of these links are the so-called "plantation melodies" or "coon songs," generally sung with banjo accompaniment, and the type of

429

dance known as "cakewalk," which became increasingly popular as a feature of minstrel shows from about 1880. We must bear in mind that while in the beginning the blackface minstrel troupes consisted of white performers with their faces blackened—who more or less faithfully imitated what they took to be typical traits of Negro music and dancing—after the Civil War and the emancipation of the slaves, with the consequent incorporation of the Negro into many phases of American life, particularly the entertainment field, Negroes themselves began to take part in the minstrel shows. While the Negro minstrel performer was still more or less bound by the long-established stereotypes of blackface minstrelsy, he nevertheless was able, through details of emphasis and interpretation, to give the songs and dances and instrumental accompaniments an authenticity and an originality that they had not previously possessed.

In an earlier chapter it was pointed out that many of the old minstrel tunes were marked by syncopation. For example, both "Old Zip Coon" and "Old Dan Tucker," among many others, contain the characteristic rhythmic figure, ♪♫♩, that became the standard cakewalk formula of ragtime music. Among the songs of Stephen Foster, particularly those in which he was most influenced by the singing and dancing of the Negro roustabouts on the Ohio River, this syncopation is also found. Willis Laurence James has observed that Foster's "The Glendy Burk" (1860) is "a true ragtime song," and that to be convinced of this one need simply pat the hands and feet while singing it, to provide the regular beat of the bass in ragtime.

It is thus a very thin gap that separates the more genuine minstrel songs of the mid-nineteenth century from the authentic ragtime style that emerged a few decades later. That gap was filled by the Negro performers, particularly the banjoists and later the pianists, who began to find an outlet for their musical talents and an expression for their racial heritage in minstrelsy, in vaudeville and variety (which soon replaced the minstrel shows), and in the entertainment world in general. As we shall presently see, some of that "entertainment" was associated with the unrespectable "underworld" that opposed no barriers of convention or prejudice to the Negro musicians and their strangely disconcerting music with its "hot" rhythm and its "blue" notes. It was the musical meeting of these two worlds—that of the honky-tonks and barrel houses, and that of the popular stage and commercial publishing—that made possible the rise of ragtime as a permanent form of American popular music. Before we go on to describe where and in what manner this development took place, we must cast a backward glance at some of the antecedents of ragtime, which are equally applicable to the background of jazz and the blues.

The entire body of Afro-American music is in fact a whole, possessing an organic unity stemming from a common cultural tradition (the basic traits of this tradition were described in Chapter 4). We are aware that Afro-American music absorbed many influences, from folk tunes of the British Isles to the French and Spanish dance music of Louisiana. We also know that it has manifested itself in various directions: the spirituals and shouts, the work and play songs, the children's songs and lullabies, the cornfield "hollers" and the blues, the banjo tunes and the many dances that go with them. In spite of superficial differences, all these manifestations, when one gets to the core of them, disregarding conventional adulteration (such as the "arranged" spirituals sung by trained choirs and concert artists), will reveal their common ancestry and close kinship. This common tie is in the "hot" quality of the music. All true Afro-American music is "hot," whether it be a spiritual, a work song, a blues, a banjo tune, a piano rag, or a jazz piece.

"Hot rhythm" on the levee

That greatly gifted writer and observer of Afro-American folkways, Lafcadio Hearn, spent several years in Cincinnati as a young man, before going to New Orleans. He took a keen interest in the music of the Negro stevedores, and in 1876 published in the Cincinnati *Commercial* an article called "Levee Life," [1] in which he vividly described the songs and dances of these workers. He also collected the words of many of the songs, but unfortunately not the music. His article was subtitled "Haunts and Pastimes of the Roustabouts, Their Original Songs and Peculiar Dances." His description is worth quoting, for it is one of the basic documents on the folk backgrounds of ragtime and jazz. He begins by setting the scene:

. . . on a cool spring evening, when the levee is bathed in moonlight, and the torch-basket lights dance redly upon the water, and

[1] Reprinted in *An American Miscellany*, vol. 1.

the clear air vibrates to the sonorous music of the deep-toned steam-whistle, and the sound of wild banjo-thrumming floats out through the open doors of the levee dance-houses. . . .

Then he tells something of their songs and dances in general:

Roustabout life in the truest sense is, then, the life of the colored population of the Rows, and, partly, of Bucktown—blacks and mulattoes from all parts of the States, but chiefly from Kentucky and Eastern Virginia, where most of them appear to have toiled on the plantations before Freedom; and echoes of the old plantation life still live in their songs and their pastimes. You may hear old Kentucky slave songs chanted nightly on the steamboats, in that wild, half-melancholy key peculiar to the natural music of the African race; and you may see the old slave dances nightly performed to the air of some ancient Virginia-reel in the dance-houses of Sausage Row, or the "ballrooms" of Bucktown. . . . Many of their songs, which have never appeared in print, treat of levee life in Cincinnati, of all the popular steamboats running on the "Muddy Water," and of the favorite roustabout haunts on the river bank and in Bucktown.

Finally he takes us into one of these "dance-houses," where on the back of a long bench, placed with its face to the wall, with their feet inwardly reclining upon the seat, sat the musicians:

A well-dressed, neatly-built mulatto picked the banjo, and a somewhat lighter colored musician led the music with a fiddle, which he played remarkably well and with great spirit. A short, stout negress, illy dressed, with a rather good-natured face and a bed shawl tied about her head, played the bass viol, and that with no inexperienced hand.

What Hearn calls a "bass viol" is doubtless the double bass or bull fiddle (generally referred to as string bass, or simply bass, in jazz terminology), which later came to be an important element in the rhythm section of the classic New Orleans jazz band. It is exasperating that Hearn does not tell us *how* this Negro woman played the string bass, instead of how well she played it. If it was used primarily to mark the rhythm, then we have the precursor of a jazz trio.

Hearn then goes on to describe the dancing:

The musicians struck up that weird, wild, lively air, known per-haps to many of our readers as the "Devil's Dream," and in which

"the musical ghost of a cat chasing the spectral ghost of a rat" is
represented by a succession of "miauls" and "squeaks" on the fiddle.
The dancers danced a double quadrille, at first, silently and rapidly;
but warming with the wild spirit of the music, leaped and shouted,
swinging each other off the floor, and keeping time with a precision
which shook the building in time to the music. The women, we noticed, almost invariably embraced the men about the neck in swinging, the man clasping them about the waist. Sometimes the men advancing leaped and crossed legs with a double shuffle, and with almost sightless rapidity.

Then the music changed to an old Virginia reel, and the dancing
changing likewise, presented the most grotesque spectacle imaginable. The dancing became wild; men patted juba and shouted, the
negro women danced with the most fantastic grace, their bodies describing almost incredible curves forward and backward; limbs intertwined rapidly in a wrestle with each other and with the music; the
room presented a tide of swaying bodies and tossing arms, and flying
hair. The white female dancers seemed heavy, cumbersome, ungainly
by contrast with their dark companions; the spirit of the music was
not upon them; they were abnormal to the life about them.

Once more the music changed—to some popular Negro air, with
the chorus—

> Don't get weary,
> I'm goin' home.

The musicians began to sing; the dancers joined in; and the dance
terminated with a roar of song, stamping of feet, "patting juba,"
shouting, laughing, reeling. Even the curious spectators involuntarily
kept time with their feet; it was the very drunkenness of music, the
intoxication of the dance.

It was something of this "intoxication of the dance," something of
this irresistible "hot" rhythm that forced you to keep time with your
feet, that the whole country was to feel when ragtime swept across
the land. Notice Hearn's remark that the white dancers were not possessed by the spirit of this music, and that only with the Negroes
did it appear as a natural, spontaneous outpouring of rhythm and
feeling. The rise of ragtime could take place only after the Negro
was given an opportunity to express himself musically outside of his
own limited milieu: on the stage and in the world of entertainment.

What is important to remember is that the fusion in ragtime of the more or less conventional "coon song" and cakewalk tradition of minstrelsy with the authentic strain of genuine Afro-American syncopated and polyrhythmic "hot" music could not have occurred unless the culturally untamed (i.e., conventionally uneducated) Negro folk had kept alive throughout the South, and more particularly along the vast Mississippi River basin, their uninhibited "hot" style of making music. The cities along the Mississippi and its tributaries were especially significant in this development because they provided employment for the Negroes on the levees and steamboats and created permanent urban communities where the kind of music and dancing described by Hearn could flourish unmolested by the entrenched forces of respectability. What Hearn saw and heard and described in Cincinnati in 1876—in effect a kind of primitive jam session—had obviously been going on for some time before that, and undoubtedly had its replica in other riverside cities. His account reveals the existence of a well-established tradition of "hot" instrumental music flourishing "beyond the pale" in the water-front dance houses of our riparian cities. It is no wonder, then, that the rise of ragtime and blues and jazz was to center around these cities, chiefly New Orleans, Memphis, and St. Louis. Later, of course, Chicago and New York became the inevitable centers of commercial exploitation and mass diffusion.

Thus far we have traced two principal currents as converging in the creation of ragtime: the blackface minstrelsy of the stage, with its concomitant output of "coon songs," and the genuine, "hot" Afro-American folk music. A third contributing current should now be mentioned: the Negro brass bands of the towns and cities, which began to spring up shortly after the Civil War. More will be said about these street bands in the chapter on jazz, in the development of which they had a vital role. Here it is sufficient to mention that Negro brass bands, under the driving impulse of "hot" rhythm, soon began to "rag" many of the marches and tunes they played. This "ragtime" band music was later imitated by such celebrated white bands as Sousa's and Pryor's, and in fact it was Sousa's band that gave Europe its first taste of ragtime. Band music, however, is more important in connection with the history of jazz, because ragtime is essentially music for piano. Ragtime may be described as the application of systematic syncopation to piano playing and composition. More precisely, it consists basically of a syncopated melody played over a regularly accented beat (2/4 time) in the bass. As previously observed, the basic rhythmic formula of ragtime is the so-called "cakewalk" figure, which, as we pointed out in discussing the compositions of L. M. Gottschalk, is also frequently met with in much of Latin American popular music, particularly that which has been strongly influenced by Afro-American elements from the Caribbean area. In view of the close connection between the cakewalk and the rise of ragtime something should be said here about the background of the former.

Cakewalk and "coon songs"

The cakewalk appears to have originated in an actual custom of plantation life in ante-bellum days. Featured in the blackface minstrel shows, it passed over into the variety acts that marked the transition to vaudeville. When the team of Harrigan and Hart presented, in 1877, a number called "Walking for Dat Cake" (music by Dave Braham and words by Harrigan), they billed it as an "Exquisite Picture of Negro Life and Customs." It was a precursor of the many cakewalk songs that flooded the nation around the turn of the century.

According to the testimony of Shephard N. Edmonds, a Negro born in Tennessee of freed slave parents,

The cakewalk was originally a plantation dance, just a happy movement they (the slaves) did to the banjo music because they couldn't stand still. It was generally on Sundays, when there was little work, that the slaves both young and old would dress up in hand-me-down finery to do a high-kicking, prancing walk-around. They did a take-off on the high manners of the white folks in the "big house," but their masters, who gathered around to watch the fun, missed the point. It's supposed to be that the custom of a prize started with the master giving a cake to the couple that did the proudest movement.[2]

The combination of cakewalk rhythm and banjo technique is a direct forerunner of ragtime.

During the 1890s variety teams such as Smart and Williams, and especially Williams and Walker, popularized the cakewalk, which quickly became a national craze. Cakewalk contests sprang up everywhere, from the biggest cities to the remotest hamlets. That high-

[2] Quoted in Blesh and Janis, *They All Played Ragtime,* p. 96.

kicking step and that tricky rhythm had captivated the country. A large part of the world was also fascinated by this American novelty.

One of the earliest and most perceptive writers on American music, the novelist Rupert Hughes, wrote in 1899:

> Negroes call their clog dancing "ragging" and the dance a "rag," a dance largely shuffling. The dance is a sort of frenzy with frequent yelps of delight from the dancer and spectators and accompanied by the latter with hand clapping and stomping of feet. Banjo figuration is very noticeable in ragtime music and division of one of the beats into two short notes is traceable to the hand clapping.[3]

There can be no question about the importance of the banjo in the genesis of ragtime. This instrument, used by the Negroes from the early days of slavery, and having undoubtedly an African prototype, was the precursor of piano ragtime music. As we observed in an earlier chapter, the original "coon songs" took the banjo as the symbol of the plantation melody, even though they were published in versions for voice and piano. When the "coon songs" were revived and attained a new and wider popularity toward the end of the nineteenth century, they still clung to the banjo as a symbol of the plantation life that was by then very much under the enchantment of distance and ignorance. One of these songs, "New Coon in Town," by J. S. Putnam, published in 1883, was specifically subtitled "Banjo Imitation." This was an adumbration of ragtime before the name itself was applied to popular music. Just as in the early plantation melodies syncopation occurs incidentally, so in the later "coon songs" of the 1880s and 1890s ragtime appears in a few measures here and there, until, by 1897, full-fledged ragtime piano numbers began to be published with a rush. In order to explain this sudden surge of published ragtime, it is necessary to take up the story of the popular pianists who created American ragtime music out of the materials and backgrounds we have been describing.

"King of ragtime"

The most famous name associated with the rise of ragtime is that of Scott Joplin (1869–1917), though there is some dispute as to

[3] Hughes in the Boston *Musical Record*, Apr. 1, 1899.

whether he actually deserves the title of "King of Ragtime." Perhaps such titles are unnecessary anyway. Joplin, a Negro, was born in Texarkana, Texas, and grew up in a household that was full of music. His mother sang and played the banjo, his father played the violin, and his brother the guitar. Scott himself was attracted by the piano (there was one in a neighbor's house). When his father managed to save enough money for the purchase of an old-fashioned square grand, Scott taught himself to play, and attracted the attention of a local German musician who gave him lessons and familiarized him with the music of the great European composers. This orthodox influence was counterbalanced by his wanderings as an itinerant musician while he was still in his teens: an experience that brought him into intimate contact with the folklore and the low-life of the South. In 1885, at the age of seventeen, he arrived in St. Louis, which became his headquarters for the next eight years. He played there in the honky-tonks on Chestnut and Market Streets, where Negro pianists were developing, with freedom and originality, the style of piano music that was soon to be known as ragtime.

In 1893 Joplin, along with many other musicians, went to Chicago for the World's Columbian Exposition, where he met some of the early Chicago ragtime players, such as "Plunk" Henry and Johnny Seymour. He also made the acquaintance of Otis Saunders, who returned with him to St. Louis and soon persuaded him to write down and publish some of the piano pieces that he was playing. The following year he went from St. Louis to Sedalia, Missouri, where he wrote his first compositions. These, however, were sentimental songs, not rags. Joplin nevertheless was still playing ragtime piano, notably at a place called the Maple Leaf Club. There, in the summer of 1899, he was heard by a man who was to become a central figure in the spread of ragtime: the music publisher John Stillwell Stark. The latter was a pioneer and ex-farmer who had settled in Sedalia around 1885 and had taken to cultural pursuits with characteristic vigor and enthusiasm. Although he embraced the genteel tradition on one side (his daughter studied music with Moszkowski in Germany), he was broad-minded enough, and his pioneer instincts were strong enough, to recognize something new and vital in American music when he heard Scott Joplin play at the Maple Leaf Club. The result was the publication, in 1899, of a composition that made history: *Maple Leaf Rag*, with its classic ragtime syncopation over the steady rhythm of the bass.

Joplin's *Maple Leaf Rag* was a huge success. Stark had given him a royalty contract, so that composer as well as publisher profited from the sales, which were enormous for those times. Stark, ready for bigger things, moved over to St. Louis, set up his own printing press, and continued to publish ragtime numbers, by Joplin and others. Later he opened an office in New York, but he was not cut out for the tin-pan-alley type of business. In 1912 he returned to St. Louis, where he continued to champion ragtime, insisting that it was both respectable and valuable. He outlived the vogue of ragtime by some ten years, for he died in 1927. John Stark was a true pioneer, a man of conviction and culture, whose name should be honored in the annals of America's music.

Scott Joplin soon outgrew the "tenderloin" district where he and so many other pianists had found employment and an opportunity to play ragtime. He moved into a large house of his own and set himself up as a music teacher. He went on composing a long succession of rags and other popular pieces, some of them in collaboration with Scott Hayden, Arthur Marshall, and Louis Chauvin. His first published rag was not the *Maple Leaf Rag*, but *Original Rags*, published in March, 1899. In all, Joplin published thirty-nine piano rags, of which seven were written in collaboration with others. There are also a number of unpublished rags in manuscript. Among his rags for piano solo are *Peacherine Rag* (1901), *The Easy Winners* (1901), *Palm Leaf Rag—A Slow Drag* (1903), *Rose Leaf Rag* (1907), *Fig Leaf Rag* (1908), *Euphonic Sounds* (1909), *Stoptime Rag* (1910), *Scott Joplin's New Rag* (1912), and *Reflection Rag—Syncopated Musings* (1917).

In 1903 Joplin wrote the book and music for *A Guest of Honor*, described as "A Ragtime Opera." It received only one concert performance in St. Louis and was never published, though Stark evidently contemplated its publication, judging by an entry in the U.S. Copyright Office. The manuscript has disappeared; so nothing is known concretely of this first attempt at an American ragtime opera.

From about 1909 Joplin lived in New York, and there he tried his hand at opera again. The work was *Treemonisha*, an opera in three acts, which he published at his own expense in 1911, in a piano score. The scene of the opera is laid "on a plantation somewhere in the State of Arkansas," and the action takes places in 1886. Treemonisha is a Negro girl who receives an education and is thus able to overcome the superstitions by which her people are bound. She is acclaimed as their teacher and leader, while the Negroes assemble and dance *A Real Slow Drag*, which forms the climax of the opera:

> Dance slowly, prance slowly,
> While you hear that pretty rag.

The score of *Treemonisha* employs ragtime, but not exclusively. Scott Joplin was trying to create an American Negro opera; he deserves credit for pioneering in this direction.

After he had painstakingly orchestrated the work, a single performance was given in Harlem, in a concert version without scenery or costumes, and with piano accompaniment. It did not reach the right audience, obtained no success, and was never heard again. The dashing of his operatic ambitions was a severe blow to Joplin. His mind began to fail, and on April 1, 1917 he died, famous and honored for his rags if not for his operas.

Other ragtime composers

Another important figure in early ragtime was the Negro pianist Thomas M. Turpin, composer of the first published Negro rag that is known, the *Harlem Rag*, which appeared in 1897. This was followed by *The Bowery Buck* (1899), *A Ragtime Nightmare* (1900), *St. Louis Rag* (1903), and *The Buffalo Rag* (1904). Turpin was definitely associated with the St. Louis sporting district and wrote most of his rags in a place called the Rosebud, which he owned and where he played the piano and imparted to other colleagues the secrets of ragtime. He died in 1922, having earned the unofficial title of "Father of St. Louis Ragtime."

James Sylvester Scott (1886–1938), also a Negro, learned to play the piano in his home town of Neosho, Missouri, and later moved to Carthage, where he got a job in Dumars's music store, playing ragtime in his spare time. Dumars thought his music was good enough to publish; so the next few years saw the publication of several James Scott numbers. Scott visited St. Louis where Stark published his *Climax Rag* in 1914. Other early Scott rags include *Frog Legs Rag*

(1906), *Kansas City Rag* (1907), *Great Scott Rag* (1909), *Sunburst Rag* (1909), *Hilarity Rag* (1910), and *Ophelia Rag* (1910). Altogether he published thirty rags for piano solo, the last of which was *Broadway Rag*, issued in 1922.

From 1914 James Scott lived as a music teacher and performer in Kansas City, continuing to compose and to develop his extraordinary technique as a ragtime pianist. *Honeymoon Rag* and *Prosperity Rag*, both published by Stark in 1916, reveal the increasing complexity of his style.

Louis Chauvin, a Negro pianist of St. Louis, who could neither read nor write music, is credited by some authorities with being one of the pioneer creative figures in ragtime, though only his *Heliotrope Bouquet* (1907) was published with his name (in collaboration with Scott Joplin). Two writers on ragtime, Simms and Borneman, assert that "many of his [Chauvin's] original tunes and syncopations were transcribed by Tom [Turpin] and later by Scott Joplin without any due credit." It is impossible to prove or disprove this statement, but it is a fact that much appropriation of unpublished material was going on in the 1890s, when musicians, both Negro and white, were racing neck-and-neck to get on the ragtime band wagon with compositions that they could call their own once the copyright had been registered. Actually, the first piano rag to be copyrighted was by a white musician, William Krell, and was titled *Mississippi Rag* (January 25, 1897). Not until December of 1897 was the first rag by a Negro composer published; that was, as previously noted, Tom Turpin's *Harlem Rag*.

If one took the date of copyright or of publication as the criterion, then precedence in the ragtime field would go to a white musician named Ben R. Harney, from Middlesboro, Kentucky (*b.* 1871), whose celebrated hit tune, "You've Been a Good Old Wagon but You've Done Broke Down," was published in Louisville in January, 1895. The following year it was brought out by Witmark in New York. This was a song, not a piano rag, but, in the words of Blesh and Janis,[4] "the piano accompaniment and the concluding instrumental 'dance' section are bona fide, if elementary, ragtime. . . . These facts establish Harney's unassailable priority as a pioneer of printed ragtime—if one disregards a mere matter of nomenclature or titling—and amply explain

---

[4] Blesh and Janis, *op. cit.*, p. 95.

his own staunch conviction that he 'originated ragtime.' " Actually, Harney was a writer of ragtime songs rather than of piano rags. Another famous early ragtime hit of his was *Mr. Johnson (Turn Me Loose)*, published in 1896.

Ben Harney undoubtedly had a lot to do with popularizing ragtime. When he appeared in New York in 1896, at the age of twenty-five, an item in the New York *Clipper* said: "Ben R. Harney . . . jumped into immediate favor through the medium of his genuinely clever plantation Negro imitations and excellent piano playing." When Harney published his *Rag Time Instructor* in 1897, he called himself "Original Instructor to the Stage of the Now Popular Rag Time in Ethiopian Song." Harney certainly did not originate ragtime, but he was a link in the chain that connected the old-time "Ethiopian business" with the folk-rooted novelty called ragtime.

Many other white musicians, nearly all from the South or Middle West, where they had ample opportunity to hear the true ragtime Negro playing and to absorb its characteristic traits at first hand, took a prominent part in the development and diffusion of ragtime. Among the most notable were George Botsford, Charles H. Hunter, Charles L. Johnson, Joseph Lamb, and Percy Wenrich. Botsford began with *The Katy Flyer—Cakewalk Two Step* in 1899 and ended with the *Boomerang Rag* in 1916. Charlie Johnson published about thirty rags, among them *Doc Brown's Cake Walk* (1899), *Dill Pickles* (1906), *Swanee Rag* (1912), *Blue Goose Rag* (1916), and *Fun on the Levee —Cakewalk* (1917). Some of his rags were published under the name of Raymond Birch. Hunter, a native of Nashville, Tennessee, almost totally blind from birth, first appeared in print in 1899 with *Tickled to Death*, followed by *A Tennessee Tantalizer* in 1900, *'Possum and 'Taters* in 1901. Hunter published a few more numbers, but died of tuberculosis in 1907. Joseph Lamb, a protégé of Joplin in New York (he was, exceptionally, an Easterner), was the author of *Excelsior Rag* and *Ethiopia Rag* (both 1909), *American Beauty Rag* (1913), *Cleopatra Rag* (1915), *Contentment Rag* (1915), and numerous others, many of which remain unpublished. Percy Wenrich, born in Joplin, Missouri, in 1880, and known as "The Joplin Kid," began imitating Negro ragtime at the age of twelve and later attended the Chicago Musical College but preferred—to use the title of one of his songs— "Wabash Avenue after Dark." He brought out *Peaches and*

Cream Rag (1905), *Noodles* (1906), *Sweet Meats Rag* (1907), *Memphis Rag* (1908), *Sunflower Rag* (1911), and others. He also wrote many successful songs, among them: "Put on Your Old Grey Bonnet" (1909) and "When You Wore a Tulip and I Wore a Big Red Rose" (1914).

Other ragtime composers who merit at least passing mention are Eubie Blake (*Charleston Rag*, c. 1899), Thomas E. Broady (*Mandy's Broadway Stroll*, 1898), Robert Hampton (*The Dogin' Rag*, 1913), Tony Jackson (*The Naked Dance*, c. 1902), Joe Jordan (*Double Fudge*, 1902), Henry Lodge (*Temptation Rag*, 1909), Arthur Marshall (*Ham and—Rag*, 1908), Artie Matthews (*Pastime Rags*, Nos. 1–5, 1913–1920), Paul Pratt (*Vanity Rag*, 1909), Luckey Roberts (*Junk Man Rag*, 1913), J. Russel Robinson (*Sapho Rag*, 1909; *Dynamite Rag*, 1910), and Euday Bowman (*Twelfth Street Rag*, 1916). Other prominent ragtime musicians—Ferdinand "Jelly Roll" Morton, Thomas "Fats" Waller, and James P. Johnson—will be discussed later, for their careers run over into the postwar period of ragtime.

Genuine ragtime music was difficult to play. But around 1900, and for several years thereafter, almost everybody in the United States wanted to play it. Harney's *Rag Time Instructor* proved unsatisfactory as a textbook. A more practical method was needed, and this came in 1903 when Axel Christensen of Chicago hired a studio and advertised: "Ragtime Taught in Ten Lessons." Pupils flocked to him, and encouraged by his success he published in 1904 Christensen's *Instruction Book No. 1 for Rag-Time Piano Playing*, which went into several revised and enlarged editions. Admitting that "It takes a skillful musician to play ragtime flawlessly," Christensen nevertheless undertook to impart the rudiments and "to teach the rawest beginner how to play ragtime in twenty lessons" (not *ten* this time!)

Far different was *The School of Ragtime—Six Exercises for Piano*, by Scott Joplin, published by John Stark in 1908. This is not a beginner's school, but a set of *études* for the advanced student. In his preface Joplin wrote:

What is scurrilously called ragtime is an invention that is here to stay. That is now conceded by all classes of musicians. That all publications masquerading under the name of ragtime are not the genuine article will be better known when these exercises are studied. That real ragtime of the higher class is rather difficult to play is a painful truth which most pianists have discovered. Syncopations are no indication of light or trashy music, and to shy bricks at "hateful ragtime" no longer passes for musical culture. To assist the amateur players in giving the "Joplin Rags" that weird and intoxicating effect intended by the composer is the object of this work.

Joplin wrote his exercises on three staves, of which the uppermost is a kind of guide and not to be played. This fundamental document of classic ragtime, consisting of the exercises and the composer's comments thereon, demands some quotation here. In his note to Exercise No. 1 the author writes:

It is evident that, by giving each note its proper time and by scrupulously observing the ties, you will get the effect. So many are careless in these respects that we will specify each feature. In this number, strike the first note and hold it through the time belonging to the second note. The upper staff is not syncopated, and is not to be played. The perpendicular dotted lines running from the syncopated note below to the two notes above will show exactly its duration. Play slowly until you catch the swing, and never play ragtime fast at any time.[5]

Slow march tempo (Count Two)

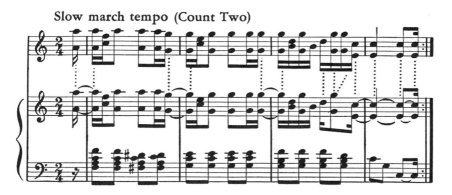

Concerning Exercise No. 3, Joplin made the following comment:

This style is very effective when neatly played. If you have observed the object of the dotted lines they will lead you to a proper rendering of this number and you will find it interesting:

[5] Excerpts from *The School of Ragtime* used by permission of Scott Joplin's estate.

Slow march tempo (Count Two)

The sixth and final exercise is preceded by the following note:

The instructions given, together with the dotted lines, will enable you to interpret this variety which has very pleasing effects. We wish to say here, that the "Joplin ragtime" is destroyed by careless or imperfect rendering, and very often good players lose the effect entirely, by playing too fast. They are harmonized with the supposition that each note will be played as it is written, as it takes this and also the proper time divisions to complete the sense intended [since the principle of the dotted lines has been illustrated in the previous examples, the upper staff is omitted in quoting Exercise No. 6]:

Slow march tempo (Count Two)

It is significant that Joplin stresses the need of a moderate tempo for ragtime. "Never play ragtime fast," he tells the student. And again, ". . . very often good players lose the effect entirely, by playing too fast." This was the classic St. Louis concept of ragtime, as exemplified by Scott Joplin.

New Orleans and New York

Important as was St. Louis in the rise of ragtime, the contribution of New Orleans must not be overlooked. That was the original center of "ragging" street bands and of the ragtime dance bands that ushered in jazz. It was also a center of ragtime piano, especially in the notorious red-light district of "Storyville," a section of the city set aside for "sporting" purposes. The leading New Orleans ragtime pianists were Antony Jackson (1876–1921) and Ferdinand "Jelly Roll" Morton (1885–1941), both of whom later went to Chicago. Morton's major role in the history of jazz will receive attention in a later chapter. Meanwhile our main concern will be with his piano rags. But first a few words about Tony Jackson.

Tony Jackson was a singer as well as a pianist, and the "composer" of several song hits, though he could not read music. His "Pretty Baby" (in collaboration with Egbert Van Alstyne) was a big hit in 1918. Among other melodies are "Don't Leave Me in the Ice and Snow" and "Miss Samantha Johnson's Wedding Day." As a ragtime player and improviser he is recalled as a fabulous performer by old-timers, but none of his rags was ever published. When queried about this, Jackson is said to have replied that he would burn them before he would give them away for five dollars apiece. The men who made money out of ragtime were not always its genuine creators.

During eight weeks in 1938, Jelly Roll Morton recorded for the Library of Congress, on 116 record sides, the story of his life, with musical illustrations at the piano. Here is a large part of the saga of ragtime, blues, and jazz, requiring the addition of many scholarly footnotes on points of historical fact, but presenting, with vivid and authentic details that otherwise would be lost to history, the background and genesis of a people's music. In Morton's recordings we can follow the transformation of an old French quadrille into the famous *Tiger Rag*, and observe the metamorphosis of *Maple Leaf Rag* into the hot, "stomping" style of New Orleans ragtime, of which Jelly Roll was the great piano exponent.

Morton did not begin to have his piano rags published until 1918, but many of them were written much earlier. The celebrated *King Porter Stomp*, for instance, dates from 1906. Other piano rags by Morton include *Frog-i-more Rag, The Pearls, Kansas City Stomps, Shreveport Stomps, Midnight Mama, Chicago Breakdown, Black Bottom Stomp, Ham and Eggs, Bugaboo, Mister Joe, Crazy Chord Rag, Buddy Carter's Rag, The Perfect Rag* (some unpublished). Through the many recordings that Jelly Roll Morton made, we can appreciate both the individual brilliancy of his style and the development of the typical New Orleans "hot" idiom.

With James P. Johnson (*b.* 1894) and Thomas "Fats" Waller, the scene shifts to New York. Johnson received lessons in harmony and counterpoint from a "long hair" professor and has worked ambitiously at compositions in the larger forms, such as the *Jasmine* (*Jazz-o-Mine*) *Concerto* for piano and orchestra and the *Harlem Symphony*, in four movements (1932), which includes a syncopated passacaglia on the hymn tune "I Want Jesus to Walk with Me." Looking upon Scott Joplin as a great forerunner, Johnson has endeavored to continue the tradition of classic ragtime with such piano pieces as *Caprice Rag* (1914), *Harlem Strut* (1917), *Carolina Shout* (1925), and many others. Mention should also be made of his syncopated *Eccentricity Waltz* (1926).

Thomas "Fats" Waller (1904–1943), a Negro born in New York, was the son of a pastor; his mother, who was musical, provided him with a high-class musical training under Carl Bohm and Leopold Godowsky. But he took to ragtime as to his natural element, composing his first rag at the age of fifteen. A man of huge bulk, irrepressible humor, and prodigious energy, he turned out over four hundred compositions in his relatively brief lifetime. In addition to his popular songs and scores for Broadway shows (*Keep Shufflin', Hot Chocolates, Early to Bed*), Waller composed many piano rags, among them: *Handful of Keys, Smashing Thirds, Fractious Fingering, Bach Up to Me,* and *Black Raspberry Jam.*

The heyday of ragtime was from about 1897 to 1910. It was in 1897 that Kerry Mills, white composer of sentimental songs, brought out, in an inspired moment, his stirring and immensely popular ragtime tune, *At a Georgia Camp Meeting*, based on the Civil War song

"Our Boys Will Shine Tonight." Contrary to a popular notion, Irving Berlin's much-publicized *Alexander's Ragtime Band* (1911) did not usher in the great age of ragtime. By that time ragtime was on the way out. Berlin's tune caught the public fancy and gave a fillip to the waning vogue of ragtime. But overexploitation by commercial interests, the high-pressure promotion of pseudo ragtime, and the mechanical repetition of routine formulas, soon brought about the decline of ragtime as a vital form of American music.

That this decline was under the circumstances inevitable may now be clearly perceived. What may also be now perceived and proclaimed is that ragtime, in its most authentic manifestations, as played and as written by both Negro and white musicians who were closest to its traditional origins, with its spurious elements sifted out by time and critical appraisal, remains as a permanent, important, and original contribution to America's music.

chapter twenty-two

Singin' the blues

Got de blues, but too dam' mean to cry.
(TRADITIONAL.)

The spirituals are the manifestation of Afro-American folk music in choral singing. The blues are the manifestation of Afro-American folk music in solo singing. When "a lonely Negro man plowing out in some hot, silent river bottom," raised his voice in a wailing "cornfield holler," he was singing the birth of the blues.[1] When a roustabout resting on the levee sang,

> Gwine down de river befo' long,
> Gwine down de river befo' long,
> Gwine down de river befo' long,

as if strengthening his lazy resolve by reiteration, he was singing the birth of the blues, with its three-line, twelve-bar pattern.

The three-line stanza seemed to develop naturally by repetition. Since the singer was giving relief to his feelings—of lonesomeness, or longing, or resentment, or sorrow—there was consolation in repeating the sentiment that he wanted to express. He began by telling what was on his mind, repeated it once for emphasis, and finished it off with a second repetition for good measure. This pattern was certainly no strain upon the singer's powers of improvisation. When the latter sought more scope, a variation in the third line resulted:

> I've never seen such real hard times before
> I've never seen such real hard times before
> The wolf keeps walkin' all 'round my door.

[1] See John and Alan Lomax, *American Ballads and Folk Songs*, p. 191.

448

This three-line stanza, consisting of statement, repetition, and "response," is the classic verse form of the blues. There are other patterns, for the blues are not stereotyped; but the above may be regarded as the norm.

Within their compact form the blues conveyed a complete mood and situation:

> Railroad blues
>
> I'm gonna lay my head on some lonesome railroad line
> I'm gonna lay my head on some lonesome railroad line
> An' let that two-nineteen train pacify my min'.

Often the verses of the blues, like those of the spirituals, were made up of current tag lines strung together in the moment of improvisation.

Although most blues have the burden of lament associated with the expression "feeling blue," they have an undertone of humor, not so much stressed as implied, that gives them a character utterly different from that of the ordinary sentimental song. Indeed, they are not sentimental at all, but combine realism and fantasy in a straightforward projection of mood and feeling.

The origin of the blues is lost in obscurity. Conjecturally, we can say that they developed concurrently with the rest of Afro-American folk song in the South of the United States. By 1870 they were probably widespread throughout that region, though assuredly not known by the name of "blues" until considerably later.

Besides being a type of folk song in their own right, and later a form of American popular music, the blues were a means of effecting the transition of Afro-American "hot" music from the vocal to the instrumental realm through the medium of piano blues and the jazz band. The blues are therefore of far-reaching significance in the development of American music.

The musical structure of the blues

Abbe Niles was unquestionably right when he remarked that "the blues architecture is admirably adapted to impromptu song and versification alike"—except that the term "architecture" is a bit pretentious for folk music. Since we have already seen something of the versification, let us now glance at the musical structure of the blues. First, as regards harmony: the harmonic scheme of the blues is merely a foundation upon which the melodic structure rests; its function is important—for without it the whole structure would collapse—but it does not constitute the creative element in the blues. It is like the form of the sonnet in poetry, providing a definite framework, capable of being varied within limits but needing the skill and inspiration of the poet to result in something creative. Keats and Hunt could not have improvised sonnets on the spur of the moment unless they had been thoroughly familiar with the sonnet as a traditional form.

To be suited to "impromptu" song, a harmonic scheme must be simple and stable, and at the same time provide scope for sufficient variation to avoid absolute sameness. The harmonic scheme of the blues fulfills these conditions. Normally only three chords are used: tonic, subdominant, and dominant seventh. The usual progression consists of the common chord of the tonic, the same on the subdominant, the chord of the dominant seventh, and back to the tonic chord. There are several variants, such as the introduction of the dominant seventh at the beginning, but essentially the harmonic foundation is "solid" enough to offer a firm base for the melodic inspiration of the singer or instrumentalist.

The usual structure of the blues consists of a twelve-bar pattern. Each line of the verse corresponds to four measures of the music. To express it in another way, there are two complete melodic statements (corresponding to the verse statement and its repetition), each ending on the tonic (or the third or fifth of the tonic chord), followed by the melodic "response" (corresponding to the third line of the verse), which also ends on the tonic. Here is an example in the widely diffused folk blues, "Joe Turner": [2]

[2] From *A Treasury of the Blues*, p. 12. Copyright 1926, 1929, by W. C. Handy and Edward Abbe Niles. Published by Charles Boni, New York. Used by permission of the copyright owners.

It will be noticed that there is a considerable gap between the end of one melodic phrase and the beginning of the next. Each statement actually occupies three rather than four measures. Abbe Niles has ably described the significance of this time interval in the melodic structure of the blues:

This is typical, and important. It affords to the improviser, for one thing, a space in which his next idea may go through its period of gestation,—and this is important to him. But to us it is of far greater interest that, assuming he isn't compelled to concentrate on what is to follow, he can utilize this space, not as a hold, but as a *playground* in which his voice or instrument may be allowed to wander in such fantastic musical paths as he pleases, returning (not necessarily but usually) to the keynote, third, or fifth, yet again before vacation is over. Regularly in folk-blues the last syllable of each line thus coincides, not only with the keynote or another element of the tonic major triad, *but with the first beat, third bar, of its corresponding four bars of music,* leaving seven quick beats or three slow ones (according to the time-signature) before the melody proper resumes its motion.[3]

This pattern can be verified by reference to the melody of "Joe Turner" quoted above. The space between the end of one melodic statement and the beginning of the next was often filled in with a simple ejaculation sung on a few interpolated notes, such as *oh, Lawdy!* As we have previously noticed, the interpolation of a brief ejaculatory refrain after each line is a common trait of Negro folk song, being frequently found both in spirituals and work songs. In the blues, the interpolated notes, whether sung or played instrumentally, came to be known as the "break" or the "jazz"; but this was after the blues had passed their archaic or folk stage. All these folk-born forms—blues, ragtime, jazz—existed in practice long before they were tagged with a name, classified, imitated, and exploited.

The "break" might be very simple or very elaborate, according to the impulse and skill of the singer or player. From the very beginning of our chronicle of America's music we have been familiar—recall the early folk psalmody of New England—with the traditional practice of melodic ornamentation. Handy says that as a child he heard Negro congregations singing "baptisin'" and "death-and-burial" songs with

[3] *Ibid.,* p. 14. From the introductory text by Abbe Niles.

all the voices weaving their own melodic threads around the notes of the tune. He transcribed one of these melodic improvisations, as re-called by him: [4]

This is interesting (though much more so would be the combination of many voices in this improvised embellishment); but Niles, who quotes this transcription, is mistaken when he writes that these hymns, in their ornamented versions, were "sung as they never were except by Negroes." The Negroes undoubtedly had their peculiar intonation, rhythm, and intervals; but the singing of tunes with improvised melodic embellishments, and the filling-in of "gaps" or holds with interpolated notes, was a firmly established practice in Anglo-American folk music long before the development of the Negro spirituals and the blues. The *manner* of jazz improvisation may be unique, but the principle has a long tradition in both the folk and the art music of Europe.

Many of the folk blues use the pentatonic scale (it will be found in "Joe Turner," above, with the addition of a minor third), but this scale, so widespread in folk music, is not what gives to the blues their peculiar melodic quality. The characteristic trait is rather the flatting of the third and seventh degrees of the diatonic scale. These are the so-called "blue notes" that have been of such significance in modern

[4] *Ibid.*, p. 23. Arranged by W. C. Handy. Copyright 1926 by W. C. Handy. Used by permission.

music. Frequently, in singing the blues, a Negro will return to the
third of the tonic chord; and as Niles remarks, this is "a fact of the first
importance to the blues because of the tendency of the untrained
Negro voice when singing the latter tone at an important point, to
worry it, slurring or wavering between flat and natural." [5] Strictly
speaking, therefore, it is not the flatted third as such, but rather this
ambivalent, this *worried* or slurred tone, that constitutes the true
"blue note."

The blues scale (diatonic, with microtonally flatted third and seventh) lies at the very core of Afro-American folk song, and its influence has permeated large sectors of American music, both in the
popular and in the fine-art idioms. To demonstrate the widespread use
of the blues tetrachord in every type of Afro-American vocal expression, Winthrop Sargeant cites the "chanting sermon" of a Negro
preacher in Alabama who in his declamation employed just two notes:
a tonic, and the "blue" third above it.[6] And the congregation would
echo him in similar fashion.

All the evidence indicates that the blues scale, and the blues intonation that goes with it, are an original and unique contribution
of the Negro race to America's music.

The primitive or archaic blues, as we have remarked, were probably sung at first without accompaniment. But as the possession of
musical instruments became more common among the Negroes, instrumental accompaniments, usually on the banjo or the guitar, later
on the piano, were added. This instrumental participation was of immense importance in the development of the blues and their transition
into jazz. The incorporation of the blues scale, blues harmony, and
melodic improvisation, into the idiom of instrumental music, from
the piano to the emergent jazz band, was an epoch-making development in the history of American music. The accompanying instrument, or instruments—for there might be several—not only provided
the basic harmony but imitated, and in a manner competed with, the
voice in melodic improvisation. The solo voice is the "leader"; the
instruments "follow the leader" but also weave semi-independent
melodic lines, while at the same time filling in the harmony and marking the beat of the rhythm. When the voice ceases at the end of a
melodic statement (i.e., a line of the verse), it is "answered" by the

[5] *Ibid.,* p. 14.
[6] Sargeant, *Jazz: Hot and Hybrid,* p. 183.

instruments, which then find themselves "on their own," free to assert their individuality boldly before the voice assumes its ascendancy again in the next vocal statement. And at the end, when the voice has finished with its third line, it is the instruments that have the final say. Since each vocal statement is answered by an instrumental statement, there is a perfect antiphonal pattern that corresponds to a fundamental device of Afro-American music.

Since the instruments, in addition to "answering" the voice, also weave their melodic lines along with it, we get the element of polyphony in the blues, with a more or less complex contrapuntal texture, depending on the number of instruments involved. And since the singer will sometimes follow a melodic line independent of the underlying harmony, we also get the element of polytonality (or more accurately, bitonality), that is, the simultaneous use of two or more keys. Thus the vocal and instrumental blues, within their deceptively simple framework, are capable of considerable complexity and variety.

It is important to stress the interplay between the vocal and instrumental elements in the blues. As we shall see later, jazz developed largely from the attempt to render the effects of Afro-American vocal intonation on modern musical instruments. When, toward the end of the nineteenth century, the piano began to be widely used for accompanying the blues, Negro pianists employed the so-called "blues tone-cluster," played by simultaneously sounding the flat and natural keys of the third and seventh, as follows:

These piano "blue notes" were the keyboard equivalent of the "slurred" or microtonal pitch used in singing.

To summarize: the blues developed originally as a form of Afro-American folk song, probably took shape gradually after the Civil War, were widely sung throughout the rural South in the final decades of the nineteenth century, and soon emerged as a (normally) twelve-bar song form with instrumental accompaniment, basically antiphonal in structure. Taken up by the Negro musicians who converged on the cities of the South and Middle West in the 1890s in search of employment, legitimate or otherwise, the *urbanized* blues branched off from the archaic or folk blues (which continued on their own course) and took a line of development that in turn branched off into two

distinct channels: the blues as popular song and the blues as jazz. Both
of these currents eventually converged in the productions of tin-pan
alley, where the blues became less blue and the jazz less hot.

Composer of "St. Louis Blues"

Many musicians and many singers, some anonymous, some legendary, some obscure, some famous, many now dead, some still living,
were responsible for the transition of the blues from a folk song of
one region and one group to a type of song known throughout the
land, widely imitated, often changed, frequently distorted, occasionally cheapened, but generally asserting its essential integrity and individuality as a musical form and as a nonsentimental expression of
feeling. Among these musicians, there is one whose name has been
particularly associated with the rise of the blues as a type of popular
music: W. C. Handy, known above all as the composer of "St. Louis
Blues."

William Christopher Handy was born in Florence, Alabama, on
November 16, 1873. His father, a Methodist preacher, was strongly
opposed to the boy's musical inclinations. "Son," he said one time, "I'd
rather follow you to the graveyard than to hear you had become a
musician." Nevertheless, young Handy managed to acquire the rudiments of music in school—and out of it also, though scarcely in an
orthodox fashion. In his own words:

We Handy's Hill kids made rhythm by scraping a twenty-
penny nail across the teeth of the jawbone of a horse that had died
in the woods near by. By drawing a broom handle across our first
finger lying on a table we imitated the bass. We sang through fine-
tooth combs. With the thumb of the right hand interlocked with
the little finger of the left, we placed the thumb of the left hand
under our chin and made rhythmic sounds by rattling our teeth. We
would put the thumb of our right hand on our goozle or Adam's
apple, yelling at the same time:

> Went down the river,
> Couldn't get across,
> Paid five dollars for an old gray horse.

. . . For drums we wore out our mother's tin pans and milk pails,
singing:

Cornstalk fiddle and shoestring bow
Broke in the middle, jumped up Joe.[7]

Then there was the eighty-year-old fiddler called Uncle Whit Walker, who not only fiddled but sang and "stomped" at the same time. "Uncle Whit could stomp the left heel and the right forefoot and alternate this with the right heel and the left forefoot, making four beats to the bar. That was real stomping." And it was real musical training for young Handy.

Later, having learned to play an old-fashioned rotary-valve cornet, Handy took to the road with a minstrel show. In 1903 he formed his own dance band in Clarksdale, Mississippi, and in 1905 transferred his activities to Memphis, where he formed a new band. In the 1909 campaign for mayor of Memphis, Handy's Band was hired by the supporters of a candidate named E. H. Crump. Handy set out to write a campaign song that would not only help elect Mr. Crump but also provide a hit tune for his own band. The result was a piece originally called "Mister Crump," but published three years later as "Memphis Blues." Regarding this composition, Handy wrote in his autobiography:

The melody of *Mister Crump* was mine throughout. On the other hand, the twelve-bar, three-line form of the first and last strains, with its three-chord basic harmonic structure (tonic, subdominant, dominant seventh) was that already used by Negro roustabouts, honky-tonk piano players, wanderers and others of their underprivileged but undaunted class from Missouri to the Gulf, and had become a common medium through which any such individual might express his personal feelings in a sort of musical soliloquy.[8]

Handy, therefore, did not claim to have originated the blues, but merely to have developed and exploited the vein of Negro folk music with which he had become familiar in his boyhood and youth. The lyrics he mostly pieced together from snatches of folk song that he picked up here and there.

In the "Memphis Blues," Handy introduced a rhythmic figure in the bass, which is that of the habanera or tango rhythm, widely dif-

[7] Handy, *Father of the Blues*, p. 15.
[8] *Ibid.*, p. 99.

fused in the music of the Caribbean and the east coast of South America: ♪♩♪♪♪ . He called it the "tangana" rhythm. A variant of this pattern, by the way, produces the rhythm of the once-popular American dance called the Charleston (♩ ♪♩). Handy also introduced the tangana rhythm into his famous "St. Louis Blues," composed in 1914. He used it in the instrumental introduction and in part of the accompaniment (middle strain).

Handy used both three- and four-line verses in "St. Louis Blues." The first two strains consist of the typical three-line verse of the folk blues, so that the first part is made up of two twelve-bar strains. But the second part consists of a four-line unit, so that we get the sixteen-bar strain that is standard for most American popular songs. This procedure of using the sixteen-bar strain in the blues was continued as a regular practice by most of the commercial composers who turned out the pseudo blues of tin-pan alley.

Handy himself stood about midway between the tradition of Negro folk music and that of tin-pan alley. He claimed that in his blues he "aimed to use all that is characteristic of the Negro from Africa to Alabama." Nevertheless, he also confesses that he took up with the "low forms" of Negro folk music hesitantly and approached them "with a certain fear and trembling" because they were not considered respectable and they did not come from books, which were the symbol and source of education. So Handy was to a certain extent another victim of the genteel tradition, which functions on many levels. Whatever strength he has as a musician, he owes entirely to the tradition of Negro folk music, some of which he absorbed in spite of himself.

From Memphis, Handy moved to Chicago and later to New York, where he formed his own music publishing company. He eventually became blind, but continued to carry on courageously with his work. In addition to those already mentioned, Handy's published blues include "Joe Turner Blues" (1915), "The Hesitating Blues" (1915), "John Henry Blues" (1922), and "Blue Gummed Blues" (1926). In spite of the much-publicized title, "Father of the Blues," W. C. Handy did not create the blues any more than Ben Harney created ragtime. But he was indubitably a pioneer of the *composed* blues as a type of American popular song. He died in New York on March 28, 1958.

The following blues cadences and connecting passages (examples furnished by W. C. Handy [9]) will serve to demonstrate the harmonic style as developed in the popular idiom:

Numerous white composers began to cultivate the blues as a type of popular song, among them Cliff Hess ("Homesickness Blues," 1916), Jerome Kern ("Left-All-Alone-Again Blues," 1920), Irving Berlin ("School-House Blues," 1921), and George Gershwin ("The Half of It, Dearie, Blues," 1924). The use of the blues idiom in the symphonic music of Gershwin and other composers of "serious" music will be discussed in the chapter titled "The Americanists." It is time now to return to the folk roots of the blues and to say something about those who in a sense were and are the real creators of the blues: the Negro singers and players through whose interpretations are heard the deep ancestral strains of this traditional song, containing the quintessence of the Afro-American spirit in music.

The great blues singers

Listening to recordings of the great blues singers is the only way that one can learn to know the real spirit and texture of these unique songs. As a word of caution, it should be remarked that many of the blues do not conform to the three-line twelve-bar pattern that was de-

[9] From *A Treasury of the Blues*, p. 21.

scribed as the norm. Folk music is not standardized, and form in the sense of pattern is not the prime factor in the blues. The intonation, the rhythm, the harmonic progression and melodic inflection, the style and the spirit: these are what make the blues be really the blues. And these qualities have to be embodied in a real blues singer before they come alive in all their power and authenticity.

We began this chapter by saying that the spirituals were the manifestation of Afro-American folk music in choral singing, and the blues in solo singing. This is true in the main, but on occasion a man or a woman alone might sing a spiritual for his or her own solace, perhaps even humming or chanting it without words; and very likely it was out of this kind of lonesome singing, just for consolation, just for the pleasure and beauty of the music, that the blues were born. An example of Negro song with guitar accompaniment, chanted without words, in which the spiritual blends into the blues, is heard in the haunting singing and playing of "Blind Willie" Johnson (*ca.* 1902–1949) in "Dark Was the Night." To hear this beautiful and somber chant is to feel the folk roots of the blues entwined very deeply indeed in the heart of the Negro race.

Another example of the organic relationship between the spiritual and the blues is to be found in "Blind Willie" Johnson's singing of "Lord, I Just Can't Keep From Crying," with guitar accompaniment and female "helpers" (women's voices as background). This is, strictly speaking, a spiritual, but its mood of lament is very close to the origin of the blues. Furthermore, this is an extraordinary number that should be heard by anyone interested in either the spirituals or the blues. The rhythm of the guitar, the husky, moving quality of Blind Willie's voice, and the graceful weaving of the women's voices in the background, create an unforgettable impression.

The true minstrels of American music were not those of the stage, but those itinerant Negro singers and players, sometimes blind like the bards of old and led by a boy, who wandered through the Southland, singing the songs learned in their childhood and others that came from later and more bitter experience of life, like the blues that were so often a lament for betrayal in love:

> Ain't got no mama now, ain't got no mama now.
> She told me late las' night, you don' need no mama no how.

"Blind Lemon" Jefferson sings this "Black Snake Moan" (the snake is an age-old sexual symbol) with guitar accompaniment and some wordless chanting in between the verses.

Lemon Jefferson (1897–1930) was born blind in a small farmhouse in Texas and grew up to be "perhaps the most exciting country blues singer of the 1920s" (Samuel Charters).[10] At the age of twenty he went to seek his fortune in Dallas, but without much success:

> "I stood on the corner and almost bust my head,
> I stood on the corner; almost bust my head.
> I couldn't earn enough money to buy me a loaf of bread."

In 1925 he went to Chicago to make his first recordings for Paramount, which billed him as "a real old-fashioned blues singer." His first release, which became a big success, included "Booster Blues" and "Dry Southern Blues." Other recordings followed, but he made little money, and that he spent on women and booze. He recorded about eighty blues before he froze to death on a wintry night in Chicago—a victim of his dissolute habits. He was sometimes bitter and often obscene, but at his best his singing was deeply moving and his guitar playing subtly effective.

Huddie Leadbetter (1885–1949), more familiarly known as "Leadbelly," had been influenced by his association with Lemon Jefferson, for whom he served as "lead man" for a time. As a recollection of those days, Leadbelly used to sing a number that he called "Blind Lemon Blues." Born in Louisiana, he acquired a vast repertoire of songs that he never forgot; and also became an extraordinary performer on the twelve-string guitar. Sentenced to death for murder, he spent many years in jail but was pardoned and lived to become sensationally successful as a folk singer.

Another blues singer who began by trying to imitate Blind Lemon Jefferson was William "Big Bill" Broonzey (1893–1959), a native of Scott, Mississippi, and one of seventeen children born to poverty and hardship. Finding his own style by many trials and errors, he began to record successfully in the 1930s, often with piano accompaniment or with a small jazz group. This was his greatest period, during which he recorded such numbers as "Big Bill Blues," "Bull Cow Blues," and "Mistreatin' Mama Blues." According to Samuel Charters, Broonzey

[10] Charters, *The Country Blues*, p. 56.

copyrighted more than three hundred blues, but "he probably would have had trouble defending his copyright. . . ." In his later years he appeared frequently as a concert performer and wrote a book called *Big Bill's Blues*.

Leroy Carr (1899–1934), from Nashville, Tennessee, was one of the most influential blues singers, who is credited with having "almost completely changed the style of popular blues singing." From 1928 until his death he recorded more than one hundred blues for Vocalion, beginning with his first big success, "How Long How Long Blues." He was often accompanied by a remarkable guitarist who called himself Scrapper Blackwell (his real name was Francis Black), while Carr himself played the piano. Among the numbers they recorded together were "Kokomo Blues" and "Trouble Blues."

Muddy Waters (*b.* 1915), whose real name was McKinley Morganfield, came from Mississippi. In his early years he recorded some fine folk blues for the Library of Congress Folk Music Archives, notably "I Be's Troubled" and "Country Blues." Later he formed his own band, with which he visited England in 1958, and thereafter became a popular entertainer.

Sam "Lightin'" Hopkins (*b.* 1912) was born in Texas and learned to play the guitar as a boy. For a long time he found it difficult to make a living, but in 1947 he made his first recordings for a small company in Houston: "Short Haired Woman" and "Big Mama Jump." These started him on the road to fame. During the heyday of his career he recorded nearly two hundred sides, including "Shotgun Blues," "Rolling Blues" ("Rollin' and Rollin'"), and "Penitentiary Blues." In the late 1950s he was living in Houston, obscurely and in poverty. He was probably the last of the country blues singers who followed the rough, primitive tradition of Blind Lemon Jefferson.

The first of the great women blues singers was Gertrude "Ma" Rainey (1886–1939), who at the age of fifteen was already married and traveling with her husband's minstrel troupe in the South. Her rich and powerful voice, and the classic line of her singing, may be heard in "Traveling Blues," which she recorded with accompaniment of tub, jug, and washboard band. She also recorded "Counting House Blues," "Jelly Bean Blues," "Moonshine Blues," "Stack O'Lee Blues," "Slow Driving Moan," and many others. Her qualities as a blues singer were eloquently described by Rudi Blesh, in his book *Shining Trumpets:*

Ma Rainey's singing, monumental and simple, is by no means primitive. It is extremely conscious in its use of her full expressive means, definitely classic in purity of line and its rigid avoidance of the decorative. . . . Rainey's voice is somber, but never harsh, and its sad and mellow richness strikes to the heart. Her vibrato, slow, controlled and broad, is one of the important and characteristic elements in her tone production, and her tones are projected by sheer power with an organlike fullness and ease. The deepest and most genuine feeling fills her every note and phrase with gusty humor or with an elegiac and sometimes almost gentle sadness.

Bessie Smith (*d.* 1937), who became known as "Empress of the Blues," also began her career touring through the South in minstrel and tent shows. Discovered by a talent scout, she began to record for Columbia with immediate success, especially among the Negroes. She soon became a commanding figure in the world of jazz, recording with Louis Armstrong, Buster Bailey, Fletcher Henderson, James P. Johnson, and other celebrated jazz musicians. Her earliest recordings, made with members of Fletcher Henderson's Orchestra, included some of the masterpieces that she made famous, among them "Cold in Hand Blues," "You've Been a Good Ole Wagon," and "Cake Walking Babies from Home" (1925). Her range of expression was extraordinary: from a pop tune like "Jazzbo Brown" to the social protest of "Poor Man's Blues," from the wistful pathos of "Young Woman's Blues" to the frank sexuality of "Empty Bed Blues," from the bitterness of "Hard Drivin' Papa" to the raucous humor of "Put It Right Here." A large, vital, handsome woman with a tremendous presence and a wonderful sense of timing, she was both a great singer and a remarkable personality. In later years she knew some hard times and made some concessions to commercialism (with what deep conviction she sang, "Nobody Knows You When You're Down and Out"); but the nearly two hundred numbers that she recorded constitute a priceless legacy of song and a timeless treasure of America's music.

Piano blues and "boogiewoogie"

The jazz pianist and composer Ferdinand "Jelly Roll" Morton was also a fine blues singer. The lyrical quality of his style is demonstrated in such recordings as "Winin' Boy" and "Mamie's Blues," in both of which he accompanies himself on the piano. In the "shouting" type of blues he performs effectively in "Michigan Water Blues" and "Doctor Jazz." Transposition of the blues from the vocal to the instrumental medium is illustrated in the recordings of "Mr. Jelly Roll" and "Wolverine Blues," which Morton made together with Johnny Dodds on clarinet and "Baby" Dodds on drums. Here the clarinet takes the place of the human voice: it *sings*. The merging of ragtime and blues in a piano solo may be observed in Jelly Roll's playing of "Tom Cat Blues," which he recorded in 1924 in the New Orleans style of "hot" piano playing.

The "boogiewoogie" style of piano blues was launched by Jimmy Yancey (1898–1951), whose wife "Mama" Yancey was also a remarkable blues singer (compare the recordings of "Pallet on the Floor" and "How Long Blues" that they made together). Boogiewoogie transfers to the piano the twelve-bar pattern of the blues with its basic harmonic structure and is characterized by a persistent rhythmic figure in the left hand, while the right hand embroiders its own rhythmic-melodic configurations. The resulting cross-rhythms are complex and exciting. The typical Yancey bass has a powerful, driving momentum. Among his recorded piano blues are "The Fives, or Five O'Clock Blues" (also recorded as "Yancey Stomp"), "Midnight Stomp" (fast blues), and "How Long Blues" (slow blues).

Continuators of the boogiewoogie style were Clarence "Pine Top" Smith (1900–1928), who first popularized the term "boogiewoogie"; and Meade Lux Lewis (*b.* 1905). Pine Top Smith, whose checkered career ended when he was shot by a stray bullet during a brawl in a night club—an institution where he spent most of his waking hours—composed "Pine Top's Boogie Woogie," "Pine Top's Blues," "Now I Ain't Got Nothin' at All," and "Jump Steady Blues." Meade Lux Lewis's masterpiece is "Honky-Tonk Train Blues," with its chromatic harmonies and compelling cross-rhythms.

The transformation of the vocal blues into the boogiewoogie idiom may be further observed in the piano playing of another Yancey follower, Albert Ammons (1903–1949), whose solo version of "St. Louis Blues," executed with tremendous drive, is a striking example of this trend.

James P. Johnson (1891–1955), mentioned in the chapter on ragtime, was also a fine performer and composer of piano blues in the classical tradition (for example, "Snowy Morning Blues," composed in 1927). Johnson, like Ellington, was a "pop" musician who aspired to create in the larger forms. Besides a four-movement *Harlem Symphony* (1932) he composed a symphonic version of "St. Louis Blues" (1936).

The blues have colored almost every aspect of America's music, from folk song to opera, from pop tune to symphony, from stomp to sonata, from spirituals to rock-and-roll, from hot jazz to western and country music. During the 1960s, the blues became a kind of obsession with modern jazz musicians seeking their roots in the past. The blues reach both into the past and into the future. Their influence is not limited to American music; their appeal is universal and will endure as long as mankind continues to feel the profound emotions or the ribald moods that they so memorably and uniquely express.

chapter twenty-three

The growth of jazz

Jazz has contributed an enduring value to America in the sense that it has expressed ourselves.
GEORGE GERSHWIN, IN REVOLT IN THE ARTS.

In 1917 the now defunct but then widely read *Literary Digest* observed that "a strange word has gained widespread use in the ranks of our producers of popular music. It is 'jazz,' used mainly as an adjective descriptive of a band." Actually, the strange word was spelled "jass" when first publicly used to designate a dance band. In 1915 a dance band from New Orleans was billed at Lamb's Café in Chicago as Brown's Dixieland Jass Band. Of the many explanations that have been suggested concerning the origin of the word—including possible French or African origin—the most reliable appears to be that "This word jazz is a corruption of the Elizabethan *jass* which had survived in the vernacular of the bawdy houses."[1] There can be little doubt that the term originally carried a sexual connotation, and Lafcadio Hearn testifies that it was used in New Orleans during the nineteenth century.

The music that came to be called "jazz" was rooted in the cultural, social, and racial conditions of the South. No single city—not even New Orleans—can legitimately claim to have been its exclusive birthplace. African survivals in American folk music, the hot rhythm of the camp-meeting spirituals and gospel songs, the form and inflection of the blues, the improvised "washboard" bands, the marching brass bands that played for funerals, parades, and picnics, were common to wide sections of the South. The early ragtime musicians who had such a strong influence on the beginnings of jazz came from various parts of the Midwest and the Southwest.

[1] Charles Edward Smith, in *The Jazz Record Book*, p. 4.

Yet New Orleans may be called the cradle and nursery of jazz. There geographic, economic, demographic, and social factors created a cultural climate favorable to the emergence of an urban folk music such as jazz. This music began to take shape and substance when the Negro, after the Civil War, had an opportunity to obtain, and to use in his own fashion, the conventional manufactured instruments of European origin, such as the trumpet or cornet, clarinet, trombone, snare and bass drums, as well as the piano. After the Civil War, dispersed Confederate military bands provided a source of secondhand instruments, so plentiful and cheap that they were within almost anyone's reach. There were many Negro marching bands in New Orleans during the nineteenth century: more than a dozen such bands took part in the mammoth funeral procession for President Garfield in 1881. Negro fraternal and benevolent associations, and various labor organizations, had their own bands. One of their functions was to furnish music for the funeral of a deceased member.

The band music that developed with the New Orleans marching bands during this period, roughly from about 1870 to 1890, belongs to the pre-history of jazz. Our knowledge of how this music sounded can only be through conjecture, based on tracing back long-established traditions and piecing together shreds of contemporary evidence. The music, we know, was mostly for street parades and funerals. The band would accompany the hearse to the cemetery, playing slow dirges, perhaps a favorite standard hymn or spiritual song. After the interment, on the way back, the band would begin to play gayer tunes in "hot" rhythm, while the people followed, dancing in the streets, often with colored umbrellas or parasols. There would be a "second line" walking beside or behind the band, fascinated by the shining brass instruments, whistling or singing the tunes, and trying to imitate the sounds with all sorts of improvised or homemade instruments. In this second line there were assuredly many youngsters who grew up to be the makers and leaders of New Orleans jazz.

When "hot" brass bands began to be used for dancing, the era of jazz was definitely ushered in. Previously it had been the custom to use string orchestras, sometimes with a piano, for ballroom dancing, and the music they played was "sweet" (i.e., not syncopated or roughly intoned). When the powerful impetus of the "hot" bands was unleashed on the dance floor, it was the beginning of a revolution in American popular music. This development took place in the 1890s.

Many people are under the impression that jazz music originated in the red-light district of New Orleans, popularly known as "Storyville," after the name of the alderman who initiated the ordinance to have this section of the city set aside for organized vice. Storyville's brothels, many of them marked by garish splendor, flourished from 1887 to 1917, when they were abolished owing to pressure from the War and Navy Departments. This period coincided with the rise of jazz, and it is true that many musicians found employment in Storyville, where cash was plentiful, prejudice rare, and the demand for entertainment unflagging. All this makes for a colorful, risqué setting that writers have not failed to exploit and to embroider with piquant details. What concerns us here, however, is the music that emerged as jazz from a wide diversity of ingredients and social conditions, of which Storyville was typical but not predominant. If it provided jazz musicians with the encouragement and support long denied to them by the more respectable elements of society, it also furnished ammunition for those who held that jazz was intrinsically and irrevocably immoral. How could anything good come out of such an atmosphere, they asked. There was a furious moralistic barrage directed against jazz; not until 1925 did the voice of a courageous preacher arise in the land to proclaim that "Jazz is not necessarily the gateway to hell."

Pioneers of jazz

The most colorful figure associated with the beginnings of jazz in New Orleans was Charles "Buddy" Bolden (1868–1931), a barber who learned to play the cornet in his spare time. In the 1890s he formed a band that was in great demand for both dances and parades; it was a small band, of five to seven pieces, which was the norm for early New Orleans jazz. It included cornet, clarinet, valve trombone (alternating with slide trombone, used for glissandi), guitar, bass, and drums. Later a second clarinet was added. During the twelve years or more of its existence, Buddy Bolden's Band—actually, at the height of his popularity he had several going on at once—included many of the important pioneers of hot jazz, among them William "Bunk" Johnson (1879–1949), the cornet and trumpet player who was with Bolden from 1895 to 1899 and who made a sensational comeback in 1940.

Concerning those days, "Bunk" Johnson reminisced in his old age: "Buddy could not read a note, but he surely played a good stiff lead and would have you maybe in six sharps before you finished. . . . We played parades and advertising wagons and, excuse me for the expression, honky tonks. . . ."[2] At the height of his fame and success, Bolden was called "King;" but from 1906 he suffered periods of mental derangement and a year later he was permanently committed to a hospital for the insane.

The jazz historian Paul Eduard Miller is sceptical about Bunk's claim that Buddy Bolden was musically illiterate. "Judging from the overwhelming consensus of reports from old-time New Orleans musicians"—Miller writes—"he was a reasonably good musician too and not all his playing was sheer spontaneity or so-called improvisation. His technique, too, was good and was acquired by a natural bent for the medium rather than protracted study, although there is little question that he was given considerable instruction on the cornet before he approached the zenith of his career as a jazz virtuoso."[3] The point is important, because the musical illiteracy and "sheer spontaneity" of the early New Orleans jazz musicians have been grossly overemphasized. Miller recognizes that the best of them were "instinctive musicians who had a flair for the right jazz phrasing and intonation," but their performance resulted from an often precarious and always exciting balance between acquired skill and intuitive expression. This is as true of the old-timers of 1965 as of the pioneers of 1895.

When "King" Bolden was struck down by insanity, his crown was inherited by another cornet player, Freddie Keppard (1883–1932), whose celebrated Olympia Band included such famous jazzmen as Louis "Big Eye" Nelson (1885–1949) and Sidney Bechet (1897–1959) on clarinet, Willy Santiago on guitar, Zue Robertson on trombone, and Joe Oliver on cornet. But there were other contenders for the royal mantle. The clarinetist T. V. Baquet led the no less celebrated Excelsior Band, which could boast of such great players as Alphonse Picou (1878–1961) on clarinet, Manuel Perez on cornet, and John Robichaux on drums. Perez and Robichaux also had bands of their own. Picou became famous for his high-register elaboration of the clarinet solo in the march called *High Society*. The cornet player Oscar "Papa" Celestin (1884–1954) was leader from 1910 of the Tux-

[2] Letter to Frederic Ramsey, Jr., quoted in *Jazzmen* (ed. Ramsey and Smith).
[3] From "Fifty Years of New Orleans Jazz," in *Esquire's 1945 Jazz Book*, p. 7.

edo Band, which played at the Tuxedo Dance Hall and was reputed to be the hottest band in town. Its personnel included the great Johnny Dodds (1892–1940) on clarinet and his brother Warren "Baby" Dodds (1898–1959) on drums.

But the greatest and most influential of the early jazz pioneers was Joseph "King" Oliver (1885–1938). Born on a plantation in Louisiana, he took up the cornet after going to New Orleans as a boy. From 1907 he played with many bands in the Crescent City, and in 1915 he formed his own band. Oliver was one of many New Orleans jazzmen who migrated to Chicago after World War I; he went there in 1918 and remained for ten years. Chicago was more of a metropolis than New Orleans and offered better opportunities for musical employment at various cafés and night clubs. Oliver soon took over an existing band and renamed it The Creole Jazz Band: in 1923 this became the first Negro jazz band to make a series of recordings, with results of paramount importance for the history of jazz. Musicians who played with King Oliver's Creole Jazz Band during these years in Chicago included the clarinetists Johnny Dodds, Jimmie Noone and Barney Bigard; the trombonists Edward "Kid" Ory and Honoré Dutrey; "Baby" Dodds on drums; the pianist Lilian Hardin; and, from 1922, a young cornet and trumpet player from New Orleans named Louis Armstrong. Although the band as a whole was the best of its kind and time, in the series of recordings that it made over the next five years the inventive genius of Louis Armstrong was responsible for the first significant advance in jazz style. His playing marked the emergence of the soloist as a creative factor; he made the solo not only a test of skill and invention but also an opportunity for imaginative and emotional expression. Even in such a banal tune as "Big Butter and Egg Man from the West," his solos have intense expressive power. Although Louis Armstrong (b. 1900), known as "Satchmo," was to have a glorious and world-wide career in the realm of jazz and popular entertainment, his most original contributions to jazz were made in those recordings of the 1920s. Scarcely less influential as a singer than as a trumpet player, it is his unique personality—warm, vital, humorous—that comes through in whatever he does. He will go down in history as "Satchmo the Great."[4]

[4] This is the title of a film on the life of Armstrong that was released in 1957. In the same year a set of four recordings was issued, titled *Satchmo, A Musical Biography*, with introductory narrations by Armstrong. The nickname "Satchmo" is a contraction of "Satchel Mouth."

As for Armstrong's patron and model, King Oliver, his fortunes rapidly declined after he went to New York in 1928. He continued to make some recordings with pick-up groups, but eventually died in obscurity in Savannah. But history has lifted him from obscurity to a pinnacle of posthumous fame. His talent brought him success; a mechanical invention—the phonograph—made him immortal. As a composer he left us several classics of jazz: "Canal Street Blues," "Chimes Blues," "Doctor Jazz," "West End Blues," and (with Louis Armstrong) "Sugar Foot Stomp" (also known as "Dipper Mouth Blues").

Ferdinand "Jelly Roll" Morton (1885–1941), previously mentioned in the chapter on ragtime, was another New Orleans musician who followed the trend to Chicago in the twenties. He was active there from 1923 to 1928, recording with a small group called The Red Hot Peppers that included Omer Simeon on clarinet, Kid Ory on trombone, and Johnny St. Cyr on guitar and banjo. These are probably the most important recordings of that time after those of King Oliver. Among the numbers they recorded are such classics as "Black Bottom Stomp," "Smoke House Blues," "Steamboat Stomp," "Buddy Bolden's Blues," and "Doctor Jazz." Jelly Roll also recorded many piano solos, including his own compositions such as "King Porter Stomp," "Winin' Boy Blues," "Mamie's Blues," and "Mister Joe." He usually sang the vocals in his own blues. Important as pianist, singer, arranger, composer, and leader, Jelly Roll Morton also made a significant contribution to the informal history and aesthetics of jazz through the series of interviews that he recorded with Alan Lomax at the Library of Congress in 1938.[5] His place in the development of jazz, if not as prominent as he himself claimed, is nevertheless considerable and his stature has increased rather than diminished since his death.

Rise of Dixieland

Dixieland music is jazz played by white musicians in a manner more or less approximating that of early New Orleans Negro jazz. A white musician from New Orleans named George V. Laine (b. 1873), usually called "Jack" or "Papa," is credited with having started the trend that came to be known as Dixieland. Forming his first band

[5] These interviews, with additional material by Alan Lomax, were subsequently published under the title *Mister Jelly Roll* (1950).

in 1888, he began to play rags by such composers as Scott Joplin and to imitate the Negro "stomps." Jack Laine's Ragtime Band consisted of cornet, clarinet, trombone, guitar, bass, and drums (played by Laine). Laine also became leader of the Reliance Brass Band, organized around 1892–93. Among the musicians who joined this band was a cornet player from New Orleans named Dominick ("Nick") La Rocca (1889–1961), soon to be famous as leader of the Original Dixieland Jazz Band.

Meanwhile, another white musician from New Orleans, the trombonist Tom Brown (1890–1958), formed a Dixieland band that was brought to Chicago in 1915, opening at Lamb's Café in June of that year. As already noted, the billing of this group as "Brown's Dixieland Jass Band" first gave general currency to the term "jazz" (as it came to be spelled). The success of Brown's band stimulated the search for more Dixieland talent from New Orleans.

In 1916 a promoter from Chicago contracted Alcide "Yellow" Nunez, the clarinetist, and four other players: Eddie Edwards (trombone), Nick La Rocca (cornet), Henry Ragas (piano), and Tony Sbarbaro (drums). This band opened at Schiller's Café under the name of Dixieland Jass Band. Reorganized with La Rocca as leader and Larry Shields on clarinet, and calling itself the Original Dixieland Jazz Band, this group went to New York in 1917 and began a sensational engagement at Reisenweber's Restaurant. At that time they made the first recordings of Dixieland jazz, including "Tiger Rag," "Reisenweber Rag," "Barnyard Blues," "At the Jazz Band Ball," "Ostrich Walk," "Bluin' the Blues," and "Clarinet Marmalade." With its visit to England in 1919, the band gave an impetus to European interest in jazz. The group disbanded in 1925, but La Rocca reorganized it in 1936 to make some recordings for Victor. In later years he complained that historians of jazz had failed to do justice to his pioneer accomplishments.

After the First World War, the most important Dixieland band in Chicago was the New Orleans Rhythm Kings, led by the New Orleans trumpet player Paul Mares (1900–1949). The band, which opened at the Friars' Inn late in 1921, included, besides Mares on trumpet, Leon Rappolo (*recte* Roppolo) on clarinet, George Brunies on trombone, and Ben Pollack on drums. In some of its recording sessions in 1923, Jelly Roll Morton acted as musical director and also played the piano in several numbers, including his own composition

"Milenburg Joys." The New Orleans Rhythm Kings added a saxophone to the melody section—a trend that was soon to be widely followed. Their recordings of "Tiger Rag" and "Milenburg [*recte* Milneburg] Joys," among others, demonstrate the authentic Dixieland style and its affinity with the traditional New Orleans style.

The next chapter in the rise of Dixieland brings on the scene a group of young musicians from the Chicago area, among whom Albert Edwin ("Eddie") Condon (*b.* 1904) may be regarded as the guiding spirit. Others in the group included Bud Freeman (tenor sax), Jimmy McPartland (cornet), and Frank Teschemacher (1906–1932), who played clarinet and saxes. All attended the same high school in Chicago and were known as the "Austin High Gang." Teschemacher organized the Chicago Rhythm Kings, in which Mezz Mezzrow played tenor sax; "Muggsy" Spanier, cornet; Eddie Condon, banjo; and Gene Krupa, drums. Condon himself, with the singer and comb player William ("Red") McKenzie (1907–1948), formed a group called the "Chicagoans," which included Jimmy McPartland on cornet, Lawrence ("Bud") Freeman on tenor sax, and Gene Krupa on drums. The recordings made by this group, beginning in December, 1927, are classics of Chicago Dixieland style.

One of the most influential Chicago bands was the "Wolverines," which in 1923 had as its star performer a young cornet player named Leon Bismarck ("Bix") Beiderbecke (1903–1931). Bix carefully studied the styles of such great Negro players as King Oliver, Louis Armstrong, and Jimmie Noone; and he in turn influenced other players, both white and Negro. As Leonard Feather observes, "He was probably the first white musician ever to be admired and imitated by Negro jazzmen." Appreciated by only a few during his lifetime, Bix became a legend after his untimely death. Famous for his beautiful tone and legato playing on the cornet, he was also a pianist and composer who pioneered in applying modern harmonies to jazz.

Eddie Condon went to New York in 1928, opened his own night club in Greenwich Village in 1946, and continued his campaign on behalf of Dixieland music in the face of changing fashions. Another musician who did a great deal to popularize Dixieland jazz was Ernest Loring ("Red") Nichols (1905–1965). Born in Ogden, Utah, he came to New York in 1923, and from 1925 was very active in making recordings with various groups of his own, of which the most celebrated was known as the Five Pennies. On most sessions the group actually consisted of six to ten players, including some of the most notable white jazzmen of that era: Jimmy Dorsey (clarinet and alto sax), Benny Goodman (clarinet), Eddie Lang (1904–1933) on guitar (one of the greatest players of this instrument), Miff Mole (trombone), and Joe Venuti (violin). Of these musicians, the most important for the history of Dixieland, because of his many recordings (a hundred or more) was Irving ("Miff") Mole (b. 1898). For several years he had his own Dixieland band in New York and from 1948 was active in Chicago. Returning to New York in the 1950s, he made more Dixieland recordings, until forced to retire by ill-health.

Some critics are convinced that there was a "Chicago style" in jazz, and have tried to describe it in various ways. According to Frederic Ramsey, Jr., the Chicago jazz players "took the Negro jazz, pushed the beat, mixed in a lot of their own feeling of gingery brashness, and came out with something they can proudly call a music of their own, Chicago jazz."[6] Another critic, George Avakian, attempted a more elaborate description of the Chicago style:

The tension, urgency and fire of Chicago style are external as well as internal matters. An "explosion" at the end of every chorus sends the succeeding one off to a catapult start; those two-bar flares are played by everyone, even in choruses which are otherwise solos. Stop-and-go devices, shifting rhythmic patterns (including a kind of double-time known as the "Chicago shuffle"), varying dynamics, and all-out finishes capped by "double endings" (the addition of two extra bars to the last chorus) are used to create a supercharged atmosphere. The ensemble holes are filled like Nature tackling a vacuum; the solos are almost agonized. Phrases are short, jagged, almost spit out. There is a Chicago tone, too—tart, slightly off-pitch, with a buzzy, rough edge. Strong notes stop mattering; driving, on-the-beat excitement is what counts.[7]

Since it was played by white musicians, Chicago-style jazz may be regarded as a type of Dixieland. Some of its leading exponents have already been mentioned. Important bands that recorded in the twenties included Charles Pierce and His Orchestra (with Muggsy Spanier and Frank Teschemacher), Bix Beiderbecke and His Gang, Paul Mares and His Friars' Society Orchestra, and, of course, the Chicago Rhythm Kings and the McKenzie-Condon Chicagoans.

[6] In Notes to Jazz, Vol. VI, Folkways Records (FP 65, Chicago, No. 2).
[7] In record liner notes for Chicago Style Jazz, Columbia Records, CL 632.

New York and the era of swing

So many jazz musicians flocked to New York in the 1920s and 1930s that this city virtually became the new capital of jazz. Even when a particular style originated elsewhere, as was the case with Kansas City "jump style," the large impact was made through New York. The musicians who came to Manhattan, both white and Negro, were from all parts of the country and of many different backgrounds. They gave new directions to the development of jazz. With the rise of big bands and more sophisticated types of musical expression, the art of the arranger and orchestrator began to assume prime importance.

James Fletcher Henderson (1898–1952), a native of Georgia who studied chemistry and mathematics at Atlanta University, came to New York not to play jazz but to do postgraduate work. But part-time piano playing with W. C. Handy soon led to full professional commitment in music, and by 1923 he was leading his own band, which for many years played at the Roseland dance hall on Broadway. The band, a large one, included many of the best sidemen, among them Louis Armstrong on trumpet and Coleman Hawkins on tenor saxophone. Its historical importance was aptly stated by Leonard Feather: "Henderson's was the first large band to acquire a wide reputation by playing jazz." Most of the dance orchestras were concerned merely with the commercial success obtained by playing popular tunes in a conventional manner. Jazz was being crowded out by commercialism—Eddie Condon complained, "The only place we could play was in our rooms, at our own request"—and its incorporation into the framework of the large dance band was achieved only by the talent of such leaders and arrangers as Fletcher Henderson and Duke Ellington.

Fletcher Henderson wrote arrangements for other bands besides his own, and indeed some of his most celebrated arrangements were made for Benny Goodman, among them "When Buddha Smiles," "King Porter Stomp," "Blue Skies," and "Down South Camp Meeting." Henderson was a pioneer in developing the kind of music that came to be known as "swing." His brother Horace (*b.* 1904) was also active as pianist, leader and arranger.

Other arrangers who influenced large-band style were Don Redman (*b.* 1900), Benny Carter (*b.* 1907), and Melvin J. ("Sy") Oliver (*b.*

1910). Redman, a child prodigy who played the trumpet at three, had conservatory training in theory and composition. In 1931 he formed his own band in association with Horace Henderson; after 1940 he worked chiefly as a free-lance arranger and composer. His band theme during the 1930s was "Chant of the Weed," which he composed. An excellent saxophone player and a good singer, Redman brought to jazz, for the first time in such a conspicuous manner, the skills of a trained composer and the attributes of an authentic jazz musician.

Benny Carter, a native New Yorker, learned to play several instruments, including clarinet and trumpet, but became best known as an alto saxophonist. He formed his first big band in 1933 and thereafter was active with various groups in France, England, California, and New York. He made arrangements for Fletcher Henderson and Benny Goodman, as well as for his own recording groups, often giving prominence to sections scored for saxophones and strings. "Sy" Oliver provided many arrangements for the very successful band of Jimmie Lunceford (1902–1947), including such famous numbers as "Four or Five Times," "Swanee River," "Organ Grinder's Swing," and "Raggin' the Scale." In 1939 he became the arranger for Tommy Dorsey's band.

James Melvin ("Jimmie") Lunceford (1902–1947) and William ("Chick") Webb (1902–1939) were leaders of two of the most important big Negro bands of the swing era. Lunceford, who began his career as band leader in Memphis, achieved prominence with his recordings for Victor and Decca in the 1930s. From about 1934 to 1944 his band, in the words of Leonard Feather, "enjoyed a unique reputation as the best-disciplined and most showmanly Negro jazz orchestra." Even after the band's decline in popularity and its leader's death, the "Lunceford style" continued to be influential during the next decade.

Chick Webb was a native of Baltimore who went to New York in 1924 and two years later formed his first band, which included Johnny Hodges and Benny Carter. Regarded as one of the greatest of jazz drummers and "one of the most dynamic figures in jazz" (Feather), Webb overcame the handicaps of physical deformity and ill-health (he died of tuberculosis) to become a dominant personality of the swing era. His partner in success was the great singer Ella Fitzgerald (b. 1918), whom he discovered in 1934 while she was singing in an amateur show in Harlem. She made her first recording with

Webb's band, "Love and Kisses," on June 12, 1935. Their biggest hit was the novelty song "A-Tisket, A-Tasket," which they recorded in 1938. After Webb's death the following year, Ella Fitzgerald took over the leadership of the band for a while. Chick Webb's band played most often at the Savoy Ballroom in Harlem but also became famous through its many recordings and national broadcasts. Radio, indeed, was an important medium for the diffusion of jazz during this period, and an influential factor in the formation of public taste.

The most creative and influential of all the big-band leaders and composer-arrangers is Edward ("Duke") Ellington (*b.* 1899). A native of Washington, D.C., he studied piano from the age of seven and at nineteen was leading his own dance band. From 1923 he was active in New York, where his first important engagement was at the Kentucky Club in 1927. Among the talented sidemen who joined him there was the trumpet player James ("Bubber") Miley (1903–1932), who specialized in the "growl" solos and "wa-wa" effects that became identified with the Ellington orchestra. From the end of 1927 until 1932, Ellington played at the Cotton Club in New York and recorded extensively. Famous soloists with the band, who made significant contributions to "the Ellington sound," included Barney Bigard on clarinet, Johnny Hodges on alto and soprano sax, and Charles M. ("Cootie") Williams on trumpet. It was for Williams that Ellington wrote *Concerto for Cootie* (recorded in 1940), one of the first attempts to apply a miniature concerto form to the idiom of jazz. Late in 1940, Williams left Ellington to join Benny Goodman's band—an event commemorated in the piece by Raymond Scott titled "When Cootie Left the Duke."

Ellington composed a number of tunes that became popular, among them "Mood Indigo," "Sophisticated Lady," "Solitude," "In a Sentimental Mood," "Daybreak Express," and "Blue Harlem." But his ambition was to write larger and more complex compositions. The duration of jazz and pop tunes was generally determined by the three minutes that it took to play one side of a 78-rpm disc. Ellington got around this limitation by using two sides of the disc for his "Creole Rhapsody" (1931) and four sides for "Reminiscing in Tempo" (1935). But he still wanted to compose works of full symphonic proportions. He did this with the suite titled *Black, Brown and Beige*, in four movements (with a total duration of fifty minutes): (1) "Work Song," (2) "Come Sunday" (spiritual), (3) "The Blues," (4) "West Indian Dance: Emancipation Celebration: Sugar Hill Penthouse." In

1943 Ellington had the immense satisfaction of conducting this work at a concert in Carnegie Hall. Among his other large compositions are *Diminuendo and Crescendo in Blue, Bluetopia, Deep South Suite, Liberian Suite, New World A-Comin'*, and *Golden Broom and Green Apple* (a suite). Ellington conducted the first performance of the last-mentioned work in a concert given by the New York Philharmonic Orchestra in July, 1965. It was reported that he made the Philharmonic swing. This was one of a series of concerts that featured such eminent composer-conductors as Leonard Bernstein, Aaron Copland, Lukas Foss, and Darius Milhaud. Ellington's appearance in this company confirmed the judgment made many years ago by the English composer Constant Lambert, who called him "the first jazz composer of distinction."

In 1939 Ellington began his long association with Billy Strayhorn (*b.* 1915), a top-notch arranger and composer with whom he was to collaborate in many important productions, among them *Such Sweet Thunder* (1917), a suite inspired by characters from Shakespeare. Strayhorn composed the number that came to be regarded as the Ellington theme: "Take the A Train." The Ellington sound has always been a result of extraordinary teamwork, and from 1939 Billy Strayhorn was the number-two man of the team. One of their most interesting efforts was the reorchestration of Grieg's *Peer Gynt* Suite.

In a professional career of more than forty years, Ellington emerges as the major jazz figure of the age, not only as composer-arranger but also as leader and pianist. If he had recorded more piano solos, he would have been famous for that alone; and his piano style has influenced such modernists as Thelonius Monk and Charles Mingus. As a composer, he covered an amazingly wide spectrum, ranging from "pop" tunes to orchestral tone poems and symphonic suites, with almost every type of jazz expression in between. The sound of the Ellington orchestra, varying somewhat through the years according to personnel and the Duke's own evolution but always retaining its distinctive, inimitable quality, is one of the great achievements of contemporary music.

Ellington, along with some of the other leaders already mentioned—notably Fletcher Henderson and Jimmie Lunceford—had a prominent role in the development of "swing." As early as 1931 he anticipated the trend by writing a piece called "It Don't Mean a Thing If It Ain't Got That Swing." But there were many competitors in the field, and it was the clarinetist and leader Benny Goodman (*b.* 1909), a white musician from Chicago, who really launched the vogue of swing with a series of recordings in 1934 followed the next year by a nation-wide tour culminating in a sensational success at Los Angeles, California. After that, Goodman, appearing as leader of both large bands and small combos (trios to septets), and displaying a remarkable technique on the clarinet, became known as the "King of Swing."

But what is meant by the term "swing" (used as adjective, noun, and verb)? No one has ever succeeded in defining it completely. To say that it is "a certain way of making the rhythm come to life" (André Hodeir) is true but not specific enough to be very helpful. Hodeir himself tried to develop his definition by mentioning such factors as the right "infrastructure" (tempo and accentuation), the right "superstructure" (rhythmic equilibrium of the phrase), relaxation, vital drive, and "getting the notes and accents in the right place." This is intelligent verbalization, especially as developed at some length in Hodeir's chapter, "The Phenomenon of Swing";[8] but it only becomes really meaningful by experiencing the music itself. Furthermore, when one comes to analyze these factors, they appear to be the essential ingredients of all authentic jazz. So perhaps Louis Armstrong was right when he declared (speaking about the early jazz versions of Joplin's rags), "If you played his music and phrased it right, you was *swinging* way back there!" When Armstrong published a book about jazz in 1936, he called it *Swing that Music* and argued that "swing" was the basic principle of New Orleans jazz. The main difference in the new swing music, he maintained, was that it used scored orchestrations, more sophisticated harmonies, and more highly trained musicians. The problem, then, may have been simply to keep the basic characteristics of jazz while incorporating these new features of bigness, complexity, and written orchestrations. Today, long after the great vogue of swing bands, musicians, when they hear modern jazz in any style, continue to ask, "Does it swing?" And the query is evidently synonymous with, "Is it really jazz?"

Many bands, many celebrated names are associated with the era of swing, which was at its height from 1935 to 1945. Among those who rode the crest of this movement were the brothers Jimmy and Tommy Dorsey, the trumpet player and band leader Harry James, the immensely popular band leader Glenn Miller (1904–1944), the

[8] In *Jazz: Its Evolution and Essence* (New York, 1956).

clarinetist and leader Artie Shaw, as famous for his many marriages as for his swinging bands—all successful entertainers rather than significant jazz figures. For the latter, we must turn, in addition to Ellington and Goodman, to such band leaders as Woody Herman and Count Basie, who managed to be successful while contributing to the evolution of jazz.

Woodrow Charles ("Woody") Herman (*b.* 1913), a native of Milwaukee, began his professional career at the age of six by singing and dancing in local theaters. Three years later he took up the saxophone and then switched to clarinet; but his important contribution has been made as a band leader. His first band, organized cooperatively in the 1930s, became known as "the band that plays the blues": its recording of "Woodchopper's Ball" (1939), a fast blues, sold over a million copies. Adapting itself to the swing trend in the 1940s, the Woody Herman Band was voted the best swing band of 1945 in the annual poll conducted by the magazine *Down Beat.* In the 1950s the band was known as "The Third Herd." Among the many notable players who appeared with Woody Herman were Stan Getz on tenor sax, Terry Gibbs on vibes, and Chubby Jackson on bass.

William ("Count") Basie (*b.* 1904), started out as a vaudeville pianist in New York. Stranded in Kansas City while on tour, he played with a jazz band there called the Blue Devils. After this broke up he joined Bennie Moten's Band, which had developed a hard-driving "jump style," characterized by four heavy beats to the bar. When Moten died in 1935, Basie took over the best of his players to form his own band. This he brought to New York the following year; after its first recordings were released in 1937, the band quickly became famous for its fast pace and vital rhythmic impulse, as well as for its remarkable soloists. These included Buck Clayton on trumpet, Dickie Wells on trombone, Lester Young on tenor sax, Jo Jones on drums, the blues singer James Rushing, and of course Count Basie himself at the piano. Outlasting the swing era, Basie and his band continued from one triumph to another, both in America and Europe. In 1957 they played a Royal Command performance for the Queen of England—the first American band to be thus honored. Throughout many successes and changing fashions, Basie remained true to the spirit of jazz and to its basic form, the blues.

Some great soloists of the swing era exerted a wide influence on jazz style. Among them were the tenor saxophonist Coleman Hawkins (*b.* 1904) and the trumpet player Roy Eldridge (*b.* 1911). The latter's influence during the 1930s has been compared to that of Armstrong in the previous decade. Eldridge played with many of the best bands of the swing era, including those of Benny Goodman, Gene Krupa, and Artie Shaw. Coleman Hawkins began to record in 1923 with Fletcher Henderson's band, with which he remained for more than ten years. Later he led a small band of his own, recording in 1939 the number that made him famous: "Body and Soul."

The greatest pianists of the swing era were Thomas ("Fats") Waller (1904–1943) and Arthur ("Art") Tatum (1910–1956). Waller was the first jazz musician to achieve mastery on both the pipe organ and the Hammond organ, both of which he adapted to an authentic jazz style. He was also a singer and song-writer who composed such enduring tunes as "Ain't Misbehavin'," "Honeysuckle Rose," and "Keepin' Out of Mischief Now." In the 1930s he made numerous recordings with a sextet, featuring his unique arrangements of popular songs. Art Tatum, who was almost totally blind, had good training in both violin and piano but decided to concentrate on the latter. He developed an unprecedented technique in the jazz field, was an inspired improviser, and had an unequalled lightness of touch. When not playing alone, he preferred to work with a trio (bass and guitar). A set of recordings, *The Genius of Art Tatum*, was issued in eleven volumes under the Verve label.

Both of these pianists influenced the piano style of Teddy Wilson (*b*. 1912), who in turn achieved a personal manner of swinging that was widely emulated by pianists during the 1940s. Wilson is also a composer, orchestrator, and band leader.

The pianist and song-writer Earl Kenneth ("Fatha") Hines (*b*. 1905) was also important during the swing era, but actually his greatest successes during that period were obtained as a band leader, especially through his nightly radio programs that were broadcast nationally. His greatest influence as a pianist came through his recordings with Louis Armstrong in the late 1920s. His own songs include "Rosetta," "My Monday Date," and "Stormy Monday Blues."

From bebop to cool

In the early 1940s jazz was in a rather explosive stage. Gifted jazzmen with original ideas were restless under the hegemony of big-band swing and eager to find something new. Then, at the beginning of August, 1942, a nation-wide ban on recording was imposed by the musicians' union in a dispute with the licensing agencies; this ban, which lasted until the fall of 1943, put a lid, as it were, on this explosive situation. The jazz seekers went on developing their new ideas, but did not immediately reach the large sectors of the public that get their jazz chiefly through recordings. When the lid was taken off, the new music hit the public with disconcerting suddenness. No one was prepared for it—not even the critics, most of whom were hostile.

The new movement originated at a night club in upper Manhattan called Minton's Play House, around 1940, when a group of progressive jazzmen began to gather there and to experiment informally with new approaches to jazz expression, in rhythm, harmony, and melody. The two leading exponents of the new style were the saxophonist Charlie ("Bird") Parker (1920–1955) and the trumpet player John Birks ("Dizzy") Gillespie (b. 1917). Parker, born in Kansas City, was destined to be the most influential figure in modern jazz—an influence not limited to his own instrument, the alto sax, but extending into all areas and all media of jazz expression, including composition and arranging. He was a creative genius; but addiction to drugs made his life extremely unstable and eventually destroyed him. He met Gillespie after coming to New York in 1939, and thereafter the two were very closely associated in the rise of the new kind of jazz that came to be known as "bebop" or simply "bop." Gillespie, a native of South Carolina, began to play trumpet under the influence of Roy Eldridge. The vogue of bebop made him a celebrity and he was able to form his own large band in 1945. His style represents the peak of bop trumpet playing, marked by a phenomenal technique.

Both Gillespie and Parker, in the early forties, were playing with a band led by Earl ("Fatha") Hines. Had it not been for the ban, Hines would probably have made the first recordings of bebop with this band. As it was, circumstances favored the relatively conservative Coleman Hawkins, who in February, 1944, assembled a band that actually made the first recordings of bebop, with a personnel that included Dizzy Gillespie and, on tenor sax, the man largely responsible for organizing the session: Albert ("Budd") Johnson (b. 1910). As composer and arranger, Budd Johnson was a key man in the transition from swing to bop, through the music he wrote for the large bands of Earl Hines, Woody Herman, Billy Eckstine, and Dizzy Gillespie.

Drumming was also very important in the transition from swing to bop. Pioneer drummers in the new style were Jo Jones (*b.* 1911), Kenny Clarke (*b.* 1914), and Max Roach (*b.* 1925). They emphasized a light, subtle use of the top cymbal instead of persistently using the old "sock" cymbal. Carrying the steady rhythm on the top cymbal, they reserved the bass drum for special (and often unexpected) punctuations. This produced a more subtle and varied effect and enabled the drummer to achieve a legato sound. As explained by Ross Russell, "The vibration of the cymbal, once set in motion, is maintained throughout the number, producing a shimmering texture of sound that supports, agitates, and inspires the line men. . . . The fluid cymbal sound is actually a 4/4 pulse. This is the rhythmic base of bebop jazz."[9]

The increasing importance of the string bass, both melodically and rhythmically, is another characteristic feature of bebop that has had significant results for modern jazz. The pioneer in the modern use of the string bass in jazz was Jimmy Blanton (1921–1942), who displayed an unprecedented skill, boldness, and inventiveness that made him the first true master of this instrument in jazz. His successor was Oscar Pettiford (*b.* 1922), who also played the cello and who had an important role in the bop movement.

The guitar did not figure prominently in the development of bebop, but it might have done so had it not been for the untimely death of Charlie Christian (1919–1942), one of the musicians who took part in the early sessions at Minton's Play House. Although he died soon afterward, his role in the emergence of the new style cannot be disregarded; as Barry Ulanov writes:

> Christian has a direct connection with bebop. He played up at Minton's in those first experimental sessions which yielded . . . the altered chords, the fresher melodic lines, the rows of even beats and contrasting dramatic aspects of bop. Some of the participants . . . credit Charlie with the name "bebop," citing his humming of phrases as the onomatopoeic origin of the term. All of the musicians who played with him then . . . insist on his large creative contributions to the music later associated with Parker and Gillespie."[10]

For the general public, the recordings made by Parker and Gillespie with a quintet in 1945 definitely established the vogue of the new movement. By this time, 52d Street in New York had become the

[9] In *The Art of Jazz*, ed. Martin T. Williams, p. 190.
[10] Ulanov, *A History of Jazz in America.*

chief center of the progressive movement, with many small combos playing at the various night spots. Musically, this was the most important street in America.

Thelonius Monk and Earl ("Bud") Powell, both among the group that gathered at Minton's, were the chief pianistic innovators in bebop jazz. But Monk achieved his greatest reputation somewhat later, while Powell became the immediate leader of the bop movement in piano and for a time was the most widely imitated jazz pianist of his generation (he was born in New York in 1924 and died there in 1966).

The significance of bebop was summarized by Ross Russell in these terms: "Bebop is music of revolt: revolt against big bands, arrangers, vertical harmonies, soggy rhythms, non-playing leaders, Tin Pan Alley—against commercialized music in general. It reasserts the individuality of the jazz musician as a creative artist, playing spontaneous and melodic music within the framework of jazz, but with new tools, sounds, and concepts."[11]

Birth of the cool—and after

Unfortunately, some of the leaders of bebop overdid the note of individualism, carrying it to external mannerisms, so that this music became identified in the public mind with goatees, berets, eccentricity, and exhibitionism. By the end of the 1940s the situation was chaotic rather than explosive, and nobody seemed to know in what direction jazz should move next. A cooling-off period was evidently in order. A trumpet player named Miles Davis (*b.* 1926), working together with the arranger Gil Evans (*b.* 1912) and the saxophonist and composer Gerry Mulligan (*b.* 1927), took the initiative in giving jazz a new direction. The password of the new music was "cool."

Miles Davis had been exposed to the progressive trends of bebop when Billy Eckstine's Band, featuring Parker and Gillespie, appeared in his home city of St. Louis. He belonged to a well-to-do Negro family and appeared to be headed for a career in classical music when he went to New York to study at the Juilliard School of Music. But he soon found his way to 52d Street, where he began to play trumpet in various combos with Parker, Hawkins, and others. Now fully committed to jazz, he joined Billy Eckstine's Band and went on tour. In 1948 he formed his own nine-piece band in New York.

[11] In *The Art of Jazz,* ed. Williams, p. 202.

Gil Evans was born in Toronto and began his professional career in California as band leader and arranger. Self-taught in music, he tells us: "I didn't learn any theory except through the practical use of it." A crucial step in his development was his association with the band leader Claude Thornhill (1909–65), for whom he began to work as arranger in 1941. Thornhill was classically trained at the Cincinnati Conservatory and the Curtis Institute of Music: he wanted to enrich the instrumental spectrum of jazz and was the first leader to use the French horn as a functioning part of a dance band. He did this in 1941, and Evans recalls that he insisted on no vibrato except when specifically indicated for expressive purposes. New sonorities resulted when "that distant, haunting, no-vibrato sound came to be blended with the reed and brass sections in various combinations." With the addition soon afterward of a tuba, the instrumentation of Thornhill's band closely resembled that of the Miles Davis band in 1949. The link was through Gil Evans, who met Miles in that year.

The third member of this cool triumvirate, Gerry Mulligan (born in New York in 1927), had joined the Miles Davis band as baritone saxophonist in 1948. A pianist, arranger, and composer, as well as an excellent sideman, Mulligan was responsible for several of the arrangements that started a new trend in jazz when Davis's nine-piece band made its memorable recordings in 1949, released under the historic title *Birth of the Cool*. On these sides, Mulligan composed "Jeru," "Venus de Milo," and "Rocker," and made the arrangement for "Godchild." He played baritone sax in all three sessions (the last recorded in March, 1950).

The instrumentation used for these recordings consisted of French horn, trumpet, trombone, tuba, alto and baritone saxes, piano, bass, and drums. In addition to Davis and Mulligan, the players included Lee Konitz on alto sax, Kai Winding and J. J. Johnson on trombone, Kenny Clarke and Max Roach on drums, John Lewis on piano, and Gunther Schuller on French horn—all key figures in the development of modern jazz. Gil Evans made the notable arrangement of "Boplicity," utilizing skillful and unusual voicings of the six wind instruments in the ensemble (indiscriminately called "horns" in jazz parlance). Miles Davis was the composer of "Deception" and the arranger of Bud Powell's "Budo."

Gil Evans and Miles Davis continued to collaborate in many productions, such as *Miles Ahead* (1957), *Sketches from Spain* (1961), and the admirable orchestral version of Gershwin's *Porgy and Bess*.

Miles Ahead marks a significant departure in the use of a large orchestra (twenty players) to further develop the concept of the cool. Of these arrangements, the English critic Max Harrison wrote: "In elaboration and richness of resource they surpass anything previously attempted in big-band jazz and constitute the only wholly original departure in that field outside Ellington's work. . . ." The instrumentation consisted of Flügelhorn, five trumpets, four trombones, two French horns, tuba, alto sax, bass clarinet, flute, clarinet, bass and drums.

Further explorations in a chamber-music type of jazz were made by Gerry Mulligan, Jimmy Giuffre, Lee Konitz, Shelly Manne, John Graas, and other musicians who worked mainly in California—whence the term "West Coast Jazz." Most of them were trained in classical music. Mulligan, in the 1950s, introduced the pianoless quartet, consisting of baritone sax, trumpet, bass, and drums. Giuffre (*b.* 1921), specializing in the clarinet but also playing tenor and baritone sax, formed a trio with Bob Brookmeyer on trombone and Jim Hall on guitar—one of the many novel chamber combinations that have been exploited by modern jazzmen. At other times Giuffre has used a drummer or a bass player; but he does not believe that a rhythm section should "necessarily be used on every tune all the time." Giuffre is also a composer in the modern idiom.

John Lewis, who played a modest role in the first "cool" recordings of 1949, was soon to emerge as one of the leading figures in modern jazz, as founder and leader of the Modern Jazz Quartet. First organized in 1951, the MJQ was permanently established in 1954, with Lewis at the piano, Milt Jackson on vibes, Percy Heath on bass, and Kenny Clarke on drums (replaced in 1955 by Connie Kay). John Lewis, the son of musical parents, received training in violin and piano from the age of seven. At the University of New Mexico he majored in anthropology but switched to music in his final year. In 1945 he continued his musical studies at the Manhattan School of Music in New York and at the same time began composing and arranging for Dizzy Gillespie. Since then he has been a prolific composer; his scores include music for the films *No Sun in Venice* (1957) and *Odds against Tomorrow* (1959). He often uses baroque or classical forms but does not neglect the blues and other traditional types of jazz expression. He has written many musical impressions of Europe (*Milano, A Morning in Paris, Piazza Navona, Spanish Steps, Versailles*) in a refined and subtle idiom that does not, however, exclude the basic rhythmic and improvisational character of jazz.

John Lewis believes that there is no essential difference between jazz and "classical" music. Hence it is not surprising that together with Gunther Schuller (*b*. 1925), a classically trained French horn player and composer, Lewis has taken a prominent part in developing what is known as "third-stream music"—a combination of jazz and classical performing groups in which each maintains its separate identity while collaborating to produce a new kind of sound. An example is Schuller's Concertino for Jazz Quartet and Orchestra, in which the Modern Jazz Quartet is joined by a large symphony orchestra. In other performances of this type the MJQ and the Jimmy Giuffre Three have joined forces with the Beaux Arts String Quartet in compositions by Lewis, Giuffre, and Schuller. The result is completely different from what used to be known as "symphonic jazz." Third-stream music is more like a dialogue between modern jazz and classical music.

Since history consists mainly of action and reaction, it is not surprising that the cool movement brought a reaction, in the late 1950s, that came to be known as "hard bop" and "funky." The reaction was toward the recuperation of a more basic, even primitive, emotional drive, such as had been characteristic of early folk-rooted jazz, with its strong injections of earthy blues and hot gospel style. Such Negro quasi-folk-singers as Ray Charles and Mahalia Jackson (the former an important pianist also), with their emphasis on "rhythm and blues," influenced the funky trend. The trumpet player Clifford Brown (1930–1956), in spite of his untimely death in a traffic accident, contributed to the movement with his fusion of cool and bop elements. The pianist and composer Horace Silver (*b*. 1928), in association with the tenor saxophonist Stan Getz and the drummer and leader Art Blakey, and with Bud Powell's style as his point of departure, set the pace for the funky trend in 1955, relying heavily on riffs and elementary chordal patterns. The Jazz Messengers led by Art Blakey (*b*. 1919)—called by Nat Hentoff "the most emotionally unbridled drummer in jazz"—and the combo led by Nat and Julian ("Cannonball") Adderley were probably the most representative bands of the funky movement. The essential feature of funky music was that it attempted to incorporate some of the technical advances of bebop—particularly its melodic and rhythmic complexities—while reverting to a more traditional harmonic framework Therefore it was, paradoxically, both progressive and regressive.

Two tenor saxophonists John Coltrane (*b.* 1926) and Sonny Rollins (*b.* 1929) were particularly identified with hard bop, and both became influential figures in the decade after 1955. Coltrane has played with Gillespie, Miles Davis, and Thelonius Monk, developing an impassioned and impetuous style characterized by extremely rapid runs. Rollins cultivated a hard tone, deliberate melodic distortion, and a general tendency to undercut sentimentality with sarcasm. He has played with Miles Davis, Max Roach, and Thelonius Monk, and from 1957 made many recordings with a trio (tenor sax, bass, and drums).

In the words of Martin Williams, "In part, the funky idiom represented an attempt by the jazzmen to rediscover their emotional roots at a time when cool jazz seemed to be jeopardizing them in favor of preciosity and contrivance."[12] In this sense, it emphasized a trend that has motivated much of the work of the most "advanced" jazz composers, such as Ornette Coleman and Charles Mingus.

Some modern jazzmen

Around 1955 the composer, bass player, and pianist Charles Mingus (*b.* 1922) appeared as a powerful force and an explosive personality in modern jazz. Born in Nogales, Arizona, he was raised in Los Angeles, where he studied piano as well as trombone and cello before switching to bass. His first professional experience was with two of the great New Orleans musicians, Kid Ory and Louis Armstrong. He then went on to work with Lionel Hampton, Art Tatum, Charlie Parker, and Bud Powell, making his contribution to bebop in 1947 with a piece called "Mingus Fingers." By this time he was becoming known as an extraordinary bass player—a reputation sustained and increased in subsequent years. In the 1950s he moved to New York, where he established the Charlie Mingus Jazz Workshop to experiment with compositional techniques. He was concerned with avoiding the use of a written score while maintaining a formal framework for each composition. His solution was to work out the lines of the composition mentally and then play the "framework" on the piano for his musicians to assimilate. He found that in this way he could project his own creative individuality while allowing a maximum of individual freedom to each of the musicians in the group. An impressive result of the Jazz Workshop was the album titled *Pithecanthropus Erectus*, contain-

[12] In *Jazz*, ed. Hentoff and McCarthy, p. 297.

ing three compositions by Mingus in addition to his version of Gershwin's "A Foggy Day." The instrumentation is for bass, alto sax, tenor sax, piano, and drums. The title piece is "a jazz tone poem" of nearly eleven minutes' duration, depicting nothing less than the evolution, superiority, decline, and destruction of Man.

The extent to which Mingus pioneered in many of the concepts and procedures of modern jazz can be appreciated through a retrospective recording titled *Prebird*, which contains a selection of his compositions from the 1940s. As summarized by Nat Hentoff:

Mingus has been one of the pioneers in occasionally disregarding traditional jazz chordal patterns in favor of modal bases for improvisation. He was also one of the first jazzmen to experiment seriously with shifting time signatures and with a rhythmic pulse that slowed down and accelerated according to the emotional changes in the piece. Moreover, in a number of his earlier works and increasingly in the past few years, there have been Mingus performances without any explicitly stated pulse at all. In addition, long before the speech-like pitches and cadences of Ornette Coleman, Mingus required his sidemen to extract unprecedented cries and other exclamatory colorations from their instruments.[13]

The recorded works of Mingus include *Tijuana Moods*, *Mingus Presents Mingus*, *The Clown*, *Mingus Ah Um*, *Mingus Dynasty*, *Mingus Mingus Mingus Mingus*, *Blues & Roots*, and *Mingus at Monterey*. In *Blues & Roots*, as the title indicates, he goes back to childhood memories ("I was born swinging and clapped my hands in church as a little boy") as evoked in "Wednesday Night Prayer Meeting"; to the folk-rooted blues ("Cryin' Blues," "Moanin' "); and to the old-time New Orleans tradition in "My Jelly Roll Soul" (a tribute to Jelly Roll Morton). In *Mingus at Monterey* (recorded at the 1964 Jazz Festival in Monterey, California), the composer emphasizes his sense of continuity with the main stream of jazz by a remarkable tribute to Duke Ellington in the form of a medley that includes "I've Got It Bad," "Mood Indigo," "Sophisticated Lady," and "Take the A Train." The major Mingus work in this album is *Meditations on Integration*, for twelve performers, lasting almost thirty minutes, in which the composer played both bass and piano. An expression of Mingus's strong feelings on racial discrimination, the work passed from

[13] "A Volcano Named Mingus," by Nat Hentoff, in *HiFi/Stereo Review*, Vol. 13, No. 6 (December, 1964).

melancholy lyricism to wild cacophony, held together by inventive dialogues and strongly defined rhythms. It reaffirmed Mingus's position, in the mid 1960s, as the most controversial and dynamic of contemporary jazzmen.

Ornette Coleman (*b.* 1930), alto saxophonist and composer, was born in Texas, lived for a while in New Orleans, then studied theory and composition by himself while working as an elevator operator in Los Angeles. In 1959 the sponsorship of a recording company enabled him to study at the School of Jazz in Lenox, Massachusetts. Settled in New York, he began to make a strong impact on the jazz world with such recordings as *The Shape of Jazz to Come* (1959), *Change of the Century* (1960), *This Is Our Music* (1961), and *Ornette!* (1962). Coleman believes in free group improvisation. When his group starts out to play, he tells us, they do not have any idea what the end result will be. He prefers a small ensemble, such as alto sax, trumpet, bass, and drums. He uses a plastic saxophone (at first because it was cheaper, later because he liked it), and his trumpet player, Donald Cherry, uses a pocket trumpet. Abandoning traditional chord patterns, Coleman makes reckless sorties into atonality, aiming at frenzy rather than form.

George Russell (*b.* 1923) is a composer, theorist, performer, and leader who has been developing concepts and techniques for jazz composition, culminating in his "Lydian Chromatic Concept of Tonal Organization." This is a twelve-tone concept in which intervals are considered in relation to a "center of tonal gravity." The system is chromatic but not atonal. It employs the concept of "pan-tonality," in which any number of different scales can be used either sequentially or simultaneously. Russell's compositions include *The Day John Brown Was Hanged* (1957), *New York, N.Y.* (1959), *Concerto for Billy the Kid* (1957; for the pianist Bill Evans), *Jazz in the Space Age* (1959; a suite in four movements), and *All about Rosie* (1957), based on Negro children's singing games from Alabama. This piece is scored for two saxes, two trumpets, trombone, flute, bassoon, piano, vibraphone, bass, harp, French horn, guitar, and drums. Russell is convinced that jazz must necessarily become more complex, but "no matter how complicated the techniques become, we can always master them and produce good art." At the same time, he believes that it is important "to preserve the intuitive nature of jazz." These ideas summarize the dilemma of modern jazz, navigating perilously between intuition and complexity.

chapter twenty-four

The Americanists

I was anxious to write a work that would immediately be recognized as American in character.

AARON COPLAND, OUR NEW MUSIC.

In the 1920s many composers in the United States were trying very hard to be "American." Some composers turned to the tribal chants of the Indians, some were attracted by the Negro spirituals, others drew on the tradition of Anglo-American folk music, and others found material in the songs of the cowboys. A few composers, among them Antheil, Carpenter, and Copland, were tapping the resources of current popular music. Gershwin, by profession a highly successful composer of popular songs, was making the transition from tin-pan alley to Carnegie Hall through the medium of so-called "symphonic jazz." That term, like everything else connected with jazz, is controversial. In no other field of American music does one have to tread more warily than in that of jazz and its manifold ramifications. Our concern in this chapter is not so much with jazz itself as with some of its by-products, particularly in the realm of symphonic music.

In a symposium entitled *American Composers on American Music*, published in 1933, Gershwin made a statement on "The Relation of Jazz to American Music" (his words were set down by the editor, Henry Cowell). He summed up his views as follows:

> Jazz I regard as an American folk-music; not the only one, but a very powerful one which is probably in the blood and feeling of the American people more than any other style of folk-music. I believe that it can be made the basis of serious symphonic works of lasting value, in the hands of a composer with talent for both jazz and symphonic music.[1]

[1] Reprinted from *American Composers on American Music*, edited by Henry Cowell, with permission of the publishers, Stanford University Press. Copyright 1933 by the Board of Trustees of Leland Stanford Junior University.

490

Although Gershwin sought—and soon found—success as a writer of popular music, he also sought, from boyhood, to familiarize himself with "classical" music and to acquire a theoretical and practical knowledge of musical composition as practised by "The Great Masters," whom he always admired and looked up to, even when they were still among the living (as in the case of Ravel and of Stravinsky, from both of whom he aspired to receive lessons after he himself had become famous). His was not a case of a "popular" composer suddenly switching to "serious" composition because of a fortuitous opportunity. There was never any such dichotomy in Gershwin's attitude toward music. In his teens, while working as a song-plugger at Remick's music store, he was heard, in an off moment, playing some preludes and fugues by Bach. A fellow-worker asked, "Are you studying to be a concert pianist?" And the answer was: "No, I'm studying to be a great popular-song writer." He had greatness in mind, not a particular kind of music.

Gershwin's parents were immigrants from Russia (the family name was originally Gershovitz) who had established themselves in New York in fairly comfortable circumstances. George was born in Brooklyn, on September 28, 1898, two years after his brother Ira (who became the author of many of the lyrics for George's musical plays). After his first exposure to operatic potpourris, George, in 1912, began more serious musical study with Charles Hambitzer, a fine pianist and composer who introduced him to the piano literature from Bach and Beethoven to Debussy and Ravel, not forgetting the Romantics—especially Chopin and Liszt—who left a deep impression upon Gershwin. To a friend, Hambitzer wrote: "I have a new pupil who will make his mark in music if anybody will. The boy is a genius. . . ." Although he began to write popular songs at the age of fifteen, at the same time that he entered the world of "tin-pan alley" through his job as song-plugger at Remick's, there was no slackening in his pursuit of musical knowledge. In 1915 he undertook the study of harmony, theory, and orchestration with the distinguished pedagogue Edward Kilenyi. In 1919—the same year in which his song "Swanee" made a tremendous hit as sung by Al Jolson—Gershwin composed a string quartet with the principal theme in blues style. In 1923, already a highly successful Broadway composer, he took lessons for several months with the celebrated composer and teacher Rubin Goldmark. In that same year the singer Eva Gauthier gave a recital in New

York in which she programmed songs by Gershwin—with the composer at the piano—along with songs by Bartók, Hindemith, Milhaud, Schoenberg, and other contemporaries. I agree with Carl van Vechten that "this was one of the very most important events in American musical history." It undermined the absolute dichotomy between "serious" and "popular" music: what counts is talent.

Notwithstanding his success in both fields, Gershwin continued his efforts to perfect his musical training: for nearly two years (1926–1927) he studied counterpoint with Henry Cowell, one of the most "advanced" musical theorists of our time. To his brother Ira, Gershwin said: "I maintain that a composer needs to understand all the intricacies of counterpoint and orchestration, and be able to create new forms for each advance in his work." This attitude he maintained even at the height of his success: as late as 1932 he began to study composition with Joseph Schillinger, with whom he worked for about four years. Few composers have been so assiduous in seeking improvement.

In 1920 Gershwin was engaged to write music for *George White's Scandals*, but he did not confine himself to the standard musical-comedy numbers: for the 1922 show he wrote a one-act "Negro Opera," called *Blue Monday* (later renamed *135th Street*). The score included "Blue Monday Blues" and a spiritual, "I'm Going to See My Mother." It was conducted by a musician named Paul Whiteman, a former symphony cellist, the son of a music educator, who had drifted into the outskirts of jazz and had formed a large band that specialized in "sweet" arrangements. Though no jazz musician himself, Whiteman had the good sense to hire the best available jazz players—and to pay them well. His principal arranger was Ferde Grofé. In 1924 the Paul Whiteman Orchestra consisted of three trumpets, three trombones, four saxophones (with Russ Gorman doubling on B flat clarinet), two pianos, four violins, two banjos, two basses, and drums. Among its most remarkable players were Frank Siegrist on trumpet, master of The Split, the Horse Whinny, the Lip Slur, the Tone Dip, the Drag, the Flutter Tongue, and the Common Mute; Willy Hall, Jack Fulton, and Roy Maxon on trombone, Russ Gorman and Hal McLean on saxes.

Impressed by what Gershwin had done in *Blue Monday*, Whiteman commissioned him to write a symphonic composition in jazz style for a special concert pretentiously titled "Experiment in Modern

Music" that he was organizing. Gershwin set to work and in three weeks completed the piano score of *Rhapsody in Blue,* finishing it on January 7, 1924. That original score, as previously stated, bore the inscription: "For Jazz Band and Piano." But Whiteman and Grofé had a different idea: they wanted the work to sound big and "symphonic." Hence in Grofé's orchestral score the *Rhapsody* is described as for "Piano Solo and Orchestra." Grofé's original orchestration (completed on February 4, 1924) included, in addition to the usual saxophones, trumpets, and trombones, a B flat clarinet, a bass clarinet, an oboe, a tuba, two French horns, accordion, celesta, two pianos, string bass, banjo, timpani, traps, and eight violins divided into two stands. In the score, the names of certain musicians are written in beside their respective instruments, and numerous special jazz effects are indicated at various points; for example, "Siegrist solo, muted Kazoo;" "Fly swatter or Brush;" "Let string snap" (banjo and bass); and at one point the tuba is directed to play with flutter tongue, "if possible." Actually, with these musicians almost anything was possible.

The "Experiment in Modern Music" took place in Aeolian Hall, New York, on February 12, 1924, with a hodge-podge program that began with *Livery Stable Blues* and concluded with Elgar's *Pomp and Circumstance March*—presumably to demonstrate the progress achieved by "modern music." The audience, which included most of the musical celebrities of that time, was apathetic until it heard the opening clarinet glissando of the *Rhapsody in Blue* (next to the last number on the program), in which Russ Gorman made the unbelievable audible, when, "halfway up the 17-note run, he suddenly stopped playing separate notes and slid for home on a long *portamento* that nobody knew could be done on a clarinet." Gershwin himself, as the soloist, exerted the charm and mastery that always characterized his piano-playing, and contributed to the immediate success of the *Rhapsody in Blue.*

Grofé went on making more elaborate orchestrations of the *Rhapsody:* a version dated Feb. 23, 1926, is scored for flute, oboe, two clarinets, three saxophones, three horns in F, two trumpets, trombones, bells, and other percussion, timpani, banjo, and strings. Since then, the *Rhapsody* has most often been performed with large symphony orchestra, and Gershwin's original inscription, "For Jazz Band and Piano," has been buried in oblivion. There was at least one attempt, made by Don Redman, to restore the *Rhapsody* to jazz. Leora Henderson, the jazz singer, recalls "that Don Redman even did an arrangement of *Rhapsody in Blue*, but later on they stopped the band from playin' it." It is a pity that such restrictions have prevented the jazzmen from having their way with the *Rhapsody*, for only they could make it into a work "for jazz band and piano."

The year after the première of *Rhapsody in Blue*, Walter Damrosch, at that time conductor of the New York Symphony, commissioned Gershwin to write a work of symphonic proportions for that orchestra. The result was the Concerto in F for piano and orchestra, first performed in New York on December 3, 1925, with Gershwin as soloist. For this work Gershwin himself did the orchestration: he was now a "serious" composer, and *noblesse oblige!* In presenting the Concerto, Dr. Damrosch made a short speech in which he contributed to the current fallacy that Gershwin had taken jazz and dressed it up "in the classic garb of a concerto," thereby making it presentable to concert audiences. What Gershwin actually had done was to write a conventional piano concerto utilizing some traits of American popular music, including the standardized or commercialized type of jazz, while the real jazz went on its own way, eventually making its entry into Carnegie Hall without benefit of any "classic garb."

The Concerto in F is in three movements: Allegro, Andante con moto, and Allegro con brio. John Tasker Howard was of the opinion that Gershwin's attempt to be formally correct in the Concerto "took away much of the natural charm that had been found in his previous *Rhapsody in Blue*." But a concerto for piano and orchestra is a work of art, not a work of nature, and the Concerto in F is a better work of art than the *Rhapsody in Blue*. When the English conductor Albert Coates, in 1930, named Gershwin's Concerto in F as one of the best musical compositions of all time—and the only one by an American to figure on his list—he displayed remarkable acumen as well as exceptional courage. Within a quarter of a century after its première, Gershwin's Concerto had firmly entrenched itself as the first work in that form by an American composer to have entered the permanent repertoire of symphonic music.

Gershwin's next symphonic work was the orchestral tone poem *An American in Paris*, first performed in New York on December 13, 1928. This is a gay and brash composition, colorfully and realistically orchestrated (the score includes taxi horns), not without its moments of sentimentality, mixed with mockery. The work has an especially effective blues section. In this tone poem the composer caught the spirit of a decade and produced a period piece that "dates" without fading. That *was* America in the 1920s—Paris included.

In 1931 Gershwin wrote the music for a film comedy called *Delicious*, in which there was a sequence of New York street scenes. For this sequence he devised a "rivet theme" to express the dynamic energy of the city, continually rebuilding itself. Around this theme he composed a work for piano and orchestra originally called *Rhapsody in Rivets*. Renamed rather tamely *Second Rhapsody* (perhaps not to frighten prospective listeners), it was first performed by the Boston Symphony Orchestra under the direction of Koussevitzky, on January 29, 1932. It utilizes mechanistic effects, dance rhythms, and tunes of the Broadway type; but the spontaneous charm of the first *Rhapsody* is lacking.

In December, 1933, Gershwin completed the brilliant *Variations on "I Got Rhythm"* for piano and orchestra, based on one of his best songs from the musical comedy *Girl Crazy* (1930). For several years he had been studying orchestration with Schillinger, and this work bears evidence of the latter's influence. The *Cuban Overture* (1934), with its conventional rumba rhythms, was the last orchestral work that Gershwin lived to complete. During these years he was also much absorbed by his big opera, *Porgy and Bess*, completed in 1935 (it is discussed in Chapter 30). Finally, we must mention the Preludes for piano, a characteristic attempt to blend blues-jazz ingredients with the romantic piano tradition.

In 1937 Gershwin was living in Hollywood, California, writing music for films. While working on a score for the *Goldwyn Follies* he was suddenly taken ill and a tumor of the brain was diagnosed. An operation proved unsuccessful, and he died on July 11, 1937.

To Gershwin might be applied the words that Sinclair Lewis wrote about himself: "It's not at all that I prefer Americanism, or advocate it; I simply am it."

Composer from Brooklyn—no. 2

Aaron Copland, like Gershwin, was born in Brooklyn (on November 14, 1900), and took harmony lessons from the same teacher, Rubin

Goldmark. All the Copland children—there were five of them—had music lessons, but only Aaron thought of taking up music seriously as a career. The idea occurred to him when he was about thirteen, and some two years later he definitely decided that he would like to become a composer. After an unsatisfactory attempt to learn harmony by correspondence, he began to study with Goldmark, an excellent teacher but very conservative in his tastes. Goldmark warned his pupil against the "moderns," which of course immediately set him on their track. Young Copland reveled in the music of Scriabin, Debussy, and Ravel, and quickly acquired the reputation of a musical radical.

Copland's next objective was Paris. Reading of the establishment of a summer music school for Americans at Fontainebleau, in 1921, he was the first to apply for admission. At the Fontainebleau School he studied composition with Paul Vidal, whom he describes as "a French version of Rubin Goldmark," only more difficult to understand. But there was another teacher at Fontainebleau, the brilliant Nadia Boulanger, whose acquaintance Copland soon made. This encounter marked a decisive moment in his career. He decided to stay in Paris as long as possible in order to continue studying with Boulanger. He was one of the first American pupils in composition of this remarkable woman whose teaching and personality have exerted such a profound influence on contemporary American music. Copland remained in Paris for three years, studying, becoming familiar with new music, and composing several vocal and instrumental works, including the score of a one-act ballet, *Grohg*. In June, 1924, he returned to the United States.

Nadia Boulanger had commissioned him to write a symphony for organ and orchestra, in which she was to appear as soloist. The work received its first performance in New York on January 11, 1925. Three years later it was revised for large orchestra without the organ, becoming Copland's First Symphony. Its three movements are: Prelude, Scherzo, Finale (Lento—Allegro moderato). Noteworthy is the use of "blues-type" music in the middle section of the Scherzo.

In his autobiographical sketch, *Composer from Brooklyn*, Copland tells us that at this time he "was anxious to write a work that would immediately be recognized as American in character." He does not explain why he had this desire, except to say that it was symptomatic of the period. The interesting point is that in trying to write music that would immediately be recognized as American in character he turned to the idioms of our popular music, and specifically to jazz, or what he conceived to be such. The award of a Guggenheim Fellowship in 1925 (the first given to a composer) gave him freedom to compose as he pleased. His first important experiment "in the American idiom" was a suite for small orchestra and piano titled *Music for the Theatre*, composed at the MacDowell Colony in New Hampshire during the summer of 1925. This suite consists of five movements: "Prologue," "Dance," "Interlude," "Burlesque," "Epilogue." Neoclassical in form and spirit, influenced by Stravinsky, it is in the movement titled "Dance" that the traces of jazz technique are most apparent.

In his Concerto for Piano and Orchestra, which he played for the first time with the Boston Symphony on January 28, 1927, Copland continued to develop the use of jazzlike rhythms, particularly in the second movement. Referring to the Piano Concerto, he afterward wrote:

> This proved to be the last of my "experiments" with symphonic jazz. With the Concerto I felt I had done all I could with the idiom, considering its limited emotional scope. True, it was an easy way to be American in musical terms, but all American music could not possibly be confined to two dominant jazz moods: the "blues" and the snappy number.[2]

This limitation of jazz to two moods is rather arbitrary. Students of jazz have found it to contain at least five well-defined moods or emotional attitudes, as follows: (1) The Blues ("simple, direct, personal sadness"), (2) The Romantic (expansive, buoyant, dramatic, imaginative), (3) The Lyric ("a highly personal expression—a singing, a brilliant soaring of the spirit . . ."), (4) The Decadent (veering between plaintive resignation and intense maladjustment), (5) The Protest ("an angry, sometimes vicious, attack on life").[3] Objectively, it would be difficult to sustain Copland's statement that "these two moods [the blues and the snappy number] encompass the whole gamut of jazz emotion."

In any case, Copland confesses that he was more interested in the letter than in the spirit of jazz. "What interested composers," he writes, "was not so much the spirit . . . as the more technical side of jazz—

[2] Copland, *Our New Music*, p. 227.
[3] See "The Main Currents of Jazz" by Miller and Crenshaw in *Esquire's 1945 Jazz Book*, pp. 25-26.

the rhythm, melody, harmony, timbre through which that spirit was expressed."[4] And he adds that "By far the most potent influence on the technical side was that of rhythm." He concludes, therefore, that only the technical procedures of jazz were of permanent value to the composer, since these "might be applied to any number of different musical styles." Referring to the polyrhythms of jazz, he writes: "The peculiar excitement they produce by clashing two definitely and regularly marked rhythms is unprecedented in occidental music. Its polyrhythm is the real contribution of jazz." This at least makes clear Copland's position as a composer with regard to jazz and its influence.

In 1929 Copland entered a competition sponsored by the RCA Victor Company, which offered an award of $25,000 for a symphonic work. He wished to submit a one-movement symphony, which he called *Symphonic Ode*, but was unable to complete it in time to meet the deadline. He therefore extracted three movements from the score of his early ballet, *Grohg*, and submitted them under the title of *Dance Symphony*. None of the works submitted won the full award, which was divided among five contestants, Copland receiving $5,000 for his symphony. No one would ever guess from the *Dance Symphony* that its composer was born in Brooklyn, but it contains ample evidence of his sojourn in Paris. It fluctuates between the impressionism of Debussy and the primitivism of Stravinsky, with more than passing recognition to Ravel. While these influences indicate the musical climate of Copland's formative years, the *Dance Symphony* nevertheless bears the mark of his individuality both in mood and texture. It is derivative but not imitative.

During this period Copland became very active on behalf of contemporary music. Together with Roger Sessions he organized the Copland-Sessions Concerts (1928–1931) for the performance of new music by American composers. He was the first director of the American Festival of Contemporary Music at Yaddo (Saratoga Springs, New York), and a moving spirit of the American Composers Alliance, the League of Composers, and the United States section of the International Society for Contemporary Music.

At about the same time (1928–1929), Copland completed his *Symphonic Ode*, which was first performed by the Boston Symphony Orchestra on February 19, 1932. Copland himself refers to this work as "fulsome" and observes that it "marks the end of a certain period

[4] Copland, *op. cit.*, p. 88.

in my development as a composer." He was now interested in writing music of a more austere character, more intellectual in conception and expression.

Austerity and imposed simplicity

To this "period of austerity" belong the Piano Variations (1930), the *Short Symphony* (1933), and *Statements* for orchestra (1934). To these should be added another work of similar tendency, the Piano Sonata, which, though not completed until 1941, was begun, according to Arthur Berger, in 1935. The trio titled *Vitebsk*, "Study on a Jewish Theme," for violin, cello and piano (1929), may also be regarded as related to this period. This work is significant also as Copland's only deliberate attempt to treat Jewish material in his music, though critics have found reflections of his Jewish background in other phases of his work, particularly in his early compositions.

Copland remarks of his compositions of this period that "They are difficult to perform and difficult for an audience to comprehend." That is undoubtedly why they represent the least-known portion of his output. On the other hand, difficulty is relative, and in the second half of the twentieth century more listeners were prepared to assimilate what seemed difficult in earlier decades. Consequently, Copland's music of this period has received increasingly wider recognition.

The Piano Variations is a work of ingenious and masterly construction, forceful in utterance, concise in expression, modern not only in manner but in essence. Conciseness is also a quality of the *Short Symphony*, which takes barely fifteen minutes to perform. For originality, for inventiveness, for vitality and expressiveness, for workmanship and beauty of detail, the *Short Symphony* is one of Copland's finest works. In 1937 the composer made an arrangement of the *Short Symphony* for sextet (string quartet, clarinet, piano).

Whatever the artistic qualities of these works, there were comparatively few listeners for this type of music, hence Copland felt the urge to reach a larger public. In his own words:

During these years I began to feel an increasing dissatisfaction with the relations of the music-loving public and the living composer. The old "special" public of the modern music concerts had fallen away, and the conventional concert public continued apathetic or indifferent to anything but the established classics. It seemed to me that we composers were in danger of working in a vacuum. Moreover, an entirely new public for music had grown up around the radio and the phonograph. It made no sense to ignore them and to continue writing as if they did not exist. I felt that it was worth the effort to see if I couldn't say what I had to say in the simplest possible terms.[5]

Thus began what Copland describes as his "tendency toward an imposed simplicity."

The works representing this tendency range from *El Salón México* (1936) to *Appalachian Spring* (1944). The prevailing trend is toward the utilization of folk material. But there is also the phase of writing occasional or "workaday" music for special purposes, such as the "play-opera" for high-school performance titled *The Second Hurricane* (1937); the *Music for Radio* (*Saga of the Prairie*), of the same year; and *An Outdoor Overture* for high-school orchestra (also arranged for band). And then there is the very practical phase of writing music for films, including *Of Mice and Men* (1939), *Our Town* (1940), and *North Star* (1943). The *Lincoln Portrait* of 1942, for speaker and orchestra, with its declamatory style and its snatches of popular songs of the Civil War period, belongs definitely within the tendency toward an imposed simplicity. The main theme of this work is based on the folk ballad "Springfield Mountain."

El Salón México was a deliberate attempt to write "tourist music." Concerning the genesis of this orchestral evocation, Copland writes:

During my first visit to Mexico, in the Fall of 1932, I conceived the idea of writing a piece based on Mexican themes. I suppose there is nothing strange about such an idea. Any composer who goes outside his native land wants to return bearing musical souvenirs. In this case my musical souvenirs must have been very memorable, since it wasn't until 1933 that I began to assemble them into the form of an orchestral work.

From the very beginning, the idea of writing a work based on popular Mexican melodies was connected in my mind with a popular dance hall in Mexico City called Salón México. No doubt I realized even then, that it would be foolish for me to attempt to translate into musical sounds the more profound side of Mexico, the Mexico of the ancient civilizations or the revolutionary Mexico

[5] Copland, *Our New Music*, pp. 228–229.

of today. In order to do that one must really know the country. All that I could hope to do was to reflect the Mexico of the tourists, and that is why I thought of the Salón México. Because in that "hot spot" one felt, in a very natural and unaffected way, a close contact with the Mexican people. It wasn't the music I heard, but the spirit that I felt there, which attracted me. Something of that spirit is what I hope to have put into my music.[6]

So Copland joined the company of Rimsky-Korsakoff and Chabrier as a composer of "tourist music," a genre to which *El Salón México* is a vividly picturesque contribution. As for the tunes he uses, he got most of them from two books: Frances Toor's *Cancionero Mexicano*, and *El Folklore y la Música Mexicana* by Rubén M. Campos. Among the melodies he borrowed are "El Palo Verde," "La Jesucita," and especially "El Mosco," which occurs twice, immediately after the introductory measures. *El Salón México* was first performed in Mexico City on August 27, 1937

Apart from this Mexican excursion, and a *Danzón Cubano* for two pianos (also orchestrated) which he wrote in 1942, Copland's main concern during this period was the folk music of the United States. During the 1940s American folk music was attracting widespread attention, as jazz had done two decades earlier, but with this difference: it was less controversial, it provoked no outbursts of moral indignation, it drew no imprecations from the righteous. When Copland experimented with jazz, he placed himself in the *avant-garde;* when he took up American folk music, he was moving with the prevailing trend, and this was in line with his strategy of coming closer to the public. In the light of historical perspective, it may also be found that Copland himself contributed something to the vogue of folk music, for doubtless there were some Americans, and many foreigners, who heard these tunes for the first time in the engaging musical scores that he wrote for the ballets *Billy the Kid* (1938), *Rodeo* (1942) and *Appalachian Spring* (1944).

Billy the Kid, written for the Ballet Caravan, was produced in New York on May 24, 1939. Three years later the composer made a symphonic suite from the ballet score. The ballet deals with the legendary desperado of the trans-Pecos country, of whom many a ballad tells:

[6] Quoted in Program Notes of the Boston Symphony Orchestra.

I'll sing you a song of Billy the Kid,
I'll sing you a song of the desperate deeds that he did,
Way out in New Mexico long, long ago,
When a man's only chance was his own fo'ty fo'.

Prominent in the score is the cowboy song "Bury Me Not on the Lone Prairie," which Copland uses in an idealized version to create a mood of pathos just before the scene of the final shooting.

Rodeo, written for Agnes de Mille, was produced by the Ballet Russe de Monte Carlo in New York on October 16, 1942. The heroine of the story is a "cow girl" who outdoes the men in broncobusting and thereby becomes socially unpopular. But all ends well when she meets her match. Along with more familiar cowboy songs, the score includes freely treated versions of "Sis Joe" and "If He'd Be a Buckaroo." From this ballet the composer extracted *Four Dance Episodes* for orchestra, consisting of "Corrale Nocturne," "Buckaroo Holiday," "Saturday Night Waltz," and "Hoedown."

Appalachian Spring (the title is from a poem by Hart Crane) was written on a commission from the Elizabeth Sprague Coolidge Foundation and was first performed by Martha Graham and her company at the Library of Congress on October 30, 1944. The original score was for chamber orchestra (thirteen instruments). The composer later arranged the music as a concert suite for symphony orchestra. The score evokes the pastoral mood of early Americana, with its scenes of tenderness between the Bride and her Intended, the folk-hymn atmosphere of the Revivalist and his Flock, the suggestions of country dances and fiddle tunes, and the sentiments of rural piety as reflected in the Shaker song "Simple Gifts" (see page 229 for the music of this song). The five variations on this Shaker tune, in a style that has been called "American Baroque," are among the most effective pages of *Appalachian Spring*.

The diatonic texture of this music is continued in Copland's Third Symphony (1946). In the four movements of this symphony, according to the composer, "any reference to jazz or folk material is purely unconscious." This is the phase of "unconscious Americanism," based on the theory that if an American composer writes his own kind of music the result will *ipso facto* be "American." The last movement of the Third Symphony opens with material taken from *Fanfare for the Common Man*, written in 1942.

The allusions to jazz and to popular dance rhythms (including those of Brazil) in the Clarinet Concerto (1948), written for Benny Goodman, certainly do not appear to be "purely unconscious," although they lack the aggressive prominence of the jazzlike features in the Piano Concerto of 1926.

The 1950s found Copland making use of twelve-tone techniques, beginning with the Quartet for Piano and Strings (1950), which has been described as "an extended essay in melodic serialism." Copland's concern with twelve-tone writing, like Stravinsky's, has been to make use of it in his own way, without any doctrinal *parti pris*. His use of dodecaphonic devices coincides, moreover, with a return to the creative climate of his earlier "period of austerity." His decision to orchestrate the *Piano Variations* of 1930 some twenty-seven years after they were composed is symptomatic. The renewed trend toward austerity reaches its culmination in a work of that same year (1957), the long, complex, and difficult *Piano Fantasy*, in which twelve-tone writing predominates. Here the aim was to fill a substantial time-canvas with a continuous flow of meaningful and closely related musical events, enhanced by pianistic virtuosity. Once again Copland was writing music "difficult to perform and difficult for an audience to comprehend." Perhaps he was merely reaping the reward of being a famous composer, no longer in need of attracting an audience. At all events, history can record the reappearance, during the decade of the 1950s, of Copland the introspective, austere, and uncompromising composer. At the beginning of the next decade, the trend was continued with the *Nonet* (1960), which, however, returns to diatonic materials in spite of its use of serial devices. The rather heavy texture of this work has been cleverly characterized (by Eric Salzman) as a kind of "total diatonicism."

Whatever may be the ultimate verdict regarding the intrinsic value of Copland's music, or the degree of attention that posterity may bestow upon his compositions, he remains historically important as a musician who by the diversity and effectiveness of his output, by his impressive impact on America's musical activity at many different points, by his versatility, his adventurousness, and his industry, has participated with extraordinary completeness in the musical events of the contemporary world, not only in the concert hall, the theater, and the classroom, but also in such typical twentieth-century media of mass communication as the radio and the motion picture. Whatever posterity may say, we can only reply: "He was a musician of our times." During the second quarter of the twentieth century, he occupied the foreground of the musical scene.

"Protagonist of the time-spirit"

"Gentlemen, a genius—but keep your hats on!" With this paraphrase of Robert Schumann's excited tribute to Chopin's Opus 1, Arthur Farwell began an article on Roy Harris written in 1931. It was in that year that Harris's Opus 1, a Sonata for piano, appeared in print. The composer could hardly be called precocious, for he was then thirty-three years old. True, he had written a few earlier works, which had already brought him a small measure of recognition; nevertheless at a comparatively mature age he still stood on the threshold of his career as a composer. Farwell, therefore, could approach his music in a spirit of discovery and with the thrill that comes from recognizing genius before it has been generally acclaimed.

Moved by the excitement of discovery, and by a certain "pride of authorship," for Harris had been a pupil of his, Farwell was by no means cautious in his tributes to this rising luminary of America's music. "It may be that he will prove to be the protagonist of the time-spirit," wrote Farwell. And this: "Harris is a straight-out classicist, challenging the entire subsequent epoch, neo-classicists and all, from the primal standpoint of Bach and Beethoven. . . ." Of the orchestral Toccata: "I regard it as one of the greatest emotional and intellectual achievements of modern times." No wonder that Walter Piston, after the publication of this article, found it appropriate to congratulate his colleague for "surviving the trying experience of having been hailed as a genius."

In the light of Harris's unbounded enthusiasm, unabashedly expressed, for his own music, one may be permitted to doubt that he found the experience of being hailed as a genius in the least trying. In the words of Henry Cowell, "Harris often convinces his friends and listeners of the extreme value of his works by his own indefatigable enthusiasm for them." In 1942 he wrote to Nicolas Slonimsky: "I have finished two movements of my Fifth Symphony, and it is wonderful beyond my wildest hopes." Such self-adulation is refreshing, but we need to pick our way carefully among the superlatives.

Roy Harris was born in Lincoln County, Oklahoma, on the anniversary of Lincoln's birth: February 12, 1898. This chronological coincidence, and the fact that the event occurred in a log cabin, are important ingredients of "the Harris legend," which makes him appear as a rugged product of the pioneer Middle West. The family moved to California while he was still a child, and it was there that Harris grew up, on his father's farm. His musical experience consisted chiefly of some sporadic piano lessons and playing the clarinet in a school band. He spent four years working as a truck driver for a California dairy company, exploring music in his spare time and finally, at the age of twenty-four, deciding that he wanted to be a composer. He then went to Los Angeles, where he studied harmony with Farwell and orchestration with Altschuler. His first recognition as a composer came when Howard Hanson conducted his Andante for Orchestra at Rochester in 1926. This was a signal to move on to Paris, where Harris joined the distinguished company of Nadia Boulanger's pupils.

In Paris he wrote a Concerto for piano, clarinet and string quartet, which was performed there in 1927. An accident that resulted in a broken spine caused him to return to the United States, necessitating a serious operation followed by a long convalescence, during which he composed his First String Quartet. After another sojourn in Paris Harris returned to New York, where his music had been performed by the League of Composers; by 1934, when his First Symphony was performed in Boston, he was on the highroad to fame. Koussevitzky's interest in his music gave him an effective start in that direction.

From the beginning, Harris took himself very seriously as a composer. He felt imbued with a sense of destiny and with a feeling of moral responsibility toward his country and his times. In an article entitled "The Growth of a Composer," published in *The Musical Quarterly* for April, 1934, he stated his artistic credo: "The creative impulse is a desire to capture and communicate feeling." This statement is crucial for the appreciation of Harris's music. His compositions have grown out of a yearning for self-expression. But at the same time he feels a cosmic urge to express something beyond himself, and then he speaks of the "search for an understandable race-expression."

Harris has been extremely articulate about his aims as a composer, both in general and in connection with specific works. He has on several occasions tried to establish verbal equations between the American character and American music, and several of his compositions purport to be musical expressions of such equations. In an essay on *Problems of American Composers*, published in 1933, he develops at some length the theory that Americans have rhythmic impulses that are fundamentally different from the rhythmic impulses of Europeans, "and from this unique rhythmic sense are generated different melodic and form values." Attempting to define this American sense of rhythm, he writes:[7]

Our sense of rhythm is less symmetrical than the European rhythmic sense. European musicians are trained to think of rhythm in its largest common denominator, while we are born with a feeling for its smallest units. That is why the jazz boys, chained to an unimaginative commercial routine which serves only crystallized symmetrical dance rhythms, are continually breaking out into superimposed rhythmic variations which were not written into the music. This asymmetrical balancing of rhythmic phrases is in our blood; it is not in the European blood. . . . We do not employ unconventional rhythms as a sophistical gesture; we cannot avoid them. To cut them out of our music would be to gainsay the source of our spontaneous musical impulses. . . . Our struggle is not to invent new rhythms and melodies and forms; our problem is to put down into translatable symbols and rhythms and consequent melodies and form those that assert themselves within us.

As regards harmonic idiom in American music, Harris has this to say:

American composers have not as yet developed any predominant type of harmonic idiom, but I have noticed two tendencies that are becoming increasingly prevalent both with our commercial jazz writers and with our more serious composers: (1) the avoidance of definite cadence, which can be traced to our unsymmetrically balanced melodies (difficult to harmonize with prepared cadences) and our national aversion to anything final, our hope and search for more satisfying conclusions; (2) the use of modal harmony, which probably comes from ennui of the worn-out conventions of the major and minor scales and our adventurous love of the exotic.

It is typical of Harris's musical metaphysics that he ascribes an alleged avoidance of definite cadence to an alleged national aversion of any-

[7] The three quotations that follow are from *American Composers on American Music*, edited by Henry Cowell. Reprinted with permission of the publishers, Stanford University Press. Copyright 1933 by the Board of Trustees of Leland Stanford Junior University. Originally published in *Scribner's*.

thing final, which in turn is equated with our hope and search for something more satisfying.

Harris has been much concerned with the "social value" of music. In the same essay he writes:

> Musical literature never has been and never will be valuable to society as a whole until it is created as an authentic and characteristic culture of and from the people it expresses. History reveals that the great music has been produced only by staunch individuals who sank their roots deeply into the social soil which they accepted as their own.

There is ample evidence to indicate that Harris considers himself to be one of those "staunch individuals" who are creating an authentic and characteristic musical expression of American culture. He has made this clear in the commentaries he has appended to several of his scores. Let us now briefly review his major works, beginning with the symphonies.

The compositions of Roy Harris

The *Symphony, 1933*, his first, was performed by the Boston Symphony orchestra on January 26, 1934, under the direction of Koussevitzky, who called it "the first truly tragic symphony by an American." The composer gave the following summary of its three movements: "In the first movement I have tried to capture the mood of adventure and physical exuberance; in the second, of the pathos which seems to underlie all human existence; in the third, the will to power and action."

The Second Symphony, performed by the same orchestra on February 28, 1936, also consists of three movements, of which the first is a sort of bravura introduction, the second (Molto cantabile) a "study in canons," and the third a "study in rhythmic developments," which is again intended to convey "a feeling of power." The emphasis on canonic writing is characteristic of Harris, with whom canon and fugue are favorite devices.

With the performance of his Third Symphony by Koussevitzky and the Boston Symphony Orchestra on February 24, 1939, Harris achieved a resounding triumph. Its success was sensational. Within a year it received ten performances by the Boston Symphony alone, in various cities. According to Leichtentritt, thirty-three performances were given by American orchestras during the season of 1941–1942, in addition to several performances abroad.

The Third Symphony is a relatively brief work, in one continuous movement, with a duration of approximately seventeen minutes. The composer has provided the following outline of its musical structure divided into five sections:

    I. Tragic—low string sonorities
   II. Lyric—strings, horns, woodwinds
  III. Pastoral—woodwinds with a polytonal string background
  IV. Fugue—dramatic
      A. Brass and percussion predominating
      B. Canonic development of materials from Section II constituting background for further development of Fugue
   V. Dramatic—tragic
      A. Restatement of violin theme of Section I: tutti strings in canon with tutti woodwinds against brass and percussion developing rhythmic motif from climax of Section IV.
      B. Coda—development of materials from Sections I and II over pedal tympani

It will be noticed that the emphasis is upon strictly musical structure, combined with generalized emotional situations devoid of programmatic or descriptive connotations.

On February 21, 1941, the Boston Symphony Orchestra gave the first performance of Harris's fourth symphony, the *Folk Song Symphony* for chorus and orchestra, in which his musical Americanism finds literal expression through the use of American folk songs. It was written, moreover, with the intent "to bring about a cultural cooperation and understanding between the high school, college and community choruses of our cities with their symphonic orchestras." The folk tunes are taken from the collections of John and Alan Lomax and Carl Sandburg. The symphony consists of five choral sections and two instrumental interludes.

After a performance of the *Folk Song Symphony* in Cleveland, Herbert Elwell wrote, "This music is nothing if not 100% U.S.A." Henry Simon aptly described it as "not so much a symphony as a little concert of Americana."

In his Fifth Symphony, performed on February 26, 1943 (inevitably by the Boston Symphony), Harris clung to his obsession of expressing the American character in music. He wanted to portray qualities "which our popular dance music, because of its very nature, cannot reveal." And the composer's comments continue:

Our people are more than pleasure-loving. We also have qualities of heroic strength—determination—will to struggle—faith in our destiny. We are possessed of a fierce driving power—optimistic, young, rough and ready—and I am convinced that our mechanistic age has not destroyed an appreciation of more tender moods. . . .

The Fifth Symphony opens with a somewhat martial introduction, followed by a chorale movement "in singing choral style, yet rhapsodic." The last movement consists of a triple fugue, that is, it is in three sections and on three subjects, with interpolated material, the whole of considerable structural complexity. This work represents an advance in technical mastery over the Third Symphony.

The Sixth Symphony (performed April 14, 1944, Boston Symphony) is another essay in musical Americana, this time based on Lincoln's Gettysburg Address, and dedicated to "the Armed Forces of Our Nation." The four movements of the symphony are titled, respectively, "Awakening," "Conflict," "Dedication," "Affirmation"—episodes that the composer conceives as making up "that great cycle which always attends any progress in the intellectual or spiritual growth of a people," and which he considers as finding "a classic expression" in the Gettysburg Address. The last movement of the Sixth Symphony, again, is cast in the structure of a fugue, by which the composer has endeavored to "reflect in architectural terms the mood of strong faith in mankind." This is an example of Harris's attempt to make musical structure serve the programmatic purpose of his symphony.

The one-movement Seventh Symphony (1952) is a richly orchestrated ragout with bits of everything that appeals to Harris, from solemn funeral marches and folksy hymnlike tunes to touches of ragtime and rumba rhythms. The Eighth Symphony followed in 1961, commissioned for the "golden anniversary" of the San Francisco Symphony Orchestra. For his Ninth (1962) the composer turned to the preamble of the Constitution of the United States and the poetry of Walt Whitman for help in being 100 per cent American while still trying "to achieve a dynamic form."

Harris also wrote what he calls a *Symphony for Voices* (In Three

Movements) for full chorus of mixed voices, on poems of Walt Whitman; a setting of Whitman's *A Song of Occupations* for eight-part mixed chorus; and a *Whitman-Triptych* for chorus of women's voices *a cappella* (*I Hear America Singing; An Evening Lull; America*). If ever there was a spiritual affinity between a composer and a poet, it is to be found in Harris and Whitman.

One of Harris's most overt expressions of musical Americanism is the Overture *When Johnny Comes Marching Home* (1934), in which he was concerned "to express a gamut of emotions particularly American and in an American manner." All in all, he is the composer who has worked hardest to be an "Americanist."

A strong case could be made for regarding the piano and chamber music of Roy Harris as being the best of his production. Besides the two Piano Sonatas, there are the Sextet for Piano and Winds; the Three Variations on a Theme for String Quartet; the Trio for Violin, Cello, and Piano; and the Piano Quintet—all works written before 1940—in which his finest qualities are concentrated.

Assorted Americanists

John Alden Carpenter (1876–1951), a pupil of J. K. Paine at Harvard, and like Charles Ives, a businessman by profession, was one of the first American composers to experiment with the use of jazz inflections. He employed ragtime rhythms in his Concertino for piano and orchestra, composed in 1915, several years before the vogue for "symphonic jazz." Another experiment in the popular idiom was the ballet or "jazz pantomime" titled *Krazy Kat* (1921), inspired by the newspaper comic strip of that name. The success of this work brought a commission from Diaghilev, the impresario of ballet, to write a score employing the American musical vernacular and depicting some typical aspect of American life. Carpenter responded with *Skyscrapers*, "a ballet of modern American life," which was produced at the Metropolitan Opera House in New York on February 19, 1926. These works were symptomatic of the "Jazz Age." They now appear to us as period pieces. Carpenter's musical Americanism was largely of the surface; his style was wholly dominated by French impressionistic influences. Although he wrote symphonies, choral works, songs, and chamber music, he will perhaps be best remembered for his amusing descriptive suite for orchestra, *Adventures in a Perambulator* (1914).

Douglas Moore (*b.* 1893) is an Americanist above all by his operas, which are discussed in Chapter 30. But he should also be mentioned here because of other contributions to musical Americana, such as *The Pageant of P. T. Barnum* (1924), a suite for orchestra in five episodes ending with "Circus Parade," *Moby Dick* (1928), symphonic poem after the famous novel by Melville; *Overture on an American Tune* (1931), a musical portrait of Babbitt, the typical American businessman of Sinclair Lewis's novel; *Village Music* (1942) and *Farm Journal* (1947), both for orchestra; *The Ballad of William Sycamore* (poem by Stephen Vincent Benét), for baritone solo, flute, trombone, and piano; and *Down East Suite,* for violin and piano.

William Grant Still has been concerned mainly with depicting the backgrounds of the American Negro in music. Born in Woodville, Mississippi, in 1893, he was raised in Little Rock, Arkansas, where his mother taught school. His racial heritage includes Indian, Negro, and European strains. Becoming a composer of "serious" music was not an easy task for Still. After considerable knocking about at odd jobs, he obtained a scholarship to study composition at Oberlin College. Later he became an arranger for W. C. Handy in New York, where he also studied composition with the modernist Edgard Varèse. Playing in theater and night-club orchestras, and arranging popular music, gave him another variety of musical experience. Out of this varied background, Still began to compose symphonic works influenced by Afro-American traditions: *Darker America* (1924); *From the Black Belt,* for chamber orchestra (1926); *Africa* (1930); *Afro-American Symphony* (1931); and the Second Symphony in G minor (1937), subtitled "Song of a New Race" and described as an expression of "the American colored man of today."

Still has written the operas *Blue Steel* (1935) and *Troubled Island* (1949). Haiti is the setting of *Troubled Island*, which deals with the life of the Emperor Dessalines, whose brief moment of power and glory had a tragic ending. The libretto is by the Negro poet Langston Hughes. The West Indies, Africa, and Harlem, provide the settings for three ballets by Still. *Sahdji* (1931) has its scene in ancestral Africa and calls for a chorus that comments on the action, also a bass chanter who recites African proverbs. *La Guiablesse* (1933), with its stage locale on the island of Martinique, uses West Indian and Louisiana Creole material. The third ballet, *Lenox Avenue* (1937), depicts scenes in the Negro section of New York; from this score the composer extracted an impressionistic *Blues* for piano. Two of Still's most impressive works are the cantata *And They Lynched Him on a Tree* (1940) for contralto, mixed chorus, orchestra, and narrator; and *In Memoriam: The Colored Soldiers Who Died for Democracy* (1943).

Ross Lee Finney (born in Wells, Minnesota, in 1906) not only used American folk songs in some of his compositions—for example, the String Quartet in G minor (1941)—but also turned to the historical heritage of America's music in *Pilgrim Psalms* (1945) and *Hymn, Fuging, and Rondo* (1943; originally titled *Variations, Fugueing, and Rondo*). He paid tribute to that early American music lover Benjamin Franklin in the cycle of seven songs for high voice with piano titled *Poor Richard* (with texts from *Poor Richard's Almanac*).

The *Pilgrim Psalms*, for tenor, soprano, orchestra of strings and brasses, and mixed chorus, are settings of fourteen tunes from the *Ainsworth Psalter*. The composer states that his treatment of these tunes "springs both from the old melodies and from my own emotional feelings." The concluding Psalm calls for the participation of the audience.

The *Hymn, Fuging, and Rondo*, for orchestra, resulted from Finney's keen interest in the music of the early New England composer William Billings. The unifying theme in this composition is derived from a hymn tune by Billings called "Berlin." The whole work, as described by the composer, is

. . . a triptych held together by, and commenting on, this early style. The first panel is a set of variations on the hymn, developed in a free melodic manner rather than harmonically. These variations are balanced by the last panel, a Rondo which is vigorous and harmonic. Between these, and linked together by a reference to the hymn, are two contrasting panels in fugato style: the first—naively, perhaps—a picture of hell-fire and brimstone; the second, pastoral and elegiac. The whole is framed by the Billings hymn.

Henry Cowell (1897–1965) also turned to the tradition of the early American hymn and the "fuging" or "fuguing" tune (the first spelling is more colloquial) for many of his most important contributions to musical Americana. Thoroughly familiar with this tradition, he assimilated its principal stylistic traits and transmuted them into a contemporary though conservative instrumental expression. Under the generic title of *Hymns and Fuguing Tunes*, Cowell, from 1942 to 1957, wrote a series of pieces for a variety of instrumental media, ranging from piano solo (No. 1) to full orchestra (No. 3). No. 1 was also arranged for symphonic band. No. 4 is listed permissively as being "for recorders or any 3 voices or instruments." No. 12 is for the unusual combination of three horns. Several of the *Hymns and Fuguing Tunes* were incorporated in Cowell's symphonies: No. 5 was expanded to become two movements of Symphony No. 10 (1952–1953); No. 6, for piano, was incorporated into the last movement of Symphony No. 4 (1946); material from *Hymn, Chorale, and Fuguing Tune* No. 8, for string quartet, was used in Symphony No. 10; while Symphony No. 9 made use of material from *Hymn and Fuguing Tune* No. 9 (1950), for cello and piano. Hence this important American tradition permeates a very substantial portion of Cowell's instrumental and symphonic production.

Of Cowell we are told that "part of his childhood was spent among fiddling and ballad-singing relatives on Kansas, Iowa, and Oklahoma farms, so that he absorbed the prevalent Irish-American idiom very early." This formative experience was followed by a life-long interest in, and study of, the folk music of the United States and other parts of the world, especially of the Near and Far East. Cowell's rural background is reflected in his *Old American Country Set* for orchestra (1937), consisting of "Blarneying Lilt," "Comallye," "Charivari" (pronounced *Shivaree*), "Meeting House," and "Cornhuskers' Hornpipe." In somewhat similar vein are *Pastorale and Fiddler's Delight* and *Saturday Night at the Firehouse*, both for orchestra.

One of our most genuine "Americanists," Cowell is also an innovator of great importance and an eclectic of universal scope; hence he figures not only in this chapter, but in Chapter 27, "Innovation and experiment," as well.

Ernst Bacon (born in Chicago in 1898) has been especially attracted by the heritage of Anglo-American folk songs, some of which he arranged in a collection called *Along Unpaved Roads*. He has also evoked the historical past of the United States in the orchestral suites *Ford's Theatre* and *From these States*. Two "folk operas," *A Tree on the Plains* (1942) and *A Drumlin Legend*, likewise have American settings.

Elie Siegmeister (born in New York City in 1909) has been a consistent Americanist both in his stage works (*Doodle Dandy of the U.S.A.; Sing Out, Sweet Land; Darling Corie*) and in his instrumental and vocal compositions. Among the former are *A Walt Whit-*

man Overture (1939), *Lonesome Hollow,* and *Sunday in Brooklyn* (for orchestra). His vocal works include *Abraham Lincoln Walks at Midnight,* for chorus; and *Strange Funeral in Braddock,* for solo voice and orchestra (1933).

Another native of New York City, Morton Gould (*b.* 1913), has cultivated a wide diversity of musical Americana, ranging from derivatives of jazz to tap dancing. His compositions in the jazz-blues orbit include *Chorale and Fugue in Jazz* (1933), *Swing Symphonietta, Boogie-Woogie Etude,* and *Big City Blues* (1950). *The Concerto for Tap Dancer and Orchestra* dates from 1952. Other types of Americana are exploited in *A Foster Gallery* (1940), *Cowboy Rhapsody* (1944), *Spirituals* (1941), *Minstrel Show* (1946), and *Fall River Legend* (1948, a ballet based on the Lizzie Borden axe murders). One of his most ambitious efforts is *A Lincoln Legend* for orchestra (1942). Even when the title does not reveal an overt Americanism, this may be proclaimed in the music itself, as is the case with Concerto for Orchestra (1945), characterized as "boisterously Americanistic."

Jerome Moross, born in Brooklyn, New York, in 1913, cultivated musical Americana most notably in his ballets: *Paul Bunyan: American Saga* (1936), *American Pattern* (1937), and especially *Frankie and Johnny* (The Scandalous Life of), commissioned by Ruth Page, who produced it for a six-weeks' run in Chicago in 1938. Acquired by the Ballet Russe de Monte Carlo in 1945, it was revived in Paris in 1950 with sensational effect. *Frankie and Johnny* puts on the stage the most celebrated and enduring of the "hard-boiled" American folk ballads: an "eternal triangle" of the underworld. The score seethes with stomps, blues, rags, fox-trots, and one-steps (for the funeral finale, when everybody gets drunk). The orchestral suite from the ballet music consists of an Introduction and Seven Dances, each of which is related to an episode of the fateful events attending the shooting of the faithless Johnny by the discarded Frankie. The shooting itself is done to the strains of a fox-trot. Throughout the ballet, a Salvation Army lass wanders on stage, beating a bass drum, tambourine, and cymbal, and commenting on the action.

Ernest Bloch's *America*

One of the most fervid manifestations of musical Americanism is the work of the Swiss-born composer Ernest Bloch (1880–1959) titled

America and described as "an epic rhapsody in three parts for orchestra." The score has the following dedication:

This Symphony has been written in love for this country/In reverence to its Past—In Faith in its Future/It is dedicated to the memory of Abraham Lincoln and Walt Whitman, whose vision upheld its inspiration.

Bloch's *America* was completed in 1927, eleven years after the composer first came to the United States. It received a mixed critical reception and has not entrenched itself very firmly in the symphonic repertoire. Nevertheless, the intent and scope of the work entitle it to more than casual attention.

The epic rhapsody *America* is an attempt to summarize and express in music the essential historical role and destiny of the United States of America. It applies the epic style to musical composition, relying on broad and massive effects, and on the impact of the work as a whole rather than on the refinements or distinction of any of its component parts. In a prefatory note to the score, the composer wrote:

The Ideals of America are imperishable. They embody the future credo of all mankind: a Union, in common purpose and under willingly accepted guidance, of widely diversified races, ultimately to become one race, strong and great.

The score has running explanatory references at the bottom of the pages, which are intended to clarify the composer's intentions. Part I begins with the year 1620. It evokes the soil, the Indians, the *Mayflower*, the landing of the Pilgrims, primeval nature, and Indian life (with quotation of Indian tribal melodies). Part II covers the period of the Civil War, 1861–1865, and bears the subheading "Hours of Joy—Hours of Sorrow." In this section there are musical quotations from "Old Folks at Home," Virginia reels, "Hail Columbia," Creole folk songs, "Dixie," "Battle Cry of Freedom," "John Brown's Body," and "Tramp, Tramp, Tramp." Part III, bearing the date 1926, evokes the spirit of the present and the future. Two Negro folk songs are quoted: "I Went to the Hop Joint" and "The Coon-can Game." There is a section reflecting the "turmoil of the present time," the speed and noise of the Machine Age.

The next episode depicts the mastery of Man over the machines, his environment, and himself. The call of America to the nations of the world leads to the climax of "The Fulfillment Through Love," and at this moment the people (i.e., the audience) rise to sing the anthem that the composer has incorporated in the score:[8]

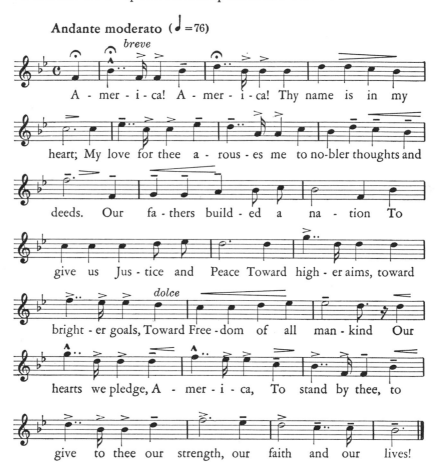

Andante moderato (♩=76)

A - mer - i - ca! A - mer - i - ca! Thy name is in my heart; My love for thee a - rous - es me to no-bler thoughts and deeds. Our fa - thers build - ed a na - tion To give us Jus - tice and Peace Toward high - er aims, toward bright - er goals, Toward Free - dom of all man - kind Our hearts we pledge, A - mer - i - ca, To stand by thee, to give to thee our strength, our faith and our lives!

As the composer explains, the symphony is based entirely upon the anthem, which "from the first bars appears, in root, dimly, slowly taking shape, rising, falling, developing, and finally asserting itself victoriously in its complete and decisive form. . . . The Anthem . . . symbolizes the Destiny, the Mission of America."

Critics tend to sneer at Bloch's *America* as the aberration of a great composer; they point to its naiveté and allege its inferiority as a work of art. They are deaf to its moral grandeur, its epic sweep,

[8] From the symphony *America* by Ernest Bloch, C. C. Birchard & Company, Publishers. Used by permission.

its emotional fervor. Whatever the ultimate verdict may be on this work, it remains as a significant historical document, reflecting a moment of history when much of the world looked to America as the best hope of mankind.

The era of Americanism was a heroic age in the musical history of the United States. Initiated around the turn of the century by such men as Farwell and Gilbert, it reached its apogee in the two decades from 1920 to 1940 and thereafter declined; by mid-century it was no longer a vital force. Its chief representatives—Cowell, Harris, Thomson, Gershwin, Copland—produced a greater number of viable works than any previous generation of American composers. Together with Charles Ives they created an American art music that was heard around the world.

chapter twenty-five

The eclectics

*All music is a tone experience. . . . . All human music should be close to us
. . . irrespective of race or epoch.*
DANE RUDHYAR IN AMERICAN COMPOSERS ON AMERICAN MUSIC.

Eclecticism, in philosophy, is a system composed of doctrines selected
from different sources. By analogy, an eclectic composer is one who
selects his material from various sources. To a certain extent all creative
artists are eclectic, because an artist does not derive his material or
develop his style solely from one source or tradition. This is particularly true of modern artists, who, to begin with, have all the sources
and traditions of the past to draw on; and in addition, thanks to the
greatly developed facilities for cultural interchange, have at their
disposal the materials and resources pertaining to all the cultural systems of the world.

Eclecticism in music, therefore, scarcely serves to define a specific
school or group of composers, especially in the United States, where
eclecticism is the norm rather than the exception. We are a nation
made from many sources and many cultures. An American composer
can be thoroughly eclectic even without seeking material beyond the
borders of his own country. He can draw on the music of the Indian
and of the Negro, on the heritage of Anglo-American folk song, on the
Hispanic tradition of the Southwest, on the tradition of rural hymnody
and on the various types of popular music, from ragtime to boogiewoogie. Many of the composers dealt with in other chapters of this
book, among them Arthur Farwell, Henry Gilbert, George Gershwin,
Henry Cowell, and Aaron Copland, are markedly eclectic, and what
we have done is simply to emphasize certain prominent trends within
their eclectic tendency, such as the folklorism of Farwell and the
Americanism of Gershwin. In this chapter we shall deal with com-

518

posers whose music represents divergent trends, and who have little in common with one another except a marked tendency toward eclecticism.

The first of these composers is Charles Tomlinson Griffes (1884–1920), whose predominant tendency might be described as exotic eclecticism. Griffes began by assimilating the technique of German song writers, veered to the impressionism of Debussy and the primitivism of Stravinsky, underwent the influence of the arch-eclectic Busoni, made more than a passing bow to the Russian "Five," turned briefly to American Indian themes, and found a congenial source of material in the music of the Far East. Throughout these avatars he maintained a personal style and developed a power of expression that entitle him to a distinctive place among the creative musicians of America. That he died before achieving his full creative development seems probable; that he suffered from material handicaps in his career as a composer is certain; and that his music reveals technical weaknesses may be conceded. Yet alone for such works as *The Pleasure Dome of Kubla Khan*, the *Poem* for flute and orchestra, and the Sonata for piano, his place is secure.

Charles T. Griffes was born in Elmira, New York, on September 17, 1884. At an early age he displayed a remarkable sensitivity for color, a trait that remained with him as a composer, for he came to associate certain keys with certain colors. His musical aptitude was at first channeled in the direction of becoming a concert pianist, and upon the advice of his teacher he went to Europe in 1903 to complete his training at the Stern Conservatory in Berlin. He remained in Germany four years, except for two brief visits to his home. He became increasingly interested in composing, in spite of the fact that his teacher tore up the first song that he submitted—perhaps because it was in French. He rebelled against the "terribly ordinary and common" modulations recommended by the pedantic professor at the Conservatory, and was happier when he managed to have some lessons in composition with the gifted Humperdinck, composer of the opera *Hansel and Gretel*.

When Griffes returned to the United States in 1907 the only immediate solution he could find for the problem of earning a living was to accept a position as music teacher at the Hackley School for boys in Tarrytown, New York. It was not a congenial situation. Of his pupils he wrote, "Oh! how they bore and weary me!" Nevertheless he was destined to remain at this school for the rest of his life.

As a composer, Griffes was befriended and encouraged by that generous and broad-visioned champion of American music, Arthur Farwell. After his early settings of German songs, he began to set poems by American and English authors, including Sidney Lanier ("Evening Song"), Sara Teasdale, and Oscar Wilde. He wrote a series of impressionistic piano pieces: *The Lake at Evening* (1910), *The Night Winds* (1911), *The Vale of Dreams* (1912), *Barcarolle* (1912), and *Scherzo* (1913).

Early in 1912 Griffes began to compose a work for piano based on Coleridge's poem "Kubla Khan." After frequent revisions over several years he finally decided that it would be more effective as an orchestral composition. In this form it was completed in April, 1916. But not until November 28, 1919, just a few months before the composer's death, did this symphonic poem receive its first performance.

Regarding this symphonic poem, Griffes wrote:

> I have taken as a basis for my work those lines of Coleridge's poem describing the "stately pleasure-dome," the "sunny pleasure-dome with caves of ice," the "miracle of rare device." Therefore I call the work *The Pleasure-Dome of Kubla Khan* rather than *Kubla Khan*. . . . As to argument, I have given my imagination free rein in the description of this strange palace as well as of purely imaginary revelry which might take place there. The vague, foggy beginning suggests the sacred river, running "through caverns measureless to man down to a sunless sea." The gardens with fountains and "sunny spots of greenery" are next suggested. From inside come sounds of dancing and revelry which increase to a wild climax and then suddenly break off. There is a return to the original mood suggesting the sacred river and the "caves of ice."

The passages in Coleridge's poem to which Griffes specifically refers consist of lines 1 to 11 and lines 32 to 36.

In 1915 Griffes composed his piano piece *The White Peacock*, based on a poem of that title by "Fiona Macleod," the pseudonym of a Scottish writer named William Sharp who, in the early years of the century, did much to stimulate what Gilman called "the Celtic impulse" among American composers, including MacDowell. Actually, there was nothing Celtic about a white peacock, and Griffes eventually included his tone poem in a set of four piano pieces entitled *Roman Sketches* (the other three pieces are "Nightfall," "The Fountain of Acqua Paola," and "Clouds"). *The White Peacock* was orchestrated by the composer for a choreographic number staged by Adolph Bolm at the Rivoli Theatre in New York, which ran for a week beginning on June 22, 1919. Both as a piano piece and as an orchestral tone poem, *The White Peacock* obtained wide acceptance.

Griffes felt a strong attraction for the music of the Near and Far East. While working on *Kubla Khan* he consulted all the works on Arabian music in the New York Public Library, and copied out some melodies that appealed to him. His tendency toward Orientalism was further developed in his settings for voice and piano of *Five Poems of Ancient China and Japan,* and in the writing of a Japaneses dance drama, *Sho-Jo,* for the dancer Michio Ito, based on Japanese melodies given to him by the singer Eva Gauthier (1917).

The *Poem for Flute and Orchestra,* finished in 1918, is one of Griffes's best works and marks the culmination of his Orientalism. It is, to be sure, an impressionistic and highly attenuated Orientalism, which strives for atmospheric coloring rather than for ethnographic authenticity (such as we find later, for example, in the music of Colin McPhee).

Griffes also turned briefly to American Indian music, in his *Two Sketches Based on Indian Themes* for string quartet. The first of these, Scherzo, was composed in 1916; the second, Lento, in 1918, utilizing for its main theme a farewell song of the Chippewa:

In February, 1917, a dance drama with music by Griffes, titled *The Kairn of Koridwen,* was produced in New York. The music was scored for piano, celesta, flute, clarinets, horns, and harp. This small combination acted as a challenge to the composer's resourcefulness, and he made the most of it. In the words of Paul Rosenfeld: "The unusual conjunction of timbres, split horn and piano, chromatic harp, chromatic flute and celesta, the happy superposition of conflicting tonalities, the knitting of strongly contrary rhythms that abound throughout the work, should make a musicians' holiday." Actually there was so much trouble over the rehearsals and the production that it gave the musicians, including the composer, a headache rather than a holiday.

Griffes's Sonata for piano, completed in January, 1918 (revised in May, 1919), although influenced by the harmonic idiom of Scriabin, is on the whole his most original as well as most ambitious and complex work. Of relatively short duration (fifteen minutes), it is divided into three movements: Feroce-Allegretto con moto, Molto tranquillo, and Allegro vivace. In general, its form is that of the classic-romantic sonata, and its originality resides in the experimental use of tonality and in the structural unity derived from the characteristic intervals that appear in its various themes. Richly expressive, exotic in harmonic color, strongly emotional, with no padding or empty rhetorical gestures, the Piano Sonata may be regarded as a peak of neoromantic expression in American music.

Of the composers of his generation, none has better withstood time's attrition than Charles Griffes. His major works are American classics; his songs are among the best we have.

Eclectics of the immediate past

Henry Kimball Hadley (1871–1937) was a native of Somerville, Massachusetts, and a pupil of Chadwick at the New England Conservatory of Music. He also received a polishing in counterpoint from Mandyczewski in Vienna, which assured his success in the United States. And he was indeed the most successful American composer of his time, judged in terms of performance, publication, acceptance, and prestige. The fact that he was very active as a conductor also helped, since he frequently conducted his own compositions, sometimes in such remote centers as Buenos Aires and Tokyo. His one-act opera *Safie* (1909) was produced at the Municipal Opera in Mainz, Germany, while he happened to be conducting there. After five years in Germany (1904–1909) he returned to the United States, where he conducted orchestras, successively, in Seattle, San Francisco, and New York. He was one of the founders of the Berkshire Music Festival.

In his five symphonies, Hadley covered the span of human life

(No. 1, *Youth and Life*), the seasons of the year (No. 2, *The Four Seasons*), the cardinal points of the compass (No. 4, *North, East, South, West*), the key of B minor (No. 3), and a large slice of American history (No. 5, *Connecticut Tercentenary*, with its three movements dated, respectively, "1635," "1735," and "1935"). His tone poems portrayed such colorful characters as *Salomé* (1905) and *Lucifer* (1913), while his orchestral suites took the armchair tourist from *San Francisco* to *The Streets of Pekin*, with side trips via the *Oriental Suite* (1903). Leaving the sea to Debussy, he devoted his orchestral palette to *The Ocean* (1921), that mighty monster that has swallowed up so many symphonic poems. Of his numerous cantatas, *Ode to Music* was performed at the Worcester Festival in England, while *Resurgam* was heard in Queen's Hall, London, under the composer's direction. Of his operas, the most ambitious were *Azora, Daughter of Montezuma* (Chicago Opera Company, December 26, 1917), and *Cleopatra's Night* (Metropolitan Opera House, New York, January 31, 1920). Hadley also wrote a quantity of chamber music and over 150 songs.

Frederick Shepherd Converse (1871–1940) was a pupil of Paine at Harvard but also studied with Chadwick in Boston and with Rheinberger in Germany. He was for many years on the faculty of the New England Conservatory of Music. He wrote three symphonies and many other symphonic works, as well as the first opera by an American to be produced at the Metropolitan Opera House, *The Pipe of Desire* (1910). In 1918 he wrote a tone poem about a land that must have seemed very exotic to a native of Newton, Massachusetts—*California*. He went on to depict other aspects of the American scene in the orchestral suite *American Sketches* (1929), but his masterpiece in this line was the symphonic poem *Flivver Ten Million* (1927). This work depicts, in successive episodes, "Dawn in Detroit," "The Birth of the Hero," "May Night by the Roadside" ("America's Romance"), "The Joy Riders" ("America's Frolic"), "The Collision" ("America's Tragedy"), and "Phoenix Americanus," an apotheosis of "the indomitable American spirit."

David Stanley Smith (1877–1949), a native of Toledo, Ohio, studied with Horatio Parker at Yale and in 1920 succeeded him as Dean of the School of Music at that university. His approach to music was intellectual and traditionalistic within the academic convention. In addition to four symphonies and other orchestral works, such as *Fête Galante* for flute and orchestra, Smith wrote a large quantity of chamber music, including eight string quartets, and several choral works, among which are *The Vision of Isaiah* (1927) and *Daybreak* (1945). In two orchestral pieces, *1929—A Satire* and the overture *Tomorrow*, dating respectively from 1932 and 1933, he recorded his impressions of the world around him—as viewed from a comfortably protective academic niche. His compositions, in which all the trends of the time are deftly assimilated, are typical of the "professors' music" of their day: correct, occasionally useful (*Ode for Commencement Day*), genteel (*Flowers*, for chamber orchestra), edifying (*Vision of Isaiah*, for chorus), and generally inconsequential.

Arthur Shepherd (1880–1958) was born in Paris, Idaho, the son of English converts to Mormonism who had emigrated to the West in the 1870s. At the age of twelve he was sent to Boston to study at the New England Conservatory of Music. In the words of William Newman: "During the five years that followed in Boston the formal part of the training was as German as it might have been at Leipzig"— where his parents had originally considered sending him. Strong eclectic inclinations saved Shepherd from accepting late German music as the sole pathway to salvation. After periods of teaching in Salt Lake City and Boston, he became assistant conductor of the Cleveland Symphony Orchestra. He then joined the music staff of Western Reserve University in Cleveland, serving as chairman of the Music Department from 1933 to 1948.

Shepherd became interested in modern French music, particularly that of Fauré and d'Indy, and in the national folklore movement led by Farwell and Gilbert. He himself confessed that he seemed to have a strong atavistic tendency toward writing tunes "with a pronounced Celtic flavor." His First Symphony, completed in 1927 and titled *Horizons: Four Western Pieces for Symphony Orchestra* (later the composer stated that he wished this work to be known as *Nature Symphony*), is an impressive embodiment of the spirit of the West in music. It consists of four movements: "Westward," "The Lone Prairie," "The Old Chisholm Trail," and "Canyons." The second movement makes use of the cowboy song known as "The Dying Cowboy" ("O bury me not on the lone prairee"). The last movement includes a chorale derived from a hymn of the Western pioneers.

In 1946 Shepherd composed a *Fantasia on Down East Spirituals*, described as "an excursion into the realm of American folk tunes." But his main preoccupation has not been with musical Americana.

His eclectic tendencies are revealed in an extensive catalogue of works in many forms, outstanding among which are his Symphony No. 2 (1940), Violin Concerto (1946–1947), String Quartet in E Minor, Quintet for piano and strings, *Triptych* for soprano and string quartet, Second Piano Sonata, Psalm 42 for chorus and orchestra, and some two dozen songs.

Marion Bauer (1887–1955), the most distinguished American woman composer of her generation, was strongly attracted toward impressionism (*Four Songs with String Quartet, Orientale* for soprano and orchestra, *Fantasia Quasi una Sonata* for violin and piano). But she also assimilated a variety of exotic elements, ranging from American Indian (*Sun Splendor* and *Indian Pipes* for orchestra) to African (*Lament on African Themes,* for chamber orchestra, 1928). She bowed to the neoclassical trend in her *Concertino* for oboe, clarinet, and string quartet (1939–1943). Active as teacher and author, she wrote *Twentieth Century Music* (1933).

Frederick Jacobi (1891–1953) was a native of San Francisco who lived in New York for most of his life. Around 1917–1918 he became deeply interested in the music of the Pueblo Indians, which he studied in Arizona and New Mexico and which he used in his *String Quartet on Indian Themes* (1924) and *Indian Dances* for orchestra (1928). In 1923 he composed *Two Assyrian Prayers,* for soprano or tenor and orchestra. Besides admirable chamber music he composed concertos for cello, for violin, and for piano with orchestra, and several Hebraic services (*Friday Evening Synagogical Service,* 1930; *Sabbath Evening Service,* 1952).

"An intensely serious composer"

Although Roger Sessions was born in Brooklyn, New York, on December 28, 1896, that borough was not his natural habitat. His parents were from New England, and he evidently inherited the intellectual precocity associated with that region, for he wrote an opera at the age of twelve and entered Harvard at the age of fourteen. After four years in Cambridge he acquired an additional cultural patina by studying composition with Horatio Parker at Yale. Thus qualified, he obtained a teaching position at Smith College and proceeded to compose. But something was lacking; he felt the need to strike a deeper vein. The opportunity came when he met Ernest Bloch and undertook further study in composition with him. This "shock of recognition"—the answer to what he had been seeking intuitively—proved decisive for Sessions. When Bloch went to Cleveland in 1921, Sessions followed him there. Four years later, when Bloch left Cleveland, Sessions went to Europe and spent the next eight years in Florence, Rome, and Berlin. Following his return to the United States he held various teaching posts, and in 1935 was appointed to the music faculty of Princeton University. Ten years later he went to the University of California in Berkeley, but in 1953 returned to Princeton. In 1959 he became one of the co-directors of the Electronic Music Center of Columbia and Princeton Universities.

One critic assures us that Sessions derives from Stravinsky, while another hailed him as an "American Brahms." If both are right, the result is an amazing conciliation of opposites, and this argues a strong character. And that is exactly what distinguishes the music of Sessions: strength of character. He has deeply absorbed certain influences, notably those of Bloch, Stravinsky, Schoenberg, and Richard Strauss. His creative personality, the interior dynamism that prompts him to emotional expression in music, is strong enough to absorb these influences and to emerge with a mode of utterance that is as personal as it is eclectic.

We may unhesitatingly agree with Mark Schubart that Sessions is "an intensely serious composer." He takes with the utmost seriousness every aspect of musical art: the theoretical, the creative, the didactic, and the interpretative. The fruits of his cogitations are found not only in his compositions and his teaching, but also in two books that he has published: *The Musical Experience of Composer, Performer, Listener* (1950) and *Harmonic Practice* (1951). The latter, of course, is a textbook intended for classroom use. In it the author acknowledges his indebtedness to Iwan Knorr, Heinrich Schenker, Paul Hindemith, and Arnold Schoenberg. Regarding the last-mentioned he writes: "It becomes always clearer that the influence of this truly extraordinary man is not limited to his most immediate or obvious followers, but has had a far-reaching effect on friend and foe alike. His *Harmonielehre*, many later writings, and above all his music, have set in motion trains of thought, as they have opened new avenues of musical sensibility, of human awareness—in a word, of musical experience—which are at the very least a challenge to all musicians of today."[1]

[1] Quoted by permission of the publisher, Harcourt, Brace and Company, New York.

The last chapter of Sessions's text on harmony, "Introduction to Contemporary Harmonic Practice," is a valuable analysis of recent trends in composition, including the problem of tonality, and should be read by anyone seriously interested in the subject. In discussing various technical problems of today, he reminds us that, now as always, "It is never a question of applying a formula, but of solving a problem, in each case, in accordance with the composer's ideas and the technical necessities which these ideas create."

To illustrate what he means by a musical "idea," Sessions takes an example from his First Piano Sonata, which was begun in 1927 while he was in Italy. In his book *The Musical Experience* he writes:

The first idea that came to me for my First Piano Sonata . . . was in the form of a complex chord preceded by a sharp but heavy up beat.

This chord rang through my ear almost obsessively one day as I was walking in Pisa. The next day, or, in other words, when I sat down to work on the piece, I wrote the first phrase of the Allegro

as you see, the chord had become simpler—a C minor triad, in fact, and its complex sonority had given way to a motif of very syncopated rhythmic character. Later it became clear to me that the motif must be preceded by an introduction, and the melody in B [example 124c] with which the Sonata begins, immediately suggested itself, quite without any conscious thought on my part.

A few days later the original complex chord came back into my ear, again almost obsessively; I found myself continuing it in my mind, and only then made the discovery that the two lower notes of the chord, F# and E, formed the minor seventh of the dominant of the key of B minor, and that the continuation I had been hearing led me back to B; that the germ of the key relationship on which the first two movements of the sonata were based were already implicit in the chordal idea with which the musical train of thought—which eventually took shape in the completed sonata—had started.[2]

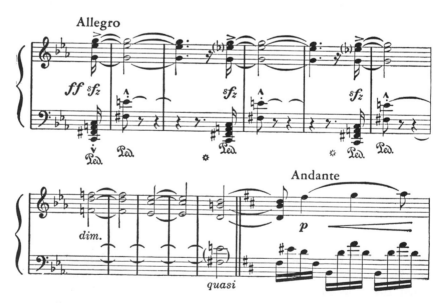

[2] Quoted by permission of the publisher, Princeton University Press. Musical examples from the First Piano Sonata, copyright 1913 by B. Schott's Söhne, Mainz, Germany; by permission of Associated Music Publishers, Inc.

Sessions goes on to say that he has pointed out these things not only to illustrate the nature of the musical idea, but also "in order to throw some light on some of the ways in which a composer's mind, his creative musical mind, that is, works." Since Sessions is generally considered to be a "difficult" composer, these insights into his creative processes are valuable in helping us understand the basis of his musical thought.

Sessions's first important work was the orchestral score he composed for a performance of Andreyev's play *The Black Maskers* given at Smith College, Northampton, Massachusetts, in June, 1923 (he taught there from 1917 to 1921). From this music he made in 1928 a symphonic suite in four movements which remained for many years his most frequently performed composition. The four movements are: (1) "Dance": stridente, sarcastico, (2) "Scene": agitato molto, (3) "Dirge": larghissimo, (4) "Finale": andante moderato un poco agitato. Sessions points out that Andreyev's play, written in 1908, deals symbolically with the theme of tragic conflict within the human soul. He quotes a passage from Andreyev's diary: "The castle is the soul; the lord of the castle is man, the master of the soul; the strange black maskers are the powers whose field of action is the soul of man, and whose mysterious nature he can never fathom."

Concerning the score of *The Black Maskers*, the composer states: "The music was conceived throughout as an expression of certain moods felt behind the incidents of the play, rather than as their descriptive counterpart." There are, to be sure, definite evocations of moods and situations depicted in the play: the suggestion of malicious laughter, cries of agony and despair, the victorious trumpetings of the black maskers as they swarm over the castle, the trumpet calls that announce the death of Lorenzo (the master of the castle), and the conflagration of the final scene, when Lorenzo finds redemption in the symbolic purity of the flames. But the music stands on its own merits: it is extremely brilliant in orchestration, emotionally powerful in its dramatic expression, rich in texture.

Other works prior to 1950 are three Chorale Preludes for organ (1926), a Concerto for violin and orchestra (1932), three *Dirges* for orchestra (1938), two String Quartets, a second Piano Sonata, two symphonies, and a one-act opera, *The Trial of Lucullus*, based on a radio play by Bertolt Brecht and first performed at the University of California at Berkeley on April 18, 1947. This opera has a moral for our times, as it deals with the humiliation of a dictatorial aggressor.

The Symphony No. 2 of Sessions, composed from 1944 to 1946, is dedicated "To the Memory of Franklin Delano Roosevelt." It is in four movements (1) Molto agitato, tranquillo e misterioso, (2) Allegretto capriccioso, (3) Adagio, tranquillo ed espressivo, (4) Allegramente. It has the dissonant contrapuntal texture, the harmonic complexity, and the rhythmic drive that are characteristic qualities of his music. Some hostile reaction was provoked by the first performance of the work at San Francisco in 1947. That is a healthy sign.

The pianist Andor Foldes, for whom the Second Piano Sonata was written, has made the following comments on this work: "The forbidding harmonies of the work and its uncompromising tonal structure will keep it from becoming very popular for the time being. . . . But regardless of its immediate acceptance, this is a work of grandeur, a composition of wide breadth and sincere, deep feeling."[3]

Sessions has passed from diatonic neoclassicism (First Symphony, 1927), through chromaticism (Second Piano Sonata) to serialism (Quintet for Strings, 1958), while always remaining the master of his musical thought. His extension of the tonal system is evident in certain works of the 1930s, such as the Violin Concerto and the String Quartet in E minor. When he adopted (and adapted) twelve-tone writing, it was without fanfare, as the result of his individual evolution, and he applied it with originality in such works as the Third and Fourth Symphonies. The decade of the 1950s was one of definitive achievement for Sessions, with the Second String Quartet (1951); the *Idyll of Theocritus* (1954), for soprano and orchestra; the Concerto for Piano and Orchestra (1956); and the Anglican Mass for unison chorus and organ (1958). In the next decade Sessions completed his Fifth and Sixth Symphonies (1964 and 1966), and the opera *Montezuma*, upon which he had been at work for many years (see Chapter 30).

The unpredictable Mr. Thomson

It would be invidious to suggest that we may tread the primrose path as we approach the music of Virgil Thomson, because this might imply that he rules over a realm of facile pleasures. This would be unfair to Thomson, who really takes music seriously, however much he may prefer to conceal the fact. Perhaps it would be more exact to say that he takes the art of composition seriously as a métier, that

[3] In *Notes* of the Music Library Association, March 1950, p. 313.

he has a meticulous sense of craftsmanship and a fastidious feeling for the *mot juste* in his music as in his prose writing (he is a remarkably productive and adept writer on musical subjects), but that he refuses to write music that takes itself too seriously and that he absolutely balks at being pompous about anything whatsoever. It may seem either too obvious or too cryptic to call him the Erik Satie of American music, yet the title is helpful as an orientation. Thomson's special achievement, as Charles Seeger remarked, is the apotheosis of the commonplace, and that brings him rather close to Satie. Thomson, moreover, has been dubbed "our most musical Francophile," and he certainly imbibed through every pore the musical atmosphere of Paris in the 1920s, over which the spirit of Satie presided like an avuncular oracle.

Virgil Thomson was born in Kansas City, Missouri, on November 25, 1896. His musical training was orthodox. He matriculated at Harvard, where he studied music with a number of impeccable professors. He even played the organ in King's Chapel, Boston. He also displayed aptitude for winning academic awards, obtaining the Naumburg and Paine Fellowships, which permitted him to go to Paris, where he studied with Nadia Boulanger and acquired a permanent taste for French culture. After graduating from Harvard in 1922 he continued there for three years as an assistant instructor and then went to Paris again, where he remained most of the time until the outbreak of World War II. In Paris he formed a friendship with Gertrude Stein, whose *Capital, Capitals* and *Four Saints in Three Acts* he set to music (see the chapter "Toward an American Opera"). He inevitably gravitated toward the circle of Jean Cocteau and "Les Six," the group of young antibourgeois composers, followers of Satie, whose irreverent attitudes and unconventional creations embodied the spirit of '26. These young composers, among them Milhaud and Honegger, were intrigued by jazz and the idioms of American popular music. For them, nothing was vulgar or commonplace. Or if it was, they transmuted everything they touched. Thomson found in them a stimulus for his own musical curiosity and eclecticism.

In February, 1926, at St. Cloud, Thomson completed his *Sonata da Chiesa* (literally, "church sonata," a term borrowed from seventeenth-century Italian instrumental music) for clarinet in E flat, trumpet in C, viola, horn in F, and trombone. Who but a disciple of Satie would have thought of inserting a tango as the second movement in this supposedly austere type of chamber music? That is the Thomson touch, and he carries it off most effectively, and discreetly, with just a suggestion of the tango rhythm in the clarinet and trumpet parts, played *con sordino*. The flanking movements are a Chorale and a Fugue, the former plentifully supplied with parallel fifths. This little work demonstrates Thomson's skillful and expressive use of dissonance within a neoclassical framework.

The lure of Paris did not cause Thomson to forget his American heritage. In his *Symphony on a Hymn Tune* (1928) he drew on the heritage of American (Protestant) hymnody, though it would be a mistake to regard this as religious music in the conventional sense. Thomson's own description of the work is as follows: "It is a set of variations on the hymn 'How Firm a Foundation'; each movement consists of a further set of variations tightened up in various ways, the first in the manner of a sonata, the second as a Bach chorale-prelude, the third as a passacaglia. The fourth is twice tightened up, once as a fugue, once as a rondo." But there are allusions also to "Yes, Jesus Loves Me," and "For He's a Jolly Good Fellow," together with snatches of Gregorian chant, cowboy tunes, marches, and other material used in a spirit of parody. Thomson's adherence to classical forms while obviously having fun with the whole thing is like the implied ridicule of someone who salutes another person too ceremoniously. The symphony, as John Cage suggests, is actually a delightful musical *collage*.

The Symphony No. 2 is a reworking for orchestra of the Piano Sonata No. 1; the orchestration was done in 1931. The work is in three movements, to be played without pause. Prevailingly diatonic, or pan-diatonic, the Symphony is characterized by the composer as full of "dancing and jollity." Yet here too there are allusions to American hymnody, presented in its social context, and to Thomson's favorite "For He's a Jolly Good Fellow."

Thomson's next two orchestral scores were written for documentary films: *The Plow that Broke the Plains* (1936) and *The River* (1937)—the latter dealing with the problem of erosion in the Mississippi valley, the former with drought and devastation in the Great Plains. Both scores were made into concert suites and as such have stood up with the best of Thomson's music; together with the music he wrote for another documentary film, *Louisiana Story* (1948), these scores rank with the most effective musical Americana written in the second quarter of our century. To them may be added the music for a ballet, *Filling Station* (1937), a "period piece" in the purest sense of the term—including an evocation of the "Big Apple."

Apart from suites made from the operas *Four Saints in Three Acts* and *The Mother of Us All*, Thomson's other important orchestral compositions are the Concerto for Violoncello and Orchestra (1950), the Concerto for Flute, Strings, Harp and Percussion (1954), and three "landscapes" written at different times but constituting a sort of tryptich: *The Seine at Night*, (1947), *Wheat Field at Noon* (1948), and *Sea Piece with Birds* (1952). These compositions are in Thomson's neoromantic manner, in which subjective feeling is fused with coloristic tone-painting, like the shrill cry of the seagulls in the third landscape. A work of symphonic proportions, though scored for band, is *A Solemn Music* (1949), written in memory of the composer's dear friend Gertrude Stein. The *Five Songs to Poems of William Blake* for baritone and orchestra (1951), including "Tiger! Tiger!" and "The Little Black Boy," are both deeply moving and consummately written for the voice.

In addition to the *Sonata da Chiesa*, Thomson's chamber music includes two string quartets (1931 and 1932) and a Sonata for Violin and Piano (1930), which are straight neoromantic works utilizing traditional forms (each has a movement in waltz tempo). Another chamber work, the *Stabat Mater* (in French) for soprano and string quartet (1931), leads us to a consideration of Thomson's religious music.

Quite apart from such musical joking as the *Variations and Fugues on Sunday School Tunes* for organ (1926–1927), or the thematic interplay of hymn tunes in the symphonies, Thomson has been one of the most consistently productive writers of religious music among contemporary American composers. The earliest work remaining in his catalogue is a *De Profundis* for mixed voices, composed in 1920 and revised for publication in 1951. During the twenties he wrote a quantity of religious music, including Three Antiphonal Psalms for two-part chorus and the *Missa Brevis* (in Latin) for men's voices (1924). Ten years later he wrote another *Missa Brevis*, for women's voices, with percussion ad lib. Also from the thirties are the *Scenes from the Holy Infancy (according to Saint Matthew)* for mixed voices (1937); *Hymns from the Old South*, also for mixed voices, are from 1949; and in 1959–1960 he composed his most important religious score, the *Missa Pro Defunctis* (Requiem Mass), for men's chorus, women's chorus, and orchestra—a work of forty-five minutes' duration. The composer directs that, "In performance, the choirs should stand on opposite sides of the orchestra in so far as such an arrangement is practicable." The work begins with a Praeludium and concludes with a Postludium, both brief. It is designed for liturgical use.

Musically, the *Missa Pro Defunctis* represents the apotheosis of Thomson's ambiguous use of the interval of a third. As the composer himself explains:

> Harmonically the work is dominated by the major third, which is used in parallel lines, in canons, in stacked-up position as augmented triads, in chromatic chords (combined with the major second), and in major chords that often run parallel and at other times are arpeggiated into bugle-calls and vocalizes. The constant presence of the major third produces constant tonal shifts in the melody and, through its frequent appearance in stacked-up form as the augmented triad, generates whole-tone harmonies as well as constant modulation. This non-stable tonality aspect—of evanescence with iridescence—resulted from the wish to express the idea, constantly present in the text, of "eternal light." Also to suggest a region neither heaven nor earth but in some outer space between the two where it may be imagined music is freed from both the frictions of twelve-tone chromaticism and gravitational "pulls" of classical harmony.

In this brief survey it has been possible to suggest only a small measure of the abundant, extraordinarily varied, and unique musical production of Virgil Thomson. It would have been pleasant, for instance, to dwell on the many delightful musical portraits that are his specialty; most of them are for piano, but some are orchestrated (including those of Aaron Copland and Pablo Picasso). When much of the pretentious music of the last forty years has fallen into oblivion, the deceptively uncomplicated music of Virgil Thomson will still be delighting both listeners and performers.

Thomson, who was music critic of the *New York Herald Tribune* from 1940 to 1954, is an extremely lucid, perceptive, and elegant writer on music. He has published four books: *The State of Music* (1939), *The Musical Scene* (1945), *The Art of Judging Music* (1948), and *Music Right and Left* (1951); in 1965 he completed his autobiography and began an opera on the life of Lord Byron.

An academic eclectic

Randall Thompson, born in New York City in 1899, studied theory with Hill and Spalding at Harvard, and composition privately with Ernest Bloch. From 1922 to 1925 he was a Fellow of the American Academy in Rome. His various teaching posts have included the University of Virginia, Princeton, and Harvard. His most important work has been done in the choral and symphonic fields, though he has also written some admirable chamber music. In his production, two works stand out: The Second Symphony (1931) and *The Peaceable Kingdom* (1936), the latter for mixed chorus *a cappella*. The Symphony is in the conventional four movements and employs the traditional forms, beginning with a sonata-allegro and concluding with a modified rondo. The suggestions of American popular idioms in the Vivace are as clever and engaging as they are discreet and skillful.

The Peaceable Kingdom consists of eight choruses from Isaiah for mixed voices *a cappella*, suggested by the painting of that title by the early nineteenth-century American artist Edward Hicks, who was also a Quaker preacher. Thompson selected the texts from Isaiah with a view to illustrating the spirit of the painting. The first chorus contrasts the reward of the righteous, who "shall sing for joy of heart," and the fate of the wicked, who "shall howl for vexation of spirit." The second chorus, "Woe Unto Them," is a dramatic admonition to those who "regard not the Lord." The third chorus continues to foretell the doom of the wicked: "Their children also shall be dashed to pieces before their eyes." The dramatic tension reaches its culmination in the next number, "Howl Ye," for double chorus with antiphony. The final section is also antiphonal, men's voices being opposed to women's voices in proclaiming the words of the prophet:

Say ye to the righteous, it shall be well with him:
for they shall eat the fruit of their doings.

Thompson's choral music includes further *Five Odes of Horace* (1924), *Americana* (1932) for mixed voices and piano or orchestra, *Alleluia* for mixed voices *a cappella* (1940), and *The Testament of Freedom* (1943) for men's voices with piano or orchestra. Each of these compositions is completely different from any of the others.

The *Odes* show his mastery of part writing and his skill in the solution of the rhythmic problems presented by the text. *Americana* is a set of five choruses with texts from the *American Mercury*, dealing with five aspects of American life—fundamentalism, spiritualism, temperance, capital punishment, optimism. Thompson's setting of *Alleluia*, written on that word alone, is a well-conceived and brilliantly executed *a cappella* choral number that has firmly established itself in the repertoire of American choirs. *The Testament of Freedom* is a setting of selected writings by Thomas Jefferson: *A Summary View of the Rights of British America* (1774); *A Declaration of the Causes and Necessity of Taking up Arms* (July 6, 1775); Letter to John Adams, Monticello, dated September 12, 1821. In this work the composer deliberately set himself to write a type of "public music" that would be as impersonal as possible and that would possess a dignified grandeur arising from simplicity of means. Hence the writing is predominantly in unison, stressing directness of expression and clarity in projection of the text.

Among Thompson's instrumental works should be mentioned his two String Quartets, the Suite for oboe, clarinet, and viola (1940), the *Jazz Poem* for piano and orchestra (1928), *The Piper at the Gates of Dawn* (1924), symphonic prelude for orchestra, and the Third Symphony (1949), which incorporates folklike material.

A dynamic New Yorker

By 1950 the United States had a generation of mature composers who were taught by other American composers rather than by European teachers. To this generation belongs William Schuman (born in New York City on August 4, 1910), who was a pupil, and to a certain extent a disciple, of Roy Harris. Primarily a symphonist in the grand, dramatic manner, he had reached his Eighth by 1963 and was doubtless aiming at the Ninth and beyond. With Harris he shares an admiration for Walt Whitman, whose *"Pioneers!"* he set to music for mixed chorus *a cappella*, and an interest in Americana, ranging from Billings to baseball. Though he can take himself as seriously as Harris (for example, in *Credendum: Article of Faith*, for orchestra, 1955), he also has the lighter touch that Harris lacks, as demonstrated in his one-act opera *The Mighty Casey* (1953), based on the well-known baseball classic, with strong injections of musical-comedy style. He has also written a *Circus Overture* for the Broadway extravaganza *The Seven Lively Arts.*

Schuman was educated at Columbia University, with some further study at the Mozarteum in Salzburg. From 1935 to 1945 he was on the faculty of Sarah Lawrence College, and then became president of the Juilliard School of Music. In 1962 he was appointed president of the Lincoln Center for the Performing Arts in New York.

A man of tremendous energy and of remarkable organizational and executive ability, he composes according to a strict schedule and frequently revises his major works over a period of several years. His principal works, in addition to the eight symphonies, include three overtures, a Piano Concerto, a Violin Concerto, four String Quartets, *A Song of Orpheus* (Fantasy for cello and orchestra), and the scores for several ballets: *Undertow* (1945), *Night Journey* (1947), and *Judith* (1949)—the last two written for Martha Graham and all three tending toward the tragic.

The Symphony No. 1 for 18 instruments (1935) and Symphony No. 2 (1937) are relatively unimportant. The Symphony No. 3 (completed in January, 1941) is in neoclassical style and consists of four movements: Passacaglia, Fugue, Chorale, Toccata. In it Schuman's tendency toward the use of bitonality and polyharmony is affirmed. This tendency is further developed in the Symphony No. 4 (completed in August, 1941), which is in three movements and closely akin in style to the Third Symphony, complex in structure and markedly contrapuntal in texture. Robert Sabin aptly said of this symphony that it is "as functional, and as beautiful, in its way, as a skyscraper or an ocean liner. Yet it is neither inhuman nor unfeeling. On the contrary, it is a direct expression of the spirit of its time in art." One should mention a jazzy injection in the last movement of the Fourth Symphony.

Schuman's Fifth Symphony, finished in July, 1943, is for strings. Its three movements are: Molto agitato ed energico, Larghissimo, and Presto leggiero. The jazzlike element, merely adumbrated in the Fourth Symphony, acquires full stylistic status in the last movement of the *Symphony for Strings*, which applies syncopation in the manner of ragtime music. The Symphony No. 6, completed on the last day of 1948, represents the peak of Schuman's achievements to date. The work is in one movement with six sections, all derived from thematic material stated at the beginning. The sections are marked Largo;

Moderato con moto; Leggieramente; Adagio; Allegro risoluto, presto; Larghissimo. Though the structure of this work reveals the composer's customary formal logic and intellectual control, its emotional impact tends to be machinelike rather than inwardly generated. The Seventh Symphony, completed in May, 1960, is in four movements: (1) Largo assai, (2) Vigoroso, (3) Cantabile-Intensamente, (4) Scherzando brioso (the composer directs that the work be played without pause: its duration is about thirty minutes). It was commissioned by the Serge Koussevitzky Foundation and the Boston Symphony Orchestra, in celebration of the orchestra's seventy-fifth anniversary. The large orchestration calls for additional woodwinds and brasses, ad libitum.

The Fantasy for cello and orchestra, *A Song of Orpheus* (beginning "Orpheus with his lute," from Shakespeare's *Henry VIII*), is based on Schuman's own setting of that song for voice and piano. In the score the words of the song are printed below the cello part, "to enable the soloist to perform the melody with the clarity of a singer's projection."

William Schuman, like Virgil Thomson, merits a place among the Americanists as well as the eclectics, because of his continual preoccupation with the American scene. In his *American Festival Overture* (1939) he gave expression to a typically American mood. In his own words:

> The first three notes of this piece will be recognized by some listeners as the "call to play" of boyhood days. In New York City it is yelled on the syllables "Wee-Awk-EE" to get the gang together for a game or a festive occasion of some sort. This call very naturally suggested itself for a piece of music being composed for a very festive occasion. . . . The development of this bit of "folk material" . . . is along purely musical lines.

In his *New England Triptych* (1956) for orchestra, Schuman incorporates and develops themes drawn from three choral works by William Billings. The first is the stirring anthem "Be Glad, Then, America"; the lyrical middle section is based on the moving lament "When Jesus Wept"; and the final section is a spirited adaptation of "Chester," the hymn tune that became the marching song of the Continental Army.

Other examples of musical Americana by Schuman include *Newsreel: In Five Shots* (1941) and *George Washington Bridge* (1950), both for band; music for the documentary film *Steel-town;* and the baseball opera mentioned above, *The Mighty Casey* (libretto adapted from E. L. Thayer's "Casey at the Bat").

Creston, Dello Joio, Swanson

Paul Creston (*recte* Joseph Guttoveggio) was born in New York City in 1906 and studied music with Randegger, Déthier, and Pietro Yon. In composition he is self-taught. He first attracted attention with his *Seven Theses* for piano (1933), which demonstrated the objective style that he was to pursue in *Five Two-part Inventions* (1937) and *Six Preludes* (1945) for piano, the Suite for violin and piano (1939), the *Partita* for flute, violin, and strings (1937), and the orchestral *Pastorale and Tarantella* (1941) and *Prelude and Dance* (1941).

In his orchestral tone poem *Threnody*, composed in 1938, Creston combines a subjective approach (personal emotion) with the abstract development of musical ideas. This work is marked by the free use of modal materials derived from Gregorian chant, a tendency that reached its culmination in Creston's Third Symphony (1951), subtitled *Three Mysteries* (the Nativity, the Crucifixion, and the Resurrection). According to the composer's statement:

> Although the work derives its inspiration from these events, historic and mystic, it is a musical parallel of the inherent emotional reactions rather than a narrative or painting. The programmatic content, such as there may be, is for the justification of drawing from the immense wealth in Gregorian chant.

Of Creston's earlier symphonies, the First (1940) is in the usual four movements, but the Second (1944) has only two movements, each divided into two sections: (1) "Introduction and Song," (2) "Interlude and Dance." The whole is conceived as an "apotheosis" of song and dance, the foundations of music. Further tributes to the dance as abstract form are *Two Choric Dances* (1938) and *Invocation and Dance* (1953), both for orchestra. Other works from the 1950s are the Fourth and Fifth Symphonies, the symphonic poem *Walt Whitman* (1951), and the *Lydian Ode* for orchestra (1956).

Creston composed a Concertino for marimba and orchestra, and three works for E flat alto saxophone: a Suite, a Sonata, and a Concerto with orchestra. He has also written a quantity of choral and chamber music, and music for organ. His idiom is conservative, with moderate use of dissonance.

Norman Dello Joio, born in New York City in 1913, studied composition with Bernard Wagenaar and Paul Hindemith, doubtless imbibing his neoclassical tendencies from the latter. He also shares Creston's predilection for Gregorian themes and conservative harmonic idioms. Like Creston, he has been organist and choirmaster in several New York churches. An exceptionally interesting contrast in the use of Gregorian material from the same source (*Mass of the Angels*) is presented in two works by Dello Joio: the Piano Sonata No. 3, and the Variations, Chaconne, and Finale for orchestra, the former composed in 1947, the latter in 1948. The treatment of the themes in the orchestral work is brilliant and colorful; in the piano sonata it is more introspective but equally imaginative. The *Fantasia on a Gregorian Theme* for violin and piano is another work in similar vein.

Dello Joio's neoclassical tendencies are fully manifested in his *Ricercari* for piano and orchestra (1946), which purports to be a kind of Scarlatti *redivivus*. Its three movements develop a single germinal idea harmonically, melodically, and rhythmically. Likewise in the neoclassical tradition are the *Sinfonietta* for piano and orchestra (1941) and the *Serenade for Orchestra* (1948). Following a similar tendency, but in a lighter vein, is the *Variations and Capriccio* for violin and piano, written to be, as the composer says, "earfully charming." More serious in mood are the orchestral *Magnificat* (1942) and *Epigraph* (1951), the latter described as "a piece written in memory of a man." Dating from the same year is the symphony *The Triumph of Saint Joan*, in three movements: (1) "The Maid," (2) "The Warrior," (3) "The Saint." (When Dello Joio's opera *The Trial at Rouen* was revised in 1959, it was given the same title as this symphony.) In 1961 the composer returned to his neoclassical vein, but with a greater depth of expression, in the *Fantasy and Variations* for piano and orchestra.

Particularly impressive are Dello Joio's choral compositions. These include *The Mystic Trumpeter* (after Walt Whitman), for full chorus of mixed voices, soprano, tenor, and baritone solos, and French horn (or piano); *A Psalm of David* for mixed chorus and piano (or brass, strings, and percussion); *Prayers of Cardinal Newman* for mixed chorus and organ (1961); and the "symphonic cantata" *Song of Affirmation* (adapted from Stephen Vincent Benét's *Western Star*), for narrator, soprano solo, mixed chorus, and full orchestra (1953). He has also written two operas: *The Trial at Rouen* (1955; revised 1959) and *Blood Moon* (1961).

Howard Swanson was born in Atlanta, Georgia, in 1909, but his parents moved to Cleveland when he was nine. After graduating from high school he got a job as greaser in a locomotive roundhouse, then as a letter carrier, and afterward as a postal clerk. After completing his studies at the Cleveland Institute of Music, he received a Rosenwald Fellowship that enabled him to study composition with Nadia Boulanger in Paris for two years. Thus, like so many other American composers of our time, he became a member of what one pun-happy critic has dubbed "the Boulangerie" (i.e., "the Bakery"). Abandoning Paris in the face of the German occupation, Swanson returned to the United States, where, to make his living, he worked for a time in the Internal Revenue Service of the Treasury Department. Finally, resolved to devote himself entirely to music, he resigned and began to compose intensively.

The next episode of Swanson's career reads like a classical American "success story." His dramatically expressive songs, in which the text, the melody, and the accompaniment are so skillfully interwoven, were introduced at a recital in New York in October, 1946, and immediately won critical acclaim. The songs were taken up by Marian Anderson and other celebrated singers, so that the composer's international reputation was quickly established. His Short Symphony, composed in 1948, was given its first performance by Dimitri Mitropoulos with the New York Philharmonic-Symphony Orchestra in November, 1950, and was later included in the repertoire of that orchestra when it played at the Edinburgh Festival in Scotland in the summer of 1951. Then the influential Music Critics' Circle of New York chose Swanson's Short Symphony as the best new orchestral work performed in that metropolis during the 1950–1951 season.

Swanson's Short Symphony is in three movements: Allegro moderato; Andante; Allegro giocoso—Andante con moto. It is predominantly neoclassical in texture, and one critic has described it as an attempt "to apply fugue principle to the sonata-allegro scheme." It is markedly eclectic in its alternating use of freely chromatic, diatonic, neoclassical, and slightly jazzlike elements (in the last movement). These disparate elements do not always coalesce, but the Short Symphony, in spite of its shortcomings, is a sincere and attractive work.

Among other major works by Swanson are *Night Music* (1950) for chamber orchestra; Symphony No. 1 (1945); *Music for Strings* (1951); *Sound Piece* (1952) for brass quintet; Concerto for Orchestra (1954); and Concerto for Piano and Orchestra (1956). His instrumental output also includes a Piano Sonata, a Suite for Cello and Piano, and *Nocturne* for Violin and Piano. Among his numerous fine songs are "The Valley" (Edwin Markham), "The Junk Man" (Carl Sandburg), "Ghosts in Love" (Vachel Lindsay), and "The Negro Speaks of Rivers" (Langston Hughes). In 1965 Swanson completed the Symphony No. 2 and the First String Quartet.

An ambivalent urbanite

The fact that Leonard Bernstein, the conductor, has become a celebrity should not be allowed to obscure the fact that he is also a composer. His sudden leap to fame as a conductor is well known: how, at the age of twenty-five (in 1943), he substituted for Bruno Walter, with only a few hours' notice, at a concert of the New York Philharmonic that was broadcast on a national network. In 1958, when he was appointed permanent director of the New York Philharmonic, he became the first American-born musician to occupy that position.

Born in Lawrence, Massachusetts, in 1918, Leonard Bernstein attended the Boston Latin School and Harvard University, where he studied composition with E. B. Hill and Walter Piston. After graduating from Harvard, he studied orchestration with Randall Thompson at the Curtis Institute of Music in Philadelphia. His training in conducting was under Koussevitzky at Tanglewood.

From the time that he played with a jazz band at the age of thirteen, Bernstein showed a keen interest in the American musical vernacular. In historical perspective, his main contribution as a composer may be found to reside in his musical shows, of which *West Side Story* (1957) is a brilliantly successful example (see Chapter 29). As a serious composer he could pose for a portrait of "The Compleat Eclectic," since, in the words of Joseph Machlis, "he has been influenced on the one hand by Stravinsky and Copland, and on the other by Mahler and Richard Strauss."[4] Among his most ambitious symphonic works are the *Jeremiah Symphony* (1942) for mezzo-so-

4 Machlis, *Introduction to Contemporary Music, p.* 575.

prano and orchestra, *The Age of Anxiety* (Symphony No. 2, 1949), for piano and orchestra, and the Symphony No. 3—*Kaddish* (1963). The first is in three movements: "Prophecy," "Profanation," "Lamentation"; the lamentations of the third movement are sung in Hebrew in the traditional style of Biblical cantillation. The Symphony No. 2 is based on W. H. Auden's poem "The Age of Anxiety," which is intended to demonstrate that once again "the times are out of joint"—with the addition of modern neuroses. As in so many of his works, Bernstein makes effective use of jazzlike writing in this score. In his *Serenade* (1954), for violin, strings, and percussion—a composition inspired by Plato's *Symposium*—Bernstein brings "exuberant jazz themes" into the last movement, presumably to emphasize that the intellectual banquet has become very gay.

Bernstein's wit and humor—so familiar to television audiences—are also revealed in such compositions as *La Belle Cuisine* (1947), a setting of four French cooking recipes for voice and piano; *Seven Anniversaries* (1943), for piano; the ballets *Fancy Free* (1944) and *Facsimile* (1946); and the one-act opera *Trouble in Tahiti* (1952), for which he wrote his own libretto (see Chapter 30). His musical comedies are discussed in Chapter 29.

If I have dubbed Bernstein "an ambivalent urbanite" it is because he is equally at home in the fields of popular and "serious" music, and because his most characteristic compositions, such as *West Side Story* and *Trouble in Tahiti*, seem wedded to the tensions and anxieties of the modern megalopolis.

New England Armenianism

One wonders whether Alan Hovhaness, American-born composer of Armenian descent, should be included among the eclectics, because he has drawn so consistently upon a single tradition—that of Armenian modal music and its traditional instruments and related lore. Yet even within this cultural area that so largely fascinates and absorbs him, there is room for considerable eclecticism, for, as Virgil Thomson observed, "He writes in the early Christian, the medieval, and the modern Armenian techniques, possibly even a little in the pre-Christian manner of that ancient and cultivated people." Moreover, Hovhaness has moved from Armenianism to assimilate other aspects of traditional music in the Near, Middle, and Far East, so that he has become increasingly eclectic in his choice of moods, modes, and materials.

Alan Hovhaness was born in Arlington, Massachusetts, in 1911. His Armenian descent was in the paternal line, for his mother was of Scottish origin, and Leon Kochnitzky is of the opinion that "the composer's Scottish heredity played as important a part in his artistic formation as his Armenian background."[5] This opinion is based on the analogy between the composer's evocation of the myths and rituals of a "long-forgotten primitive people" and the famous "Ossianic" poems of the Scotsman Macpherson, both being taken as evidence of a cult for archaism and mystification. The theory is ingenious, but we are more concerned with the results of this influence than with its antecedents. It appears, in any case, that Hovhaness did not become "Armenian-conscious" until reaching the age of thirty. By that time he had received his musical training at the New England Conservatory of Music—which nevertheless did not prevent him from seeking new paths of his own.

Hovhaness is the most prolific American composer of his generation. By 1963 he had written his Symphony No. 16 (Opus 202) and capped it with a Symphony for Metal Orchestra (Opus 203), for six flutes, three trombones, and percussion. The latter is typical of this composer's constant search for unusual instrumental effects. In a work for piano and orchestra titled *Lousadzak* ("The Coming of Light"), written in 1945, Hovhaness imitates the effects of such ancient Armenian instruments as the *tar*, *kanoon*, *oud*, and *saz*. Of these, the *kanoon* is a zitherlike instrument on which sustained tones are simulated by rapid repetition of single notes—one of the characteristic procedures in the music of Hovhaness, together with the weaving of melodic arabesques in the manner of Near Eastern vocalization. His interest in the exploitation of timbre through percussion ensembles is manifested in such a work as the Percussion Sextet (Opus 135), for timpani, two drums, tamtam, marimbas, and glockenspiel.

Although he occasionally uses a functional title, as in the Concerto No. 5 for Piano and Orchestra (1953), Hovhaness tends to favor the descriptive or evocative title that prepares the listener for an exotic auditory experience: *Tzairek* ("Evening Song"), for violin, flute, drums, and strings; *Avak the Healer*, for soprano, trumpet, and strings; the symphony *Anahid* (named for an ancient Armenian goddess); *Pe-El-Amarna* ("City of the Sun"), for orchestra; *Arevakal* ("Coming

---

[5] See the very interesting discussion of Hovhaness's "Armenianism" in *The Tiger's Eye* (Westport, Conn.), No. 3 (March, 1948), pp. 59–65.

of the Sun"), concerto for orchestra; *Haroutiun* ("Resurrection"), for trumpet and string orchestra. In his *Magnificat,* for chorus and orchestra, the composer "tried to suggest the mystery, inspiration, and mysticism of early Christianity." A cantata, *Shepherd of Israel* (1953), for cantor, recorder (or flute), strings, and trumpet (ad libitum), was written after he learned that the young composers of Israel were interested in musical materials and modes of expression akin to those that attracted him. Hovhaness turned to the Far East in his Japanese cantata, *Fuji* (Opus 182), for female chorus, flute, harp, and strings.

Toward improvisation—and beyond

Lukas Foss was born in Berlin in 1922 and came to the United States at the age of fifteen after some musical study in Paris. He continued his studies at the Curtis Institute of Music in Philadelphia (composition, orchestration, piano, conducting) and emerged at the age of eighteen not only well equipped as a composer, but also highly proficient as a pianist and conductor. As a composer he attracted immediate attention with a cantata, *The Prairie* (text by Carl Sandburg), for soloists, full chorus, and orchestra, completed when he was only twenty-one. Foss continued to cultivate his strong vein of vocal composition with two Biblical cantatas: *Song of Anguish* (1945), from the Book of Isaiah, for baritone and orchestra; and *Song of Songs* (1946), for soprano and orchestra. These were followed by one of his most impressive works, *A Parable of Death* (1952), on texts by Rainer Maria Rilke, for tenor solo, narrator, mixed chorus, and orchestra; and by *Psalms* (1956), for chorus and orchestra.

On the instrumental side, he wrote the exuberant *Symphony in G* (1944), followed by the somewhat neoclassical Oboe Concerto (1947–1948), the String Quartet in G (1947), and the Piano Concerto No. 2 (1951–1952), which was revised a year later. It is frankly a virtuoso concerto in the grand manner, and Foss has frequently shone as soloist in its performance. A peak in his achievement as an instrumental composer was the *Symphony of Chorales* (1958), of which the four movements are based on tunes from the chorales of Johann Sebastian Bach—the whole conceived as a tribute of admiration for the famous Bach specialist and humanitarian, Dr. Albert Schweitzer.

Meanwhile, Foss had joined the music faculty of the University of California in Los Angeles, and there, in 1957, had organized the Improvisation Chamber Ensemble (piano, clarinet, cello, percussion), with himself as pianist and musical director. The purpose of the group was "to revive the classical art of improvisation in modern terms." Each of the four musicians in the ensemble receives a chart indicating the basic ideas to be followed in a particular piece—a germinal motive, a tonal scheme, a rhythmic pattern—and these are worked out during numerous rehearsals. In actual performance, of course, the results vary somewhat on each occasion; in a recording, on the other hand, the performance remains forever fixed: one might call it "frozen improvisation." Foss acknowledges the precedent of the "jam session" in jazz, but maintains that there is more advanced planning in his type of improvisation (as there is also in modern jazz, for that matter). He admits that this ensemble improvisation is primarily "a performer's music," and describes it as "a sporting kind of thing, a spiritual game."

One of the functions of the Improvisation Chamber Ensemble was to perform improvised interludes between the movements of Foss's *Time Cycle*, for soprano and orchestra, when it was first performed in 1960—a later version was written for soprano and chamber ensemble consisting of piano, clarinet, cello, and percussion, without any interludes or improvisation. *Time Cycle*, which marks a turning point in Foss's development as a composer, uses texts by Auden, Housman, Kafka, and Nietzsche—all on the theme of Time.

Time Cycle signals Foss's intention to utilize "non-musical" effects for expressive purposes. In the fourth song, Nietzsche's "O Mensch, gib Acht" ("O Man! Take Heed," from *Thus Spake Zarathustra*), the score has the following Note to Conductor: "Such orchestra men as are not playing at the given moment, may, at the conductor's discretion, be called upon to whisper the twelve numbers of the clock strokes (in the language of the country of performance). . . . The '1' should be barely audible, but the whispering increases with each number to what may be termed a 'loud whisper' for the 12th stroke of the clock."[6]

In his next work, *Echoi* (1961–1963), for four soloists (clarinet, cello, percussion, and piano), Foss carries non-musical effects much further and also allows for considerable indeterminacy or randomness in performance. On page one of the score there is a box containing

[6] From the score of *Time Cycle*, copyright by Carl Fischer, Inc., New York. Used by permission.

his principal signs for unorthodox effects. For example, notes without stems and a wavy line indicate an area of "no coordination"; $\boxed{f \diagup p}$ = random, aperiodic assortments of *forte* and *piano;* $\boxed{^{legato}\diagdown_{stacc.}}$ = random, aperiodic assortments of legato and staccato, $\boxed{\flat\text{'} \hspace{2mm} \text{'} \hspace{2mm} \text{'}}$ = random succession of patterns (what is between two ' is to be left intact). In *Echoi I* (Tempo rubato e presto), the composer tells us in a footnote that "Exact simultaneity between players is desired only when indicated (dotted line). Elsewhere the music is so composed as to allow each entrance to occur an [eighth-note] earlier than notated. This will make a free delivery possible, and render all coordination via counting impossible."[7]

Further on there is a permissive footnote for the percussionist: "Stems without notes mean that the percussionist may hit any of the drums available on this line (muffled gong, bongo, timbali), but not always the same—vary." Near the end of *Echoi I* a passage for percussion has the direction: "Do not count; the number of notes is arbitrary, a mere approximation." And again: "The distribution here is merely an example of the desired randomness." More permissiveness is prescribed in *Echoi III* (on a childhood tune): "The placement and number of grace notes is random here for the duration of the *Presto*—a mere indication of the density and asymmetry required."

There are some special instrumental effects. In *Echoi III* the percussionist is directed to play the bongo with a "Jeté DeLancey," a footnote explaining that DeLancey was "the percussionist who initiated the effect of holding the mallet at one end of the drum and bouncing the other." On the same page the clarinetist is directed to play in the manner of Duffalo, "who developed the effect of blowing while gently moving the bell over the timpano surface at varying speeds and angles. . . ." In *Echoi IV* a passage for piano has the following footnote: "A staggering (drunken) unevenness of eighth notes is particularly apropos when a phrase is repeated. If the identical *poco rubato* is then applied to each repeat, the pianist will achieve the desired 'obsessive' effect, which is best likened to a 'stuck' phonograph needle, and which should be made increasingly obvious as the piece progresses."

The maximum randomness is provided in *Echoi IV,* through a page of "interpolation" inserted as a foldout in the score. According

[7] These and other quotations are from the score of *Echoi,* copyright by Carl Fischer Inc., New York. Used by permission.

to the composer's directions: "The music on these pages is interrupted six times by the percussionist hitting an anvil at moments of his choice, at which point the players, without losing a second's time (rather like a jumping phonograph needle), shift to the interpolation page. The interpolations are—in turn—ended (interrupted) by anvil strokes which command the immediate return (jump back) to the main music. . . ."

The last three or four minutes of *Echoi IV* make use of a tape recorder and two loudspeakers. The taped portions are prerecorded. These portions of the score use the direction "Tape Imitation," which signifies to the player: "Alternate between moments of silence and imitation of your taped part as you hear it coming from loudspeaker No. 1." On the last page the pianist is directed to "hit a random assortment of dull, pitchless, amusical sounds (wood of the piano, drum sides, music stands, etc.)"—and a footnote emphasizes the non-musical character of the desired sounds: "Do not 'play' on an instrument—illegitimate sounds only."

The point to be made here is that Foss has utilized many of the devices and procedures introduced and developed over the past fifty years or so by the innovators and experimentalists whose works and ideas are discussed in Chapters 27 and 31 of this book, beginning with Henry Cowell and continuing with John Cage. When Cage and his followers introduced these devices they were regarded as odd-balls and destroyers of tradition. But when Lukas Foss directs his percussionist to use the "large lid of a garbage can," no one raises an eyebrow or mutters something about "The anarchy of the 'garbage-can' school." That is because Foss's academic credentials, musical antecedents, and institutional connections (after leaving UCLA he became conductor of the Buffalo Philharmonic Orchestra) are impeccable. The composer of *A Parable of Death* and *Symphony of Chorales* could never be identified with the beatnik fringe or the neo-Dadaists. The mere fact that he could describe non-musical sounds as "illegitimate" proves that he is on the right side of the fence even when he strays into forbidden pastures.

chapter twenty-six

The traditionalists

Will you seek afar off? You surely will come back at last,
In things best known to you finding the best, or as good as the best.
WALT WHITMAN, A SONG OF OCCUPATIONS.

Tradition implies continuity; its opposite is discontinuity. In the words of Ernst Krenek: "Tradition is the continuity of ideas expressed through the repetition of procedures. If we apply the term to the creative aspect of music, it designates adherence to compositional procedures of the past, especially of the immediate past. It is the continuation of things created in the past, but still alive in the present."[1]

In this broad sense, all composers would be "traditionalists" except the extreme innovators and the experimentalists, and there would be only two main classifications: those who believe in continuity, and those who do not. Both categories would allow for a wide range of variables. Among the experimentalists there is a considerable distance between the complex manipulations of the composer-engineer in his electronic laboratory and the neo-Dadaist who releases a butterfly in the concert hall and calls this act a "composition." Similarly, among those who "adhere to compositional procedures of the past," there is a wide distance between those who rely mainly on repetition and those who couple continuity with invention. The "traditionalists" of this chapter, then, have only this in common: that they do not break with the past. How closely they adhere to it is a matter of degree, and varies from individual to individual.

Post-romantic currents

The post-romantic tradition in American music, of which MacDowell and Paine were the most notable exponents, received a

[1] "Tradition in Perspective," *Perspectives of New Music*, I, 1 (Fall 1962), p. 27.

549

considerable impetus in the second quarter of the twentieth century from the wholehearted adherence of Howard Hanson, whose five symphonies epitomize the post-romantic movement of that period in the United States. Not content with letting his music speak for itself—which it does with an eloquence that could not be mistaken—Hanson proclaimed his allegiance in the title of his Second Symphony (1930), called "Romantic," and capped it with a dogmatic declaration at the time of its first performance:

> The symphony represents for me my escape from the rather bitter type of modern musical realism which occupies so large a place in contemporary thought. Much contemporary music seems to me to be showing a tendency to become entirely too cerebral. I do not believe that music is primarily a matter of intellect, but rather a manifestion of the emotions. I have, therefore, aimed in this symphony to create a work that was young in spirit, lyrical and romantic in temperament, and simple and direct in expression.[2]

If Hanson had reissued this "Romantic Manifesto" in 1960, it still would have found an echo in many minds—even though people might be thinking of a different kind of "modern musical realism." The hue and cry contra "cerebral" music is as strong, if not stronger, than it was thirty years ago. The romantic attitude is perennial because it is popular, and any attack on intellectualism, such as the denunciation of "cerebral" music, always finds a ready response. Hanson renewed the attack when his Third Symphony came out (1938), affirming that it, too, "stands as an avowal against a certain coldly abstract, would-be sentimental music professed by certain composers of high gifts." He wanted "warm-blooded music" instead of "cold-blooded music."

Hanson was born in Wahoo, Nebraska, on October 28, 1896. He studied at the Institute of Musical Art in New York, and in 1921 obtained the American Prix de Rome for composition. After his three years in Rome he became director of the Eastman School of Music in Rochester, New York, which he made an important center for the study and performance of American music, chiefly through the American Composers' Orchestral Concerts, inaugurated and conducted by him. A descendant of Swedish-American pioneers, Hanson showed partiality to the Nordic temperament in music, and perhaps aspired

[2] Quoted in Bagar and Biancolli, *The Concert Companion*, p. 319.

to be the American Sibelius. His First Symphony (1922), entitled "Nordic," reveals the influence of Sibelius, especially in the first movement, which "sings of the solemnity, austerity, and grandeur of the North, of its restless surging and strife, of its somberness and melancholy." His Third Symphony was written in commemoration of the 300th anniversary of the first Swedish settlement on the shores of the Delaware in 1638 and was "conceived as a tribute to the epic qualities of the Swedish pioneers in America." Hanson's Fourth Symphony (1943) is dedicated to the memory of his father, and each of its four movements bears the name of a section of the *Requiem* or Mass for the Dead: "Kyrie," "Requiescat," "Dies Irae," "Lux Aeterna."

Hanson also wrote five symphonic poems; a Concerto for organ and orchestra (1926); a Concerto for organ, strings, and harp (1943); a Concerto for piano and orchestra (1948); *The Lament for Beowulf* (1925); *Three Poems from Walt Whitman* (from "Drum Taps") for mixed chorus and orchestra; and the opera *Merry Mount* (1925).

The midwestern composer Leo Sowerby (born in Grand Rapids, Michigan, in 1895) was a Fellow of the American Academy in Rome at the same time as Howard Hanson (1921–1923). He applied conventional procedures of tone-painting in his symphonic poem *Prairie* (1929), based on Carl Sandburg's poem of that title, and in the orchestral suite *From the Northland* (1922), with its evocation of "Forest Voices," "Cascades," "Burnt Rock Pool," and "The Shining Big-sea Water." The locale is ostensibly the countryside around Lake Superior, but its woods and cascades are suspiciously close to the pines and fountains of Rome.

Sowerby also wrote the overture *Come Autumn Time*, an orchestral setting of the popular fiddle tune "The Irish Washerwoman," several cantatas, chamber music, and some fine music for organ, notably the *Classic Concerto* for organ and orchestra (or piano), and *Canon, Chaconne, and Fugue* (1951) for organ alone.

Bernard Rogers, like Howard Hanson, has had a long association with the Eastman School of Music, where he began to teach composition in 1929. Born in New York City in 1893, Rogers studied briefly with Arthur Farwell, but his principal teachers were Ernest Bloch and Nadia Boulanger. He is an amateur painter, and this interest is reflected in his music. For example, his tone poem *Fuji in the Sunset Glow* and *Three Japanese Dances* (1925) were inspired by Japanese prints; and *The Supper at Emmaus,* for orchestra (1937), was suggested by Rembrandt's famous painting. The orchestral suite *Characters from Hans Christian Andersen* (1944) is subtitled "Four Drawings for small orchestra" and each piece or "musical drawing" uses a different medium: (1) pen and ink, (2) soft charcoal, (3) gouache (impressionistic), (4) brush and ink. The composer calls these pieces "acoustical illustrations."

There is a pictorial-narrative element in Rogers's oratorio *The Passion* (1944)—probably his most important work—depicting in six scenes the Passion of Our Lord. He has also written two biblical cantatas: *The Raising of Lazarus* (1931) and *The Exodus* (1932); four programmatic symphonies; *Elegy to the Memory of Franklin D. Roosevelt* for small orchestra; *Soliloquy* for flute and strings (1921); and three operas. He is the author of a valuable treatise on orchestration.

Among the pupils of Bernard Rogers, none achieved greater prominence than David Diamond, composer of eight symphonies, who also happens to be an amateur painter. Born in Rochester, New York, in 1915, he was taken to Cleveland at the age of twelve. When his family, in 1930, returned to Rochester, he enrolled in the Eastman School of Music. After further study with Roger Sessions in New York, he became a pupil of Nadia Boulanger in Paris.

During the 1930s, Diamond began to compose in the mildly dissonant, neoclassical style of the period: *Partita* for oboe, bassoon, and piano; Concerto for String Quartet; *Elegy in Memory of Maurice Ravel,* for strings and percussion; and the Stravinskian *Psalm* (1937) for full orchestra. The following decade was extremely productive: he wrote the Second, Third, and Fourth Symphonies; the Concerto for Two Solo Pianos; *Rounds* for string orchestra; two string quartets; *The Enormous Room* (after e.e. cummings), for orchestra; and several Shakespearian scores (*Music for Romeo and Juliet, Overture to The Tempest, Timon of Athens*). These works employed the rhetoric of romanticism in a diatonic idiom.

The decade of the 1950s was one of transition for Diamond, marked by increasing chromaticism and complexity. In 1951 he settled in Florence, Italy, and took up painting seriously while continuing to compose. The works of this decade include a Concerto for Piano and Orchestra; Quintet for clarinet, two violas, and two cellos (both 1950); String Quartet No. 4 (1951); *Sinfonia Concertante* (1954–1956); and the Sixth and Seventh Symphonies. Two other compositions of this period, *The World of Paul Klee* (1957) for orchestra, and the Quintet for Woodwinds (1958), marked Diamond's passage into twelve-tone territory. His Eighth Symphony was completed in 1962.

Samuel Barber: neoromantic

Samuel Barber was born in West Chester, Pennsylvania, in 1910. At the age of thirteen he entered the Curtis Institute of Music in Philadelphia, where he studied composition with Rosario Scalero. In 1935 he was awarded the American Prix de Rome for composition. His First Symphony (in one movement) received its première by the Augusteo Orchestra in December, 1936, while he was a Fellow of the American Academy in Rome. In 1938 Toscanini conducted the first performance of Barber's *Essay for Orchestra* (Opus 12), and the *Adagio for Strings*, an arrangement of the slow movement of the String Quartet (Opus 11) composed in 1936. This was the kind of well-made music, conventional and melodic, that Toscanini liked to conduct and that concert-goers liked to hear. It confirmed the overt romantic trend of such earlier works as *Dover Beach* for voice and string quartet (1931), Sonata for cello and piano (1932), Overture to *The School for Scandal* (1932), and *Music for a Scene from Shelley* (1933).

Barber describes his *Symphony in One Movement* as "a synthetic treatment of the four-movement classical symphony"; that is to say, the customary four movements are "telescoped" and follow one another without interruption. Barber revised this symphony in 1943. This is characteristic of his procedure, for he also revised the Second Symphony in 1947. An English critic, Arthur Jacobs, visiting the United States in 1951, had this to say about Barber's Second Symphony:

> The symphony is in that neo-Romantic style which makes Barber more readily comprehensible to conventionally-educated European musicians than are many other American composers. This is music that it seems appropriate to describe in terms of rhetoric— statement and counterstatement, question and answer, repetition and summarization. . . . It harnesses modern discords to basically 19th-century modes of construction.[3]

The same could be said of most of Barber's music, but more particularly that written up to 1939, culminating with the Concerto for Violin

[3] In *Musical America*, April 15, 1951.

and Orchestra of that year. After 1940 he became somewhat more venturesome in his use of dissonance and in his treatment of tonality The Second Essay for Orchestra, composed in 1942, contains a poly-tonal fugue (*Molto Allegro ed energico*) that points toward bolder tonal procedures in such works as the *Symphony Dedicated to the Air Forces* (1944), in which the harmonies are more dissonant, the melodic lines more angular; the *Medea Suite*, with its heightened chromaticism (originally written for a ballet in 1946, it was recorded for full orchestra in 1955); and the Sonata for Piano (Opus 26, 1949), which employs twelve-tone writing. To this period belong some of Barber's best works, notably *Knoxville: Summer of 1915*, for soprano and orchestra (1947; on a text by James Agee); *Mélodies passagères* (1951), a cycle of five songs on poems of Rilke (in French translation); and the impressive *Prayers of Kierkegaard* (1954), for soprano solo, mixed chorus, and orchestra.

Barber paid tribute to the neoclassicism of the 1940s with his *Capricorn Concerto* (1944), in the style of the eighteenth-century *concerto grosso*, for flute, oboe, trumpet, and strings. In the following year he composed the attractive Concerto for Cello and Orchestra (1945). From 1956 to 1957 he composed the opera *Vanessa*, which is discussed in Chapter 30. The effective Concerto for Piano and Orchestra was written in 1961–1962. When his dramatic scena for soprano and orchestra, *Andromache's Farewell*, was first performed in New York City (1963), a critic wrote that Barber's music "is basically very conventional—conventional even in its dissonances." No doubt it is this conventional quality that has made Barber's music so widely acceptable.

An earlier work by Barber should be mentioned as being much less conventional: *A Stopwatch and an Ordnance Map* (1940), a setting of Stephen Spender's poem about the death of a soldier in the Spanish Civil War, for men's voices and three kettledrums (with optional brass).

Assorted romanticists

Robert E. Ward, born in Cleveland, Ohio, in 1917, received his bachelor's degree from the Eastman School of Music in 1939, then continued his studies at the Juilliard School of Music, where he became a member of the faculty in 1946. He also studied with Copland at the Berkshire Music Center. A romantically inclined traditionalist, he has written three symphonies and other orchestral works: *Jubilation Overture* (1946), *Concert Music* (1948), *Fantasia* for brass choir and timpani (1953), *Euphony for Orchestra* (1954); as well as a setting of "Hush'd Be the Camps Today" for chorus and orchestra (1941). His operas, *He Who Gets Slapped* (1956) and *The Crucible* (1961), are discussed in Chapter 30.

Paul Nordoff, born in Philadelphia in 1909, studied composition with Rubin Goldmark in New York. His first important work was a Secular Mass (1934), for mixed chorus and orchestra. He wrote the scores for two ballets produced by Martha Graham: *Every Soul Is a Circus* (1938) and *Salem Shore* (1944). His orchestral compositions include Prelude and Three Fugues (1932), two Piano Concertos, a Violin Concerto, a Symphony, and a Suite for chamber orchestra. His Quintet for Piano and Strings won a Pulitzer Prize in 1940.

William Bergsma, born in Oakland, California, in 1921, identified himself with the East when he switched from Stanford University to the Eastman School of Music. In 1946 he joined the faculty of the Juilliard School of Music, where he remained until 1963, when he was appointed director of the School of Music at the University of Washington—which brought him back to the Pacific Coast. The earliest work in his catalog is the *Paul Bunyan Suite* for orchestra (1937; revised 1945), followed by a suite from the ballet *Gold and the Señor Comandante* (1941; revised 1963). His First Symphony dates from 1949; *The Fortunate Islands,* for string orchestra (1947; revised 1956), was written after a sojourn in the West Indies. Other orchestral works include *A Carol on Twelfth Night* (1954), *Chameleon Variations* (1960), *Celebration: Toccata for the Sixth Day* (1962), and *Documentary* (1963).

Bergsma's chamber music includes three String Quartets, Suite for Brass Quartet (1940; revised 1945), Concerto for Wind Quintet (1958), and *Fantastic Variations on a Theme from "Tristan,"* for viola and piano (1961). His most important choral work is *Confrontation* (from the Book of Job), for four-part chorus and orchestra (1963). In 1956 he completed the three-act chamber opera *The Wife of Martin Guerre.*

Ned Rorem, born in Richmond, Indiana, in 1923, studied at the Curtis Institute in Philadelphia, at the Berkshire Music Center, and with Bernard Wagenaar at the Juilliard School of Music, besides being a private pupil of Aaron Copland and Virgil Thomson. From 1949 to 1958 he lived in France and Morocco, and from 1959 to 1961 was composer-in-residence at the University of Buffalo. Although he has written three symphonies, two piano concertos, *Design for Orchestra* (1955), *Sinfonia* for Fifteen Wind Instruments (with optional percussion), ballet scores, and chamber music, he has been especially devoted to writing for the voice. By 1963 he had written over two hundred songs, many of them revealing the influence of his sojourn in France. His choral music includes several hymn anthems, *The Corinthians* (mixed voices and organ), and *The Poet's Requiem* (1955) for soprano solo, mixed voices, and orchestra, on texts by Cocteau, Gide, Kafka, Rilke, and others. Typical of his lyrical vein is the *Mourning Scene from Samuel* (1947), for voice and string quartet, taking its text from II Samuel 1: 19–27 ("The beauty of Israel is slain upon thy high places: how are the mighty fallen!").

When Peter Mennin, in 1962, succeeded William Schuman as president of the Juilliard School of Music, he crowned a career that from its inception had proceeded in a long crescendo of success. Author of six symphonies by the time he was thirty, most of them commissioned, winner of distinguished awards, beginning with the George Gershwin Memorial Award in 1945 at the age of twenty-two, Mennin received a Ph.D. from the University of Rochester and then joined the faculty of the Juilliard School in 1947. A native of Erie, Pennsylvania, where he was born in 1923, he obtained his early musical training at the Oberlin Conservatory before going on to the Eastman School of Music. From 1958 to 1962 he was director of the Peabody Conservatory of Music in Baltimore.

Mennin's first six symphonies were composed from 1942 to 1953 (it was the Second that obtained for him the Gershwin Memorial Award), but there was a hiatus of ten years before the completion of the Seventh (in 1963). In the interim he composed other large symphonic works, notably the Concerto for Cello and Orchestra (1956) and the Concerto for Piano and Orchestra (1957), both in the grand line of the virtuoso concert piece. Among the symphonies, the Fourth (1949), titled *The Cycle*, was written for chorus of mixed voices with orchestra, on a text by the composer dealing with the cosmic forces of the world. From the same year is *The Christmas Story*, a cantata for mixed voices, soprano and tenor soli, two trumpets in C, two trombones, timpani, and strings, which received its radio première on Christmas Eve, 1949. For *a cappella* mixed chorus Mennin composed *Settings of Four Chinese Poems by Kiang Kang-Hu* (1948), in translations by Witter Bynner.

Mennin's first characteristic orchestral work was the *Concertato* (1952), based on *Moby Dick;* his most recent (up to 1963) was *Canto for Orchestra* (1963), commissioned by the Association of Women's Committees. The fact that Mennin's Cello Concerto was described in the *Cincinnati Enquirer* as "melodious, sober, high-minded," doubtless goes far to explain why he repeatedly receives commissions of this kind. For the rest, the secret of his success as a composer is an open book; it is epitomized in a phrase from the *Louisville Courier-Journal,* printed after the première of his Symphony No. 6: "The new symphony compels attention from the portentous introduction through the triumphant finale." There can be no more emphatic affirmation of the post-romantic spirit than to proceed from the portentous to the triumphant.

The modern romanticists will have the last word in this chapter, as they did the first; but before arriving at that "triumphant finale" we should turn our attention to another phase of traditionalism that was also important—and probably more characteristic—in this period: neoclassicism, whose presiding genius was Igor Stravinsky. And, if we may use the expression, the midwife of American noeclassicism was Nadia Boulanger, through whom successive generations of American composers were introduced to Stravinsky's brain-child (literally the offspring of "cerebralism," according to Howard Hanson's notion). The neoclassical doctrine is summarized in the title of a work by Stravinsky's self-avowed disciple, Arthur Berger's *Ideas of Order.*

Neoclassicism at Harvard

Stravinsky lived in France from 1920 to 1939, and it was from Paris that his influence radiated. During those years a steady stream of young American musicians flowed to and from Paris, where they imbibed the Stravinskian influence at its source. Chief among the composers of the older generation to do this were Aaron Copland and Walter Piston, both of whom had a decisive role in the development of neoclassicism in the United States (later, in the 1940s, the presence of Hindemith at Yale was also a factor in the promotion of this movement). When Stravinsky came to Harvard in 1939 to deliver his famous lectures on *The Poetics of Music,* he found himself in what by then had become the stronghold of neoclassicism in America. And although Stravinsky, when he decided to remain in the United States and become an American citizen, chose to make his home in Los Angeles, much of his tutelary spirit abided in Cambridge. The man who first brought neoclassicism to Harvard and nourished its growth there for many decades was Walter Piston.

Piston did not, at first, contemplate a career in music. His boyhood was spent in Rockland, Maine, where he was born on January 20, 1894. Having decided that he wanted to be an artist, he enrolled in the Massachusetts School of Art, from which he graduated in 1914. After working as an artist for some time, he decided that it would be wise to have a college education, so he matriculated at Harvard, and it was there that he became seriously interested in music as a profession. He proved to be a brilliant student, in spite of his dissatisfaction with "the standardized academic routine which taught harmony and counterpoint according to outmoded and unimaginative textbooks." In after years, when he became a professor at Harvard, he replaced these "outmoded textbooks" with new and excellent ones of his own writing: *Principles of Harmonic Analysis* (1933), *Harmony* (1941; revised 1948), *Counterpoint* (1947), and *Orchestration* (1955). In the meantime, after graduating from Harvard in 1924, he spent two years in Paris as a pupil of Nadia Boulanger. Upon his return he joined the Harvard music faculty and in 1951 was appointed Naumberg Professor of Music. He retired in 1960.

Piston began as a neoclassicist in the 1920s with such works as *Three Pieces* for clarinet, flute, and bassoon (1926), *Symphonic Piece* (1927), and Suite for orchestra (1929)—his first fully characteristic composition. This score contains deft and discrete allusions to the American musical vernacular, the blues in particular. It calls for "snare drum with wire brush" in the manner of the jazz bands of the period. Although Piston has never been a doctrinaire Americanist, he often draws upon American popular idioms, unobtrusively but effectively, as in the first movement of the Second Symphony, with its syncopated rhythms.

Piston's neoclassicism reached its apogee during the 1930s, with the Sonata for flute and piano (1930), Suite for oboe and piano (1932); Concerto, Prelude, and Fugue, for orchestra (1934); Trio for violin, cello, and piano (1935); the First and Second String Quartets (1933 and 1935); and particularly the *Concertino* for piano and chamber orchestra (1937). Dating from the same year, his First Symphony displays the height of his involvement with dissonant counterpoint and complex fugal writing.

In 1938, Piston wrote the music for a ballet, *The Incredible Flutist*, which he converted two years later into a Suite for orchestra. This colorful and entertaining score was for a long time his most frequently performed composition. It also marks his first incursion into programmatic or descriptive music, and by its very prominence serves to emphasize Piston's consistent adherence to the principle of "absolute" or "formal" composition, which in his case extends to the exclusion (with a rare exception) of literary texts for musical setting. He is first and last an instrumental composer, and his eight symphonies, of which the Eighth was completed in 1965, are a monument to his belief in the power of absolute music. Scarcely less significant in this respect are his String Quartets (of which the Third dates from 1947), the Piano Quintet of 1949, and the two Violin Concertos (1939 and 1959–1960)—particularly the Second, commissioned by the Ford Foundation for Joseph Fuchs. Nor must we overlook the typically neoclassical works of the 1940s, such as the *Sinfonietta* for orchestra (1941), the *Divertimento* for nine solo instruments (1946), and the Second Suite for orchestra (1948).

Many are the prominent American composers who studied with Piston at Harvard—and who in most cases were sent afterward to study with Nadia Boulanger in Paris. It was through this Harvard-Paris axis that the formation of a "Stravinsky school" occurred in the United States—not perhaps as highly organized as the term "school" might imply, but sufficiently well characterized to be accepted as a conceptual reality.

The "Stravinsky school"

It was Copland who first spoke of a "Stravinsky school" in the United States (while deploring that it had been saddled with the term "neoclassicism," which he happened to dislike) and mentioned among its members Arthur Berger, Irving Fine, Alexei Haieff, Harold Shapero, Lukas Foss, and John Lessard.[4] To these, Berger himself—who became the leader and chief spokesman of the group—later added the names of Ingolf Dahl, Charles Jones, Paul Des Marais, Leo Smit,

[4] In *Stravinsky in the Theatre*, ed. Minna Lederman (New York, 1949).

and Louise Talma.[5] The original nucleus consisted of Berger, Fine, and Shapero, all of whom had been pupils of Piston at Harvard and of Boulanger in Paris.

Arthur Berger was born in New York City in 1912. After undergraduate studies at New York University he received his M.A. at Harvard. He was for a number of years active as music critic in New York City, and in 1953 was appointed Professor of Music at Brandeis University, in Waltham, Massachusetts. With his move to Waltham, it was Brandeis rather than Harvard that became the stronghold of the Stravinskian cult in the United States. In all fairness, it should be recorded that Berger does not favor the term "neoclassicism," because in his opinion it "carries implications of pseudo-classicism, academicism, conservatism." While this may be true enough in certain contexts, it is no less true that the best "neoclassical" compositions are not characterized by any of these negative qualities. In my own judgment, the term is useful, valid, and affirmative in its creative implications.

Recovering soon from an early bout of atonalism, Berger by 1941 had written a Quartet for Woodwinds in C major, wherein he achieved that personal compromise between chromatic and diatonic writing that eventually led one critic to dub him "a diatonic Webern." Other works of the 1940s, when he remained fairly close to the Copland-Stravinsky orbit, include the *Serenade Concertante* (1944; revised 1951), for violin, woodwind quartet, strings, two horns, and trumpet; the *Partita* for piano (1947); and Three Pieces for String Quartet (1945). Yet even in these works there is no mere subservience to a Stravinskian "manner," but rather a taking off from the "eternal principles" that Berger sought and found (to his own satisfaction) in the music of Stravinsky. The composer and critic Lou Harrison was perspicacious enough to perceive this when he wrote of the Three Pieces for String Quartet that the music "bears the surface evidence of a thorough-going devotion to Stravinsky, but he (Berger) has taken that composer's devices into a farther land where the broken items of discontinuity are evenly distributed throughout the design"— whence, no doubt, the reference to Webern mentioned above.

Thanks to Stravinsky's own advance into twelve-tone writing,

[5] "Stravinsky and the Younger American Composers," *The Score* (London), June, 1955. Reprinted in *The American Composer Speaks*, ed. Chase.

Berger could adopt dodecaphonic methods and still remain faithful to the Master. This he did in *Chamber Music for Thirteen Players* (1956) and in the String Quartet of 1958. He was not, of course, the first of the American "Stravinskians" to take this direction. Irving Fine, for one, had done it as early as 1952.

Irving Fine (1914–1962) first attracted attention with *The Choral New Yorker* (1944), settings for chorus of poems from *The New Yorker* magazine. During the 1940s he wrote a number of works in a dissonant but still prevailingly diatonic idiom: *Toccata Concertante for Orchestra* (1947), Music for Piano (1947), *Partita for Wind Quintet* (1948). It was with his String Quartet of 1952 that Fine definitely turned to twelve-tone writing. His last completed work was the Symphony of 1962. At the time of his death he was director of the School of Creative Arts at Brandeis University.

Harold Shapero (born 1920 in Lynn, Massachusetts) started out as a twelve-tone composer but soon turned to neoclassical diatonicism with the String Quartet No. 1, written while he was still an undergraduate at Harvard (1940). He continued along the same direction in the Serenade in D for string orchestra (1945), the Piano Sonata for Four Hands (1941), and Trumpet Sonata (1942). In the Symphony for Classical Orchestra (1948) he demonstrated that admiration for Stravinsky was compatible with an affinity for Beethoven—an affinity also revealed in his sonatas and variations for piano.

Shapero's early interest in jazz was revived when he wrote a jazz-like piece called *On Green Mountain* (*Chaconne after Monteverdi*), for thirteen players (1953). His larger compositions include *Credo for Orchestra* (1955), *Concerto for Orchestra* (1958), and a cantata with Hebrew text for the American Jewish Tercentenary Celebration (1955). In 1952 he joined the music faculty of Brandeis University, continuing the association with Berger and Fine that had been formed at Harvard.

Of the remaining "Stravinskians," the one who is considered by Berger to have "brought with him a certain authenticity as a Stravinsky heir," is Alexei Haieff, who was born in Siberia in 1914. Because of this background, Berger believes that he has been able "to venture closer to the letter of the master than the rest of us." Haieff's adherence to the letter and the spirit of Stravinskian neoclassicism is revealed in such works at the *Serenade* (1942), for oboe, clarinet, bassoon, and piano; the *Divertimento* (1944), for small orchestra; the Sonata for Two Pianos (1945); Violin Concerto (1948); Piano Concerto (1952); and Ballet in E (1955) for orchestra.

John Lessard, born in San Francisco in 1920, came into the Stravinsky circle through having been a pupil of Boulanger in Paris. Of all the members of "The Club," he has been the most consistently neoclassical in such works as the Quintet (1943), for violin, viola, cello, flute, and clarinet; *Cantilena* (1946), for oboe and strings; Octet for Winds (1954); Concerto for harpsichord and chamber orchestra (1959); and *Symphonie Concertante* (1952), for flute, clarinet, bassoon, and string orchestra.

Instead of studying first at Harvard and then with Nadia Boulanger, Paul Des Marais (born in 1920) reversed the procedure. He studied with Nadia Boulanger in 1941–1942 (while she was teaching in the United States), then, after his discharge from the armed forces in 1945, entered Harvard. After teaching there for several years, he joined the music faculty of the University of California at Los Angeles.

Up to 1953, Des Marais's musical style was (by his own admission) "strongly classical and deeply influenced by the music of Stravinsky." The principal works of this period are the two Piano Sonatas (1947 and 1952), the Suite for baritone and piano (1951), *Theme and Changes* for harpsichord (1953), and a six-part Mass for unaccompanied mixed voices (1949). Thereafter the Stravinskian influence became less pronounced in his work. New directions are revealed in the compositions written after 1958, beginning with *Psalm 121* for unaccompanied mixed voices (1959). The works of this period, while remaining strongly tonal, utilize serial technique in an extremely free manner, as in the *Capriccio* (1962), for two pianos, percussion, and celesta. The composition titled *Organum 4* (1963–1964), for mixed voices, organ, and percussion, detaches itself from traditional forms and "consists rather of music that unfolds around slowly-moving pedal points."

Even Berger admits that the influence of Copland was as strong—and perhaps more immediate—as that of Stravinsky among the circle of Americans whom we are discussing. Ingolf Dahl (*b.* 1912) feels that the influence of Charles Ives and of American folk music was also operative in his case. Born in Hamburg, Germany, of Swedish parents, Dahl received his musical training in Cologne and Zurich, specializing on the flute. He came to the United States in 1938 and became an American citizen in 1943, making his home in Los Angeles. He had some master classes in composition with Nadia Boulanger in California.

Although Berger characterized Dahl's early style as "post-Romantic chromaticism," he himself prefers to describe it as "an expressionistically oriented dissonant and polyphonic style." Typical of this phase is the *Allegro and Arioso* for woodwind quintet of 1940–1943, of which the second movement is dodecaphonic, though not rigorously so. The Quintet for Brass Instruments of 1944 marks a change toward what the composer calls "a more liberated, aerated, open, and tonal music." The emphasis on diatonic writing continues in other works of this decade, which also exploit the technical and sonorous possibilities of various solo instruments: Concerto for Saxophone and Orchestra (1949; revised 1953); Concerto for Two Clarinets and Orchestra (1952; commissioned by Benny Goodman); *Variations on a Swedish Folktune*, for solo flute (1945); *Concerto a Tre* (1946), for violin, cello, and clarinet; and the *Divertimento* for Viola and Piano (1948).

Beginning with the *Sonata Seria* of 1953, for piano, Dahl's music moved toward a synthesis of compositional elements, equally distant from diatonic neoclassicism on the one hand, and from total chromaticism on the other. While striving to preserve the clarity of outline, closed forms, thematic development, and tonal feeling associated with neoclassicism, the composer also freely uses serial organization, not always based on the use of twelve-tone rows: he sometimes uses a six-tone row with definite tonal possibilities, as in the *Sinfonietta* for Concert Band (1960), which is in A flat major. The synthesis of this period finds its fullest expression in the Piano Quartet of 1957, the *Sonata Pastorale* of 1959 for piano, and the Piano Trio of 1962.

The MacDowell Colony for artists in Peterborough, New Hampshire, became a sort of outpost for the Stravinsky circle through the presence there, from time to time, of Berger, Fine, and Shapero. It was through meeting these composers at the MacDowell Colony, as well as through the influence of her teacher Nadia Boulanger, that Louise Talma became a member of "The Club." Born in Arcachon, France, in 1906, Louise Talma received her musical training at the Institute of Musical Art in New York City, at Columbia and New York Universities and at the Fontainebleau School of Music in France, where she also taught solfège during four successive summers (1936–1939). In 1938 she joined the music faculty of Hunter College of the City University of New York, becoming Professor of Music in 1952. She was the first woman to receive a Guggenheim Fellowship for musical composition twice in succession (1947 and 1948).

The compositions of Louise Talma's Stravinskian phase include *Four-handed Fun* (1941), for piano (four hands); Piano Sonata No. 1 (1943); *Alleluia* (1944), for piano; *Toccata for Orchestra* (1944); and an oratorio, *The Divine Flame* (1946–1948), for mixed chorus and orchestra, with mezzo-soprano and baritone soli (based on the Bible and the Missal). This was a transitional work, as was also a setting of *The Leaden Echo and the Golden Echo* (Gerard Manley Hopkins), for double chorus, soprano solo, and piano (1950). It was after hearing Irving Fine's twelve-tone String Quartet of 1952 that Louise Talma felt attracted for the first time to dodecaphonic composition ("I never much liked the dark, brooding, introspective character of the twelve-tone classics," she says). Hearing it used "with the clarity and elegance" of Fine's work, she became a convert to serial writing, beginning with the Six Etudes for Piano (1953–1954), followed by the Piano Sonata No. 2 (1955), *Passacaglia and Fugue for Piano* (1955–1962), String Quartet (1954), and Sonata for Violin and Piano (1962). Her twelve-tone vocal works include *La Corona* (seven sonnets by John Donne) for *a cappella* chorus (1954–1955); *Cantata* (1963) for tenor, clarinet, cello, piano, and percussion; and an opera in three acts, *The Alcestiad* (libretto by Thornton Wilder), which received its first performance at the opera house in Frankfurt, Germany, on March 1, 1962. This event marks the first production at a major European opera house of a work by an American woman composer.

Although Lukas Foss and Charles Jones were mentioned by Copland and Berger as belonging to "the Stravinsky school," their relationship to the group is marginal. Foss was discussed in the preceding chapter, and Jones will be discussed below, together with other composers who exemplify some of the traits associated with neoclassicism, combined with considerable formal and tonal freedom.

Toward a "new" neoclassicism

The neoclassical element in the music of Charles Jones relates more to the formal (structural) aspect than to any diatonic allegiance, since he has tended increasingly toward chromaticism. Jones, who was born in Ontario, Canada, in 1910, joined the faculty of the Juilliard School of Music and (during the summer) of the Aspen Music School in Colorado. He favors closed forms in many of his instrumental compositions, such as the Toccata for Piano Solo (1955), the Sonata for violin and piano (1956), Chorale Prelude for solo violin (1957), Sonata Piccola (1960) for piccolo, harpsichord, or piano, Concerto for Four Violins and Orchestra (1963), two symphonies (1958 and 1962), and five String Quartets. His major vocal works are a cantata, *The Seasons* (1959), for speaker, soprano, baritone, and chamber ensemble; and a setting of *Piers the Plowman* (1963), for tenor solo, chorus, and orchestra.

Although Andrew Imbrie (born in New York City in 1921) studied for one summer with Nadia Boulanger in France, his chief musical mentor was Roger Sessions, with whom he studied both at Princeton (as an undergraduate) and at the University of California. In 1947 he was appointed to the faculty of the latter university, although he spent the academic year 1947–1948 in Rome as a Fellow of the American Academy. Recognition came to him immediately when his First String Quartet received the New York Music Critics' Circle Award in 1944. Among other compositions of this decade are the *Ballad in D for Orchestra* (1947); the *Divertimento* (1948) for flute, bassoon, trumpet, cello, and piano; the Trio (1946) for violin, cello, and piano; and a setting of Walt Whitman's *On the Beach at Night* (1948), for four-part mixed chorus and orchestra.

When Imbrie's Second String Quartet (1953) was first performed in New York, Virgil Thomson wrote: "Its style is neoclassic with high chromaticism and dissonance saturations"—an excellent description of Imbrie's music as a whole. Twelve-tone procedures are used freely in the Concerto for Violin and Orchestra (1951–1954)—which Alfred Frankenstein called "the most important composition of its kind since the violin concerto by Alban Berg"[6]—and in the Third String Quartet (1957), consisting of three movements played without interruption, in a dense and dissonant contrapuntal texture that manages to make room for a strong and intense lyricism. Discussing Imbrie's string quartets, his fellow-composer Ingolf Dahl wrote:[7] "The quality of these works arises out of the combination of clear, classically oriented form (in the sense of balance of contrasted sections) with

[6] In *The San Francisco Chronicle*, April 24, 1958. Alfred Frankenstein is one of the keenest of contemporary American critics.

[7] In *The Musical Quarterly*, XLVI, 1 (Jan., 1960).

the spontaneity of those welcome comments in which the music bursts out of the established patterns in free declamation." The same observations might be applied to the impressive Sonata for Piano (1947), with its characteristic chromatic-diatonic tensions.

Imbrie's admiration for Whitman is evidently enduring, for in 1961 he returned to that poet with a setting of *Drum Taps* for mixed chorus and strings. Other works of the 1960s include the one-act opera *Three against Christmas* (1960–1961), *Psalm 42* for male chorus and organ (1962), and incidental music for James Schevell's play *Voices of Mass and Capital A* (San Francisco, 1962). Like his teacher Sessions, Andrew Imbrie is "an intensely serious composer" who does not believe in compromising, nor in turning away from the great traditions of the past, whether they stem from Beethoven or from Schoenberg. "For we must compose," he once said, "with the assumption that if we fashion our ideas with conviction and force, they will reach their goal through the ear of the listener."[8] One can only hope that this confidence in the listener's ear is not misplaced.

Daniel Pinkham, born in Lynn, Massachusetts, in 1923, is a musician of exceptional versatility who has been active as composer, conductor, harpsichordist, organist, and pianist. His own many-sided accomplishments as an executant have influenced his attitude toward composing. As he has said: "I have always been interested in making music technically accessible, and delight in trying to achieve sonorities by combining instruments in a way that is at once idiomatic for the individual performer and yet new in ensemble sound."[9]

Pinkham studied with a distinguished list of teachers, beginning at Harvard with Piston and continuing with Aaron Copland, Arthur Honegger, Samuel Barber, and Nadia Boulanger. With them, of course, he studied composition—there is another and longer list for his studies in organ, harpsichord, piano, and conducting. He became organist of historic King's Chapel in Boston, and together with the violinist Robert Brink has concertized extensively in programs of chamber music for violin and harpsichord.

Unlike some contemporary composers, Pinkham apparently does not object to having his music labeled "neoclassical." On this point

[8] In an address to the American Symphony Orchestra League, San Francisco, June 21, 1963.

[9] Statements by the composer published with the score of his *Fanfare, Aria and Echo,* for two horns and timpani (C. F. Peters Corporation, New York, 1963).

he writes: "Some have called my music neoclassical. Certainly my association with Baroque music as a performer has left its influence as far as form is concerned. My early association with singers and choruses has left me with an enthusiasm for lyricism and a singing line."

With this background, it is not surprising to find a large emphasis on choral music in Pinkham's output. His choral works include *Easter Cantata* for mixed chorus, brass instruments, celesta, timpani, and percussion; *An Emily Dickinson Mosaic*, cantata for female voices and small orchestra; *Festival Magnificat and Nunc Dimittis*, for mixed voices and organ with optional brass; *Requiem* (Mass) for alto and tenor soli, mixed voices, and accompaniment of two trumpets, two horns, two trombones, and contrabass; and *Christmas Cantata* (*Sinfonia Sacra*), composed in 1957. For orchestra he has written Symphony No. 1 and *Catacoustical Measures*. Among other instrumental works are the *Partita for Harpsichord; Piano Concertino; Concertante*, for organ, celesta, and percussion; and *Concertante No. 2*, for violin and strings (1958).

An "elite" composer

Under this caption *Time* (May 28, 1956) served notice to its readers that Elliott Carter had "arrived," while implying that his music was more to be admired than loved. Years earlier, the composer Lazare Saminsky, writing about Carter's first important score, the ballet *Pocahontas* (1939), observed that "The cognoscenti were impressed by the poised vigor of the music, its sure craft, its finish." Carter has remained a composer for the cognoscenti, but his circle of admirers has widened as his work has grown in power and originality, so that by 1960 he was regarded by many critics as the most important American composer of his generation (he was born in 1908).

Carter was a pupil of Piston and others at Harvard, and later of Nadia Boulanger in Paris (1932–1935). In 1939 he composed a Suite for Quartet of Alto Saxophones, consisting of three four-part canons, which revealed two traits of his writing: a penchant for unusual instrumental groups, and a partiality for canonic textures. The First Symphony (1942), imbued with "New England thought and feeling," reflects his admiration for Charles Ives. In his *Holiday Overture* (1944) he went over the heads of the cognoscenti, appealing directly to the average "music lover." The music for a ballet called *The Minotaur* (1947), with its blending of archaic and modern elements, gave the first measure of his orchestral power and inventiveness.

Meanwhile, he had composed the Piano Sonata of 1946, which, to Virgil Thomson's practised ear, sounded "completely original." This originality of style and concept found further confirmation in the Woodwind Quintet and the Sonata for Cello and Piano, both composed in 1948. In this Sonata, Carter employs a compositional procedure that he calls "metric modulation." This involves "the coordination of all the tempi of the work and their interrelation by notated changes of speed. . . . The large circle of speed changes is completed when the Sonata concludes by returning at the very end to the speed of the first movement." This concept of the changes and relations of speed as an element of formal construction became a fundamental phase of Carter's compositional procedure.

Structurized tempi are used as organizational components in both the First String Quartet (1951) and the Second String Quartet (1958–1959). The first movement of the former consists of a contrapuntal fantasia having four main and several subsidiary themes, each with its own speed. In the variations of the last movement the themes become slightly faster at each repetition. The Second Quartet consists of six movements played without interruption. In the words of the composer:

The four instruments are individualized, each being given its own character embodied in a special set of melodic and harmonic intervals and rhythms that result in different patterns of slow and fast tempi with associated types of expression. Thus, four different strands of musical material of contrasting character are developed simultaneously throughout the work.

Other important works of this decade are Eight Etudes and a Fantasy for Woodwind Quartet (1952); Sonata for flute, oboe, cello, and harpsichord (1952); and the *Variations for Orchestra* (1953–1955). The last-mentioned provides a good illustration of Carter's "reinvention" of traditional forms. Instead of simply presenting a different aspect of the theme in each variation, Carter was interested "in adopting a more dynamic and changeable approach." Hence, the principle of variation is often applied within each piece or section of the work, so that "in some, great changes of character and theme occur, in others, contrasting themes and characters answer each other back and forth or are heard simultaneously. . . . Thus the old notion of 'unity in diversity' presents itself to us in an entirely different guise. . . ."

Carter's first work of the 1960s was the Double Concerto for harpsichord and piano with two chamber orchestras (1961). This is an antiphonal work in which each of the two small contrasting ensembles is led by one of the soloists. As the composer explains: "In addition to being isolated in space and timbre, the antiphonal groups are partially separated musically by the fact that each emphasizes its own repertory of melodic and harmonic intervals. . . . Each of these intervals is associated, for the most part, with a certain metronomic speed, with the result that the speeds and their relationships also differ for the two groups. . . . The form is that of confrontations of diversified action-patterns and a presentation of their mutual interreactions, conflicts, and resolutions, their growth and decay over varying stretches of time."

In 1966 Carter completed one of his most important works, the Concerto for Piano and Orchestra, again demonstrating his capacity for creative invention. He is a traditionalist because he believes strongly in continuity—both historical and structural—but he uses invention to enlarge the boundaries of tradition.

A romantic at Harvard

In 1961, Leon Kirchner, an avowed romanticist, succeeded Walter Piston, the leading American neoclassicist, as Professor of Music at Harvard University. It is true that the first Professor of Music at Harvard, John Knowles Paine, was a romanticist; but then, in his time almost everybody was. Today it is rather exceptional. What is historically significant, however, is not the exceptional quality of being a romantic composer (there are always several on the scene), but the circumstance of Kirchner's going to Harvard, the stronghold of American neoclassicism for more than three decades. Like Howard Hanson thirty years earlier, Kirchner's voice has been raised in denunciation of musical "abstraction" and "cerebralism." The targets of his dislike are "the quasi-arithmeticians, the new aesthetic engineers of music (who) worship and make a fetish of complexity." As a result, he affirms, "Idea, the precious ore of art, is lost in the jungle of graphs, prepared tapes, feedbacks, and cold stylistic minutiae." Like Hanson, he wants "warm-blooded music," repudiating the "coldly stylistic."

Kirchner, too, issued his "Romantic Manifesto," in the guise of an artistic credo that emphasizes the arch-romantic concept of the creation of a personal cosmos through artistic self-expression:

An artist must create a personal cosmos, a verdant world in continuity with tradition, further fulfilling man's 'awareness,' his 'degree of consciousness,' and bringing new subtilization, vision and beauty to the elements of experience. It is in this way that the Idea, powered by conviction and necessity, will create its own style, and the singular, momentous structure capable of realizing its intent.

Kirchner's music certainly conveys the impression of being "powered by conviction and necessity." Critics have spoken of its "rhapsodic glow," its "span of creative tension," its "personal intensity," its "context of conflict and urgency," and its "emotional impact and explosive power"—a veritable catalog of romantic traits.

Leon Kirchner was born in Brooklyn, New York, on January 24, 1919. Taken to California at the age of nine, he lived there most of the time until his appointment at Harvard. He studied theory at the University of California in Berkeley, and composition with Bloch, Sessions, and Schoenberg. An excellent pianist, he has appeared frequently as soloist in his own compositions, notably the Concerto for Piano and Orchestra No. 1 (1953), his most important work prior to 1960.

In his early years Kirchner wrote a quantity of music that he later discarded. Hence the catalog of his acknowledged compositions begins with a *Duo* for Violin and Piano dating from 1947, and continues with the Piano Sonata of 1948 and the String Quartet No. 1 (1949). Aaron Copland, reviewing the *Duo*, affirmed that Kirchner's principal claim to originality resided in "the daringly free structural organization of his compositions" and situated him as "belonging to the Bartók-Berg axis of contemporary music." Charles Jones, writing of the String Quartet, observed that its chromaticism was more Wagnerian than Viennese—again a confirmation of Kirchner's post-romantic bent.

Kirchner's prestige was fully consolidated during the 1950s, when he wrote the *Sinfonia in Two Parts* (1950, commissioned by Rodgers and Hammerstein); the *Sonata Concertante* for violin and piano (1952); the *Piano Trio* (1954); the *Toccata* for strings, solo winds, and percussion (1955); *Scenes from an Opera* (1956–1957); String Quartet No. 2 (1958); and the Piano Concerto mentioned above (first performed in 1956). The following decade began with a Concerto for violin, cello, ten winds, and percussion; this was followed by the Concerto for Piano and Orchestra No. 2 (1963), commissioned by the Ford Foundation for the pianist William Masselos.

This chapter began with discussion of "an avowed romanticist" of the 1930s and concludes with presenting "an ardent romanticist"[10] of the 1960s. The reader should bear in mind that unlike objects may be compared on the basis of a single trait that they have in common. Hanson and Kirchner are both romanticists: there the similarity ends. Apart from differences of temperament and technique, we observe, in Kirchner's post-Schoenbergian romanticism, the changing "shape of time" whereby individual talents are "conditioned" by their position in the temporal sequence of history. Chromatic dissonance, for example, is characteristic of the music of our time, no matter what formal tendency it follows. Yet, throughout all its assimilation of dissonance, chromaticism, serialism—what you will—the essential romantic attitude persists, both by what it rejects and by what it affirms, as a reminder that beyond the stylistic and technical transformations of art, a flame is handed down and endures.

[10] Kirchner is given this label in the notes for the Epic recording of his Piano Trio and *Sonata Concertante*.

chapter twenty-seven

Innovation and experiment

*Why with the time do I not glance aside
To new-found methods and to compounds strange?*
SHAKESPEARE, SONNET LXXXVI.

The first great innovator in American music was Charles Ives. His experiments with polytonality and atonality, with quarter-tones and tone clusters, with spatial distribution, and with the simultaneous projection of heterogeneous and independent musical events, are by now familiar to all students of American music. Ives used atonality as early as 1907 and 1908, independently of any European developments. But his innovations were the result of intuitive solutions for immediate and specific expressive problems, hence they did not lead to a fully elaborated theory such as we find in Schoenberg. Ives wrote copiously in prose, but with more emphasis upon homespun metaphysics and transcendental idealism than upon theory and method. Accumulating one *trouvaille* after another, he was an innovator without a system.

Ives's near contemporary and long-surviving friend, Carl Ruggles (born in 1876, still living in 1966), though much more limited in creative scope and originality, spent the first twenty years of his adult life searching for a "system," and having once found it (by trial and error, one supposes) devoted the rest of his many years to composing and revising a handful of works strictly within his personal canon.[1] Eschewing variety and abundance, he sought a circumscribed perfection based on a quest for the Sublime. If his works, like his listeners,

[1] It is understood that Ruggles discarded or repudiated his compositions prior to 1918, including an opera, *The Sunken Bell*, after the drama by Gerhart Hauptmann.

572

were few, they were at least entirely his own. Engrossed in his private creative world, he let others theorize and propagandize for him.[2]

Ruggles's admirers and apologists are distinguished, enthusiastic, and articulate: they include Charles Seeger, Henry Cowell, John Kirkpatrick, Lou Harrison. Portraying the man as well as the musician, they succeeded in creating an almost fabulous character in the best Yankee tradition—a man described by Cowell as "irascible, lovable, honest, sturdy, original, slow-thinking, deeply emotional, self-assured and intelligent," and whom Seeger called "the most delightful character in contemporary American life." Whatever the ultimate fate of his music, Ruggles will probably go down in history because of a few well-placed anecdotes, such as this one, told by Henry Cowell:

> One morning when I arrived at the abandoned school house in Arlington (Vermont) where he now lives, he was sitting at the old piano, singing a single tone at the top of his raucous composer's voice, and banging a single chord at intervals over and over. He refused to be interrupted in this pursuit, and after an hour or so, I insisted on knowing what the idea was. "I'm trying over this damned chord," said he, "to see whether it still sounds superb after so many hearings." "Oh," I said tritely, "time will tell whether the chord has lasting value." "The hell with time!" Carl replied. "I'll give this chord the test of time right now. If I find I still like it after trying it over several thousand times, it'll stand the test of time, all right!"[3]

One wonders which chord that was: perhaps the tremendous chord that concludes the coda of *Portals*—rising majestically and mysteriously as if in answer to the quotation from Walt Whitman, "What are those of the known but to ascend and enter the unknown?"—which Seeger called "one of the most exquisite pages in all modern music."[4]

Ruggles, of old New England stock, was born in Marion, Massa-

---

[2] This refers to public and formal pronouncements; in private, Ruggles was an inveterate theorizer. Seeger speaks of "the reams of theoretical explanations, bizarre and, from a scholarly point of view, preposterous, that Ruggles is accustomed to regale his listeners with. . . ." (*American Composers on American Music*, p. 31).

[3] Prefatory Note to Harrison's monograph, *About Carl Ruggles*, p. 3.

[4] In his essay on Ruggles first published in *The Musical Quarterly*, XVIII, 4 (Oct., 1932) and reprinted in *American Composers on American Music* (1933), edited by Cowell (reissued in 1962).

chusetts, on March 11, 1876.[5] He learned to play the violin, and at the age of nine appeared as a local prodigy in a concert given for President Cleveland. He studied music at Harvard and then went West, founding and directing a symphony orchestra in Winona, Minnesota. From 1923 to 1933 he was active in New York, at first with the International Composers Guild and later with the Pan-American Association of Composers, both in association with Edgard Varèse. Apart from these activities, Ruggles lived as an independent creative artist, occupying for many years a converted schoolhouse in Vermont, which provided him with a huge music room. He needed plenty of space, for he liked to write his scores with colored crayons on large sheets of heavy butcher's paper spread over the floor. As a second avocation, he enjoyed a rather remarkable success as a painter. He also enjoyed his rôle as a living legend.

The corpus of works upon which Ruggles's fame depends is small. It consists of *Angels* (1921, for muted brass); *Toys* (1919, for voice and orchestra or piano); *Portals* (1926, for strings); *Evocations* (1934–1943, for piano solo); and four orchestral scores: *Men and Mountains* (1926), *Sun-Treader* (1932), *Organum* (1945), and *Affirmations* (1957). Most of these have been revised at least once and some exist in several versions. The 1954 revision of *Evocations*—subtitled "Four Chants for Piano"—was edited by John Kirkpatrick, who also recorded them for Columbia. The four "Chants" are: (1) Largo (1937), (2) Andante con Fantasia (1941), (3) Moderato Appassionato (1943), (4) Adagio Sostenuto.

Speaking of Ruggles's generalized artistic taste, Seeger writes: "It is a narrow taste, very particular, and quite of the absolutist type, with no gradations." This is reflected in the music, which moves within a firmly defined aesthetic orbit. Because of its textural complexity and the self-imposed limitations of Ruggles's compositional procedure—such as the nonrepetition of notes in the melodic line[6]—the music may give the impression of being intellectually conceived and controlled. Certainly the intellectual factor is present; but Seeger points

---

[5] The tradition that he numbered at least one whaling captain among his New Bedford ancestors is apparently apocryphal. Ruggles told John Kirkpatrick that his grandfather was a steamboat captain on the Mississippi River.

[6] The rule was not always strictly observed, especially in the inner parts; and a later critic, George Perle, has observed that Ruggles made deliberate use of repetition "either at the beginning or the conclusion of a phrase, as a means of formal and cadential articulation."

out that the form of the compositions "is mainly rhapsodic," and that in the ratio between organization and fantasy, "there is a vast preponderance of fantasy." He even goes so far as to say, "here is pure intuition."

Ruggles was attracted by rhapsodic and mystical poets. *Men and Mountains* carries a quotation from William Blake: "Great things are done when men and mountains meet." The second movement of this work is titled, "Men, rhapsodic proclamation for horns and orchestra." The music critic Lawrence Gilman saw Ruggles—somewhat exaggeratedly—as "a mystic, a rhapsodist, a composer who sees visions and dreams fantastic dreams." Perhaps he was, perhaps he did; but he was also a shrewd Yankee artisan who knew that it takes the right notes in the right places to move men and mountains in music.

In 1932 Nicolas Slonimsky conducted the first performance of *Sun-Treader*, the largest and most important of Ruggles's orchestral works. But that was in Paris: American admirers of Ruggles's music had to wait thirty-four years for this splendid score to be performed in the United States. The belated American première took place in Portland, Maine, on January 24, 1966, with the Boston Symphony Orchestra under the direction of Jean Martinon. The occasion was a three-day festival in honor of Ruggles, sponsored by Bowdoin College, which included an exhibition of his paintings and a lecture by Virgil Thomson, as well as performances of his major works. The composer himself, nearing his ninetieth birthday, was not strong enough to attend the festival, so that even his extraordinary longevity did not afford him the privilege of ever hearing a performance of his most important orchestral work.

The composer Lou Harrison, in his monograph on Ruggles, has written perceptively about the quality of his counterpoint:

It is characterized by an absolute lack of negative spacing in the voices, which is to say that no voice is ever given over to repetitious arpeggiation or figuration of any kind at all. Each voice is a real melody, bound into a community of singing lines, living a life of its own with regard to phrasing and breathing, careful not to get ahead or behind in its rhythmic cooperation with the others, and sustaining a responsible independence in the whole polyphonic life.[7]

[7] *About Carl Ruggles*, pp. 7–8.

The phrase "a community of singing lines" seems to me most felicitous in describing both the texture and the spirit of Ruggles's music.

Ruggles lived long enough to become a classic in his life-time. To the *avant-garde* of the 1960s he is not a precursor but a representative of the main tradition of Western music. John Cage wrote of him: "His work is not experimental at all but in a most sophisticated way attached to the past and to art." Granted that this be so, we can still believe that the music of Carl Ruggles is attached to a past and to an art that will endure.

To seek new paths

John J. Becker (1886–1961) is the "forgotten man" of modern American music. In 1965 only one of his works—the *Concerto Arabesque* for piano and orchestra—was available in a recording, and much of his music remained unpublished and seldom or never performed. Of his seven symphonies, the Third (*Symphonia Brevis*) had to wait twenty-nine years for its first performance. It was then (in 1958) performed under the direction of Leonard Bernstein in New York. The work, wrote Wallingford Riegger, "demonstrates how entirely the composer has shaken off the shackles of Europe and followed his own code." And Riegger spoke of "the extraordinary orchestral weaving of dissonant blends into a mounting climax unparalleled in the annals of music-making."[8]

Becker was born in Henderson, Kentucky, and received his musical training at the Wisconsin Conservatory. In 1943 he became music director and composer in residence at Barat College of the Sacred Heart in Lake Forest, Illinois. He was active as lecturer, writer, and conductor, stimulating the performance of new music in the Midwest. He composed his First Symphony in 1912, his Seventh (*The Sermon on the Mount*) in 1947. His religious works include *Missa Symphonia* (1933) for male chorus *a cappella; Mass in Honor of the Sacred Heart,* and *Moments from the Passion* (1945), both for men's or women's voices *a cappella.* In his sacred music, Becker was concerned with a renovation of the Palestrinian polyphonic style in a modern dissonant texture. One of his most important secular vocal works is the setting of Whitman's *Out of the Cradle Endlessly Rocking* (1929), for soprano, tenor, mixed chorus, and orchestra. For the stage he wrote

[8] In *Bulletin of the American Composers Alliance*, X, 1 (1959).

Dance Figure (1933), on a poem by Ezra Pound, for solo voice, dance group, and large orchestra; and *A Marriage with Space* (1934), for solo and mass recitation, solo and group dancers, and large orchestra. These works pointed toward new techniques in the musical theater.

Becker summed up his credo as a composer in the dictum: "Laws are made for imitators; creators make their own laws." Elaborating this idea, he wrote:

> It is every composer's duty to add to the already existing musical resources. Regardless of the great orchestral works of the past, the undiscovered possibilities for new ways in the development of orchestral forms and sounds are beyond comprehension. The true creative artist must never be satisfied. He must seek new paths constantly, for only by seeking will he find for himself the way to musical truth and beauty.[9]

Describing some of his orchestral devices, Becker mentioned "the juxtaposition of contrasting instruments, that is, instruments which have no relationship to each other as far as their orchestral color is concerned." Another device is that of "long sustained sections of seconds, scored for instruments of the same color." In his Third Symphony (1929) he produced "an effect like the cutting of steel" by having "the top line of a dissonant counterpoint or chordal movement in the orchestra doubled by the piano played with a percussive stroke." He was one of the early explorers of percussion music, with his dance score *Obongo* (1933) for twenty-nine percussive instruments. In a series of *Soundpieces* for strings and other instruments he developed abstract structures in sound. He composed for the films and for the theater: all in all, a vast production that remains to be fully explored and evaluated.

An eclectic innovator

Henry Cowell (1897–1965) is a striking example of how beneficial it can be for a composer to be exposed, during his formative years, to experiences that open the way to uninhibited exploration of the means of musical expression. Born in Menlo Park, California, Cowell grew up under conditions of poverty in and around San Francisco, with no regular exposure to European concert music. He became acquainted with the ecclesiastical modes (through a neighborhood organ-

[9] *Musical America* (Feb., 1950), p. 214.

ist), with Oriental music (through Chinese neighbors), and with Irish-American folk songs (through his parents) during the impressionable years of adolescence. He began to compose at the piano "on his own," relying on intuition and experimentation. Thus it was that at the age of fifteen—on March 10, 1912—he gave a public concert in San Francisco of his own music for piano, including the now-famous piece titled *The Tides of Manaunaun*, in which he used "tone clusters" as a means of suggesting the surge and roar of the tides.[10] These "tone clusters" are aggregates of adjacent tones played simultaneously. What people saw was a youth playing the piano (at times) with his forearm or fist; of course he attracted attention, and soon Cowell became known as "The Cluster Man"—a tag that stuck to him for the rest of his life.

But young Cowell was fortunate also in having come under the influence of a remarkable teacher and theorist, Charles Seeger (then at the University of California in Berkeley), who convinced him that systematic study of traditional compositional procedures was necessary. So Cowell began to study theory with E. G. Strickland and counterpoint with Wallace Sabin, while at the same time having weekly sessions with Seeger, who encouraged his experimental inclinations and urged him to find a theoretical basis for his innovations.[11] Later Cowell studied composition for three years in New York, chiefly with R. Huntington Woodworth and Percy Goetschius. In 1931–1932 he studied comparative musicology with Erich von Hornbostel in Berlin—an experience that greatly stimulated his life-long interest in non-European musical cultures. From 1923 to 1933 he made five concert tours as a pianist in Europe, playing his own compositions.

It was in a series of piano pieces composed between 1912 and 1930 that Cowell made his most original and far-reaching innovations.[12]

[10] About two years later, the pianist and composer Leo Ornstein (*b.* 1895), then living in Philadelphia, was using tone clusters in his *Wild Men's Dance* (1914) and other pieces for piano. He evidently hit upon this device quite independently, but for the same reason: to fill an expressive need. As he wrote: "I found myself using clusters for the necessary percussion effects and to meet the much deeper need to project the dark brooding quality . . . in prehistoric man" (private communication).

[11] This is precisely what Cowell did in his book *New Musical Resources*, written in 1919 though not published until 1930.

[12] A representative selection, with Cowell at the piano, will be found in the Folkways recording *Piano Music by Henry Cowell*, accompanied by an informative booklet, to which I am indebted for some biographical data.

In addition to using tone clusters, Cowell began to manipulate the strings of the piano directly, either with the hands or with a mallet or other device. He first did this in a piece called *Aeolian Harp* (1923), later in *The Banshee* (1925) and *Sinister Resonance* (1930).

In *The Tides of Manaunaun*, Cowell combined a modal melody, of the kind to which he was so partial, with tone clusters extending over one and two octaves, thus: [13]

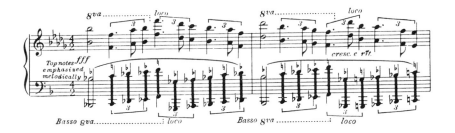

Cowell directs that the tone clusters are to be played with the forearm, with the flat of the hand, or with the fist, depending upon the length of the cluster. In the piece called *Tiger* (1928) there are clusters so large that they must be played with both forearms together. But it is not a question of "banging" the keyboard: "In legato passages, the keys should be pressed down rather than struck, in order to obtain a smooth tone quality and a unified sound." In most cases, the weight of the forearm "is enough to produce the tones without the need for adding muscular effort." When the fist is used, it should remain half-open, "not clenched tightly." At times the keys are pressed silently and held down "in order that the open string may be subjected to sympathetic vibrations."

As for using the piano strings directly, this is exemplified in *Aeolian Harp*, where the notation looks deceptively simple—until one encounters such terms as "inside," "outside," and "sw." One turns then to the explanation: "All of the notes of 'Aeolian Harp' should be pressed down on the keys, without sounding, at the same time being played on the open strings of the piano with the other hand." The symbol "sw." (either "with back of thumbnail" or "with flesh of finger") indicates that the strings should be swept in the manner directed,

[13] From *Piano Music by Henry Cowell*, with Playing Instructions. New York: Associated Music Publishers, Inc. Used by permission.

either from the lowest to the highest note of the chord, or *vice versa*. When the strings are to be plucked, the familiar abbreviation "pizz." is used. The terms "inside" and "outside" indicate the position where the strings are to be played, either near the center or near the tuning pegs.

In *Aeolian Harp* the composer wanted to achieve a mysterious, poetic quality; in *The Banshee* he wanted an eerie, unearthly, shrieking and wailing sound. The latter piece requires two players, one standing at the crook of the grand piano, the other sitting at the keyboard and holding down the damper pedal throughout the duration of the work. *The Banshee* is played entirely on the open strings of the piano, and each of the encircled capital letters, from A to L, designates a specific way of playing the strings. The three basic ways are (1) with the flesh of the finger, (2) with the flat of the hand, and (3) with the back of the fingernail. These are used in various combinations; for example, the letter H indicates that the string is to be swept up and back from the lowest to the highest note, but starting at the same time from above and below, crossing the sweep in the middle. The letter G indicates that when the finger (using the back of the nail) is half way along the string, the player should start a sweep along the same string with the flesh of the other finger, thus partly damping the sound.

In *Sinister Resonance* (1930) the music is played on the piano keyboard, but the timbre is altered by the player's manipulation of the strings with his fingers, producing stopped tones, muted tones, and harmonics. Cowell's expansion of the sound-producing possibilities of the piano has proved to be one of the most fruitful experiments of contemporary music. The technique—applied by each new composer in his own way—has become virtually standard procedure in the new music since 1960.[14] Indeed, the term "piano strings" (in German, *Klaviersaiten*) has become part of the current instrumental terminology. It will be found, for instance, in the instrumentation of the published score of Cowell's *Synchrony* (1930), where a footnote explains that "The 5 lowest strings of a grand piano [are] played on directly with a padded gong-stick."

In *Synchrony*—written in the form of an overture with introduc-

---

[14] A striking example, among many that could be cited, is the *Fantasy for Pianist* by Roger Reynolds (cf. Chapter 31,) in which both tone clusters and direct manipulation of the piano strings are used.

tory trumpet solo and polytonal textures—Cowell used orchestral tone clusters, as he had been doing, in fact, for the past fifteen years or so, beginning with *Some More Music* (*ca.* 1915) and reaching full exploitation in the Concerto for Piano and Orchestra (1929). Tone clusters had ceased to become merely a certain kind of sound effect. As Hugo Weisgall observed: "Cowell soon came to think of them as creating a system of harmony based on the interval of a second instead of a third."[15] Thus did Cowell transform a *trouvaille* into a theory.

John Cage, in his "History of Experimental Music in the United States,"[16] pays high tribute to Cowell as an innovator and a precursor of the modern experimental movement:

> His early works for piano . . . by their tone clusters and use of the piano strings, pointed towards noise and a continuum of timbre. Other works of his are indeterminate in ways analogous to those currently in use by Boulez and Stockhausen. For example, Cowell's *Mosaic Quartet*, where the performers, in any way they choose, produce a continuity from compositional blocks provided by him. Or his *Elastic Musics*, the time lengths of which can be short or long through the use or omission of measures provided by him. These actions by Cowell are very close to current experimental compositions which have parts but no scores, and which are therefore not objects but processes providing experience not burdened by psychological intentions on the part of the composer.

Elsewhere in this book mention has been made of Cowell's achievements as an Americanist and as an explorer of exotic cultures; whatever may be the value that posterity assigns to those achievements, there can be no doubt of Cowell's place as a musical innovator of the first magnitude.

Of time and space

Ruth Crawford Seeger (1901–1953) wrote a number of scores that anticipated some of the procedures of the post-1950 experimental music. She was the first woman composer to receive a Guggenheim

[15] "The Music of Henry Cowell," in *The Musical Quarterly*, XLV, 4 (Oct., 1949).

[16] Originally published in the *Darmstädter Beiträge* (1939). Reprinted in *Silence* (1961), pp. 67–75.

Fellowship, which enabled her to study in Berlin and Paris. Her compositions include Two Movements (1926) for chamber orchestra; Four Diaphonic Suites (1930) for two cellos, two clarinets, oboe, and flute (in various combinations); and Three Songs (on poems by Carl Sandburg) for contralto, oboe, piano, and percussion (1931–1932).

Her most important work is a String Quartet written in 1931. The third movement employs a procedure that has been termed "contrapuntal dynamics," whereby each voice or part makes use of independent dynamic values, as in the following example:[17]

The composer and theorist George Perle has pointed out that the fourth movement of this quartet is "a remarkable adumbration" of the compositional procedure known as "total organization," in which each "parameter" of the music (rhythm, melody, dynamics, duration) is systematically related to all the others. Perle is right when he insists that Ruth Crawford Seeger has a definite place among the independent innovators in American music.[18]

On April 10, 1927, in New York's Carnegie Hall, there took place the first performance in the United States of a composition titled *Ballet Mécanique*, written by a young composer named George Antheil. The report in the next day's *New York Times* carried these headlines:

---

[17] From *New Music, A Quarterly of Modern Compositions* (Jan., 1941), p. 12.
[18] "Atonality and the Twelve-note System in the United States," in *The Score* (London), No. 27 (July, 1960).

Antheil Art Bursts on Startled Ears—First Performance of Ballet Mécanique in This Country Draws Varied Response—Hisses, Cheers Greet Him—Concatenation of Anvils, Bells, Horns, Buzzsaws Deafens Some, Pleases Others.

For an American composer to draw hisses and cheers from a Carnegie Hall audience was in itself quite an achievement, and the novelty of the situation immediately made Antheil a celebrity.

George Antheil (1900–1959) was trained at the Philadelphia Conservatory of Music and later studied composition with Ernest Bloch. During the 1920s he spent some time in Berlin, Vienna, and Paris, appearing as a pianist and contributing to such *avant-garde* reviews as *transition* and *Der Stijl*. He was befriended and aided by Ezra Pound, who in 1925 wrote: "One has in the case of Antheil a man capable of *making* something."[19] Antheil had just given proof of this by composing, the previous year, the score of *Ballet Mécanique*, written to accompany an abstract film by Fernand Léger. It was his first important work; although he was to write six symphonies, several operas, and a quantity of other music, it is as the composer of *Ballet Mécanique* that he will go down in history.

Antheil must have been aware of this, for in later years he was eager to explain the importance and significance of this early work. Writing to Nicolas Slonimsky in 1936, he protested that his intentions had been completely misunderstood. He had never intended to "grind out pictures of the machine age" or to project "a kind of Buck Rogers fantasy of the future." As he explained:

I personally consider that the Ballet Mécanique was important in one particular and that is that it was conceived in a new form, that form specifically being the filling out of a certain time canvas with musical abstractions and sound material composed and contrasted against one another with the thought of time values rather than tonal values. . . . In the Ballet Mécanique I used time as Picasso might have used the blank spaces of his canvas. . . . My ideas were the most abstract of the abstract.[20]

Does this make Antheil a precursor of the "abstract composers"—as Virgil Thomson once called them—of the 1950s: John Cage and com-

[19] *The Letters of Ezra Pound, 1907–1941*. Ed. D. D. Paige (New York, 1950), p. 196. Pound's *Antheil and the Treatise on Harmony* was published in 1924.
[20] Quoted in Slonimsky, *Music Since 1900*, 3rd ed. (New York, 1949), p. 288.

pany? They, at least, have not claimed him as an ancestor. But he certainly anticipated some of their ideas and procedures, notably the use of "noise components with a continuum between pitch and non-pitch," and the concept of the score as a time-space canvas to be filled with musical abstractions (i.e., sounds divorced from tonal and thematic implications).[21] One has only to compare, for example, the statement by Morton Feldman: "To me my score is my canvas, my space. What I do is try to sensitize this area—this time-space."

In the 1950s, when Carlos Surinach recorded *Ballet Mécanique* with the New York Percussion Group, Antheil, in his notes for the recording, once more explained the aesthetic significance of the score. He compared it with modern architecture in its use of new materials and new methods of musical engineering, and drew an analogy with the "cantilever" principle. The work, he said, "devotes itself entirely to the TIME-SPACE principle, or the theory that TIME rather than TONALITY or anti-tonality is the main, basic 'canvas' of music." But how much of this was hindsight? At all events *Ballet Mécanique* remains to the present day "a very notorious piece, much talked about but little played," as the composer himself once described it.

One of Antheil's students in composition was Canadian-born Henry Brant (Montreal, 1913), who during the 1930s did very much what his teacher had done a decade earlier: flirting with jazz and using the American vernacular in a satirical vein, as in the *Whoopee Overture*, *The Great American Goof* (ballet), and *Five-and-Ten-Cents-Store Music*. This phase of his work may be said to have ended with the Symphony in B flat (significantly sub-titled "The Thirties"), though Brant has never hesitated to make use of the vernacular when-ever it suited him, even in his later, more complex compositions.

Brant's innovational contributions have to do with (1) exploitation of novel instrumental combinations (he has an amazing flair for original instrumentations), and (2) the spatial distribution of his performing groups so as to achieve "directional sound." This latter phase began in 1950, with *Millennium 1* (for eight trumpets, bells, and cymbals),

---

[21] Eric Salzman, in *The New York Times*, March 4, 1962, calls *Ballet Mécanique* "One of the classic, germinating works" of the 1920s and asserts that "it seems more significant than ever today in the light of what has happened since." He was reviewing a recording made by Robert Craft and the Los Angeles Contemporary Music Ensemble.

and continued through *Voyage Four* (1964), described as "a spatial concert piece for eighty-three instrumentalists and one singer led by three conductors."

Brant achieves his "antiphonal placing" by locating his performers in various parts of the auditorium, including the aisles, the balconies, and the wings. It is essential that the listener perceive the sound as coming from different directions. Sometimes he combines this spatial distribution with a "polyphony of tempos," as in *Millennium 2*, in which as many as twenty-four different tempi occur simultaneously. Since history consists largely of the testimony of eye (and ear) witnesses, let me quote an account of the première of this work by an American musician who was present:

I saw half the brass-players of the city ranged along the sides of the orchestral section of the Great Hall at Cooper Union, trumpets on one side, trombones on the other, while the stage was occupied by an ensemble of French horns, tubas, and percussion. Toward the end of the piece there was an abrupt halt in the proceedings and a single high soprano voice floated through the house: the girl, as it turned out, was concealed in the wings and singing into a microphone. The effect was uncanny, beautiful, and—for some of the audience—explosive.[22]

Champion of corporeal music

Harry Partch, born in Oakland, California, in 1901, was the first American to reject *in toto* the accepted values and norms of the classical-romantic European tradition. Self-taught in music, he developed his own aesthetic system and its concomitant theory and practice. As he tells us: "Having decided to follow my own intuitive path I began to write music on the basis of harmonized spoken words, for new instruments and in new scales. . . ."[23] These early works attempted to break down the barrier between art and reality. They include *San Francisco Newsboy Cries, Letter from Hobo Pablo, U.S.*

[22] Russell Smith, "The New Music," in *Harper's Magazine* (April, 1959). Used by permission of Harper & Row, publishers.

[23] Partch, *Genesis of a Music* (1949). Unless otherwise identified, all the quotations in this section are from the same source. Although his book was not published until 1949, we are told that the first draft was finished twenty years earlier.

Highball: Account of Hobo Trip, and *Account of the Normandy Invasion by an American Glider Pilot* (based on a recorded transcription). To this type of music, based on "harmonized spoken words," Partch gave the name *corporeal,* as opposed to what he calls *abstract* music, essentially instrumental and formalistic (like the sonata), which he sees as operative in "a realm of unreality" unrelated to any specific "here and now."

Corporeal music is essentially monophonic (using one voice) and it is based on the principle that, "Of all the tonal ingredients a creative man can put into his music, his voice is at once the most dramatically potent and the most intimate." By this, Partch does not, of course, mean his own particular voice, but "his conception as expressed by the human voice—and [this] means *one* voice." This "essentially vocal and verbal music" is characterized as being "vital to a time and place, a here and now. . . . Corporeal music is emotionally 'tactile.' It does not grow from the root of 'pure form.' It cannot be characterized as either mental or spiritual."

In attempting to give practical existence to his musical concepts, Partch found himself up against the power of what Walter Bagehot called "the single consecrated code"—entirely dominated by the values of abstract music. As Partch puts it: "Our musical system of today builds from the frame of an inherited keyboard and from inherited forms and instruments of Europe's eighteenth century. . . . The door to further musical investigation and insight has been slammed shut by the inelastic and doctrinaire quality of our one system and its esthetic forms."

Rejecting the twelve-tone tempered scale, Partch devised a scale that divided the octave into forty-three microtones. He then had to invent and make a set of new instruments to play the music using this scale. In 1941 he completed the construction of an instrument called the chromelodeon, being a reed organ with a forty-three-tones-to-the-octave scale spreading over three and one-half keyboard octaves. This was followed by the kithara, consisting of seventy-two strings in chords of six each in a lyre-type body; the surrogate kithara, with six strings, each on two long resonating boxes (mostly for sliding tones); harmonic canons, with forty-four strings and a movable bridge for each string; and various percussion instruments: diamond marimba (thirty-six blocks with bamboo resonators), bass marimba (eleven Sitka spruce blocks over redwood resonators), cloud-chamber bowls (tops and bottoms of pyrex carboys). A few conventional instruments, such as the electric guitar, were also adapted to his purpose. Visually, as well as aurally, the whole ensemble is one of fantastic beauty.

For these instruments, with voice, Partch wrote a type of work that he called "Satyr-play Music for Dance Theatre." One of these, titled *Ring around the Moon*, is described as "a satire on the world of singers and singing, music and dance; on concerts and concert audiences. . . ." More important is his setting of *King OEdipus* (in the William Butler Yeats version), produced at Mills College, California, in 1952. Concerning this score, Partch wrote: "My idea has been to present the drama expressed by language, not to obscure it, either by operatic aria or symphonic instrumentation. Hence in critical dialogue, music enters almost insidiously, as tensions enter." Two other stage works followed: *The Bewitched* (1957), "a farce for our times," and *Revelation in the Courthouse Square* (1961), based on the *Bacchae* of Euripides. In both of these the visual element is very important; that is to say, the instruments and their performers are an integral part of the spectacle. One is reminded of John Cage's query and answer regarding the "new" music: "Where do we go from here? Towards theatre. That art more than music resembles nature." That is what Partch had aimed at with his corporeal music: not art imitating nature, but music *becoming* nature.

Composition as process

John Cage was born in Los Angeles, California, in 1912. He studied composition with Cowell, with Adolph Weiss, and with Schoenberg. In spite of this double exposure to dodecaphonic influences, Cage soon concluded that twelve-tone writing was "no longer necessary." He probably learned a great deal more from Cowell, whose unorthodox ways of extracting strange sounds from a piano he found fascinating. He was also deeply impressed by Cowell's course on comparative musicology (study of non-European musical cultures), which he attended at the New School for Social Research in New York. From this it was only a step to Zen Buddhism, which profoundly influenced his aesthetic views. After teaching in Chicago and Seattle, Cage moved to New York in 1943. A twenty-five-year retrospective concert of his music given at Town Hall, New York City, on May 15, 1958, demonstrated that he had gathered a large and enthusiastic following. In 1961 his writings and lectures were assembled in a single volume and published under the title *Silence*.[24]

In 1937 Cage delivered a lecture, "The Future of Music: Credo," in which he predicted that "the use of noise to make music will continue and increase until we reach a music produced through the aid of electrical instruments which will make available for musical purposes any and all sounds that can be heard." Instead of the opposition between consonance and dissonance, the point of disagreement in the immediate future would be "between noise and so-called musical sound." Percussion music he regarded as "a temporary transition from keyboard-influenced music to the all-sound music of the future," because "any sound is acceptable to the composer of percussion music: he explores the academically-forbidden 'nonmusical' field of sound insofar as is manually possible."

As a percussion composer, Cage began to explore this "academically-forbidden" domain of sounds with *Construction in Metal* (1939), scored for orchestral bells, five thundersheets, twelve-gong gamelan, eight cowbells, three Japanese temple gongs, four automobile brake drums, eight anvils, four Turkish and four Chinese cymbals, four muted gongs, water gong, suspended gong and tamtam, plus a piano muted by metal cylinders manipulated on the strings by an assistant to the pianist (the pianist also sweeps the bass strings with a timpani stick). Structurally the work is based on a rhythmic method analogous to the Indian Tala, in which "the whole has as many parts as each unit has small parts, and these, large and small, are in the same proportion."

To facilitate further exploration of the world of percussive sound, Cage in 1938 invented what he called the "prepared piano." This is simply an ordinary grand piano certain of whose strings have been muted at specified points by the insertion of miscellaneous small objects, such as bolts, nuts, screws, hairpins, and bits of rubber, plastic, wood, glass, etc. Cage says that the choice of objects is very much like picking up shells on the beach: a matter of taste. But once the objects have been chosen, their application to the strings of the piano

[24] *Silence: Lectures and Writings by John Cage* (Wesleyan University Press, Middletown, Connecticut). Quotations by Cage are taken from this source, by permission of the publisher.

is carefully specified. The preparation of the piano, which may take as long as three hours, differs for each piece or set of pieces. Of the prepared piano, Cage writes:

The result is a gamut of sounds moving from lower to higher octaves without the correspondence of pitch characteristics of scales and modes. These sounds are of different timbres and of a decibel range comparable to that of the harpsichord. In effect, the prepared piano is a percussion ensemble under the control of a single player.

Cage's most extended work for prepared piano alone is a set of sixteen Sonatas and four Interludes, composed between 1946 and 1948. Each of the twenty pieces is a self-contained unit with its own structural pattern, and the organizing principle is that of unchanging phrase lengths within a given unit. The sonata type is that of the two-part form with repetitions. The expressive content is drawn from the "permanent emotions" of Indian philosophy: the heroic, the erotic, the wondrous, the mirthful, sorrow, fear, anger, the odious, "and their common tendency toward tranquility." Other compositions for prepared piano include *Amores* (1943), *Daughters of the Lonesome Isle, Mysterious Adventure* (both 1945), and *Music for Marcel Duchamp* (1947).

At the time when he wrote the *Sonatas and Interludes,* Cage regarded composition as "an activity integrating the opposites, the rational and the irrational, bringing about, ideally, a freely moving continuity within a strict division of parts." But as his musical thinking developed, integration and continuity no longer seemed important. He experienced a tendency "away from ideas of order to ideas of no order." He wanted form to be free—not only from preconceived "ideas of order," but also from the personal taste and volition of the composer.

The first step in this direction was the use of chance operations. This occurred in *Music of Changes* (1951), for piano, in which "the note-to-note procedure, the method, is the function of chance operations. . . . At each small structural division . . . chance operations determined stability or change of tempo." Therefore the structure itself became *indeterminate,* since "it was not possible to know the total time-length of the piece until the final chance operation, the last toss of coins affecting the rate of tempo, had been made." The toss of coins refers to the method established in the Chinese *I-Ching*

(Book of Changes), by which three coins are tossed six times (originally used for the obtaining of oracles).[25]

Music of Changes marks a turning point in Cage's work, because it demonstrated that structure could be indeterminate. Therefore, "being indeterminate, though still present, it became apparent that structure was not necessary, even though it had certain uses." Consequently, in *Music for Piano* (1953–1956) and subsequent works, "structure is no longer part of the compositional means." At this stage composition became for Cage "an activity characterized by process and essentially purposeless." This is what he means by the term "composition as process."

In *Music for Piano* another method of chance operation was used: the notes to be played were determined by imperfections in the paper upon which the music was written. The number of imperfections to be used was in turn determined by chance. This was a considerable step forward in the achievement of indeterminacy, or the preparation of the unpredictable. But to carry the principle further it was necessary to replace conventional scores with charts.

Charts were used in *Sixteen Dances* for flute, trumpet, violin, cello, and percussion; and in the Concerto for Prepared Piano and Chamber Orchestra, both composed in 1951. These works further exploit the "static gamut of sounds" that Cage originated in the prepared piano, with no two octaves repeating relations. As explained by the composer:

> The elements of the gamut were arranged unsystematically in charts and the method of composition involves moves on these charts analogous to those used in constructing a magic square. . . . Of the sixty-four elements in a square chart eight times eight . . . thirty-two were sounds, thirty-two silences.

This is a reminder that Cage composes as much with silences as with sounds. As a basis for the use of charts, the elements of sound are classified according to five characteristics: frequency, amplitude, duration, timbre, and an order of succession. Once these five characteristics have been classified, they can be manipulated by a number of ingenious chance operations so as to yield many unpredictable combinations.

The apotheosis of "no ideas of order" is achieved in the *Concert*

[25] The reader in search of an oracle may wish to consult the English translation: *The I Ching or Book of Changes*. The Richard Wilhelm Translation Rendered into English by Cary F. Baynes. Foreword by C. G. Jung. London: Routledge & Kegan Paul Ltd. 2 vols.

for Piano and Orchestra (1957–1958), which has no master score. Instead,

Each part is written in detail, both specific directives and specific freedoms being given to each player, including the conductor. . . . The pianist's part is a "book" containing 84 different kinds of composition, some, varieties of the same species, others, altogether different. The pianist is free to play any elements of his choice, wholly or in part and in any sequence. The orchestral accompaniment may involve any number of players on more or fewer instruments, and a given performance may be extended or shorter in length. Indeed, I regard this work as one "in progress" which I intend never to consider as in a final state, although I find each performance definitive.[26]

The aim of all these "chance" procedures, according to Cage, is "to make a musical composition the continuity of which is free of individual taste and memory (psychology) and also of the literature and 'traditions' of the art. The sounds enter the time-space centered within themselves, unimpeded by service to any abstraction. . . ." The composers of this music must "find ways and means to remove themselves from the activities of the sounds they make." Composition is therefore not an act of will, but simply "an act of which the outcome is unknown." That is what Cage means by the term "experimental." To the question "What is the purpose of writing music?" he replies: "One is, of course, not dealing with purposes but dealing with sounds."

During the 1950s, a number of younger composers—among them Morton Feldman, Earle Brown, and Christian Wolff—associated themselves with Cage in exploring various possibilities of "experimental" music. But since these composers came into prominence during the 1960s, they will be discussed in the final chapter of this book. Cage himself exerted his greatest influence during the fifties. By the new *avant-garde* he is already regarded as an "old master"—a sort of triune embodiment of Erik Satie, Tristan Tzara, and Marcel Duchamp, none of whom he personally resembles, but whose aesthetic ideas he has assimilated and renovated.[27]

[26] From the booklet accompanying the recording of *The 25-Year Retrospective Concert of the Music of John Cage*, produced and distributed by George Avakian.

[27] For a personal portrait of Cage and his relation to the contemporary art movement, the reader should consult *The Bride and the Bachelors* by Calvin Tomkins (New York, 1965).

Tape-recorder music

In the early 1950s, John Cage, working together with Earle Brown and David Tudor, and with the technical assistance of Louis and Beebe Barron, began to create a number of pieces for tape recorder using various chance methods of composition. The first of these (January, 1952) was *Imaginary Landscape* No. 5 (duration: 4 minutes), described as "a score for making a recording on tape, using as material any 42 phonograph records." This was followed by *Williams Mix* (same duration), for eight tracks of tapes, which utilizes approximately 600 recordings as raw material. In both pieces, "The composing means were chance operations derived from the *I-Ching*." Then, in 1958, working in the Studio di Fonologia of the Italian Radio in Milan, Cage composed the *Fontana Mix*, which calls for "parts to be prepared from the score for the production of any number of tracks of magnetic tape, or for any number of players, any kind and number of instruments." To obtain "a composition indeterminate of its performance," graphs are used; each graph unit equals a unit of time.[28] As the composer explains:

> There are ten transparent sheets with points, ten drawings having six differentiated curved lines, a graph having one hundred units horizontally, twenty vertically, and a straight line, the last two on transparent material. A sheet with points is placed over a drawing with curves (in any position). Over these the graph is placed and the straight line is used to connect a point within the graph with one outside.

Discussing the technique of composing for tape, Cage writes:

> Since so many inches of tape equal so many seconds of time, it has become more and more usual that notation is in space rather than in symbols of quarter, half, and sixteenth notes and so on. Thus where on a page a note appears will correspond to when in a time it is to occur. A stop watch is used to facilitate a performance.

At about the same time, Otto Luening (*b.* 1900) and Vladimir Ussachevsky (*b.* 1911)[29] began to write music for tape in combination

[28] Since then, "time-space" notation has been widely used in the new music (see Chapter 31).

[29] Ussachevsky was born in Hailar, China, and came to the United States

with conventional instruments. Both of these composers had long years of experience in writing conventional music before they became interested, around 1951, in tape music. In producing their tape music they have worked both individually and in collaboration with each other. Luening began by using the flute as the basis for his first tape-recorder pieces: *Fantasy in Space, Low Speed,* and *Invention* (all 1952). Although the possibilities of the flute are extended by tape manipulation, these pieces are essentially conventional, being aimed, in the composer's own words, at audiences "conditioned to impressionistic, virtuoso and tonal music." Luening's experiments with flutes and tape culminated in the *Sonority Canons for Four Live Flutes and Thirty-Three Recorded Flutes* (1960).

In 1954, Luening and Ussachevsky, in collaboration, composed two works for tape recorder and orchestra: *Rhapsodic Variations* and *A Poem in Cycles and Bells.* Regarding the former, a critic wrote: "It is full of the newest sounds, of great enveloping winds and otherworldly chirps, often tremblingly brilliant, and continuously integrated with orchestral textures of the most forthright clarity. . . . It is provocative music and amazingly secure with its new materials."[30] But the "newest sounds," like the newest styles, soon lose their novelty. In 1965 no one would call this music in the least "provocative"; it may have been novel, but it was not experimental.

At the Princeton Seminar in Advanced Musical Studies in 1959, Ussachevsky described his method of composing *A Piece for Tape Recorder* (1956).[31] The raw material consisted of non-electronic and electronic sounds. The former comprised a gong, a piano, a single stroke on a cymbal, a single note on a kettledrum, the noise of a jet plane, a few chords on an organ. The electronic sounds were: four pure tones produced on an oscillator, and a tremolo produced

---

in 1930. He studied at the Eastman School of Music and at Columbia University. The first joint concert of tape music by Luening and Ussachevsky took place in November, 1952, at the Museum of Modern Art in New York. In 1959 Luening and Ussachevsky began to work with the RCA Electronic Sound Synthesizer at Columbia University. Milton Babbitt, one of the most important experimental composers in the United States, whose work is discussed in Chapter 28, joined Luening and Ussachevsky as one of the co-directors of the Columbia-Princeton Electronic Music Center in 1959 (see Chapter 31).

[30] Lester Trimble (*b.* 1923), American composer and critic, writing in the *New York Herald Tribune,* Dec. 4, 1955.

[31] Ussachevsky, "Notes on a Piece for Tape Recorder," in *Problems of Modern Music,* ed. Lang (New York, 1960).

by the stabilized reverberation of a click from a switch on a tape recorder. According to the composer: "The over-all structure seeks to effect a gradual transition from a type of sound material that possessed a certain clearly recognizable musical quality to the type of sound that is more closely identified with a complex noise spectrum. It was my hope that this transition would appear natural, and that the sense of unity could be preserved through a motivistic affinity."

Since 1952 the use of the tape recorder in musical composition has become widespread, for the manipulation of both non-electronic and electronic sounds. Hence it no longer seems necessary to speak of "tape-recorder music" as such, except perhaps in a strictly experimental sense.[32] Cage was unquestionably right when he said that, "Whether one uses tape or writes for conventional instruments, the present musical situation has changed from what it was before tape came into existence." In addition to its immense versatility as a compositional medium—giving the composer, as Ussachevsky says, "a chance to hear and to shape his sound material as he proceeds"—the tape recorder has made possible, for the first time, an absolute correlation between time and space.

Master of organized sound

Most of the innovators we have discussed were concerned in one way or another with the "liberation of sound"—but none looked toward twentieth-century science as the means to accomplish this liberation. That prescience was the unique distinction of Edgard Varèse, who as early as 1917 declared:

Our musical alphabet is poor and illogical.

Music, which should be alive and vibrating, needs new means of expression, and science alone can infuse it with youthful vigor.

I dream of instruments obedient to my thought and which, with their contribution of a whole new world of unsuspected sounds, will lend themselves to the demands of my inner rhythm.[33]

[32] Hiller and Isaacson, in their book *Experimental Music* (New York, 1959), draw attention to experiments in marking film sound tracks directly with a stylus to produce sound patterns, thus creating another type of tape music. By this procedure, "The composer will work with unmagnetized tape while sitting at his desk, and by applying to the tape specific magnetic dyes will transfer pitch or a theme from his creative innards [*sic*] to the tape. . . ." For the pertinent references, see Hiller and Isaacson, *op. cit.*, p. 44.

[33] Printed in the French magazine *391*, número 1 (New York, June, 1917). Here translated from the original French.

Edgard Varèse was born in Paris of French and Italian parentage, on December 22, 1883 (not 1885 as usually stated).[34] From the age of nine to nineteen he lived in Italy and at seventeen, overcoming paternal opposition, he began to study music with Giovanni Bolzoni, head of the Turin Conservatory. Refusing to take up engineering as a career, as his father wished, Varèse returned to Paris and continued his musical training there, at the Schola Cantorum and the Conservatoire National. From 1907 to 1913 he lived in Berlin, conducting and composing several large works, including an opera (these scores were subsequently lost or destroyed). In Berlin he met the musician who was to have the most decisive influence on his future: Ferruccio Busoni.[35]

Although as a composer Busoni was far from radical—he was a proponent of what he called "The New Classicism"—as a theorist and aesthetic thinker he was far in advance of his contemporaries. His little book, *A New Esthetic of Music*, published in the same year that Varèse arrived in Berlin, contained such dicta as: "The function of the creative artist consists in making laws, not in following laws already made"; and, "Music was born free, and to win freedom is its destiny." These affirmations immediately struck a responsive chord in Varèse's mind and continued to vibrate therein for the rest of his life.[36] Not only through Busoni's book, but also through personal association and conversation with the Master, the young Varèse was stimulated to "feats of prophetic imagination" in mentally delineating the music of the future.

Another crucial experience came with the reading, when Varèse was about twenty, of a definition of music by the nineteenth-century physicist, mathematician, and philosopher Hoëne Wronsky, as "the corporealization of the intelligence that is in sounds." This was to him "the first perfectly intelligible conception of music" that he had encountered. It was this definition that first caused him to start thinking

[34] Varèse's given name often appears without the final "d" in works of reference and even in some of his published scores; but he himself used the (French) form, "Edgard."

[35] Ferruccio Busoni (1866–1924), famous pianist and composer, published his *Entwurf einer neuen Aesthetik der Tonkunst* in 1907. It was subsequently translated into English as *Sketch of a New Esthetic of Music* (New York: G. Schirmer, 1911).

[36] In 1939, for example, Varèse gave a speech in Los Angeles, on the theme of freedom in music, affirming that "The very basis of creative work is experimentation." The text of this speech is printed in *The American Composer Speaks* (1966), ed. Chase.

of music as "spatial—as moving bodies of sound in space." He studied the work of Helmholtz *On the Sensations of Tone* and was fascinated by the author's description of his experiments with sirens.[37] Later Varèse made some experiments of his own and found that he could obtain "beautiful parabolic and hyperbolic curves of sound, which seemed to me equivalent to the parabolas and hyperbolas in the visual domain."

Varèse came to the United States at the end of 1915, primarily as a conductor, and soon decided to make his permanent home in New York (he became an American citizen in 1927). Here he started anew his work as a composer, building on the theories he had imbibed from Busoni, Helmholtz, and Wronsky, welded by his own creative intuition. The scores that he produced during this period (1918–1936) constitute a unique and epoch-making *oeuvre*. These works are: *Amériques*, for large orchestra (1918–1921; revised 1926); *Offrandes*, for soprano, chamber orchestra, and percussion (1921–1922); *Hyperprism*, for two woodwinds, seven brasses, and percussion (1922–1923); *Octandre*, for chamber ensemble of winds and brasses with four percussion players (1923); *Intégrales*, for chamber ensemble with four percussion players (1924–1925); *Arcana*, for symphony orchestra (1926–1927); *Ionisation*, for percussion ensemble and two sirens (1931); *Ecuatorial*,[38] for bass voice, four trumpets, four trombones, piano, organ, percussion, and two theremins[39] (1933–1934; revised in 1961 with ensemble of bass voices instead of solo bass, and two *Ondes Martenot*[40] instead of the theremins); and *Density 21.5*, for flute solo,

[37] Hermann Ludwig Ferdinand von Helmholtz (1821–1894), Professor of Physiology at Heidelberg, published in 1862 the great work that is known in English as *On the Sensations of Tone as a Physiological Basis for the Theory of Music*.

[38] In many reference works this title is spelled *Equatorial* but the score has *Ecuatorial* (Spanish spelling).

[39] A space-controlled electronic instrument invented in 1919 by the Russian-born physicist Leon Theremin (*b.* 1896), which was first demonstrated in the United States in 1927. The sounds are produced by two high-frequency electric circuits, employing oscillating radio tubes. The frequency is varied by the movement of the performer's right hand moving backward and forward within a range of about three feet.

[40] An electronic instrument developed by the French musician Maurice Martenot, patented in 1922. The sound is produced by the same principle as that of the theremin, but the manner of operation is different, using a keyboard of five octaves. The player manipulates a variable condenser to obtain the desired pitch, controls the timbre by a set of buttons, and the volume by pressing a key. Martenot first brought this instrument to the United States in 1931.

written in 1936 for Georges Barrère and his platinum flute—21.5 being the density of platinum.

To understand the music of Varèse, and to evaluate its extraordinary significance, one has to start from the premise that it is a body of organized sound *sui generis*, as remote from the chromaticism of Schoenberg as from the diatonicism of Stravinsky. Occupying a "third position" in twentieth-century music, it was the first truly "revolutionary" music of our time, because its creator rejected most of the premises upon which Western composition had been based for centuries. In the words of Marc Wilkinson: [41]

He feels that importance should be given to the Pythagorean *comma*, and has never accepted the otherwise unshaken tonal principle of the tempered fifth, or the tradition of sequence by transposition. To his ear, thirteen fifths do not equal seven octaves, and as he does not, in theory, accept a scale of equal intervals (whether in relation to the octave or not), it follows that, so far as his own music is concerned, melodic or harmonic patterns cannot be transferred from one octave to another without altering their functions completely, that modulation in a tonal sense is unthinkable, and the twelve-tone method quite unmotivated.

Given these postulates, what kind of music ensues? First of all, we must recognize that Varèse's theory was in advance of the practical realities of Western composition prior to about 1950. The instruments of which he dreamt were not the obsolete artifacts of the eighteenth and nineteenth centuries that constitute the "modern" symphony orchestra. Yet, to have his music performed at all he had to make do with those instruments (in part, at least), while awaiting the advent of the electronic synthesizer that would be completely obedient to his thought and to the demands of his inner rhythm. His astonishing achievement was the creation of "a whole new world of unsuspected sounds" prior to the invention of the tape recorder and the electronic synthesizer. He lived to utilize those media too; but that is another phase in the development of his creative universe. We speak now of the works composed between 1918 and 1934.

[41] "An Introduction to the Music of Edgar (*sic*) Varèse," in *The Score* (London), No. 19 (March, 1957), p. 5. This contains an excellent analysis of *Density 21.5.* and a detailed description of *Intégrales*. The reader should also consult the article by Chou Wen-chung, "Varèse: A Sketch of the Man and His Music," in *The Musical Quarterly*, LII, 2 (April, 1966).

Varèse created his world of "organized sound" by relying in large measure on a wide array of percussive instruments, including those of indeterminate pitch. Timbre—the quality or "color" of a tone—is the paramount element in the music of Varèse; and this in turn depends on the harmonics (overtones) produced by each instrument. Hence timbre, through the overtone series, becomes "a means of exploring the sounds in between the whole and half tones of customary pitch."[42] The contrast of timbres replaces traditional harmony and polyphony. As regards form, Varèse has said: "Form is the result of a process; each of my works discovers its own form."[43]

In his instrumentation, Varèse generally avoids the strings, favoring brass and woodwind together with percussion. Typical of this combination is *Intégrales,* scored for small orchestra (no strings) and a large percussion section requiring four players. Thirty-two percussion instruments are used, including Chinese blocks, sleigh bells, slap stick, chains, string drum (or lion's roar), and twigs (to be played on shell of bass drum). All of these instruments are used with great subtlety, clarity, and precision, to achieve what Wilkinson aptly calls "an indivisible vertical structure, shimmering over the full extent of the delineated sound-space."

With *Ionisation,* Varèse turned exclusively to percussion effects: it is scored for a percussion ensemble of thirteen players, and makes use of typical Caribbean instruments (bongos, cencerro, claves, güiro, maracas), as well as three hand-operated sirens equipped with "thumb brake" (instantaneous stopping mechanism). Varèse used the latter, not for realistic sound effects, but, as previously explained, for their simulation of hyperbolic and parabolic "sound curves" in space.

With the coming of magnetic tape and electronic equipment, Varèse was able to add another dimension to his music, bringing it nearer to his theoretical concepts. In the score of *Deserts* (1949–1954) there are three interpolations of electronically organized sound, recorded stereophonically on two magnetic tapes. These electronic

---

[42] Sidney Finkelstein, in the liner notes for an EMS recording of music by Varèse (Vol. I of the *Complete Works* that never got any further).

[43] Nicholas Slonimsky may have had tongue in cheek when he said that *Ionisation* is in "sonata form" (*Music Since 1900,* p. 340): Varèse's comment on being told of this was, "So what? It proves nothing." Nevertheless, the reader should consult the excellent analysis of *Ionisation* by Slonimsky (to whom the work is dedicated) in the score published by G. Ricordi & Co. (New York).

segments are interpolated at indicated points in the work, but are never heard simultaneously with the instrumental sections. The latter are scored for flutes, clarinets, horns, trumpets, trombones, tubas, piano, and percussion (five players). The transition from one type of sound to another is so skillfully managed as to be almost imperceptible. Regarding the electronic interpolations, Varèse wrote: "The first and third are based on industrial sounds (sounds of friction, percussion, hissing, grinding, puffing), first filtered, transposed, transmuted, mixed by means of electronic devices and then composed to fit the pre-established plan of the work. . . . The second interpolation is for an ensemble of percussion instruments."

The advent of electronic media meant, among other things, the domination of space. Varèse took full possession of the spatial domain when he composed the *Poème électronique* (1957–1958) for the Philips Pavilion (designed by Le Corbusier) at the Brussels World's Fair. Recorded on a three-track magnetic tape, the sound was distributed over a system of 425 loudspeakers located on the inside walls of the pavilion, designed so as to have no right angles. Here at long last Varèse was able to realize his conception of music as "bodies of sound moving in space," actually making his organized sounds follow the parabolas and hyperbolas that had captured his youthful imagination.[44]

Varèse did not believe that electronics would supplant the traditional musical instruments, but rather supplement them. What he cherished in the electronic medium was its liberating power: "Electronics has given music a new dimension and a new freedom. My music is based on the movement of unrelated sound-masses which I always conceived as moving simultaneously at different speeds, and I looked forward to the time when science would provide the means of realization. Now thanks to electronics such unrelated metrical simultaneity is at last possible."[45]

Although Cage paid tribute to Varèse as the man who "fathered forth noise into twentieth-century music," he objected to the "man-

[44] A recording of *Poème électronique* was released by Columbia; but only those who heard it in the Philips Pavilion could appreciate its full effectiveness as a "spatial composition." The reader should consult the richly documented book *Le poème électronique* (Paris: Aux Editions de Minuit, 1958), which describes and illustrates in detail both the work of Le Corbusier and of Varèse, with facsimiles, diagrams, photos, etc.

[45] In 1961, Varèse, with the technical assistance of Bülent Arel, revised the organized sound interpolations of *Deserts*, working at the Columbia-Princeton Electronic Music Center.

nerisms" of his style, because "they draw attention to Varèse and his imagination," thus making it "quite difficult to hear the sounds just as they are." This is true: Varèse was never obsessed by sound for sound's sake. He had a truly humanistic conception of music. In explaining the title of *Deserts*, he said:

"Deserts" means to me not only the physical deserts of sand, sea, mountain, and snow, of outer space, of empty city streets; not only those stripped aspects of nature that suggest barrenness, aloofness, timelessness, but also that remote inner space no telescope can reach, where man is alone in a world of mystery and essential loneliness.

Concerning *Ecuatorial* (which is based on a text from the *Popul-Vuh*, the sacred book of the ancient Maya-Quiché), he wrote: "The execution should be dramatic and incantatory, guided by the imploring fervor of the text." The title *Amériques* was for him not merely geographic, but "symbolic of discoveries—new worlds on earth, in the sky, or in the minds of men." And in 1940, speaking of the "architecture" of music, he said:[46]

As the architect bases his structures on a perfect knowledge of the materials he uses—their resistance, their reaction, their tensile strength—the composer today should, in building his sonorous constructions, have a thorough knowledge of the laws governing the vibratory system in the atmospheric domain, and of the possibilities that science has already abundantly placed, and continues to place, at the service of his imagination. The last word is: Imagination.

Varèse sought and found new technical means and organizational concepts—those of the twentieth century—to enlarge the scope of the creative imagination in musical expression. At the time of his death in New York on November 6, 1965, his influence had made itself felt, deeply though without fanfare, on many of the most talented of the younger composers, both in the United States and abroad. As one of them wrote: "Varèse never formulated an 'ism,' never founded a school. He simply inspired."

[46] In *The Commonweal*, Dec. 13, 1940.

chapter twenty-eight

Twelve-tone trends

Composing with twelve tones is not nearly as forbidding and exclusive a method as is generally supposed.
ARNOLD SCHOENBERG, "MY EVOLUTION" (THE MUSICAL QUARTERLY, 1952).

On April 11, 1941, Arnold Schoenberg, Viennese-born composer and theorist, creator of the method of composing with twelve tones, became an American citizen. He was then sixty-six years old and had been living in the United States with his family since 1933. Until 1925 he had taught and composed in Vienna, becoming known for several works of post-romantic tendency, such as *Verklärte Nacht* ("Transfigured Night"). But, as he drew further away from tonality, he became a controversial figure, often arousing violent opposition through his alleged undermining of the "eternal" laws of musical beauty. Withal, his reputation and prestige were such that in 1925 he was appointed to succeed Busoni as Professor of Advanced Composition at the Prussian Academy of Fine Arts in Berlin. As a Jew, his situation in Berlin became precarious after Hitler seized power. Anticipating the inevitable, Schoenberg left Germany in May, 1933, going first to Paris and then to the United States. In the fall of the following year he settled in Los Angeles, California, where he remained until his death on July 13, 1951, at the age of seventy-six. From 1936 to 1944 he taught composition at the University of California in Los Angeles.

Schoenberg described the twelve-tone method as follows:

The method of composing with twelve tones substitutes for the order produced by permanent reference to tonal centers an order according to which, every unit of a piece being a derivative of the tonal relations in a basic set of twelve tones, the *Grundes-*

601

gestalt [fundamental form] is coherent because of this permanent reference to the basic set.[1]

The "twelve tones" are those of the chromatic scale (obtained by playing all the white and black keys on an octave of the piano keyboard). The composer begins by arranging these twelve tones in a series or row. Once arranged in a special order, with no tones repeated, this tone-row provides the material, both melodically and "harmonically" (i.e., vertically), out of which the entire composition is made. Since no note is to be emphasized more than another, it is essential that, in the composition, all twelve notes of the series be sounded before any one of them is repeated. The tone-row may be used in its entirety or in fragments, and in any of the following basic forms, derived from traditional contrapuntal devices:[2]

    I. Its original form (symbol: O).

    II. Its retrograde or "backwards" form (symbol: R).

    III. Its inverted or "upside-down" form (symbol: I).

    IV. Its retrograde inversion or "upside-down backwards" form (symbol: RI).

Since each of these forms of the tone-row may be transposed to each of the twelve tones of the chromatic scale, a total of forty-eight possible

[1] From an essay entitled "My Evolution," originally written in 1949 for the Mexican periodical *Nuestra Música*, later delivered as a public lecture at the University of California at Los Angeles, and published in the *Musical Quarterly* for Oct. 1952 (copyright by G. Schirmer, Inc.). Other quotations from Schoenberg used in this chapter are from the same source.

[2] The tone-row given in this illustration is that used by Schoenberg in his Suite for piano (Opus 25).

patterns is available to the composer who employs this method of composition.

Before he formulated the twelve-tone method, Schoenberg achieved what he called "the emancipation of dissonance" in such works as the Chamber Symphony (Opus 9), the *Two Ballads* (Opus 12), the Second String Quartet (Opus 10), and the Piano Pieces (Opus 11 and Opus 19)—compositions written between 1906 and 1911. On the formal side he did away with developments. On the harmonic side, in the String Quartet, according to the composer, "there are many sections in which the individual parts proceed regardless of whether or not their meeting results in codified harmonies." Hence, "the overwhelming multitude of dissonances cannot be counterbalanced any longer by occasional returns to such tonal triads as represent a key." Such was "the emancipation of dissonance," which came to be called "atonality" (though Schoenberg himself disliked the term). Faced with this "overwhelming multitude of dissonances" that he himself had unleashed, Schoenberg sought a new principle of organization, one that would provide unity and coherence along with variety and flexibility, while not rescinding the freedom of dissonance—that is, the free circulation of all twelve tones of the chromatic scale on an equal basis. It was thus that, in the Five Piano Pieces of Opus 23, Schoenberg began "working with tones," until, in the Suite for Piano (Opus 25) and the Wind Quintet (Opus 26), both dating from the year 1924, the material is organized entirely on the basis of tone-rows, and the method of composing with twelve tones takes definite shape.

After his arrival in America, Schoenberg continued to apply the twelve-tone method in such works as the Violin Concerto (1936), the Fourth String Quartet (1936), the Piano Concerto (1942); the *Ode to Napoleon Buonaparte* (1942), for reciter with string quartet (or orchestra) and piano (on a poem by Lord Byron); and *A Survivor from Warsaw* (1947), for narrator, men's chorus, and orchestra. But, curiously, he also returned to tonal writing in several works, such as a setting of the *Kol Nidre* and *Variations on a Recitative for Organ* (1941). Regarding this return to tonality, Schoenberg wrote: "A longing to return to the older style was always vigorous in me; and from time to time I had to yield to that urge." He was like an explorer who has discovered a new continent that thrills and fascinates him, but who feels now and then a longing to revisit the homeland with its familiar habits and comforts.

This nostalgia for the past, this deep attachment to the traditions of Western European music, was actually very strong in Schoenberg. He denied being a "revolutionist," and he was right. The "emancipation of dissonance," through the increasing encroachment of chromaticism since Wagner's time, was bound to happen: Schoenberg saw that this was logically inescapable and he went along with that inevitable process of historical change. But the composer who spoke of being unable to "counterbalance" (i.e., to counteract, to oppose successfully) "the overwhelming multitude of dissonances" reveals the mentality of the inhabitant of a peaceful and tranquil country that has been overrun by invading barbarians. His elaboration of the twelve-tone method was a defence against the "anarchy" of atonality (his dislike of that term is symptomatic). It was, in the words of Ernst Krenek, "a form of reaction against the bold, shocking, initial ventures into the atonal territory around 1910."

In order to realize how far indeed Schoenberg was from being a "revolutionist," one may cite not only his persistent "longing to return to the older style" (which asserted itself formally as well as tonally, with his partiality for classical and pre-classical structures, such as rondo, variations, suite, etc.), but also, and more decisively, his adherence to the tempered system which permitted the division of the octave into twelve "equal" parts. When one realizes that Varèse had repudiated this system at least as early as 1916, and that he never accepted it in theory even when reduced to applying it in practice, one can have no doubt as to which was the truly "revolutionary" musician of our era.

In this connection, it is enlightening to share the view of an American composer born in 1917, who is therefore able to look back upon the Schoenbergian impact with the double perspective of time and place. According to Lou Harrison:

> Schoenberg's ear correctly told him that there is no hierarchy of intervals in equal temperament, and he devised an "order of succession" method to enable him to make any further use of that tuning. As a European he was, it turned out, not able to do the obvious—i.e., *retune*,—for Europeans have so heavily invested in this absurdity[3] that they are stuck with it, or else must proceed on to noise [which is what Italian Futurism did].[4]

[3] Harrison's Note: "A *surd* is a mathematical term for a ratio that will never 'come out' right, as is true of the 'relationships' of equal temperament. The word surd is Latin for deaf, and ab-surd is, obviously, from deafness."

[4] From an unpublished communication of August 7, 1963.

In the light, therefore, both of the problem of "just intonation" (i.e., the rejection of equal temperament) and of "total serial organization" in composition (which will be discussed later in this chapter), the Schoenbergian concept of composing with twelve tones appears as essentially traditional and conservative. This doubtless accounts for its widespread acceptance after a period of initial resistance, so that by 1950 so-called "serial" or "dodecaphonic" methods of composing had become commonplace. The situation was aptly summarized by Krenek:

> The conservative tendency in dodecaphony is tied up with the adherence to classical structural concepts, which in turn is a consequence of the persistent belief in the indispensability of thematic development. As long as the essential nature of the twelve-tone row is seen in its unifying power, whereby all and any parts of the musical design are brought into the closest possible motivic relationships, the twelve-tone technique remains the most efficient way of applying classical methods of design in a changed, nonclassical idiom.[5]

This goes far to explain why, during the 1940s and 1950s, a large number of American composers of the most diverse backgrounds and interests, ranging from Samuel Barber to Morton Gould, and from Aaron Copland to Ross Lee Finney, were able to come to terms readily (and in Finney's case, he would have us believe, almost "unconsciously") with twelve-tone writing, without finding themselves committed to any "revolutionary" principles. That both neoclassicism and dodecaphonism were fundamentally reactionary is confirmed by Stravinsky's adoption of twelve-tone writing in the 1950s, thus signalling to all his disciples that this was a "safe" line to follow.

One of the favorite procedures has been the combining of the twelve-tone technique with tonal organization, for which Schoenberg himself, and some of his early Viennese associates, set the example. Schoenberg used this compromise in the Piano Concerto and the *Ode to Napoleon Buonaparte*. An earlier example is that of Alban Berg's Violin Concerto (1935), which utilizes a tone-row so constructed that it includes major and minor triads as well as the whole-tone scale, as follows:

[5] "Tradition in Perspective," in *Perspectives of New Music*, I, 1 (Fall, 1962), p. 34.

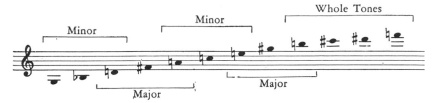

Alban Berg (1885–1935) and Anton Webern (1883–1945) were the two most famous and influential pupils of Schoenberg in Vienna, each of whom soon acquired a personal following. The posthumous influence of Webern—i.e., beginning with the period immediately after the end of World War II—has been greater than that of either Berg or Schoenberg. The American conductor and composer Robert Craft, writing from the point of view of his generation (he was born in 1923), asked rhetorically,[6] "How were we to know that in twenty years our age would be characterized by a majority of the youngest Western European composers as 'the age of Webern'?" And the English critic Peter Evans,[7] writing in 1961, noted that Webern "has now been accepted by a whole school of composers as a yardstick, a level of musical language [now he is quoting Karl Heinz Stockhausen] 'below which no composer can with a clear conscience be active.'" By 1960 it was customary to speak of "pre-Webern" and "post-Webern" tendencies in contemporary composition. But before going on to deal with post-Webern trends in American music, we must discuss some of the earlier twelve-tone composers of the United States, beginning with Adolph Weiss and Wallingford Riegger.

American twelve-tone pioneers

Adolph Weiss (born in Baltimore in 1891) was the first native-born American to be officially inscribed as a student of Schoenberg in the latter's master-class at the Berlin Academy of Fine Arts (1924–1927). A bassoonist by profession, he received his basic musical training in New York and Chicago, and played with various orchestras before

---

[6] In his notes for the complete recorded works of Webern produced by George Avakian.

[7] In *Proceedings of the Royal Musical Association*, 88th (1961–1962). The quotation from Stockhausen is taken from the latter's article "For the 15th of September, 1955," in *Die Reihe* (English ed.), II (1958–1959).

joining the Los Angeles Philharmonic Orchestra. For his own instrument he wrote a prize-winning Concerto for Bassoon and String Quartet. After his studies with Schoenberg he began to compose with twelve tones in such works as the Chamber Symphony for ten instruments (1928), *Sonata da Camara* for flute and viola (1930), and Quintet for Wind Instruments (1932). In his scherzo for orchestra titled *American Life* (1929) he does not use a twelve-tone row, but builds the composition on the basis of the augmented fourth ("quartal harmony").

The notion long prevailed that the early twelve-tone composers were arid cerebralists concocting music according to abstruse formulae. It is true that Weiss, for example, is a "numerologist" who writes all his compositions in columns of figures and then transcribes them into conventional notation. According to Lester Trimble,[8] "It is a startling experience to observe the composer at the piano, playing a new, untranscribed composition from an enigmatic page of small dots, lines, and numbers." Yet Trimble also assures us that: "His attitude toward composition is fun-loving and spontaneous, and he is visibly enamored of pure musical fantasy." After all, conventional musical notation is needlessly complicated, hermetic, inaccurate, and generally unsatisfactory; the only reason we consider it "normal" is because it is familiar (a "bad habit," as Varèse would say). More and more composers are, like Weiss, finding other symbols and devices for the graphic presentation of their musical ideas.

In 1956, while touring the Orient as a member of the Los Angeles Philharmonic Orchestra, Weiss began to compose Five Pieces for Violin and Piano, based on Japanese Court music. Whether writing twelve-tone works or carrying on a musical flirtation with the Orient, Weiss remains essentially a composer of the "old school," wedded to thematic delineations, motivic interlockings, literal restatements, and poetic connotations. All this is demonstrated in one of his major compositions, the *Theme and Variations for Orchestra* (1936). There are twelve variations, which follow the sequence of stanzas in Whitman's poem "When Lilacs Last in the Dooryard Bloom'd." According to the composer: "The spiritual content of the poem fixed the sequence of musical ideas as well as the form of the composition." Once again

---

[8] In notes for the recording of Weiss's Trio for Clarinet, Viola, and Cello (Composers Recordings, Inc.).

we are reminded that twelve-tone writing is simply a technique, a compositional device; the purport of the music remains a function of the composer's temperament and traditional allegiance. Perhaps this is what Henry Cowell had in mind when he wrote that Adolph Weiss "has utilized a Schoenbergian idiom to express his outlook on life which is quite different from Schoenberg's and is philosophically American." How refreshing to find an "Americanist"—if only "philosophically"—among the Schoenbergian dodecaphonists!

Wallingford Riegger (1885–1961) was one of the few prominent American composers to be born in the "Deep South" (in Albany, Georgia). But while he was still a child his family moved to Indianapolis; and then, when he was fifteen, to New York City, where he was to spend most of his life, and where he died after being knocked down in the street by two fighting dogs. After graduating from New York's Institute of Musical Art in 1907, he had two years of advanced study at the Berlin Hochschule and remained in Germany as a conductor until the entry of the United States in World War I.

Riegger's early compositions, such as the Piano Trio in B minor (1921), were lushly romantic—which means that he was then writing the kind of music most readily acceptable to publishers, performers, and (presumably, though no one polled their opinion) audiences. The story goes that his publisher, on the strength of these early works, accepted his *Study in Sonority* "sight unseen"—and was unspeakably shocked when he discovered that it was full of dissonances! Riegger had indeed completely altered course: he was now steering for the rough seas of atonalism and dodecaphony. The *Study in Sonority*, for ten violins or any multiple thereof, completed in 1927, was written in a strongly dissonant contrapuntal idiom; instead of adhering to the traditional tonal relationships, the composer invented, as Cowell observes, "a chord to play the part of tonic and another to play that of dominant." This method of "inventing" non-tonal "centers of attraction" was extensively used by a number of American composers during the 1930s.

Riegger's adherence to the method of composing with twelve tones is foreshadowed in his orchestral score titled *Dichotomy*, composed in 1931–1932, in which he uses two different tone-rows, one consisting of eleven tones, the second of thirteen (ten different tones and three recurring ones). This work, which closes with a passacaglia, is one of the most original American compositions of its time. Concerning it, the composer wrote:

Among the special things I should like to point out is what I call "cumulative sequence," a device by no means original with me, but used perhaps more consciously and to a greater degree in my work than elsewhere. . . . This is the old Three Blind Mice idea, keeping the original motive and *adding* a sequence, above or below, instead of moving the motive itself. I also use something I call "organic stretto," e.g., the telescoping of different sections, instead of the subject with itself, as in the fugue. It is like beginning a subordinate theme before the principal theme is established.[9]

In his First String Quartet (Opus 30) Riegger uses the twelve-tone technique in its strict or "classical" form, according to the purest Schoenbergian canon. Each of the four movements of this quartet employs the basic tone-row of twelve tones in one of the four fundamental forms prescribed by Schoenberg: in its original form (first movement); in its retrograde form, or "backwards" (second movement); in its inverted form, or "upside down" (third movement); and in its retrograde inversion form, or "upside-down backwards" (fourth movement). Clear and prominent statement of the tone-series at the outset, combined with ingenious variety of texture and a lively expressiveness, makes this an attractive and satisfying work.

In general Riegger uses the twelve-tone method rather freely. He is by no means a dogmatic Schoenbergian. Expressiveness and strength of texture are what he seeks above all. There is in his music a fundamental honesty, both of concept and workmanship, that is best described by the word "integrity." He avoids the sensational, the cliché, and the cheap effect. His qualities of originality, invention, clarity, discipline, and expressiveness, are amply revealed in his Third Symphony, the work that brought him a wider fame when performed in 1948. In this symphony, traditional and tone-row procedures are combined, and the sense of tonality is not abandoned. This is a strong and sincere work, splendidly orchestrated, which serves to place its composer in the very front rank of contemporary American musicians.

Among other compositions by Riegger are *Canons for Woodwinds* (1931), *Fantasy and Fugue* for orchestra and organ (1930–1931);

[9] Quoted by Henry Cowell in *Musical America*, Dec. 1, 1948.

Music for Brass Choir for ten trumpets, four horns, ten trombones, two tubas, and timpani (Opus 45, 1948–1949); *Passacaglia and Fugue* for orchestra (1942); Duo for Three Woodwinds (1943); *New and Old* (twelve pieces for piano, 1945); New Dance for piano and chamber orchestra (1944); Music for Orchestra (1955); Fourth and Fifth Symphonies; Variations for Piano and Orchestra (1953); and Variations for Violin and Orchestra (1959).

Perhaps the best capsule summary of Riegger's aesthetic position was formulated by Henry Cowell, who said he was "a romantic who admires strict forms."

Harrison Kerr (*b.* 1899) is one of the many American composers who studied with Nadia Boulanger in Paris. His evolution has been from a rather conventional idiom (in his student days) to a prevailingly *un*tonal (rather than *a*tonal) texture utilizing twelve-tone elements in a manner that is closer to the practice of Berg than of Schoenberg. Much of his music is marked by chromaticism, quartal harmonies (based on superimposed fourths), dissonant counterpoint, and free use of changing meters. The compositions of Kerr in which the twelve-tone technique is most prominent are the String Quartet (1937), the Suite for flute and piano (1940–1941), the Second Symphony (1943–1945; especially the slow movement), the Second Piano Sonata (1943), and the Violin Concerto (1950–1951). With few exceptions, the application of the twelve-tone method in these works is very free. Kerr, like Riegger, is essentially a romantic.

George Tremblay (*b.* 1911), the Canadian-born composer who studied with Schoenberg in Los Angeles, has also used the twelve-tone method with complete independence and personal freedom. He tells us that he "never accepted as final the academic conception of the twelve semitones of the piano octave as the only basis for true 'serial' composition." For instance, in the work for string quartet titled *Modes of Transportation* (1940), "the melodic lines are harmonized by tones identical with those in the melodies, reinstating the octave as an essential interval in the complex of harmonic sounds." Other variants include the use of multiple and auxiliary rows, and of what Tremblay calls "interceptive rows," wherein different segments of the basic row are introduced as passing and auxiliary notes. Tremblay's compositions, from the jazzlike *Prelude and Dance* of 1935 to the String Quartet No. 4 of 1963, are all instrumental and mostly for chamber groups. His larger works include a Symphony in One Movement (1949) and a Symphony in Three Movements (1952). His concern with contra-puntal textures is evident in the Quartet for Piano and Strings (1958), which abounds in canonic devices. A lighter, humorous touch is re-vealed in the *Serenade* of 1956, which reverts to jazzlike effects.

From Schubert to Schoenberg—and beyond

Ernst Krenek, like Schoenberg, was born in Vienna (in 1900) and eventually settled in California. A resident of the United States since 1938, he held academic appointments at Vassar College and at Hamline University before moving on to Los Angeles. In an autobiographical sketch published in 1942, Krenek reviewed his musical evolution and attempted to explain his "apparently aimless meanderings through styles." This is the pertinent passage:

> After a few initial attempts in the exalted late romantic manner of my teacher, Franz Schreker, I turned soon to the more aggressive idiom of atonality, whose main organizing agency was elemental rhythmic force. I became interested in jazz, in the early twenties, and I had my greatest success when I used some jazz elements in my opera *Jonny spielt auf!* . . . I was not satisfied with either rhythmically stiffened atonality or semi-primitive jazz, and in about 1928 I went back to the early romantic vocabulary of Schubert. I was called both surrealist and reactionary, while I personally had the feeling that I was making up for things which I had missed when I had been in school. Another about-face, this time slow and deliberate, took place: through concentration, condensation, sophistication of the Schubert style, I came directly to Schoenberg's twelve-tone technique. This move seemed particularly logical to me. During the last years, I have devoted much work to the practi-cal development and the critical interpretation of that technique, as well as to creative writing and theoretical studies.[10]

Anyone wishing to become acquainted with the twelve-tone tech-nique in all its "classical" purity and strictness, but in a comparatively simple form not too difficult to grasp, might well begin by acquiring a knowledge of Krenek's *Twelve Short Piano Pieces*, written in 1938, which are a sort of *Gradus ad Parnassum* of twelve-tone writing. Considerably more formidable is the Second Concerto for Piano and

[10] From *The Book of Modern Composers*, ed. David Ewen (Alfred A. Knopf, Inc., New York, 1942), p. 354.

Orchestra, composed in 1937 with strict employment of a twelve-tone row in its four basic forms. When this work received its first American performance by the Boston Symphony Orchestra on November 4, 1938, an old lady in the audience was overheard remarking to her husband, "Conditions in Europe must be dreadful."

Apart from the historical opera *Charles V* (1933), Krenek's most ambitious effort to employ the twelve-tone technique in a large-scale work is his Fourth Symphony (1947), a carefully constructed composition designed to depict the conflict between the Ideal and the Real. It was the composer's intention to present in this work "a very high amount of logical coherence and intelligible significance." But these qualities are more appreciated in mathematics and in philosophy than in music, which for most people remains a language of emotions. Hence Krenek's symphony was not received with enthusiasm.

Krenek's Third Concerto for Piano and Orchestra, composed in 1946, is not a twelve-tone composition but is based on traditional tonality. It is in five movements, played without interruption, and in each movement a different section of the orchestra enters into dialogue with the solo instrument. The score makes occasional excursions into jazzlike effects.

Among Krenek's major compositions since 1954 are three orchestral scores: *Eleven Transparencies, Quaestio temporis, From Three Make Seven; Sestina* for soprano and chamber ensemble; Sonata for Harp; Six Motets, on texts by Kafka, for *a cappella* chorus; *The Bell Tower*, chamber opera based on the story by Herman Melville; and an oratorio, *Spiritus Intelligentiae*, for voices and electronic sounds.

Stefan Wolpe is another European-born exponent of twelve-tone music, who settled in the United States about the same time as Krenek and eventually became an American citizen. Born in Berlin in 1902, Wolpe received his musical training in that city. His musical development was strongly influenced by Busoni and later by Anton Webern, whom he met after going to Vienna in 1933. He was active in Palestine for several years before going to the United States. From 1939 to 1944 he taught at the Settlement Music School in New York City.

Wolpe, like Krenek, assimilated many styles and experimented with many techniques before turning to the twelve-tone method. And then he transformed the latter for his own purposes instead of adopting it literally. According to Abraham Skulsky:[11]

[11] In *Musical America*, Nov. 1, 1951, p. 6.

Stefan Wolpe was the first composer to develop a newly organized harmonic system from the twelve-tone principles of Schoenberg. He employs harmonic zones or regions that result from each
of the individual contrapuntal lines; the inner relationship between
the harmonic zones is established by what he calls spatial organization.

Wolpe began to experiment with these spatial relationships in his
Studies on Basic Rows (1934), originally for piano and later orchestrated, in which he systematically exploited the intervallic relations
derived from the twelve-tone technique. The *Passacaglia*, for example,
"is built progressively on all the intervals from the minor second to
the major seventh." What all this amounts to is an early attempt at
"chromatic integration."

The Toccata for Piano in Three Movements (1941) used tone-rows
somewhat in the manner of the earlier Studies. Wolpe continued to
develop his personal dodecaphonic style in such works as the Sonata
for Violin and Piano (1949); *Enactments* for Three Pianos
(1951–1953); Quartet for oboe, cello, percussion, and piano (1955);
Quintet with Voice (1957); and *Form for Piano* (1959). The Quartet
for trumpet, saxophone, piano, and drums (1950) reveals his interest
in jazz.

Wolpe, who spent four years in Jerusalem, found inspiration in
Hebrew folklore and culture, as evidenced in his *Twelve Palestinian
Songs, Ten Songs from the Hebrew*, the oratorio *Israel and His Land*
(1939), and a ballet on the life of Moses, *The Man from Midian*
(1942).

The case of Ross Lee Finney (*b.* 1906) shows how a composer
may turn to twelve-tone writing, not by adopting a doctrinaire attitude, but simply as the consequence of a natural evolution. Although
he studied briefly with Alban Berg in 1931, Finney was at first strongly
opposed to dodecaphonism because of his deep commitment to tonality.
Nearly twenty years passed before he understood that "the twelve-tone
technique is not actually in opposition to tonal functionalism but is
a technique concerned with chromatic integration." In his Second
Sonata for Cello and Piano (1950), Finney used a highly chromatic
dissonant texture; but he was still seeking a method of structural organization that would enable him to write in a contemporary idiom
without sacrificing personal lyricism. This he found in the Sixth String
Quartet, completed later in the same year, which turned out to be

a strict twelve-tone work—in spite of which the composer titled it String Quartet in E! If Schoenberg occasionally felt a longing to return to the land of tonality, Finney evidently was reluctant to leave it at all.

Concerning his music, Finney wrote: "No work that I have ever written has sprung from logic; music springs, I am sure, from musical ideas and gestures. The real problem, therefore, and the one that concerns me more and more, is to find a *lyric* expression within the bounds of organization that seem to me important."[12] This essential lyricism is a constant in the twelve-tone compositions of Finney, which include a Piano Trio (1954), Seventh and Eighth String Quartets (1955 and 1960), Second and Third Symphonies (1959 and 1963), String Quintet (1958), Piano Quintet No. 2 (1962), *Variations on a Theme of Alban Berg* for piano (1952), and *Variations on a Row by Luigi Dallapiccola* for orchestra (1957). In 1961 Finney composed *Three Pieces for Strings, Winds, Percussion, and Electronic Tape*, in which the tape consists entirely of electronically generated sounds, "sometimes closely related to the twelve-tone series that controls the other instruments, sometimes very freely organized, with little pitch significance." With the establishment, in 1963, of an electronic music studio at the University of Michigan (where he is composer in residence), Finney planned to make increasing use of electronic elements in his compositions.

George Perle (*b.* 1915), like Finney, began with a fundamental objection to the twelve-tone method because "it failed to rationalize harmonic events." Nevertheless, he decided to investigate the possibilities of serial writing with the aim of finding a "dodecaphonic functionality" to replace diatonic functionality. This search led to the development of his "twelve-tone modal system." The works written in this system include a Piano Sonata (1950), Fourth and Fifth String Quartets (1948 and 1960), three Symphonies (1948, 1950, 1952), *Rhapsody for Orchestra* (1953), and *Three Movements for Orchestra* (1960).

Perle began composing in a "free" atonal style with such monophonic pieces as Sonata for Solo Viola (1942), Three Sonatas for Solo Clarinet (1943), and Sonata for Solo Cello (1947). He reverted to atonality in several later works, notably the Quintet for Strings, (1958), two Wind Quintets (1959 and 1960), and *Monody No. 1* for Solo Flute (1960). The Third String Quartet (1947) is one of the few compositions in which Perle employs strict twelve-tone meth-

---

[12] In a letter to the author, dated Feb. 22, 1954.

ods. Important also as a theorist, he is the author of *Serial Composition and Atonality* (1962).

Dodecaphonic romanticism

Ben Weber and George Rochberg are among the dodecaphonic composers who believe, with Schoenberg, that twelve-tone music is a continuation of "The Great Tradition" of Western European music, stemming from Bach and Mozart and carried on through Beethoven, Brahms, and Wagner.[13] Rochberg is convinced that music must turn away from abstraction and become again "completely melodic, singing in character, and passionate in expression." Weber too believes in the supremacy of melodic expression. "I tend to use the twelve-tone row melodically," he says, "and my rhythms are determined by my melody."

Ben Weber, born in St. Louis, Missouri, in 1916, was under family pressure to study medicine and turned his major attention to music only after a year of premedical study at the University of Illinois. From 1939 to 1941 he was active with the "New Music Group" in Chicago; from 1945 he made his home in New York City. During the 1940s he wrote a number of works, mostly for piano or for chamber ensembles, in both twelve-tone and free atonal textures, which established his reputation for fine workmanship combined with an exceptional lyric quality that often verged on expressionism. In the ensuing decade he wrote the Concerto for Piano, Cello, and Winds (1950); the highly expressionistic *Symphony in Four Movements on Poems of William Blake*, for baritone and small orchestra (1954); the Concerto for Violin and Orchestra (1954); *Prelude and Passacaglia for Orchestra* (1955); and the *Rapsodie Concertante* for Solo Viola and Chamber Orchestra. From time to time he has written tonally organized non-dodecaphonic works, such as Three Songs for Soprano and Strings, and *Concert Aria after Solomon* (1949), for soprano and chamber ensemble, which are "very directly romantic."

In 1960 Weber's important position in American music was confirmed by a commission from the Ford Foundation to write a Concerto

---

[13] In a pamphlet written in 1931, titled *National Music*, Schoenberg stated that his "teachers" were "in the first place Bach and Mozart, and in the second place Beethoven, Brahms, and Wagner." See the article by Michael Steinberg, "Tradition and Responsibility," in *Perspectives of New Music*, I, 1 (Fall, 1962), p. 154.

for Piano and Orchestra. The work (Opus 52) has a slow movement, Andantino con rubato, inscribed "In memoriam Dimitri Mitropoulos—1960." (It was Mitropoulos who, in 1954, conducted a performance of Weber's *Prelude and Passacaglia* (Opus 42) that drew both cheers and hisses from the audience.) In the Piano Concerto, Weber affirms his allegiance to the post-romantic dodecaphonism of Schoenberg. The first movement is in the character of a fantasia with a well-defined reprise; the second is a set of passacaglia variations; and the third follows the classical rondo pattern. One can agree with Frank O'Hara that, "The originality of Ben Weber's work is not conceptual or technical, but rather emotional and perceptual." The composer himself appeared to confirm this view when he told Lou Harrison: "Probably the process of introspection which governs most of my personal existence is very closely related to the impulses of perception which prompt me to write music." There is indeed a long and noble tradition of musical composition springing from "impulses of perception." To it Ben Weber belongs.

George Rochberg is another romantic of the Schoenbergian persuasion. Born in Patterson, New Jersey, in 1918, he studied compositon at the Mannes School (now College) of Music in New York, and at the Curtis Institute of Music in Philadelphia, where he taught from 1948 to 1954. The year 1950–1951, however, was spent as a Fellow of the American Academy in Rome. In 1961 he was appointed chairman of the music department of the University of Pennsylvania, in Philadelphia. A theorist and critic of high ability, he is the author of a dozen important articles and a monograph, *The Hexachord and Its Relation to the Twelve-Tone Row* (Philadelphia, 1955).

Rochberg wrote a quantity of music prior to 1948 that he prefers not to mention; most of it was oriented toward classical forms. Immersion in the music of Bartók and Stravinsky led to the writing of his First Symphony (1948–1949) and First String Quartet (1950–1952). But tonality did not provide the answers he was seeking; hence he turned to Schoenberg and plunged headlong into the twelve-tone system with the *Twelve Bagatelles for Piano* of 1952. His compositions thereafter have been consistently dodecaphonic. For a brief period (1957–1960) he submitted to the prevailing cult for Webern and even ventured into the post-Webern pointillism. But, just as by 1952 he had gotten Bartók and Stravinsky "out of his system," so by 1962 he had absorbed all that really interested him in the Webern orbit, and instinctively drew back from the path leading to "chance" music and electronic composition.

In addition to those mentioned above, Rochberg's instrumental compositions of the 1950s include a Chamber Symphony for nine instruments (1953), *Serenata d'Estate* for six instruments (1955), *Sonata-Fantasie* for piano (1956), *Cheltenham Concerto* for small orchestra (1958), and—his most important work of that decade—the Symphony No. 2 (1956), which won the Naumberg Recording Award in 1961 after having been performed with acclaim by the Cleveland Orchestra and the New York Philharmonic. From the dramatic opening measures (Declamando, fortissimo) to the soulful Mesto and Adagio sostenuto sections of the close, this is a manifestation of what Rochberg describes as "a new Romanticism, one which expresses itself fully in the language of the twentieth century. . . ."

With the composition for orchestra titled *Time-Span* (1960), Rochberg paid his tribute to space-time. Like his fellow-romanticist Ben Weber, he turned to the poems of William Blake in *Four Blake Songs* (1961), for soprano and chamber ensemble. In the String Quartet No. 2 (1959–1961) he included a section for soprano voice singing selections from the *Ninth Duino Elegy* of Rilke (in English translation). The composer tells us that originally he thought of calling this work "Fantasias and Arabesques," which gives an idea of its character. He also states that "one of the fundamental conceptions (of the Second Quartet) is the notion of tempo simultaneity, first introduced into contemporary music by Charles Ives. Two basic speeds, plus their doubles, are employed throughout the work. Combinations of these speeds result in the intensification of the expressive structure, creating at the same time a play with the possibilities of order-disorder."[14] But Rochberg is careful to add that he maintains strict control over his order-disorder dichotomy, leaving nothing to chance—or to the performers.

In 1962 Rochberg began to compose a large-scale work for soloists, chorus, and orchestra, employing texts, both liturgical and secular, from the Latin, the Hebrew, the German, the Italian, and the English (a selection from *The Trojan Women* of Euripedes is also used, but in English translation). Rochberg believes that twelve-tone music is in the process of transformation, but is convinced that total abstraction

[14] From the composer's notes for the recording of the String Quartet No. 2, issued by Composer's Recordings, Inc.

is not the ultimate answer. Rather, he thinks, "it will transform itself into something which permits composers the large gesture and allows them to construct simpler surfaces, pushing the complexities of structure and construction below the surface of sound, somewhat analogous to the relationship between surface and interior which obtains in the music of Mozart, Beethoven, Brahms."[15] There speaks the true disciple of Schoenberg.

Toward total serialization

Milton Babbitt, in the 1950s and 1960s, became the leading theoretical spokesman for those composers who were seeking to develop all the compositional possibilities inherent in the twelve-tone method, and to combine them with the technical resources made available by electronics. Babbitt was born in Philadelphia (in 1916) but was raised in Jackson, Mississippi, where from a very early age he displayed an equal addiction to music and to mathematics. When he matriculated at New York University in 1931 he intended to study mathematical logic; but the discovery, two years later, of Schoenberg and Webern, swung his major interest toward music. He began teaching at Princeton in 1938, at the same time studying composition there with Roger Sessions, whose influence upon him was decisive. A growing interest in electronic composition led to his appointment, in 1959, as one of the four co-directors of the Electronic Music Center of Columbia and Princeton Universities, located in New York City.[16] Believing that a composer should have the same intellectual freedom that the scientist enjoys, Babbitt once wrote a challenging article called "Who Cares If You Listen?"[17]

"I believe in cerebral music," Babbitt told an interviewer,[18] "and I never choose a note unless I know why I want it there." He was drawn to twelve-tone writing because with it "we can structuralize rhythm as we cannot in tonality," and he regards rhythm as the central problem of contemporary music. From about 1947, when he began to write the first works to which he attaches any importance, Babbitt aimed at the "total structuralization" of a composition by serial means:

[15] In a communication to the author under date of July 23, 1963.
[16] The other co-directors were Roger Sessions, Otto Luening, and Vladimir Ussachevsky.
[17] Published in *High Fidelity* Magazine (Feb., 1958).
[18] Anthony Bruno, in *Musical America*, February 1951.

"The twelve-tone set [his term for the row or series] must absolutely determine *every* aspect of the piece." As he explains it: "My new works . . . were concerned with embodying the extensions, generalizations, and fusions of certain techniques contained in the music of Schoenberg, Webern, and Berg, and above all with applying the pitch operations of the twelve-tone system to non-pitch elements: durational rhythm, dynamics, phrase rhythm, timbre, and register, in such a manner as to preserve the most significant properties associated with these operations in the pitch domain when they are applied in these other domains."[19]

The *Three Compositions for Piano* (1947) and *Composition for Four Instruments* (1947–1948) are the first works in which the operations of the twelve-tone method are applied to all the components or "parameters" of the composition, in the manner that is known as "total serialization." These were followed by *Composition for Twelve Instruments* (1948), two String Quartets (1948 and 1954), Woodwind Quartet (1953), *Partitions for Piano* (1957), *Composition for Tenor and Six Instruments* (1958–1960), and *Sounds and Words* (1960). After 1960 Babbitt's growing interest in the Electronic Sound Synthesizer led to the composing of such works as *Composition for Synthesizer* (1961); *Vision and Prayer* (1961) for soprano and synthesized accompaniment (text by Dylan Thomas); *Ensembles for Synthesizer* (1961–1963); and *Philomel* (1963), for soprano, recorded soprano, and synthesized accompaniment. His *Composition for Synthesizer* was the first extended musical composition produced entirely on the RCA Electronic Sound Synthesizer at Columbia University.

Mel Powell, born in New York City in 1923, shares Babbitt's interest in electronic composition. But the path he took to this terrain was utterly different. He began his musical career as a jazz pianist and arranger, joining Benny Goodman's band in 1941. Deciding that he wanted to be a "serious" composer, he studied with Hindemith at Yale. During the 1950s he wrote a number of works in a diatonic,

---

[19] In notes for the recording of *Composition for Four Instruments*, issued by Composer's Recordings, Inc. Babbitt's theories are too abstruse for detailed elucidation in a general work such as this. The interested reader should consult the following articles by Babbitt: "Twelve-Tone Invariants as Compositional Determinants," *The Musical Quarterly* (April 1960); "Set Structure as a Compositional Determinant," *Journal of Music Theory* (April 1961); and "Twelve-Tone Rhythmic Structure and the Electronic Medium," *Perspectives of New Music* (Fall, 1962).

neoclassical vein, such as *Divertimento* for violin and harp, *Divertimento for Five Winds*, and Trio for piano, violin, and cello. He had previously essayed some twelve-tone writing, and he returned to this method with the Piano Quintet of 1957—but now in the post-Webern manner, with the note-to-note procedure based on intervallic relationships rather than on pitches. This trend was continued in *Eight Miniatures for Baroque Ensemble* (1958), *Stanzas for Chamber Orchestra* (1959), and *Filigree Setting for String Quartet* (1960), in which the principle of "total serialization" is applied.

Powell's first electronic composition was *Electronic Setting* (1960). His enthusiasm for this new medium led to the creation, in February, 1962, of the Electronic Music Studio at Yale, where he had been appointed to the music faculty. The first composition completed in the new studio was Powell's *Events* (1963). Mel Powell is among those composers who believe that "the science-art interaction" is crucial for creative music in today's world.

Salvatore Martirano, born in Yonkers, New York, in 1927, is a twelve-tone composer who up to 1963 had resisted the lure of tapes and computers, preferring to obtain his unusual effects by pushing the limits of vocal and instrumental expression beyond their conventional boundaries. A pupil of Herbert Elwell, Bernard Rogers, and Luigi Dallapiccola, he was a Fellow of the American Academy in Rome from 1956 to 1959, and in 1963 joined the music faculty of the University of Illinois. His Octet for flute, bass-clarinet, contra-alto clarinet, marimba, celesta, violin, cello, and contrabass (1962) was commissioned by the Koussevitzky Foundation in the Library of Congress, while the Fromm Foundation commissioned his *Underworld* (1963), for eleven solo instruments. Earlier works include an *a cappella* Mass for mixed voices (1952–1955), *Contrasto* for orchestra (1954), and the highly original and strikingly effective score for mixed chorus and instrumental ensemble, on four songs from Shakespeare, titled *O,O,O,O, that Shakespeherian Rag* (after a line in T. S. Eliot's *The Waste Land*), composed in 1958.

Today the tone-row—and by extension the whole principle of serialization—is no longer the symbol of a particular group or movement, but rather a compositional device that musicians of many different persuasions have found useful.

chapter twenty-nine

Popular currents

Probably there is no term more abused and more often mistaken in its real meaning than 'popular music.'
JOHN PHILIP SOUSA, MARCHING ALONG.

To the average mind," wrote Sousa in his autobiography, "popular music would mean compositions vulgarly conceived and commonplace in their treatment." Needless to say, he protested against that snobbish concept—and with reason, for, as Rupert Hughes wrote in 1900, "There is probably no composer in the world with a popularity equal to that of Sousa." Hughes had the temerity to include Sousa, "The March King," in his book, *Famous American Composers*, and the courage to attack the musical snobbishness that would regard a march as inferior, *per se*, to the "passionate love-ditties" or the "vague contemplation" of the symphonic poetasters. His defense of Sousa's marches is spirited: "The music is conceived in a spirit of high martial zest. It is proud and gay and fierce, thrilled and thrilling with triumph. Like all great music it is made up of simple elements, woven together by a strong personality. . . . The glory of Sousa is that he was the first to write in this style; that he made himself a style; that he has so stirred the musical world that countless imitations have sprung up after him."

Whatever may have been the previous accomplishments of American music, it had never before induced emulation. This was Sousa's achievement: to create a kind of American music that was universally admired and imitated. True, he did not invent the military march, any more than Beethoven invented the symphony; it is not a question of form, but of style, of individuality. A march by Sousa is as distinctive as a Beethoven symphony.

One of the many misconceptions about popular music is that a wide gulf separates it from "fine art" music; that all musicians must stand upon one shore or the other, with this gulf between them. But musical practitioners themselves—especially those on the popular side—have not, as a rule, been conscious of any such separation. The best of them, like Sousa, or Gershwin, or Victor Herbert, or Duke Ellington, studied "music" (not "popular" music), and then, by intuitively developing their talents, wrote the kind of music that became "popular" because it found favor with many people (which is the only reasonable meaning of "popular" in this context). But they never conceived of popular music as being essentially a different *kind* of music. They instinctively knew—although not given to conceptual formulations of this sort—that music is a continuum, which they could enter at any of several points. And this is exactly what most of them did: Sousa wrote symphonic poems as well as military marches and operettas; Herbert wrote a grand opera and a symphonic concerto as well as operettas; Ellington wrote symphonic poems and suites as well as straight jazz pieces; and Scott Joplin, the "King of Ragtime," tried his hand at opera. Sousa's compositional inclinations were awakened when, as a boy, he heard Theodore Thomas conduct an orchestral transcription of Schumann's *Traumerei*. He did not say to himself, "That is not my kind of music, I am going to be a popular composer." What he *did* say—many years later, in his autobiography—was, "Artistic snobbery is so ridiculous."

As a lad of eleven, John Philip Sousa stood enthralled as the Grand Army of the Republic, with bands playing and banners waving, marched along the thoroughfares of Washington in the victory review that marked the end of the War Between the States. On an April evening in 1898, when the Spanish War fever was running high, he and his band gave a concert at the Metropolitan Opera House, where the playing of *The Star-Spangled Banner* and *Dixie* sparked "an extraordinary demonstration" of patriotic fervor. From 1917 to 1919, world-famous, full of honors and glory, he served as bandmaster in the United States Navy. In between, from 1880 to 1892, he had been leader of the United States Marine Band, which he completely remade into a performing group of high excellence, and then, as leader of his own band, had toured the world in triumph. *Semper Fidelis, The Washington Post, High School Cadets,* the *Stars and Stripes Forever*—who had not heard and responded to the stirring sounds of a "Sousa march"? Here and there a snobbish taste-maker or a crusty critic might take exception; in London, a prominent critic wrote: "After one hour of Sousa I could have fallen asleep with the battle in *Heldenleben* falling sweetly on my ears as a soothing lullaby." The Americans, he complained, "apparently like great noises." Had he forgotten the words of the Psalmist, "Make unto the Lord a joyful sounding noise"? The power of annoying a critic is one of the lesser but gratifying attributes of music.

Born in Washington, D.C. on November 6, 1854, of Portuguese and Bavarian parentage, John Philip Sousa studied violin with John Esputa there, and also learned to play several other instruments on the side, including the E flat alto horn! He was spared the benefits of European training because he balked at being under an obligation to the wealthy philanthropist W. W. Corcoran. Later he wrote, "I feel I am better off as it is . . . for I may therefore consider myself a truly American composer." His practical training was gained through a variety of realistic experiences in the world of professional music: with a "Quadrille Band" for society dances, an early stint with the U.S. Marine Band, as first violin at Ford's Opera House in Washington, touring the "sticks" with a variety show, playing under Offenbach when the latter toured with an orchestra in the United States, and finally, as the leader of "Sousa's Band."

From 1880, when his first musical comedy, *Our Flirtation*, was produced, Sousa directed much of his effort to the popular theater. His light opera, *Désirée* (1884), introduced to the public the celebrated singing actor DeWolfe Hopper, who later produced Sousa's most successful operetta, *El Capitan* (1895). Two other operettas, *The Bride Elect* (1897) and *The Charlatan* (1898), confirmed Sousa's place as a pioneer composer in the history of the American popular stage. He wrote his own lyrics.

Although much of his activity involved music as "entertainment," the concert programs of his band often featured music by the "great composers," and Sousa asserted that theirs (or some of it) was really the best "popular music" in the world. When asked in an interview, "What makes a composition popular?" he replied: "Its measure of inspiration." He was accepted as a co-partner by the most eminent American conductors of his time: Theodore Thomas and Walter Damrosch. With the former he played at the dedication of the Chicago World's Fair in 1892, combining forces for a performance of J. K. Paine's *Columbus March and Hymn*, with Damrosch he appeared in a joint concert at New York's Carnegie Hall in 1893. He set to music a poem by James Whitcomb Riley, *The Messiah of Nations*, for a cantata performed at the Panama-Pacific Exposition in 1915. True, he lives by his marches; but in his long lifetime (he died in 1932), he participated in many phases of America's music. Of all those included in Rupert Hughes' *Famous American Composers*—names renowned at the turn of the century—John Philip Sousa is the one whose fame endures through the powerful appeal of his music.

Sousa gave permanent prestige and universal resonance to the tradition of band music that had long flourished in the United States. His most notable predecessor was Patrick Sarsfield Gilmore (1829–1894), a native of Dublin who migrated to America. Forming his own band at Boston in 1859, he won national acclaim by his sensational participation in the National Peace Jubilee of 1869 and the World's Peace Jubilee of 1872. For the latter he assembled a chorus of twenty thousand voices and an orchestra of two thousand players, reinforced by electrically discharged cannon, anvils, and bell chimes. In 1878 he took his band on a tour of Europe. According to Sousa, this band of about sixty-six musicians was "equipped to a greater degree of musical perfection and artistic merit than any known organization of that day." He also adds that sixteen of the instruments included in Gilmore's Band had no place in his own band in 1924. Among these were two piccolos, three E-flat clarinets, one soprano saxophone, two Flügelhorns, and four French horns. Gilmore's most popular composition was the Civil War song "When Johnny Comes Marching Home," which he published in 1863 under the pseudonym of "Louis Lambert."

The most celebrated band musician after Sousa was Edwin Franko Goldman (1878–1956), a native of Louisville, Kentucky, who went to New York to study composition with Dvořák when the latter was teaching at the National Conservatory of Music. He also studied the cornet and was for ten years solo cornettist in the orchestra of the Metropolitan Opera. In 1912 he organized the New York Military Band and six years later founded the symphonic band that made him famous through the series of annual concerts that he gave in New York City as well as on tour. He was a prolific composer of marches and an influential force in American band music. His best-known march is *On the Mall*. He was succeeded as leader of the Goldman

Band by his son, Richard Franko Goldman (born in 1910), who is also a composer and a critic of repute.

Heyday of the operetta

The popular musical theater in America, although it eventually developed strongly characteristic features, began, as was to be expected, with imitations or adaptations of standard European models. The most widely copied of these models was Viennese operetta, though there was also some influence from French and English comic opera (especially Gilbert and Sullivan). An American pioneer in this field was Willard Spenser (1852–1933), whose two-act comic opera *The Little Tycoon*, produced in Philadelphia on January 4, 1886, was subsequently performed thousands of times all over the country. A close competitor was Woolson Morse (1858–1897), who turned out *The Merry Monarch* (1890), *Panjandrum* (1893), *Dr. Syntax* (1894), and his greatest success, *Wang* (1891), starring DeWolf Hopper as Wang, the Regent of Siam—a setting evoked (according to one critic) by "loud cymbals plus cacophony."

Three European-born composers achieved popularity at this time: Gustave Luders (1866–1913) with *The Prince of Pilsen* (1903), Ludwig Englander (1859–1914) with *A Madcap Princess* (1904), and Gustave Kerker (1857–1923) with *The Belle of New York* (1908). Other foreign-born musicians were to follow and to fill the American scene with their successes: Victor Herbert, Rudolf Friml, Sigmund Romberg. In the meantime, a native-born American was to make his mark with one of the most enduringly successful operettas of the era.

Reginald De Koven (1859–1920) made it a point to acquire the special training needed for composing comic operas. He was born in Middletown, Connecticut, and at the age of ten was taken to England, where he graduated from Oxford University in 1879. He then studied composition in Stuttgart, in Frankfurt, in Vienna with Genée, and in Paris with Delibes. From these two masters he learned the technique of comic opera, and began to apply his knowledge in *The Begum* (1887) and *Don Quixote* (1889). Meanwhile he had married an American and settled in Chicago. There, on June 9, 1890, he produced the greatest success of his entire career, the romantic comic opera in three acts, *Robin Hood*. It was performed by a company called The Bostonians, who kept it as their chief support for many years. The score contains De Koven's two most enduring songs, "Brown October Ale" and "Oh, Promise Me." The work achieved more than three thousand successive performances and established De Koven's reputation so firmly that he could live on it ever after. Not that he didn't try hard enough to repeat the success of *Robin Hood*. He kept on writing comic operas, turning out a total of twenty, but none even remotely approached the success of that early effort. The work that came nearest to it was *The Highwayman*, produced in New York, in 1897 and revived there, with better success, twenty years later. *Rob Roy* was produced in 1894 and *Maid Marion* in 1901, the latter a sequel to *Robin Hood*. De Koven tried his hand at grand opera with *The Canterbury Pilgrims*, libretto by Percy Mackaye, produced in New York on March 7, 1917. He also wrote what he called an American "folk opera," *Rip Van Winkle*, produced in Chicago shortly before he died (January 2, 1920).

De Koven's contemporary, Victor Herbert (1859–1924), far surpassed him in the number and permanence of his successes. Herbert was born in Dublin, Ireland, and received his musical training, primarily as a cellist, in Germany, where he was sent to study from the age of seven. In 1882 he played with the Johann Strauss Orchestra in Vienna, and from 1883 to 1886 was a member of the court orchestra in Stuttgart, where he studied composition with Max Seifritz. In 1886 he married the Viennese singer Thérèse Förster and came to the United States as a cellist at the Metropolitan Opera House. Later he held the same position with the Theodore Thomas Orchestra and the New York Philharmonic Society. From 1898 to 1904 he was conductor of the Pittsburgh Symphony Orchestra and thereafter conducted his own orchestra in New York.

In 1893 Herbert was persuaded to write a comic opera, *Prince Ananias*, for The Bostonians, who produced it in New York the following year. Its reception was sufficiently encouraging for Herbert to feel that he should continue in this path. There followed in rapid succession *The Wizard of the Nile* (1895), *The Serenade* (1897), *The Fortune Teller* (1898), *Babes in Toyland* (1903), *Mlle. Modiste* (1905), *The Red Mill* (1906), *Little Nemo* (1908), *Naughty Marietta* (1910), *Sweethearts* (1913), *The Princess Pat* (1915), *The Century Girl* (1916), *Eileen* (1917), *The Velvet Lady* (1919), and *The Dream*

Girl (1924)—the list does not pretend to be complete. This is the most distinguished and most enduringly successful corpus of light opera produced by an American composer—and Victor Herbert may be considered such by virtue of his early identification with the American milieu.

Victor Herbert's mellifluous melodies and skillful orchestrations, united to better-than-average librettos, have kept the best of his light operas alive for many decades. And many of his songs have enjoyed an independent life apart from their theatrical context. *Mlle. Modiste*, produced in New York on December 25, 1905, with Fritzi Scheff in the title role, contains the largest number of hit tunes, with "The Time and the Place and the Girl," "Love Me, Love My Dog," "I Want What I Want When I Want It," and, above all, "Kiss Me Again." *Naughty Marietta*, produced on November 7, 1910, includes "I'm Falling in Love with Someone" and "Ah, Sweet Mystery of Life." *The Red Mill* has proved to be one of Herbert's most enduring works, combining an effective plot, fast action, a picturesque setting, and attractive tunes, such as "The Isle of Our Dreams" and "Because You're You."

Rudolf Friml (*b.* 1879), a native of Prague who studied composition there with Dvořák, was headed for a career in "serious" music, but defected when opportunity beckoned on Broadway. Scoring an immediate hit with *The Firefly* (1912), he continued with *High Jinks* (1913), *Katinka* (1915), and many others. Never shedding his affinity with the style and spirit of the traditional Viennese operetta, he achieved his greatest success in three works of this type: *Rose-Marie* (1924), with its "Indian Love Call"; *The Vagabond King* (1925), containing "Song of the Vagabonds" and "Love Me Tonight"; and *The Three Musketeers* (1928), with its "March of the Musketeers."

Another European-born composer whose best vein was that of operetta is Sigmund Romberg (1887–1951), a native of Hungary who came to the United States in 1909. After several years of hack work for musical shows, his big opportunity came with *Maytime* (1917), which was so successful that two New York productions ran simultaneously. Its memorable songs were "Will You Remember?" and "Road to Paradise." Much more versatile than Friml, Romberg adapted himself to all types of the American popular theater; but romantic operetta was his forte, as he proved with three of the most enduring successes in this field: *Blossom Time* (1921), with music based on themes by

Franz Schubert; *The Student Prince in Heidelberg* (1924), certainly a classic of its kind (its songs include "Deep in My Heart, Dear" and "Just We Two"); and *The Desert Song* (1926), a perennial favorite in spite of its hackneyed "sheik plot." Scarcely less successful were *The New Moon* (1928), a catch-all of Romberg song hits ("One Kiss," "Wanting You," "Lover, Come Back to Me"); and *Up in Central Park* (1945), with its evocation of the Currier and Ives era. His last work, *The Girl in Pink Tights*, posthumously produced in 1954, was built around the story of the first American "musical extravaganza," *The Black Crook* (1866), which, by combining an old-fashioned melodrama with the dancing and lively charms of a French ballet troupe stranded in New York, marked the beginning of musical comedy in America. Throughout his career, Romberg provided evidence to support his conviction that "Nothing succeeds like a popular tune—especially a romantic tune."

Rise of musical comedy

Operetta and comic opera are the older, traditional types of the popular musical theater. They come closest to the pattern of opera, while at the furthest remove from this pattern are the musical extravaganza (or spectacle) and the revue, which do not have a story line but consist of independent "numbers" or tableaux. The most celebrated continuous example of the American musical spectacle were *The Ziegfeld Follies*, first presented in 1907 as a "mélange of mirth, music, and pretty young girls," and becoming virtually a national institution ("Glorifying the American Girl") over the next twenty-four years. Beginning in 1921, *The Music Box Revue* set an unmatched standard for that type of entertainment, although it lasted for only four seasons. Its theme song, "Say It with Music," was by Irving Berlin.

Musical comedy contains elements of operetta and spectacle, as well as of vaudeville (in the early years), but the blend, though difficult to define precisely, is somewhat different. Less consistent musically than operetta, it often has the extravagance of the spectacle but clings to the thread of a plot, however tenuous or absurd this may be. In the course of time, musical comedy evolved into the musical play, not limited to outright comedy, which is usually called simply a "musical."

During the early years of the twentieth century, the most thoroughly indigenous strain in American musical comedy was represented by the brash and versatile George M. Cohan (1878–1942), assisted by his remarkable family ("The Four Cohans"). He wrote the music, the books, and the lyrics for most of his shows, beginning with *The Governor's Son* in 1901 and ending with *Billie* in 1928. Most of them were topical, full of local color, expressing "The American Idea" (as he titled one of his shows) in a popular idiom that suited the rising tide of optimism and mass entertainment. Such songs as "The Yankee Doodle Boy," "I Want to Be a Popular Millionaire," "Any Place the Old Flag Flies," and "I'm a Popular Man," expressed the spirit of the time—and the place. For Cohan, Broadway was the hub of the universe; he might get as far as *Forty-Five Minutes from Broadway* (1906), but he would prefer to have been *The Man Who Owns Broadway* (1909), and his theme song was surely "Give My Regards to Broadway." George M. Cohan was a dynamic figure whose productions epitomize an era in American social history. And he it was who wrote the favorite song of the First World War: "Over There."

Jerome Kern (1885–1945) came to musical comedy with an entirely different background. Born in New York, he attended the College of Music there and then went to Europe for further study in composition. He also acquired some theatrical experience in London. Back in New York, he obtained a foothold in the musical theater by injecting new songs into well-worn operetta importations which were then flooding the American stage. The first show for which he wrote all the music was *The Red Petticoat* (1912) and his first big success came with *Very Good Eddie* (1915). Other hits followed: *Oh, Boy!* in 1917, *Sally* in 1920, *Stepping Stones* in 1923, *Sunny* in 1925, *The Cat and the Fiddle* in 1931, *Music in the Air* in 1932, and *Roberta* in 1933. These shows contained such songs as "Till the Clouds Roll By," "In Love with Love," "The Night Was Made for Love," "The Song Is You," and "Smoke Gets in Your Eyes," which are among the many melodies that have made Kern's music endure.

But it was with *Show Boat* (1927) that Jerome Kern really made theatrical history. In a period dominated by the leg-show, the lavish spectacle, the inane plot, he decided to set a literate work to music, a new novel by Edna Ferber that touched on such controversial subjects as miscegenation and the hard lot of the southern Negro. Though originally billed as a "musical comedy," *Show Boat* has been variously described as an operetta, a musical play, and "almost a folk opera."

My own conclusion now is that it was really a "musical play," probably the first example of a new genre in the American theater that is best characterized by turning an adjective into a substantive: the *musical*. I agree with Cecil Smith's judgment: "No other American piece of its vintage left so large a permanent musical legacy, and certainly no other surpassed it in quality." Historically, it marked the trend toward literary sources in the making of the American musical.

George Gershwin (1898–1937), whose background and achievements in the realm of "serious" music were described in Chapter 24, got off to a rather slow start with his first two musical comedies, *La! La! Lucille* (1919) and *Sweet Little Devil* (1924), in which his lack of technical preparation was apparent. He hit his stride with *Lady, Be Good* (1924), *Tip-Toes* (1925), *Oh, Kay* (1926), *Funny Face* (1927), and *Girl Crazy* (1930). With *Strike Up the Band* (1930) he and his brother Ira (who wrote the lyrics for most of his shows) turned to political and social satire that pulled none of its punches. It was hard-hitting, often bitter, very effective, and quite amusing. Gershwin was to continue this vein of satire, though with less propaganda and more humor, in *Of Thee I Sing* (1931), which spoofed the folklore of an American presidential election and its aftermath in the White House. In 1932 *Of Thee I Sing* was awarded the first Pulitzer Prize ever bestowed for a musical play, as "the original American play performed in New York which shall best represent the educational value and power of the stage." George and Ira Gershwin went on to display once more the satirical power of the musical comedy stage with *Let 'em Eat Cake* (1933). The libretto was by Kaufman and Ryskind, and, as Brooks Atkinson wrote, "Their hatreds have triumphed over their sense of humor." This could scarcely be called musical *comedy*. Gershwin, in any case, was ready to leave the field of musical comedy, for by this time he had established his reputation as a "serious" composer. In the same year (1933) he turned out one more piece in the genre that he had cultivated with such success, *Pardon My English*, an inconsequential affair, and when he returned to the lyric theater it was with a far more ambitious effort, *Porgy and Bess* (1935). The story of that work is told in the chapter "Toward an American Opera."

Cole Porter (1892–1965), whom Cecil Smith calls "the genteel pornographer" of musical comedy, was born in Peru, Indiana. He graduated from Yale in 1913; then, after study at the Harvard Law

School, he enrolled at the music school there and finally polished off his musical training at the Schola Cantorum in Paris, where Vincent d'Indy presided over a musico-mystical-aesthetic regime that was almost monkish in its austerity. It was not there that Porter acquired his encyclopedic knowledge of sex, which he displayed to a delighted public in his first complete musical-comedy score, *Fifty Million Frenchmen* (1929), for which he also wrote the sophisticated lyrics (a practice he was to continue in other works). Porter's next show, *The New Yorkers* (1930), was allegedly a "sociological musical satire" (that was a fashion of the 1930s), but it proved to be chiefly a vehicle for Jimmy Durante. Porter, at all events, continued to turn out one show after another. The list includes *The Gay Divorcée* (1932), *Anything Goes* (1934), *Jubilee* (1935), *Red Hot and Blue* (1936), *Leave It to Me* (1938), *Du Barry Was a Lady* (1939), *Panama Hattie* (1940), *Let's Face It* (1941), *Something for the Boys* (1943), *Around the World* (1946; a failure), and *Kiss Me Kate* (1948; a huge success, based on Shakespeare's *The Taming of the Shrew*). This last show included such characteristic Porter songs as "I Hate Men," "Wunderbar," and "So in Love Am I." The songs of Cole Porter are thoroughly idiosyncratic. They have a wide range of expression, from deft parody ("Wunderbar") to erotic feeling ("Night and Day") and exotic evocation ("Begin the Beguine").

Vincent Youmans (1898–1946) was a composer who might have left an even stronger impression than he did on the musical-comedy stage had not illness cut short his career. His masterpiece was *No! No! Nanette*, produced in 1923, which contains those memorable songs, "Tea for Two" and "I Want to Be Happy." The score of *Hit the Deck* (1927) included one of his biggest hits, "Hallelujah." Another lasting success, the balladlike "Without a Song," made its appearance in *Great Day* (1929). In the 1930s he wrote the music for *Smiles*, *Through the Years*, and *Take a Chance*. This last featured two of his most effective songs, "Eadie Was a Lady" (sung by Ethel Merman), and "Rise and Shine" (which brought the frenzy of revivalism to the musical-comedy stage).

Irving Berlin (*recte* Isidore Balin), born in Russia in 1888, was brought to America as an infant and grew up in New York's lower East Side. He got a job as a singing waiter at a place known as "Nigger Mike's" in Chinatown. Thereafter he began an extraordinarily successful career as a song-writer, turning out such hits as "Alexander's Ragtime Band," "Everybody's Doin' It," "When that Midnight Choo-Choo

Leaves for Alabam," "When My Baby Smiles at Me," "A Pretty Girl Is Like a Melody," "What'll I Do?" "All Alone," "Blue Skies," "Remember," and many others.

In August, 1918, on leave from the Army, Irving Berlin produced a soldier show called *Yip, Yip, Yaphank*, for which he wrote the tunes and the lyrics and which included the hit song, "Oh, How I Hate to Get Up in the Morning." Twenty-four years later this song was heard again in another soldier show put together by Berlin, *This Is the Army*, produced on July 4, 1942, with immense success. This had been originally conceived as an up-to-date version of *Yip, Yip, Yaphank*, but turned out to be something quite different. Its theme song, "This Is the Army, Mr. Jones," quickly captured the nation.

Apart from these two soldier shows, Berlin's most important contributions to American musical comedy were made with *Face the Music* (1932) and *As Thousands Cheer* (1933), both with librettos by Moss Hart and both highly topical in their allusions to the current depression, political affairs, and contemporary celebrities. *Face the Music* had police corruption in New York as the target of its satire, while *As Thousands Cheer* directed its shafts at everything from the White House to the Metropolitan Opera. One sketch was titled "Franklin D. Roosevelt Inaugurates Tomorrow." Berlin's next musical show, *Louisiana Purchase* (1940), also exploited the vein of political satire, with the demagogue "Huey" Long as its target. Six years later, Berlin climaxed his career with a tremendous success, *Annie Get Your Gun*, which included the song hits "Doin' What Comes Naturally," "Show Business," and "They Say It's Wonderful." Ethel Merman starred in the role of Annie Oakley, the sharpshooting girl of Buffalo Bill's Wild West Show, who learns that "You Can't Get a Man with a Gun." In 1954, Irving Berlin received a citation of merit from President Eisenhower as the composer of "God Bless America" and other patriotic songs.

Rodgers, Hart, and Hammerstein

American musical comedy may be said to have reached maturity in the series of shows for which Richard Rodgers wrote the music, at first in literary partnership with Lorenz Hart and later with Oscar Hammerstein 2d.

Richard Rodgers was born in New York City in 1902, the son

of a physician. The usual legend of musical precocity is attached to his infancy: "He began picking out tunes on the parlor piano at the age of four." While attending Columbia University he met his librettist, Lorenz Hart, with whom he wrote the varsity show of 1918, *Fly with Me*. He left college at the end of his second year but continued to study composition at the Institute of Musical Art while writing many amateur shows with Hart. Professional success seemed so remote that he was on the point of taking a job as salesman for a clothing concern. Then, in 1925, the Theatre Guild invited him to write music for the *Garrick Gaieties*, and he was launched on Broadway.

The first noteworthy Rodgers and Hart production was *A Connecticut Yankee* (1927), based on Mark Twain's fantasy of a Yankee at the court of King Arthur, with lyrics that combined the archaic with the slangy. There followed *Present Arms* (1928), glorifying the Marines; *Jumbo* (1935), an extravaganza combining all kinds of entertainment, from circus to opera; *On Your Toes* (1936), with its remarkably realistic ballet by Balanchine, *Slaughter on Tenth Avenue*; *Babes in Arms* (1937), a tribute to youth; and *I'd Rather Be Right* (1937), a political satire in which they collaborated with George Kaufman and Moss Hart. The series continued with *I Married an Angel* (1938), *Too Many Girls* (1939), and—especially memorable for its maturity—*Pal Joey* (1940), based on some hard-boiled stories by John O'Hara concerning a plausible young heel who climbs to success by making love to a society woman, only to be let down when she tires of him. In the course of the show all the bromides and clichés of the entertainment business are cleverly satirized. The importance of this work is its portrayal of character and its social-psychological realism. After one more show, *By Jupiter* (1942), the partnership of Rodgers and Hart was dissolved (Hart died in 1943). They had collaborated on twenty-nine shows (nine of them made into motion pictures) and had written a total of nearly four hundred songs.

A new musical-comedy team was formed when Rodgers began to collaborate with Oscar Hammerstein 2d, initiating a partnership that was to be no less memorable than its predecessor, since it produced such masterpieces as *Oklahoma!* (1943), *Carousel* (1945), *South Pacific* (1949), *The King and I* (1951), and *Me and Juliet* (1953).

Oklahoma! was an adaptation of the regional play by Lynn Riggs *Green Grow the Lilacs*, which had been produced by the Theatre Guild in 1931. It reached the St. James Theatre in New York on

March 31, 1943, and remained there for nearly six years. It achieved a total of 2,202 performances, the longest run of any musical show in the history of Broadway up to that time. On the road it endeared itself to the entire nation. It contained such attractive songs as "O What a Beautiful Morning," "People Will Say We're in Love," and "The Surrey with the Fringe on Top." It also had a dramatic plot and a stunningly effective ballet sequence with choreography by Agnes de Mille that surpassed anything hitherto seen on the American stage.

With *Carousel*, based on the play *Liliom* by the Hungarian dramatist Ferenc Molnar, Rodgers and Hammerstein took an important step forward into the realm of musical theater rather than musical comedy. The scene of the play was shifted to New England, with plenty of local color; but its essential dramatic and psychological ingredients were faithfully maintained and projected with considerable musical skill. Entire scenes were developed musically, instead of through spoken dialogue alternating with interpolated songs. The songs, when they occurred, were very good (for example, "If I Loved You" and "What's the Use of Wond'rin'?"); but *Carousel* has continued to hold the stage, not as a collection of songs strung on a thin plot, but as a fully integrated musical play.

For their next successful production, Rodgers and Hammerstein again turned to the work of a well-known writer, in this case *Tales of the South Pacific* by James Michener, which provided them with an exotic setting for the romance of the American army nurse who falls in love with an island planter. The array of hit songs in *South Pacific* ranged from the love duet "Some Enchanted Evening" to the hilarious sailors' chorus, "There Is Nothing Like a Dame." Their next show moved into a still more exotic setting, for *The King and I* is based on the book *Anna and the King of Siam*, which recounts the experiences of an English girl who was engaged as a teacher for the children of the King of Siam. The last work on which Rodgers and Hammerstein collaborated was also one of their biggest successes: *The Sound of Music* (1959), based on the life of the Trapp Family Singers. Hammerstein's death in 1960 terminated the partnership.

The musical marches on

Another promising partnership, that of Richard Adler and Jerry Ross, resulted in two notable hits, *The Pajama Game* (1954) and *Damn*

Yankees (1955), before it was abruptly terminated by the untimely death of Ross at the age of twenty-nine. Leonard Bernstein, equally at home in the classical and popular fields, demonstrated his versatility with two zestful, tuneful, and brilliantly orchestrated musical comedies, *On the Town* (1944) and *Wonderful Town* (1953), then moved into a more sophisticated atmosphere with *Candide* (1956), based on Voltaire's tale of the youth who believed everything was for the best in this best of all possible worlds. The score covers a wide range of parody, from Italian grand opera to Gilbert and Sullivan, and makes use of set pieces, or numbers, in a clever and witty manner—perhaps too clever for popular success. With *West Side Story* (1957), a retelling of the Romeo and Juliet story in terms of today's underprivileged youth in upper Manhattan, Bernstein turned out another brilliant score which nevertheless depended for much of its effect on the extremely dramatic choreography of Jerome Robbins, who directed the production. Withal, *West Side Story*—tough, contemporary, realistic, compassionate—is a landmark in the American musical theater.

Harold Arlen (*b.* 1905) obtained success as a song-writer ("Blues in the Night," "That Old Black Magic") before achieving a hit on Broadway with *Bloomer Girl* (1944), a period piece on the life of the American feminist Amelia Bloomer. His next two shows had West Indian settings: *House of Flowers* (1954), with book and lyrics by Truman Capote; and *Jamaica* (1957), which was a personal triumph for the Negro singer Lena Horne.

Frank Loesser (*b.* 1910) made his mark with one of the smashing successes of Broadway, *Guys and Dolls* (1950), based on stories by Damon Runyon dealing with small-time characters—entertainers, gamblers, salvationists—in the Big City: a lively and colorful "fable of Broadway," with a remarkable ballet by Michael Kidd. Loesser then moved nearer to the "musical play" with *The Most Happy Fella* (1956), based on Sidney Howard's play *They Knew What They Wanted*. This was musical drama rather than musical comedy, though it did not renounce the attraction of a popular tune. Returning to the vein of musical comedy, Loesser in 1961 produced the biggest hit of his career thus far, *How to Succeed in Business without Really Trying*, a fast-moving satire of big business, office politics and sex, and high-pressure advertising.

Harold Rome (*b.* 1908) studied architecture at Yale but was diverted into music by the Depression, finding that he could make more money by writing songs than by drafting blueprints. In 1937 the International Ladies Garment Workers Union invited him to write the music and lyrics for a revue to be staged by members of the union. The result was *Pins and Needles,* a clever political satire with left-wing tendencies. Rome continued the political-social vein in *Sing out the News* (1938) and *Call Me Mister* (1946), both of the topical-revue type. Thereafter Rome turned to the musical-comedy framework, as in *Wish You Were Here* (1952), about the ways of love at an adult summer camp; *Fanny* (1954), drawn from the trilogy of plays by the French author Marcel Pagnol, was a more fully developed musical play with strong characterization and songs that projected authentic emotions.

Jule Styne, born in England in 1905, came to the United States as a child prodigy on the piano and then attended the Chicago Musical College. After writing some successful songs he invaded Broadway victoriously with *High Button Shoes* (1947), *Gentlemen Prefer Blondes* (1949), *Bells Are Ringing* (1956), *Gypsy* (1959), and *Do, Re, Mi* (1960). All were tremendously successful; perhaps the most memorable is *Gentlemen Prefer Blondes,* after the celebrated novel by Anita Loos about gold-digging flappers in the 1920s. The score contains such classic songs as "Diamonds Are a Girl's Best Friend" and "A Little Girl from Little Rock."

Meredith Willson (*b.* 1902) had a career in classical music, as flautist and composer, before turning to musical comedy. Almost immediately he obtained a smash hit with *The Music Man* (1957), a nostalgic evocation of life, love, and music in a small midwestern town in the year 1912. This was followed by *The Unsinkable Molly Brown* (1960), based on the "true life story" of an American country girl who reaped a fortune from the gold mines of Colorado, made a social splurge in Europe, and survived the sinking of the *Titanic* in 1912.

The German-born composer Kurt Weill (1900–1950), who came to the United States in 1935 after achieving a considerable success in Europe—notably with *The Three-Penny Opera* (a modern version of *The Beggar's Opera*)—made several impressive contributions to the American musical theater. After *Johnny Johnson* (1936), a "war fable" by dramatist Paul Green, Weill obtained his first big success with *Knickerbocker Holiday* (1938), for which Maxwell Anderson wrote the libretto and the lyrics (based on Washington Irving's *Father Knickerbocker's History of New York*). His next production, in collaboration with Moss Hart and Ira Gershwin, was *Lady in the Dark* (1941), which featured Gertrude Lawrence in the role of a successful but unsatisfied magazine editor who seeks the advice of a psychoanalyst to solve her personal problems. Much of the action is concerned with depicting the lady editor's vivid dream sequences. The score marked another milestone toward the maturity of the musical play. Weill's *One Touch of Venus* reverted to a more conventional pattern, but in *Street Scene* (1947), based on Elmer Rice's play of the same name, with lyrics by Langston Hughes, he achieved a musicodramatic work that far transcended the limitations of musical comedy. It comes very close to being an American opera—and a very fine one too.

Weill's last work, again in collaboration with Maxwell Anderson, was "a musical tragedy," *Lost in the Stars* (1949), based on the novel of South African life by Alan Paton, *Cry, the Beloved Country*. And again the conventions of the popular musical show were cast aside, while retaining the vitality and direct appeal of the popular idiom. The continuous musical development of opera is present, but without the dead weight of archaic traditions. Weill was moving in a significant direction, but death cut short his career. His *Three-Penny Opera*, in an English version and adaptation by Marc Blitzstein, was revived in New York in 1954 and had a tremendously long run of over three years. His early opera *Rise and Fall of the City of Mahagonny* (1930), with a somewhat surrealistic American setting laid in Alabama, exposing contemporary corruption and hypocrisy, was also revived posthumously in 1965, but with moderate success. It was one of the first European operas to make use of jazz idioms. Weill also composed an American folk opera, *Down in the Valley* (based on the folk song of that name), for performance by schools and amateur groups.

Frederick Loewe, born in Vienna in 1904, received a thorough musical training in piano and composition: when he came to the United States in 1923 it was with the intention of pursuing a career in so-called serious music. This actually involved him in a nomadic and precarious existence, until he finally turned to writing popular songs. A crucial encounter was his meeting with the writer Alan Jay Lerner in 1942. They decided to collaborate but got off to a slow start: only with their fourth attempt did they achieve a real success. This was *Brigadoon* (1947), described as "a whimsical musical fantasy." At once it was apparent that twin luminaries had again appeared in the American musical theater. For the first time a musical comedy received the award of the Drama Critics' Circle as the best play of the year. But this was only a beginning, a sort of dress rehearsal for the greatest musical triumph of the century: *My Fair Lady*, produced on March 15, 1956. Based on Bernard Shaw's play *Pygmalion*, it was the most literate musical comedy ever written, and musically one of the most sophisticated, with a kind of Viennese elegance and élan in a splendor of elaborate settings, gorgeous costumes, and delightful choreography. Rex Harrison as Professor Higgins, Julie Andrews as Liza, and Stanley Holloway as Mr. Doolittle, made theatrical history in this musical play that captivated the entire world. On June 13, 1961, it broke the long-run record previously held by *Oklahoma!* A screen version starring Audrey Hepburn as Liza repeated the triumphs of the stage show. As a paradigm of musical comedy, *My Fair Lady* will continue to be both a delight and a challenge to coming generations.

American musical comedy—we may also use the terms musical show or simply "musical," as a noun—in its more ambitious manifestations has often approached the status of opera or musical drama. This has enriched its musical and dramatic vocabulary; but we must not forget that the American musical show, as distinct from its European predecessors, acquired its special character as an expression of the American vernacular—in music, in speech, in dancing, in social context. The lifeblood of the American musical comes from the vitality of the vernacular. Many of our best operas—*Porgy and Bess, The Mother of Us All, Regina*—have drawn upon the same source. It may be that the great works of the American lyric theater will emerge at the point where opera and musical show converge; but thus far it is the latter that has proved to be more vigorous and original. Whatever may eventually emerge, it is certain that the American musical theater will continue to be vital, varied, enterprising, and changeful.

chapter thirty

Toward an American opera

Take care of the professional line and the artistic line will take care of itself.
VIRGIL THOMSON, THE STATE OF MUSIC.

The editor of *Harper's Magazine*, writing in 1859 about the arts in America, concluded that "what is fine in the buildings of the old countries we can borrow; their statues and their pictures we will be able in good time to buy." That was the theory of the fine arts that prevailed in America for many generations: a theory that art imitated or imported from Europe was better than anything we could produce ourselves, and that the best hope for us was to imitate faithfully and borrow extensively. Few people were ready to listen to Emerson when he said: "It is in vain that we look for genius to reiterate its miracles in the old arts; it is its instinct to find beauty and holiness in new and necessary facts, in the field and roadside, in the shop and mill."

During the nineteenth century, composers such as Fry and Bristow tried to create American grand opera by a slavish imitation of the Italian models then in vogue. The choice of an American subject like the legend of Rip Van Winkle did little to mitigate the imitativeness of their music. Toward the end of the century, when the prevailing mode was Wagnerian music drama, Walter Damrosch's setting of *The Scarlet Letter* (1896) was aptly characterized as "the *Nibelungen* of New England." After an excursion into French poetic drama with *Cyrano de Bergerac* (1913), Damrosch many years later turned again to an American subject in *The Man Without a Country*, with a libretto by Arthur Guiterman after the story by Edward Everett Hale, produced at the Metropolitan Opera House on May 2, 1937; but he succeeded only in producing another conventional grand opera made from a European stereotype.

It may be objected that Damrosch, Breslau-born and European-trained, was musically too close to his native Germany to have a feeling for American elements in opera. But the native-born American composers of opera were just as conventional and just as imitative, as proved by the earliest American operas produced at the Metropolitan Opera House: *The Pipe of Desire* (1910) by Frederick S. Converse; *Mona* (1912) by Horatio Parker; *Cleopatra's Night* (1920) by Henry Hadley. Resounding public successes were achieved by the two operas of Deems Taylor, *The King's Henchman* (February 17, 1927), with a libretto by Edna St. Vincent Millay, and *Peter Ibbetson* (February 7, 1931), after the novel by Du Maurier (previously dramatized by Constance Collier). The former received fourteen performances in three seasons, the latter sixteen performances in four seasons. These records have never been surpassed by any other American composer whose works have been given at the Metropolitan Opera House.

Howard Hanson's opera *Merry Mount*, produced on February 10, 1934, achieved a total of nine performances. Based on a fictional account of happenings at Thomas Morton's colony at Merry Mount, the plot of the opera deals with the downfall of a Puritan pastor who, in attempting to save the soul of a beautiful sinner, loses his own and brings death to both himself and her. Olin Downes described the music as "at times conventional and noisily effective," and added: "It displays neither originality nor any special aptitude for the theater." This remark would apply to most American operas produced at the Metropolitan. Deems Taylor's operas displayed some aptitude for the theater—which accounts for their relative success—but they completely lacked originality—which may account for their subsequent neglect.

With dogged persistence, but with even more dismal results, the Metropolitan, on January 11, 1947, produced another American opera, *The Warrior*, music by Bernard Rogers, libretto (dealing with the story of Samson and Delilah) by Norman Corwin, a prominent radio dramatist. In spite of the reputation of both composer and librettist, the work was a flat failure: dull, stilted, and lifeless. Rogers, a composer with an excellent technical background, revealed, like so many of his predecessors, a lack of feeling for dramatic values in the musical theater. Corwin, who could certainly write effectively when he chose, became self-conscious and pretentious, as so many people do when they approach opera from the outside.

There is general agreement that opera should be good theater. It should also be good music; and theater and music should be thoroughly integrated, so that neither overbalances the other and each contributes structurally to the effectiveness of the whole. Many American operas have been condemned for not being good theater. On the other hand, when a particularly effective dramatic work has been set to music, the complaint is sometimes made that the music is more or less superfluous. Something of the sort occurred with Louis Gruenberg's operatic version of Eugene O'Neill's drama, *Emperor Jones*, produced at the Metropolitan Opera House on January 7, 1933. The play deals with a Negro Pullman porter who goes to an island in the West Indies and makes himself "Emperor" there. The mysterious and primitive forces of the island prey on his mind, and he becomes demented, while the terrors of the jungle close in around him. As Olin Downes remarked after the première, Gruenberg showed dramatic instinct and intuition for the theater, and it is this which makes his work a landmark among American operas produced at the Metropolitan. He utilized a modern orchestral idiom and drew on the dramatic resources of Afro-American rhythms and songs, as in the spiritual "Standin' in the Need of Prayer," and in the writing for chorus. Moreover, he had the wisdom to choose a subject dealing with recognizable human beings in the world of today, involved in a comprehensible dramatic situation charged with inherent psychological tensions. Critics may question the extent to which the music enhances the intrinsic dramatic power of the play, and the degree of merit that the score possesses as music. But the significance of *Emperor Jones* is that here at last an American opera appeared that was both musical and dramatic.

Gruenberg has written two other operas. The first was *Jack and the Beanstalk*, to a libretto by John Erskine, subtitled "A Fairy Opera for the Childlike," which was produced by the Juilliard School of Music in New York on November 19, 1931. The other is an opera written especially for radio performance: *Green Mansions*, after the novel by W. H. Hudson, produced by the Columbia Broadcasting System on September 17, 1937. Radio and television have played a role of considerable importance in the development of American opera. In fact, these media, together with the university workshops and the Broadway theater, have made possible the emergence of an American tradition in the lyric theater.

It may not be irrelevant to note that Gruenberg had worked for some time with the stylization of Afro-American material, as in *The Daniel Jazz* and *The Creation* (both for high voice and eight solo instruments), and *Jazz Suite* for orchestra. *Emperor Jones* was a continuation of this vein. The point is of interest because, when we reach the first indisputable masterpiece of the American lyric theater, Gershwin's *Porgy and Bess*, we find that it resulted from a similar interest in Afro-American material, combined with the cultivation of so-called "symphonic jazz" and the background of the Broadway musical show.

Gershwin's *Porgy and Bess*

Somewhere around 1929 Gershwin read the novel called *Porgy*, by Du Bose Heyward, dealing with Negro life in Charleston, South Carolina. He was attracted by the subject, saw at once its dramatic, human, and musical possibilities, and wished to make an opera of it. When the novel was made into a play, Gershwin was closer to getting the libretto that he wanted. The libretto was finally fashioned by Heyward, with the composer's brother Ira collaborating on the lyrics (as he had done for many of George's Broadway shows). The summer of 1934 was spent by Gershwin on Folly Island, about ten miles from Charleston, absorbing the music and the folkways of the Negroes. He attended services of the Gullah Negroes on nearby islands, and took part in their "shouting." He noted the cries of the street vendors in Charleston, with their fascinating melodic inflections.

Gershwin spent nine months orchestrating *Porgy and Bess*. To Rouben Mamoulian he wrote: "It is really a tremendous task scoring three hours of music." Gershwin was not doing another musical "show," he was writing a full-sized opera, and he took the job very seriously. Partly because the work was cut (by about one-fourth) for its original production, and partly because of Gershwin's use of some tunes in the Broadway manner, the notion prevailed that *Porgy and Bess* was just a super musical play rather than a "real opera." But as Alexander Steinert remarked: "It belongs in an opera house, played by a large orchestra, for which it was written." *Porgy and Bess* may not be orthodox grand opera, but it *is* opera, and some day it may be given in the large opera houses of America, as it has been given, with tremendous acclaim, in those of Europe.

It is customary to speak of *Porgy and Bess* as a folk opera. But neither this description nor any other appears on the title page of the published score. Since Gershwin does not use folk tunes to any appreciable extent (there are some traditional street cries in the score), there is no need to call his work a folk opera. *Porgy and Bess* is simply an American opera in three acts and nine scenes. If anyone doubts its operatic proportions, let it be observed that the manuscript score contains 700 pages of closely written music.

The action takes place in Catfish Row, a Negro tenement section on the Charleston water front, and on the nearby island of Kittiwah. The time is the recent past. The central figures are Porgy, a crippled Negro beggar who rides in a small cart drawn by a goat, and Bess, who comes to live with him after her man Crown, a powerful stevedore, commits murder and flees to Kittiwah Island. A character named Sportin' Life, who peddles dope, tries to induce Bess to accompany him to New York. She refuses and remains with Porgy. In the second act the people of Catfish Row are mourning for Robbins, the man killed by Crown in a crap game. But this is also a day of gaiety, for there is to be a picnic on Kittiwah Island. Bess is persuaded to go along, though her heart tells her she should stay with Porgy. As she is about to leave the island after the picnic, she hears the voice of Crown, who has been hiding and waiting to find her alone. She tries to resist him, but in the end yields, for he still attracts her strongly; and he keeps her on the island when the others leave.

After a few days Bess returns to Catfish Row, ill and delirious. Recovering, she confesses to Porgy that she has agreed to meet Crown and go away with him. His domination over her is strong, but at heart she fears him. Her real love, as she now admits, is for Porgy, and as the latter sings "You got Porgy, you got a man," he promises to protect her from Crown. Following a terrific storm, Crown suddenly returns. In the third act he reappears, attempts to enter the room where Bess is, and is intercepted and strangled to death by Porgy. When the police come to investigate, they receive no help in identifying the killer. But Porgy is taken to jail as a witness. Meanwhile, Sportin' Life again tempts Bess with "happy dust" and the lure of New York. This time, feeling alone and defeated, she succumbs and goes off with Sportin' Life. When Porgy comes back and learns that Bess has gone to New York, he calls for his goat and cart, and sets off to find her.

There are many goods tunes and memorable songs in *Porgy and Bess.* The fact that some of these songs are couched in the Broadway idiom does not invalidate their status as operatic material. We have only to think how close to the spirit of Italian popular song are many of the tunes in the operas of Verdi. Gershwin was writing an American opera, dealing with a certain segment of the American folk, and his use of the popular-song idiom, integrated into the action and the score, was entirely appropriate. The songs in *Porgy and Bess* are so excellent, and so much a part of America's music, that it is fitting to review them briefly.

"Summertime" is the lovely lullaby sung in the opening scene by Clara, wife of the fisherman Jake (who is later lost in the storm). "Gone, Gone, Gone" is a mourning-spiritual for the death of Robbins, with the call-and-response pattern faithfully reflected in solo and chorus, and with the typical melodic inflections of Negro singing. "My Man's Gone Now" is Serena's lament for her murdered husband, remarkable for its expressive use of syncopation and for the wailing glissando chorus, accompanied by a chromatic crescendo in the orchestra. "It Takes a Long Pull to Get There," sung by Jake and the fishermen, is a stylization of the Negro work song in call-and-response form, with the characteristic grunt at the end of the chorus as the men pull at the net: *to get there, huh!* It shows also the blend of work song and spiritual, as the singer first says, "I'm going out to de Blackfish banks," and at the end, "But I'll anchor in de Promise' Land."

A tune in Gershwin's best popular style is "I Got Plenty o' Nuthin'!" Porgy's song of insouciance, when he is feeling carefree and happy with love. A complete contrast is the "Buzzard Song," sung by Porgy when a great bird flies low over Catfish Row, bringing an ill omen. This is a truly dramatic aria (including high notes) both in itself and in the function it performs in the opera, marking a transition to tragedy. "Bess, You Is My Woman Now" is the love duet sung by Porgy and Bess just before she goes to the picnic, and it is in the operatic tradition. Then comes the irresistible syncopation of "Oh, I Can't Sit Down" sung by the people as they leave for the picnic, while The Charleston Orphans' Band plays on stage.

At the picnic the Negroes are dancing and making music on mouth organs, combs, bones, washboard, and washtub. Sportin' Life sings his big humorous song, "It Ain't Necessarily So" ("De t'ings dat yo' li'ble to read in de Bible"), with effective help from the chorus. When Crown appears, he and Bess sing the duet, "What You Want wid Bess," in which she expresses her loyalty to Porgy while Crown asserts his domination over her.

The cries of the street vendors—the Strawberry Woman, the Honey Man, and the Crab Man—are the folklore gems of the opera. Another spiritual, "Oh, Doctor Jesus," sung while the people are praying during the storm, over the continuous humming of men and women, reveals again the degree of skill achieved by Gershwin in the stylization of Afro-American material. Sportin' Life's "temptation song," "There's a Boat Dat's Leavin' Soon for New York," marked *Tempo di Blues,* is the product of a top-notch Broadway song writer. Finally there are the last two songs of Porgy, the first when he is seeking for Bess after his return from jail, "Bess, Oh Where's My Bess?" and the second when he starts for New York in his goat cart, in a mood of exaltation that approaches the religious fervor of the spirituals: "Oh Lawd, I'm On My Way."

Porgy and Bess was first performed at the Colonial Theatre in Boston on September 30, 1935, under the auspices of the Theatre Guild, directed by Rouben Mamoulian and conducted by Alexander Smallens. On October 10 it was brought to the Alvin Theatre in New York, where it ran for sixteen weeks, followed by a road tour of three months. It was revived in 1938 and in 1942, and was taken on a tour of Europe in 1952 with an all-Negro cast that performed it with immense success in the leading capitals. A revival at the Ziegfield Theatre, New York, in 1953 was tremendously successful. *Porgy and Bess* has proved its vitality as a work for the theater, its validity as a work of art, and its stature as an American opera.

In the American vein

American composers, since the nineteenth century, had tried to present American subjects in operatic form, but perhaps they had tried too hard to emulate the style of "grand opera," with results that were imitative, stilted, artificial, and pretentious. Gershwin, adapting the operatic tradition to familiar material and to his own background as a composer, avoided these pitfalls. An American subject was not the open sesame to operatic success; but, other factors being equal, it could facilitate the path to that integrity of form and style, that integration of content and expression, which make for successful works of art. Douglas Moore, a composer who had frequently occupied himself with the American scene, found in a story by Stephen Vincent Benét a bit of American folklore, as well as some deeper reflection of the American spirit, that appealed to him strongly. The result was the one-act opera *The Devil and Daniel Webster*, produced in New York on May 18, 1939. In this work the composer follows the tradition of *opéra comique* in having spoken dialogue alternating with singing. There are "set numbers," such as the duet between Mary and Jabez, the latter's narrative of his deal with the Devil, and Scratch's ballad, "Young William Was a Thriving Boy." Then there is Daniel Webster's song, "I've Got a Ram, Goliath," in the manner of the tall-tale, bragging, frontier ballad. Webster's stirring oration in the trial scene is in the form of "melodrama," i.e., spoken rhythmically over an orchestral accompaniment. The action then sweeps quickly to a boisterous climax in which the Devil is driven out of New Hampshire.

Beginning with his musical setting—fanciful and humorous—of Philip Barry's play *White Wings*, in 1949, Douglas Moore devoted his main creative effort to the lyric theater. In 1951 he completed the tragic opera in three acts *Giants in the Earth*, after the somber novel by O. E. Rolvaag, dealing with the hardships and spiritual conflicts of a pioneer family in the Dakota Territory. Ten years later another ambitious opera, *The Wings of the Dove*, based on the novel by Henry James, was produced in New York. But it was an intervening work, *The Ballad of Baby Doe*, produced by the New York City Opera Company in 1956, that brought Moore his greatest success as an operatic composer. The libretto, by John Latouche, tells the true story of Baby Doe Tabor, which had its main setting in Leadville, Colorado, from 1880 to 1935. In that year the aged and impoverished Baby Doe froze to death in a shack near the "Matchless Mine" that had brought sudden wealth to her husband and which she had promised him never to abandon. Tabor himself, after becoming the richest man in Colorado and divorcing his first wife to marry the young and beautiful Baby Doe, lost all his wealth in 1895 and died four years later. There was an episode of glitter and glamor when Tabor, as interim Senator, took his new wife to Washington; but the scandal ruined his political career. These are good operatic ingredients, and Moore has made the most of them, aided by an excellent libretto. Working within a traditional framework, he has skillfully organized his musical resources, tempering them to the tastes of the growing public for opera made-in-America.

The team of Thomson and Stein

Virgil Thomson deserves a special niche in the halls of American opera. His contributions to the American lyric theater are unique and memorable. On February 8, 1934, an enterprising organization called "The Friends and Enemies of Modern Music," produced in Hartford, Connecticut, Thomson's opera, *Four Saints in Three Acts,* with libretto by Gertrude Stein. It was sung by an all-Negro cast and created a sensation. In the same month it was brought to New York for a run of several weeks at the Forty-fourth Street Theatre. Broadcast performances in 1942 and 1947, and a highly successful revival at the Broadway Theatre in New York in April, 1952, demonstrated that the appeal of this work was the result not merely of novelty but also of its intrinsic musical merit and stagecraft. Taken on its own terms—as it must be taken—*Four Saints in Three Acts* is a lovely work. No one familiar with the writings of Gertrude Stein and the compositions of Virgil Thomson need be told that this is not a conventional opera. The composer has summarized the intent of the work in these words:

> Please do not try to construe the words of this opera literally or to seek in it any abstruse symbolism. If, by means of the poet's liberties with logic and the composer's constant use of the simplest elements in our musical vernacular, something is here evoked of the child-like gaiety and mystical strength of lives devoted in common to a non-materialistic end, the authors will consider their message to have been communicated.[1]

Thomson's delightful music greatly facilitates our participation in the unlogical landscape of words and images created by Stein's untrammeled text. The score incorporates elements from a variety of religious traditions, ranging from Gregorian chant to American folk hymnody (Thomson is thoroughly familiar with the shape-note tradition of the fasola folk). Thomson sets English words to music with marvelous clarity, precision, and fidelity to the spoken language. In spite of the deceptive simplicity of his musical idiom, his score is full of subtleties and of imaginative touches that reveal a high order of creative inspiration. *Four Saints in Three Acts* is an opera completely *sui generis,* and a masterpiece.

[1] Introducing a broadcast performance in 1942.

Another product of the Stein-Thomson collaboration was the opera *The Mother of Us All*, commissioned by the Alice M. Ditson Fund of Columbia University and produced at the Brander Matthews Theatre on May 7, 1947. The central figure of this opera is Susan B. Anthony, pioneer leader in the struggle for woman suffrage in the nineteenth century. The cast includes many other historical figures, several of them anachronistic: Daniel Webster, Anthony Comstock, Ulysses S. Grant, John Adams, Lillian Russell, Andrew Johnson, Thaddeus Stevens—also Virgil T(homson) and "G. S." (none other than Gertrude Stein, of course). To explain everything that happens in this opera would take too long. Daniel Webster pursues (discreetly) Angel More; John Adams courts Constance Fletcher, but cannot kneel to propose because he is an Adams; General Grant is stubborn; Jo the Loiterer marries Indiana Elliot and then changes names with her; and in the midst of it all, Susan B. Anthony carries on her Cause, and in the last scene but one the chorus sings:

> Susan B. Anthony was very successful we are all very grateful to Susan B. Anthony because she was so successful, she worked for the vote for women and she worked for the vote for colored men and she was so successful they wrote the word male into the constitution of the United States of America, dear Susan B. Anthony.[2]

In the last scene the cast gathers around the statue of Susan B. and her comrades in the suffrage fight. At the end, Susan B.'s voice is suddenly heard from the statue and attempts to expound what it is all about (previously she had said, "I am not puzzled but it is very puzzling"). Her final message is summed up in these words: "Life is strife, I was a martyr all my life not to what I won but to what was done." If this is still puzzling, try listening to the music.

The same qualities of clarity and felicity in the setting of English are evident in this score, equally manifested in the treatment of recitative and in the arias and choruses. The musical materials utilized by Thomson are heterogeneous: revival hymnody, gospel tunes *à la* Salvation Army band style, modal melodies, popular-song idiom, and so forth. He employs the calculated cliché and the deliberate commonplace with an amazing effect of freshness. The whole score has style,

[2] Stein, *Last Operas and Plays*, p. 83. Used by permission of Rinehart & Co., publishers.

and it is unmistakably the Thomson style. It is also unmistakably American.

Blitzstein and Bernstein

The proletarian novel of the 1930s had its counterpart in the opera of "social significance" with its themes of the class struggle and social justice. Two such operas were written by Marc Blitzstein (born in Philadelphia, 1905), a pupil of Scalero, Boulanger, and Schoenberg. The first of these was *The Cradle Will Rock*, first performed in a concert version in New York in 1937 (with piano) and ten years later brought to the stage at the City Center in New York with the original orchestration. The second was *No for an Answer*, produced at the Mecca Auditorium in New York on January 5, 1941. Regardless of the ideological content, these operas had the merit of coming to grips with problems of our times and in the musical language of our times. Moreover, they revealed a flair for the theater that was further manifested in a later, nonpolitical work: Blitzstein's operatic version of Lillian Hellman's play *The Little Foxes*, produced in 1949 in New York City, under the title of *Regina*, for a run of fifty-six performances.

Blitzstein's *Regina* began to make operatic history when it was revived by the New York City Opera Company on April 2, 1953. Some concessions were made to operatic dogma with the deletion of spoken dialogue or its transformation into recitative; but even so, this is a work that "defies classification" according to conventional standards. One critic, taking up the defiance, labeled it a "jazz opera." Now, it is true that the score calls for the appearance on stage of a jazz band and a jazz singer, who perform at the big party given by Regina to celebrate the business deal that symbolizes the money-greed of this unsavory family. But one might just as well call Mozart's *Don Giovanni* a "dance opera," because it employs a dance orchestra on stage. Not so, says the jazz labeller, because Blitzstein's score is full of syncopated rhythms and because many of its airs have the cut of "Broadway ballads." True, the colored servant Addie sings a slow blues to console the unhappy alcoholic Birdie; true, the dissipated Leo sings a syncopated ditty to show that he's "the life of the party"— but what could be a better expression of his character? As for the blues, they are a classical form of American music, which long ago acquired artistic status. Blitzstein also uses the waltz and the galop, which presumably do not make this a "dance opera." He also introduces his own versions of a Negro spiritual and a revival hymn ("Do You Love Everybody?"), both employed with complete appropriateness and dramatic effect. In contrast to these popular elements, and equally appropriate in context, is an instrumental intermezzo (for a scene change), played on stage, in the style of Louis Moreau Gottschalk (Andante rubato), which could symbolize the genteel veneer that covers the corruption of these people. Who is to say that any of these ingredients is not "operatic"? The composer decides; form, style, content—all depend on the choice he makes from the material available to him. Art is not a matter of legislation (aesthetic or other), but of creation; that is, of free will and invention. In *Regina*, Marc Blitzstein has created an American type of opera; it is a viable work, a masterpiece of its kind. His next opera, *Sacco and Vanzetti*—commissioned by the Ford Foundation for the Metropolitan Opera Company—was left unfinished at his death in 1964. Only the first and second acts were substantially completed.

Leonard Bernstein is another composer who has explored new possibilities in American opera with his one-act work in seven scenes *Trouble in Tahiti*, first performed at Brandeis University in July, 1952, and produced for television (which seems to be its most suitable medium) on November 16 of the same year. Writing his own libretto, Bernstein has exposed the troubled heart of Suburbia, U.S.A., under the chamber-of-commerce patter ("Sweet in the spring, healthful in winter") and the come-on of the real-estate agent ("Out of the hubbub, less than an hour by train"). His protagonists are a youngish couple with one child, whose marriage has ill withstood the attrition of time, the inroads of routine, and the withering of early illusions. Not their up-to-date kitchen, not the washing machine, nor the colorful bathrooms, nor the Sheraton sofa, nor the little white house with flagstones, can lift them out of their limbo of bickering and boredom. She takes to the analyst's couch, he bolsters his ego with sports and business; they fail miserably in their attempts to communicate with each other. The atmosphere of Suburbia is established by "The Trio" (two men and a girl), described as "a Greek chorus born of the radio commercial," who sing generally "in a whispering, breathy *pianissimo*, which comes over the amplifying system as crooning." The work is scored for double woodwinds, two horns, two trumpets, two trombones, tuba, percussion, harp, and single strings. The time is "Now," the place: "Any American city, and its suburbs."

In an aria that she sings while visiting a hat shop, Dinah (the wife) tells the story of "a terrible, awful movie" she has just seen, called "Trouble in Tahiti." Although she begins by denouncing it as "escapist technicolor twaddle," before long she is carried away by the mood of the theme song, "Island Magic"—a captive of escapism in spite of herself. In the end, she and her husband can think of nothing better, to escape from further bickering and boredom, than to go to the movies. The picture they see is "Trouble in Tahiti"—"the bought-and-paid-for magic, waiting on a Silver Screen."

Menotti and Barber

If some artists make their mark by creating new expectations, others achieve success by satisfying—perhaps with a slight touch of novelty—expectations that already existed. The term "opera" arouses in most minds certain expectations associated with melodramatic plots, strong emotions, violent death, love duets, impressive arias, and elaborate sets. For a long time, American composers tried their best to provide these ingredients, with only partial success. It took a native of Italy, Gian-Carlo Menotti, to demonstrate that a skilful blending of nineteenth-century operatic ingredients, spiced with some twentieth-century harmonies and some up-dated elements of *verismo*, would meet with an immediate response from American audiences.

Born in Cadigliano, Italy, in 1911, Menotti studied for two years at the Milan Conservatory before coming to the United States in 1928. He completed his musical studies at the Curtis Institute of Music in Philadelphia and began his career with an *opera buffa* called *Amelia Goes to the Ball*, for which he wrote his own libretto (as he was to do for all subsequent works). This was produced in Philadelphia in 1937 and at the Metropolitan Opera House in New York on March 3, 1938. It earned him a commission from the National Broadcasting Company for a radio opera, *The Old Maid and the Thief* (1939). In 1942 he was back at the "Met" with a one-act tragic opera, *The Island God*. But it was a "musical tragedy" in two acts, *The Medium* (1946), that made him famous; in the spring of 1947 it had an unprecedented run on Broadway. Thereafter it enjoyed continuous success, with many performances in America and Europe, and a film version made under the composer's direction.

Menotti adhered to tragedy in his next work, *The Consul*, a musical drama in three acts, which began its Broadway run at the Ethel Barrymore Theatre on March 15, 1950. The action takes place in a large European city and the time is the present. The principal characters are John Sorel and his wife Magda. The scene alternates between the shabby apartment of the Sorels and the office of an unspecified Consulate. John Sorel is a patriot, a friend of freedom and therefore an enemy of those who have the power in his country. He and his wife are trying to obtain visas so that they can escape to a free nation. Sorel, pursued by the secret police, is forced to go into hiding. Meanwhile Magda joins the crowd of persistent, frustrated people who haunt the Consulate seeking visas. The Consul himself never appears and is too busy to see anyone. Magda's urgency and anguish are of no avail against the solid wall of indifference and routine.

There can be no question about the theatrical effectiveness of *The Consul*. That can be taken for granted in the works of Menotti. He knows all the tricks of the trade and can apply them with unfailing cleverness. The opening of the first act, with a phonograph playing a sentimental French song backstage while John Sorel, injured, stumbles into the room and is greeted by a frantic Magda, is but one of many clever devices in the score. The treatment of the recitative, always a difficult matter in English opera, is one of the most satisfactory features of *The Consul*.

In 1951 Menotti was commissioned by the National Broadcasting Company to write the first opera designed especially for television production: *Amahl and the Night Visitors*. This chamber opera was suggested by Hieronymus Bosch's painting "The Adoration of the Magi." A crippled shepherd boy sees a star shining brightly in the night sky and excitedly tells his mother about it. She reproves him for "imagining things." He goes to bed, and soon the Three Kings arrive, bearing gifts for a newborn child. While the Kings sleep, the mother, wishing to help her crippled son, attempts to steal some of the gold but is discovered by a servant. When the Kings offer to let her keep the gold, since the newborn child does not really need it, she becomes remorseful. So that he also may give a gift, the boy offers his crutch. He then finds himself miraculously healed and accompanies the Three Kings on their journey.

One of Menotti's most ambitious and controversial operas, *The Saint of Bleecker Street*, was produced in New York, at the Broadway Theatre, on December 27, 1954. Its setting is that section of lower Manhattan popularly known as "Little Italy," and all the characters are Italian-Americans living in that tumultuous neighborhood. In Menotti's plot, racial, religious, social, and emotional tensions are worked up explosively for the intended effects of tragedy. The protagonists are a young girl who feels a strong religious vocation and who dies just as she is about to take the veil; her brother, whose possessive love for his sister is as strong as his hatred of the religion she professes; and the brother's fiancée, whom he stabs to death in a fit of rage after she taunts him with his exaggerated love for his sister. A New York critic aptly summed up the qualities of this work: "It is a pastiche, but a pastiche of enormous talent and theatrical magic."

Unfortunately, in Menotti's next opera, *Maria Golovin* (1958), there was more pastiche than talent, and the theatrical "magic" was very close to hocus-pocus. Granted that Menotti is master of his means, the limitations of those means have become increasingly apparent. To American composers of opera he taught some useful lessons: he gave them a formula for success, and, more importantly, he proved that success is not enough.

When Samuel Barber decided to try his hand at opera, he turned to his friend Menotti for a libretto. The result was *Vanessa*, a grand opera in four acts, first performed at the Metropolitan Opera House, New York, on January 15, 1958 (it was the first American opera given there since Rogers' *The Warrior* in 1947). The plot revolves around a beautiful, selfish and worldly woman, of middle age but still highly attractive, who falls in love with, and eventually marries, the son of her former lover. Meanwhile, the latter has seduced Vanessa's niece, Erika, who is too "noble" to make a fuss about this unhappy episode. As Vanessa and her young husband go off to a gay life in Paris, Erika, a mournful personification of the sacrificial victim, remains alone, brooding and waiting, in the elegant house that Vanessa has bequeathed her as a consolation prize.

Barber evidently set out to write an elegant grand opera for the "carriage trade," and in this endeavor he succeeded, with able assistance from his librettist, Menotti. The plot, to be sure, is rather thin; but the music is luscious. What conventional skill can do, Barber has accomplished; *Vanessa* was to the late 1950s what *The King's Hench-man* was to the late 1920s: the American opera at the "Met" that everybody was talking about. Barber's next opera, *Antony and Cleopatra,* was commissioned for the opening of the new Metropolitan Opera House at Lincoln Center, in September 1966.

More from the American scene

Although in their choice of subjects American opera composers (and their librettists) have often demonstrated their belief in the adage that "distance lends enchantment"—in both time and place—there is still an impressive roster of works dealing with the American scene, beginning with Bristow's *Rip Van Winkle* in the nineteenth century, including the "Indianist" operas of Cadman and Nevin, and continuing to the present with no sign of abatement. Some of the most notable of these overtly "American" operas have already been described in this chapter; but the list is long, and a further sampling, at least of representative titles, is in order.

The composer Vittorio Giannini (1903–1966) drew on American literature for *The Scarlet Letter* (1938), on American history (the Aaron Burr conspiracy) for *Blennerhasset* (1939), and on rural life for *The Harvest* (Chicago, 1961). Otto Luening turned to Longfellow's famous poem for his four-act opera *Evangeline* (1948). A small midwestern town is the setting for *A Provincial Episode* by Max Wald (1889–1954). Lukas Foss came very near to creating an American "folk opera" when he brought to the lyric stage Mark Twain's classic of frontier humor, *The Jumping Frog of Calaveras County* (1950). Norman Dello Joio allowed himself to be operatically seduced by the charms of an octoroon actress from old Louisiana, somewhat to the detriment of his second opera, *Blood Moon* (1961). Jack Beeson (born in 1921) depicted the "amorous misadventures of a lady evangelist" in *The Sweet Bye and Bye* (1957). The catalogue could be indefinitely extended; but I wish to discuss in more detail three operas dealing with the American scene that seem particularly significant for the period since 1950.

Although Aaron Copland, in 1937, wrote a workaday little opera for high school performance, *The Second Hurricane,* it was not until the 1950s that he ventured—surely not without some trepidation—to attempt a full-scale opera. This was *The Tender Land,* in three acts, commissioned by Richard Rodgers and Oscar Hammerstein 2d for the League of Composers' thirtieth-anniversary year. It was first produced at the New York City Center of Music and Drama on April 1, 1954; in a revised—and improved—version it was given at the Berkshire Music Center on August 2 of the same year. The action takes place on a lower-middle-class farm in the Midwest; the time is the early thirties. The outwardly simple plot involves the emotions and family stresses that beset a young girl on the day of her graduation from high school. The characters are all everyday, ordinary Americans. The work received a tepid reception; but its genuine merits should not be overlooked. No one has pin-pointed these merits better than the composer-critic William Flanagan, himself an operatic writer of distinction: "The score of *The Tender Land* contains pages—and a lot of them—that are among Copland's best; the enchanted tune that opens the opera and reappears for frequent and telling metamorphoses; the stunning quintet that closes the first act; the meticulously controlled romanticism of the love music; and the Mother's extravagantly lyrical closing aria . . . which is Copland at the very peak of his remarkable expressive powers."

A composer of the next generation, Carlisle Floyd (born in Latta, South Carolina, in 1926), whose musical formation owes more than a little to Copland, sprang into sudden fame when his opera *Susannah* received the New York Music Critics' Circle citation following its New York production in September, 1956. Drawing upon the musical folklore as well as the mores, the mental climate, and the setting of his native region, and using religious revivalism as emotional leaven, Floyd was able to develop a situation involving strongly developed characters and leading to a tragic dénouement without straining either his plot or his musical resources. The latter were well within the orbit of conventionality, but effectively disciplined for the purposes of theater. *Susannah* definitely marked the appearance of a composer to be reckoned with in American opera.

Robert Ward (born 1917), a pupil of Copland, began his operatic career with *He Who Gets Slapped* (1956, after the play by Andreyev), but made a greater impression with his opera *The Crucible* (1961), based on the play by Arthur Miller dealing with the witchcraft craze in early New England; the libretto is by Bernard Stambler. Commissioned by the New York City Opera Company under a grant from the Ford Foundation and produced on October 26, 1961, *The*

Crucible was awarded the Pulitzer Prize and the New York Music Critics' Circle citation for opera. Unfolding in four acts, with a large cast and a full orchestra, this is a work that builds up to musical-emotional climaxes in the traditional manner while allowing for considerable realism in portrayal of character. A typically effective climax is that of Act I, when Abigail, accused of commerce with the Devil, confesses her sins while the chorus sings a hymn, "Jesus, My Consolation." With each act, indeed, the composer demonstrates that he has learned the art of bringing down the curtain—*al colpo della Tela.* At the end, when John Proctor is going to the gallows, a self-confessed lecher, the drum-roll sounds, "The new sun is pouring down on Elizabeth's face" (his wife), and the curtain falls on a tremolando fortissimo, followed by a pizzicato pianissimo of one note.

Operas such as *Baby Doe, The Tender Land, Susannah,* and *The Crucible* demonstrate that dealing with an American subject is far from being a handicap to the composer. But it *is* a limitation—as any prescription of time and place would be—and American composers have inevitably asserted their freedom of choice by looking further afield for plots and settings. The fact that Carlisle Floyd's operatic version of *Wuthering Heights* (1958) was generally held to be less successful than *Susannah* does not necessarily indicate the inspirational superiority of the native scene. At most it indicates the difficulty of dominating so large and complex a theme, with all its weight of literary tradition. Serving as his own librettist, the composer was handicapped by excessive fidelity to Emily Brontë's text. But Floyd has an appetite for ambitious projects, as he manifested again with his next opera, *The Passion of Jonathan Wade,* produced by the New York City Opera Company in October, 1962.

Sessions and Weisgall

Among the older American composers, Roger Sessions turned to an "American" subject—in the broad historical sense—with his opera in three acts and eleven scenes, *Montezuma,* composed in 1960–1963 but planned as far back as 1935, when the composer asked Antonio Borghese to write a libretto based on *The True History of the Conquest of Mexico,* by the Spanish soldier-chronicler Bernal Díaz (who appears as narrator in the opera). Other principal characters are Montezuma, last "Emperor" of the Aztecs (tenor), the conquistador Alvarado (tenor), Hernán Cortés (baritone), and the latter's Indian mistress, Malinche (soprano). There is a double women's chorus in addition to the standard mixed chorus. Having received no encouragement for the production of his grand opera in the United States, Sessions accepted an invitation to have the work produced at the West Berlin Opera, in April, 1964. On this occasion it was sung in German. The music uses the twelve-tone procedures that characterize Sessions's later scores.

Just as Menotti brought to the United States the tradition of Italian turn-of-the-century opera stemming from Mascagni and Puccini, so his almost exact contemporary, Hugo Weisgall (born in Czechoslovakia in 1912), became the chief American exponent of the expressionist trend in twentieth-century opera, taking off from Schoenberg and Alban Berg. Weisgall came to the United States at the early age of eight, so that his formative experience as well as his musical training were acquired in this country—specifically, at the Peabody Conservatory in Baltimore and as a pupil of Sessions in composition (he also obtained a Ph.D. in Germanic Literature at Johns Hopkins University). But no other American composer has so consistently explored the domain of expressionism which, in music at least, is so closely identified with Central Europe.

Up to 1960, Weisgall showed a preference for one-act operas: *The Tenor* (1950; libretto by Karl Shapiro and Ernst List, after Wedekind), *The Stronger* (1952, based on the play by Strindberg), and *Purgatory* (1958), which uses as a libretto the unaltered text of William Butler Yeats's last play. These operas have certain features in common: the use of a small orchestra, very few characters (only one singing role in *The Stronger*, two in *Purgatory*), and a psychological approach to motivation and characterization (his choice of libretti is, of course, crucial in this respect). Weisgall has no use for the outward trappings of opera: his scenes are a quiet uptown bar in New York, a hotel room, a ruined house in Ireland ("and a bare tree in the background"). Each opera is an exploration (and revelation) of the subconscious. With his penchant for symbolism and psychological drama, it is not surprising that for his most ambitious opera to date, Weisgall turned to Pirandello's play *Six Characters in Search of an Author* (1953–1956), fashioned into a libretto by Denis Johnston (produced by the New York City Opera on April 26, 1959). This is a full-scale opera in three acts, with full orchestra and a large cast of characters, as well as a chorus (ad libitum). But the emphasis is still inward, for the search is that of each human being for his own identity in a world of appearances. Operatically, the theme is probably over-complex. But Weisgall has followed the difficult path of expressionism with courage, conviction, and skill.

In the second half of the twentieth century, American opera is still in search of a public, but it does not need to seek composers: they are present in large numbers, with a wide variety of skills and styles and aims. This, too, has been the era of subsidized opera in the United States (by the Ford Foundation chiefly), so that both composer and public have a firmer ground for communication and acceptance.

chapter thirty-one

The scene in the sixties

The creative imagination, at its most vital, has revealed itself through many and often surprising channels.
ROGER SESSIONS IN PROBLEMS OF MODERN MUSIC (1960).

The headnote for this chapter is from a paper prepared for the Princeton Seminar in Advanced Musical Studies held in the summer of 1959 under the direction of Roger Sessions. The seminar enabled some twenty-five young American composers to meet with older colleagues—among them Varèse, Krenek, Copland, Carter, Babbitt, Ussachevsky—to discuss problems and trends of modern music. Paul Fromm, founder and president of the Fromm Music Foundation, which has given such strong support to contemporary music, drew attention, in his foreword to the published discussions and papers of the seminar,[1] to what he called "the plight of the loneliest individuals in contemporary music—the young professional composers." Elaborating this idea, he wrote:

Their expectations of acceptance by society, raised by the fellowships and prizes available to them as students, prove unfounded; while at the same time they have lost the stimulating contact with their fellow-students that enriched their school days. Although they are aware of everything that really is contemporary, they have no one with whom to share this awareness. Their chances of entry into public musical life have been barred by the insurmountable barrier of their own originality and the hostility of individuals and institutions who deny the public anything that cannot be standardized.

Awareness of what is really contemporary—not merely a slightly modernized rehash of the past—and creative commitment to this con-

[1] *Problems of Modern Music*, ed. Lang (New York: W. W. Norton, 1960), p. 18.

temporary world are indeed almost insurmountable obstacles to the new composers facing the commercially dominated "professional musical world" of the narrowly standardized (and therefore profitable) concert repertoire, the star personality system, and hostility to whatever upsets comfortable habits of listening and performing. Music that is truly creative—i.e., new and original—cannot be geared to a public conditioned by the mass media of communication.

Potentially there is an audience for new music—not a mass audience, but a significant segment nonetheless. The problem is that any audience, large or small, can hear only the music that is performed for it; and the majority of professional performers, as Milton Babbitt said, "shun and resent" the new music. What is the remedy for such a situation? Should the modern composer retreat to an ivory tower or an electronic studio, communicating only with a small circle of his peers? Something of the sort was suggested by Babbitt in an article provocatively titled "Who Cares If You Listen?"[2] Yet in the end, Babbitt was forced to admit, even though by implication, that such a disdainful isolation could not be the ultimate solution: he warned his readers that if the new, serious, advanced music is not supported, "music will cease to evolve, and, in that important sense, will cease to live."

Composers, too, must live in order to write music and thereby perhaps provide certified "masterworks" for the standard repertoire of the future. Materially, most American composers have solved this problem by becoming university teachers. It is a truism that the American university is the traditional haven of the artist; what is significant is the increasingly important rôle of the university as a creative and disseminating center for the *contemporary* arts, providing not only material security for the artist but also a stimulating atmosphere based on awareness of the really contemporary values, and an opportunity for communication based (in the case of music) on adequate performance resources and the ability to attract limited but receptive audiences. The composer himself—often doubling as performer—has been the most active agent in this development. With backing from the foundations, the universities have proved receptive to his initiatives and have welcomed their new rôle as patrons of the new as well as guardians of the past. The movement in this direction is nation-wide

---

[2] Published in *High Fidelity*, VIII, 2 (Feb., 1958). Reprinted in *The American Composer Speaks*, ed. Chase.

and rapidly growing. Should the present decade accomplish no more than the expansion and consolidation of this trend, its contribution to our musical culture would be of incalculable value.

Computers and synthesizers

The university's modern rôle as a research center has also been extended to include music—the medium of aesthetic expression most profoundly affected by recent developments in the electronic production and manipulation of sound. A pioneer in this field is the University of Illinois, where in 1955 Lejaren A. Hiller, Jr., and Leonard M. Isaacson began to experiment with computer programs for producing music.[3] The immediate result was the *Illiac Suite for String Quartet,* completed in 1956. The authors were careful to explain that this was not primarily intended as a work of art but rather as "a research record—a laboratory notebook." Their experiment was done for the ultimate purpose of determining whether the use of high-speed digital computers might eventually "lead to new and different ways of composing music which would interest the contemporary composer."

In 1963, Hiller and Robert A. Baker collaborated in producing the *Computer Cantata,* for which they used an IBM 7090 computer in conjunction with "a completely generalized programming scheme for musical compositions," familiarly known as MUSICOMP (MUsic Simulator-Interpreter for COMpositional Procedures).[4] Again, the purpose was experimental (in a scientific sense) rather than aesthetic or creative. The texts for the vocal sections of the cantata, incidentally, are described as "stochastic approximations to spoken English derived from a synthesis by a computer of stochastic phoneme sequences." The aim of this type of experimentation is to investigate the process of musical composition "in terms of the extracting of orderly structures out of random materials by a process of selection and rejection."

The idea of using computers for the production of music has aroused widespread interest during the present decade. To cite only one instance among many, at the end of 1965 the University of Alabama received a research grant to support the development of a com-

[3] A detailed description of this project will be found in the book *Experimental Music: Composition with an Electronic Computer,* by Hiller and Isaacson (New York: McGraw-Hill, 1959).

[4] Hiller and Baker, "*Computer Cantata:* A Study in Compositional Method," in *Perspectives of New Music,* III, 1 (1964).

puter program for producing—not composing—music. In this case the computer is simply a tool for the composer: "The numbers which the computer provides are translated into sound by a digital-to-analog converter which results in an ordinary magnetic tape recording." This project is particularly interesting because its director, the composer David Cohen (*b.* 1927), believes that "this particular method of executing 'electronic' sounds should be available to composers other than those dedicated to a more-or-less post-Webern style." Describing himself as belonging to what he calls "the radical center,"[5] Cohen's aim is to make electronic media acceptable and useful to "main-stream" or traditional composers instead of being largely the monopoly of an experimental group "who approach music with a scientific, mathematical, or electronic orientation." Hence his project includes the preparation of a manual describing in a non-technical way the use of the computer program and supplying examples of the kinds of timbre available. Thus he hopes to encourage composers of many different backgrounds and aesthetic views to make use of "this exciting contemporary medium."

There is, in fact, a widespread and rapidly growing "grass-roots" movement throughout the nation in the use of electronic media, including digital computers, for making music. "Do-it-yourself" manuals are available for the musician who wishes to have his own electronic studio, and musical periodicals carry advertisements for electronic instruments just as they would for pianos and organs—all guaranteed "to meet the requirements of contemporary composers." This vulgarization of electronic music media is certainly a characteristic development of the present decade.

Meanwhile, the most complex and costly electronic equipment is available in only a few centers throughout the world, three of which are located in Cologne, Milan, and New York. The Columbia-Princeton Electronic Music Center was established in Manhattan in 1959 with the assistance of a grant from the Rockefeller Foundation. Two

[5] Under the heading of "Music from the 'Radical Center,'" in *Perspectives of New Music*, III, 1 (Fall-Winter, 1964), Cohen describes a compositional procedure that lies between "conventional tonal organization" and the total procedural control advocated by a large segment of the *avant-garde*. He believes that the "radical center" represents "a vital force in today's music." Cohen's own output includes an admirable Symphony No. 1 (1965), based on the idea of musical palindromes (of which the verbal paradigm is: "Able was I ere I saw Elba"). The most "revolutionary" feature of this symphony is that the last movement begins and ends on a C major triad!

co-directors were appointed from each of the sponsoring universities: Roger Sessions and Milton Babbitt from Princeton, Otto Luening and Vladimir Ussachevsky from Columbia. One of the three studios in the Center houses the RCA Electronic Sound Synthesizer, while the others contain equipment for sound generation and modification. During the 1960s the Center attracted composers from all over the world, among them Bülent Arel from Turkey, Halim El-Dabh from Egypt, and Mario Davidovsky from Argentina. Edgard Varèse worked there during the last years of his life. In May, 1961, Columbia presented the first public concert of music produced at the Center, with compositions by Arel, El-Dabh, Davidovsky, Babbitt, Luening, and Ussachevsky.[6] The last-mentioned was represented by the Prologue to *Creation*, the first part of a projected choral work for four full choruses which may be performed either as a combination of live performers and pre-recorded chorus, or entirely as a recorded work on multiple tracks of tape. Babbitt's *Composition for Synthesizer* is a purely electronic work, created entirely on the RCA Electronic Sound Synthesizer, and is concerned with various aspects of programming and control. Luening's *Gargoyles* is a work for violin and synthesized sound, consisting of a theme and variations. Thus the Electronic Music Center lends itself to a wide variety of aims that reflect the personal interests, styles, and creative objectives of the composers involved.

Sight, sound, and space

The tendency to popularize tape and electronic music—in the "pop art" sense—and even to make it, on occasion, an adjunct of "op art," is manifested in the activities of the ONCE Group in Ann Arbor, Michigan. The Group was founded in 1960 as an informal association of composers, performers, film-makers, theatrical designers, and other artists. The composers (most of them performers also) included Robert Ashley, George Cacioppo, Philip Krumm, Gordon Mumma, Roger Reynolds, and Donald Scavarda. The annual ONCE Festivals, begun in 1961, have featured their compositions along with a catholic selection of *avant-garde* music—including the neo-Dadaist wing (George Brecht, LaMonte Young, Peter Jennings)—from other sections of the

---

[6] The music of this concert was recorded and released by Columbia Records. Another recording of compositions from the Center, by Arel, Davidovsky, and Ussachevsky, was issued by Son Nova.

country (and some foreign composers too). The broad scope of the Festivals is indicated by the 1964 programs, which included participation of the Judson Dance Theatre of New York with the painter-choreographer Robert Rauschenberg, the Brandeis University Chamber Chorus under the direction of Alvin Lucier, the University of Illinois Chamber Players directed by Jack McKenzie, and, representing jazz, the Bob James Trio with the versatile Eric Dolphy.

Robert Ashley has carried to extremes the "pop art" trend of the ONCE Group, in the sense of assimilating commonplace elements from everyday life. His *in memoriam Kit Carson* (1964) is an "opera" without music—it consists simply of such miscellaneous sounds as one might hear at a party, with radios, phonographs, and television sets being turned on and off in the midst of snatches of banal conversation. It has been aptly described as "audio-visual-theatrical 'pop art.'" Such productions are symptomatic of the "anti-art" trend that is very much a part of the scene in the 1960s.

Donald Scavarda's *Landscape Journey* (1964) illustrates the combination of sight and sound that characterizes much of the work done by the ONCE Group. It is scored for clarinet, piano, and multiple film projection. As described by an ear-and-eye witness: "Its form resembles a simple rondo where the A sections are built of slowly moving sound-patterns whereas the B segments are represented by a soundless visual play of fast-moving colors and shapes on two screens."[7]

Emphasis on the visual elements in musical composition and performance—insisted upon by such innovators as Partch and Cage—has become increasingly prominent during the 1960s. It is manifested not only in the projection of various kinds of images, but also in the graphic aspect of the new "time-space" scores, and even in the prescribed actions and movement of the performers. These factors are present in an extraordinary work by a former member of the ONCE Group, Roger Reynolds, titled *The Emperor of Ice Cream* (1962). This is an elaborately complex, quasi-surrealistic audio-visual setting of the poem of that title by Wallace Stevens. It is described as "a chamber work in which the singers occasionally play percussion instruments and the performers continually cue one another." Choreography, costumes, and lighting are important elements in the total sound-spec-

---

[7] *The Musical Quarterly*, L, 4 (Oct., 1964), "Current Chronicle," which contains an interesting account of works performed at the 1964 ONCE Festival.

tacle. The score—in itself a fascinating work of graphic art—indicates not only the sounds but also the movements and configuration of the singers and instrumentalists on stage. The scoring is for four male and four female singers, piano, vibraphone, percussion, and double bass. The time-space correlation is accomplished by having the vertical dimension of each page be proportional to the width of the stage, while each page, from left to right, represents twenty seconds in time. All performers are identified by symbols, the instruments by signs and abbreviations. The performers' movements are indicated by diagonal dotted lines. The location of stave and other notational markings on the page (top to bottom) indicates the position of the performer (left to right) when a particular sound is realized. All this might be merely clever and ingenious were *The Emperor of Ice Cream* not an emotionally and artistically valid and effective setting of a powerful and moving poem about death.

Roger Reynolds was born in Detroit in 1934 and obtained his degree in engineering physics at the University of Michigan before deciding to make music his career. He then studied composition with Ross Lee Finney and Roberto Gerhard. In 1962 a Fulbright grant took him to the Electronic Music Studio in Cologne. One of his four works performed at the 1962 ONCE Festival—a composition for chamber orchestra titled *Wedge* (1961)—was acclaimed by H. Wiley Hitchcock as "the most powerful new work of the entire festival." In this score, as the composer explains, "There are two relatively independent 'layers' of organized sound: one assertive and episodic, the other reflective and continuous." For this reason it has been compared to Ives's *The Unanswered Question*. Ives is indeed one of the composers whose influence Reynolds acknowledges, the others being Varèse and Cage. In *Wedge*—as in several other scores—the composer freely uses clusters as well as direct manipulation of the piano strings. The work literally begins with a bang (of the keyboard cover against the body of the piano) and ends with a brief but stunning crescendo. The vibraphone (that "in" instrument of the sixties) is almost always used with the motor turned off: it is intended to sound "quasi-xylophonic, brilliant, *secco*, and steely." Gunther Schuller described *Wedge* as "a work in which the worlds of Varèse, Cage, and jazz meet in a fascinating amalgam."

By the end of 1965 Reynolds had produced some fifteen scores, including *A Portrait of Vanzetti* for narrator, winds, percussion, and

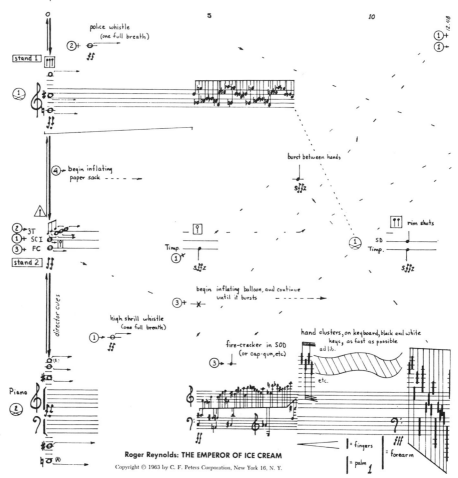

Roger Reynolds: THE EMPEROR OF ICE CREAM
Copyright © 1963 by C. F. Peters Corporation, New York 16, N. Y.

magnetic tape; *Gathering,* for flute, oboe, clarinet, French horn, and bassoon; *Fantasy for Pianist* (1964); and *Quick Are the Mouths of Earth* (1965), for chamber orchestra. Concerning this last, the composer writes:

There are three types of spatial interplay between the instrumental groups: clusters of marked entrances occurring across the entire span of the ensemble; the passing of similar materials from group to group; or, the continuous flow of one sound (a particular pitch or noise) from right to left, etc.

This work does not involve improvisation, but it does make use of

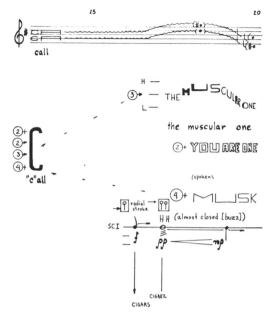

"instrumental and notational techniques that are inherently somewhat indeterminate."

Fantasy for Pianist, which requires the performer to work strenuously "inside" the piano, has to do—the composer tells us—with "fixation, resonance, ornamentation, and the unexpected." We may perhaps say that the musical world of Roger Reynolds is an emotional and intellectual ordering of the unexpected.

Degrees of indeterminacy

Various kinds of ordering of the unpredictable have been the concern of several composers who were associated with John Cage in

New York during the 1950s, particularly Morton Feldman, Christian Wolff, and Earle Brown. Of these, Feldman, a native New Yorker (*b.* 1926), was the first to meet Cage, in the winter of 1949–1950. Cage encouraged him to have confidence in his musical intuitions. This was a welcome change from studying composition with Wallingford Riegger and Stefan Wolpe. Feldman also became a close friend of the painter Philip Guston, who introduced him to abstract expressionism. "The new painting," he later wrote, "made me desirous of a sound world more direct, more immediate, more physical than anything that had existed heretofore."[8] Thus, he made the discovery "that sound in itself can be a totally plastic phenomenon, suggesting its own shape, design, and poetic metaphor." His desire, then, was not to "compose" in the traditional sense, "but to project sounds into time, free from a compositional rhetoric that had no place here." In his persistent search for a direct, plastic quality in his music, Feldman has replaced "compositional rhetoric" with what he describes as "a totally abstract sonic adventure."

According to this conception, "sounds no longer had an inherent symbolic shape"; therefore it was possible to allow for indeterminacies in regard to pitch. In *Projections* (1951) the composer designated, not the exact pitch, but only the register (high, middle, or low); he also designated durations and dynamics. The same principle was applied in two orchestral works of the same year, *Intersection No. 1* and *Marginal Intersection*, in which scores are replaced by graphs. Within the given time structure, the performers were free to choose their entrances, as well as the actual pitches and dynamics.

Between 1953 and 1958 Feldman abandoned the graph because it gave too much freedom to the performer. He had never thought of the graph as "an art of improvisation," hence it was disconcerting to find performers using it in this manner. When he returned to the graph with two more orchestral works, *Atlantis* (1958) and *Out of "Last Pieces"* (1960), he used "a more vertical structure where soloistic passages would be at a minimum." The instrumentation of *Out of "Last Pieces"* includes amplified guitar, harp, celesta, vibraphone, and xylophone, all of which play sounds from any register that the performer chooses. "All other sounds are played in the high registers

---

[8] The quotations in this section are from Feldman's notes for the recording of his *Durations* (Time Records 58007).

of the instruments, except for brief sections in which low sounds are indicated. Dynamics throughout are very low."[9] In this work Feldman fully achieves his ideal of "a totally abstract sonic adventure," analogous to an abstract painting, devoid of "compositional rhetoric" and dramatic connotations.

Feldman also wanted to achieve a textural freedom "in which each instrument is living out its own individual life in its own individual sound world." This was the particular achievement of his work in the 1960s—when he again abandoned the graph—beginning with *Durations* (1960–1961), a series of five pieces for various instrumental combinations. In all the works of this period, the actual sounds to be played, as well as the dynamics, are indicated by the composer. A device that he uses in two chamber works, *de Kooning* and *Chorus and Instruments*, is that of having each instrument enter as the previous sound fades. This is a result of Feldman's concern, since 1963, with exploring different aspects "of the duration and subsequent decay of a sound"—perhaps a reflected influence from electronic music, in which this aspect is an important factor. This preoccupation with sound duration and decay continues in such pieces as *Vertical Thoughts* (1–5) for soprano and ten instruments, *The King of Denmark* for percussion solo (in which the performer uses only his fingers or hands to play a large battery of percussion instruments), *Piano Piece* (1964), *Numbers* for nine instruments, and *Four Instruments* (violin, cello, chimes, piano). In *Numbers*, the conductor determines the duration of each sound; in *Four Instruments*, "each instrumentalist functions as a conductor as he determines the duration of the sound he is playing (very slow) and the entrance of the player following him."

In 1965 Feldman wrote a piece for chorus called *Christian Wolff*, which in the eighteenth century might have been titled "Ode for an Absent Friend." Wolff (born in France in 1934) was the youngest member of the Cage group. Brought to the United States at the age of seven, he studied piano and flute, but received no formal training in composition. At Harvard, where he obtained his doctorate, he majored in the classics. He was attracted by Cage's doctrine of the liberation of sounds—the idea that these should not be "subservient

---

[9] From notes for the recording of *Out of "Last Pieces"* by the New York Philharmonic under the direction of Leonard Bernstein (Columbia ML 6133).

to some evident intention—e.g., one's feelings, dramatic purposes, adherence to traditional clichés or conventions."[10] He began to use the prepared piano (though with fewer preparations than Cage generally used), and to experiment with rhythmic structures during the 1950s. He was also concerned with strictly limiting the number of pitches used in each piece. In *Nine*, for example, there are not only nine instruments but also nine pitches. In the *Duo for Violins* there are only three pitches. As the composer explains: "In these pieces I thought of making 'melodies' not in lines but out of sound complexes. Such a complex might be two notes that sound simultaneously and then one released; the sound of the second tone continuing after the release of the first seemed a separate entity."

With *Duo for Pianists* (1957), Wolff began to include free elements in his compositions, leaving certain choices to the performer. From this point he actually became more interested in writing for performers than for listeners, and in the concomitant search for spontaneity. As he puts it: "The point is partly to enliven the music by having it in the process of making as though for the first time whenever it is played (or even rehearsed). It is practically impossible, because of the free elements, to make a piece sound the same twice in succession. Thus a piece would always include a quality of taking place for the first time, as opposed to having performances be simply reproductions—for which, in the end, machines seem better suited."[11]

The use of silence as a factor of indeterminacy was another idea that Wolff took over from Cage. The idea is that silence may be used "to make a piece more transparent in the sense that sounds from the environment (stray noises during performance) could be accommodated and would not be felt as interruptions. A piece could then become a kind of frame, having its own particular articulation, but through which one could also simply listen to all the sounds going on at a certain time in a certain place."

Wolff continued to use indeterminacies of various kinds in such pieces as *For Five or Ten People* (1962); *In Between Pieces* (1963), for any three instruments; *For 1, 2, or 3 People* (1964), for any means of sound production, instrumental or not (this includes electronic means—"provided the sounds can be made at the performance itself,

---

[10] This and other quotations in this section are from a private communication.
[11] Several of Wolff's pieces have been recorded (Time Records); but of course these are "simply reproductions" that remain forever static.

no pre-recording permitted"); and Septet (1964), for any seven instruments and a conductor. These are all based on various complex systems of choice and of coordination. In the Septet, for example, there are three kinds of coordination: with another specified player, with any next sound (regardless of who plays it), and with the conductor's signal.

Earle Brown was born in Lunenberg, Massachusetts, on December 26, 1926. He majored in engineering and mathematics at Northeastern University and later studied composition privately with Roslyn B. Henning and Kenneth McKillop. From the latter he acquired a knowledge of the "Schillinger System of Musical Composition," developed by the Russian-American theorist, composer, and mathematician Joseph Schillinger (1895–1943), author of a work titled *The Mathematical Basis of the Arts* (posthumously published in 1948). One of Schillinger's ideas was "to transform musical qualities into time-space structures." Brown found the Schillinger system valuable because "it exposes one to an extremely iconoclastic, mathematically analytical, and constructivist point of view." He also admired its "quantitative and qualitative analysis of SOUND, the physical *material* of the art, and the suggestions of innumerable bases for 'objectively' controlling and generating the material within whatever 'aesthetic' context one chooses." He parted company, however, with the excessive mathematical rigidity of Schillinger's system.

Brown met Cage in Denver (where he was teaching the Schillinger System) and decided to move to New York in 1952, where he worked with Cage and Tudor on the project for music for magnetic tape. Although he received ideas from both Cage and Schillinger—a neat reconciliation of opposites!—Brown tells us that his major aesthetic influences came from two plastic artists: the painter Jackson Pollock and the sculptor Alexander Calder. As he writes:

The earliest, strongest and still the predominant influence on my conceptual attitude toward art and "poetics" were the works of Alexander Calder and Jackson Pollock, which I remember seeing first in 1948 or 1949, and the Max Ernst book, *Beyond Painting*, which I read in 1950 and which was in a sense the verbal confirmation of what I felt in the Calder and Pollock works: the function of non-control and the "finding" of aspects of the work within the process of "making" the work. The integral but unpredictable "floating" variations of a mobile, and the contextual rightness of

Pollock's spontaneity and the directness in relation to the materials and his particular image of the work show an awareness of the "found object" tradition as well as establishing unique and personal conditions of control of the totality. The momentary resolution of this dichotomy seems to me the "subject" (as distinct from *object*) of today's art, common to all the arts.[12]

The problem of the composer, as distinct from that of the painter, was to provide not only for his own creative spontaneity and "immediacy of involvement," but also for the performer's. Calder's mobiles, with their "constant and virtually unpredictable but inherent change," suggested to Brown the construction of units of rhythmic groups "with assigned intensities but 'open' timbre possibilities," which could then be modified and assembled rather arbitrarily by various devices, "accepting the fact that all possible assemblages are inherently possible and valid." It is important to bear in mind that Brown rejects "chance" as a compositional procedure. His principle is that of controlled indeterminacy "through varying realizations of the given material."

During the 1950s, in such works as *Folio Pieces* (1952–1953), *Music for Cello and Piano* (1955), and *Hodograph I* (1959) for six instruments (including marimba and vibraphone), Brown developed various graphic devices intended to encourage and facilitate the concept of mobility. These "invented notations of a highly ambiguous graphic nature, subject to numerous different but inherently valid realizations," permitted the music "to be performed in any direction from any point in the defined length of time." Brown called this *time notation* because, instead of depending on any rational method of measurement, it relies "upon the performer's actions relative to their 'time sense' of the graphic spatial relationships." In the 1960s, time notation has come to be widely used by the new composers.

Continuing his exploration of "open form," Brown composed two of his most important works, *Available Forms I* (1961) for eighteen instruments (commissoned by the city of Darmstadt), and *Available Forms II* (1962) for large orchestra with four hands (i.e., two conductors), commissioned by the Rome Radio Orchestra. Concerning the "open form" principle of these works, the composer wrote:

[12] From notes by the composer for recordings of his music (*Hodograph I, Music for Cello and Piano, Music for Violin, Cello and Piano*) issued by Time Records.

The title of the work refers to the availability of many possible forms which these composed elements may assume, spontaneously directed by the conductors in the process of performing the work. The individual musical events are rehearsed, the performances are not. The conductors work independently of one another but are of course dependent and related by their mutual knowledge of the combinatorial sound possibilities and by their intuitive and aural responses to the materials (events) and to each other's sound-forms as they develop in the process of performing.

No two performances will arrive at the same formal result but the work will retain its identity from performance to performance through the unchanging basic character of the events.[13]

The composer adds that he does not believe in "a final best form" for the musical events from which these works are created.

During 1964–1965, Brown composed several "closed form" works, including *Calder Piece* for four percussionists and a mobile by Calder (which, in effect, functions as "conductor" of certain sections of the form); *Corrobborree*, for three pianos (1964); and a String Quartet (1965). This last is "organized around a scale of sound values between the least characteristic (basically inarticulate and having a high noise coefficient) and the most characteristic sound of strings (basically articulate and elegantly musical)." These works use both specific and rational time notation as well as graphic notations which the composer prefers to describe as "generalized or statistical notations." Summing up his artistic credo, Brown said: "I remain devoted to the potential of human collaborative intention and attempt to compose in a manner which expands and intensifies the artistic and communicative aspects of this dream."

Improvisation and open style

Among the younger composers who have gone in for time notation and works in open style is Larry Austin (*b.* 1930). A native of Oklahoma, Austin studied composition with Milhaud, Imbrie, and Shifrin; in 1958 he joined the faculty of the University of California in Davis. There he has been particularly active in developing what he calls "total art improvisations." Together with the pianist-composer Richard Swift and other virtuoso performers, Austin—who himself plays trum-

[13] From program notes of the New York Philharmonic Society, Feb. 1964.

pet and Flügelhorn—organized the New Music Ensemble in 1962. The ensemble consists of seven performers, who double on several instruments; one of them is a soprano, her voice being simply another instrument. In its "free group improvisations" the ensemble does not use plans or charts, but relies entirely on its "compositional feeling for structure from the smallest musical gesture to the total composition." Its musical vocabulary is strictly contemporary. There are no prearranged pitch patterns: "any and all pitch combinations are admitted, but for the most part duplication of pitches is avoided." This procedure keeps to a minimum "all references to conventional diatonic modes." The aim is to achieve "total improvisation" within an implicit context that acts as a deterrent to chaos. The New Music Ensemble—which has issued several recordings under its own label (NME)—exemplifies "spontaneous composition" in a highly skilled, stylistically consistent, completely contemporary, and often witty and entertaining manner.

Austin's concern with improvisation is doubtless related to his interest in jazz, which in turn has motivated several of his compositions: *Homecoming: A Cantata for Soprano and Jazz Quintet* (1959), *Fantasy on a Theme by Berg for Jazz Band* (1960), and *Improvisations for Symphony Orchestra and Jazz Soloists* (1961). This last was performed by the New York Philharmonic in February, 1964, on which occasion the composer provided the following comment:

At strategic points throughout the work are brief moments in which the individual performers—at times orchestral, at times jazz, at times both—invent rhythmic designs on given pitches within specified spans of time. I believe this "uncontrolled" element injects moments of creative tension in the work not readily obtained in a situation completely controlled by the composer. I strive to involve the performer and the listener in active music making.[14]

During 1964 and 1965, Austin combined these various compositional interests in several works in "open style." This phase began with *Continuum for a Number of Instruments* (1964), based on "the relative motion of sounds in time," thus doing away with conventional bar-lines and meters. This was followed by *Quartet in Open Style* (1964),

[14] Program notes of the New York Philharmonic Society. The *Improvisations* were recorded by the Philharmonic under the direction of Leonard Bernstein (Columbia ML 6133). Not to be outdone, Bernstein included "Four Improvisations by the Orchestra" in this recording.

Open Style for Orchestra with Piano Soloist (1965), *Changes:* Open Style for Trombone and Magnetic Tape (1965), *Catharsis:* Open Style for Two Improvisation Ensembles, Tape, and Conductor (1965), and *The Maze:* A Theatre Piece in Open Style for Three Percussionists, Tape, Projections, and Conductor (1965). In these scores, space equals time, and the relation is indicated in various ways. In *Changes*, small vertical lines are used to mark the space-time units: "Each centimeter of visual space from left to right represents one second of time, there being 20 seconds per system, three systems per page, and a total of nine pages, or nine minutes." This method also allows exact synchronization of the tape portions (two loudspeakers) with the trombone part. In Austin's most ambitious "open style" composition to date, the Open Style for Orchestra with Piano Soloist, each page of the huge score consists of a system of coordinates with thirty space-time units to the page. The direction "1cm = 60" means that one centimeter equals one second of time, and therefore each vertical line corresponds to one "conductor's beat." (Actually, the conductor's beat-pattern is in five throughout the work.) The total "length" of the work is 460 centimeters.

Austin's most far-out venture with open style is *The Maze*, written for "any small grouping of from three to nine instruments and/or voices," with two tracks of tape. Its duration is sixteen minutes (i.e., the length of the tape). This is "an abstract theatre piece," which calls upon the improviser-performers for "interpretive movement as well as interpretive sound." Lighting, stage properties, costume, and make-up are an integral part of the work.

In Austin's *Catharsis*, the "score" consists of one large sheet in which there are no notations, only verbal instructions, visual guidelines, and indications of elapsed time. The performers are simply instructed to do certain things over a specified time span. For example, the brass instruments: "At random, play two bell-tones (*szfp* > *ppp*) during a 15-second time span." In the *tutti*, "All instrumentalists quickly and quietly play a flurry of notes in a five-second time span." At one point the small ensemble is directed to "improvise in opposition to the tape," and later to "improvise a wide variety of ten-second gestures, quietly at first but later rising in volume." While it is perfectly legitimate for Austin to describe such works as being in "open style," it is important to bear in mind that the term does not always imply improvisation. In Earle Brown's "open form" works, for instance, there is no improvisation, only a degree of indeterminacy in the formal structure.

The musical "theater piece," first shaped by Harry Partch and given a new dimension of indeterminacy by Cage, has become a definite genre in these times—perhaps the twentieth-century version of "the complete art-work" that Wagner advocated. Austin's California colleague, Morton Subotnick—teaching at nearby Mills College in Oakland—is another cultivator of this genre. A native of Los Angeles (*b.* 1933), he studied composition with Kirchner and Milhaud. Co-founder and concert director of the San Francisco Tape Center, Subotnick since 1960 has consistently used tape in combination with traditional instruments, beginning with Four Preludes for Piano Solo and Piano and Tape (1960–1964). His Serenade No. 3 (1965) combines tape with flute, clarinet, violin, and piano in a fully integrated chamber ensemble. This piece employs both exact notation and spatial notation (with no "beat"); and one page, just before the end (lasting forty seconds), allows for a degree of indeterminacy. Each player may begin to play at any point within a given "box," but then he must proceed in order from left to right and top to bottom.

Subotnick's first theater piece, titled *Mandolin* (1963), was written for violin, tape, and light projections. The second, titled *Play!* (1964), is for woodwind quintet, piano, tape, and 16-mm film. When this piece was performed in Seattle, the composer and critic Henry Leland Clarke described it as "film and chamber·music that beats the theatre of the absurd at its own game." And he concluded his review by saying, "Since it most completely realized the composer's intentions, *Play!* may be pronounced the most serious number on the program." So "serious," indeed, are Subotnick's intentions, that in 1966 he was headed, not for a loft in lower Manhattan (that modern temple of the Absurd), but for a pillar of the Establishment—in this instance the St. Louis Symphony Orchestra, which commissioned his *Play! No. 3* (for orchestra and tape).

A clarinetist as well as a composer, Subotnick—like Larry Austin, Robert Erickson, and Richard Swift—represents the new generation of composer-performers who in the 1960s have made California a lively area of *avant-garde* activity.

Many other composers in the sixties share an interest in jazz, among them Meyer Kupferman of New York (*b.* 1926), who has had experience as a performer and arranger of jazz. Self-taught in composition,

Kupferman has a long list of works to his credit, including four symphonies, chamber music, film scores, and two operas with libretti by Gertrude Stein: *In a Garden* and *Doctor Faustus Lights the Lights*. But his most important compositional project was begun in 1960 with the "Cycle of Infinities," a series of pieces for various performing groups or soloists, both instrumental and vocal, all of which are based on the same twelve-tone row. By the end of 1965, the number of works in the cycle had reached fifteen. Many are of concert-length duration, divided into six or eight movements, and further divided by an intermission. More than half of the "Infinities"—the composer tells us—"are seriously involved with jazz elements—not improvised, but written out in what I would call 'a tightly organized approach' to the integration of jazz rhythms, stylistic factors, articulation, and so on—in the complex language of contemporary compositional methods. *Infinities 8*, for example, is a string quartet of twenty-two minutes' duration based on jazz elements. The score for this is written so precisely that all the jazz-like materials can be negotiated by non-jazz or symphonic players. . . ." All the works in the cycle require performers of virtuoso ability, and the composer, working in consultation with individual players, has explored the limits of virtuosity through new instrumental techniques.

Compositional techniques in the "Infinities" have been only marginally involved with electronics. Various "echo" devices—using the sympathetic vibrations of piano strings, monitored and amplified by contact microphones and several loudspeakers—have been employed to provide an "electronic atmosphere" for unaccompanied instrumental or vocal works. For example, the "echo" device, utilizing the sounds of two pianos, is employed in *Infinities Four* and *Infinities Six* (both 1962), the former for soprano, the latter for small chorus (with texts from Rimbaud's *Une Saison en Enfer*). *Infinities Four* also employs what the composer calls the "fixed duo" technique, whereby the soloist pre-records a first part for an entire program and then performs a second part against the tape (in duo form) during the concert performance.

The cyclical character of the "Infinities" is emphasized not only in the use of an identical tone-row throughout, but also in that "individual movements of different *Infinities* can be extracted and performed separately, or in pairs; or, more importantly, in a 'mixed assembly' of various combinations."

When *Infinities Three* (1961), for saxophone, bass, and drums, was first performed at the Coolidge Auditorium in the Library of Congress, jazz critic John Wilson called it "a fascinating example of totally ordered composition that, in skilled hands, comes out as buoyant jazz." *Infinities Thirteen* (1965), described as a "Quartet for Eight Instruments" (i.e., four players who double on a second instrument), is not an outright jazz piece, but after a moderately slow first movement that emphasizes elaborate woodwind solos, there is a very fast, hard-driving second movement marked "Jazz Beat," which exploits the melodic and rhythmic virtuosity of post-Parker jazz. The *Infinities Jazz Concerto* is a composite work combining cello, three saxophones (doubling on flute and clarinet), and bass. Such works, among many others by various composers that could be cited, provide evidence that jazz is still a vital factor in contemporary American art music.

"The new liberalism"

Billy Jim Layton (*b.* 1924) is another composer who acknowledges that his work has been deeply influenced by jazz. A native of Texas, his early musical experience was as a performer in school bands and jazz combos. After attending the New England Conservatory, from which he graduated in 1948, he pursued graduate studies at Yale and at Harvard, where his teachers in composition were, respectively, Quincy Porter and Walter Piston. At Harvard he also acquired a Ph.D. in musicology. Stylistically, the most important single influence on his music is that of Elliott Carter. But even more important was "the anonymous tutelage of the vernacular."[15] As Layton writes:[16]

> I should like to emphasize that there is one influence upon my music which is greater than that of any single composer, not excluding the great masters of the past. This is the popular music with which I grew up. I began as a school band and jazz musician, playing clarinet and saxophone, and arranging for various dance orchestras in Texas in the thirties and early forties. This was the heyday of swing, of course, with its wonderful combination of big band ensemble and solo improvisation, and the experience with this music has left an indelible mark upon my musical responses

[15] This phrase is borrowed out of context from a book on modern music by the Argentine composer and critic Juan Carlos Paz.
[16] In a private communication.

and imagination. In my compositions this jazz element sometimes rises to the level of an overt reference; more often it is submerged beneath the surface, but it is nearly always there.

A major confluence of these jazz-inspired elements occurs in Layton's *Dance Fantasy for Orchestra*, Opus 7 (1962–1964), which the composer describes as a kind of ballet score without scenario or choreography. The work was motivated by "a strong urge to write music which would have the direct, primary qualities of gesture which one associates with music for the theatre, and a desire to turn away from the speculative and the theoretical." Following the first performance of the *Dance Fantasy*, a critic wrote of it:[17]

The succession of stylistic patches from such diverse sources as Carter, jazz, Ives, Boulez, and Copland, and a range of textures and sonorities from the bubbling woodwind riffs of the opening to the orchestral "white noise" of the climax to the immediately following prairie-sunset stillness, seems a daring attempt to assimilate everything in music into a personal language where each "style" would function as a macrocosmic element.

Doubtless on the defensive because of the obvious eclecticism of the *Dance Fantasy*, Layton attempted to justify his aesthetic position in an explanatory note:[18]

Some listeners will be troubled by the mixture of elements or passages of a decidedly contemporary nature with other elements which relate in an obvious way to certain familiar traditions. Actually, this eclectic quality is found in all of my music. Far from trying to subdue this tendency, I consciously promote it. In fact, I regard a far-ranging frame of reference as one of the foundations of my aesthetic. There is no question that certain great masters were notable for the purity and elegance of their language; but such concerns have always seemed to me somewhat alien to my own way of thought. Indeed, I believe it is fair to say that a preoccupation with purity of style is not very characteristic of the American mentality in general.

During his rather prolonged student years, Layton produced a large number of works that he later discarded from his catalog. His ac-

---

[17] Benjamin Boretz, in *The Nation*, Dec. 7, 1964.

[18] For the first performance of the *Dance Fantasy* by the New Haven Symphony Orchestra, Oct. 27, 1964.

knowledged Opus 1 is the Five Studies for Violin and Piano (1952); each study develops a particular aspect of composition (rhythm, meter, harmony, melody, form, sonority), in a manner that is artistically effective as well as technically interesting. Opus 2 is *An American Portrait* (1953), subtitled "Symphonic Overture for Orchestra," which follows the tradition of the "American overtures," popularized by such composers as Harris, Copland, and Schuman. Opus 3 consists of *Three Dylan Thomas Poems* (1954–1956), for mixed chorus and brass sextet. Opus 4, written at Rome in 1955–1956, is the work that made Layton famous: the String Quartet in Two Movements. Although immediately performed in Rome and later in Zurich, the Quartet was not heard in the United States until 1960, when the Claremont Quartet played it in New York. The two following works were Three Studies for Piano (1957) and *Divertimento* (1958–1960), for six solo instruments and percussion.

The two movements of Layton's String Quartet, Opus 4, are strongly contrasted, the first being intensely dramatic, the second—a Theme with Interlude and Five Variations—more lyrical and introspective. Yet each movement also has its internal contrasts, for the transition from great emotional intensity to introspective lyricism is characteristic of Layton's music. When the dissonance saturation and the almost savage reiteration become nearly unbearable, the tension is suddenly released by a passage of tranquil beauty. Although the instruments are pushed to their extreme limits, and quarter-tones are occasionally used, the Quartet remains within the mainstream of the modern tradition. The composer tells us that his aim in writing this work was "to achieve the widest range of expression possible without lapsing into incoherence, by always maintaining the strongest formal control." It has been compared with Carter's First Quartet, and the comparison is valid in establishing the general aesthetic and technical character of the work. But Layton assures us that he wrote his Quartet before having heard Carter's; what is important is that the Quartet in Two Movements stands on its own merits as a forceful, expressive, and beautifully crafted composition.

An English critic has suggested that Layton's music "in its feeling and style points the way to a possible future mainstream for American music."[19] Layton himself thinks of such a mainstream as issuing from what he calls "The New Liberalism." Today, he writes, "there is

[19] Anthony Payne, in *The Musical Times*, Nov. 27, 1964.

need for a new, rich, meaningful, varied, understandable, and vital music which maintains contact with the great tradition of humanism in the West."[20] Not since the heroic days of Roy Harris has such an affirmative voice been heard in American music.

A passionate expressionist

Among the composers who came directly under the influence of Edgard Varèse is Ralph Shapey (b. 1921), who as a conductor became known as a brilliant interpreter of Varèse's music. This relationship is all the more interesting because Shapey's music has been labeled "post-Schoenbergian," and he himself has acknowledged the tremendous impact that Schoenberg's music had upon him as a youth. In Philadelphia, where he was born and raised, he attended, at the age of sixteen, the world première of Schoenberg's Violin Concerto. He knew nothing then of the twelve-tone method, but the music appealed to him emotionally: "I was enthralled, and I was completely taken by the magnificence of it—that music for the first time could speak on the level that I heard in my mind."[21]

Shapey went on to study composition with an exponent of twelve-tone writing—but one who was also a very eclectic and adventurous musician: Stefan Wolpe. He adopted the twelve-tone method when it suited him, but at the same time maintained a complete independence. When he was asked, in 1965, "Do you consider yourself a serialist?" he replied: "I consider myself everything."

This open-minded attitude enabled Shapey to reconcile the influences of Schoenberg and Varèse in a typically American—rather than Hegelian—synthesis. The influence of Varèse appears not only in his music but also in his thought and terminology. For example, Shapey describes his symphonic work Ontogeny (a Varèse-like title!) as "a pattern of processes in Time through which the inherent potentialities of sound proceed to be freely realized." Then there is his partial definition of music as "an object in Time and Space: aggregate sounds structured into concrete sculptural forms"; and of the composer as "an architect of sound, time, space, and flux." Among his compositional

[20] From Layton's article, "The New Liberalism," in Perspectives of New Music, III, 2 (1965).

[21] Quoted from an interview with Easley Blackwood, in the Chicago Daily News, Sept. 25, 1965.

procedures he mentions "imposed discipline by ritualistic reiteration" and "the voice projected as an instrument, using syllables in organized sound-structures."

The first score that embodies Shapey's current concepts is *Ontogeny for Symphony Orchestra* (1958), described by a critic as " 'sound-color' music of an amazing complexity, rhythmic force, atmospheric and uninhibited outcry in all sorts of timbre, especially the percussive." This was followed by *Evocation* (1959), for violin with piano and percussion; *Rituals* (1959), for symphony orchestra; and some twenty chamber works. In two of these works—*Dimensions* for soprano and twenty-three instruments(1960) and *Incantations* for soprano and ten instruments (1961)—Shapey employs the human voice as an instrument, using syllables instead of a literary text.

When *Incantations* was first performed in New York, one critic described it as "a composition of abstract expressionism that seems to lay bare the most secret and elemental doubts, yearnings, torments, and despairs of the human soul trapped in the chaos of the urban jungle." Such an interpretation is of course largely subjective, but it leaves no doubt as to the expressive power and emotional impact of the music. Of the four movements in the work, it is the third (entirely instrumental), with its headlong frenzy, that might evoke images of the soul caught in a mechanistic urban chaos. Musically, however, this seeming "chaos" is tightly organized and carefully controlled in its extreme metrical complexity. The "disciplined reiteration" of which the composer speaks is fully operative in this movement. Each part appears as "a self-involved unit of individual proportions," and the whole is conceived as a web of "varied phrases resulting from the juxtaposition of designs." The entire movement is maintained at a constant dynamic level (*sempre forte*), until a crescendo at the very end. This is followed by the dreamlike Recitative of the final movement, hummed *sotto voce* by the soprano with the *pianissimo* punctuation of tom-toms, gongs, and cymbals. Here, in this poetic dream-sequence, the term "incantation" may be interpreted almost literally, to suggest the "magical" power of music. *Incantations* is scored for soprano, cello, trumpet, alto saxophone, French horn, and percussion. In the first and second movement, the cello engages in a sort of dialogue with the voice, and both parts include microtonal intervals.

Shapey's attitude toward composing is deliberately "problematical," in the sense that he practices a kind of creative "brinkmanship," so that his music often "trembles on the brink of meaning" (to borrow a phrase from Dr. Johnson). A previously quoted critical comment describes his work as "abstract expressionism"—which elicits the query, "Why 'abstract'?" If there is any significance attached to the term "expressionistic" in music, then I believe it may legitimately be applied to the compositions of Ralph Shapey. He has the courage of his obsessions, no matter how far they may carry him, and he has dared "the great gesture" of complete emotional involvement at a time when intellectualization is the order of the day. In one of his most remarkable scores, the *Discourse for Four Instruments* (1961), the three movements are marked, respectively, "With great gesture," "With intense wildness," "With tenderness." There is a kind of admirable bravado in thus going against the current.

Another composer who has gone his own way, sometimes but not always using tone-rows, is Seymour Shifrin (*b.* 1926). A native of Brooklyn, he studied composition with Luening, Schuman, and Milhaud. For a number of years he taught at the University of California in Berkeley, and in 1966 was appointed to the music faculty of Brandeis University. He has written mostly chamber music, an exception being the Three Orchestra Pieces (1960). Concerning his Serenade for Five Instruments (1956), Andrew Imbrie wrote: "One is fascinated by the highly expressive and exposed melodic shapes, interrelated in a supple and elastic rhythmic context." These qualities are also evident in such scores as the String Quartet No. 2 (1962), and *The Odes of Shang* (1963), for small chorus, piano, and percussion (the translations from the Chinese are by Ezra Pound). In the latter work there is a highly sensitive use of timbre within a frame of discreet Orientalism. Shifrin's output of the sixties also includes a Phantasy for Piano (1961); *Satires of Circumstances* (1963–1964), on poems of Thomas Hardy, for soprano and chamber ensemble; and String Quartet No. 3 (1965–1966).

Merging of East and West

Orientalism is nothing new in Western music: from the *chinoiseries* of the eighteenth century to the work of such present-day composers as Cage, Cowell, Harrison, and Hovhaness, it has produced a copious musical literature. But a really profound "meeting of East and

West"—on the philosophical, aesthetic, and technical levels—has rarely been achieved. Perhaps it required a composer from the East, but one with thorough mastery of Western musical traditions and techniques, to accomplish this creative synthesis. Such a composer is Chou Wen-chung, who came to the United States from China in 1946 and has devoted his creative efforts to what he calls a *"re-merger"* of Eastern and Western musical concepts and techniques. Born in Chefoo in 1923, Chou Wen-chung studied at the National Chungking University before coming to the United States. In this country he studied composition with Nicolas Slonimsky, Otto Luening, and (from 1949 to 1954) with Edgard Varèse. He became an American citizen in 1958.

In an article explaining his aesthetic views and the evolution of his music, Chou wrote:[22]

> Like the Chinese calligrapher and painter, I have always regarded the technique of a composer as a spontaneous manifestation of his gradually crystallizing esthetic concepts. This is perhaps in agreement with the Confucian concept: *Music* is "born of emotion;" *tones* are the "substance of music;" melody and rhythm are the "appearance of tones." Greatness of music lies not in "perfection of artistry" but in attainment of "spiritual power inherent in nature."
>
> Since in my opinion Chinese poetry and painting, among all art forms, seem to have come closest to the idea of knowing the power inherent in any individual thing and of using things as things, I first tried in my early works to convey through sound the qualities of Chinese poetry and painting, and to achieve this end with the same economy of means. In these works, I was influenced by the same philosophy that guides every Chinese artist, be he poet, painter, or musician: affinity to nature in conception, allusiveness in expression, and terseness in realization.

These aesthetic concepts are embodied in Chou's first orchestral score, *Landscapes* (1949), in which each of the three movements is based on a traditional Chinese melodic pattern (*ch'u tiao*); each of these, in turn, is associated with a poem evoking a particular type of landscape. The music attempts to evoke the impression of dots,

---

[22] "Toward a *Re*-merger in Music," in *Contemporary Composers on Contemporary Music* (New York: Holt, Rinehart and Winston, 1967). This and other quotations from the same source are used by permission of the author and the publisher.

lines, delicate shadings, open space, and motion. In two subsequent orchestral works—*All in the Spring Wind* (1952–1953), *And the Fallen Petals* (1954)—there occurred "a marked change in the use of tonal material and instrumental resources." As explained by the composer:

> Line, mass, and their interaction, together with such elements as articulation, duration, intensity and timbre, are organized into an integrated body of sound that ebbs and flows—in the manner of a tonal brushwork in space—with ever-changing motion, tension, texture, and sonority. It seems to me that these works reflect not only the fundamental concept of the Chinese painter in general, but also that of the Chinese musician in particular. The ancient Chinese musician believed that each single tone or aggregate of tones is a musical entity in itself and a living spark of expression as long as it lasts. Therefore, it was also believed that the meaning in music lies intrinsically in the tones themselves, that maximum expressiveness can be derived from a succession of tones without resorting to extraneous procedures.

As a result of these experiences and reflections, Chou Wen-chung became increasingly interested in the analogy with the art of Chinese calligraphy, "in which the controlled flow of ink—through the interaction of movement and energy, the modulation of line and texture—creates a continuum of motion and tension in a spatial equilibrium." These principles were applied in a work for piano, *The Willows Are New* (1957), where the thematic material is based on a traditional composition for *ch'in*, the ancient Chinese zither. They were further developed in *Metaphors* (1960) for wind symphony orchestra, and in *Yu Ko for Nine Players* (1965), adapted from the "Yu Ko for Ch'in" by Mao Ming-chung (*ca.* 1280). The latter work is scored for piano, violin, alto flute, English horn, bass clarinet, trombone, and a battery of twenty percussion instruments. "In this adaptation," writes the composer, "I have magnified, as closely to the original as possible, these inflections in pitch, articulation, timbre, dynamics, and rhythm to a more perceptible level by expanding the articulations and timbres possible on each instrument used, and by controlling the microtonal modifications in pitch according to the nature of each instrument."

The work titled *Cursive* (1963), for flute and piano, further explores the analogy with Chinese calligraphy. The title refers to the type of script in which the joined strokes and rounded angles result in expressive and contrasting curves and loops. In this score, the composer explains,

The cursive concept has influenced the use of specified but indefinite pitches and durations, and the use of regulated but variable tempo and intensity. Throughout the score, the piano is treated as a combination keyboard, string, and percussion instrument, while the flute is required to use controlled microtonal modifications in pitch. An attempt is made to treat the individual sound as a "living matter" through inflections in its production and control.

The same principle of treating each individual sound as "a living matter" is embodied in the composition titled *Riding the Wind* (1964), for wind symphony orchestra with large percussion section (six players). The work has for its motto some verses from the Chinese poet Lieh Tzu (fifth century B.C.):

I am borne hither and thither like a dry leaf torn from a tree.
I know not whether the wind is riding on me or I the wind.

The work is characterized by a "counterpoint of dynamics," with continually varying inflections in all the voices, the production and decay of each tone being always carefully and beautifully controlled.

In 1966 Chou Wen-chung completed a chamber concerto for piano, winds, and percussion, titled *Pien*—the Chinese term for a mutable mode (the word means "to change," "to transform"). As the composer explains,

These modes are based upon three disjunct segments of the octave that are either unbroken (a minor third) or broken (a major and a minor second, i.e., the minor third interpolated with a *pien*-tone). These segments are reciprocally mutable according to whether the movement is ascending or descending; the order of the two seconds also depends on the direction of movement. In other words, each segment in the ascending order is reflected in mutation in the descending order—the intervals being mutually complementary, the pitches being mutually exclusive.

In these days when composers are writing so much about the *process* of musical composition, the reader may be inclined to scepticism concerning all such theoretical explanations. Let it therefore be said, most emphatically, that Chou Wen-chung is first and foremost an extremely gifted and sensitive creative artist, whose compositions reach aesthetic heights comparable to those attained by the great Chinese artists in painting, poetry, and calligraphy.

A merging of Eastern and Western traditions in music is also to be found in the work of the Egyptian-American composer Halim El-Dabh, who was born in Cairo in 1921 and came to the United States in 1950. As a youth he assimilated the traditional Egyptian music of his environment and also learned to play several native instruments. He studied piano at the Sulcz Conservatory in Cairo (1940–1941); but at the University of Cairo he specialized in agricultural engineering. Not until 1949 did he decide to embark upon a career in music. From 1950 to 1954 he studied music at various places in the United States, including the New England Conservatory and Brandeis University; among his teachers in composition were Aaron Copland and Irving Fine. He achieved prominence as a composer when his "dance epic" *Clytemnestra*, commissioned by Martha Graham, was performed in New York in 1958.

Clytemnestra, described as "an epic dance drama for voices and orchestra," is a large-scale work lasting nearly two hours and consisting of a Prologue, Two Acts, and an Epilogue. The score calls for the intoned voices of a dramatic soprano and a dramatic baritone with falsetto range. When this work was taken on tour by the Martha Graham Dance Company in 1958, a critic wrote that it conveyed an impression of "archaic Oriental music, functional, effective, a good blend of modern technique in composition with an ancient heritage." El-Dabh has also written two ballet suites on classical subjects: *Agamemnon* and *Iphigenia;* and a cantata titled *Leiyla*, for mezzo-soprano solo, male chorus, piano, celesta, xylophone, double bass, and timpani.

Many of El-Dabh's compositions are for percussion ensembles, some employing conventional Western instruments (e.g., *Juxtaposition* No. 1, for two timpani, xylophone, and marimba), others featuring a variety of Eastern instruments, particularly the Derabucca Drum. He has explained and illustrated the technique of the latter in a four-page pamphlet titled *The Derabucca: Hand Techniques in the Art of Drumming.*[23] His *Sonics* No. 7 and No. 10 are scored for Derabucca or multiple drums. In these pieces no fixed pitch indications are given,

[23] Published by C. F. Peters Corporation (New York, 1965).

the positions of the notes on the staff representing *relatively* higher and lower pitches. Each piece consists of three sections: The Constant, The Variable, and the Finale. Improvisation is always allowed in The Variable, and exceptionally in the Finale, if the performer so chooses. The players are asked to "treat the percussion instruments with extreme musical sensitivity." In some pieces, the composer allows wide latitude in the choice of instruments "within the limits of the tone-qualities indicated in the score." In *Tabla-Dance*, for example, "the leader of the group may choose any number of drums and jingles of any kind, shape, or origin that will produce the quality of sound called for in the score." The composer suggests a pair of Indian drums, the *Tabla-Bahya*, because "the wooden, cylindrical *Tabla* will provide clear tones, and the brass, semi-spherical *Bahya* will provide deep tones;" the *Mrdanga*, a long, cylindrical, two-headed drum (muffled); and a *Khanjeri* or *Duff* (Indian and Arabian tambourines), "which can provide for both the drum and jingle sounds." El-Dabh's percussion pieces also provide for several versions that can be performed by a varying number of players; *Tabla-Tahmeel* No. 1, for instance, can be performed by three to fourteen players; *Hindi-Yatt* No. 1, by three to twelve players. Most of these pieces are short (three to five minutes) and unpretentious, and perhaps intended primarily as "performer's music."

A Cuban in California

If we turn our eyes—and ears—toward Latin America, we find that there has been a considerable exchange of influences with the United States, in both the popular and erudite fields of composition. Since about 1950, however, there has been less emphasis on the typical, exotic, or native aspects of Latin American art music; both Carlos Chávez of Mexico and Alberto Ginastera of Argentina have long outgrown their nationalistic phases. The younger generation of Latin American composers identify themselves with current international trends in serial and electronic composition. Such is the case, for instance, with Mario Davidovsky of Argentina, who in 1965 was working at the Columbia-Princeton Electronic Music Center; and with Aurelio de la Vega, formerly of Cuba, who in 1959 joined the faculty of San Fernando Valley State College in California (he became an American citizen in 1966).

Aurelio de la Vega, born in Havana in 1925, studied theory with Frederick Kramer and composition with Ernst Toch. He has been very active as teacher, lecturer, writer, and proponent of new music. He established his reputation as one of the leading composers of the Americas with such works as the Symphony in Four Parts (1960), the Quintet for Winds (1959), and *Structures* (1962), for piano and string quartet. His *Coordinates for Magnetic Tape* (1963), described as "an electronic piano concerto," was first performed at the Ojai Festival (California) in 1964. It is in three movements: "Polynomial," "Acoustical Measurements," "Vectors." The work "features the juxtaposition of recorded, transfigured piano sounds against an 'orchestra' of electronically derived sounds." *Exametron* (1965), for flute, cello, and four percussion players, derives its title from the fact that the number six controls the entire work: "six players, six main sections, a series of six notes, six basic tempos, six dynamics, six basic densities regarding the aural concept, and six cross-relations among the parts." The composer writes further about the work:

In general, *Exametron* is a lyrical piece and thus represents my current musical preoccupations. Although the piece is rigorously serialized, I have tried to maintain an atmosphere of spontaneity throughout. [Of the several perpetual-variation sections, two are *ad libitum*.] The two non-percussion instruments are treated soloistically at times, and at others blend with the percussion ensemble as subsidiary voices. As in my other works, I am much concerned here with linear conception, detail work, lyrical lines, rhythmic activity, recurring melodic leaps, sound production, extreme ranges and timbres, and a certain virtuoso approach to the aural material.[24]

De la Vega began to employ twelve-tone writing consistently with the String Quartet in Five Movements, dating from 1957. In the Cantata for Two Sopranos, Contralto and Chamber Orchestra (1958) he combined twelve-tone organization with tonal elements arising from the harmonic implications of the basic row (a pattern of major and minor thirds). In *Structures* for piano and string quartet, he introduced aleatory elements (*Mobile* No. 1 and *Mobile* No. 2) in two movements that alternate with the three movements in fixed structure. In 1965, de la Vega completed a large orchestral work in three movements,

[24] From program notes for the Monday Evening Concerts, Los Angles, October 11, 1965.

titled *Analigus,* of which the score is entirely notated with new graphic symbols.

Toward a new synthesis

The younger generation of composer-performers in New York is well represented by Harvey Sollberger and Charles Wuorinen, both born in 1938. The former is a flutist, the latter a pianist. Sollberger, who was born in Grand Rapids, Iowa, studied composition with Beeson and Luening at Columbia University. Wuorinen, a native New Yorker, also studied with these teachers, as well as with Ussachevsky. Both of them joined the music faculty of Columbia University. Sollberger's compositions of the sixties include Solos for Violin and Five Instruments, Grand Quartet for Flutes, Composition for Viola and Piano (all 1962), Two Oboes Troping (1963), Chamber Variations for Twelve Players and Conductor (1964), and *Musica Trans-alpina* (1965–1966) for soprano and baritone with chamber ensemble.

Wuorinen attracted wide attention with his Third Symphony, completed when he was twenty-one, which Wilfrid Mellers characterized—with some exaggeration—as "a shatteringly sensational, brash, technicolored piece that brings Copland, Harris, and Riegger up to date with superb irreverence." This ignores the mood of deep reverence in the finale, which includes a chorale treatment of a fragment from *La Déploration de Johannes Ockeghem* by Josquin des Préz. At all events, the many scores written prior to 1960 are significant primarily as heralding a remarkable new talent in American music, rather than as works upon which Wuorinen's reputation will ultimately rest. His more recent works include *Duuiensela* for piano (1962), the Piano Variations and Chamber Concerto for Cello and Ten Players (both 1963), Chamber Concerto for Flute and Ten Players (1964), Chamber Concerto for Oboe and Ten Players (1965), Orchestral and Electronic Exchanges (1964–1965), and a Piano Concerto (1965–1966) in one movement. This is a twelve-tone work "as respects pitch and temporal organization"; that is to say, the "temporal organization is the direct temporal analogue of the twelve-pitch-class system."

Wuorinen's Orchestral and Electronic Exchanges, for orchestra and synthesized sound, received its first performance in July, 1965, as part of the French-American Festival organized by the New York Philharmonic under the artistic direction of Lukas Foss, who conducted the work. The composer's program note explains the nature and purpose of the score:[25]

The title seemed appropriate in view of the basic structural dynamics of the composition: the presentation of all of the basic material in the tape part, and the surrounding of each section of this tape part with orchestral commentaries and variations. Thus, although there is little "dialogue" (i.e., complex polyphony) between tape and orchestra, a process of "exchange" is, in a very real sense, taking place: for on the one hand, the total orchestral gesture is naturally dependent upon what the tape utters, while on the other hand, the tape (although completely fixed) will be perceived differently in the orchestral context which its material generates than it would be in isolation.

These relationships are possible because . . . the frequency materials of tape and orchestra are essentially the same: the tempered twelve-part division of the octave. Thus, subject only to speed of articulation and rhythmic complexity, the tape and orchestra may share the same material. . . .

The casual listener will immediately notice that the electronic part avoids most if not all attempts at the production of "new" sounds, "effects," and timbres. The purpose of the tape in this work is, on the contrary, to make possible the completely accurate realization and presentation of very complex *pitch* and *rhythmic* situations and relationships—which, as realized with the Synthesizer, possess a stability and clarity unavailable with conventional instruments. The tape part, then, *displays* certain musical relationships, and the playing of the tape can therefore be in no sense thought of as a performance. The orchestra, however, *performs,* using the same material as the tape has displayed. It is this contrast between the *performed* and the *displayed,* which provides *Exchanges* with its basic character.

Wuorinen, both by his chronological situation and his technical-temperamental equipment, is the type of composer who may bring about a new creative synthesis between traditional and electronic media in musical composition. In his Third Symphony he gave ample proof of his ability to communicate in terms of traditional compositional rhetoric, which aims at a direct emotional-dramatic effect. If he can preserve this power of communication while developing his

[25] From program notes of the New York Philharmonic Society, July 30, 1965.

present concern with "large-scale structural articulation derived from set structure, and the articulative devices associated with . . . the formal procedures of Stravinsky and Varèse . . ."—then he may indeed assume for his generation a commanding position and prestige comparable to those achieved by the leading American composers of the three preceding generations.

There is every reason to believe that the 1960s will go down in history as one of the most dynamic decades in the annals of American music. Creatively, composers have consolidated the new technological resources—particularly in the electronic media—developed during the previous decade. While the establishment of the Columbia-Princeton Electronic Music Center in New York was certainly a development of major importance, internationally as well as nationally, the dynamism of the sixties is more significantly illustrated by the rapidly increasing number of smaller electronic studios throughout the United States. The general acceptance of electronic media in musical composition will surely be regarded as a characteristic trend of the sixties.

Another significant trend, as pointed out at the beginning of this chapter, has been the formation of groups for performing contemporary music. Here the composer-performer, with the backing of universities and foundations, has taken the initiative in breaking through the restrictions of the musical Establishment based on the standard repertoire of familiar works. As stated in the prospectus of one of these groups, such initiatives are founded on "the firm belief that the artist of today can and must extend his expressive vocabulary to include imaginative use of the materials of today." The activity of these new performing groups, which have sprung into existence in all parts of the country, offers what is probably the most impressive and far-reaching development of this decade. Instead of waiting to pick up crumbs of recognition from the Establishment, the composers and performers have established their own professional world based on creative values and freedom of invention rather than upon routine repetition. Communicating with an ever-widening audience, they may yet succeed in bringing about a revolution of values in America's world of music.

A note on recordings

The usefulness of discographies is offset by their ephemerality. Their chief value, which is timeliness, appears to best advantage in periodical publications that aim at currentness. These have a practical function: they tell the reader what recordings are actually available at the time of publication. One month, or six months, or one year later, some, many, or all of these recordings may no longer be available; that is to say, their manufacturers will have discontinued making them, they will have been "withdrawn" from the catalogue, and only a few remainders may be left on the shelves of dealers. In the case of the standard repertoire, the consequences of this situation are not too serious, because there are always numerous recordings available of the "classical" works. The prevailing criterion is strictly economic: when a record fails to sell in sufficient quantity, it is withdrawn. Obviously, by the law of supply and demand, it follows that those titles for which there is the least demand are the first to be withdrawn and the last to be replaced. The field of contemporary music is most generally affected by this rule, since only those composers who have "big names" can count on being well represented in the record catalogues. In spite of the growing interest in contemporary American art-music, very few American composers qualify as "big names" in the books of the recording companies. Among them are Barber, Bernstein, Copland, Cowell, Schuman, and (belatedly) Charles Ives. But it is American music of the past that suffers most severely from the application of commercial criteria: a historical discography of early American music—prior, say, to 1910—would consist very largely of items, ranging from Puritan Psalmody and New England fuguing tunes and anthems to works of the "Boston Classicists" at the turn of the century, that have been withdrawn from circulation. In other words, such a discography would be almost entirely obsolete—which is why it has not been attempted here. And even a current discography would, for the reasons explained, soon become obsolete.

What, then, should the reader do, if he wishes to acquire a representative collection of American music on records? First of all, he should take as his *vade mecum* the *Schwann Long Playing Record Catalog*, which in 1966 was in its eighteenth year of publication. This is a monthly guide to current recordings, which may be obtained at all record dealers. Its main listing is alphabetical, by composers; but there are also listings under Collections, Ballets, Operas, Music Shows, Folk Music, Popular, and Jazz. One of its most valuable features is the designation (by a diamond-shaped symbol) of those items that are to be discontinued by the manufacturer. Thus forewarned, the reader may hasten to acquire the doomed items in which he is most interested, before they are lost and gone—not forever, perhaps, in all cases, but probably for a very long time at best.

The most important single source for recordings of American art-music is Composers Recordings, Inc. (CRI), founded in 1955. Within the next ten years, more than 250 works by some 150 composers had been issued under the CRI label. The catalogue includes composers of the immediate past, such as Griffes, Carpenter, Jacobi, Mason, Powell, as well as present-day composers of the most divergent tendencies, from Barber to Cage, from Partch to Babbitt. It offers a truly representative and ever-increasing cross-section of contemporary art-music in the United States, in all forms from opera to song, from symphony to sonata. What is of fundamental importance is that the CRI releases are permanently maintained in the catalogue. Hence both the historical and practical values of the collection are enormously enhanced by its cumulative character.

Folkways Records and Service Corporation of New York is an important source for miscellaneous musical Americana, especially folk, ethnic, and popular music. Its catalogue includes many items of historical interest, such as traditional ballads and topical songs associated with different periods of American history, from Colonial times to the Civil War. One of its major contributions is a historical anthology of jazz in twelve volumes, edited by Frederic Ramsey, Jr. The "Ethnic Folkways Library" is strong in American Negro and Indian tribal music. The Folkways catalogue tends to have more stability than those of the larger recording companies. Historically, one of its most valuable items is *The New England Harmony: A Collection of Early American Choral Music*, selected and annotated by Alan C. Beuchner.[1]

[1] An earlier recording, *The American Harmony: Hymns and Fuguing Tunes*,

The Library of Congress in Washington, through its Archive of Folk Song, has issued a copious selection of authentic folk and ethnic music of the United States, including songs, ballads, dances, and instrumental pieces. These are drawn from field recordings made by experts, and are accompanied by authoritative booklets. The catalogue includes a large quantity of American Indian music, as well as a great variety of songs and ballads from the Anglo-American tradition. A complete listing, classified by subjects, and with an index of titles, is available (Superintendent of Documents, U.S. Government Printing Office, Washington, D.C.). The records may be ordered directly from the Recording Laboratory of the Library of Congress.

The Society for the Preservation of the American Musical Heritage, Inc., a non-profit entity founded in 1958 by Karl Krueger for the purpose of producing and distributing recordings of American music—from Colonial times to the twentieth century—not otherwise available. Its catalog includes Early American Psalmody and Catholic Mission Music in California, music by professional immigrants of the eighteenth century, anthems by Billings and Read, and compositions by Gottschalk, Fry, Bristow, William Mason, Sidney Lanier, J. K. Paine, MacDowell, Foote, Chadwick, Farwell, Gilbert, and Griffes, among others. Many of these recordings were distributed gratis to colleges, universities, music schools, and public libraries in the United States and abroad. In 1965, however, this service was discontinued and the recordings were made available on the basis of membership and subscription (open to individuals as well as institutions).

In the realm of jazz, the discography is of course enormous and has been very thoroughly documented. Most of the works listed in the bibliography of jazz in this book include discographies. The latter have a special significance in jazz, independent of their current availability, because of the great importance of the performers. Hence discographies of jazz with personnel listings are of permanent historical value. Discontinued jazz recordings of the past are continually being reissued, mostly in the form of anthologies covering either an entire period or the career of a single jazz musician. The reader interested in recordings of jazz will have no difficulty save that of choice—a commodity rarely offered to the *aficionado* of American art music.

---

originally issued by Washington Records, with commentary by Irving Lowens, is unfortunately out of print. Cf. "William Billings and the Yankee Tunesmiths," by H. Wiley Hitchcock, in *HiFi/Stereo Review* (February, 1966).

Bibliography

The general bibliography that precedes those for specific chapters is not meant to be exhaustive but is intended as a representative list of titles on American music and as a guide for the reader who may wish to pursue further special phases of the subject.

The bibliographies for the individual chapters serve largely as a list of sources, supplementing with complete bibliographical data the brief references given in the footnotes.

Since there is overlapping in the subject matter of certain chapters, several titles are necessarily repeated. In the case of such repetitions, only the author and title are mentioned, and the reader is referred to the chapter in which the complete listing of the imprint occurs. Thus, the entry: Sonneck, Oscar G. *Early Opera in America* (5), means that the complete listing of this work will be found in the bibliography for Chapter 5.

General bibliography

Barzun, Jacques. *Music in American Life.* New ed. Bloomington: Indiana University Press, 1962.

Bio-bibliographical Index of Musicians in the United States of America from Colonial Times. New ed. Washington, D.C.: Music Division, Pan American Union, 1956.

Chase, Gilbert (ed.). *The American Composer Speaks* (A Historical Anthology, 1770–1965). Baton Rouge: Louisiana State University Press, 1966.

Copland, Aaron. *Copland on Music.* Garden City, N.Y.: Doubleday & Co., Inc. 1960.

———. *Our New Music; Leading Composers in Europe and America.* New York: McGraw-Hill Book Company, Inc., 1941.

Courlander, Harold. *Negro Folk Music, U.S.A.* New York: Columbia University Press, 1963.

Cowell, Henry (ed.). *American Composers on American Music.* A Symposium, with a New Introduction by the Author [*sic*]. New ed. New York: Frederick Ungar Publishing Company, 1962. (Originally published in 1933.)

Edmunds, John, and Gordon Boelzner. *Some Twentieth Century American*

697

Composers: A Selective Bibliography. With an Introductory Essay by Peter Yates. 2 vols. New York: The New York Public Library, 1959. (Includes excellent photographic portraits.)

Ellinwood, Leonard. *The History of American Church Music.* New York: Morehouse-Gorham Co., Inc., 1953.

Elson, Louis C. *The History of American Music.* New York: The Macmillan Company, 1904. Rev. ed., 1915. (Also new edition, revised to 1925 by Arthur Elson.)

——. *The National Music of America and Its Sources.* Boston: L. C. Page & Company, 1899. (Also new edition, revised to 1924 by Arthur Elson.)

Encyclopédie de la Musique et Dictionnaire du Conservatoire. Ed. by Albert Lavignac and Lionel de la Laurencie. Paris: Delagrave, 1913–1931. Part I, vol. 5 (1922) includes a section on music of the United States by Esther Singleton.

Farwell, Arthur, and W. Dermot Darby. *Music in America.* Vol. 4 of *The Art of Music.* New York: The National Society of Music, 1915.

Fisher, William Arms. *One Hundred and Fifty Years of Music Publishing in the United States.* Boston: Oliver Ditson Company, 1933. (A revision and extension of the author's *Notes on Music in Old Boston,* 1918.)

Goss, Madeleine. *Modern Music-makers: Contemporary American Composers.* New York: E. P. Dutton & Co., Inc., 1952.

Haywood, Charles. *A Bibliography of North American Folklore and Folksong.* New York: Greenberg, 1951. New edition in 2 vols., New York: Dover Publications, 1961.

Howard, John Tasker. *Our American Music: A Comprehensive History from 1620 to the Present.* New York: Thomas Y. Crowell Company, 1965. (Originally published in 1931.)

——. *Our Contemporary Composers: American Music in the Twentieth Century.* New York: Thomas Y. Crowell Company, 1941.

Hubbard, W. L. (ed.). *History of American Music.* Volume 8 of *The American History and Encyclopedia of Music.* Toledo, Ohio: Irving Squire, 1908–1910.

Hughes, Rupert. *Contemporary American Composers.* Boston: L. C. Page & Company, 1900. (Also new edition, revised to 1914 by Arthur Elson under the title *American Composers.*)

Lahee, H. C. *Annals of Music in America; a chronological record of significant musical events, from 1640 to the present day . . .* Boston: Marshall Jones Company, 1922.

Lang, Paul Henry (ed.). *One Hundred Years of Music in America.* New York: G. Schirmer, Inc., 1961.

Lavignac, Albert. *Music and Musicians.* New York: Henry Holt and Company, 1899. Includes chapters on music in the United States by H. E. Krehbiel, who edited the 4th rev. ed. in 1903.

Lowens, Irving. *Music and Musicians in Early America.* New York: W. W. Norton & Company, Inc., 1964.

Madeira, L. C. (comp.). *Annals of Music in Philadelphia and History of the Musical Fund Society from Its Organization in 1820 to the Year 1858.* Edited by Philip H. Goepp. Philadelphia: J. B. Lippincott Company, 1896.

Marrocco, W. Thomas, and Harold Gleason. *Music in America. An Anthology from the Landing of the Pilgrims to the Close of the Civil War, 1620–1865.* New York: W. W. Norton & Company, Inc., 1964.

Mason, Daniel Gregory. *The Dilemma of American Music.* New York: The Macmillan Company, 1928.

———. *Music in My Time.* New York: The Macmillan Company, 1938.

———. *Tune In, America! A Study of Our Coming Musical Independence.* New York: Alfred A. Knopf, Inc., 1931.

Mathews, W. S. B. (ed.). *A Hundred Years of Music in America.* Chicago: G. L. Howe, 1889.

Mellers, Wilfrid. *Music in a New Found Land. Themes and Developments in the History of American Music.* London: Barrie & Rockliff, 1964; New York: Alfred A. Knopf, Inc., 1965.

Reis, Claire. *Composers in America; Biographical Sketches of Contemporary Composers with a Record of Their Works.* Rev. and enlarged edition. New York: The Macmillan Company, 1947.

Ritter, Frédéric Louis. *Music in America.* New York: Charles Scribner's Sons, 1883.

Rosenfeld, Paul. *An Hour with American Music.* Philadelphia: J. B. Lippincott Company, 1929.

Sessions, Roger. *Reflections on the Music Life in the United States.* New York: Merlin Press, 1956.

Slonimsky, Nicolas. *Music Since 1900.* 3rd ed., revised and enlarged. New York: Coleman-Ross Co., Inc., 1949.

Sonneck, Oscar G. *Miscellaneous Studies in the History of Music.* New York: The Macmillan Company, 1921. Includes "The History of Music in America."

———. *Suum Cuique; Essays in Music.* New York: G. Schirmer, Inc., 1916. Includes "A Survey of Music in America."

Stevens, Denis (ed.). *A History of Song.* London: Hutchinson, 1960; New York: W. W. Norton & Co., Inc., 1961. (The chapter on art-song in the United States is by Hans Nathan.)

Stevenson, Robert. *Protestant Church Music in America: A Short Survey of Men and Movements from 1564 to the Present.* New York: W. W. Norton & Co., 1966.

Sward, Keith. "Jewish Musicality in America." *Journal of Applied Psychology,* XVII, 6 (Dec., 1933), 675–712.

Upton, William Treat. *Art-song in America; A Study in the Development of American Music.* Boston and New York: Oliver Ditson Company, 1930. (A supplement was issued by the same publisher in 1938.)

Wolfe, Richard J. *Secular Music in America, 1801–1825.* A Bibliography. 3 vols. New York: The New York Public Library, 1964.

For one, Puritan psalm singers

Bradstreet, Anne. *The Works of Anne Bradstreet in Prose and Verse.* Edited by John H. Ellis. Charlestown, Mass.: A. E. Cutter, 1867.

Cotton, John. *Singing of Psalms a Gospel Ordinance: Or a Treatise wherein are handled these four particulars. I. Touching the duty itself. II. Touching the matter to be sung. III. Touching the singers. IIII. Touching the manner of singing.* Boston, 1647.

Covey, Cyclone. *The American Pilgrimage.* New York: Collier Books, 1961.

Fisher, William Arms. *Ye Olde New England Psalm Tunes (1620–1820), with historical sketch.* Boston: Oliver Ditson Company, 1930.

Haraszti, Zoltán. *The Enigma of the Bay Psalm Book.* Chicago: University of Chicago Press, 1956.

——— (ed.). *The Bay Psalm Book. A Facsimile Reprint of the First Edition of 1640.* Chicago: University of Chicago Press, n.d. [1956].

Lowens, Irving. "The Bay Psalm Book in 17th-Century New England." In *Music and Musicians in Early America.* New York: W. W. Norton & Company, 1964.

MacDougall, Hamilton C. *Early New England Psalmody, 1620–1820.* Brattleboro, N. H., Stephen Daye Press, 1940.

Playford, John. *An Introduction to the Skill of Musick* (11th ed.). London, 1687.

———. *The Whole Booke of Psalms: With the Usual Hymns and Spiritual Songs, Together with all the Ancient and Proper Tunes sung in Churches, with some of Late Use . . .* (4th ed.). London, 1698.

Pratt, Waldo Selden. *The Music of the Pilgrims.* Boston: Oliver Ditson Company, 1921.

———. *The Music of the French Psalter of 1562.* New York: Columbia University Press, 1939.

The Psalms, Hymns, and Spiritual Songs, of the Old and New Testament: Faithfully Translated in English Meetre. For the use, Edification and Comfort of the Saints in publick and private, especially in New-England (9th ed.). Boston: Printed by B. Green and J. Allen, for Michael Perry, 1698.

Ravenscroft, Thomas. *The Whole Booke of Psalmes: With the Hymnes Evangellical and Songs Spirituall. Composed into four parts by Sundry Authors. . . .* Printed at London, 1621. 2d ed., 1633.

Scholes, Percy A. *The Puritans and Music in England and New England.* New York: Oxford University Press, 1934. Contains a wealth of valuable material and copious bibliographical references.

Sewall, Samuel. *Diary,* ed. by Mark Van Doren. New York: Macy-Masius, 1927. Also edition of the Massachusetts Historical Society in three volumes, 1876–1882.

Smith, Carleton Sprague (ed.). *Early Psalmody in America.* Series I. *The Ainsworth Psalter.* Psalm 65, with settings by Claude Goudimel. New York: The New York Public Library, 1938.

Warrington, James. *Short Titles of Books Relating or Illustrating the History and Practice of Psalmody in the United States.* Privately printed, Philadelphia, 1898.

For two, New England reformers

Chauncey, Nathaniel. *Regular Singing Defended, and proved to be the only true way of singing the songs of the Lord. . . .* New London: Printed and sold by T. Green, 1728.

Curwen, J. Spencer. *Studies in Music Worship*. First Series (2d ed.). London: J. Curwen & Sons, 1888.

Gould, Nathaniel D. *History of Church Music in America*. Boston: A. N. Johnson, 1853.

Hood, George. *History of Music in New England*. Boston: Wilkins, Carter and Company, 1846.

Kouwenhoven, John A. "Some Unfamiliar Aspects of Singing in New England." *The New England Quarterly*, VI, 3 (Sept. 1933), 567-588.

Lowens, Irving. "John Tufts's Introduction to the Singing of Psalm-Tunes (1721-44): The First American Music Textbook." In *Music and Musicians in Early America* (1). (The complete text of Tufts's book is reprinted in the Appendix.)

Mainzer, Joseph. *The Gaelic Psalm Tunes of Ross-shire, etc*. Edinburgh, 1844.

Metcalf, Frank J. *American Psalmody (1721-1820)*. New York: C. F. Hartmann, 1917.

Morison, Samuel Eliot. *Harvard College in the Seventeenth Century*. Cambridge: Harvard University Press, 1936.

Patrick, Millar. *Four Centuries of Scottish Psalmody*. New York: Oxford University Press, 1949.

Staples, Samuel E. *The Ancient Psalmody and Hymnology of New England*. Worcester, Mass.: C. Jillson, 1880.

Symmes, Thomas. *Utiles Dulci. Or, A Joco-Serious Dialogue, concerning regular singing: calculated for a particular town (where it was publicly had, on Friday, Oct. 12, 1772.) but may serve some other places in the same climate*. Boston: Printed by B. Green, for S. Gerrish, in Cornhill, 1723.

Tufts, John. *A Very Plain and Easy Introduction to the Singing of Psalm Tunes*. Boston, 1721. Facsimile edition published by Harry Dichter. Philadelphia: Musical Americana, 1954.

Walter, Thomas. *The Grounds and Rules of Musick Explained, or An Introduction to the Art of Singing by Note*. Boston: Printed by J. Franklin, for S. Gerrish, near the Brick Church in Cornhill, 1721.

For three, Singing dissenters

Andrews, Edward D. *The Gift to Be Simple. Songs, Dances and Rituals of the American Shakers*. New ed. New York: Dover Publications, 1962.

Benson, Louis F. *The English Hymn: Its Development and Use in Worship*. Richmond: John Knox Press, 1962. (Reprint of 1915 edition.)

Bost, George H. *Samuel Davies: Colonial Revivalist and Champion of Religious Tolerance*. (Doctorial dissertation.) The University of Chicago, 1944.

Chauncey, Charles. *Seasonable Thoughts upon the State of Religion in New England. . . .* Boston: Printed by Roger and Fowle for Samuel Eliot in Cornhill, 1743.

Church Music and Musical Life in Pennsylvania in the 18th Century. Publications of the Pennsylvania Society of the Colonial Dames of

America, IV. 3 vols. Philadelphia: Printed for the Society, 1926–1947.

Da Silva, Owen. *Mission Music of California*. Los Angeles: Warren F. Lewis, 1941.

David, Hans T. *Musical Life in the Pennsylvania Settlements of the Unitas Fratrum*. Winston-Salem, N.C.: The Moravian Music Foundation, 1959. (Reprinted from *Transactions of the Moravian Historical Society*, vol. 13, 1942.)

Foote, Henry W. *Three Centuries of American Hymnody*. Hamden, Conn.: Shoe String Press, 1961. (Reprint of the 1940 edition.)

Gerson, Robert A. *Music in Philadelphia*. Philadelphia: Theodore Presser, 1940.

Grider, Rufus A. *Historical Notes on Music in Bethlehem, Pa. (1741–1871)*. Winston-Salem, N.C.: The Moravian Music Foundation, 1957. (Reprint of the original edition published at Philadelphia in 1873.)

Hall, Thomas C. *The Religious Background of American Culture*. Boston: Little, Brown & Company, 1930.

Hess, Albert G. "Observations on the Lamenting Voice of the Hidden Love." *Journal of the American Musicological Society*, V, 3 (1952), 211–223.

Hymns on the Great Festivals and other occasions. London: Printed for M. Cooper at the Globe in Pater-noster-Row and sold by T. Trye near Grays-Inn Gate, Holborn, etc., 1746. (Contains musical settings of Wesleyan hymns by John Frederick Lampe.)

Jackson, George Pullen. *White and Negro Spirituals*. Locust Valley, N.Y.: J. J. Augustin, Inc., 1943.

Learned, Marion D. *Life of Francis Daniel Pastorius, the Founder of Germantown*. Philadelphia: W. J. Campbell, 1908.

McCorkle, Donald M. "John Antes, American Dilettante." *Musical Quarterly*, XLII, 4 (Oct., 1956).

Rau, Albert G., and Hans T. David. *A Catalogue of Music by American Moravians, 1742–1842*. Bethlehem, Pa.: The Moravian Seminary and College for Women, 1938. (Includes 24 plates of selected compositions and facsimiles.)

Sachse, Julius F. *The German Pietists of Provincial Pennsylvania, 1694–1708*. Philadelphia, 1895.

———. *The Journal of Johannes Kelpius, Magister of the Hermits of the Ridge in Pennsylvania, 1694–1708*. Philadelphia, 1893. (Photographically reproduced from the original in the Historical Society of Pennsylvania.)

———. *Music of the Ephrata Cloister*. Lancaster, Pa.: Published by the Author, 1903.

Stevens, Abel. *The History of the Religious Movement of the 18th Century, Called Methodism*. 3 vols. New York: Carlton and Porter, 1858–1861.

Sweet, William Warren. *Religion in the Development of American Culture, 1765–1840*. New York: Charles Scribner's Sons, 1952.

Wesley, John. *A Collection of Psalms and Hymns*. Charles-town, S.C.: Printed by L. Timothy, 1737.

———. *The Journal of the Rev. John Wesley*. Edited by Nehemiah Curnock. 8 vols. London: R. Culley, 1909–1916.

For four, African exiles

Alberts, Arthur S. *Tribal, Folk and Cafe Music of West Africa.* Recorded and edited. Text and Commentaries by Melville Herskovits, Duncan Emrich, Richard Waterman, and Marshall Stearns. New York: Field Recordings, 1950.

Ballanta (-Taylor), Nicholas G. J. *St. Helena Island Spirituals.* New York: G. Schirmer, Inc., 1925.

Bancroft, Frederic. *Slave-Trading in the Old South.* Baltimore: J. H. Furst Co., 1931.

Brandel, Rose. *The Music of Central Africa.* The Hague: Martinus Nijhoff, 1962.

Captain Canot; or, Twenty Years of an African Slaver. Written out and edited from the Captain's Journals, Memoranda, and Conversations, by Brantz Mayer. New York: D. Appleton & Company, Inc., 1854.

Curtis, Natalie. *Songs and Tales from the Dark Continent.* New York: G. Schirmer, Inc., 1920.

Donnan, Elizabeth (ed.). *Documents Illustrative of the Slave Trade to America.* Washington: Carnegie Institution, 1930–35.

DuBois, William E. B. *Black Folk: Then and Now; An Essay in the History and Sociology of the Negro Race.* New York: Henry Holt and Company, Inc., 1939.

Epstein, Dena J. "Slave Music in the United States before 1860: A Survey of Sources." *Notes of the Music Library Association,* XX, 2 (Spring, 1963) and XX, 3 (Summer, 1963).

Fisher, Miles M. *Negro Slave Songs in the United States.* Ithaca: Cornell University Press, 1953.

Gaines, Francis P. *The Southern Plantation: A Study in the Development and the Accuracy of a Tradition.* New York: Columbia University Press, 1924.

Gorer, Geoffrey. *Africa Dances; a Book about West African Negroes.* London: Faber & Faber, Ltd., 1935.

Hare, Maud (Cuney). *Negro Musicians and Their Music.* Washington: The Associated Publishers, Inc., 1936.

Harrison, William P. *The Gospel Among the Slaves.* Nashville: Publishing House of the M. E. Church, 1893.

Herskovits, Melville J. *The Myth of the Negro Past.* New York: Harper & Brothers, 1941.

Jones, A. M. *Studies in African Music.* London: Oxford University Press, 1959.

Jones, Charles C. *The Religious Instruction of the Negroes in the United States.* Savannah: Purse, 1842.

Klingberg, Frank J. *An Appraisal of the Negro in Colonial South Carolina.* Washington: The Associated Publishers, Inc., 1941.

Kolinski, Mieczyslaw. "La música del Oeste Africano." *Revista de Estudios Musicales,* I, 2 (Dec., 1949), 191–215.

Krehbiel, Henry E. *Afro-American Folksongs.* New York: G. Schirmer, Inc., 1914.

Letters from the Rev. Samuel Davies and Others; Shewing the State of Religion in Virginia, South Carolina, &c. Particularly Among the Negroes. London: J. and W. Oliver, 1759.

Merriam, Alan P. "African Music." In Bascom and Herskovits, eds., *Continuity and Change in African Cultures* (Chicago: University of Chicago Press, 1958).

Mordecai, Samuel. *Virginia, Especially Richmond, in By-Gone Days.* 2nd ed. Richmond: West and Johnston, 1860.

Phillips, Ulrich B. *American Negro Slavery.* Baton Rouge: Louisiana State University Press, 1966. (Originally published in 1918.)

———. *Life and Labor in the Old South.* Boston: Little, Brown & Company, 1929.

———. (ed.) *Plantation and Frontier Documents: 1649–1863.* Cleveland: The A. H. Clark Company, 1909.

Stampp, Kenneth M. *The Peculiar Institution: Slavery in the Ante-Bellum South.* New York: Alfred A. Knopf, Inc., 1956.

Ward, W. E. "Music of the Gold Coast." *The Musical Times* (London), LXXIII (Aug., Sept., Oct., 1932).

Waterman, Richard A. "African Influences on the Music of the Americas." In Sol Tax, ed., *Acculturation in the Americas* (Chicago: University of Chicago Press, 1952). Proceedings of the 29th International Congress of Americanists, Vol. II.

———. *African Patterns in Trinidad Negro Music.* Doctoral Dissertation. Department of Anthropology, Northwestern University, Evanston, Illinois, May, 1943. Includes material from a valuable unpublished work by M. Kolinksi, *Die Musik Westafrikas* (see above, under Kolinski).

Wesley, John. *The Journal of the Rev. John Wesley, A.M.* (3)

For five, Gentlemen amateurs

Berman, Eleanor D. *Thomas Jefferson among the Arts.* New York: The Philosophical Library, 1947.

Fithian, Philip Vickers. *Journal & Letters of Philip Vickers Fithian, 1773–1774: A Plantation Tutor of the Old Dominion.* New edition. Williamsburg, Virginia: Colonial Williamsburg, Inc., 1957. Edited, with an Introduction, by Hunter Dickinson Farish.

Franklin, Benjamin. *Complete Works.* Edited by John Bigelow. 10 vols. New York & London: G. P. Putnam's Sons, 1887–1888.

———. *Quatuor pour 3 violons et violoncelle, transcription de Guillaume de Van.* Paris: Odette Lieutier, 1946.

Hastings, George E. *The Life and Works of Francis Hopkinson.* Chicago: The University of Chicago Press, 1926.

Hopkinson, Francis. *Seven Songs for the Harpsichord or Forte Piano.* Philadelphia, 1788. Facsimile edition published by Harry Dichter. Philadelphia: Musical Americana, 1954.

King, A. Hyatt. "The Musical Glasses and Glass Harmonica." *Proceedings of the Royal Musical Association* (London). Session LXXII, 1945–1946, pp. 97–122.

Lichtenwanger, William. "Benjamin Franklin on Music." In *Church Music and Musical Life in Pennsylvania* . . . , vol. 3, part 2, pp. 449–472. (3)

Maurer, Maurer. "A Musical Family in Colonial Virginia." *Musical Quarterly*, XXXIV, 3 (July, 1948).

Molnar, John W. "A Collection of Music in Colonial Virginia: The Ogle Inventory." *Musical Quarterly*, XLIX, 2 (April, 1963).

Smith, Carleton Sprague. "The 1774 Psalm Book of the Reformed Protestant Dutch Church in New York City." *Musical Quarterly*, XXXIV, 1 (Jan., 1948). (Refers to Francis Hopkinson.)

Sonneck, Oscar G. *Early Concert Life in America*. Leipzig: Breitkopf & Härtel, 1907. Reprinted by Musurgia, New York, 1949.

——. *Early Opera in America*. New York: G. Schirmer, Inc., 1915. Reprinted by B. Blom, New York, 1963.

——. *Francis Hopkinson, the first American poet-composer; and James Lyon, patriot, preacher, psalmodist; two studies in early American music*. Washington, D.C.: Printed for the Author by H. L. McQueen, 1905. Reprinted by Da Capo Press, New York, 1966.

——. "The Musical Side of Our First Presidents." In *Suum Cuique; Essays in Music*. New York: G. Schirmer, Inc., 1916.

Wright, Louis B., and Marion Tinling (eds.). *The Great American Gentleman: William Byrd of Westover in Virginia; his secret diary for the years 1709–1712*. New York: G. P. Putnam's Sons, 1963.

For six, Professional emigrants

Drummond, Robert R. "Alexander Reinagle and His Connection with the Musical Life of Philadelphia." *German-American Annals*, n.s., V, 5 (1907), 294–306.

Howard, John Tasker (ed.). *A Program of Early American Piano Pieces*. New York: J. Fischer & Brother, 1931. (Compositions by Carr, Pelissier, Reinagle, Taylor, and others.)

Johnson, H. Earle. *Musical Interludes in Boston, 1795–1830*. New York: Columbia University Press, 1943.

Konkle, Burton A. *Joseph Hopkinson, 1770–1842, Juror, Scholar; Inspirer of the Arts; Author of Hail Columbia*. Philadelphia: University of Pennsylvania Press, 1931.

Krohn, Ernst C. "Alexander Reinagle as Sonatist." *Musical Quarterly*, XVIII, 1 (Jan., 1932).

Lowens, Irving. "Benjamin Carr's *Federal Overture* (1794)." In *Music and Musicians in Early America*. (1)

——. "James Hewitt: Professional Musician." *Ibid.*

Mates, Julian. *The American Musical Stage before 1800*. New Brunswick, N.J.: Rutgers University Press, 1962. (Mostly about Benjamin Carr.)

Maurer, Maurer. "The 'Professor of Musick' in Colonial America." *Musical Quarterly*, XXXVI, 4 (Oct., 1950).

Milligan, Harold V. (ed.) *Pioneer American Composers. A Collection of Early American Songs*. 2 vols. Boston: The Arthur P. Schmidt Company, 1921.

Parker, John R. (ed.). *The Euterpeiad: or Musical Intelligencer. Devoted to* the Diffusion of Musical Information and Belles Lettres. Boston, 1820–1823. Reprinted by Da Capo Press, New York, 1966.

Parker, John R. *Musical Biography; or, Sketches of the Lives and Writings of Eminent Musical Characters*. Boston, 1824.

Redway, Virginia Larkin. "The Carrs, American Music Publishers." *Musical Quarterly*, XVIII, 1 (Jan., 1932).

———. *Music Directory of Early New York City; A File of Musicians, Music Publishers and Musical Instrument-makers in New York directories from 1786 through 1835*. New York: The New York Public Library, 1941.

Reinagle, Alexander. *Four Piano Sonatas*. Edited by Frederick Freedman. New York: Da Capo Press, 1966.

Sonneck, Oscar G. *Bibliography of Early American Secular Music*. Revised and enlarged by William Treat Upton. New edition with preface by Irving Lowens. New York: Da Capo Press, 1964.

———. *Early Concert Life in America*. (5)

———. *Early Opera in America*. (5)

Williams, George W. "Charleston Church Music 1562–1833." *Journal of the American Musicological Society*, VII, 1 (1954), 35–40.

For seven, Native pioneers

Barbour, J. Murray. *The Church Music of William Billings*. East Lansing: Michigan State University Press, 1960.

Behrend, Jeanne (ed.). *Choral Music of the American Folk Tradition*. First and Second Series. Philadelphia: Elkan-Vogel Company, Inc., 1954–1956.

Belcher, Supply. *The Harmony of Maine: being an original composition of psalm and hymn tunes, of various metres . . . with a number of fuging pieces and anthems. Together with a concise introduction to the grounds of musick, and rules for learners. For the use of singing schools and music societies*. Boston: Thomas and Andrews, 1794.

Billings, William. *The Continental Harmony*. Boston: I. Thomas and E. T. Andrews, 1794. Facsimile reprint edited, with an Introduction, by Hans Nathan. Cambridge: The Belknap Press of Harvard University, 1961.

———. *The New-England Psalm-Singer; or American Chorister. Containing a Number of Psalm-Tunes, Anthems and Canons. In Four and Five Parts*. Boston: Printed by Edes and Gill, n.d. [1770].

———. *The Singing Master's Assistant, or Key to Practical Music, being an Abridgement from the New-England Psalm-Singer; together with several other Tunes, never before published*. Boston: Printed by Draper and Folsom, 1778.

Britton, Allen P. *Theoretical Introductions in American Tune-Books to 1800*. Unpublished doctoral dissertation, University of Michigan, 1949. Ann Arbor, Michigan: University Microfilms, No. 1505.

Brooks, Henry M. *Olden-Time Music*. A compilation from newspapers and books. Boston: Ticknor & Co., 1888.

Cheney, Simeon Pease. *The American Singing Book . . . the biographical department containing biographies of 40 of the leading composers, book-makers, etc., of sacred music in America.* . . . Boston: White, Smith & Co., 1879.

Cheney, Simeon Pease. *Brother Cheney's Collection of Old Folks Concert Music, a very careful selection of the old fugue tunes and anthems together with a few new pieces.* . . . Boston: White, Smith & Co., 1879.

Daniel, Ralph T. *The Anthem in New England Before 1800.* Evanston: Northwestern University Press, 1965.

Gilman, Samuel. *Memories of a New England Village Choir . . . By a Member.* Boston: Crosby, Nichols & Co., n.d.

Goldman, Richard Franko (ed.). *Landmarks of Early American Music, 1760–1800.* New York: G. Schirmer, Inc., 1943.

Law, Andrew. *The Musical Primer, or the First Part of the Art of Singing: Containing the Rules of Psalmody . . . together with a number of Practical Lessons and Plain Tunes.* New Haven: 1780.

Lowens, Irving. *Music and Musicians in Early America.* (1) (See especially "The Origins of the American Fuging-Tune.")

Lyon, James. *Urania, or a choice Collection of Psalm-Tunes, Anthems and Hymns from the most approved Authors, with some entirely new; in two, three and four Parts.* . . . Philadelphia: 1761.

Marrocco, W. Thomas. "The Set Piece." *Journal of the American Musicological Society,* XV, 3 (1962), 348–352.

Metcalf, Frank J. *American Writers and Compilers of Sacred Music.* New York and Cincinnati: Abingdon Press, 1925.

Moore, John W. *A Dictionary of Musical Information . . . and a list of modern musical works published in the United States from 1640 to 1875.* Boston: Oliver Ditson & Co., 1876.

Sonneck, Oscar G. *Bibliography of Early American Secular Music.* (6)
———. *Early Concert Life in America.* (5)
———. *Francis Hopkinson and James Lyon.* (5)

Standish, L. W. *The Old Stoughton Musical Society.* Stoughton, Mass.: The Society, 1929.

For eight, Progress and profit

Birge, Edward B. *History of Public School Music in the United States.* Boston: Oliver Ditson Company, 1928.

Hastings, Thomas. *Dissertation on Musical Taste; or General Principles of Taste Applied to the Art of Music.* New York: Mason Brothers, 1853. (First edition published at Albany in 1822.)

John, Robert W. "Elam Ives and the Pestalozzian Theory of Music Education." *Journal of Research in Music Education,* VIII (1960), 45–50.

Johnson, H. Earle. *Hallelujah, Amen! The Story of the Handel and Haydn Society of Boston.* Boston: Bruce Humphries, 1965.

Lucas, G. W. *Remarks on the Musical Conventions in Boston.* Northampton, Mass.: The Author, 1844.

Mason, Henry L. *Hymn-Tunes of Lowell Mason; A Bibliography.* Cambridge: Harvard University Press, 1944.

———. *Lowell Mason, An Appreciation of His Life and Work.* New York: The Hymn Society of America, 1941.

Mason, Lowell (ed.). *The Boston Handel and Haydn Society Collection of Church Music . . .* (10th ed.). Boston: Published by Richardson, Lord and Holbrook, 1831.

Mason, Lowell. *The New Carmina Sacra: or Boston Collection of Church Music. . . .* Boston: Published by Rice and Kendall, Late Willkins, Carter and Company, 1853.

Mason, William. *Memories of a Musical Life.* New York: Century Company, 1901.

Perkins, Charles C., and John S. Dwight. *History of the Handel & Haydn Society of Boston.* Boston: A. Mudge & Sons, 1883.

Proceedings of the Musical Convention Assembled in Boston, August 16, 1838. Boston: Kidder and Wright, 1838.

Rich, Arthur L. *Lowell Mason, "The Father of Singing among the Children."* Chapel Hill: The University of North Carolina Press, 1946.

Scanlon, Mary B. "Thomas Hastings." *Musical Quarterly,* XXXII, 2 (April, 1946).

Seward, T. F. *The Educational Work of Lowell Mason.* Boston: [1879?]. This 32-page book contains (1) Seward's "The Educational Work of Dr. Lowell Mason," pp. 1–21; (2) "Published Works of Dr. Lowell Mason," pp. 22–23; (3) A. W. Thayer's "Lowell Mason," pp. 24–32, this last item reprinted from *Dwight's Journal of Music.*

For nine, The genteel tradition

Brink, Carol. *Harps in the Wind, The Story of the Singing Hutchinsons.* New York: The Macmillan Company, 1947.

Damon, S. Foster (ed.). *Series of Old American Songs.* Providence: Brown University Library, 1936.

Fatout, Paul. "Threnodies of the Ladies' Books." *Musical Quarterly,* XXXI, 4 (Oct., 1945). (Includes numerous musical examples.)

Heaps, Willard A. *The Singing Sixties; The Spirit of Civil War Days Drawn from the Music of the Times.* Norman: University of Oklahoma Press, 1960.

Hewitt, John Hill. *Shadows on the Wall.* Baltimore: Turnbull Brothers, 1877.

Hill, Richard S. "The Mysterious Chord of Henry Clay Work." *Music Library Association Notes,* 2nd ser., X, 2 (March, 1953), and X, 3 (June, 1953).

Hutchinson, John W. *The Story of the Hutchinsons.* 2 vols. Boston: Lee and Shepard, 1896.

Jordan, Philip D. *Singin' Yankees.* Minneapolis: The University of Minnesota Press, 1946.

———, and Lillian Kessler (eds.). *Songs of Yesterday.* New York: Doubleday, Doran & Company, 1941.

Luper, Albert T. (ed.). *Civil War Music.* Special issue of *Civil War History,* IV, 3 (Sept., 1958), containing a series of monographs on this subject.

Root, George Frederick. *The Story of a Musical Life.* Cincinnati: The John Church Company, 1891.

Russell, Henry. *Cheer! Boys, Cheer! Memories of Men and Music.* London: John Macqueen, Hastings House, 1895.

Silber, Irwin (ed.). *Songs of the Civil War*. New York: Columbia University Press, 1960.

For ten, The fasola folk

Aiken, Jesse B. *The Christian Minstrel*. Philadelphia, 1850.
———. *Harmonia Ecclesiae; or, Companion to the Christian Minstrel*. Philadelphia, 1853.
———. *The Imperial Harmony*. New York and Chicago: Bigelow & Main, 1876.
———. *The True Principles of the Science of Music, with a rare collection of a few of the best tunes that are published*. Philadelphia: J. B. Aiken, 1893.
Buchanan, Annabel Morris. *Folk Hymns of America*. New York: J. Fischer & Brother, 1938. Fifty folk-hymn settings from 17 states; with introduction, notes, bibliography, and analyses of modes and tunes.
Davisson, Ananias. *Kentucky Harmony. Or A Choice Collection of Psalm Tunes, Hymns and Anthems . . .* (4th ed.). Harrisonburg, Va.: Printed and sold by the Author, 1821.
Eskew, Harry. "William Walker, 1809–1875: Popular Southern Hymnist." *The Hymn*, XV, 1 (Jan., 1964).
———. "Joseph Funk's 'Allgemein Nützliche Choral-Music' (1816)." In *Thirty-second Report*, Society for the History of the Germans in Maryland. Baltimore, 1966.
Everett, Lemuel C., and A. B. Everett. *The New Thesaurus Musicus; or United States Collection of Church Music . . .* Richmond: Published by the Authors, 1859. (Originally published in 1856.)
———. *The Progressive Church Vocalist . . .* (3rd ed.). New York: Mason Brothers, 1855.
Funk, Joseph, and Sons. *The New Harmonia Sacra: A Compilation of Genuine Church Music*. 22nd ed. Harrisonburg, Va.: H. A. Brunk, 1959.
Hamm, Charles. "Patent Notes in Cincinnati." *Bulletin*, Historical and Philosophical Society of Ohio, XVI, 4 (Oct., 1958), 293–310.
Hauser, William. *The Olive Leaf . . . A Collection of Beautiful Tunes*. Wadley, Jefferson County, Georgia, 1878.
Jackson, George Pullen. *Another Sheaf of White Spirituals*. Gainesville: University of Florida Press, 1952.
———. *Down East Spirituals and Others*. Locust Valley, N.Y.: J. J. Augustin, Inc., 1939.
———. *Spiritual Folk-Songs of Early America*. Locust Valley, N.Y.: J. J. Augustin, Inc., 1937. Reprinted by Peter Smith, 1965.
———. *The Story of the Sacred Harp*. Nashville: Vanderbilt University Press, 1944.
———. *White Spirituals in the Southern Uplands*. New edition, with an introduction by Don Yoder. Hatboro, Penna.: Folklore Associates, 1964. Also reprint of 1933 edition by Dover Publications, New York, 1965.
———. *White and Negro Spirituals*. (3)
Lowens, Irving. *Music and Musicians in Early America*. (See General Bibliography.)

McIntosh, Rigdon M. *Light and Life: A Collection of New Hymns and Tunes for Sunday-schools, prayer meetings, and revival meetings.* Boston: Oliver Ditson Company, 1881.

———. *Tabor; or, the Richmond Collection of Sacred Music.* New York: F. J. Huntington & Company, 1866.

Original Sacred Harp. Denson Revision. Cullman, Alabama: Sacred Harp Publishing Company, 1960.

Seeger, Charles. "Contrapuntal Style in the Three-Voice Shape-Note Hymns." *Musical Quarterly,* XXVI, 4 (Oct., 1940).

Swan, M. L. *New Harp of Columbia.* Nashville, Tenn.: L. D. Schultz, 1921. Facsimile reprint of the 1867 edition of *Harp of Columbia.*

Walker, William. *The Christian Harmony.* Spartanburg, S.C., 1866. Rev. ed. Philadelphia: E. W. Miller, 1901.

———. *The Southern Harmony, and Musical Companion.* New ed. Philadelphia: E. W. Miller, 1854. (Facsimile reprint by the Federal Writers Project, Works Progress Administration, New York, 1939.) New reprint by Pro Musica Americana, Los Angeles, 1966, with Introduction by Glenn C. Wilcox.

White, B. F., and E. J. King. *The Sacred Harp,* 1844. Republished as *The B. F. White Sacred Harp,* Cooper Revision. Troy, Alabama: Sacred Harp Book Company, 1949. (See also above, under *Original Sacred Harp.*)

Wyeth, John. *Wyeth's Repository of Sacred Music, Part Second.* (2d ed.). *Together with a plain and concise Introduction to the Grounds of Music. . . .* Harrisburg, Pa.: By John Wyeth, Printer and Bookseller, 1820. (Facsimile reprint, with a New Introduction by Irving Lowens. New York: Da Capo Press, 1964.)

For eleven, Revivals and camp meetings

Andrews, Edward D. *The Gift to Be Simple.* (3)

Asbury, Samuel E., and Henry E. Meyer. *Old Time White Camp Meeting Spirituals.* Austin, Texas: The Texas Folklore Society, 1932.

Belden, Albert D. *George Whitefield—the Awakener; a Modern Study of the Evangelical Revival.* Nashville, Tenn.: Cokesbury Press, 1930.

Bellinger, Lucius C. *Stray Leaves from the Portfolio of a Local Methodist Preacher.* Macon, Georgia: Printed for the Author by J. W. Burke & Co., 1870.

Candler, Warren A. *Great Revivals and the Great Republic.* Nashville, Tenn.: Publishing House of the M. E. Church; South, Smith & Lamar, Agents, 1904.

Cleveland, Catherine C. *The Great Revival in the West, 1797–1805.* Chicago: University of Chicago Press, 1916.

Davidson, Robert. *History of the Presbyterian Church in the State of Kentucky.* New York, 1847.

Dow, Lorenzo. *History of Cosmopolite; or, The Four Volumes of Lorenzo's Journal . . .* New York: J. C. Totten, 1814.

Eller, Paul H. *Revivalism and the German Churches in Pennsylvania,*

1783–1816. Chicago, Privately Published, 1935. (Distributed by University of Chicago Libraries.)

Goen, C. C. *Revivalism and Separatism in New England, 1740–1800*. New Haven: Yale University Press, 1962.

Hillman, Joseph. *The Revivalist: A Collection of Choice Revival Hymns and Tunes* . . . Rev. L. Hartsough, musical editor. Troy. N.Y.: *c.* 1869.

Johnson, Charles A. *The Frontier Camp Meeting*. Dallas: Southern Methodist University Press, 1955.

Keller, Charles R. *The Second Great Awakening in Connecticut*. New Haven: Yale University Press, 1942.

Maxson, Charles H. *The Great Awakening in the Middle Colonies*. Chicago: University of Chicago Press, 1920.

McDowell, Lucien L. *Songs of the Old Camp Ground*. Ann Arbor, Michigan: Edwards Brothers, 1937.

Mecklin, John M. *The Story of American Dissent*. New York: Harcourt, Brace & Co., 1934.

Sellers, Charles C. *Lorenzo Dow, the Bearer of the Word*. New York: Milton, Balch & Co., 1928.

Smith, Timothy Lawrence. *Revivalism and Social Reform in Mid-Nineteenth-Century America*. New York: Abingdon Press, 1957.

Sweet, William Wallace. *Revivalism in America, Its Origin, Growth, and Decline*. New York: Charles Scribner's Sons, 1944.

Thompson, Charles L. *Times of Refreshing. A History of American Revivals from 1740 to 1877*. Chicago: L. T. Palmer & Co.; Philadelphia: W. R. Thomas, 1877.

Weisberger, Bernard A. *They Gathered at the River; the Story of the Great Revivalists and Their Impact upon Religion in America*. Boston: Little, Brown & Co., 1958.

For twelve, the Negro spiritual

Allen, William Francis, Charles P. Ware, and Lucy McKim Garrison (eds.). *Slave Songs of the United States*. New York: A. Simpson and Company, 1867. Reprinted by Peter Smith, New York, 1951. Rev. ed., Oak Publications, 1965.

Aptheker, Herbert (ed.). *A Documentary History of the Negro People in the United States*. New York: The Citadel Press, 1951.

Ballanta (-Taylor), Nicholas G. J. *St. Helena Island Spirituals*. (4)

Bolton, Dorothy G., and H. T. Burleigh (eds.). *Old Songs Hymnal*. New York: Century Company, 1929.

Botkin, B. A. *Lay My Burden Down: A Folk History of Slavery*. Chicago: University of Chicago Press, 1945.

Burlin, Natalie Curtis. Hampton Series of Negro Folk-Songs. 4 books. New York: G. Schirmer, Inc., 1918–19.

Chase, Gilbert. "A Note on Negro Spirituals." In *Civil War History*, IV, 3 (Sept., 1958).

Courlander, Harold. *Negro Folk Music, U.S.A.* New York: Columbia University Press, 1963.

Epstein, D. J. "Slave Music in the United States before 1860: A Survey of Sources." (4)

Fenner, Thomas P., and F. G. Rathbon. *Cabin and Plantation Songs as Sung by the Hampton Students.* New York: G. P. Putnam's Sons, 1874.

Fisher, Miles M. *Negro Slave Songs in the United States.* (4)

Gordon, Robert W. "The Negro Spiritual." In *The Carolina Low-country.* New York: The Macmillan Company, 1931, pp. 191–222. Also contains "Some Songs the Negro Sang," arranged by Katherine C. Hutson, pp. 225–327.

Grissom, Mary Allen. *The Negro Sings a New Heaven.* Chapel Hill: The University of North Carolina Press, 1930.

Hallowell, Emily (ed.). *Calhoun Plantation Songs.* Boston: C. W. Thompson & Company, 1901.

Hatfield, Edwin F. (compiler). *Freedom's Lyre; or, Psalms, Hymns and Sacred Songs, for the slave and his friends.* New York: S. W. Benedict, 1840.

Jackson, G. P. *White and Negro Spirituals.* (3)

Jackson, L. P. "Religious Development of the Negro in Virginia from 1760 to 1860." *Journal of Negro History,* XVI (1931), 168–239.

Johnson, Guy B. *Folk Culture on St. Helena Island, South Carolina.* Chapel Hill: The University of North Carolina Press, 1930.

Kemble, Francis Anne. *Journal of a Residence on a Georgia Plantation in 1838–39.* New edition. New York: Alfred A. Knopf, 1961.

Krehbiel, H. E. *Afro-American Folksongs.* (4)

Marsh, J. B. T. *The Story of the Jubilee Singers, with Their Songs.* Boston: Houghton, Osgood & Company, 1880.

McIlhenny, Edward A. *Befo' de War Spirituals.* Boston: Christopher Publishing House, 1933.

Murphy, Jeannette Robinson. "The Survival of African Music in America." *Popular Science Monthly,* LV (Sept., 1899), 600–672.

Odum, Howard W., and Guy B. Johnson. *The Negro and His Songs.* Chapel Hill: The University of North Carolina Press, 1925. Reprinted by Folklore Associates, 1964, with a Foreword by Roger D. Abrahams.

Parrish, Lydia. *Slave Songs of the Georgia Sea Islands.* Music transcribed by Creighton Churchill and Robert MacGinsey. New York: Creative Age Press, Inc., 1942.

Parsons, Elsie Clews. *Folk Tales of the Sea Islands. Memoirs of the American Folklore Society,* No. 16. Cambridge, Mass.: The Society, 1923. (Includes eighteen songs.)

Scarborough, Dorothy. *On the Trail of Negro Folk-Songs.* Cambridge: Harvard University Press, 1925. Reprinted by Folklore Associates, 1963, with a Foreword by Roger D. Abrahams.

Seward, Theodore F. *Jubilee Songs as Sung by the Jubilee Singers of Fisk University.* New York: Bigelow & Main, 1872.

Waterman, Richard A. " 'Hot' Rhythm in Negro Music." *Journal of the American Musicological Society,* I, 1 (1948).

White, Newman I. *American Negro Folksongs.* Cambridge: Harvard University Press, 1928. Reprinted by Folklore Associates, 1965, with a Foreword by Bruce Jackson.

Work, John W. *American Negro Songs.* New York: Howell, Soskin Publishers, 1940.
Consult also the bibliography for Chapter 4.

For thirteen, The Ethiopian business

Burleigh, Henry T. *Negro Minstrel Melodies.* New York: G. Schirmer, Inc., 1910.
Damon, S. Foster (ed.). *Series of Old American Songs.* (9)
Galbreath, C. B. *Daniel Decatur Emmett, Author of Dixie.* Columbus, Ohio: F. J. Heer, 1904.
Loesser, Arthur. *Humor in American Song.* New York: Howell, Soskin, Inc., 1941.
Nathan, Hans. *Dan Emmett and the Rise of Early Negro Minstrelsy.* Norman: University of Oklahoma Press, 1962.
Paskman, Daily, and Sigmund Spaeth. *"Gentlemen, Be Seated!" A Parade of the Old-Time Minstrels.* New York: Doubleday, Doran & Co., 1928.
Rice, Edward LeRoy. *Monarchs of Minstrelsy, From "Daddy" Rice to Date.* New York: Kenney Publishing Co., 1911.
Rourke, Constance. *American Humor.* New Edition. New York: Doubleday & Company, 1953.
White, Newman. *American Negro Folksongs.* (12)
Wittke, Carl. *Tambo and Bones, a History of the American Minstrel Stage.* Durham: Duke University Press, 1930.
Consult also the bibliography for Chapter 14.

For fourteen, America's minstrel

Foster, Morrison. *My Brother Stephen.* Indianapolis: Privately printed for the Foster Hall Collection, 1932.
————. *Songs and Musical Compositions of Stephen Collins Foster.* Pittsburgh, 1896.
Foster, Stephen Collins. *Songs, Compositions and Arrangements.* Foster Hall Reproductions. Indianapolis: Privately printed for the Foster Hall Collection by J. Kirby Lilly, 1933.
Fuld, James J. *A Pictorial History of the First Editions of Stephen C. Foster.* Philadelphia: Musical Americana, 1957.
Gombosi, Otto. "Stephen Foster and 'Gregory Walker.'" *Musical Quarterly,* XXX, 2 (April, 1944).
Howard, J. T. *Stephen Foster, America's Troubadour.* New edition. New York: Thomas Y. Crowell Company, 1953.
Jackson, George P. "Stephen Foster's Debt to American Folk-Song." *Musical Quarterly,* XXII, 2 (April, 1936).
Milligan, Harold V. *Stephen Foster, A Biography.* New York: G. Schirmer, Inc., 1920.
Morneweck, Evelyn Foster. *Chronicles of Stephen Foster's Family.* 2 vols.

Pittsburgh: Published for the Foster Hall Collection by the University of Pittsburgh Press, 1944.

Sonneck, Oscar G., and Walter Whittlesey. *Catalogue of the First Editions of Stephen C. Foster.* Washington, D.C.: The Library of Congress, 1915.

Walters, Raymond W. *Stephen Foster: Youth's Golden Gleam; a Sketch of His Life and Background in Cincinnati, 1846–1850.* Princeton: Princeton University Press, 1936.

For fifteen, The exotic periphery

Allen, William Francis, *et alter* (eds.). *Slave Songs of the United States.* (12)

Arpin, Paul. *Life of Louis Moreau Gottschalk.* Translated from the French by H. C. Watson. New York, 1852.

Asbury, Herbert. *The French Quarter.* New York: Alfred A. Knopf, Inc., 1938.

Cable, George W. "Creole Slave Songs." *The Century Magazine*, XXXI, 6 (April, 1886).

———. "The Dance in Place Congo." *Ibid.*, XXXI, 4 (Feb., 1886).

Carpentier, Alejo. *La Música en Cuba.* México, D.F.: Fondo de Cultura Económica, 1946.

Fors, Luis Ricardo. *Gottschalk.* Havana, 1880.

Gottschalk, Louis Moreau. *Notes of a Pianist,* edited by his sister, Clara Gottschalk. Philadelphia: J. B. Lippincott, 1881. (New edition, edited with notes by Jeanne Behrend. New York: Alfred A. Knopf, 1964.)

Grenet, Emilio (ed.). *Popular Cuban Music,* Havana, 1939.

Hearn, Lafcadio. *Two Years in the French West Indies.* New York: Harper & Brothers, 1890.

Hensel, Octavia. *Life and Letters of Louis Moreau Gottschalk.* Boston: Oliver Ditson Company, 1870.

Krehbiel, H. E. *Afro-American Folksongs.* (4)

Lange, Francisco Curt. "Vida y Muerte de Louis Moreau Gottschalk en Rio de Janeiro (1869)." *Revista de Estudios Musicales* (Mendoza, Argentina), Año II, Nos. 4, 5–6 (1950–1951).

Lindstrom, Carl E. "The American Quality in the Music of Louis Moreau Gottschalk." *Musical Quarterly*, XXXI, 3 (July, 1945).

Loggins, Vernon. *Where the World Ends; The Life of Louis Moreau Gottschalk.* Baton Rouge: Louisiana State University Press, 1958.

Peterson, Clara Gottschalk. *Creole Songs from New Orleans.* New Orleans: L. Gruenwald Company, 1902.

Whitfield, Irène Thérèse. *Louisiana French Folk Songs.* Baton Rouge: Louisiana State University Press, 1937.

For sixteen, Europe versus America

Armstrong, W. G. *A Record of the Opera in Philadelphia.* Philadelphia: Porter and Coates, 1844.

Goodrich, A. J. *Complete Musical Analysis.* Cincinnati: The John Church

Company, 1889. (Includes analyses of works by Paine, Pratt, Buck, Gilchrist, and Gleason.)

Hipsher, Edward E. *American Opera and Its Composers.* (30)

Howe, M. A. De Wolfe. "John Knowles Paine." *Musical Quarterly*, XXV, 3 (July, 1939).

Huneker, James G. *The Philharmonic Society of New York and Its 75th Anniversary.* New York: The Society, 1917.

Krehbiel, H. E. *Notes on the Cultivation of Choral Music and the Oratorio Society in New York.* New York: E. Schuberth and Company, 1884.

———. *The Philharmonic Society of New York.* New York and London: Novello, Ewer and Company, 1892.

Lanier, Sidney. *Music and Poetry: Essays upon Some Aspects and Inter-relations between the Two Arts.* New York: Charles Scribner's Sons, 1898.

Lowens, Irving. "William Henry Fry: American Nationalist." In *Music and Musicians in Early America.* (1)

Mason, William. *Memories of a Musical Life.* New York: Century Company, 1902.

Mathews, W. S. B. (ed.) *One Hundred Years of Music in America.* (See General Bibliography.)

Mattfeld, Julius. *A Hundred Years of Grand Opera in New York (1825–1925).* New York: The New York Public Library, 1927.

Mims, Edwin. *Sidney Lanier.* Boston: Houghton Mifflin Company, 1905.

New York Philharmonic Journal, ed. by Edward Jerome Hopkins. New York: The Society, 1868–1885.

Starke, Aubrey H. *Sidney Lanier: A Biographical and Critical Study.* Chapel Hill: University of North Carolina Press, 1933.

———. "Sidney Lanier as a Musician." *Musical Quarterly*, XX, 4 (Oct., 1934).

Thorpe, Harry C. "Sidney Lanier: A Poet for Musicians." *Musical Quarterly*, XI, 3 (July, 1925).

Upton, William Treat. *The Musical Works of William Henry Fry in the Collection of The Library Company of Philadelphia.* A Research Bulletin of The Free Library of Philadelphia. Philadelphia, 1946.

———. *William Henry Fry, American Journalist and Composer-Critic.* New York: Thomas Y. Crowell Company, 1954.

Consult also the *Dictionary of American Biography* for articles on Bristow, Buck, Fry, Gilchrist, Gleason, Paine, Pratt.

For seventeen, A romantic bard

Brown, Rollo W. *Lonely Americans.* New York: Coward-McCann, Inc., 1929.

Butler, Nicholas Murray. "Columbia and the Department of Music." *The New York Times,* Feb. 8, 1904. Reprinted by Columbia University, 1904.

Currier, T. P. "MacDowell as I Knew Him." *Musical Quarterly*, I, 1 (Jan., 1915).

Erskine, John. "Edward MacDowell." *Dictionary of American Biography,* vol. 12, pp. 24–27.

Erskine, John. "MacDowell at Columbia: Some Recollections." *Musical Quarterly*, XXVIII, 4 (Oct., 1942).

Gilbert, Henry F. B. "Personal Recollections of Edward MacDowell." *New Music Review*, II, 132 (1912).

Gilman, Lawrence. *Edward MacDowell, A Study*. New York: John Lane Company, 1908.

MacDowell, Edward. *Critical and Historical Essays*. Edited by W. J. Batzell. Boston: The Arthur P. Schmidt Company, 1912.

Matthews, J. Brander (ed.). *Commemorative Tributes to Edward Mac-Dowell*. New York: American Academy of Arts and Letters, 1922.

Page, Elizabeth F. *Edward MacDowell, His Work and Ideals*. New York: Dodge Publishing Company, 1910.

Porte, John F. *Edward MacDowell, A Great American Tone Poet*. London: Kegan Paul, Trench, Trubner & Co., 1922.

Rosenfeld, Paul. *An Hour with American Music*. (See General Bibliography.)

Sonneck, Oscar G. *Catalogue of the First Editions of Edward MacDowell*. Washington, D.C.: The Library of Congress, 1917.

———. *Suum Cuique*. (5) Includes "MacDowell vs. MacDowell."

For eighteen, The Boston classicists

Chadwick, George W. *Commemorative Tribute to Horatio Parker*. New Haven: Yale University Press, 1921. Also in American Academy of Arts and Letters Publication No. 23 (New York, 1922).

Engel, Carl. "George W. Chadwick." *Musical Quarterly*, X, 3 (July, 1924).

Howe, M. A. De Wolfe. *The Boston Symphony Orchestra*. Boston: Houghton Mifflin Company, 1914.

Hughes, Rupert. *Contemporary American Composers*. (See General Bibliography.)

Klein, Sister Mary Justina. *The Contribution of Daniel Gregory Mason to American Music*. Washington, D.C.: Catholic University of America Press, 1957.

Langley, Allen L. "George Chadwick and the New England Conservatory of Music." *Musical Quarterly*, XXI, 1 (Jan., 1935).

Leichtentritt, Hugo. *Serge Koussevitzky, the Boston Symphony Orchestra, and the New American Music*. Cambridge: Harvard University Press, 1946.

Mason, Daniel Gregory. "Arthur Whiting." *Musical Quarterly*, XXIII, 1 (Jan., 1937).

———. *Music in My Time, and Other Reminiscences*. New York: The Macmillan Company, 1938.

Semler, Isabel Parker. *Horatio Parker; a Memoir for his grandchildren, compiled from letters and papers . . . in collaboration with Pierson Underwood*. New York: G. P. Putnam's Sons, 1942. Includes "Works of H. W. Parker, compiled by Oliver W. Strunk."

Smith, David Stanley. "A Study of Horatio Parker." *Musical Quarterly*, XXVI, 3 (July, 1940).

Spalding, Walter Raymond. *Music at Harvard*. New York: Coward-Mc-Cann, Inc., 1935.

Spalding, Walter Raymond. *Music: An Art and a Language*. Boston: The Arthur P. Schmidt Company, 1920.

Tuthill, Burnet C. "Mrs. H. H. A. Beach." *Musical Quarterly*, XXVI, 3 (July, 1940).

For nineteen, Nationalism and folklore

Baker, Theodore. *Über die Musik der Nordamerikanischen Wilden*. Leipzig: Breitkopf & Härtel, 1882.

Burton, Frederick R. *American Primitive Music, with special attention to the songs of the Ojibways*. New York: Moffat, Yard & Company, 1909.

Carter, Elliott. "American Figure, with Landscape." *Modern Music* (May-June, 1943). (Deals with Henry F. B. Gilbert.)

Clapham, John. "The Evolution of Dvořák's Symphony 'From the New World.'" *Musical Quarterly*, XLIV, 2 (April, 1958).

Curtis, Natalie. *The Indians' Book*. An offering by the American Indians of Indian lore, musical and narrative, to form a record of the songs and legends of their race. New York and London: Harper & Brothers, n.d. [1907].

Densmore. Frances. *The American Indians and Their Music*. New York: The Women's Press, 1926.

Downes, Olin. "An American Composer." *Musical Quarterly*, IV, 1 (Jan., 1918). (Deals with Henry F. B. Gilbert.)

Farwell, Arthur. "An Affirmation of American Music." Reprinted in *The American Composer Speaks*, edited by Chase. (See General Bibliography.)

Fillmore, John C. *The Harmonic Structure of Indian Music*. New York: G. P. Putnam's Sons, 1899.

Fletcher, Alice C. *Indian Story and Song from North America*. Boston: Small, Maynard & Co., 1900.

Gilman, Benjamin Ives. "Zuñi Melodies." *A Journal of American Ethnology and Archaeology*, I (1891), 63–91.

———. "Hopi Songs." *Ibid.*, V (1908).

Howard, J. T. *Charles Sanford Skilton*. New York: Carl Fischer, Inc., 1929.

Nettl, Bruno. *North American Indian Musical Styles*. Philadelphia: American Folklore Society, 1954.

Salter, Sumner. "Early Encouragements to American Composers." *Musical Quarterly*, XVIII, 1 (Jan., 1932).

Seeger, Charles. "Nationalism, Traditionalism and the American Composer." In *Report of the Second Inter-American Conference on Ethnomusicology*. Held at Bloomington, Indiana, April 24–28, 1965. Bloomington: Indiana University Press, 1966.

Upton, William Treat. *Anthony Philip Heinrich*. New York: Columbia University Press, 1939.

Waters, Edward N. "The Wa-Wan Press: An Adventure in Musical Idealism." In *A Birthday Offering to Carl Engel*, edited by Gustave Reese. New York: G. Schirmer, Inc., 1943.

For twenty, Composer from Connecticut

Bellamann, Henry. "Charles Ives: The Man and His Music." *Musical Quarterly*, XIX, 1 (Jan., 1933).

Copland, Aaron. "One Hundred and Fourteen Songs." *Modern Music*, XI, 2 (Jan.-Feb., 1934).

Cowell, Henry and Sidney. *Charles Ives and His Music*. New York: Oxford University Press, 1955.

Hall, David. "Charles Ives: An American Original." *HiFi/Stereo Review*, XIII, 3 (Sept., 1964).

Ives, Charles. *Essays before a Sonata*. Edited by Howard Boatwright. New York: W. W. Norton & Company, Inc., 1961.

———. *Symphony No. 4*. With a Preface by John Kirkpatrick. New York: Associated Music Publishers, 1965. (This is a facsimile edition of the performance score used for the première of the work in New York on April 26, 1965.)

Mellers, Wilfrid. "Realism and Transcendentalism: Charles Ives as American Hero." In *Music in a New Found Land*. (See General Bibliography.)

Rosenfeld, Paul. *Discoveries of a Music Critic*. New York: Harcourt, Brace & Company, Inc., 1936.

Schonberg, Harold. "America's Greatest Composer." *Esquire*, L, 6 (Dec., 1958).

Taubman, Howard. "Posterity Catches Up with Charles Ives." *The New York Times Magazine* (Oct. 23, 1949).

Yates, Peter. "Charles Ives." *Arts and Architecture*, LXVII, 10 (Feb., 1950).

For twenty-one, The rise of ragtime

Blesh, Rudi, and Harriet Janis. *They All Played Ragtime: The True Story of an American Music*. New rev. ed. New York: Alfred A. Knopf, Inc., 1959.

Borneman, Ernest, and Bartlett D. Simms. "History and Analysis of Ragtime." *The Record Changer* (Oct., 1945).

Campbell, S. Bronson. "Early Great White Ragtime Composers and Pianists." *Jazz Journal*, II (May, 1949).

———. "Ragtime Begins." *The Record Changer*, VIII (March, 1948).

Charters, Ann (ed.). *The Ragtime Songbook*. New York: Oak Publications, 1965.

Confrey, Zez. *Modern Course in Novelty Piano Playing*. New York: Mills Music Company, Inc., 1923.

Gardner, Carl E. "Ragging and Jazzing." *Metronome* (New York), XXXV, 10 (1919).

Hearn, Lafcadio. *American Miscellany; articles and stories now first collected by Albert Mordell*. 2 vols. New York: Dodd, Mead & Company, Inc., 1924.

Hughes, Rupert. "A Eulogy of Ragtime." *The Musical Record* (Boston), No. 447 (April, 1899).

Witmark, Isidore. *The Story of the House of Witmark: From Ragtime to Swingtime*. New York: Lee Furman, Inc., 1939.

For twenty-two, Singin' the blues

Bradford, Perry. *Born with the Blues*. New York: Oak Publications, 1965.

Charters, Samuel B. *The Country Blues*. New York: Rinehart, 1959.

Ellington, Duke. *Piano Method for Blues*. New York: Robbins Music Corporation, 1943.

Gombosi, Otto. "The Pedigree of the Blues." *Proceedings of the Music Teachers National Association*, 40th ser., 70th year. Pittsburgh: Published by the Association, 1946.

Greene, Maude. "The Background of the Beale Street Blues." *Bulletin of the Tennessee Folklore Society*, VIII (1941).

Handy, William Christopher (ed.). *A Treasury of the Blues*. With an historical and critical text by Abbe Niles. New York: Published by Charles Boni, distributed by Simon and Schuster, 1949. (Originally published in 1926.)

———. *Father of the Blues: An Autobiography*. New York: The Macmillan Company, 1941.

Jones, LeRoi. *Blues People: Negro Music in White America*. New York: William Morrow, 1963.

Keil, Charles. *Urban Blues*. Chicago: University of Chicago Press, 1966. Important study by a jazz musician and anthropologist.

Lomax, John A. and Alan. *Negro Folk Songs as Sung by Lead Belly*. New York: The Macmillan Company, 1936.

Mezzrow, Milton, and Bernard Wolfe. *Really the Blues*. New York: Random House, 1946.

Oliver, Paul. *Conversations with the Blues*. New York: Horizon Press, 1965.

Silverman, Jerry (ed. and arr.). *Folk Blues*. New York: The Macmillan Company, 1958.

For twenty-three, The growth of jazz

Armstrong, Louis. *Swing that Music*. New York: Longmans, Green & Co., Inc. 1936.

———. *Satchmo: My Life in New Orleans*. New York: Prentice-Hall, 1954.

Balliett, Whitney. *The Sound of Surprise*. New York: E. P. Dutton & Co., 1959.

Blesh, Rudi. *Shining Trumpets: A History of Jazz*. New York: Alfred A. Knopf, Inc., 1946. (Revised edition, 1958.)

Borneman, Ernest. *A Critic Looks at Jazz*. London: Jazz Music Books, 1946.

Brunn, H. O. *The Story of the Original Dixieland Jazz Band*. Baton Rouge: Louisiana State University Press, 1960.

Charters, Samuel B. *Jazz: New Orleans 1885–1957*. New York: Walter C. Allen, 1958.

Condon, Eddie, and Thomas A. Sugrue. *We Called It Music*. New York: Henry Holt & Company, Inc., 1947.

Delaunay, Charles. *New Hot Discography* (2nd ed.), edited by W. E. Schaap and George Avakian. New York: Criterion Music Corporation, 1948.

Feather, Leonard. *The Book of Jazz*. Rev. ed. New York: Horizon Press, 1965.

———. *The Encyclopedia of Jazz*. New edition. New York: Bonanza Books, 1962.

———. *Inside Jazz*. New York: Consolidated Music Publishers, Inc., 1949. (Originally published as *Inside Be-bop*.)

Finkelstein, Sidney. *Jazz: A People's Music*. New York: The Citadel Press, 1948.

Gammon, Peter. *Duke Ellington and His Music*. New York: Roy Publishers, 1958.

Goffin, Robert. *Jazz, from the Congo to the Metropolitan*. New York: Doubleday, Doran & Company, 1944.

———. *Horn of Plenty: The Story of Louis Armstrong*. New York: Allen, Towne & Heath, 1947.

Goodman, Benny, and Irving Kolodin. *The Kingdom of Swing*. Harrisburg, Pa.: Stackpole Sons, 1939.

Green, Benny. *The Reluctant Art: The Growth of Jazz*. New York: Horizon Press, 1963.

Grossman, William L., and J. W. Farrell. *The Heart of Jazz*. New York: New York University Press, 1956.

Hadlock, Richard. *Jazz Masters of the Twenties*. New York: The Macmillan Co., 1965.

Harrison, Max. *Charlie Parker*. New York: A. S. Barnes and Co., 1961.

Hentoff, Nat (ed.) *Jazz; New Perspectives on the History of Jazz by Twelve of the World's Foremost Jazz Critics and Scholars*. New York: Rinehart, 1959.

Hobson, Wilder. *American Jazz Music*. New York: W. W. Norton & Company, 1939.

Hodeir, André. *Jazz: Its Evolution and Essence*. Translated by David Noakes. New York: Grove Press, 1956.

Horricks, Raymond. *Count Basie and His Orchestra, Its Music and Its Musicians*. With Discography by Alun Morgan. New York: Citadel Press, 1957.

James, Michael. *Miles Davis*. London: Cassell and Company, 1961.

Keepnews, Orrin, and Bill Grauer. *A Pictorial History of Jazz*, New York: Crown Publishers, 1955.

Lambert, George. *Duke Ellington*. New York: A. S. Barnes and Co., 1961.

Lomax, Alan. *Mister Jelly Roll*. New York: Duell, Sloan & Pearce, Inc., 1950. (Paperback ed., Grove Press, 1956.)

McCarthy, Albert J. *Louis Armstrong*. New York: A. S. Barnes and Co., 1961.

Merriam, Alan P. *A Bibliography of Jazz*. [Compiled] with the assistance of Robert J. Benford. Philadelphia: American Folklore Society, 1954.

Morgan, Alun, and Raymond Horricks. *Modern Jazz; A Survey of Developments Since 1939*. London. V. Gollancz, 1957.

Panassie, Hugues. *The Real Jazz*. New York: Smith & Durrell, 1942.

Ramsey, Frederic, and Charles Edward Smith. *Jazzmen.* New York: Harcourt, Brace & Company, Inc., 1939. (Paperback ed., Harvest, 1959.)

Sargeant, Winthrop. *Jazz: A History.* New edition. New York: McGraw-Hill Book Co., Inc., 1964. (Originally published as *Jazz: Hot and Hybrid,* 1938.)

Shapiro, Nat, and Nat Hentoff (eds.). *Hear Me Talkin' to Ya; The Story of Jazz by the Men Who Made It.* New York: Rinehart, 1955.

Stearns, Marshall W. *The Story of Jazz.* New York: Oxford University Press, 1956.

Toledano, Ralph de (ed.). *Frontiers of Jazz.* New York: Oliver Durrell, Inc., 1947.

Ulanov, Barry. *Duke Ellington.* New York: Creative Age Press, Inc., 1946.

———. *A Handbook of Jazz.* New York: The Viking Press, Inc., 1957.

———. *A History of Jazz in America.* New York: The Viking Press, Inc., 1952.

Williams, Martin T. (ed.). *The Art of Jazz; Essays on the Nature and Development of Jazz.* New York: Grove Press, 1960.

———. *Jelly Roll Morton.* London: Cassell and Co., Ltd., 1962.

For twenty-four, The Americanists

Armitage, Merle. *George Gershwin, Man and Legend.* New York: Duell, Sloan and Pearce, 1958.

Berger, Arthur. *Aaron Copland.* New York: Oxford University Press, 1953.

Ewen, David. *A Journey to Greatness. The Life and Music of George Gershwin.* New York: Henry Holt & Company, 1956.

Farwell, Arthur. "Roy Harris." *Musical Quarterly,* XVIII, 1 (Jan., 1932).

Gershwin, George. *George Gershwin's Song Book.* New York: Simon and Schuster, 1930.

Goldberg, Isaac. *George Gershwin, A Study in American Music.* New edition. Supplemented by Edith Garson. With Foreword and Discography by Alan Dashiell. New York: Frederick Ungar Publishing Co., 1958.

Jablonski, Edward, and Lawrence D. Stewart. *The Gershwin Years.* With an Introduction by Carl Van Vechten. Garden City, N.Y.: Doubleday, 1958.

Slonimsky, Nicolas. "Roy Harris." *Musical Quarterly,* XXXIII, 1 (Jan., 1947).

Smith, Julia F. *Aaron Copland: His Work and Contribution to American Music.* New York: E. P. Dutton & Company, 1955.

Weisgall, Hugo. "The Music of Henry Cowell." *Musical Quarterly,* XLV, 4 (Oct., 1959).

(Consult also the works by Copland, Cowell, and Mellers in the General Bibliography.)

For twenty-five, The eclectics

Briggs, John. *Leonard Bernstein: the Man, His Works, and His World.* Cleveland: World Publishing Co., 1961.

Broder, Nathan. "The Music of William Schuman." *Musical Quarterly*, XXXI, 1 (Jan., 1945).
Cowell, Henry. "Paul Creston." *Musical Quarterly*, XXXIV, 4 (Oct., 1948).
Downes, Edward. "The Music of Norman Dello Joio." *Musical Quarterly*, XLVIII, 2 (April, 1962).
Glanville-Hicks, Peggy. "Virgil Thomson." *Musical Quarterly*, XXXV, 2 (April, 1949).
Hoover, Kathleen, and John Cage. *Virgil Thomson: His Life and Music.* New York: Thomas Yoseloff, 1959.
Maisel, Edward M. *Charles T. Griffes; The Life of an American Composer.* New York: Alfred A. Knopf, Inc., 1943.
Newman, William S. "Arthur Shepherd." *Musical Quarterly*, XXXVI, 2 (April, 1950).
Schreiber, Flora R., and Vincent Persichetti. *William Schuman.* New York: G. Schirmer, Inc., 1954.
Schubart, Mark A. "Roger Sessions." *Musical Quarterly*, XXXII, 2 (April, 1946).

For twenty-six, The traditionalists

Alter, Martha. "Howard Hanson." *Modern Music*, XVIII, 2 (Jan.-Feb., 1941).
Austin, William. "The Music of Robert Palmer." *Musical Quarterly*, XLII, 1 (Jan., 1956).
Broder, Nathan. *Samuel Barber.* New York: G. Schirmer, Inc., 1954.
Carter, Elliott. "Walter Piston." *Musical Quarterly*, XXXII, 3 (July, 1946).
———. "Shop Talk by an American Composer." *Musical Quarterly*, XLVI, 2 (April, 1960).
Citkowitz, Israel. "Walter Piston—Classicist." *Modern Music*, XIII, 2 (Jan.-Feb., 1936).
Diamond, David. "Bernard Rogers." *Musical Quarterly*, XXXIII, 2 (April, 1947).
Goldman, Richard Franko. "The Music of Elliott Carter." *Musical Quarterly*, XLIII, 2 (April, 1957).
Riker, Charles. *The Eastman School of Music: Its First Quarter Century, 1921–1946.* Rochester: The University of Rochester, 1948.
Ringer, Alexander. "Leon Kirchner." *Musical Quarterly*, XLIII, 1 (Jan., 1957).
Skulsky, Abraham. "Elliott Carter." *Bulletin of the American Composers Alliance*, III, 2 (Summer, 1953).
Tuthill, Burnet C. "Howard Hanson." *Musical Quarterly*, XXII, 2 (April, 1936).

For twenty-seven, Innovation and experiment

Antheil, George. *Bad Boy of Music.* New York: Doubleday, Doran & Co., 1945.
Becker, John L. "Finding a Personal Orchestral Idiom." *Musical America* (Feb., 1950).

Buchanan, C. L. "Ornstein and Modern Music." *Musical Quarterly,* IV, 2 (April, 1918).

Cage, John. *Silence.* Middletown, Conn.: Wesleyan University Press, 1961. (The collected lectures and writings of Cage.)

Carter, Elliott. "Expressionism and American Music." *Perspectives of New Music,* IV, 1 (Fall-Winter 1965), 1–13.

Chou Wen-chung. "Varèse: A Sketch of the Man and His Music." *Musical Quarterly,* LII, 2 (April, 1966).

Cowell, Henry. "The Music of Edgard Varèse." *Modern Music* (Jan.–Feb., 1928).

———— (ed.). *American Composers on American Music.* (See General Bibliography.)

————. *New Musical Resources.* New York: Alfred A. Knopf, 1930.

Dunn, Robert (ed.). *John Cage.* New York: Henmar Press, Inc., 1962. (Includes catalogue of works, recordings, bibliographies, and an interview between Cage and Roger Reynolds.)

Harrison, Lou. *About Carl Ruggles.* New York: Published by Oscar Bardiansky at the Alicat Bookshop in Yonkers, 1946.

Hiller, Lejaren A., and Leonard M. Isaacson. *Experimental Music: Composition with an Electronic Computer.* New York: McGraw-Hill Book Co., 1959. (Includes full score of the *Illiac Suite.*)

Partch, Harry. *Genesis of a Music; Monophony: the Relation of Its Music to Historic and Contemporary Trends; Its Philosophy, Concepts, and Principles; Its Relation to Historic and Proposed Intonations; and Its Application to Musical Instruments.* Madison: University of Wisconsin Press, 1949.

Pound, Ezra. *George Antheil and the Treatise on Harmony.* Paris, 1925.

Schuller, Gunther. "Conversations with Varèse." *Perspectives of New Music,* III, 2 (Spring-Summer, 1965).

Seeger, Charles. "Carl Ruggles." *Musical Quarterly,* XVIII, 4 (Oct., 1932).

Waldman, Frederick. "Edgard Varèse: An Appreciation." *Juilliard Review,* I (Fall, 1954).

Weisgall, Hugo. "The Music of Henry Cowell." (24)

Wilkinson, Marc. "An Introduction to the Music of Edgar [*sic*] Varèse." *The Score* (London), No. 19 (March, 1957).

Yates, Peter. "The Music of Harry Partch." *American Record Guide,* No. 21 (Jan., 1955).

For twenty-eight, Twelve-tone trends

Babbitt, Milton. "Who Cares If You Listen?" In *The American Composer Speaks,* edited by Chase. (See General Bibliography.)

Bruno, Anthony. "Two American Twelve-tone Composers." *Musical America,* 71 (Feb., 1951). Deals with Babbitt and Weber.

Goldman, Richard Franko. "The Music of Wallingford Riegger." *Musical Quarterly,* XXXVI, 1 (Jan., 1950).

Hill, Richard S. "Schoenberg's Tone-Rows and the Music of the Future." *Musical Quarterly,* XXX, 4 (Oct., 1944).

Krenek, Ernst. "A Composer's Influences." *Perspectives of New Music,* III, 1 (Fall-Winter, 1964).

Leibowitz, René. *Schoenberg and His School: The Contemporary Stage of* the *Language of Music*. Translated from the French by Dika Newlin. New York: The Philosophical Library, 1949.

O'Hara, Frank. "About Ben Weber." *Bulletin of the American Composers Alliance*, V, 2 (1955).

Perle, George. *Serial Composition and Atonality*. Berkeley: University of California Press, 1962.

———. "Atonality and the Twelve-note System in the United States." *The Score* (London), No. 27 (July, 1960), 51–66.

Rochberg, George. *The Hexachord and Its Relation to the Twelve-Tone Row*. Bryn Mawr, Pa.: Theodore Presser, 1955.

Rubsamen, Walter. "Schoenberg in America." *Musical Quarterly*, XXXVII, 4 (Oct., 1951).

Rufer, Josef. *Composition with Twelve Notes*. Translated by Humphrey Searle. New York: The Macmillan Company, 1954.

Schoenberg, Arnold. "My Evolution." *Musical Quarterly*, XXXVIII, 4 (Oct., 1952).

———. *Style and Idea*. New York: The Philosophical Library, 1950.

Skulsky, Abraham. "Stefan Wolpe." *Musical America* (Nov. 1, 1951).

For twenty-nine, Popular currents

Burton, Jack. *The Blue Book of Broadway Musicals*. Watkins Glen, N.Y.: Century House, 1952.

DeKoven, Mrs. Reginald. *A Musician and His Wife*. New York: Harper & Brothers, 1926.

Ewen, David. *Complete Book of the American Musical Theater*. New York: Henry Holt & Company, Inc., 1958.

———. *Richard Rodgers*. New York: Henry Holt & Company, Inc., 1957.

———. *The World of Jerome Kern; a Biography*. New York: Holt, Rinehart and Winston, 1960.

———. *The Story of Irving Berlin*. New York: Henry Holt & Company, Inc., 1950.

———. *The Life and Death of Tin Pan Alley: The Golden Age of American Popular Music*. New York: Funk and Wagnalls, 1964.

Fuld, James J. *American Popular Music, 1875–1950*. Philadelphia: Musical Americana, 1955. (A reference work.)

Green, Stanley. *The World of Musical Comedy*. Foreword by Deems Taylor. New York: Ziff-Davis Publishing Company, 1960.

———. *The Rodgers and Hammerstein Story*. New York: The John Day Co., 1963.

Lewine, Richard, and Alfred Simon (compilers). *Encyclopedia of Theatre Music; A Comprehensive Listing of More than 4000 Songs from Broadway and Hollywood: 1900–1960*. New York, Random House, 1961.

Lewiton, Mina. *John Philip Sousa, the March King*. New York: Didier, 1944.

Marks, E. B. *They All Had Glamour. From the Swedish Nightingale to the Naked Lady*. New York: Julian Messner, Inc., 1944.

McSpadden, Joseph W. *Operas and Musical Comedies*. Enlarged ed. New York: Thomas Y. Crowell Company, 1951.

Morehouse, Ward. *George M. Cohan, Prince of the American Theatre.* Philadelphia: J. B. Lippincott, 1943.

Raph, Theodore (ed.). *The Songs We Sang: A Treasury of American Popular Music.* New York: A. S. Barnes, 1965.

Rodgers, Richard (ed.). *The Rodgers and Hart Song Book.* New York: Simon and Schuster, Inc., 1951.

Smith, Cecil. *Musical Comedy in America.* New York: Theatre Arts Books, 1950.

Sousa, John Philip. *Marching Along, An Autobiography.* Boston: Hale, Cushman and Flint, 1928.

Spaeth, Sigmund. *A History of Popular Music in America.* New York: Random House, 1948.

———— *Tin Pan Alley: A Chronicle of American Popular Music.* Introduction by George Gershwin. With a Supplement . . . by Edward Jablonski. New York: Frederick Ungar Publishing Co., Inc., 1961.

Stambler, Irwin. *Encyclopedia of Popular Music.* New York: St. Martin's Press, 1965.

Taylor, Deems. *Some Enchanted Evenings.* New York: Harper & Brothers, 1953. (Deals with Rodgers, Hart, and Oscar Hammerstein II.)

Waters, Edward N. *Victor Herbert, a Life in Music.* New York: The Macmillan Company, 1955.

Woollcott, Alexander. *The Story of Irving Berlin.* New York: G. P. Putnam's Sons, 1925.

For thirty, Toward an American opera

Brinnin, John Malcolm. *The Third Rose: Gertrude Stein and Her World.* New York: Grove Press, Inc., 1961.

Davis, Ronald L. *A History of Opera in the American West.* Englewood Cliffs, N.J.: Prentice-Hall, Inc., 1965.

Graf, Herbert. *Opera and Its Future in America.* New York: W. W. Norton & Company, Inc., 1941.

————. *Opera for the People.* Minneapolis: University of Minnesota Press, 1951.

Hamm, Charles. "Opera and the American Composer." In *The American Composer Speaks,* edited by Chase. (See General Bibliography.)

Hipsher, Edward E. *American Opera and Its Composers.* Philadelphia: Theodore Presser Company, 1927.

Hoover, Kathleen, and John Cage. *Virgil Thomson; His Life and Music.* (25)

Howard, J. T. *Deems Taylor.* New York: J. Fischer & Brother, 1927.

Johnson, H. Earle. *Operas on American Subjects.* New York: Coleman-Ross Company, Inc., 1964.

Kolodin, Irving. *The Story of the Metropolitan Opera, 1883–1950.* New York: Alfred A. Knopf, Inc., 1953.

Lahee, H. C. *Grand Opera in America.* Boston: L. C. Page & Company, 1902.

Mattfeld, Julius. *A Handbook of American Operatic Premières.* Detroit: Information Services, Inc., 1963.

Rosenfeld, Paul. *A Musical Chronicle.* New York: Harcourt, Brace & Company, Inc., 1923. Includes "The Fate of Mona."

Stein, Gertrude. *Last Operas and Plays*. New York: Rinehart & Company, Inc. 1948.
Thomson, Virgil. *The Musical Scene*. New York: Alfred A. Knopf, Inc., 1945. Includes "Blitzstein's Operas."

For thirty-one, The scene in the sixties

Babbitt, Milton. "An Introduction to the R.C.A. Synthesizer." *Journal of Music Theory* (Winter, 1964).
Childs, Barney, and Elliott Schwartz (eds.). *Contemporary Composers on Contemporary Music*. New York: Holt, Rinehart, and Winston, 1967.
Hiller, Lejaren A. "Electronic Music at the University of Illinois." *Journal of Music Theory* (Spring, 1963).
———, and Robert A. Baker. "*Computer Cantata:* A Study in Compositional Method." *Perspectives of New Music* (Fall-Winter, 1964).
———, and Leonard M. Isaacson. *Experimental Music*. (27)
Judd, F. C. *Electronic Music and Musique Concrète*. London: Neville Spearman, 1961.
Knowles, Alison, Philip Corner, Benjamin Patterson, and Tomas Schmit. *The Four Suits*. New York: Something Else Press, 1965. Includes thirteen compositions by Philip Corner, plus four "Finales."
Krenek, Ernst. "New Developments in Electronic Music." *Musical America* (Sept., 1955).
Lang, Paul H. (ed.). *Problems of Modern Music*. New York: W. W. Norton, 1960.
Layton, Billy Jim. "The New Liberalism." *Perspectives of New Music* (Spring-Summer, 1965).
Meyer, Leonard B. "The End of the Renaissance?" *Hudson Review*, XVI (1963), 169–86.
———. "Meaning in Music and Information Theory." *Journal of Aesthetics and Art Criticism*, IV, 3 (1957).
Mumma, Gordon. "An Electronic Music Studio for the Independent Composer." *Journal of the Audio Engineering Society*, XII, 3 (July, 1964).
Pierce, J. R. "A Portrait of the Machine as a Young Artist." *Playboy* (June, 1965).
Reynolds, Roger. "Indeterminacy: Some Considerations." *Perspectives of New Music*, IV, 1 (Fall-Winter 1965), 136–140.
Salzman, Eric. "Music from the Electronic Universe." *High Fidelity* (August, 1964).
Schillinger, Joseph. *The Mathematical Basis of the Arts*. New York: The Philosophical Library, 1948.
Tenney, James. *META+HODOS: A Phenomenology of Twentieth Century Musical Materials and an Approach to the Study of Form*. New Orleans: Inter-American Institute for Musical Research of Tulane University, 1964.
Vega, Aurelio de la. "Electronic Music: Tool of Creativity." *Music Journal* (Sept., Oct., and Nov., 1965).
(See also *The American Composer Speaks*, in the General Bibliography, for statements by Babbitt, Brown, Cage, Carter, Sessions).

Index